DIRECTOR
CLARENCE M. KELLEY

D1622709

ASSOCIATE DIRECTOR
NICHOLAS P. CALLAHAN

CONTINUED ON BACK ENDLEAF

LABORATORY DIVISION

ASSISTANT DIRECTOR
JAY COCHRAN, JR.

FRONT OFFICE:

PUBLICATIONS, PLANNING AND
EVALUATION UNIT
FORENSIC SCIENCE TRAINING UNIT

CRYPTANALYSIS-GAMBLING-TRANSLATION SECTION:

CRYPTANALYSIS
GAMBLING EXAMINATIONS
POLYGRAPH
SECURITY OF FBI COMMUNICATIONS
TRANSLATIONS

DOCUMENT SECTION:

CHARRED PAPER EXAMINATIONS
HANDWRITING AND HANDPRINTING
INDENTED WRITING
INK AND PENCIL EXAMINATIONS
OBLITERATED WRITINGS
PAPER EXAMINATIONS
PHOTOGRAPHIC EXAMINATIONS
PORTRAIT PARLE EXAMINATIONS
PRINTING
RUBBER STAMP, CHECKWRITER, AND
OTHER MECHANICAL DEVICES
SHOEPRINT EXAMINATIONS
TIRETREAD EXAMINATIONS
TYPEWRITING
MISCELLANEOUS

RADIO ENGINEERING SECTION:

FM AND CW RADIO SYSTEMS ENGINEERING
EQUIPMENT DEVELOPMENT
TESTING AND EVALUATION
MOBILE AND PORTABLE RADIO SYSTEMS
COMMUNICATIONS AND INVESTIGATIVE
SUPPORT
RADIO FREQUENCY LIAISON COMMITTEES
EVIDENCE EXAMINATIONS
ACOUSTIC ANALYSIS

PHYSICS AND CHEMISTRY SECTION:

BIOCHEMICAL
BIOLOGICAL
EXPLOSIVES
FIBERS AND HAIRS
GENERAL CHEMICAL
GLASS FRACTURES
GUNPOWDER TESTS
GUNS AND AMMUNITION
INSTRUMENTAL ANALYSIS
METALLURGICAL
MINERALOGICAL
NEUTRON ACTIVATION ANALYSIS
NUMBER RESTORATION
PHARMACOLOGICAL
RESEARCH
TOOLMARKS
TOXICOLOGICAL
WOOD
X-RAY

EXTERNAL AFFAIRS DIVISION

ASSISTANT DIRECTOR
DONALD W. MOORE, JR.

PRESS SERVICES OFFICE

FUGITIVE PUBLICITY PROGRAMS
NEWS RELEASES
TOP TEN FUGITIVE PROGRAM

CORRESPONDENCE AND TOURS:

CORRESPONDENCE – CITIZEN INQUIRIES
CORRESPONDENCE REVIEW
MAILING LISTS
DISTRIBUTION OF REPRINTS
TOURS OF FBIHQ
SPEECH MATTERS

RESEARCH SECTION:

FBI LAW ENFORCEMENT BULLETIN
INVESTIGATOR
SPECIAL PROJECTS
LIBRARY
BUREAU-WIDE INFORMATION PROGRAM
YOUTHFUL CRIMINALITY
RADIO-TV NEWS MEDIA CONTACTS

COMPUTER SYSTEMS DIVISION

ASSISTANT DIRECTOR
ANDREW J. DECKER, JR.

UNIFORM CRIME REPORTING SECTION:

UNIFORM CRIME REPORTS
LAW ENFORCEMENT OFFICERS KILLED OR
ASSAULTED STATISTICS
NATIONAL BOMB DATA STATISTICS

NATIONAL CRIME INFORMATION CENTER SECTION:

NATIONAL CRIME INFORMATION CENTER
COMPUTERIZED CRIMINAL HISTORIES
SYSTEMS DEVELOPMENT
NCIC CCH OPERATIONS
NCIC CCH CRIMINAL HISTORY CONVERSION

DATA PROCESSING SECTION:

ACCOUNTING REPORTS
COMPUTER SYSTEMS:
DATA PROCESSING
TELEPROCESSING
OPERATIONS RESEARCH
SYSTEMS ANALYSIS
PAYROLL
RETIREMENT RECORDS
STATISTICAL TABULATIONS
VOUCHERS

FIELD OFFICES

ALBANY	DALLAS	MEMPHIS	PORTLAND
ALBUQUERQUE	DENVER	MIAMI	RICHMOND
ALEXANDRIA	DETROIT	MILWAUKEE	SACRAMENTO
ANCHORAGE	EL PASO	MINNEAPOLIS	ST. LOUIS
ATLANTA	HONOLULU	MOBILE	SALT LAKE CITY
BALTIMORE	HOUSTON	NEWARK	SAN ANTONIO
BIRMINGHAM	INDIANAPOLIS	NEW HAVEN	SAN DIEGO
BOSTON	JACKSON	NEW ORLEANS	SAN FRANCISCO
BUFFALO	JACKSONVILLE	NEW YORK	SAN JUAN
BUTTE	KANSAS CITY	NORFOLK	SAVANNAH
CHARLOTTE	KNOXVILLE	OKLAHOMA CITY	SEATTLE
CHICAGO	LAS VEGAS	OMAHA	SPRINGFIELD
CINCINNATI	LITTLE ROCK	PHILADELPHIA	TAMPA
CLEVELAND	LOS ANGELES	PHOENIX	WASHINGTON, D.C.
COLUMBIA	LOUISVILLE	PITTSBURGH	**TOTAL 59**

FBI

By Sanford J. Ungar

FBI

THE PAPERS & THE PAPERS: An Account of the Legal and Political Battle over the Pentagon Papers

THE ALMOST REVOLUTION: France–1968 (with Allan Priaulx)

Sanford J. Ungar

FBI

An Atlantic Monthly Press Book

Little, Brown and Company — Boston – Toronto

FIRST EDITION

T 03/76

Portions of this book appeared originally in *The Atlantic*.

Quotations from *I Lived Inside the Campus Revolution* by W. T. Divale
are reprinted with permission of Henry Regnery Company Publishers.

Excerpts from Bernard De Voto's October 1949 column
in *Harper's* magazine reprinted by special
permission of *Harper's* magazine.

ATLANTIC–LITTLE, BROWN BOOKS
ARE PUBLISHED BY
LITTLE, BROWN AND COMPANY
IN ASSOCIATION WITH
THE ATLANTIC MONTHLY PRESS

LIBRARY OF CONGRESS CATALOGING IN PUBLICATION DATA

Ungar, Sanford J
FBI.

"An Atlantic Monthly Press book."
Bibliography: p.
Includes index.
1. United States. Federal Bureau of Investigation.
HV8138.U53   353.007'4   75–38638
ISBN 0–316–88744–7

Designed by Susan Windheim

Published simultaneously in Canada
by Little, Brown & Company (Canada) Limited

PRINTED IN THE UNITED STATES OF AMERICA

To
Max Ungar (1895–1956)
and
Sy Barash (1926–1975)

List of Illustrations

Contents

CONTENTS

Preface

*For me, it would be impossible to be totally candid with you, be-
cause for twenty-two years I was taught to be guarded. . . . I
don't think I can be totally candid with anybody, because of my
training. I have to be very concerned about what I say. . . . I can't
even be candid with my wife. . . . We're so concerned about hurting the FBI's image . . . and also, if I say something wrong, my
career could be finished.*
— *The assistant-special-agent-in-charge of a major
FBI field office*

IN THE FALL OF 1973, I approached Clarence M. Kelley, who had been
director of the FBI for only a few months, with a request that the
Bureau cooperate with me on a book that I was planning to write
about it. At the time, I had a leave of absence from the staff of the
Washington Post, for which I had covered legal and judicial affairs —
including the Justice Department and the FBI — and a fellowship at
the Adlai Stevenson Institute in Chicago. I had been encouraged by
friends in government and the press to use the opportunity to study
the Bureau in depth. The idea was to write about this powerful and
intriguing institution at a period of transition in its history, to trace and
evaluate the contributions of J. Edgar Hoover, and to look closely at
events since his death — but to do so at a distance from the day-to-day
developments in Washington. Kelley had a reputation for openness as
chief of police in Kansas City, and he was asserting publicly that he
welcomed greater scrutiny of the FBI. Intermediaries, including
people who knew him well, assured me that he would be receptive to a

project for an objective, outsider's look at the Bureau — neither a piece of propaganda in its behalf nor a brief for dismantling the institution, but an unbiased inquiry into the nature of the FBI, how it works, who peoples it, and what it does.

It was not unusual for journalists to ask the Bureau's cooperation with books and articles, nor for them to get it. But there was invariably a firm condition: that the FBI's "experts" review the materials before publication to assure that they were "accurate" and did not somehow violate security. And such assistance and review was generally provided only to certified Bureau "friends," writers who were personal pals of Hoover or had otherwise demonstrated their fidelity to the FBI point of view. Others, including disgruntled or disrespectful former agents and anyone else who wanted to write about the Bureau, were usually left out in the cold. Much of what was published about the FBI, therefore, suffered from feast or famine. I asked that Kelley break with that tradition and cooperate without any strings attached.

My proposal, I was told, was reviewed at a luncheon in the director's office attended by officials from the Bureau's External Affairs Division, which is responsible for watching over the FBI image. They had pulled together a dossier of my writings, and they confidently pronounced that these demonstrated I was an "enemy" of Mr. Hoover and, *ipso facto*, of the Bureau. They fought the idea of helping me. The External Affairs men and other traditionalists in the FBI hierarchy noted other drawbacks: I had worked for a "liberal" newspaper that was on Hoover's "no-contact list" because it was presumed to be dedicated to the destruction of the FBI, and my work had appeared in other unacceptable publications. I was too young to have the proper perspective. And, as shocking as anything else, I had a beard, for some in the Bureau the telltale mark of bomb-throwers and others not to be trusted. Another theory that was circulated, revealed to me later, was that I had somehow been in league with former Acting Director L. Patrick Gray III, about whom I had written, but then had abandoned and pilloried as soon as he became embroiled in the Watergate scandals. Who could say what I would now write? The strongly expressed advice of the professionals was to refuse my request; but Kelley, according to sources close to him, said, "The man is going to write a book whether we help him or not, so we are going to help him." He granted many of my requests for access to Bureau offices and officials. Some skeptics suggested that Kelley's attitude was not shaped entirely by altruism and openness, that he had his own selfish motives for going along — perhaps hoping that the book would enhance his own image and reputation. Indeed, as time passed and he became less independent of the Bureau hierarchy, Kelley did seem to waver and to appear less enthusiastic about the project; I became convinced that had my initial approach to him come later in his tenure, he might have followed the insiders' advice and declined to help. His standing orders, however, were that External Affairs cooperate with me.

With the FBI External Affairs Division's begrudging variety of cooperation, one needs no other problems. In direct contravention of instructions from the director's office, agents were often sent along to sit in on my sessions with assistant directors and other Bureau officials (they were only there to help answer questions, they insisted). I was misled and occasionally told untruths about when Kelley would testify at congressional hearings and whether they would be open to the press and public. At one point, my schedule of interviews with Bureau officials was canceled in midstream, because the assistant FBI director in charge of External Affairs decided I was going too far and asking too many "personal" questions. Top officials from External Affairs would sometimes show up unexpectedly at what I had expected to be private interview sessions with Kelley. ("It helps us," explained one; "it lets us know what his latest thinking is.") On one occasion, the assistant director persistently interrupted Kelley and turned the interview into a fountain of old-fashioned FBI clichés, to the director's own obvious annoyance. At times, when calls went out to field offices to advise that I would be visiting, they were in the form of warnings; at least one agent was told by the division that I had "sweet-talked" the director into going along with my project. External Affairs followed my visits with phone calls to ask about me and occasionally ordered up reports on my excursions into the field, asking for lists of everyone who spoke to me and for descriptions of the questions I asked. As a result, cards with my name and description appeared in the "indices" of some of the field offices I visited. One high-ranking Bureau official advised me that External Affairs was just waiting for me to trip up — hoping that I would remove a document from somebody's desk or commit some other indiscretion that would justify cutting off my access to the FBI.

These nuisances — the External Affairs actions seldom rose to the level of actual harassment — became something of a joke among some Bureau people, including Kelley. Sometimes he addressed the problem head-on, for example, on the occasion when, at the director's invitation, I attended a meeting he held with two special-agents-in-charge in Kansas City (described more fully on pages 572–577). As the session concluded and the men prepared to leave, Kelley turned to them and asked whether there was anything they wanted to discuss out of my presence. "Oh no, not a thing," they both insisted. Had my attendance at the conference created any "barrier" or other problem, the director wanted to know. "Absolutely not," said the visitors almost in unison; I had been most welcome and they were pleased that I had joined them. "Well," Kelley told them, "you gentlemen will probably have calls when you get home, asking 'How did you get along with that beard? How was Ungar?' I hope your answers will be the same then as they have been now."

The fact is, of course, that the roadblocks thrown up by External Affairs were relatively easy to circumvent. Many Bureau officials, including Kelley, met and spoke with me without the knowledge of the division. If it was uncomfortable or clumsy for some of them to do so on Bureau premises, we met in restaurants, bars, their homes or mine. Ultimately I visited eleven field offices — Alexandria, Chicago, Detroit, Jackson, Kansas City, Los Angeles, Miami, Minneapolis, New York, San Francisco, and Tampa — and many of the smaller resident agencies under their jurisdiction. I also visited the FBI "legal attachés" in Paris, London, and Bonn. These did not necessarily represent an ideal cross section or a random sample, but the offices included a wide variety of situations and specialties. I attended several regional management symposia of FBI officials convened by Kelley during his early months on the job, and many of the contacts made under those circumstances led to other fruitful ones. I also interviewed dozens of former agents and Bureau and Justice Department officials. Although I was not permitted official access to Bureau files or documents, I managed to see some things unofficially.

My reception in the field was warm and gratifying. I met hundreds of agents. Only a few of them were outwardly hostile — one actually ran in the other direction when he saw me coming around the corner in his field office — and most welcomed the opportunity to talk candidly and openly of their work and their feelings about the Bureau. In a few instances, I was even treated as if I were the bearer of secret knowledge of Kelley's plans (which I was not) and some agents queried me — without success — about his attitudes and policies. Some people may have attempted to convey messages to the director through me, but I never privately transmitted any such message; it is entirely possible, however, that I have inadvertently accomplished the purposes of certain reformist groups within the FBI through what I have written and the impressions I have passed along in this book. On occasion, Kelley did ask for my observations about matters of ongoing controversy, and although I was concerned to preserve my integrity as an outsider, I acknowledged my misgivings, for example, about some aspects of Bureau policy and actions in the "security" field, misgivings which are plainly evident in the book. My only commitment to the director was to seek the FBI's point of view in response to criticisms, and I hope I have obtained and adequately portrayed both sides of most of the issues. The only advice I can recall offering to him was that the Bureau should be far more open and that its press policy should change drastically.

I was concerned at several junctures about the risk of accepting too much cooperation from the FBI and thereby compromising my independence. This concern could reach absurd extremes, as when I called my publisher one night to ask whether he thought it fell within allowable limits to accept a ride in a Bureau car from Los Angeles to Barstow, California; we decided that it really would be foolish for me to follow the FBI vehicle in a rented car. As it turned out, that ride and other similar experiences contributed significantly to my research. I tried scrupulously to avoid any situation where anyone in the Bureau felt that he or she might be buying favorable treatment in the book by being helpful to me. Some dedicated and devoted FBI people have a strange sense of the meaning of "objectivity," however, and I fear that they will feel that my description or analysis of situations is a betrayal, after they have been so "nice" to me. That is a regrettable, but perhaps inevitable, circumstance.

On some subjects and events involving the FBI, there seems to be no objective truth, only a number of competing versions that reflect different individuals' views of the facts, often selfish or expediently shortsighted. Where this is the case, I have attempted to construct the most accurate, meaningful picture possible from conflicting sources and the other available data. Even so, there may be other versions, other revisions of the FBI's internal history, that I have neglected, and some of these matters will perhaps be clarified further only with the passage of time. One Bureau official acknowledged to me with embarrassment that he had on an earlier occasion, at the suggestion of higher-ups, lied to me; how many times this may have happened but was not acknowledged one can only speculate.

The book is, at best, incomplete — as one agent suggested to me, it's a snapshot of a train that has begun to move fast. Efforts have been made to keep it as comprehensive and up to date as possible, but the new climate of disclosure surrounding the intelligence community and the Bureau's growing, albeit reluctant, openness have made this difficult. In a few instances, I obtained exclusive information about some aspect of the FBI only to have it become general knowledge a few months later; there were several areas in which I felt that the FBI began to open up with others only after I had broken the ground in the course of my book research.

I have honored the request of many sources for anonymity or confidentiality; some will deny that they have ever spoken to me. As is often the case in reporting about government institutions, honoring such requests was the only way to obtain some of the most valuable material. If anything, I have bent over backward to protect the younger agents who were candid with me; even if the Bureau is changing, many agents feared old-Bureau-style recriminations for their frankness in touchy areas — a fear that may well be justified. Often, I have simply omitted names where they are unnecessary. Where names have been changed, this fact is indicated in the text.

My first year's work on this book was made possible by a generous fellowship from the Adlai Stevenson Institute and by a leave of absence from the *Washington Post*. Through that year and beyond, I have had the support and encouragement of the editors of *The Atlantic Monthly*. Several people assisted me with research, but I am especially grateful to Daniel Pollock and Art Brodsky for bailing me out in the final stages. My family, friends, and colleagues in Chicago, including those at the Public News Center of WTTW-TV, were important sources of strength. Certain FBI agents and employees, who shall remain nameless here, helped in unusual, selfless ways. Ruth Muller, in preparing the manuscript, made order out of chaos. My editor, Michael Janeway, gave unselfishly and unstintingly of his time and ideas; if any credit is due, he deserves a very large share. But most of all, I was aided and abetted, coaxed and cajoled, egged on and spurred on, critiqued and improved, by Beth Ungar. This is in every sense her book, too.

SANFORD J. UNGAR
Washington, D.C.
November 1975

Note on Usage

MOST OF THE TERMS AND TITLES USED in this book are consistent with the official style and hierarchy of the FBI. Thus, some may require explanation. An assistant-to-the-director is not just any assistant to the man who runs the Bureau, but one of its highest-ranking officials, just below the associate director and above the assistant directors. (The two assistants-to-the-director are now also called deputy associate directors. See organization chart.) All agents are known as "special agents" in formal Bureau parlance, but the word "special" has generally been dropped here, except where it forms a part of a significant job title — as in special-agent-in-charge (also known as an SAC) or assistant-special-agent-in-charge (also known as an ASAC). The SACs and ASACs run the fifty-nine field offices, the major administrative units in the FBI's nationwide organization, and supervise the resident agencies in their territory (see endpapers). Although the largest resident agencies (RAs) may have nearly as many agents assigned to them as the smallest field offices, the bureaucratic distinction is important and has been preserved here. In this book, "the Bureau" may refer generally to the entire FBI (as it does for most outsiders) or specifically to FBI headquarters in Washington (as it does for most agents). The title or assignment attached to any individual Bureau official or agent here is the one that he or she had when interviewed or observed; except where relevant to the events being related or the point being stressed, no attempt has been made to keep up with the subsequent transfers, promotions, demotions, or retirements of everybody mentioned in the book. The "Director" refers specifically and exclusively to J. Edgar Hoover, whereas the "director" may be any of his successors in the job. Other terms, abbreviations, acronyms, and Bureau usages are explained in the Glossary.

FBI FIELD OFFICES

PACIFIC TIME ZONE

MOUNTAIN TIME ZONE

BELLINGHAM
EVERETT
BREMERTON
56 TACOMA
OLYMPIA
WENATCHEE SPOKANE
YAKIMA
COEUR D'ALENE
KALISPELL
GREAT FALLS
GLASGOW
MINOT

ASTORIA LONGVIEW
VANCOUVER
46 RICHLAND
LEWISTON
MISSOULA
HELENA

SALEM
PENDLETON
BOZEMAN
BILLINGS
MILES CITY
BISMARCK

EUGENE
BEND
10

COOS BAY
BOISE

MEDFORD
KLAMATH FALLS
TWIN FALLS
IDAHO FALLS
POCATELLO
RIVERTON
CASPER
RAPID CITY
PIERRE

EUREKA
REDDING
SUSANVILLE
CHICO
ELKO
OGDEN
ROCK SPRINGS
CHEYENNE
SCOTTSBLUFF
NORTH PLATTE

YUBA CITY
RENO
50 PROVO
FT. COLLINS
GRANT

SANTA ROSA VALLEJO
SAN RAFAEL
48 CARSON CITY
SOUTH LAKE TAHOE
BERKELEY
OAKLAND
53 HAYWARD STOCKTON
SAN MATEO MODESTO
PALO ALTO SAN JOSE MERCED
SANTA CRUZ
MONTEREY SALINAS
FRESNO
VISALIA
BOULDER
17
GLENWOOD SPRINGS
GRAND JUNCTION
COLORADO SPRINGS
COLBY
HAYS

BAKERSFIELD
CEDAR CITY
DURANGO
PUEBLO
GARDEN CITY

SANTA MARIA
LANCASTER
27
FARMINGTON

SANTA BARBARA
SAN FERNANDO VALLEY PASADENA
PORT HUENEME WEST COVINA BARSTOW
LOS ANGELES INTERNATIONAL AIRPORT **29** VICTORVILLE REDONDO BEACH
LONG BEACH RIVERSIDE
SANTA ANA
PALM SPRINGS
KINGMAN
FLAGSTAFF
LOS ALAMOS
GALLUP SANTA FE
2
AMARILLO
CLINTON
WOODWARD
ALTUS

PRESCOTT
44 MESA
ROSWELL
CLOVIS
LUBBOCK
WICHITA

52 ESCONDIDO
EL CENTRO
YUMA
TUCSON
SAFFORD
ALAMOGORDO
LAS CRUCES
HOBBS
MIDLAND
ABILENE

NOGALES
19
SAN ANGELO

ALASKA

BERING TIME ZONE
FAIRBANKS

4

FREDERICKSBURG
DEL RIO

20
HAWAII

ALASKA-HAWAII TIME ZONE
JUNEAU

GUAM
YUKON TIME ZONE
ALASKA-HAWAII TIME ZONE
LAREDO
MCAL

PACIFIC TIME ZONE

NOTE: WHEN IT IS 6:00 P.M. MONDAY IN EASTERN TIME ZONE, IT IS 9:00 A.M. TUESDAY IN GUAM.

FIELD OFFICES

1 ALBANY	7 BIRMINGHAM	13 CINCINNATI	19 EL PASO	25 KANSAS CITY	32 MIAMI
2 ALBUQUERQUE	8 BOSTON	14 CLEVELAND	20 HONOLULU	26 KNOXVILLE	33 MILW/
3 ALEXANDRIA	9 BUFFALO	15 COLUMBIA	21 HOUSTON	27 LAS VEGAS	34 MINNE
4 ANCHORAGE	10 BUTTE	16 DALLAS	22 INDIANAPOLIS	28 LITTLE ROCK	35 MOBIL
5 ATLANTA	11 CHARLOTTE	17 DENVER	23 JACKSON	29 LOS ANGELES	36 NEWA
6 BALTIMORE	12 CHICAGO	18 DETROIT	24 JACKSONVILLE	30 LOUISVILLE	37 NEW
				31 MEMPHIS	38 NEW

RESIDENT AGENCIES

ATLANTIC TIME ZONE

EASTERN TIME ZONE

ATLANTIC TIME ZONE

STAMFORD
BRIDGEPORT
WATERBURY
HARTFORD
NEW LONDON
DANBURY

BABYLON
KINGSTON
GARDEN CITY
POUGHKEEPSIE
ST GEORGE
SUFFERN
WHITE PLAINS
JFK INTERNATIONAL AIRPORT
MONTICELLO

ATLANTIC CITY
RED BANK
PISCATAWAY
CAMDEN
PARSIPPANY
TRENTON
HACKENSACK

ST. THOMAS
CHARLOTTE AMALIE

VIRGIN ISLANDS
(SAN JUAN OFFICE)

ST. CROIX

PUERTO RICO

AGUADILLA   FAJARDO
PONCE

FBI Headquarters

State Capital & Field Office Hq. City

State Capital & RA

State Capital & RA - No Office Space

Field Office Hq. City

Resident Agency

Resident Agency - No Office Space

Field Division Boundaries

State Lines Overlapped by Field Division Districts

Time Zone Boundaries *

* NOTE: ARIZONA, HAWAII AND PORTIONS OF INDIANA DO NOT OBSERVE DAYLIGHT SAVING TIME.

JULY 10, 1975

39 NEW YORK	46 PORTLAND	53 SAN FRANCISCO
40 NORFOLK	47 RICHMOND	54 SAN JUAN
41 OKLAHOMA CITY	48 SACRAMENTO	55 SAVANNAH
42 OMAHA	49 ST. LOUIS	56 SEATTLE
43 PHILADELPHIA	50 SALT LAKE CITY	57 SPRINGFIELD
44 PHOENIX	51 SAN ANTONIO	58 TAMPA
45 PITTSBURGH	52 SAN DIEGO	59 WASHINGTON, D.C.

Prelude

I

Winning One
for the Director

By the time we found him, Gargano was suffering so badly from gangrene and loss of blood that he was almost dead. It was too bad we didn't get there a little later.
— An FBI agent who worked on the Northlake bank robbery case

THERE WAS AN UNSEASONABLY EARLY SNOW in the Chicago area on Friday morning, October 27, 1967. It had the effect of slowing all movements down, but the situation was further complicated in the western suburb of Northlake at about 10:30 A.M., when the police department received an anonymous call advising that a gasoline truck had overturned and spilled its contents on the street at the outskirts of the town. Most of Northlake's 35-man police force, concerned that the combination of snow and gasoline would cause dangerous traffic conditions, raced to the area mentioned in the call to investigate the accident; but they could find nothing out of the ordinary.

It soon became clear that the phone call had been a hoax. About ten minutes later, as the police cars were on their way back to the station, three men wearing disguises walked into the Northlake Bank — a long, low modern structure that stood alone at the side of a major thoroughfare — ordered everyone to lie on the floor and collected almost eighty-four thousand dollars from the tellers' drawers into a large bag. They were heavily armed, with handguns as well as automatic rifles, some of which, it would later be learned, had been stolen a week earlier in a holdup at the National Guard Armory in Salem, Illinois, some three hundred miles to the south. The bank robbery alarm was

3

flashed to the policemen returning from the scene of the fictional accident, and they were immediately diverted to the bank. Two police cars, one marked and one unmarked, arrived in the bank's parking lot just as the robbers, behind their schedule, were coming out through a set of double glass doors. There was a bitter gun battle in front of the bank in which two policemen, one a plainclothes detective and the other a uniformed officer, were immediately killed. One of the bank robbers, later identified by the Federal Bureau of Investigation from his fingerprints as Ronald Del Raine, was shot through the neck and shoulders and abandoned for dead by his two companions. But as they were entering their getaway car, one of those two was shot in the shoulder by an off-duty policeman from the suburb of Schaumburg who had heard the shooting and commotion from a nearby dry cleaning shop. When the getaway car was later recovered in a factory parking lot about four blocks from the bank — where the "switch car" had apparently been parked during the robbery — it was riddled with bullets and the passenger side of its interior was covered with blood.

Word of the bank robbery and police killings spread quickly over the police radio, and officers from what seemed like every police department in Chicago's vast suburbs converged on the Northlake Bank, all offering to help solve the case. So did the FBI, which had automatic jurisdiction because the bank was federally insured, and which, by common practice for decades, coordinates most such bank robbery investigations. Once the Chicago Field Office of the Bureau learned that two policemen had been killed, it ordered all available agent cars to the scene. Some had an easier time getting there than others. One pair of agents, an old-timer experienced in bank robbery cases and a new man who was just being broken in on the office's specialized bank robbery squad, had their brakes fail on the expressway while en route and had to be picked up in another car on its way to Northlake.

One of the first Bureau agents at the bank was Joe Burke, and he still says that he "will never forget" what he saw: "The windows of the bank were all shot out, and there was glass everywhere. . . . There were pools of blood in the parking lot, and somebody was just starting to wash down the area. . . . It was an amazing sight." The bodies of the two dead policemen were still in the parking lot, and two other officers who had been wounded, as well as Del Raine, were being taken off to the hospital. Inside the bank it was chaos. Perhaps a hundred people were milling around — victims of the robbery, both bank employees and customers; policemen; and the usual assortment of gawkers, the curiosity-seekers drawn by the excitement. Members of the press were beginning to arrive. Finally one husky man with red-

4

dish hair stood on one of the counters and banged on an ashtray until the noise subsided. "I'm Stratton from the FBI," he said in a rough monotone, "and we're going to start conducting an investigation."

Ramon W. Stratton was not just a run-of-the-mill agent. At the age of thirty-nine, he had already been affiliated with the Bureau for twenty-four years. He was recruited at sixteen from his high school graduating class in Knappa, Oregon, when wartime responsibilities had left the FBI shorthanded, to become a clerk in the Portland Field Office. After attending college and law school at night while he worked as a clerk, he entered training and became an agent in 1953. For just over a year he was assigned to Houston (where he often drove to work with an up-and-coming assistant-special-agent-in-charge named Clarence Kelley) and then to New York, where he spent eight years, mostly assigned to a squad responsible for tracking down interstate fugitives. But Stratton's real opportunity to shine came when he was assigned to Alaska. As the resident agent in Juneau, where he picked up the nickname "Snowshoes," he cracked a gambling ring that had organized a system of illegal cash payoffs on pinball machines in local bars; the case he built was strong enough to obtain a conviction under a new law that prohibited "interstate transportation in aid of racketeering" (ITAR to the Bureau). For some reason, J. Edgar Hoover was especially impressed with the accomplishment. The Director wrote to Stratton praising him for his outstanding investigative talents and promoted him to be the only "street agent" in all the Bureau with the rank and compensation level of GS-14. (Most agents working "on the bricks" were classified as GS-13s, and the higher grades were ordinarily reserved for those in supervisory positions.)* As fast as fortunes can rise in the FBI, however, they can also fall, and early in 1965 Stratton was informed that he was to be punished on the basis of a report that he had told a "dirty story" at a recent police school where he was teaching on the Bureau's behalf. As normal, or appropriate, as that might have seemed to most people, in the netherworld of the FBI, run according to Hoover's regulations and predilections, it was a sin. Without any hearing or opportunity to defend himself, he was suspended for a month without pay in the midst of the Alaskan winter. The punishment also included an immediate, unrequested transfer to Chicago once he was back on the payroll.

In Chicago, despite an abrasive manner that sometimes alienated those above him, Stratton was soon named the field office's "bank

---

* Today there are only seventeen "street agents" in the entire FBI with the rank of GS-14. The basic pay for a GS-13 agent in 1975 was $21,816, for a GS-14, $25,581; but most agents are in higher "steps" within those grades.

robbery coordinator." In a big city where crime was growing and spreading rapidly, that was an important responsibility; he often had to take charge of major cases, size them up under the pressure of a crisis, and deploy large numbers of agents sensibly but quickly. For, as anyone in the Bureau is quick to say, in most instances the longer a case goes unsolved, the harder it becomes to solve.

Ray Stratton stayed at the Northlake Bank, along with other agents and a host of policemen, for about twelve hours on that Friday in October. Then he went back downtown to the field office. He doesn't remember getting to sleep at all until Saturday night. It did not take long for FBI headquarters in Washington to declare the case a "special" — a case on which particular and urgent efforts would be made — and Stratton asked Special-Agent-in-Charge Marlin W. Johnson to release about a hundred and fifty agents for duty on the Northlake case in the days that followed. Johnson balked at first, concerned that this would leave the flanks exposed in other important areas of the field office's work; but the intense interest in the case, reflected both in spectacular newspaper publicity and, more importantly, in phone calls straight from the Director's office in Washington, brought him around to grant Stratton's request. Some agents interviewed everyone who had been in the vicinity of the robbery, and others lined up in a long row to conduct a step-by-step search of the crime scene. Every little item that was found, whether a scrap of metal or a fleck of paint, was logged and saved as potential evidence. Some typical problems cropped up early on. The Northlake Police Department, for example, persisted in putting out its own police radio broadcasts on the case that were not cleared with the FBI. Some of the information in them the Bureau considered plainly unreliable, such as the names of the accomplices that the injured robber left at the scene, Del Raine, had later allegedly given to a Northlake policeman. (The names proved to be phony, and Del Raine eventually denied to the FBI that he had ever given such a false story as he lay injured outside the bank.) As a result, the Bureau put out its own separate broadcasts on the case, signed simply STRATTON, FBI. Whatever resentments some of the other local law enforcement organizations might have felt against the aggressive, publicity-snatching federal contingent, it seemed clear that they were more likely to trust the FBI's word on the case than that of the Northlake police.

One important break came early. As Stratton checked to see what the first police officers on the scene had done, he discovered that members of the suburban Melrose Park department — which did not enjoy a particularly good reputation with the FBI at the time — had

6

picked up all of the spent cartridges that were fired from the bank robbers' guns. Once they were turned over to the Bureau, an agent from the Chicago Field Office was immediately dispatched with them on a flight to Washington, so that they could be examined by the FBI Laboratory. Word came back on Saturday morning: some of the shells were identical to those submitted for examination only a few weeks earlier after the armed robbery of an A&P supermarket in Canton, Ohio, in which two policemen had been injured. An FBI informant there had subsequently linked that robbery to two men with long criminal records, Henry Michael Gargano and Clifton Orneal Daniels. The modus operandi in the two cases seemed similar. Gargano and Daniels now became the prime suspects in the Northlake case. It was a textbook example of Hoover's principles of scientific law enforcement at work. By Saturday night agents filed formal complaints against all three men in United States District Court in Chicago, and warrants were issued for the arrest of Gargano and Daniels.

The manhunt took some bizarre turns, reminiscent of the FBI's gangster-chasing days of the 1930s, when a growing Bureau had sought and captured or killed characters like John Dillinger — a parallel that was not lost on the Chicago newspapers. A doctor on the city's South Side, Theodore Roosevelt Mason Howard, reported that a woman had come to him, flashed $5,000, and offered more, if only he would treat her "brother," who had been shot in the shoulder while escaping from the Northlake Bank. Dr. Howard refused, but provided her with some pain-killing pills for the man, then called the Bureau. The woman was identified as Mary Frances Cook, who worked as a stripper at a Chicago night spot under the name of "Sheer Folly" and had recently been Gargano's girlfriend. (During one subsequent interview, Cook took off her clothes while talking with an FBI agent, a situation of which the Director surely would have disapproved had he known.) When agents searched her apartment, they found a photograph of her with Gargano and the fingerprints of several other people. One man whose prints were in the apartment ran off to Providence, Rhode Island, as soon as he heard that the FBI was looking for him. Located there, he was arrested and brought back to Chicago as a possible witness in the Northlake case. It turned out, however, that he was just another of Cook's boyfriends and knew nothing about the Bank robbery; he apparently ran away only because he was worried about having violated the conditions of his own parole and did not want the Bureau to find out. At one point, agents did an aisle-by-aisle, car-by-car search of all the parking lots at Chicago's O'Hare Airport and they found a car that had been left there by Daniels before the bank robbery, but still no leads as to the whereabouts of the two men. Gargano's father was contacted and persuaded to make a public appeal to his son to surrender, to no avail.

But over the weekend, the Chicago Field Office had a lucky tip: a man contacted the Bureau and said he knew of a phone call made by Gargano shortly after the robbery. In exchange for a small amount of money and a promise of "perpetual protection" of his identity, the man revealed that the call had been made from a coin telephone at a particular intersection in the western suburb of Bellwood, only a few miles from Northlake. Convinced that Gargano's injury would have prevented him from going far to make a phone call, Stratton organized a building-by-building search of the neighborhood in the vicinity of the telephone booth. Starting from a hub, agents fanned out and attempted to talk with someone who lived in, or was otherwise connected with, each building. Finally, on Tuesday, October 31, they came upon a garage behind a house in Bellwood. Parked inside it was a car with heavy bloodstains and a number of weapons, including some that were used in the Northlake bank robbery — obviously the "switch car." In the loft apartment above the garage, the agents found bloody water in the toilet and tub, along with materials that had apparently been used by a sister-in-law of Gargano to create a makeshift dressing for his wounds. According to the people who lived in the house, the men who rented the apartment some weeks earlier had left in a hurry. The agents were frustrated at being too late. But once they searched the apartment thoroughly, they were also relieved: it was stocked with Browning automatic rifles, other weapons, and thousands of rounds of ammunition. Slits for the gun barrels had been cut in the windows and in the door at the top of a narrow stairway leading to the apartment. As one agent put it later, "They would have blasted anyone who tried to come up. . . . If we had gotten there on time, we probably would have lost some agents."

In the meantime, another agent in the field office had been assigned to dig out all the records on a previous case, in which Gargano was convicted of bank robbery and sentenced to federal prison in 1956, to look for any possible leads that might help solve the Northlake bank robbery. The Bureau believes strongly in the principles of criminal recidivism, and so it keeps voluminous documentation on almost every case it has ever investigated. This file revealed that the last time around Gargano had been located and arrested, after an extensive manhunt, at a rundown cabin in the woods at Fish Lake, Indiana, owned by his grandfather. The Chicago agents immediately contacted their counterparts in Indianapolis. Fish Lake, near La Porte, was in the territory of the Gary Resident Agency, but all of the agents there were involved in the investigation of a voting fraud case that had been declared an urgent priority by the Department of Justice, so the matter was referred instead to the South Bend Resident Agency on Tuesday. At first checking out the shack from a distance, three FBI agents found that a car with Illinois license plates (rented at O'Hare, it was later learned) was parked outside and there were other signs of activity around the cabin that were unusual for late October. The agents recruited local La Porte County sheriff's deputies and Indiana state policemen as reinforcements and returned. After the officers and agents announced their presence by loudspeaker, Mary Cook and another woman, Antoinette Leonardo, who was Gargano's sister and Del Raine's girlfriend, emerged. They were followed by Daniels, who said that Gargano was too weak to come out on his own. FBI agent Gene Norris, the same man who had arrested Gargano there more than ten years earlier, shouted that he was coming in. "If I wasn't so weak, I'd kill the first guy through the door," Gargano replied, showing none of the legendary kinship for the agent who had previously taken him into custody. Norris found the man lying in bed with two guns, but unable to lift them. Gargano was taken off to the hospital and the others to a local jail, pending their transfer into the hands of federal marshals.

It was less than five days — one hundred and two hours, to be exact, the Bureau proudly pointed out — between the sounding of the alarm at the Northlake Bank and the arrest of Gargano and Daniels. Two days later, on November 2, a federal grand jury in Chicago indicted them and Del Raine for bank robbery and the killing of the two police officers during their escape. It was the kind of performance the FBI likes to flaunt, and the local authorities and press could not praise the Bureau enough for its good old-fashioned roundup of the culprits. "It's too bad you can't do this on every case," Stratton would say some years later, reminiscing; "but if you did, there would never be time for anything else."

J. Edgar Hoover lost no time exploiting the Northlake case to make his own rhetorical points. Speaking on November 1 at the graduation ceremonies of the eightieth session of the FBI National Academy, the Bureau's police training school, he pointed out that Gargano and Daniels had met and become friends while they were both in the federal penitentiary at Marion, Illinois, serving time for bank robbery. They had both been released on parole earlier in 1967. Del Raine, similarly, had been paroled in 1966 from his own sentence for bank robbery. "The bleeding hearts of this country have had their

9

say too long," the Director declared in an attack on the parole system, "and we need, therefore, to get back to the fundamentals in the enforcement of law and order and the protection of the law-abiding citizen and his right to walk on safe streets." Hoover's anger, on this case as on others, fed into sentiment that was building in Congress for tough new anticrime legislation.

This was one case where the Bureau looked forward eagerly to court proceedings in which its side would easily prevail, and the agents were delighted when a federal judge turned down the defendants' motion to waive a jury trial in Chicago on the basis of the heavy publicity surrounding the bank robbery and investigation. In anticipation of the trial, Stratton coordinated the collection of a vast reserve of evidence, enough to require a large separate room of its own in the Chicago Field Office. As in many of the Bureau's favorite cases, however, the trial was never to be. On July 16, 1968, when the three prisoners were scheduled for a routine court appearance, the FBI had a tip from inside the jail that they were armed and planning an escape. Gargano, called to the telephone on a ruse, was pounced on by agents and marshals, who found that he was carrying a .38 caliber revolver; Del Raine, seized in his cell, was found to be concealing a sharpened kitchen knife. It turned out that they had been planning to shoot U.S. District Court Judge Edwin A. Robson and to attempt to escape. Instead, when they were brought before Robson that day, all three changed their pleas to guilty. He sentenced each of them to one hundred and ninety-nine years in federal prison. The three women who had helped them all subsequently pleaded guilty to being accessories after the fact and received sentences ranging from a year's probation (the stripper) to a year in prison (Gargano's sister).

A separate FBI investigation of the escape attempt revealed that a plumber working at the Cook County Jail had smuggled the gun in to Gargano for $10,000 from the bank robbery loot. Joseph Tierney, chief U.S. Marshal for the Northern District of Illinois and a Democratic stalwart in Chicago, resigned his post after the Bureau found that his men had failed to search the prisoners when they were transferred into federal custody from the county jail for their court appearance on that July day.

At some point the Bureau developed the idea that Gargano, facing a lifetime behind bars, might be prepared to talk about other unsolved criminal cases with which he was familiar, and in June 1969, again back at Marion, he was interviewed in the penitentiary by a hapless agent from the Springfield Field Office, As the agent was constrained to put it in the FBI's stilted language, Gargano "stated that at no time had he ever indicated a willingness to furnish any information about any prior criminal activities and stated further that he was not desirous of revealing any information along this line to the FBI or any other law enforcement agency."

The case was, as the Bureau likes to say, closed. In its way, it would be remembered with both fondness and horror.*

* Gargano escaped from the Marion penitentiary again in October 1975. But the FBI was denied the pleasure of recapturing him this time; he was taken into custody by Greene County, Indiana, sheriff's deputies.

II

Scenes of Bureau Life

WHAT SHALL IT BE?
LAW & ORDER
or
CHANGE & CHAOS
— *Poster in Los Angeles Field Office,*
Federal Bureau of Investigation

CHRISTMASTIME IN LOS ANGELES . . .

Eight women, well dressed in the style of a-special-occasion-at-work-today, trying to act demure but tittering nervously, file into the office of Special-Agent-in-Charge Elmer F. Linberg for a solemn morning ceremony. The setting is formal. There is an American flag in the corner. Photographs on the wall give equal billing to J. Edgar Hoover and Clarence M. Kelley, with no hint that there was a turbulent fourteen-month hiatus between their reigns over the FBI. The desk is stocked with a substantial collection of books written by or in praise of the FBI. Off to the side is a blue plastic wastebasket with a white stripe around the top, the indication that it is an authorized depository for "confidential" trash, which must be burned or otherwise disposed of in a secure manner.

Carol A. Harvey, forty, has spent half her life as a "clerical employee" of the Bureau and now, on the twentieth anniversary — to the day — of her employment, she is being honored by her bosses and her peers. Miss Harvey had completed two years of college in Pasadena back in 1953 when, at the urging of two men she knew who were planning to apply later for training as special agents, she looked into job opportunities with the Los Angeles Field Division. Here she has been ever since, in her first full-time job and her only one.

According to one agent who has recruited clerks in the Los Angeles area, the FBI is looking for "that special kind of person" with "that sparkle in the eye." Miss Harvey, who has a prim appearance but an enthusiastic manner, seems to have filled the bill. She has advanced steadily within the office. At first, holding a GS-2 rank on the civil service scale, she pushed a messenger buggy, then moved on to "searching" — checking the local indices for previous references in the files to names appearing in new investigations and communications. Later she would handle the office mail, the confidential files themselves, and then serve for eight years as a radio dispatcher of the office cars. "That was my favorite job," she confides; "you have to enjoy it to do it well. You must keep cool when it's really busy. If you're running a bank robbery [dispatching agent cars, already on the street, to the scene of a crime just committed], someone's life could depend on it." For the past four years, she has been supervising some sixty employees working with the office files, an important job because "paperwork" — how to create it, handle it, digest it, and dispose of it — is at the heart of everything in the FBI.

After clearing his throat several times, Linberg reads aloud a letter that has come in from Washington for Miss Harvey:

PERSONAL

Miss Carol A. Harvey
Federal Bureau of Investigation
Los Angeles, California

Dear Miss Harvey:

Twenty years ago you entered on duty with the Federal Bureau of Investigation. I wish to take this opportunity to extend my heartiest congratulations on your anniversary and to present to you the Bureau's Twenty-Year Service Award Key.

I am constantly aware of the fact that the Bureau's progress through the years has been made possible by the wholehearted willingness with which our many loyal and conscientious associates have dedicated themselves to the greater interest of our organization. I want you to know that I am not unmindful of your selfless contributions in this regard.

I trust that through your continued association with the Bureau you will assist in handling our increasing obligations.

With best wishes and kind regards,

Sincerely,
[signed]   Clarence M. Kelley
Director

13

Linberg does not say it, of course, but he realizes — and perhaps Miss Harvey, after all these years, shares the secret — that this is but one of several routine form letters sent out from FBI headquarters like clockwork on the appropriate occasions. Every employee gets one after ten, twenty, and twenty-five years of service. (On the thirtieth anniversary, the employee gets not merely a letter, but a teletype from the director, sent over the Bureau's encrypted communications network.) Other letters note the birth of an agent's child or a statistically significant wedding anniversary. All are perfectly typed, because clerical errors, under the standard established by Hoover over nearly half a century, are theoretically not tolerated.

Miss Harvey's letter, like those the twenty thousand other employees of the Bureau receive on special occasions, bears Director Kelley's signature, or a very good replica of it. Given the number of congratulatory letters, he probably did not really sign it; more likely, the job was done by a machine like the ones that sign senators' and congressmen's names, or by an expert forger who works in the FBI Laboratory. But the thought is there, as is the cultivation of institutional fealty. These matters, Linberg tells a visitor in an aside, are "important in building up morale. It is part of the Bureau's overall employee relations program. . . . Many employees wear their service keys with pride." Indeed, if Miss Harvey follows the practice of most of her colleagues, she will frame the letter and treasure it. The service key will probably be mounted as a pin or go onto a charm bracelet with the others — all formally gifts from the FBI Recreation Association, an employee organization whose funds come from the two-dollar annual "voluntary" contribution of every FBI employee* and from such special grants as a share of the royalties from a book once ghostwritten for Hoover.

Standing behind his desk, Linberg accompanies the presentation with a little speech. He pays homage to the steady and sturdy leadership of Hoover over the years, the kind of unwavering devotion and discipline that became a model for exemplary workers like Miss Harvey, and he adds, to the nods and smiles of his little audience, that it is "good that Mr. Kelley is moving slowly in making changes." An office photographer takes a group picture and one of the beaming Miss Harvey with each of her friends. Everyone will get copies, and some of the pictures may appear in *The Investigator,* official publication of the Recreation Association. One of the women has also brought her own camera, and the celebration ends in a flurry of flashbulbs.

Carol Harvey's anniversary is one of several special events in the

* An estimated 98 percent of FBI employees contribute to the FBIRA.

field office on this particular day. A little card at the Information Desk indicates that an agent is retiring after thirty years ("So Long, Gang — Thanks for Carrying Me All These Years, Jerry Moore"). And chief clerk Eileen Ryan is stepping down after forty-two years of faithfully serving the Bureau. She became chief of the Los Angeles clerical force just at the time Carol Harvey was joining it (her departure now leads to Miss Harvey's promotion to "assistant chief clerk"), and before that she spent twenty-two years in the Chicago Field Office. There have already been several parties for Miss Ryan, and now the agent responsible for the office's press relations wonders how he can "capitalize" on Miss Ryan's retirement in order to give the FBI's local image a shot in the arm. And well he can, because she is an old-school type, an almost theatrical character, who still has "that sparkle in the eye." She knows the stories, good and bad, but tells only the former and smiles a coy and titillating smile as she reviews the latter in her mind. "It's good to go out when you're at your peak," says Miss Ryan, thumbing through a book she will use to study for the Law School Admission Test although she is in her sixties. Like other stalwarts, Miss Ryan is proud of the FBI and of the young agents she helped along in their early days who now have major responsibilities. She singles out as the most important Bureau accomplishment during her tenure the computerization of records, and praises the assistance newly provided by the California Law Enforcement Telecommunications System, a statewide data bank that feeds into the federal network. One day, she says brightly, perhaps within five years, all of the FBI's indices will be computerized, and it will be possible to "type right into Washington" and obtain an instant summary of all the FBI's information about, and references to, an individual. "It's going to make it more and more difficult to be a criminal," she predicts with a wink.

Elmer Linberg is a slight, unassuming-looking man, a native of the Pennsylvania coal country who worked his way up the hard way and who owes much of his status and station in life to the FBI. This is his third tour of duty in Los Angeles; his Bureau career spans thirty-three years, eight of them in Mississippi during the years of the civil rights strife. Despite his title, he is not really *the* special-agent-in-charge, but one of three. The three are actually all assistants to the local chief who, because Los Angeles is such a large and important office, has recently been advanced to the title and rank of assistant director of the FBI. New York is the only other office so organized. (The thirteen other assistant directors are all at headquarters in Washington.) Linberg's bailiwick is the office's criminal section, handling

15

such matters as kidnappings, extortions, crimes aboard aircraft, and interstate transportation of stolen motor vehicles.

Linberg is in charge of today's ceremony for Carol Harvey by default. The other top men in the field office, like many of the agents, are taking vacation days, not because the law enforcement business has fallen off during the holiday season (it hasn't), but rather because they, like most other federal employees, would lose their annual leave time if they fail to use it up before the year is out. The assistant-director-in-charge is in Texas visiting his family. He will be leaving Los Angeles soon anyway, because he is caught up in one of the chain-reaction transfers that hit the upper- and middle-management ranks of the Bureau every few months. He will go to the FBI Academy in Quantico, Virginia, to head up the agency's Training Division, still as an assistant director; his predecessor there, said to be unimaginative and unresponsive to new trends in education, has been kicked upstairs to become one of the two assistants-to-the-director, in a Kelley revival of an important Hoover-era administrative position — higher ranking than the fifteen assistant directors. Coming to take over in Los Angeles is the man who has been special-agent-in-charge in Philadelphia. The assistant director in charge of the Office of Planning and Evaluation at headquarters had an opportunity to keep his rank by coming to run the Los Angeles office, but he preferred to stay in the East because of a serious illness in his family, so he accepted a cut in pay and rank by going to Philadelphia instead. The new man who will head the Office of Planning and Evaluation is coming from San Antonio, where he was special-agent-in-charge, and the Bureau grapevine has it that Kelley's desire to bring him to headquarters is what started it all.

The day is not all pomp. Calls come in on two bank robberies. Eight FBI cars respond to the first, at a Wells Fargo branch office on Sunset Boulevard in Hollywood, but the culprit seems to have gotten away in a yellow Volkswagen. The agents, working with local police, will interview every employee of the bank, as well as the victim-teller, pick up the film from the surveillance camera, and develop enough of a report to permit comparison with the modus operandi of other known or wanted bank robbers in the area. Ninety minutes later, it is reported that another holdup has just occurred at a savings-and-loan association on Santa Monica Boulevard. Squad supervisor Jim Cassagnola reaches a teller at the savings-and-loan by telephone while the robbery is still in progress; suddenly he looks up from the phone, a smile on his face, and declares, "The PD [police department] is on the scene and they've got him in custody." The crowd that has gathered in the corridor outside Cassagnola's office cheers and applauds. "This is only the second time in my career when I've heard of the bandit being caught in the bank," says Cassagnola. Four Bureau cars have arrived at the savings-and-loan, and one agent is dispatched to interview the suspect at the police station. Under an agreement with the local California authorities, the case will automatically be prosecuted in federal court.

Bank robbery is a big business in Los Angeles, because there are so many small branch banks and there is so much money around. The recent average has been one a day for every day in the year in the territory covered by the Los Angeles Field Division — north in a strip along the coast nearly to Monterey, south almost to San Diego, east to the Nevada and Arizona borders. The biggest year was 1968, when there were 381 bank robberies in the territory, as compared with only 96 during all of 1962. That's why the agents call it "the bank robbery capital of the world." There were ten false alarms earlier in the day before the two "good" ones. Cassagnola is proud of the statistics, which show that over the ten-year period from 1963 to 1973 the solution rate for bank robberies in the Los Angeles Field Division has been 82.8 percent.

Later in the afternoon, there is a surge of activity in Linberg's office when two agents, experts in the field of interstate transportation of obscene matter (ITOM), return from seizing a copy of *The Devil in Miss Jones* at a Beverly Hills movie theater. It was nothing dramatic, they report; they merely executed a search warrant they had obtained from a federal magistrate after watching the film several times. The theater was expecting the agents, and the entire process took only forty-five minutes; there were no arrests and there would be no formal announcement of the raid. The agents would now await the development of evidence concerning the distributor in New York, but they are frankly skeptical about the prospects for a conviction. They had obtained only three ITOM convictions thus far in the new fiscal year. Nonetheless, supported by the United States attorney for the Central District of California and the appropriate authorities at the Justice Department in Washington, they feel it is important to press their efforts against films they regard as offensive.* While the case develops,

---

* As one expert who handles ITOM cases at FBI headquarters puts it, the Bureau's general definition of hard-core pornography is "anything that depicts an actual penetration situation or an oral copulation . . . or focuses on the genital area and shows ejaculation." Each field office has some leeway, however, and its choices are based in part on the attitude of the local U.S. attorney toward obscenity. Before proceeding against any film, agents are expected to "view" it and report their observations on a Form 302.

of course, the theater will obtain and exhibit another print of *The Devil in Miss Jones.*

But these developments seem minute, and the activity around them inconsequential, in the sepulchral emptiness of the vast field office. The large bullpens, where agents normally sit, four to a phone, at identical government-issue steel desks, are nearly empty. Agent "workboxes," containing only what is absolutely needed on pending cases (the rest is in the files, open or closed), are tucked away in specially fortified closets.

It is a proud office, Los Angeles, which has survived embarrassing publicity involving former Special-Agent-in-Charge Wesley G. Grapp, who monitored and sometimes recorded agent phone calls and allegedly traded on the FBI's name to obtain large unsecured loans from southern California banks. With Grapp out of the way — he retired, rather than accept banishment to the provinces as a "street agent" — Los Angeles is a desirable assignment again. The work, according to the classic FBI definition, is good. And the statistics are great. Ask any supervisor, and he can produce a sheet from his desk drawer which shows that in Fiscal Year 1973 alone, 2,740 fugitives were "located" in the territory — more, it is chauvinistically contended, than by the New York and Chicago offices combined. There are thirteen thousand "cases" of one sort or another pending at any given time. "A lot of people come to Los Angeles to commit a crime," remarks Chester St. Vincent, a legendary supervisor who is thought to have handled perhaps more major cases than anyone else now in the active service of the FBI.

The office occupies four floors of a modern federal building near the UCLA campus in the Westwood section; it has a full-time nurse and an intricate security system that includes closed-circuit television at every entrance. The size, Linberg acknowledges, sometimes requires "the big corporate approach," unlike the traditional FBI office where everyone is supposed to be one big happy family; but the bosses have tried to remedy this during the holiday season with elaborate Christmas decorations and a dinner dance on board the *Queen Mary.*

Change, as Linberg notes, is coming in small doses. Coffee is now permitted at the desks. Senior officials, and others with special permission, may take their Bureau cars home at night. Two female agents have arrived and are being assigned work much like their male counterparts. There is a subtle shift away from "security" work, with more agents taking on responsibilities for criminal cases. The office is atwitter with the news that permission has just been granted by headquarters to assign a full-time stenographer to the resident agency in Santa Ana; this means that agents assigned there will no longer have to tie up their phone lines into Los Angeles every time they want to dictate a report or memorandum, and that someone will be available to answer the phone in Santa Ana if all the agents are out working on cases. The plan is also to branch out and station some of the Los Angeles agents in "satellite" offices in the suburbs, but there had been trouble finding office space. That problem was remedied in Van Nuys, however, when the local police department found room for the FBI after an agent who is an expert on sex crimes helped solve some mysterious rape cases. There is no federal jurisdiction over rape, except on a federal reservation, so the action was merely catalogued, and justified, in the category of "police assistance."

But some things don't change. The new credentials being issued to agents, carrying color photographs for the first time, have the words "U.S. Department of Justice" below, rather than above, "Federal Bureau of Investigation."

"I intend to stay, at least for a while," says Carol Harvey, speaking of her warm feelings toward the FBI. "I can't think of a better place to be. . . . The people are unbelievable; you don't find them like that anywhere else." It is an attitude that many people, on all levels of this field office, express.

Although only a clerk, Miss Harvey met Hoover on several occasions when he stopped in to "inspect" the Los Angeles office during his annual trip to vacation in La Jolla. "We here in this office felt his presence," she recalls; "it was amazing how many people he would remember each time from previous years." She became concerned over the embattled position Hoover was in during his last years. "I didn't approve of [the criticisms of Hoover]. If there were some things, possibly — well, he was not the youngest man, but he had done such a beautiful job over the years and that should not be knocked down. He ran a tight ship, and I feel that was necessary in an agency of this kind."

Has there been a decline in the performance of the FBI since Hoover's death? "No, I don't think so. People are well trained enough to function perfectly well on their own momentum. . . . Mr. Kelley seems good. He plans his moves before he makes them. Perhaps he will provide the kind of strong, silent leadership which we were used to." As for L. Patrick Gray III, who served as acting director for fifty-one weeks after Hoover's death and ultimately resigned when it was discovered that he had burned documents related to the Watergate scandals — "I was impressed with Mr. Gray when I met him, too," says Miss Harvey. "At the time, I think everybody was. He was a dynamic speaker . . . you paid attention, you listened. . . . We were all very hopeful at the time, but became quite disillusioned with events later on."

Musing about the changing role of women in the FBI, Miss Harvey says, "I have no desire ever to become an agent. . . . I am perfectly willing to let the man carry the gun. I am not a great believer in Women's Lib. There are plenty of jobs that women can do to assist. . . . But times do change, and you have to go along with it. This is a whole new generation. . . ."

Carol Harvey turns to her visitor. "I appreciated meeting you today," she says softly, "and I hope you will speak well of us."

◆

Three months later in Quantico, Virginia . . .

The whisper in the audience is that "if Mr. Hoover could see this, he would turn over in his grave." A class of twenty-seven new agents has just completed training and, with appropriate ceremony, is being sent out across the length and breadth of the land to slay the dragons. What is unusual is that the group includes a number of blacks, two women, and several Mexican-Americans and others with Spanish surnames. There is even a graduate of Boalt Hall, the law school of the notoriously left-wing Berkeley campus of the University of California. ("I was one of the few Republicans there," says Russell Atkinson rather defensively; "I favor law enforcement. . . . I am pretty conservative in outlook.") As they parade across the stage in the auditorium of the FBI Academy here — some wearing bright, modish clothes and platform shoes, smiling and hamming it up for relatives who have come to watch — they look almost like a caricature of "the new Bureau," which is meant to be less regimented, more relaxed, and a better reflection of the population it serves. The "class counselor" is also a young black agent, and his final pep talks are full of encouragement rather than the traditional warnings to new agents about last-minute mistakes that could cause them to be busted out of their new career.

Training has taken sixteen weeks and has been in spanking new classrooms outfitted with educational technology so sophisticated — videotapes, dial-up cassette machines, and the like — that many of the instructors, almost all agents themselves, do not yet understand how to use it. The curriculum has been updated, with the old unit on how to handle "ambush" situations dropped as out of date, for example, and a new one added on basic interviewing technique, an area in which agents have recently been found lacking. So the trainees have been required to interview each other in long sessions and then to watch instant replays on videotape. They have done simulated investigations in a "crime scene laboratory" and even watched the operation of a crooked gambling table. They have all qualified in the gym — some of them, admittedly, only in the last weeks of training — and worked hard on the Bureau's own unique firearms course, which teaches, among other things, that one always shoots to kill. On their last day they were up in the "sniper tower" on the firearms range, learning how to handle potential urban disrupters.

These people are probably as enthusiastic today as any who have ever entered in service with the FBI. Charles Gabriel, of Syracuse, New York, has a cousin who is an agent, and he says unabashedly that "I have geared my whole life to my ambition of joining the Bureau"; on receiving his credentials, he becomes one of a handful of Jewish agents. Several members of the class have already been working in law enforcement, and Albert Rodriguez, a thirty-two-year-old policeman from San Antonio, explains that "as long as I am going to make a career of this kind of work, I thought I should get to the top law enforcement agency in the world, one with pride and integrity." Ralph Young, a black police detective from Pittsburgh, is the third generation in his family to serve with that department. "It's the only profession I know," he says in explaining his decision to move on and join the FBI; "I want to be with the best. The Bureau is the best." Young and classmate William Vanderpool, an alcoholic control board officer from Florida, are special cases: both, as young officers, attended the FBI National Academy, the Bureau's special three-month training course for members of local law enforcement agencies. Sufficiently inspired by that exposure, they went home and completed college degrees in order to qualify for agents' training. Although they will have to go through the same informal initiation period in their first assignments as anyone else, as former policemen they are considered especially valuable material for the FBI. Vanderpool has turned down two better-paying job offers to choose the Bureau; others in the class have taken a pay cut by leaving the Marine Corps for the FBI.

21

The women seem to have made their decision largely out of curiosity. Mary Denn, of Utica, New York, was "not that happy in education" (she was a counselor at a women's college) and felt "ready for something much different." Sheila Horan, of Hartford, for her part, was a graduate student in education and psychology and decided that law enforcement "just seemed like a good field at this point for women." Her mother, once over the initial surprise at her daughter's application and acceptance to become an agent, "was so excited that she wanted to join me." Each woman has made it through training without any obvious physical or emotional scars ("I was no lonelier than anyone else," says Denn), but looks ahead with some trepidation to arrival in a medium-sized field office where she will be the first female agent to serve.

On the whole, says Martin McNerney, who is in charge of new agents' training, "this is a real fine class. We get an opportunity to pick and choose and be very selective, and this is a good group." Only one prospective agent, also a former police officer, had dropped out — in the first week, when he was apparently unable to meet the physical requirements. As McNerney talks, a young man arrives with a plastic bag to empty his confidential wastebasket; the trash collector, McNerney points out proudly, is a graduate of Southern Methodist University who is putting in three years as a "clerical employee" at Quantico — his means of qualifying for agents' training.

The new agents have already been issued their weapons and given their first office assignments. Today's is really only a symbolic exercise during which they will receive their credentials; but with families present and cars packed and ready to go, it is a somewhat emotional occasion, a true turning point in the lives of these people. Delivering a sort of commencement speech is "Mr. National Academy," James V. Cotter, who has run the police-training program for more than a decade. "In a few minutes, gang, you're gonna receive the very cherished credentials that identify you as a special agent of the Federal Bureau of Investigation . . . that make you dedicated, envied, and admired," says Cotter, a sentimental man who loves the Bureau and its ways. "Your badge is the majesty of the law . . . no longer will you have the freedom to let your personal feelings and prejudices affect your actions . . . have patience with policy, but have the courage to suggest change . . . it's now time to join the varsity, even as a rookie." Cotter pauses for a moment to ask for contributions to help the family of a policeman slain in Dayton, Ohio, a day earlier. Later, he turns to the audience, points to the class, and says, "Look well at these young people . . . the future of the organization is vested in their Fidelity, Bravery, and Integrity."

◆

A few weeks later in St. Paul . . .

The scene is peculiar for a federal courtroom. Agents rush in, deliver documents to the prosecutors, and then rush out to transmit requests for more. Defense legal workers hold an urgent meeting in a corner and send a delegate to the attorneys on their side with a new idea. The open sarcasm and bitterness between the two sides is far more dramatic than the testimony, which drones on and is frequently interrupted by conferences at the bench, supposedly confidential but perfectly audible to everyone in the room — especially whenever the judge, in a stage whisper, proclaims himself "sick and tired" of something. There is not an empty seat, but hardly anyone seems to be listening to the proceedings; instead, there is a low murmur rather like that in a baseball stadium.

"I've never been in a case like this, Your Honor," complains William Kunstler, chief defense counsel. "Well, believe me, I've never been in a case like this before, either," replies U.S. District Court Judge Fred Nichol with a wave of his robe. The prosecutors just glower, at each other and at everyone else.

It is the Wounded Knee case, the trial of Dennis Banks and Russell Means, leaders of the American Indian Movement, on charges of conspiracy, burglary, larceny, assault on federal officers, impeding federal officers in the course of a civil disorder, and theft of motor vehicles — the first of several scheduled trials growing out of AIM's seventy-one-day siege of the hamlet of Wounded Knee, South Dakota, in 1973. It is an emotional case that raises touchy questions of old broken treaties, poor relations between whites and Indians, and internal Indian disputes. But it is some time since the jury has been in the courtroom, since the last substantive testimony was taken. The trial has been interrupted for a special hearing on defense motions charging misconduct by the FBI.

The Bureau has been bedeviled by a series of damaging revelations and allegations: Agents had added notations and otherwise altered a document that was a potential piece of evidence. At a Wounded Knee roadblock, agents had listened in on a party-line extension telephone and reported on conversations coming from the occupied village, and the defense is calling this wiretapping. There are

23

charges that the FBI has "invaded" the defense camp, interfering with privileged communications between defendants and their attorneys.* The Bureau seems generally to have held back from the prosecution, and therefore from the court and the defense, many documents that are relevant to the case; some are being turned over months after they were supposed to have been presented in compliance with a court order.

As a result, one agent after another is paraded to the witness stand to face questioning by the dreaded Kunstler — in agent lore, to survive his cross-examination is almost the equivalent of surviving an airplane hijacking crisis — and by conspiracy theorist Mark Lane. Some agents, the old-timers who are afraid to go beyond testimony that has been specifically authorized in advance, seem frightened and almost pathetic; others, mostly young agents whose mettle was tested at Wounded Knee and who consider the hearing a waste of time, seem cocky and impudent. Both groups sometimes give answers that are literal to the point of evasiveness. Kunstler, meanwhile, has turned his anger at the FBI into a crusade that runs parallel to the trial. Just a few days ago, for example, he told the St. Paul Rotary Club that unless the Bureau is controlled, any organization or social club could become the subject of FBI harassment in the manner of AIM and other radical groups. The Rotarians were receptive to the argument.

Judge Nichol, too, is adding fat to the fire. Ever since he arrived here from Sioux Falls, after the defense was granted a change of venue, he has been quite vocal. In one report from the trial that circulated widely around the nation, he declared that the FBI has "deteriorated badly"; he says frequently that he is not sure the agency can be trusted. The judge has ordered that all Bureau files relating to the case be brought to a central location and kept intact, lest they be tampered with. Nichol was appointed to the bench by President Lyndon B. Johnson, at the urging of Senator George S. McGovern (D–South Dakota), and he delights in making allusions to the Watergate scandal that is unfolding in Washington and hurting the Republicans. Each time he seems to tar the FBI with a Watergate brush.

In a small FBI office one flight up from the courtroom, a duplicating machine clicks away to keep up with the judge's orders to supply newly discovered documents. Phone calls come from and go to FBI headquarters in Washington. In this office and across the street in an apartment rented by the Bureau — strategically located for a bird's-

---

* A year later, Douglass Durham, an Indian who served as AIM's chief of security during the Wounded Knee trial, declared that he had been working as an FBI informant at the same time.

24

eye view of comings and goings at the courthouse and of demonstrations connected with the trial — agents complain that they are being unjustifiably accused and mishandled.

The FBI, in a word, is on trial.

Back on the other side of the Mississippi River, on the third floor of the federal building in downtown Minneapolis, things are quieter, if not much calmer. The central attraction in the waiting room of the FBI field office is the J. Edgar Hoover Practical Pistol Course Trophy, a marksmanship award, which was returned to Minneapolis in 1973 after an eight-year tour of other field offices. There is a poster with pictures of the FBI Employee Service Awards, a display board with photographs of the current Ten Most Wanted fugitives (six of them elusive underground members of the New Left), and a map that pinpoints the headquarters cities of all fifty-nine field divisions in the country and the locations of the smaller offices in Minnesota and North and South Dakota that report to Minneapolis. The overcrowded decorations help distract attention from a threadbare carpet that is taped together in places.

Special-Agent-in-Charge Joseph Trimbach has a tall stack of papers on his desk and several concentric black circles around his eyes; he says he has not had a decent night's sleep in two weeks. He presides over the field division that has the largest geographical responsibility and, for the moment, some of the FBI's biggest problems. "We are not operating as a normal field office, and we haven't for some time," he explains; rather, the office is stumbling from one crisis to another, with the Wounded Knee situation a brooding presence that will not go away.

Trimbach had arrived in Minneapolis — his first assignment as an SAC — on February 12, 1973, and the next day he was sent to Rapid City, South Dakota, to head up a federal antiriot investigation of an earlier AIM-inspired demonstration in Custer. One job assigned to his task force of twenty-five agents was to guess what the militant Indians' next move would be on the Pine Ridge Sioux Reservation. The question was answered fourteen days later, when AIM occupied Wounded Knee and took eleven hostages. Trimbach's investigation and intelligence mission turned into a combat role, and he was sent reinforcements from most areas of the country, primarily young agents who, instead of their usual discreet assignments, found themselves fighting in trenches on land they were unfamiliar with and untrained to defend. What most people, including Judge Nichol, do not seem to understand, Trimbach complains, is that "these agents were operating in a

25

wartime atmosphere," performing a job that might ordinarily be assigned to the military if the opposing forces were not Indians. If these
agents violated the rulebook — by, for example, picking up a telephone on which they might learn something about what "the enemy"
would do next — it was because they felt their lives were threatened,
he insists. And, he says, if the memoranda they dictated to stenographers after coming off twelve-hour or longer shifts were not perfectly
accurate and did not conform to the usual standards, it was because
they were thinking about getting some precious sleep rather than
about preparing a perfect case for later prosecution.

After a few weeks, Pat Gray relieved Trimbach of his duties at
Wounded Knee and sent in another special-agent-in-charge. The command was subsequently rotated several more times among ranking
Bureau personnel from various offices, while Justice Department officials negotiated with AIM leaders for an end to the occupation. Responsibility for the case was formally returned to the Minneapolis
Field Office only in late May. Thus, Trimbach points out, there is no
single "case agent" who is familiar with all the relevant materials and
paperwork, as would usually be true. Even as he speaks, a special
detail of agents is poring through five thousand bound folders, containing some 316,000 separate entries, all related to Wounded Knee, in
a search for other items that might have to be turned over in the
proceedings before Judge Nichol. Trimbach insists that nothing has
been intentionally withheld from the court.

The special-agent-in-charge speaks of the dedication in his office
to the Wounded Knee case. Two young women, clerical employees
from San Francisco who were temporarily dispatched to help the FBI
contingent during the siege, have now been transferred to Minneapolis, at their own request, because of a desire to see the case through
and the malefactors punished. Trimbach knows the prospects for the
conviction of Means and Banks have faded, but he worries now that
Judge Nichol, in a fit of pique and with a new tirade against the
Bureau, will dismiss the charges before all the government's evidence
has even been presented. "If that case is thrown out," he says, a look of
gloom on his face, "there are people in this office who will cry."

Other problems have intruded during Trimbach's brief tenure —
"PINAP," for example, the Bureau's official nickname for the 1972
kidnapping of Virginia Piper, wife of a wealthy Minneapolis investment banker. Piper paid a million dollars, then the highest kidnap
ransom ever, for her release. Trimbach inherited that case, but it is still
not solved, although an entire squad of a dozen agents, working from
their own designated room, continues to follow up every minute lead.

A few months back, when some of the ransom money began to surface in southern Minnesota, Trimbach thought his men might be only a few days, or even hours, behind the kidnappers; but then the press printed stories about the appearance of the currency and — in Trimbach's view as a direct result — the kidnappers were scared off. By now, he speculates, the rest of the ransom may have been sold off to the Mafia at a discount and shipped overseas to foreign bank accounts and vaults. But the squad will be kept on the case for the indefinite future; the FBI expects its people to solve big ones like that.

Some months previously two escapees from a county jail in northern Minnesota held an entire family hostage in their farmhouse at Wadena. After the situation became especially dramatic because of nationwide television coverage, Assistant-Special-Agent-in-Charge Phil Enlow managed to negotiate the release of most of the family's children. But the crisis was finally defused not by any grand FBI strategy, but when one of the gunmen fell asleep.

More recently, just as all hell was beginning to break loose in the St. Paul courtroom, there was yet another kidnapping, of Eunice Kronholm, wife of another Minneapolis banker. The field office's resources were mobilized on that case, too — one stenographer tells of working through the weekend and helping on a nighttime surveillance, without a cent of extra pay — but it turned out to be a case more to the FBI's liking. Mrs. Kronholm, after persuading her kidnappers to watch a telecast featuring the Reverend Billy Graham, had talked her way into an early release. When she stumbled into a suburban grocery store and called home to say that she had been freed, Trimbach and Enlow, rather than call the local police department in the area of the grocery store to pick her up, jumped in a car and drove the thirteen miles to do it themselves. That way, the FBI didn't have to split the credit and attention on the case. Three suspects have now been arrested and all of the ransom recovered but for $100, which one of the kidnappers spent on a new suit so that he might look good for his arrest. Mrs. Kronholm and her family, at a press conference after her release, roundly praised the FBI; this week, after testifying before the appropriate state and federal grand juries, she is touring the field office to thank personally the agents who worked on the case.

The only embarrassing sidelight of the Kronholm affair is that newspaper reporters, able to monitor the FBI's radio communications about the ransom drop on citizens'-band short-wave radios, had followed the agent posing as banker Kronholm to the drop-off point and then published stories and maps with the details before Mrs. Kronholm was released. Trimbach thinks this may have endangered the victim's life, and the incident has set off a dispute with the local press over the proper guidelines for covering breaking crime stories involving the FBI.

But then, most things that Trimbach touches these days seem to turn sour. He has been pilloried by Kunstler for a quiet visit to the editors of the St. Paul newspapers, requesting an opportunity to respond to any attacks made on the FBI outside the courtroom during the Wounded Knee trial. And twitted by Judge Nichol, because the teletypes and memoranda sent out asking agents to notify Trimbach if they had eavesdropped on the controversial telephone at the Wounded Knee roadblock warned that the matter could result in dismissal of the case — in the judge's words, "a not-so-subtle way of discouraging the agents from coming forward." And resented by agents in his own office, for remaining aloof and unconcerned about their day-to-day problems. Even a program about the FBI that he recently encouraged a Minneapolis television station to do was disappointing to Trimbach, "because it was not one hundred percent pro-FBI."

The next morning, Trimbach is gone — summoned to Washington overnight for a summit conference between Justice Department and FBI officials over how to comply with Judge Nichol's order that all of the Bureau's files on the Wounded Knee case, including those that reveal the identities of confidential informants, be turned over for inspection by the federal prosecutors handling the case. Nichol wants the files reviewed for any other possible FBI improprieties and for materials the defense lawyers may be entitled to have. That is not the way it usually works in cases developed by the FBI. It is a time-honored practice, astonishingly enough, that the Bureau unilaterally decides what items will be useful to the prosecutors, separates them from the file, and makes only them available.

It is this court order that has provoked the greatest concern in the FBI ranks; as one veteran in the Minneapolis office puts it, "If they get a wedge in this case, it will set a dangerous precedent for all law enforcement agencies." The FBI's "raw files" are not routinely inspected by the lawyers who try federal cases, and the names of the much-treasured confidential informants, unless they are to be witnesses in open court, are never revealed without the informants' express permission. One problem, of course, is that the informants themselves are often underworld figures, and the circumstances under which they provide the information are cloudy. Some informants, motivated by money, will say what they think the agents want to hear. On other occasions, agents may use the term "confidential informant" as a cover for some extralegal or illegal method of obtaining information. The Bureau has rarely trusted such inside details to prosecutors, who often, as in the Wounded Knee case, include young attorneys who may exploit the publicity to build a reputation or launch a political career.

The Washington meeting, according to later accounts, is a tense one, with the Justice Department representatives, from Attorney General William Saxbe down to the assistant United States attorneys from South Dakota, arguing that the special circumstances might merit making an exception to the rule. But the FBI representatives, including Director Clarence Kelley, are adamant, and they insist that individual pledges of confidentiality and protection to informants and sources cannot be broken in wholesale fashion. Already, they claim, Nichol's order and the threat that the files could be turned over in open court have brought calls to Minneapolis and other field offices from informants, unconnected with Wounded Knee, who fear that they may need protection if their relationship with the Bureau is exposed.*

Finally, an uneasy compromise is hammered out: the prosecutors will see the general files on the Wounded Knee case, but without any informants' names. If a particular bit of information seems crucial to the attorneys, they will ask the Bureau for the name of the person who provided it, and the FBI will decide, on an individual basis, whether to reveal it. But whether or not the Justice Department officials or the judge realize it, the FBI has reached its own internal conclusion: should an informant decline to agree that his name will be revealed, or should the Bureau determine for its own reasons of security that it should not be, the FBI has no intention of giving the information to the prosecutors or anyone else — even at the risk of precipitating dismissal of the entire case for defying the judge's order. And the Bureau men feel secure in their conclusion. They know that it would be virtually impossible for anyone else, unauthorized, to get into the informant files; that the Justice Department, embattled as it is because of Watergate, would not want to risk a public confrontation with the FBI over the issue; and that in the event of such a confrontation, the Bureau has powerful resources for stirring congressional and public support for its firm position.

The FBI usually has its way.

* The reason for the Bureau's extreme testiness on this occasion became clear only later — it feared that Douglass Durham's dual role would be revealed in the midst of the trial, sabotaging the prosecution.

"We're going to learn a lot more about the FBI before this thing's over," says Judge Nichol in an informal conversation alone in his chambers.

The judge acknowledges that he has seen nothing to indicate a deliberate, purposeful attempt by the Bureau to deceive or defy him. But he is deeply troubled. "There may be something wrong with the [FBI's] system," he observes; "almost every day something new comes in that was just turned up. . . . They're not as careful as they were twenty-three years ago, when I was an assistant United States attorney and depended on them. . . . Their 302s [forms on which agents report the results of interviews] are not as careful, not as accurate. Time after time, in this case and others, defense counsel make mincemeat out of them and call attention to their errors. . . . The thing that gripes my ass is that they think they can't make mistakes. Goddammit, they do make mistakes . . . and guys like Kunstler can destroy them."

Nichol allows as how he has little faith in Kunstler, Lane, or the other defense lawyers, "who started out harassing me pretty bad, trying to get me to explode at them." But too often, the judge continues, "the FBI are like the Indians. They take the view that if you're not with them a hundred percent, you're against them. Trimbach and Enlow probably think that I'm out to get them. Well, no, I'm not. As a matter of fact, I would like to see them shape up. . . . From all that I can find out, Clarence Kelley is trying to do a fine job, and I have no evidence to the contrary . . . but I do think some of the steam has been taken out of the FBI."

One of the things that upsets him most, Nichol says, is the disclosure of "counterintelligence programs" conducted by the Bureau against New Left and black organizations during the late 1960s. "The faking of evidence, harassment, that is going pretty damn far. . . . I don't think the FBI are venal . . . but I don't want to live in a police state. That [threat] is more likely to come in this country from fascists, from big corporations, than from the communists and leftists. . . . The interlocking directorships of corporations, why they are more powerful than United States senators, maybe even than the President sometimes. The FBI is not worried at all about those people."

Some Bureau agents, meanwhile, are conducting their own whispering campaign against the judge — suggesting, for example, that he cannot possibly be objective because of his wife's involvement in Indian rights causes. But Nichol would have the last word. He denounced the FBI in court for permitting a key prosecution witness in the trial, Louis Moves Camp, to drink heavily while in Bureau custody, and for attempting to influence a district attorney in Wisconsin to drop a rape charge that was pending against the witness. Finally dismissing all charges against Means and Banks on September 16, 1974, after one juror had a stroke and the government refused to accept a verdict rendered by the remaining eleven, Nichol said, "It's hard for me to believe that the FBI, which I have revered for many years, has fallen to that low an estate."

"Half the stuff that went on out there [at Wounded Knee] is not even on paper," says an agent who was assigned there during the confrontation with AIM, as he and his friends gather in a bar near the field office after a rough day in court. Another agrees: "Wounded Knee is totally atypical. It is unlike anything the FBI has ever encountered before or will confront in the future." They feel misunderstood. Unappreciated. Poorly represented in the courtroom by prosecutors who do not themselves really seem to understand the circumstances under which the agents had worked at Wounded Knee. Savagely attacked by defense attorneys who they feel are exploiting the trial to keep AIM and themselves in the news. Abused by a judge who seems to jump to conclusions about the Bureau, all negative, and scarcely exercises any control over his courtroom.

It is the FBI against the world, as the world is seen from the Twin Cities, and there seems no easy way out. The problem is complicated by the fact that the case involves American Indians, who have been neglected and mistreated by whites for centuries and readily stir sympathy when up against the monolithic federal government. "There was nothing to negotiate at Wounded Knee," says Trimbach with a long sigh. "It was merely an illegal act that had to be stopped. . . . It's not our function to analyze whether their cause is just or not."

◆

Early summer in Quantico . . .

A brassy Marine Corps Band, from the base just down the road, is on the stage playing marches to welcome the audience that packs into the auditorium for the "graduation exercises" of the ninety-seventh session of the FBI National Academy. The audience includes excited families, well-braided military officers, and even members of foreign diplomatic missions. It is a glorious, sunny day at this stark new complex of Bureau buildings (its detractors call the architectural style "penitentiary modern") tucked away in the Virginia woods forty-one miles south of Washington. This is what the FBI likes to call "the West Point of law enforcement," and today is a festive occasion for the two

31

hundred and fifty policemen who have just completed three months of special training and will return home to certain advancement.

The invocation, by a navy chaplain, suggests that policemen are "co-workers with God" in keeping domestic peace and order. There are introductions of distinguished guests — an alderman from Chicago, the director of the Secret Service, and Quinn Tamm, director of the International Association of Chiefs of Police, once head of FBI training programs himself, later a Bureau pariah because of an ugly dispute with Hoover, but now, with the Director gone, welcome to set foot on FBI property again. It is noted that one member of the class, Robert M. Henderson, of the Kodiak, Alaska, Police Department, is, as fate would have it, the eight-thousandth graduate of the National Academy since its inception in 1935. The man elected spokesman for the class, David L. Allan of Her Majesty's Inspectorate of Constabulary for Scotland, one of about a dozen students from overseas, speaks of the academy's "imaginative and thoughtful curriculum," of the general international need "to reshape and improve training programs to help the policeman understand the man on the street," and of the importance of wives and families to law-enforcement officers. Allan also announces that the class has raised money to contribute two new entrance signs for the Quantico facility, "to announce to the world that the ninety-seventh session was proud to be here."

The main speaker of the day, introduced by Director Clarence M. Kelley as "a dedicated and determined friend of law enforcement," is U.S. Attorney General William B. Saxbe. There has been an undercurrent of tension between Saxbe's office and certain quarters in the Bureau in recent days, because of indications that the attorney general, who has gained a reputation for saying the wrong (and sometimes inaccurate) thing at the worst time, intends to comment on some controversial aspects of FBI policy rather than deliver a speech full of platitudes typical of such an occasion. Efforts have been made by the FBI to dilute the attorney general's intended remarks, but the concerned Bureau officials, scattered in the audience, are not sure just where the matter stands.

Saxbe's initial words pose no problem: he commiserates that the policeman's tasks "seem to grow more and more complex on almost a weekly basis," and declares to the class that "you can be truly proud of your profession. You are doing a good job, often amid trying circumstances. You stand in the front lines protecting the rights, lives, and property of Americans against the evildoer." But before long Saxbe turns his attention to the controversial "counterintelligence programs" that were employed by the FBI against leftist, black, and other dissi-

32

dent groups in the 1960s, only recently revealed. "Among enforcement agencies, there is a great need for proper intelligence programs and for proper investigative programs," Saxbe concedes; "the goal, of course, is to determine whether criminal statutes have been violated." He continues:

In the particular operations to which I refer, however, additional facets were added. Memoranda released . . . by the FBI show that the program also sought to "expose, disrupt, misdirect, discredit, or otherwise neutralize" a number of organizations and their members.

Among the various activities called for were leaks of detrimental information as well as efforts to spread dissension through partially false and entirely fabricated documents.

Now it should be recognized that these are typical military intelligence–type activities. It also should be stressed that the FBI did not set up such efforts out of whim or caprice but rather from its real and deep concern for the Nation's security.

But I believe we have to clearly define the elements of the programs. We can all agree, I am certain, that intelligence material is vital for the protection of the Nation and its citizens. The concern arises when a program goes beyond intelligence-gathering and develops tactics of disruption.

But are disruptive tactics something that should occur in the Department of Justice — without the knowledge of the Attorney General? I think not.

Are disruptive tactics something that should occur in the Department of Justice — even with the Attorney General's knowledge? Again, I think not.

The national security can be protected without resorting to such practices.

When you return to your various police departments, I hope you will take the word with you and pass it along that the dirty tricks are over — not only in campaign tactics, but in law enforcement as well. The public is demanding that we find ways to enforce the laws that do not violate standards of decency and fairness.

At one point Saxbe pauses to look across the podium at his host. "Director Kelley and I are in total agreement that the Department of Justice will not allow nor will the FBI carry out any improper activities," he says.

The silence is heavy over the auditorium. "My point in discussing certain FBI programs is not to criticize a man who is no longer here to defend himself," says the attorney general with a tone of reassurance.

J. Edgar Hoover had a long and notable career in the Federal service and left as his legacy the greatest investigative agency in the world. I will leave

33

attempts to make ultimate judgments to others who are more comfortable in that field. The purpose of my remarks is to stress that all of us with criminal justice responsibilities must continually examine and reexamine every aspect of our work to make certain it is fair — as well as legal. There is no person who should be immune from criticism and no practice that should be shielded from healthy skepticism.

Most members of the audience applaud, the polite but persistent applause of people who may not really have been listening. But the FBI officials, including Assistant Director John J. MacDermott of the External Affairs Division and his assistant, George Quinn, who would have to field queries about the attorney general's apparent abandonment of the Bureau, sit with their hands folded and stare icily into space.

The ceremony proceeds, with "Mr. National Academy," Inspector James V. Cotter, reading the roll of graduates while Kelley presents diplomas. An FBI photographer diligently clicks off a picture of each policeman with the director; every graduate will get an "autographed" copy. The Marine Band takes up its refrains again, and the crowd spills out into the sunshine.

Later in the day, a ranking FBI official muses about the Saxbe speech and offers what is probably a representative Bureau reaction. "When you invite someone into your home," he asks, "do you expect him to take a crap on the living room floor?"

*

How It Began

III

Building a Monolith

Imagine if you can 300,000 square feet of space lined with seem-ingly endless rows of green metal filing cases containing the life histories of millions of people. There has never been anything like it before in the history of mankind. Yet, by an ingenious system which has proved a lifesaver in these days of incredibly quick ex-pansion, the Bureau's trained personnel can identify any incoming fingerprints in less than three minutes if a previous record is on file in these miles of metal cases.
— *J. Edgar Hoover, in his Introduction to* The FBI
in Peace and War, *by Frederick L. Collins, 1943*

THERE HAD TO BE SOMETHING WRONG if the Director was late coming downstairs for breakfast. For he was a man who lived according to a routine so rigid that it was almost a ritual. The evening before, he had left the office right on schedule and had dinner at the home of his close friend, associate director and alter ego Clyde A. Tolson, then returned to his own house near Rock Creek Park in Northwest Washington. But by 8:30 A.M. on May 2, 1972, his driver had already arrived to take him back to FBI headquarters, where he habitually arrived at exactly 9, and J. Edgar Hoover had still not emerged from his bedroom. The driver, Tom Moten, and Hoover's longtime housekeeper, Annie Fields, hesitated about taking any action; the Director was not the sort of man who liked to be reminded of things or corrected by others. Besides, he customarily slept in the nude. But finally Moten, accompanied by the gardener and houseman, James Crawford, went upstairs and found him sprawled naked and lifeless on the floor alongside his bed. The

37

housekeeper summoned his personal physician, who pronounced Hoover dead at seventy-seven years of age, apparently of a sudden heart attack.

Hoover's death was uniquely peaceful and, some would say, timely. He missed his opportunity to move triumphantly with the FBI into its own cavernous new building across Pennsylvania Avenue from the Justice Department (the new FBI home was quickly named the J. Edgar Hoover Building after his death), but he also avoided having to face the fact that an administration — that of Republican Richard M. Nixon — had finally decided that Hoover, after running the FBI for forty-eight years, should be replaced once Nixon was safely reelected. "I think his passing was a godsend," says Richard G. Kleindienst, for a time Hoover's nominal boss and an ardent admirer of the Director, without a trace of hostility, "a godsend for him, for the country, for his reputation, and for the Bureau. It was a happy death, an easy one. He had a long and useful life and did not have to suffer indignity."

But still the Director's death came as a shock, to his admirers and detractors alike. It was the kind of news item that made common people pause from what they were doing and brood about its meaning. It was the lead story in almost every newspaper in the United States and a prominent one in the overseas press as well, the occasion for editorial outpourings. "J. Edgar Hoover was America's symbol of tough law enforcement. There he stood granite-like through the vicissitudes of half a century protecting his country against all enemies — be they internal gangsters or external predators," said the Johnson City, Tennessee, *Press-Chronicle* in a typical eulogy; "J. Edgar Hoover set a lifetime example of steadfastness that made him almost the dictionary definition of the word," editorialized the Spokane, Washington, *Chronicle*. Although few verbalized it, many wondered and worried what the effects of Hoover's death might be on the FBI and, indirectly, on the nation. He had worked under eight presidents and sixteen attorneys general, building the Bureau and himself into institutions that were theoretically and demonstrably above the political fray that produced presidents and attorneys general. Just what had he built, and how did he do it? There was a public impulse now to look inside, to evaluate the Bureau more searchingly. Did Hoover's death mean that the FBI, the fortress, would also pass on? Would it continue to bear his imprint? And how would it do without him? The Watergate break-ins, six weeks away, would provide a test, and part of the answer.

Although there had been an attorney general personally serving the President from the earliest days of the American Constitution, the

Department of Justice was formally created only in 1870. It had no separate investigative service, and the job of doing any detective work associated with federal cases fell to the regional United States attorneys themselves. The United States marshals, in addition to their responsibility for processing and serving the orders of federal courts, were expected to track down and apprehend offenders, if necessary with the help of locally recruited posses. Both the federal attorneys and the marshals were political appointees with little or no law-enforcement experience, and the administrators in Washington were unsympathetic to them. As former Attorney General Homer Cummings and Carl McFarland pointed out in their landmark 1937 study, *Federal Justice,* a deputy marshal was paid the same fee of one dollar for the capture of a fugitive in those early days of the department, no matter how easy or difficult the task was. If a sought-after fugitive was killed while resisting arrest, the deputy did not receive the fee; what is more, he was expected to pay the burial expenses for the quarry he had killed. Sometimes federal officers were prosecuted in the state courts for killing or injuring the people they had been sent out to capture.

In 1871, Congress did make available to the new Justice Department a fund of $50,000 for the detection and prosecution of federal crimes, and both the amount and the authorized list of expenditures were expanded in the years that followed. The money was generally used to hire part-time outsiders, including the Pinkerton Detective Agency, but Congress banned that practice in 1892. After that decision the investigative services were usually performed by federal bank examiners and agents discreetly borrowed from the Customs Bureau, the Interior Department, and the Treasury Department's Secret Service. The Justice Department also had a small corps of "examiners," appointed by patronage, who mostly inspected the records of court clerks and other regional officials. But the department's capacity was feeble, and in 1903, when a family wrote to request help in finding their kidnapped daughter, Acting Attorney General James C. McReynolds characteristically replied, "You should furnish me with the names of the parties holding your daughter in bondage, the particular place, and the names of witnesses by whom the facts can be proved."

It was Charles J. Bonaparte, grandson of the French emperor's brother and President Theodore Roosevelt's attorney general, who finally complained in 1907 that "a Department of Justice with no force of permanent police in any form under its control is assuredly not fully equipped for its work." He appealed to Congress to authorize the department to name "a small carefully selected and experienced force

39

under its immediate orders," which could be regularly depended upon for investigations. Instead, however, Congress reacted with an amendment that prohibited the use by the Justice Department of any Secret Service personnel borrowed from the Treasury Department — apparently in part because the Secret Service agents' work in a land fraud investigation had led to the indictment and conviction of several members of Congress.

Bonaparte responded boldly with an action that has been subject to differing interpretations ever since — as either defiance of Congress or proper exercise of discretion; by an order issued July 26, 1906, he organized a small separate Justice Department force under the direction of Chief Examiner Stanley W. Finch. Most of the people he hired were Treasury agents who had worked for Justice. In his annual report for the year, Bonaparte asserted the value of having the new agents' activities directed and controlled within the department and recommended that the attorney general "be justly held responsible for the efficiency and economy of the service rendered by the force." Early the next year, President William Howard Taft's attorney general, George W. Wickersham, confirmed the action and logically named the unit the Bureau of Investigation. Its jurisdiction was to be over matters not specifically assigned to other agencies. In 1910, Cummings and McFarland recounted, Wickersham reported that the Bureau's most significant work had to do with

the national banking laws, antitrust laws, peonage laws, the bucket-shop law, the laws relating to fraudulent bankruptcies, the impersonation of government officials with intent to defraud, thefts and murders committed on government reservations, offenses against government property, and those committed by federal court officials and employees, Chinese smuggling, customs frauds, internal revenue frauds, post office frauds, violations of the neutrality laws . . . land frauds and immigration and naturalization cases.

But the new Bureau also got an unusual assignment in 1910, when Congress passed the White Slave Traffic Act, also known as the Mann Act (for its author, Congressman James Robert Mann of Illinois), which forbade interstate transportation of women "for the purpose of prostitution or concubinage," a law that President Taft signed over bitter protests that it violated states' rights. Finch complained before a congressional committee that "unless a girl was actually confined in a room and guarded . . . there was no girl, regardless of her station in life, who was altogether safe." He explained that by sending letters to postmasters and chiefs of police, the Bureau was able to pinpoint communities with particularly active prostitution rackets; in those towns it hired attorneys to help keep tabs on the brothels, taking a census and watching for new out-of-state arrivals. Initially the focus of enforcement, in line with Justice Department policy, was on cases where commercialism was involved, and many instances were discovered in which young girls had been cruelly exploited. But the Supreme Court took a broad view of the new law, and in one opinion it said that "pecuniary gain" need not be proved for the act to be employed in punishing "immorality." Many cases, in fact, involved only one or two couples who crossed a state line under unlucky circumstances, and one early defendant was heavyweight boxing champion Jack Johnson, who ended up in jail as a result of a trip with his fiancée, a former prostitute. To put a federal law enforcement service in charge of monitoring the moral behavior of the citizens was always a questionable and controversial step — and it was never clear that Congress had really meant to go that far — but the most important long-range impact of the Mann Act on the Bureau was that it meant an increase in manpower over its humble beginnings.

The next significant expansion of the Bureau came in the years leading up to and during American involvement in World War I. The initial concern, after the war began in Europe in 1914, was over violations of the stiff American neutrality laws, from the alleged plans of Hindus living on the West Coast to stir an uprising against the British in India to German efforts to arouse American opinion against aiding the Allies. No one agency had clear jurisdiction in this area, and the laxity of security was dramatized on July 30, 1916, when, as a result of sabotage, two million tons of dynamite exploded on Black Tom Island in New York Harbor, a transfer point for supplies to be shipped to Europe. Other similar incidents followed, and by the time the United States entered the war against Germany in April 1917, the nation was stirred to an extraordinary patriotic fervor. Volunteer vigilante organizations sprouted with the intention of keeping the country on the right track, and one, in Missouri, issued formal warnings and threats to those it considered to be "speaking or acting in a disloyal way." Although President Woodrow Wilson quashed a proposal within the Justice Department to institute courts-martial for civilians who interfered with the military effort, his administration did obtain from Congress broad expansions of the Espionage Act, including one that covered "seditious utterances." The Bureau, its strength increased from three hundred to four hundred agents, was given responsibility for apprehending those "enemy aliens" considered to be dangerous and for watching others thought to be potentially harmful, as well as for en-

41

forcing the new conscription law. It also monitored, and pursued with a vengeance, a radical organization that was suspected of sabotage and of counseling resistance to the draft, the Industrial Workers of the World (IWW).

To the consternation of many national leaders, the Justice Department and its growing Bureau fell into association with one of the most prominent vigilante organizations, the American Protective League. In 1917 its founder, Chicago advertising executive A. M. Briggs, persuaded Finch's successor as chief of the Bureau, A. Bruce Bielaski, that a volunteer organization of loyal citizens should help the overloaded Bureau with its wartime work, and Bielaski in turn convinced Attorney General Thomas W. Gregory that this would be a good idea. With the prestige of official sanction, the APL grew spectacularly — until it had two hundred and fifty thousand members in chapters spread across the country. They paid a dollar to get a badge that first said Secret Service Division and later (after the Treasury Department protested about possible confusion with its real Secret Service) Auxiliary to the U.S. Department of Justice. Besides reporting on people it considered suspicious, the APL performed such services as investigating the background of everyone the American Red Cross planned to send overseas. Because of its militant antiunion stand, the APL was widely suspected of involvement in the lynching of Frank H. Little, an IWW leader in Montana.

One of the most extensive and shocking uses of the league was to help the Bureau of Investigation in 1918 with dragnet "slacker raids," intended to haul in young men who had failed to register for the draft. Thousands of people were arrested, especially in New York and Chicago, and jailed overnight for the simple offense of not having a draft card in their possession at the time they were approached by police, Bureau agents, APL auxiliaries, or specially deputized off-duty soldiers and sailors. Only one in every two hundred of them turned out to be genuine draft-dodgers, and that record left the Bureau's image somewhat tarnished. Even after a contrite Attorney General Gregory responded to criticism by disavowing the practice of using outsiders to conduct the raids in May 1918, the abuse was repeated in September of the same year. It became clear that the Bureau, perhaps out of mere enthusiasm for its tasks, was getting out of control.

Among the onerous wartime laws passed by Congress was the Alien Act of 1918, "an act to exclude and expel from the United States aliens who are members of the anarchistic classes," including those who advocated the overthrow of the government by force or violence, the assassination of public officials, or the unlawful destruction of

42

property. These are categories subject to a broad range of definitions and interpretations, of course, but some contemporary politicians saw no need for subtlety in the matter. The Alien Act found an eager enforcer in the person of Attorney General Gregory's successor, A. Mitchell Palmer, a Pennsylvania lawyer and Democratic politician who had been Alien Property Custodian during the war. Palmer was stirred to outrage and to fear over the nation's postwar fate by a series of bombings around the country in 1919, including some in Washington. Most of them were attributed to anarchist organizations. One of the bombs exploded on a spring night in front of Palmer's own home in the Georgetown section of the capital (and across the street from Assistant Secretary of the Navy Franklin D. Roosevelt's house), seriously damaging Palmer's house and the neighboring buildings. The blast mutilated beyond identification the unknown people who planted the bomb; left behind were the same anarchist leaflets that had been found at the scene of other explosions. Palmer reacted by declaring war on the radicals. He named William J. Flynn, the former director of the Secret Service, to take over the Bureau and involve it more actively in the fight against subversion. Francis P. Garvan became an assistant attorney general in charge of a new General Intelligence Division that would concentrate on radical and subversive activities. Garvan's direct assistant was a twenty-four-year-old up-and-coming Justice Department lawyer named John Edgar Hoover.

During its first three and a half months in existence, the GID compiled personal histories of some sixty thousand individuals thought to be radicals; before long the special indices grew to include more than two hundred thousand names. The division's translators also perused some five hundred foreign-language newspapers, in order to keep up with "radical propaganda." Palmer, apparently eager to build a personal reputation and eventually to succeed the ailing President Wilson in the White House, appealed for peacetime sedition legislation. But when he did not get it, he relied instead on the 1918 Alien Act and used the Bureau to conduct one of the most extraordinary adventures in American legal history, the "Red raids," which later came to be known as the "Palmer Raids," the attorney general's personal monument. The first test raid in late 1919 was against the Federation of the Union of Russian Workers; it resulted in a relatively small number of deportations and many mistaken arrests. But Palmer was spurred on by a favorable reception among the public and in the press, and he determined to try the same dragnet tactics, reminiscent of the slacker raids, on the Communist and Communist Labor parties, which had been carefully watched by the GID. On the night of January 2, 1920, the Bureau swept down on suspected radicals in thirty-three different cities; an estimated ten thousand people were arrested, many of them new immigrants who barely spoke English and had simply chosen an unfortunate place to gather that evening for recreation or night classes. They were confused and frightened to find themselves arrested as criminal anarchists and then held in squalid cells. Some of the "aliens" who were picked up were actually American citizens; but in the deplorable conditions in which the victims of the Palmer Raids were held, it was some time before they could make themselves known and heard.

As it was later revealed in congressional and independent investigations of the raids, most of the victims of Palmer's zeal were arrested without warrants, and as a result, the majority were released, either before or after prosecution.

There was concern about the raids in and out of government; at a cabinet meeting shortly afterward the sickly Woodrow Wilson turned to his attorney general. "Palmer," he said, "do not let this country see red."

One reason for the failure of the raids was that Assistant Secretary of Labor Louis R. Post, who had authority over the deportation proceedings, refused to accept Palmer's argument that the radicals had been engaged in a conspiracy against the nation. Although some well-known anarchists were deported, Post threw out many of the cases and publicly questioned the motives and tactics behind the raids and the Bureau's performance. Palmer was unrelenting. He denounced Post for a "habitually tender solicitude for social revolution and perverted sympathy for the criminal anarchists of the country" and claimed that the Labor Department official had "utterly nullified the purpose of Congress in passing the deportation statute" and "set at large among the people the very enemies whom it was the desire and intention of Congress to be rid of." There was a short-lived move to impeach Post, but the real culmination of the affair came during a Senate investigation in early 1921. The worst accusations about the raids were shown to be true, and the most persuasive indictment of them came from the outgoing attorney general's own testimony in defense of his and the Bureau's actions. Palmer suggested that the Fourth Amendment guarantee against unreasonable searches and seizures did not apply to aliens, and he insisted that the overzealous agents should be understood and forgiven for their excesses. "I apologize for nothing that the Department of Justice has done in this matter. I glory in it," Palmer testified; "if . . . some of my agents out in the field . . . were a little rough or unkind, or short or curt, with these alien agitators whom they observed seeking to destroy their homes, their religion, and their country, I think it might well be overlooked." Palmer never made it to the presidential nomination, but he remained a hero to many people.

In the end, the Palmer Raids had a threefold legacy: they did succeed in substantially weakening the spirit and the organizational abilities of communists and other extreme left-wing groups in the United States, and they demonstrated that the use of methods that stretched and went beyond the law were a great help and an efficient tool in undermining "subversives." At the same time, the raids brought substantial additional disrespect upon the growing Bureau of Investigation and a cloud of distrust over the supposedly impartial Department of Justice. They also established the vague and dangerous precedent that the line may sometimes be blurred between straightforward law enforcement and the use of the judicial processes to achieve political ends.

But it remained for the corrupt administration of President Warren G. Harding to bring the Bureau into notoriety. Although Flynn staged a lobbying campaign to remain as chief of the Bureau, Attorney General Harry M. Daugherty, a political crony of Harding from Ohio, selected a man touted as a "famous international sleuth," William J. Burns, as the new director. Actually, Burns like Flynn was a former head of the Secret Service who, on his retirement in 1909, had established the William J. Burns National Detective Agency. The agency had some well-publicized successes in solving notorious murder and bombing cases, and Burns had pulled off a neat trick in the years before the American entry into World War I — investigating both German activities in this country for the British and British activities for the Germans. A prior indication of the investigative techniques that Burns might condone in the Bureau was his surreptitious entry into a New York law office to make copies of documents for a client, an incident that led to his conviction on a misdemeanor charge. To the Harding administration, however, that seemed to be taken as a qualification rather than as a blot on his record, and it became widely known that Bureau men, under Burns's leadership, randomly wiretapped, broke into offices and shuffled through personal files, and kept tabs on people's private lives. The most likely targets were "enemies" — persons who criticized Daugherty, the Department of Justice, and the Bureau of Investigation; senators who asked too many questions; and other competing government departments. What little standards there might have been for agents' performance were thrown out, and Bureau investigators sometimes beat prisoners in order to obtain confessions.

To a Bureau that was already ideologically politicized Burns added a partisan twist. He kept records of the party affiliations and political connections of individual agents and added to the force on the basis of specific recommendations from friendly congressmen. Among the new people carrying agents' badges, selected in the manner of small-town honorary deputy sheriffs, were a New York producer who had brought a burlesque show to Washington and a drunk who performed a lunchtime sideshow outside the Justice Department head-quarters. Others turned out to be ex-convicts, and one had even been convicted of murder. But the most sensational recruit was a particular star of the Harding era, Gaston Bullock Means, a con man who was in the midst of an extraordinary career during which he swindled people out of hundreds of thousands of dollars. As one biographer of Harding has noted, Means boasted in middle age that he had been accused of every imaginable crime, from petit larceny to murder, but convicted of none. At one point early in World War I he had even operated as a German spy. No sooner had Means become a "special employee" of the Justice Department, for ninety days at seven dollars a day, than he was selling copies of department reports to underworld figures and offering to "fix" federal prosecutions for an appropriate price. Suspended at one point, he ignored the order to leave, stayed at his desk, and was quietly rehired by Burns on the Bureau payroll because Burns valued his contacts with the underworld. When Means did eventually leave, he took along forged documents and had great financial success in bootlegging circles with his offers to intervene to help obtain liquor permits and quash indictments. Years later he swindled funds from the wife of a wealthy Washington newspaper publisher, Mrs. Ned Mc-Lean, with a spurious offer to solve the Lindbergh kidnapping case.

The Bureau was thrust into the middle of another crisis situation in the early 1920s when railway unions rebelled against pay cuts ordered by the government's Railway Labor Board. Hundreds of thousands of workers went out on strike, management hired strikebreakers, and in some areas there was sabotage to prevent the trains from running. Attorney General Daugherty obtained a sweeping injunction from federal district court in Chicago that banned any "acts or words" that would interfere with railroad operations. Cast in an unusual if not necessarily unwilling role, Bureau agents were sent out to enforce the injunction, and they infiltrated the ranks of the strikers to search for evidence of violations. Some twelve hundred unionists were arrested and many of them convicted of contempt of court, and the Bureau was largely credited with breaking the back of the railroad strike, an accomplishment of which Daugherty and Burns were proud.

In the same period, the Bureau also pursued the newly revived

Ku Klux Klan. The federal agents were given the assignment at the urgent request of the governor of Louisiana, who complained that the Klan was holding vast areas of the state in a grip of terror. Often working under cover, the Bureau penetrated the Klan and — because there were no directly applicable federal statutes — searched out a few local officials not tied to the Klan who were willing to accept the evidence gathered by the federal investigators and use it to prosecute in state court. The Bureau also managed to arrest one leading Klansman for violating the White Slave Traffic Act. Once the Bureau had finished its unorthodox campaign against the Klan, the organization, like the communist parties before it, was substantially weakened.

Both the special task of quelling the railroad strike and the assault on the Klan fell to the well-established General Intelligence Division, still under the supervision of Hoover, who was by now assistant director of the Bureau under Burns. As its most important business, however, the GID was still preoccupied with the threat of subversion, and Burns took every opportunity to warn Congress about "the danger of this radical element in this country." Attorney General Daugherty was, if anything, more paranoid than even his predecessor Palmer about the threat from the Left, and he declared that the railroad strikers were being encouraged by "Red Agents of the Soviet Government," who were getting instructions directly from Moscow. But Daugherty took his accusations even further, charging, for example, that his radical enemies were out to destroy him by such reckless tactics as putting poison gas into a bouquet of flowers on a platform where the attorney general was speaking.

The Red smear was one tactic among many used by the Bureau against freshman Senator Burton K. Wheeler of Montana, a Democrat who had been elected in 1922 with the assistance of the left-leaning Montana "Non-Partisan League" and who was to run for Vice-President on the Progressive party ticket in 1924 with Senator Robert La Follette. Shortly after his arrival in Washington Wheeler took on the corrupt Department of Justice in speeches on the Senate floor. The Republican National Committee promptly counterattacked against the newcomer and, apparently using material provided by the Bureau, claimed that during his earlier term as United States attorney in Montana, Wheeler had permitted the state to become "a hotbed of treason and sedition." At the same time, Bureau agents hid in the bushes outside Wheeler's Northwest Washington home to spy on him, ransacked his Capitol Hill office, and tried to lure him into a compromising situation with a woman in an Ohio hotel room. Eventually, as a reprisal for the Senate investigation of the Justice Department which

47

Wheeler was mounting, the department got a federal grand jury in Montana to bring an indictment against Wheeler for allegedly using his influence to obtain oil and gas leases for a prospector who was a friend and client. In the swirl of controversy that resulted, Burns later acknowledged before a Senate committee that the Bureau had been baldly used in an effort to bring a vendetta against Wheeler, to discredit the senator before he could release his revelations about the Justice Department; another witness testified that Bureau agents had candidly acknowledged they were out to "frame" Wheeler. The strategy failed — Daugherty left office in disgrace, implicated in the Teapot Dome scandal; and when Wheeler came to trial in Montana, he was acquitted — and the Bureau had fallen to the lowest ebb yet in its sixteen-year history.

It was against this backdrop that J. Edgar Hoover, the young man on the make in the Justice Department, took over the Bureau of Investigation. Some months after Calvin Coolidge assumed the presidency on the death of Harding, he demanded the resignation of Attorney General Daugherty and replaced him with Harlan Fiske Stone, a fellow New Englander, a distinguished New York lawyer and former dean of the Columbia University Law School. Stone had been a critic of the Palmer Raids and other recent Justice Department policies, and one of his first moves was to get rid of Burns and look for a successor. He failed in his search for an outsider with broad law enforcement experience and a good reputation, so he turned instead, apparently on the recommendation of Secretary of Commerce Herbert Hoover (no relation), to "young Hoover" — only twenty-nine — for a tryout in the job. In an oft-quoted — though some say apocryphal — conversation in the attorney general's office on May 10, 1924, Stone offered Hoover the position. As related by the Bureau's authorized historian, Don Whitehead, and others over the years, Hoover said, "I'll take the job, Mr. Stone, on certain conditions."

"What are they?" the attorney general asked.

"The bureau must be divorced from politics and not be a catch-all for political hacks. Appointments must be based on merit. Second, promotions will be made on proved ability and the Bureau will be responsible only to the Attorney General," Hoover replied brashly.

As this account has it, Stone was delighted with the terms, and said, "I wouldn't give it to you under any other conditions. That's all. Good day."

Hoover, riding into his new role in the classic image of a white knight on a shining steed, lost no time in cleaning out one of the most discredited agencies of government. He fired the agents with criminal records and drove out many of those who had no qualifications but their politics, using a technique that would later become standard in the Bureau: frequent short-notice transfers from one office to another. Among others, Gaston Means was permanently banned from the Bureau's offices. Within days, Hoover and Stone agreed on a basic policy statement that included a pledge to make the Bureau "a fact-gathering organization" whose "activities would be limited strictly to investigations of violations of federal laws." In a public statement intended to assuage feelings over the recent controversies, Stone declared that

the Bureau of Investigation is not concerned with political or other opinions of individuals. It is concerned only with their conduct and then only with such conduct as is forbidden by the laws of the United States. When a police system passes beyond these limits, it is dangerous to the proper administration of justice and to human liberty, which it should be our first concern to cherish. Within them it should rightly be a terror to the wrongdoer.

Hoover, too, sought to make it clear that despite his background in the GID,* the preoccupation with radicals was a relic of the past. "It is, of course, to be remembered that the activities of Communists and other ultra-radicals have not up to the present time constituted a violation of the federal statutes," the new Acting Director said in an early memorandum, "and consequently, the Department of Justice, theoretically, has no right to investigate such activities as there has been no violation of the federal laws."

While housecleaning, Hoover established qualifications for agents, apparently for the first time, and improved upon the cursory training that had been set up under Burns. Those with legal or accounting backgrounds would be preferred, unless there were other "outstanding" qualities that came to the Bureau's attention. Hoover established a career service in which the salaries and retirement benefits would be better than in any comparable agency, in the federal government or elsewhere. It would be spoken and thought of as distinct from, although always lodged within, the Justice Department. Promotions at all levels were to be based on a merit system and the special-agents-in-charge of regional field offices were to be given greater authority and

* Hoover, and other Bureau officials speaking in his behalf, would try in later years to dissociate the Director from the Palmer Raids and other unsavory activities of the early GID. But the record seems clear that Hoover played a significant part in the development and implementation of the Bureau's strident antiradical policies and actions.

J. Edgar Hoover served every President from Calvin Coolidge through Richard Nixon, gaining more power and influence all the time. The tradition of a private relationship between the President and the FBI Director began under Franklin D. Roosevelt, who gave the Bureau extraordinary wartime powers and delighted in receiving gossip from FBI files during private White House sessions with Hoover.

Here the Director is shown at a ceremony on May 18, 1934, where Roosevelt signs six of the special crime bills, passed by Congress with hardly a dissenting vote, that made federal crimes of bank robbery and other offenses previously punished only by the states; the bills led to a dramatic expansion of the Bureau, stimulated its celebrated "gangbuster" days, and established much of the investigative jurisdiction that it still has today. To the left of Hoover is Attorney General Homer Cummings, who pushed for the legislation; to the right is Senator Henry Ashurst (D-Arizona), who helped steer it through Congress; to the right of Ashurst is Joseph B. Kennan, assistant attorney general in charge of the Justice Department's Criminal Division.

President Harry S Truman congratulates Hoover after award-
ing him the Medal of Merit at a White House ceremony
on March 8, 1946; to the President's left are other medal recipients, Colonel J. Monroe Johnson, director of the Office of
Transportation, and John J. Pelley, president of the American
Railroad Association.

Hoover received many honors and awards in his time, and in
another White House ceremony on May 27, 1955, President
Dwight D. Eisenhower pinned the National Security Medal on his
lapel in recognition of "brilliant leadership" in the field of law
enforcement. (In the background between Hoover and Eisenhower
are Secretary of Health, Education and Welfare Oveta Culp
Hobby and Secretary of the Treasury George Humphrey; to the
President's right is Secretary of State John Foster Dulles.)

Shortly after President John F. Kennedy took office in 1961, the Director posed with him and his brother, Attorney General Robert F. Kennedy. So popular was Hoover by that time that President Kennedy made the announcement of his retention as head of the FBI one of his first postelection declarations; but the Director sparred incessantly with Robert Kennedy, his nominal boss at the Justice Department, accusing him of trying to weaken the Bureau by requiring it to hire members of minority groups as agents. As soon as President Kennedy was assassinated in 1963, Hoover began circumventing Robert Kennedy and dealing directly with Lyndon B. Johnson, the new President.

Johnson was one of Hoover's best political friends in Washington; here he congratulates the Director in 1965 after announcing that the mandatory federal retirement age of seventy had been waived to permit Hoover to remain in his job.

Another long-standing friend of the Director, from the Red-hunting days of the late 1940s and early 1950s, was Richard M. Nixon; sometimes the two attended baseball games together. On November 14, 1968, Hoover became one of the first government officials summoned to Nixon's transition headquarters in New York after he had been elected President. Later, Nixon was the first President in decades seriously to consider replacing Hoover, but the Director saved him the trouble when he died in his sleep on May 2, 1972.

discretion; an "inspection" system, later much imitated in other parts of the federal service, was established to monitor performance in the field. Conscious of the misbehavior and corruption common in other federal agencies, Hoover also introduced the severest of behavioral standards. With Prohibition still in effect, he wrote in a memo to the field that "I am determined to summarily dismiss from this Bureau any employee whom I find indulging in the use of intoxicants to any degree or extent upon any occasion. . . . I, myself, am refraining from the use of intoxicants . . . and I am not, therefore, expecting any more of the field employees than of myself."

Stone was pleased with Hoover's early performance, and after seven months he named his protégé permanent Director of the Bureau, a position that required no formal confirmation. The attorney general undoubtedly had no idea just how permanent the job would become for Hoover, but as long as Stone lived he remained a staunch defender and supporter of Hoover's performance. Although elevated to the Supreme Court after only eleven months in the Justice Department, Stone kept in close touch with the Director, sometimes dropping in by the back door to ask Hoover for an accounting of his "stewardship." In the 1930s, according to a man who worked closely with Hoover at the time, Stone, despite his reputation for probity, had private and discreet access to Bureau documents relating to German activities in the United States during World War I. At one point Stone wrote to Felix Frankfurter asserting that Hoover had

removed from the Bureau every man as to whose character there was any ground for suspicion. He refused to yield to any kind of political pressure; he appointed to the Bureau men of intelligence and education, and strove to build up a morale such as should control such an organization. He withdrew it wholly from extra-legal activities and made it an efficient organization for investigation of criminal offenses against the United States.

For his own part, Hoover idolized Stone and considered him his mentor. He quoted him often. Only one formal portrait of an attorney general hung in the Director's office: Stone's.

For the first several years after Hoover's appointment to the directorship, the Bureau fell into a period of benign obscurity, a merciful relief from its earlier notoriety. The Hoover management was quiet and conservative, and the time was one of consolidation and review. One of the Director's primary boasts in his annual report for 1927, for example, was that he had reduced the force of agents by sixteen men. Field offices were cut back and their territorial jurisdiction conformed to the outlines of federal judicial districts. Costs were reduced, and yet, the Director could explain, the Bureau was becoming "efficient"; it was accomplishing more. But once established on an even keel by Hoover, the Bureau would grow and prosper. It attracted wider notice and was assigned broader responsibilities. As it grew, it was renamed, first the Division of Investigation, which seemed to put it on a par with the legal divisions of the Department of Justice; and then in 1935 the Federal Bureau of Investigation, a name that, in effect if not by design, seemed to denote it as the most important among many federal investigative agencies, one big enough to have its own internal complement of "divisions."

The Director had a particular knack for making the Bureau seem indispensable to the people, and to the nation's police. There was already an Identification Division in the Bureau when Hoover took over, but it was a rather chaotic combination of records based on the old Bertillon system of identifying people by a complex set of body measurements (length and width of head, left foot, left little finger, etc.) and of fingerprint files that had been maintained by the International Association of Chiefs of Police and turned over to the Justice Department under Daugherty; others came from files at the federal penitentiary in Leavenworth, Kansas. Although the Bureau had possession of 810,188 fingerprint records, no money had been appropriated for it to operate an identification service. Hoover, however, went to Congress in 1924 and quickly obtained the funds. In 1930 Congress also settled a dispute over who should manage fingerprint files (some police officials favored giving control to the Department of the Interior) by formally authorizing a Division of Identification and Information within the Bureau that would include the fingerprints of law-abiding citizens as well as criminals. The ever-growing criminal file was an obvious boon to law enforcement. Fugitives using aliases were often identified when they were arrested on new charges. Many persons applying for jobs as policemen around the country were found to have criminal records themselves when their fingerprints were checked against FBI files. As the value of the service increased, so did the number of "subscribers," until thousands of government and police agencies were contributing duplicates of all the fingerprints they took. Thousands of people applying for jobs with the Works Progress Administration (WPA) in the late 1930s were matched with criminal records, and were not hired.

Even visitors who toured FBI headquarters in Washington were for a time invited to submit to voluntary fingerprinting and have their cards placed in a special noncriminal file along with those of John D.

55

Rockefeller, Jr., and other patriots who had done so. The tour guides pointed out that having one's prints on file with the FBI could prove to be of inestimable value if one were suddenly seized with amnesia or injured beyond ready identification in a traffic accident. Visitors went home with a card carrying the print of a single finger and the legend: "Souvenir print. Federal Bureau of Investigation, United States Department of Justice. J. Edgar Hoover, Director. Patents pending." Sometimes the souvenirs were framed, or shown around back home, with the result that social and fraternal organizations would invite the nearest special-agent-in-charge to come by and conduct a wholesale fingerprinting session of their members for addition to the files in Washington.

By July 1974, when the Identification Division celebrated its own fiftieth anniversary (the anniversary of Hoover's obtaining the money from Congress to launch a formal fingerprint identification service), it had in all of its files combined some 159,000,000 fingerprints, with the files growing at the rate of another 3,000 sets of prints a day. More than 7,300 agencies were regularly contributing fingerprints, and the division employed over 3,000 of its own people, including the 1,300 "fingerprint technicians" who scoured the files to make "idents" of unknown suspects.

Another feature that permitted the FBI to score successes and win gratitude in Hoover's early days was its laboratory, established in 1932 and initially patterned after a small crime laboratory that had been set up at Northwestern University to help the Chicago Police Department. As it developed, the FBI Lab was featured as a cornerstone of "scientific law enforcement"; in both federal and local investigations it solved cases by identifying and analyzing blood, hair, firearms, paint, handwritings, typewriters, inks, and other mysterious bits of evidence or clues. The appearance of an efficient, articulate FBI representative on a witness stand, equipped with attractive charts and spouting technical jargon, was often credited with helping a prosecutor win a conviction. At the same time, the Bureau collected at headquarters a national fraudulent check file and a modus operandi file that helped police figure out whether new crimes were being committed by people who already had established records and identifiable patterns of behavior. Later, the FBI would also begin compiling the Uniform Crime Reports and thus become regarded as the single authoritative source in the country on just how bad crime was becoming where at any particular time. It would develop a list of the "Top Ten," the nations' most wanted fugitives from justice, encouraging every citizen to be on the lookout for these dangerous characters and to remember that even a new neighbor might be wanted by the police somewhere else for committing a heinous crime. And it formed a "disaster squad" within the Identification Division which offered its services to identify the victims of plane crashes and other accidents anywhere in the country (and overseas as well, if Americans were believed to be among the victims and if the government of the country where the accident occurred invited or approved of the FBI's assistance) — sometimes a gruesome service to perform, but one that earned the Bureau a great deal of appreciation.

Before long, Hoover seemed to have turned the once-corrupt Bureau into a corps of incorruptibles. What irregularities did occur — and there were remarkably few — were handled internally and quietly, and the Bureau, unlike other agencies whose factions sometimes went public to settle intramural problems, developed a strong bias against airing its "dirty linen" in public. In the view of the average citizen, a view nourished by official Bureau policy, the special agent — Melvin Purvis was a popular example — was an iron man, almost robotlike in his dedication to the common good, his capacity to solve a mysterious crime, and his ability to walk the straight and narrow path. What is more, the FBI came to be seen as a bulwark of American democracy, the fearless protector and defender of the status quo in troubled times, the agency that would stand behind its country, right or wrong. In the days when many other organizations, official and private, were indifferent or uncertain about their policy toward the rise of fascism in Europe, Hoover was seeking to put the FBI in the forefront of the fight against the Nazis. His stand against Hitler was taken long before it was in vogue, a fact that was not to be forgotten in Congress. (And yet, when the government moved to intern Japanese-Americans on the West Coast during World War II, the Director opposed the internment as unnecessary for the nation's security.)

With the new authority for internal security and some overseas operations that was granted as World War II approached, the FBI was for the first time since the 1920s back in the business of hunting "subversives." It was ready for more menacing enemies than gangsters: ideology was once again its concern. The Bureau's own ideology had its roots in Hoover's early experience in the radical-baiting GID, and it later impaired the agency's objectivity.

Organizationally and bureaucratically, Hoover was a genius. Early in his tenure he inaugurated the tradition that everything, small and large, would be done in the Director's name. It was always J. Edgar Hoover personally who announced every breakthrough, who outlined the Bureau's options, and who went to the ramparts to denounce the nation's enemies. The labors of thousands of other people were produced and presented in his name; the bright young men who worked closely with him in the early years — people like James S. Egan, Harold Nathan, and Edward A. Tamm — were virtually unknown to the public. For whatever egotistical motives that policy may have had, it also made the Director personally responsible whenever something went wrong, reluctant though he may have been to admit it. The system minimized buck-passing and scapegoating, externally if not internally. It also had the advantage of making Hoover directly responsible to Congress, which revered him, hung on his every word, and swallowed his spectacular statistics as fast as he could dish them up. The more Hoover and the Bureau were asked to do, the more money they were given to do it. The more money they got, the higher the caseload went and the better the statistics became. There was rarely a limit. Nothing was ever thrown away or lost, or so it seemed. The Bureau's files grew to become an enormous resource, more or less sacrosanct, a comprehensive repository of information (and allegations and gossip) probably unequaled anywhere else in the world.

Hoover's method of collecting information and running the Bureau made him a hero to some and the personification of evil to others, but above all an enduring national celebrity. How a person felt about Hoover almost became a reliable yardstick of his politics. Some of the Director's most vocal and unrelenting supporters, ironically, barely knew him; but their instinct for survival told them that they could get great mileage out of even a single photograph taken with Hoover or a properly lavish word of praise for him at the right time. Senator Robert C. Byrd (D–West Virginia), for example, became one of the most outspoken and knowledgeable defenders of the Hoover image when it was under attack in the 1960s; but asked about Hoover later, Byrd acknowledged that they were "not close" at all — that, in fact, they scarcely knew each other and that Byrd largely "just admired him from afar." More people developed doubts about Hoover as the years went on, and many became convinced that, contrary to his claims (as in the controversy about wartime internment of the Japanese-Americans), he had no genuine sensitivity to civil liberties and in fact encouraged ideological witch-hunts; but to the end those critics were a distinct minority among Americans.

Hoover's external success was for decades mirrored inside the Bureau. Because they were proud to serve an organization with such a sterling reputation, because they became such instant pillars in their communities, and perhaps because they struggled through together under unquestioned and often unreasonable discipline, the agents developed an extraordinary and unusual esprit de corps which has often been compared to that of the United States Marine Corps. As John P. Mohr, long a close administrative aide to Hoover, put it, "You knew what a special agent looked like. You were proud of him. You could trust him." Some would claim that the all-too-predictable white shirt, fedora hat, spit-shined shoes, and well-polished car became too much of a trademark and eventually even limited the Bureau's effectiveness, but Mohr insists that was never the case — that any disadvantage was more than compensated for by the public confidence that such uniformity inspired. For the average FBI agent, the Bureau became his extended family, his source of many political and social values, his most enduring fraternal connection. Agents depended upon each other almost indiscriminately and took heart from the singleness of purpose, character, and even personality that they seemed bound to discover in their colleagues. If an agent symbolically left the fold by publicly criticizing or embarrassing the Bureau, his colleagues generally turned against him with a vengeance.

The seemingly eternal presence of Hoover as Director and his tendency to institutionalize the smallest success as a model for the future shaped the FBI in these years. He had created the Bureau of bureaus, and he wanted to control it absolutely. He was building a monolith; once it was perfect, there was no room for change. And Hoover was perhaps the country's greatest expert at keeping himself in place; he developed a special relationship with each of the eight presidents he served and was far more powerful than many of the sixteen attorneys general. Though he served at the pleasure of the President, no President exercised his prerogative to select a new director. He claimed a role for himself as an adviser to the nation's top policymakers, a provider of inside information and insight that helped cut through the confusion of a crisis. Just as he had once (in 1923, while still assistant director of the Bureau and chief of the GID) prepared the brief on Bolshevik tactics when they seized power in Russia that was a central element in Secretary of State Charles Evans Hughes's successful argument before the Senate Foreign Relations Committee that the United States should not recognize the new Soviet regime in Russia, he would advise President Herbert Hoover that the "bonus army" of desperate and destitute veterans that descended on Washington in 1932 was made up mostly of "criminals or communists" — advice that may have led the President to his disastrous authorization of military action to clear the demonstrators out of the capital.

Hoover's career as Director was almost terminated at the end of nine years. President Franklin D. Roosevelt, on his election in 1932, turned to the Senate for some of his important cabinet appointments. He selected Senator Thomas J. Walsh of Montana, the scourge of Teapot Dome, as his attorney general. Now Walsh's junior colleague from Montana was none other than Burton K. Wheeler — the victim of the Harding Justice Department's vendetta. This meant that the Walsh appointment did not bode well for Hoover. Walsh associated the Director with the improprieties of the Bureau in the Wheeler case (in which Walsh, in a dramatic gesture, had served as trial counsel for his Senate colleague). The new attorney general was thought certain to pick his own director. But Walsh died days before Roosevelt was inaugurated, and the post of attorney general went to Homer Cummings, a Connecticut lawyer.

There was one more threat, in the person of James A. Farley, Roosevelt's postmaster general and chief dispenser of patronage, who allegedly wanted to get rid of Hoover in favor of Val O'Farrell, who had a private detective agency in New York and wrote a crime column for a newspaper there. Another widespread report had it that the Bureau would be merged with other federal investigative agencies and run by an official from the Interior Department. Hoover mounted a vigorous campaign to save his job, including some informal Bureau efforts, it was later alleged, to find blotches in Farley's background and personal life. Another part of that campaign was a visit to Wheeler, who had substantial influence with Roosevelt and had been told, according to his own later accounts, that he could prevent Hoover's reappointment if he so desired. Wheeler, like Walsh, had seen Hoover sit by Daugherty's side during the Senate investigation of the Justice Department, and he suspected that the young chief of the GID had been a more willing and valuable assistant to Burns than was commonly supposed. Wheeler also knew that the prosecutor at his own Montana trial had made nightly progress reports by telephone back to Hoover in Washington (ironically, a hotel switchboard operator loyal to the embattled senator had listened in and provided Wheeler with the details). But Hoover, in his private meeting with Wheeler, insisted that he had nothing substantial to do with the case against the senator and had only followed through on work previously done in the department. "I didn't believe him," Wheeler said later in an interview, "but I decided not to block him . . . besides, I thought Farley's man would be no damn good, too political." Wheeler thus not only endeared himself to Hoover, he was transformed from a Bureau "enemy" into a bona fide Bureau "friend." From that time on, even after he left the Senate

Mr G —

Please get me another copy

of Sanford Unger's

FBI

[initials]

Ordered
1-28-86

in 1947, he could feel free to, and occasionally did, call upon the Bureau to provide him with discreet information.

Once Hoover weathered the advent of the New Deal, his job was never seriously threatened again. Homer Cummings was quite taken with the Director and so for the most part were his successors as attorney general in the Roosevelt cabinet, Frank Murphy, Robert H. Jackson, and Francis Biddle; but even had they not been, Hoover had protection. Roosevelt, for his part, made Hoover an ally in peace and war.

It was during FDR's tenure that Hoover, for all his declarations that the FBI was directly responsible only to the attorney general, began going around his nominal superior and submitting materials for Roosevelt's personal interest, including juicy tidbits about members of his cabinet and other prominent figures, and details of substantive cases. The technique was well established, in any event, by July 1945, when Tom C. Clark became attorney general under Roosevelt's successor, Harry S Truman. "President Truman would tell me about things the Bureau was doing that I didn't even know about," Clark recalled; "he was obviously getting them directly." Clark complained to Hoover, and "he reluctantly gave me copies of some of the things he was sending over to the White House . . . but not all of them. Some information was then just passed by word of mouth." At one point, Clark discovered, on the basis of a tip from an aide to a Senate investigating commitee, that the Bureau was keeping a "secret file" on him while he was attorney general. When he confronted Hoover on the subject, the Director claimed not to know anything about it; "but I was satisfied that Hoover's boys were very loyal and scared," Clark said. "They wouldn't have set up a file on the attorney general without [Hoover's] knowledge." Clark read through his file — "There wasn't anything but general stuff and newspaper clippings," some dealing with his alleged reluctance to investigate Democratic vote frauds in Kansas City — and then returned it to the Bureau archives.

Clark probably got to know Hoover as well as any attorney general did. They had become friends during World War II, when Clark held lower positions in the Justice Department and Hoover adopted the Texan as a confidant. "Mr. Hoover was always critical of attorneys general," especially Murphy and Biddle, Clark recalled. Ultimately Clark and Hoover had a falling out, too, just after Clark had been designated as attorney general, over the postwar *Amerasia* spy case, when Clark learned that the Bureau had surreptitiously obtained a key and searched the apartment of one of the defendants without a warrant. "I told Hoover that I thought this was wrong, that we would have to dismiss the charges," Clark said; "he was furious. That probably started the deterioration of our [official] relationship." Nonetheless, if things became more tense between Hoover and Clark within the Department, the two men became friends again during Clark's service on the Supreme Court and until the Director's death. That friendship was not disrupted by the disputes between Hoover and Clark's son Ramsey, attorney general in the late 1960s, not even when Hoover later called Ramsey Clark a "jellyfish."

Relations between Truman and Hoover were, for the most part, good, although the President became angered when the Director sought to have the newly established Central Intelligence Agency put under his control in addition to the Bureau. Later, after his retirement, Truman summed up his feelings about Hoover during his extensive interviews with biographer Merle Miller:

To tell you the truth, I never gave him all that much thought. He was, still is, inclined to take on, to try to take on more than his job was, and he made quite a few too many speeches to my mind, and he very often spoke of things that, strictly speaking, weren't any of his business, but then a lot of people do that, especially in Washington. As long as he did his job, I didn't pay too much attention to him. One time, they brought me a lot of stuff about his personal life, and I told them I didn't give a damn about that. It wasn't my business. It was what he did *while* he was at work that was my business.

The Director apparently had little personal contact with President Dwight D. Eisenhower, although he was close to Attorney General Herbert Brownell and threw his considerable influence behind the Eisenhower administration by making a rare public appearance before a congressional committee to testify in support of the administration's position during the furor over whether Truman's assistant secretary of the treasury, Harry Dexter White, had been a communist agent.

It was President John F. Kennedy who confirmed the primacy and importance of the Director more than anyone had in years, when he announced, immediately after his election in 1960 — even before choosing an attorney general — that J. Edgar Hoover would be retained as head of the FBI. The attorney general, of course, was to be the President's younger brother, Robert F. Kennedy. Before the President's brother took the job, he went to pay court to the Director, an old friend from the younger Kennedy's days on the staff of Senator Joseph McCarthy's investigating committee. Hoover initially welcomed the notion of having a protégé (and the son of an old friend, Joseph P.

Kennedy) as his new "boss" in the Justice Department. But Hoover was aging, and this "boss" meant to be a real boss. The relationship turned poisonous, especially after President Kennedy's assassination in 1963. The Democratic years of 1961 through 1968 were, for the most part, difficult ones for the Bureau and the Justice Department. Many FBI officials seemed to concentrate their working hours on undercutting Attorneys General Robert Kennedy, Nicholas deB. Katzenbach (whom they called "Katzenjammer"), and Ramsey Clark. But Hoover's staying power remained intact; he held open his direct lines to Presidents Kennedy and Lyndon B. Johnson. His real trouble came later, from the people whom the Director felt closer to than anyone since the Roosevelt era, the administration of his old friend Richard M. Nixon.

But the Director probably died without ever knowing about that trouble. He seemed confident that he had held the line in good times and bad and that he would leave behind a Bureau that was solid as a rock, an agency that had become as powerful as any in the world, an institution that by the 1960s and 1970s one way or another touched or affected almost every American's life at some point, an enterprise so strong that it had utterly lost the capability to recognize and examine its weaknesses.

"When Mr. Hoover died, the Bureau — the old Bureau — died too," said an outsider who later came in with Clarence Kelley; "it had to."

How the Bureau Works

IV

Criminal Jurisdiction

[W]hen we reflect upon the present condition of affairs in this country, and remember that there are, as I am reliably advised, more gangsters under arms in the United States at this hour than there are men under arms in the entire United States Army, we realize the necessity for taking drastic measures to deal with gangsters.

— *Senator Henry F. Ashurst (D-Arizona), March 29, 1934, during Senate debate on "crime bills" proposed by the Roosevelt administration*

BOB LEE, TWENTY-NINE YEARS OLD, tall, sharply dressed, and newly moustachioed, strides into the Tampa federal courthouse for the return of a verdict. He tries to look dispassionate and unconcerned, but his composure is shaken slightly by the hostile glances and angry whispers of the family he must pass between the elevator and the courtroom. ("The little kids looked at me like I was Simon Legree," he later recounts to his colleagues in the Tampa Field Office; "they hated me because I was trying to put Dad in jail.")

The case has special interest for Lee because the crime that the father and son defendants are accused of is assault on a federal officer engaged in the performance of his duties, and the federal officer-victim is Lee himself. Some months earlier, in a rural area near Tampa, the agent and his partner were in the process of serving a fugitive warrant on the father, who was wanted on a criminal charge in another state, when the man and his teenage son allegedly turned on Lee and attacked him to try to prevent the arrest. Had the man gone along peacefully, his arrest probably would have been the last he saw of the federal agents; ordinarily, the federal charge — "unlawful flight to avoid prosecution" or, in the case of a bail jumper or escaped prisoner, "unlawful flight to avoid confinement" — is immediately dropped and the prisoner returned for trial on the pending local charges. But the FBI takes seriously any physical resistance to its agents, and Lee and his partner, once they had subdued the man and taken him into custody, went straight to the United States attorney and filed their own charges.

The trial of the assault case has taken two days, with the agents as the key prosecution witnesses, and now the jury comes in to announce it has acquitted the son but convicted the father. As the other children sob in the front row of the courtroom, the judge declares that the man, who says that he wants to make Tampa his home, will remain free pending sentencing, but he adds that "if you jump bail, agents of the FBI and other federal agencies will begin looking for you . . . and they'll find you . . . and you'll be in worse trouble than you are now."

Back in the field office, a relatively small one where camaraderie runs high among the younger agents, Lee is received warmly and treated like someone who has had some special trauma in his life. The conversation in the bullpen is lively, with most of the agents agreeing that the worst development is that the father was "OR'd" (freed on his own recognizance). "That's the same scumbag who tried to hurt my body," says Lee in a tone of disgust; "he can jump again, and I'll be sent out into a field at night to wait for him." Others reassure him: "Oh well, one [conviction] is better than none." "Batting .500 isn't bad." "We told the truth; they didn't." "You should've seen the act — the kids were crying and looking up at the judge." Lee is resigned to it all: "Well, I don't get paid any more for a guilty than a not guilty. My world's not going to change." Then a smile, a sigh, and a mocking remark to the woman agent at the next desk: "It's such an exciting life." The group drifts off to a nearby bar to cheer up Lee.

Bob Lee (full name: Robert E. Lee) is from Tennessee, where he worked for the state Law Enforcement Planning Agency after leaving the Marine Corps and before joining the FBI. In the Tampa Field Office, he is assigned, along with a black agent, to "the road trip," which means that he gets a variety of assignments from different squads in the office, mostly involving visits to small rural communities. ("I can talk to these people . . . say 'Howdy' and ask them how their tomatoes are doing . . . and find out what I need to know.") Because he is recently divorced, there is a possibility that Lee, like other young single agents, will be transferred to a major urban field office, such as New York. But he hopes not, since he does most of his work in Tampa for the "fugitive squad" and he finds that "the best work there is" in the FBI. He enjoys his assignment enough to have listed Tampa as his "office of preference"; he likes talking to simple folk in trying to track down fugitives, making frequent arrests, and having a rapid turnover of cases.

Lee would not have that exciting caseload — and would probably not be an FBI agent at all — were it not for some dramatic and extraordinary developments back in the 1930s.

During the last years of Prohibition and the start of the Depression, the United States was seized by an unprecedented wave of violent and well-publicized crimes. The names of the most notorious gangsters were as well known by the average citizen as those of movie stars or politicians, and entire communities — small towns as well as big cities — lived in dread of when the menace might strike them. Generations later movies like *Bonnie and Clyde* recalled the names, the menace, and the sensationalism that accompanied them then as now. The gangsters were mobile and, for the most part, clever; they took advantage of the limited jurisdiction of local and state police forces by fleeing quickly across city, county, and state lines.

Perhaps the most frightening new crime of the era was kidnapping, which invariably extended beyond the reach of any single jurisdiction. "It is a crime," former Congressman Cleveland A. Newton told the House Judiciary Committee in February 1932,

which during the past years has grown by leaps and bounds, because it is a most profitable racket, and in many respects the safest racket of all the dangerous forms of crime — we find that there are usually from seven to ten persons involved in every kidnapping; it takes about that many to "put on the job." It is the kind of crime where criminals are efficient, and where they are experienced, and where they lay their plans in advance for the purpose of covering up the crime. It is practically impossible to get direct evidence against the individual so that it is necessary to use the laws of conspiracy.

Whereas at one time kidnapping had been a crime largely perpetrated by gangsters on each other — for example, by rival groups of bootleggers and gamblers — the latest victims were what Newton called "people of respectability, members of the best families," at least in his hometown of St. Louis. That city's police chief, Joseph A. Gerk, told the committee that two hundred and eighty-two kidnappings had been reported nationally in 1931 alone, and that there might have been as many more cases that were unreported and unknown because the victims, once returned safely, were afraid to talk. Gerk complained that corrupt "peace officers" in some jurisdictions refused to cooperate with kidnap investigations and that they might be helping to hold the abduction victims pending the payment of ransom. "And all of this, gentlemen, is not in Manchuria," declared an alarmed Walter B. Weisenberger, president of the St. Louis Chamber of Commerce; "it is not in Soviet Russia, or in Africa — it is in St. Louis, U.S.A., in the year 1932, and in the land of liberty. And you have a thing like that existing in one of the largest cities of this country today, so that these people, in securing protection for their loved ones who are threatened, can only do it by an organized vigilance committee, such as existed in the old days in the West."

Newton, Gerk, and Weisenberger were testifying in support of a bill introduced by their congressman, Democrat John J. Cochran, "forbidding the transportation of any person or persons in interstate or foreign commerce, kidnapped or otherwise unlawfully detained" — in effect, making kidnapping a federal crime. For all the terror and concern over kidnapping, there was by no means an overwhelming national consensus in favor of such legislation, which was regarded in some quarters as a dangerous incursion on the police powers reserved to the states in the federal Constitution. President Herbert Hoover's embattled administration, although it had the early equivalent of a tough law-and-order position, was reluctant to rock the boat in an election year. Some members of the House Judiciary Committee received the testimony with skepticism and wondered aloud whether the more appropriate action might not be merely to clean up and strengthen local law enforcement.

Nonetheless, an unusual combination of forces supported the idea of a more ambitious federal role. In the late 1920s, for example, conservative businessmen and former public officials had formed a group they called the National Crime Commission, which supported "vigorous measures" to halt the crime wave and urged tough and uncompromising punishment of those caught and convicted. A 1927 conference held by the group in Washington attracted prison officials, academic students of crime, and representatives of organizations ranging from the American National Retail Jewelers' Association to Rotary International and the Salvation Army; one member of the NCC's executive committee was the defeated Democratic vice-presidential candidate of 1920, soon to become governor of New York, Franklin Delano Roosevelt. The NCC's appeal was largely emotional, but alongside it was the more sober and scholarly warning from the National Commission on

Law Observance and Enforcement, named by President Hoover and chaired by former Attorney General George W. Wickersham, that crime had become a genuinely national problem and that the country faced a threat from lawlessness. It stressed the need for a strong federal presence in law enforcement. For quaint, even incredible, as it may seem now, the fact was that in 1932 many citizens, officials, and scholars believed that, except in specific and isolated cases — such as "white slave traffic" — the detection and prosecution of crime was none of the federal government's business.

However, force was gathering behind the development of a novel legal theory that the commerce clause of the Constitution, which provided for federal regulation of interstate and foreign trade, could be broadly employed in what was just coming to be called the "war" against crime. "The use of the federal power," wrote J. P. Chamberlain later in the *American Bar Association Journal*, "was based on the theory that it was only by the use of both federal and state power that the evil complained of could be regulated in view of the ease of distribution through facilities of interstate commerce." This had essentially been the logic behind the Mann Act of 1910, officially aimed at controlling interstate prostitution, a law that made a federal crime of a traditionally local one and gave major responsibilities to the Bureau of Investigation. It was upheld as constitutional by the Supreme Court in separate cases in 1913 and 1917. Similarly, in 1919, Congress passed the Dyer Act (named for its principal sponsor, Congressman Leonidas C. Dyer, a Republican from Missouri), forbidding interstate transportation of a stolen motor vehicle and receipt or disposal of any such vehicle. In a landmark 1925 opinion by Chief Justice William Howard Taft upholding the Dyer Act, a unanimous Supreme Court said in language than now seems as defensive as it does dated:

Congress can certainly regulate interstate commerce to the extent of forbidding and punishing the use of such commerce as an agency to promote immorality, dishonesty or the spread of any evil or harm to the people of other States from the State of origin. In doing this it is merely exercising the police power, for the benefit of the public, within the field of interstate commerce. . . . It is known of all men that the radical change in transportation of persons and goods effected by the introduction of the automobile, the speed with which it moves, and the ease with which evil-minded persons can avoid capture, have greatly encouraged and increased crimes. One of the crimes which have been encouraged is the theft of the automobiles themselves and their immediate transportation to places remote from homes of the owners. . . . The quick passage of the machines into another State helps to conceal the trail of the thieves, gets the stolen property into another police jurisdiction and facilitates the finding of safer places in which to dispose of the booty at a good price. This is a gross misuse of interstate commerce.

Spurred on by such endorsement, the federal government made ample and successful use of the Dyer Act, through United States attorneys and regional Bureau agents, to punish car thefts.

If prostitutes and cars were proper subjects for legislation, argued Weisenberger before the House Judiciary Committee, "under the Federal laws, it should be made a crime to steal a child from the mother's breast and take it away from the State." It was only a small expansion of federal authority that was sought, insisted the bill's proponents, and not a general "centralization of power in the Federal Government." As Congressman Cochran, sponsor of the antikidnapping bill, explained his credentials, "Ever since I have been a Member of Congress, I have openly opposed Federal aid measures. I am opposed to them today — with the exception of rivers and harbors — and I am perfectly willing to vote today or any other day, to set a date to discontinue Federal aid to the States in connection with good roads." But in light of the kidnapping threat, Cochran argued, an exception to the purist position was justified.

The turning point came in March 1932, when the twenty-month-old son of aviation pioneer Charles A. Lindbergh was kidnapped from the family's New Jersey home. The case attracted attention across the country and around the world, as the Lindbergh family paid a $50,000 cash ransom in the hope of recovering their first child. As long as there was a chance that the Lindbergh baby would be found alive, Congress deliberately delayed action on the pending legislation lest it provoke the kidnapper to a reckless reaction. But after the child was discovered dead, a variation of the Cochran proposal, now dubbed the "Lindbergh Kidnap Law," was passed and signed by a reluctant President Herbert Hoover — still a states-rights man on crime, only now bowing to a strong wind. A companion bill made it a federal crime to send a ransom demand or a kidnapping threat through the mails.

Jurisdiction under the new law fell to the Bureau of Investigation, but the impact was hardly felt overnight. Agents, unless they violated the rulebook, were not permitted to make arrests themselves, but were supposed to call on a United States marshal or a policeman to take a fugitive or other criminal they had located into custody; although many agents armed themselves in self-defense, they were not formally authorized to carry weapons. The Bureau could only enter kidnapping cases after it was firmly established that the kidnap victim had been transported across a state line, which was often too late to be of much help in solving the case. The Lindbergh case, in fact, was not broken until September 1934, more than two and a half years after the actual abduction of the child, when Bruno Richard Hauptmann, a carpenter from the Bronx, was arrested after spending one of the gold certificates included in the ransom. (The Bureau claimed primary credit for solving the controversial case, but to this day there is dispute over whether that credit more properly should have been shared with the New Jersey State Police, the New York City Police Department, and U.S. Treasury agents.)

The crime wave continued unabated through 1933, as the gangsters who violated Prohibition, newly repealed after the fifteen-year experiment, looked for other things to do. Bank robberies and kidnappings competed for the national spotlight, and there were plenty of both. One incident that especially shocked the country's conscience was the "Kansas City Massacre": a group of Bureau agents and policemen were escorting Frank Nash, a convicted and escaped mail robber who had been recaptured in Hot Springs, Arkansas, out of Kansas City's Union Station for the trip back to prison in Leavenworth, when the convict and four of his guards were slain in broad daylight by a gang of underworld figures, including Charles "Pretty Boy" Floyd, who had intended to free Nash. Shortly thereafter, Charles F. Urschel, a wealthy oilman, was kidnapped during a bridge game at his home in Oklahoma City by Alfred L. Bates and George "Machine Gun" Kelly, the man who allegedly nicknamed Bureau agents "G-men" during his later capture. John Dillinger, the enigmatic and often romanticized gangster, released from prison in a bitter mood in May 1933, went on a fourteen-month spree during which he robbed at least a dozen banks; stage-managed and supplied the guns for the escape of some friends from the Michigan City, Indiana, prison; led raids on midwestern police stations and city halls; and twice broke out of jail in spectacular fashion. Lester Gillis, alias "Baby Face" Nelson, escaped from prison and killed three Bureau agents before he finally died himself in a shootout. Clyde Barrow and Bonnie Parker also terrorized the Midwest with their exploits. The Barker-Karpis gang, its separate wings led by Kate "Ma" Barker and Alvin "Old Creepy" Karpis, operated virtually unchallenged, robbing banks, killing policemen, and kidnapping wealthy business executives. As Roosevelt's attorney general, Homer Cummings, declared in a speech before the Daughters of the American Revolution, "We are now engaged in a war that threatens the safety of our country — a war with the organized forces of crime."

J. Edgar Hoover led the Bureau into the breach, using what little interstate jurisdiction it already had. Agents pieced together the background of the Kansas City Massacre and identified the culprits, eventually catching them. The Director himself took the midnight phone call from Mrs. Urschel about her husband's abduction on the Bureau's newly installed special emergency kidnap line; the Bureau assembled tiny clues and fragments of the victim's own recollections, once he was safely returned, to track down the place where he had been held, a Texas farm owned by Machine Gun Kelly's in-laws. After a number of embarrassing failures, Bureau agents finally surrounded Dillinger on a Chicago street and killed him. Much was made of the fact that under the law as it stood the Bureau had no jurisdiction in the search for this "Public Enemy Number One" until he stole a car in Indiana and drove it across the state line into Illinois, thus violating the Dyer Act. Some of the others, like Ma Barker, her son Fred, and Karpis — dubbed "Public Rat Number One" by Hoover — took longer to find, but eventually they were killed or captured and hauled in amid great ballyhoo. It was Hoover's glory, and he made the most of it. The Bureau was busting gangs, and the gangbusters were ready for their reward.

The Bureau's success, and its flair, lent strength to the Roosevelt administration's desire to build upon the Lindbergh Law and get the federal government far more involved in investigating and punishing crimes of violence through legislation under the commerce clause. The new kind of crime that was the heritage of the nation's experiment with Prohibition, it was argued, demanded a new and aggressive response, and the resources previously spent on enforcement of Prohibition by the federal agency specifically assigned that fool's errand should be redirected to other, genuinely pressing problems. The Seventy-third Congress, elected with Roosevelt in the Democratic landslide of 1932, was more willing than its predecessor. When Attorney General Cummings requested the passage of some ambitious new laws in 1934, there was none of the uproar and few of the objections that had accompanied the original antikidnapping law proposal. Senator William H. King, a Democrat from Utah, did express a strong demurrer during floor debate on March 29 over a bill that would make it a crime to flee from one state to another in order to avoid testimony or prosecution:

I appreciate the importance of legislation which is within the purview of the Federal Government to deal with racketeering and gangsters. The criminal records of gangsters and racketeers have aroused the country and led to a demand for their control. Undoubtedly, if the States exercised the authority

74

possessed by them and zealously enforced their criminal laws, many of the crimes which have shocked them would not have been committed. However, I am sure that the States and their officials will be more earnest in the future in curbing the crimes referred to and punishing law violators. Referring to the bill which we are now discussing . . . any State has the power to deal with these questions, and to enact laws providing that any person charged with a felony who flees from a State shall be guilty of an offense and be subject to prosecution therefor. . . . By this measure we are taking a position that the States are incompetent to deal with matters with which they have complete authority to deal and which are exclusively within their jurisdiction. . . . I shall not object to the consideration of this bill. I shall vote against it, however, because I believe it will be abused in its administration. I doubt its constitutionality; and I have not any doubt on earth that in the hysteria now existing, and that which may follow, persons will be imposed upon, will be arrested and prosecuted under the Federal law, where the facts and circumstances will not warrant it. We are assuming that the States are wholly impotent to deal with questions which properly arise under their authority. We are challenging the competency of the States to govern their own affairs. We are substituting a Federal criminal code for the criminal codes of the States.

That was, in effect, what the Roosevelt administration was asking Congress to do, but Senator King was nearly alone in his protests. When the same bill and others in the package came up on the House floor five weeks later, they stirred so little controversy that one of the party leaders said he had granted leave for the day to "a good many men who are not specially interested in these matters."

For the most part, members of both houses accepted the reasoning advanced in memoranda sent to Capitol Hill by Cummings. On the bill forbidding interstate flight to avoid prosecution or testimony, he argued:

While this bill would undoubtedly extend Federal criminal jurisdiction in a marked degree, yet it would afford an opportunity for the apprehension of the roving class of criminals who are responsible for so many of the crimes of violence in our country. Although drastic in nature, it is my opinion ultimately some relief must be provided for those who suffer from offenses committed by criminals who flee from the scene of crime [sic] beyond the jurisdiction of the State wherein the crime is committed and eventually escape punishment entirely. I advocate the most serious consideration for this act.

In the House, Congressman D. D. Glover (D-Arkansas) declared that "the passage of those acts will be the finest day's work that Congress has ever done during my experience." Expressing his own spirit for the fight and sounding very much like some of his successors of later decades, Glover continued:

After the passage of these acts there will be no excuse on the part of those whose duty it is to enforce the law to say "We have not the power to handle the situation." Then, we shall have the right to expect of them the enforcement of the law to the letter. I am glad to see Congress giving every aid possible to those who have the duty of enforcing the law. It was my privilege to serve as prosecuting attorney of my district and I know how difficult it is to enforce the law against criminals without public sentiment backing up our officials. I am glad that Congress has heeded the public sentiment that has been so often expressed in the United States recently for law enforcement against crime. I am sure that whatever else is necessary to strengthen the hands of those whose duty it is to enforce the law, that power, so far as Congress is able to give it, will be given our officials. We hope also that the States will follow this lead and will so strengthen the State laws that both the States and the Nation may cooperate together in a great way in putting down the crime we have, that is so prevalent in the United States.

On one day, May 18, 1934, without even taking a record vote, Congress voted final passage of six of the laws requested by Cummings; three more were adopted in June. In addition to the Fugitive Felon Act that forbade escape across state lines to avoid prosecution, the laws gave the Bureau a broad range of enforcement powers and protected its agents. Stiff penalties were enacted for the killing or assaulting of federal officers. The Lindbergh Law was amended to create a presumption of interstate transportation of the victim after seven days (thus getting the Bureau into a case automatically), to cover cases where there was no ransom demand, and to add the death penalty. It became a federal crime to extort money or other valuables by telephone or any other means subject to interstate regulation, and to interfere with interstate business and trade by threats or any other form of intimidation. Employees of federal penitentiaries were formally forbidden to assist in any way the escape of prisoners. Robbery of any national bank or member bank of the Federal Reserve System became a federal violation; and, in a parallel to the Dyer Act, so did interstate transportation of stolen property worth $5,000 or more. The Bureau was also given secondary jurisdiction under the National Firearms Act, and it was made clear that agents had full arrest power* and

---

* But a formal warrant was always deemed necessary until 1951, when Congress granted agents the authority for arrests without a warrant when they were actual witnesses to the commission of a felony.

the authority to carry any kind of arms. As a special incentive to build support for the new offensive, in the last days of the 1934 session Congress also appropriated $25,000 to be spent by the attorney general on rewards for the capture of fugitives and another $25,000 on rewards for information leading to the arrest of fugitives by the authorities. Significantly, the penalty for violating any of these new federal laws was at least five years in prison or five thousand dollars' fine or both — more than under most state laws. Federal prosecutors were also empowered to step in and take charge of any of these cases whenever they wanted, even if jurisdiction was shared with a state.

In the course of a few days, Congress enacted one of the most important, if least recognized, New Deal reforms. It gave the federal government a comprehensive criminal code for the first time; the Bureau now had not only a mandate, but vast new authority.

Federal criminal procedure was also tightened up to make things easier for the government. In the meantime, at the urging of congressmen who were impressed by the Bureau's work, Hoover and Cummings floated a proposal to have the Bureau run a national police training school for local law enforcement officers. The Attorney General's Crime Conference of December 1934 liked the idea, and seven months later the National Academy was functioning with a first class of twenty-three police officers.

As one historian of federal law enforcement, Arthur C. Millspaugh, put it in a 1937 Brookings Institution study, the legislation and other decisions of the early 1930s meant that "the metamorphosis of the Bureau of Investigation was complete. It had sloughed off its chrysalis. Its agents, the 'G-men,' no longer 'examiners,' were now armed, trained, mobile, active in the pursuit of criminals, rapidly developing a legend of invincibility, and kept in the spotlight, sometimes to their embarrassment, by a remarkable propaganda policy."

The legislation of the 1930s formed a solid base for the Bureau's criminal jurisdiction, and those laws even today account for a major percentage of the agency's activities and its beloved statistical accomplishments. But they also served as an important precedent, which would lead Congress in other times of alarm or crisis to heap new responsibilities on Hoover, often still relying on the commerce clause of the Constitution. Harry and Bonaro Overstreet, in their sympathetic *The FBI in Our Open Society* (thousands of copies of which have been distributed by the FBI), note that the 1960s was another period when Congress created many areas of actual or potential criminal jurisdiction for the Bureau. In a period of a few weeks, for example, seven statutes were adopted — including a vague-sounding prohibition on "interstate travel or transportation in aid of racketeering" — to fight the major gambling operations of organized crime.* Other federal laws passed during the 1960s forbade interstate bribery schemes to influence the outcome of sports events; broadened the category of people protected by the law against assault on federal officials; made it an offense to "destroy or mutilate a Selective Service registration card"; prohibited false statements in connection with application for loans insured by the Federal Housing Administration; banned the manufacture or marketing of cigarettes in packages without a health warning; and for the first time specifically made it illegal to kill or assault the President and Vice-President, giving clear responsibility for assassination investigations to the FBI. Meanwhile, Congress also gave the Bureau substantial assignments in the Civil Rights Act of 1964, with its stress on equal access rights to public accommodations, and in the Voting Rights Act of 1965. Eventually, the waiting period for presumption of interstate flight in kidnapping cases was shortened to only twenty-four hours, so that the Bureau was bound to be involved in investigating all but the simplest, most quickly solved abductions.

Even when no specific legislative assignment has been made, the FBI's jurisdiction can be invoked. Every year since 1921, the annual appropriations act for the Department of Justice has included a vague grant of investigative authority for the Bureau. As now codified in Section 533 of Title 28 of the U.S. Code, it says that "the attorney general may appoint officials . . . to detect and prosecute crimes against the United States . . . [and] to conduct such other investigations regarding official matters under the control of the Department of Justice and the Department of State as may be directed by the attorney general."

The FBI today lists publicly more than eighty categories of criminal jurisdiction, from "admiralty matters" and "government and Indian reservation matters" to the "Switchblade Knife Act" and "interstate obscene or harassing telephone calls." The "classifications," as they are called, used to identify cases and handle them administratively in groups, are derived from hundreds of individual statutes for which the FBI has enforcement responsibility. Some of the jobs are obviously trivial, such as protecting the Smokey Bear symbol used in national forest fire-prevention campaigns and guarding against fraudulent use of the Peace Corps "name, seal or emblem"; but others, including investigation of "crimes aboard aircraft," can involve unanticipated

* For an account of the Bureau's work in the field of organized crime, see Chapter XVII.

78

volumes of work and danger, for example, during an epidemic of airplane hijackings. Certain predictable areas, however, still account for much of the bureau's work: of the 37,891 fugitives it reported "locating" during Fiscal Year 1974, 22,224 were wanted for desertion, harboring deserters, or enticing others to desert from the armed forces; 2,465 were escaped federal prisoners and parole or probation violators; 3,478 had fled across state lines to avoid prosecution, confinement, or testimony; 2,260 were wanted for Selective Service Act violations; 1,233 for interstate transportation of stolen property; and 1,045 for interstate transportation of stolen motor vehicles or aircraft.

On some occasions, Hoover chose to fend off attempts by the FBI's enthusiastic supporters in Congress to extend the agency's authority into both minute areas of crime (such as "interstate transportation of stolen dogs") and more ambitious ones, in the simplistic belief that an evil touched by the Bureau would instantly disappear. Throughout his career Hoover railed against the danger of converting the Bureau into a "national police force," and his prestige on Capitol Hill was so substantial that he was generally permitted to pick and choose which assignments would be appropriate and desirable for the FBI to take on. It was a cozy and coy game: when he consented to accept an important new assignment, or to expand an old one, he also often managed to have it accompanied by an increase in appropriations and an authorization of new additional manpower. Part of the gimmick was to avoid new areas so difficult that they might drag down the statistics on which the Bureau has built its image; and thus the Bureau has never had anything beyond the most peripheral involvement in the nation's fight against illegal narcotics activity. That responsibility, on the federal level, has fallen to a string of specialized agencies, including the Bureau of Narcotics and Dangerous Drugs, now united in and succeeded by a separate branch of the Justice Department called the Drug Enforcement Administration.

Other aspects of federal law-enforcement responsibility have also remained outside the Bureau's scope over the years, although there is often overlap. The Secret Service, working within the Treasury Department, has two primary responsibilities: personal protection of the President, Vice-President, people running for or retired from those offices and their immediate families, as well as visiting heads of state and other foreign dignitaries in the United States designated for special protection; and enforcement of the laws against counterfeiting. The Postal Inspection Service investigates many crimes involving illegal use of the mails and other related irregularities. The Bureau of Customs polices the nation's frontiers, and the Immigration and Natu-

79

ralization Service has responsibility for enforcing the immigration statutes and regulations. The Internal Revenue Service investigates tax violations, and the Alcohol, Tobacco and Firearms Bureau of the Treasury Department has jurisdiction over most offenses involving weapons and illegal whiskey and cigarette marketing.

Despite these exceptions, however, FBI agents have become involved in so many areas of enforcement over the years that they are in effect federal policemen, frequently drawn into matters where the lines between state and federal authority are blurred, and sometimes serving the same symbolic — if less visible — role as the old-fashioned cop on the beat, protecting the denizens from the evil, often unknown forces that are deemed to threaten them, and assuming themselves to have a broad and open mandate on the public's behalf. Some 65 percent of FBI agent time is spent investigating criminal matters, and this is a responsibility agents tend to take very seriously indeed.

E. T. "Easy" Zinn, a former Memphis policeman who has served as an agent in large and small field offices as well as at FBI headquarters, is as deeply plunged into the Bureau's criminal jurisdiction as anyone could be. His latest assignment, and newest step up the FBI career ladder, is as an assistant-special-agent-in-charge (ASAC) of the New York Field Office. The office is so large that it is administered by an assistant director, four special-agents-in-charge (SACs) and five ASACs. Zinn's bailiwick is New York's General Criminal (as opposed to Organized Crime) Division, to which hundreds of agents are assigned. Unlike Bob Lee and other agents assigned to smaller offices like Tampa, who tend to have a wide variety of cases, the New York agents are channeled into specialties, and each one usually becomes an expert on two or three specific, sometimes minutely defined, violations of federal law. Because New York is such a major port, for example, the field office needs people trained to investigate allegations of "crime on the high seas," such as murders on merchant ships and an extortion–bomb threat against the ocean liner *Queen Elizabeth II*. At the same time, entire squads can be kept busy hunting down stolen stocks and bonds.

New on the job and with his direct boss off in San Francisco temporarily helping with the investigation of the disappearance of Patricia Hearst, Zinn is bewildered but busy. Only a few days after he arrived he was awakened by the office in the middle of the night with the report that a large apartment building on Second Avenue had been ripped apart by an explosion. Although there were early indications that a gas leak caused the blast, Zinn raced to the scene on the chance that there would be evidence of a bombing or some other federal crime involving the crossing of state lines. Since the ASAC/Criminal personally supervises the squad responsible for investigating bombings and destruction of aircraft, Zinn was also notified when a bomb exploded at Kennedy Airport. (Agents were available on the spot there, since the New York office has a resident agency with several men based at the airport.)

In a city like New York, say Zinn and Robert Hartman, a unit supervisor in charge of fugitive cases, the work is "good" — plentiful and often exciting — but at times hopelessly complicated and frustrating. Bank robbers who know their way around can disappear into a subway in minutes, and "there is a lot of dirty legwork" in trying to pick up their trail or to piece together several crimes around a common modus operandi. Most agents going out on the street in New York travel by bus or subway; there is one Bureau car available for about every five agents, but instead of being downstairs or across the street, as in many field offices, most of them are parked some fifteen blocks away. The General Criminal Division has trained several of its agents as "stick men," who have special skill in speed driving and can weave their way through New York traffic easily in a chase situation. They are on call for emergencies. It has also broken with Bureau tradition and encouraged some agents to grow beards or moustaches that may be useful for undercover work and surveillances in everything from difficult fugitive cases to kidnap investigations.

Despite the frustrations, Zinn asserts, "the men love this work. . . . You've got action going all the time. . . . A lot of second-office agents come here and catch on quickly, working with older men on their squad." The usual pattern has been for agents to seek transfer away from New York as soon as possible; but now, Hartman points out, "there are quite a few twenty-year fellows around." He has been in the New York Field Office about that long himself, and though it was not always so, it is now listed as his "office of preference." He debunks the conventional wisdom that New York is an unfortunate place to be assigned and prefers the Bureau line that "if you're a good agent in Mobile, you can be here, too."

Zinn, forty-seven, eager on the job after some twenty-five years in what he likes to call "police work," is of the breed that insists it is a privilege and a pleasure to serve in any position for the Bureau anywhere. But he is particularly enthusiastic about his new challenge in New York. Zinn is not one to glamorize the job or to innovate, but rather stresses the importance of routine and often plodding traditional investigative techniques, such as the "neighborhood investigation." "Periodically, in law enforcement, you get a break or some luck," he says, insisting that that is how the average criminal case is solved, by the Bureau as by other agencies. "If new techniques can be devised within the framework of our jurisdiction, I'm all in favor of it," he adds in a tone that indicates he has his doubts. "Previously we could go in and flood most situations with manpower, but now we are dealing with a different type of criminal. He is more educated, both formally and informally by the media," Zinn says. He pauses and sighs. "It's just not the criminal of the thirties that we're dealing with."

V

"Applicant Work" and Civil Investigations

If any citizen knows of the presence of a single Communist or other subversive person in any Federal job, let him furnish that information, and the evidence which supports his belief, to the Attorney General or to the FBI. Any information that may be furnished in response to this request will be promptly investigated and will be acted upon if the allegations are found to be true.
— President Harry S Truman, speaking before
the Federal Bar Association in Washington,
April 24, 1950

IN OCTOBER 1974 PRESIDENT GERALD R. FORD NAMED a new man, Andrew E. Gibson, to become the Federal Energy Administrator, a position at the center of American efforts to develop meaningful policies to deal with the energy shortage. Gibson was a man unknown to the public whose nomination was not expected to stir particular controversy; there was no reason to believe that he would be any better or worse than anyone else at sorting through the tangle of oil industry profits and fuel consumption. But Gibson became quickly known, and promptly disqualified, when it was discovered that the President's choice was receiving nearly $900,000 in severance pay from an oil transport company that might be affected by his actions in the government — an impermissible circumstance, especially at a time of great sensitivity to ethics in government after the scandals of the Nixon administration. The White House was embarrassed. Because of Ford's eagerness to fill the important job speedily, he had neglected to ask for a "background check" on Gibson by the FBI. Such a check, it was suggested, surely would have revealed such an obvious conflict of interest.

This President, however, was no more hapless than his recent predecessors. For over twenty years, points out William V. Cleveland, assistant director of the Bureau in charge of its Special Investigative Division, "each and every [President] has had his fingers burned, until he has learned that it's a very wise thing to have us check people out." Dwight Eisenhower had himself photographed at the White House with a prospective top aide only a short time before that aide had to withdraw for what one FBI official later called "the very best of reasons" — homosexuality. John Kennedy named a prominent black attorney to become a commissioner of the District of Columbia, only to discover that the man had not paid his income tax for several years. Lyndon Johnson learned about the problems of his personal assistant, Walter Jenkins, after police arrested Jenkins on a sodomy charge in a YMCA restroom in the capital. Richard Nixon, determined to put his own brand of conservatives on the Supreme Court, plunged in first with the nomination of Clement F. Haynsworth, Jr., then with that of G. Harrold Carswell; had anyone asked the FBI to investigate, the President might have learned before their abortive confirmation hearings that there were suggestions of financial conflicts in Haynsworth's background and evidence of white supremacist sentiment in Carswell's. (The FBI took much of the heat for the failure to discover this information, but J. Edgar Hoover, enamored as he was of the Nixon White House, never pointed out publicly that the Bureau was not asked for a background check of these nominees until after some of the negative publicity about them had broken.)

Until the fumble on the Gibson nomination, this run of presidential bad luck had seemed to be over. The FBI, in fact, was very much in the news for its comprehensive investigations of Gerald Ford and Nelson Rockefeller, the first two persons nominated for Vice-President under the terms of the Twenty-fifth Amendment. In Rockefeller's case, it was the Bureau that discovered the vast gifts and loans he had made to other public figures and his personal employees, as well as a Rockefeller family project in 1970 to underwrite a derogatory campaign biography of Arthur Goldberg, who was then trying to unseat Rockefeller as governor of New York. Some people, unaware that the FBI has no authority to investigate candidates for elected public office, looked admiringly at the checks on Ford and Rockefeller and said they wished the same had been done before the election of Spiro Agnew, who resigned after admitting that he had not paid taxes on money kicked back to him by Maryland contractors.

For veteran Bureau agents, it was ironic that the tables had turned. The public was applauding and pleading for more of the same kind of work that had once given the FBI a bad name — prying into backgrounds, looking for skeletons in the closet, checking on academic performance and social life and personal finances. Whatever it might be called on the outside, nosiness or foolishness, within the Bureau this is known as "applicant work," often boring and plodding, frequently assigned to new and unsophisticated agents. It now consumes only about 5 percent of agent time, but still accounts for a major part of the Bureau's image.

The original civil service rules issued by the federal government in 1884 stated that no inquiry could be made concerning the "political or religious opinions or affiliations of any applicant" for jobs covered by the new merit system. That protection was strengthened by the Lloyd–La Follette Act of 1912, which guaranteed civil service employees the right to be presented with the charges against them and an opportunity to reply before they could be removed or disciplined.

But as the old fears over the nation's security from subversion returned in the years leading up to World War II, the guardians of public safety looked this time among government employees for their "radical" bogeymen; and as Hoover made it clear on many occasions after President Roosevelt gave him responsibility for protecting the nation's internal security, membership in or sympathy with "organizations such as the German-American Bund and the Communist Party" simply could not be viewed as being in the category of legitimate "political activities." From the moment it was formed in 1938, the House Committee on Un-American Activities warned that the New Deal had peppered the government with "subversive" or otherwise "disloyal" employees. Chairman Martin Dies, a congressman from Texas, claimed that these employees were generally members of "front organizations of the Communist Party" and demanded they be dismissed. Congress appropriated $100,000 in 1941 specifically for an FBI investigation of, among others, more than a thousand federal employees on a special list provided by the Dies committee. (Two were eventually dismissed and another one disciplined, as the only results of the special inquiry.) Congress had encouraged the new paranoia with a provision in the 1939 Hatch Act that made it illegal for any employee of a federal agency or contractor "to have membership in any political party or organization which advocates the overthrow of our constitutional form of government." All appropriation acts passed in 1941 and for many years thereafter included a prohibition on using the money "to pay the salary or wages of any person who advocates, or who is a member of an organization that advocates, the overthrow of the Government of the United States by force or violence."

"Loyalty" was rarely, if ever, defined, but it was the primary concern of special wartime regulations issued by the Civil Service Commission and of the newly established Interdepartmental Committee on Employee Investigations. Particularly "sensitive agencies" like the military were permitted to dismiss outright, without any formal procedures, anyone considered to be "a security risk." It was President Truman, however, who, hounded by his critics and driven to show that he was as concerned as the next fellow about subversion, advanced the issue to hysterical proportions after the war. On March 22, 1947, he issued Executive Order 9835, otherwise known as the Loyalty Order, requiring that "there shall be a loyalty investigation of every person entering the civilian employment" of the federal government and a review of those already holding jobs, from file clerks and mailmen to the highest positions. A Loyalty Review Board was established to coordinate the effort, and whenever an initial check turned up anything suspicious, the FBI was to conduct a full-fledged investigation. Congress appropriated eleven million dollars for the first year of loyalty review, most of it going to the Bureau. The Federal Employee Loyalty Program was handsomely launched, and state and local governments were encouraged to set up their own miniature loyalty programs patterned after the federal one.

The project began with the fingerprinting of millions of people already on the federal payroll, who were also required to complete background questionnaires for the FBI's use. Each agency had a special board to examine its own people. "Disloyalty" could be spotted if the employee's or applicant's "activities and associations" included sabotage, treason, "advocacy of revolution or force or violence to alter the constitutional form of government of the United States," "intentional, unauthorized disclosure . . . of documents or information of a confidential or non-public character" obtained through government employment, "acting so as to serve the interests of another government in preference to the interest of the United States," and "membership in, affiliation with or sympathetic association with any foreign or domestic organization, association, movement, group or combination of persons, designated by the Attorney General as totalitarian, fascist, communist or subversive." The "attorney general's list" of organizations, originally drawn up in 1943 by Francis Biddle but now updated and issued with the executive order, was a dizzying array of names, from the Military Virtue Society of Japan and the National Blue Star

Mothers of America to the Connecticut State Youth Conference and the Ku Klux Klan. If no such "derogatory information" was found concerning an employee or applicant for a federal job in the Bureau's initial screening, he or she was in the clear; if something turned up, however, a more complete investigation was ordered.

Loyalty investigations wreaked havoc in the State Department, where 425 people were dismissed between 1947 and 1953 simply on the grounds that they were alleged homosexuals and therefore thought to be security risks. Individual careers were ruined, especially among China experts, who were accused of having communist sympathies when they predicted — correctly — that Mao Tse-tung's revolution would ultimately prevail over the Nationalists led by Chiang Kai-shek. John Stewart Service, for example, became a cause célèbre before the loyalty review board; narrowly cleared, he was later fired anyway by Secretary of State Dean Acheson. Acheson made a controversial decision to retain Service's colleague John Carter Vincent, the subject of a negative finding by the board; but as soon as President Eisenhower's secretary of state, John Foster Dulles, took over, he dropped Vincent. O. Edmund Clubb was a similar victim.

Some government employees who were victims of the loyalty scare eventually managed to beat the charges. Wolf Ladejinsky, an expert on Asian land reform, was removed from the Agriculture Department in 1955 by Secretary Ezra Taft Benson simply because he had three sisters in the Soviet Union — only to be rehired for duty in Vietnam by Harold Stassen of the Foreign Operations Administration. Milo Radulovich lost his commission as a lieutenant in the Air Force because his sister was allegedly subversive; after presentation of his case on nationwide television by Edward R. Murrow, he was reinstated.

The loyalty programs were an extraordinary development in a nation that claimed to be devoted to free thinking and freedom of association. Dignity was conferred upon some of the most outlandish accusations in the files of the House Committee on Un-American Activities, and the federal loyalty-screening apparatus was assumed to be infallible; there was no provision for appeal of its decisions to the courts. Contrary to the constitutional protections prevailing in the courts, if there was a "reasonable doubt" as to a person's "loyalty," the decision went against him; thus was the nation protected from "subversion." Some agencies merely decided not to hire qualified and talented people, or dismissed them on another pretext, rather than face a furor on Capitol Hill or with the loyalty boards; some people withdrew their applications rather than submit to the ordeal. Many of those

87

adjudged to be "disloyal" were in effect blacklisted from any decent employment — the government notified others of the findings against them, although not of the quality of the evidence used to reach that finding.

Meanwhile, there developed in the special regulations drawn up by the "sensitive agencies" a separate category of "non-subversive" information which could also result in one being declared "a security risk" to the government. This idea was institutionalized and extended throughout the government under an expansion of the loyalty program launched with Executive Order 10450, issued by President Eisenhower on April 27, 1953. It was named the Federal Employee Security Program and is still officially in effect. Among the factors that could be disqualifying under its provisions were "any behavior, activities, or associations which tend to show that the individual is not reliable or trustworthy"; "any deliberate misrepresentations, falsifications, or omission of material facts"; "any criminal, infamous, dishonest, immoral, or notoriously disgraceful conduct, habitual use of intoxicants to excess, drug addiction, or sexual perversion"; "an adjudication of insanity, or treatment for serious mental or neurological disorder without satisfactory evidence of cure"; and "any facts which furnish reason to believe that the individual may be subjected to coercion, influence, or pressure which may cause him to act contrary to the best interests of the national security." Dulles used the new program as the vehicle for dismissing another of the embattled China experts, John Paton Davies, Jr., who was said to lack "judgment, discretion and reliability." Hoover boasted of how successfully this program turned up government employees who had not previously acknowledged their criminal records. One of its main effects, however, was also a hunt within the government for homosexuals, people with emotional disorders, and others who might be considered outside the boundaries of normality and therefore somehow potential targets for blackmail.

The new "full background investigation" (also known as a "full field investigation") that was part of some loyalty-security inquiries was big business for the FBI and also the source of considerable controversy. Suddenly Bureau agents, many of them clumsy and inexperienced at the work, were knocking on doors, asking people about themselves and about their neighbors, friends, and relatives on behalf of Uncle Sam. "Loyalty" remained an elusive concept, of course, and some agents tried to find their way by looking into people's reading habits and personal political opinions. They asked whether individuals read liberal journals like *The New Republic*, whether they had supported the 1948 presidential candidacy of Henry Wallace, how they felt about the merits of the American and Soviet social and economic systems, and explored their positions on issues such as racial segregation and socialized medicine. Some of the reports included unreliable gossip and the minutest of trivia, and in keeping with Bureau policy on all cases, the sources of information were always kept secret, even if there was a finding against an employee or applicant and he wanted to appeal (although there were also carefully arranged leaks to congressional committees and the press). Some critics charged that the investigators took on a prosecutor's bias and set up informal quotas for themselves on the amount of subversion, disloyalty, or other questionable conduct that had to be turned up to prove that the program was working successfully. Hoover invariably replied to the critics with indignant outrage, asserting that agents were well trained, did not ask improper questions, sought out both sides of any dispute, noted the biases of any informants, paid scrupulous attention to civil rights, and reported only the facts.

Although the Civil Service Commission and individual government agencies had first responsibility for many aspects of the loyalty-security programs, the Bureau also invested enormous resources in the effort. In an article in the *Northwestern University Law Review* in 1954, the Director reported that the Bureau had processed more than five million "loyalty forms," most of them eventually to be marked "No Disloyal Data," but many resulting in extensive follow-up field investigation. Although the FBI had no formal responsibility for the adjudication of loyalty cases, Hoover noted that of those investigated under the original Truman program, five hundred and sixty were "removed from or denied Federal employment on grounds relating to loyalty" and 6,828 left their jobs or withdrew their applications before the investigations were complete — the implication being that they saw the handwriting on the wall. The percentages were minuscule, but in the eyes of some, the accomplishments were considerable.

However controversial its role in the loyalty-security programs may have been, the Bureau seemed to win the confidence of Congress and the public that it was qualified to be the arbiter — or at least the provider of information — about who should be trusted to enter the sacred ranks of government. This was one of the roles that gave the FBI considerable power and discretion, but also involved it in drudgery that it sometimes had to fight to escape. When Congress passed the Foreign Assistance Act of 1948, setting up a program of postwar economic aid to Europe, it included a clause requiring that anyone to be employed in the program must be "investigated as to loyalty and security by the Federal Bureau of Investigation." The

Atomic Energy Act, adopted in 1946, called for a Bureau check on the "character, associations and loyalty" of every employee of the Atomic Energy Commission and anyone who would come into contact with its restricted data. That was a responsibility the FBI took seriously, and with some enthusiasm at first; but the fascination wore off, as the Bureau found itself looking into the background, say, of truck drivers who delivered goods to an atomic installation. In 1952 Congress agreed that only the "highly sensitive" AEC security clearances had to be handled by the Bureau and that the more routine ones could be done by the Civil Service Commission, until and unless "subversive derogatory" information was uncovered. That change gradually brought the number of atomic energy checks made by the Bureau down from a high of one hundred thousand a year to about four thousand. Similar clauses requiring a Bureau role in investigating applicants were written into the laws authorizing American participation in the World Health Organization and the International Labor Organization and establishing the National Science Foundation, as well as the Federal Civil Defense Act of 1950 and the Mutual Security Act of 1951, among many others.

In a more recent example, the drafters of the legislation establishing the Peace Corps in 1961 sought to require a full FBI background check of every person who applied to work for the agency as an overseas volunteer. The Bureau protested, but the Kennedy administration asserted that in order for the unusual program to get off to a good start, and to convince those who were skeptical of its value, the FBI's imprimatur on the first batch of volunteers was essential. Finally, Hoover entered into an informal agreement with the first Peace Corps director, R. Sargent Shriver, brother-in-law of the President and of the then attorney general, that the Bureau would do a full investigation of the first one thousand volunteers. Later the FBI entered the picture only if the Civil Service Commission first turned up a "subversive derogatory" tidbit.

The theory of the FBI's role has always been that it operated on the most objective of criteria, that it provided facts which others — the loyalty review boards, Civil Service Commission, and the agencies of government — could use to make decisions about the suitability of a person for employment. As the Director repeatedly put it, "At no time does the FBI make any recommendations, express opinions or grant clearances." In practice, of course, agents were not always so objective, and they frequently relied upon stereotypes as guidelines to make their work easier. They were more likely, for example, to suspect and interrogate harshly a man with a beard or long hair than one of their own close-shaved and -cropped variety. Loud or unconventional clothes were distrusted, as were once esoteric fields of study such as anthropology. Often, anyone of liberal views was assumed to be one step on the spectrum toward communism, and "liberal" was a derogatory term in the Bureau context. (It still is, for some older agents.)

On paper, Hoover was true to his word. He seldom tried directly and on the record to block someone's employment; but there are numerous examples of his efforts to do so behind the scenes, especially within the Department of Justice. Everyone knew that Hoover took it upon himself to "clear" people. Sometimes he would straightforwardly telephone an assistant attorney general and declare himself opposed to the hiring of a certain candidate for a job on the basis of the FBI background investigation. Even Robert C. Mardian, the hard-line assistant attorney general for the department's Internal Security Division during the Nixon administration (who was later convicted in the Watergate cover-up trial), hardly a slouch on the issue of subversion, had his trouble along these lines in 1970, when Hoover intervened and attempted to block the employment as an assistant to Mardian of a young lawyer who had previously worked with the assistant attorney general in another capacity at the Department of Health, Education and Welfare. The problem was that the lawyer, Daniel J. McAuliffe, who sometimes wore "mod" clothes including a wide, flashy American flag tie, had once signed an anti–Vietnam war petition while at HEW, and Hoover was adamant that such "radicals" and "protesters" should not be infesting the Justice Department. Mardian was finally able to hire his man only by having Attorney General John N. Mitchell overrule Hoover.

Inevitably, the Bureau's "applicant work" led to overuses and abuses. So infatuated was President Lyndon Johnson with the ability of the FBI to run quick file checks on people he was considering for presidential appointments that he would sometimes call Hoover or one of his aides directly from his airplane when he was taking off from Washington for Texas. In what came to be known in Bureau circles as an *Air Force One* Special, Johnson would rattle off four or five names and ask that information about them be waiting for him by the time he got to his ranch. On the basis of this preliminary check, the President would then tell the Director the names of the people on whom he wanted a full background investigation to be run. The Nixon administration, for its part, seemed inclined to use the pretext of an "applicant" investigation as a way of finding out more about its "enemies." In one well-publicized instance, an assistant to H. R. Haldeman, Nixon's chief of staff, ordered up a prompt background investigation of Daniel

Schorr, a CBS television correspondent who was often critical of the administration. When the Bureau, with characteristic speed, had interviewed twenty-five of the correspondent's family and acquaintances within seven hours and Schorr learned about the investigation, the White House quickly concocted the cover story that he was being considered for an appointment with the Council on Environmental Quality, but then it canceled the inquiry. The Bureau went along with the story, and Bureau officials have insisted that they had no reason to disbelieve it or to question the administration's plans and suspect its motives when the White House asked for a check on Schorr.

The FBI still performs several categories of "applicant work." It conducts a full field investigation of everyone seeking a job with the Bureau, from agent down to messenger. It does "name checks" — an average of 10,000 a day — in its extensive fingerprint records and criminal and security files at the request of other government agencies (and views this strictly as a "service function"). Some investigations, including those of prospective employees of the Atomic Energy Commission, the National Aeronautics and Space Administration, and the Arms Control and Disarmament Agency, are done on the basis of laws passed by Congress.* Others, including what remains of the Federal Employee Security Program ("security forms" are still processed — 367,656 in Fiscal Year 1974 — and "subversive derogatory" information referred by the Civil Service Commission), are authorized specifically by presidential executive orders. The Bureau is also expected to do a full background investigation of anyone convicted of a federal crime who later applies for a presidential pardon. But most of those that now attract public attention are based on orders and authorizations of the attorney general or on informal agreements between the Bureau and the White House, begun by Eisenhower upon his election in 1952. (The FBI had earlier investigated about three hundred prospective appointees for Truman.) They include the investigations of those who will hold professional positions in the Justice Department, prospective cabinet members, federal judges, and other presidential appointees, including members of the White House staff. Under an authorization given by Attorney General Herbert Brownell in 1953, the FBI also conducts "applicant-type investigations" of staff members of some congressional committees — Senate and House Appropriations, Senate and House Judiciary, Senate Armed Services, Senate Foreign Relations, and the Joint Committee on Atomic Energy.

Most of the special inquiries for the White House, more interest-

* The FBI is reimbursed by some executive agencies for the applicant work it does for them.

ing to the average agent than the traditional loyalty investigation and more important for the Bureau's sense of self-esteem, are pursued with gusto. The Special Investigative Division, which handles them, has established strict standards for speed (fifteen days for the average major presidential appointment, for example, and thirty days for a member of the White House staff) and exhaustiveness, especially in light of the recent aggressive roles of congressional committees and the press in turning up potentially damaging information about a nominee's background. "We can't afford to have some congressman bring something up in the middle of a hearing that we didn't find in our own investigation," says one official of the division, "so we cover the man's entire life." So thorough have some of the investigations become that presidents have occasionally delayed asking for them, lest the identity of the nominee be leaked prematurely to the press by someone who has been visited in the course of the investigation. Congressional committees or executive agencies frequently complain that the filling of a position has been delayed by the FBI investigation, but the Bureau invariably denies that; it points with pride to the fact that it can do in two weeks what it often takes the Civil Service Commission or Departments of State and Defense two months to complete.

No longer quite so jealous of its applicant work, however, the Bureau has made steady efforts in recent years to cut it back and to hand more responsibility over to the Civil Service Commission, which it regards as the "proper agency" for monitoring the background and qualifications of most government employees. The FBI finally persuaded the attorney general's office, for example, to relieve it of responsibility for investigating most clerical employees of the Justice Department; as a result, its personnel investigations for the department have dropped from an average of ten thousand a year in the 1960s to a recent average of about six thousand. But just as the percentage of time spent on applicant-type investigations was declining, Agnew and then Nixon resigned, and the country was in the extraordinary position of using the Twenty-fifth Amendment to fill the vice-presidency twice in one year. This launched two of the most comprehensive investigations in Bureau history. According to the statistics, the background check on Gerald Ford involved three hundred and fifty agents in thirty-three field offices, who conducted a thousand interviews and wrote 1,500 pages' worth of reports. Investigating his wealthier and more worldly successor, Nelson Rockefeller, required the efforts of three hundred and fifty agents from thirty-six domestic field offices and two overseas. They conducted 1,400 interviews and wrote reports coming to 2,248 pages. In each case, an agent familiar with the

93

investigation was assigned to sit with senators and congressmen on the committees reviewing the nominations who wanted to read the reports in detail before deciding how to vote, both to protect the files and to answer their questions.

Policymakers in the Bureau and the Justice Department as well as their statisticians have had a chance to scale back the role of applicant work. It has apparently been years since anyone has been denied a federal job on national security grounds, and the attorney general's list of subversive organizations no longer exists. While homosexuality and alcoholism once automatically excluded people from jobs, the modified standard is that such factors must be shown to affect the employee's work materially before he is fired or disqualified. But still the Bureau probes for such details of people's lives.

Another 1 percent of agent time is spent on civil investigations on behalf of the federal government. Early cases, many of them eventually to be resolved in the U.S. Court of Claims, grew out of American involvement in World Wars I and II. Private contractors, for example, sued for additional fees from the military or another agency, protesting that government actions or regulations prevented fulfillment of a contract within the time or budget contemplated. Agents were also sent out to investigate the disability claims of some veterans and their families under war-risk and national service life insurance.

The Bureau often acts for the government in suits arising under the Federal Tort Claims Act, which made the United States liable, much as a private citizen is, to claims for compensation for personal injuries or property damage as a result of alleged negligence. Other laws under which the Bureau has investigated cases include the Renegotiation Acts, whereby the government could reclaim excessive profits from contractors, the False Claims Statute, and the Surplus Property Act. Coming out of the wars it was also involved in investigations of matters involving admiralty law and claims against the alien property custodian. In more recent years, FBI civil investigations have often grown out of such programs as federal housing and Medicare, wherever fraud is suspected and a civil suit is brought instead of, or in addition to, a criminal case.

Civil investigations have traditionally been tedious and unsensational. They may take countless hours of agent time, and in the end the agent may be cast in the unsympathetic role of having to testify in court on behalf of an impersonal bureaucracy against the claims of a disabled veteran. But some cases have tested sophisticated accounting skills, and many of them have been valued by the Bureau for their

94

contributions to the annual statistics. Because the Bureau counts as a "savings" to the government any claim disallowed by a court and the amount by which the government's cost for any service or contract is reduced in a case investigated by the Bureau, those statistics can be sensational — and sensationalized. If the FBI investigates a case in which a citizen sues the government for $25,000 and then settles for $500, the Bureau will credit itself with a "savings" of $24,500. Don Whitehead reported in *The FBI Story* that in the first ten years after the war the FBI had saved the government more than six hundred million dollars "by exposing false claims and fraud against the government, auditing renegotiated contracts, proving ability to pay fines, and establishing the nonliability of the federal government in personal-injury and property-damage claims." That accounting system has been preserved and still figures prominently in the Bureau's annual calculation of its worth to the country.

As Hoover explained it in a 1950 article for the *Syracuse Law Review*, "The Government has many interests to protect. Unless these interests are zealously guarded, it would stand to lose many millions of dollars each year. The Department of Justice and the FBI might be likened, in this connection, to a vast shield, attempting to protect the best interests of the Government."

VI

Counterintelligence

There is certainly still a communist empire that we have to cope with, regardless of détente. . . . They are not only trying to subvert our economic system, but our whole way of life. . . . We must show them we are watching.
— *Supervisor of a "security" squad in an FBI field office in a major city*

ANTHONY (NOT HIS REAL NAME) is an "ethnic Russian" who lives in a large American port city. Born in one of the small independent countries absorbed into the Soviet Union during World War II, he immigrated to the United States and became a citizen, but retained close ties and kept up contact with the members of his family who stayed behind. Unlike many of his fellow countrymen in the United States, he was never active in the "captive nations" movement that agitates for the "liberation" of their homelands from Soviet rule; rather, he kept to himself, holding down a good government job and following an uncontroversial routine that attracted no particular attention.

Some time ago Anthony traveled to the Soviet Union as a tourist for six weeks; his planned itinerary went beyond the run-of-the-mill Intourist program and included visits to relatives in out-of-the-way places, some of which required that he seek special permission from the authorities. The moment he arrived in Moscow he had an unexpectedly warm reception. The man who greeted him and treated him as a distinguished guest of the country, it turned out, was a representative of the KGB, or the Committee on State Security.* He had an astonishing acquaintance with Anthony's background, family, habits, interests, and livelihood. The host also had some suggestions for ways that life could be made easier for Anthony's relatives. Before Anthony knew just what was happening, he had been whisked off for some full-fledged recruiting.

Contrary to his original plan, the first two weeks of Anthony's visit to the Soviet Union were spent on intensive training in secret writings, inks, cryptanalysis, and basic code systems — an orientation course on how he might be able to help Soviet intelligence upon his return to the United States. Anthony showed enough interest and willingness in the early stages of his visit to convince his KGB trainers that he could be trusted to cooperate. For the next several weeks, Anthony went ahead with his original schedule, and he found that arrangements had been expedited for him by his new friends. He had happy visits with his relatives. Then, in the last few days before his flight home, he received additional training. It was not explained exactly what he would be expected to do to help, but special interest was shown in his job, where he might be exposed to the kinds of background information useful in establishing false identities and complete personal histories. He was shown a long list of American scientists, technicians (the aerospace industry was of particular interest), and military officials of Slavic origin, and asked whether he knew, or could make contact with, any of them. He acknowledged that he was familiar with some of the names. He was given enough money, in American dollars, to pay for his travel to a first meeting with his "principal," in a North American city distant from his home, as well as an "open code" he could use to advise whether he would be there on schedule.† The KGB officials warned Anthony that the FBI would probably interview him shortly after his return, briefed him on what to say in that event, and asked that he notify an appropriate contact in the States if the Bureau approached him.

For the first few weeks after his return, Anthony ruminated nervously about his adventure with the KGB. He was puzzled about why

* The KGB, as presently constituted, coordinates most intelligence functions in a single agency. Estimated to have as many as half a million employees, it is the Soviet equivalent of the FBI, the Central Intelligence Agency, the National Security Agency, the United States Information Agency, and others, all rolled into one.
† An open code involves statements like "the swimming match is canceled" to indicate an inability to keep a meeting, and gives simple code names to items of interest; an aircraft carrier, for example, might be called a "lamp" and a gun a "house." It is a relatively unsophisticated method of communication.

and how they had selected him in the first place, curious about what he would be asked to do, and worried that if he did the wrong thing it could result in harm to his family in the Soviet Union. Finally, though, he approached a man well known in his émigré community to unburden himself — an agent in the local FBI field office whose specialty is "nationalities intelligence." It seemed clear to the Bureau, on debriefing Anthony, that he had been recruited for the specific purpose of helping the KGB develop false identities for the "illegals" it sends abroad, intelligence operatives who do not have the "legal" cover of diplomatic posts and must instead use assumed names and professional facades. In fact, the FBI probably would have interviewed Anthony after a time; his background, age, job, life-style, and the "hostage situation" of his relatives still living in the Soviet Union made him a natural for a possible approach by the KGB. In the normal course of events, the Bureau would have learned about his extended visit and asked him if anything unusual had happened on his trip and whether he had seen or heard anything that might be of value to the American intelligence and counterintelligence community.

The Bureau advised Anthony to follow the game plan as much as possible, to go ahead with the "meet" with his "principal," in the hope that this would lead the FBI to other members of the Soviet intelligence network and to clues concerning its major interests of the moment. The FBI's hope was that the agents assigned to Anthony would be able to monitor and control his activities sufficiently so that he could function effectively as a double agent, appearing to work for the KGB but actually feeding it false or useless materials and remaining loyal to the United States. Concerned that Anthony might be under surveillance by other foreign agents, the Bureau became cautious about the circumstances under which it met with him, and began setting up rendezvous in hotel rooms where FBI agents had registered under false names after "dry-cleaning" themselves with trips to the movies or sporting events. But one of the immediate problems was to figure out how the KGB had "targeted" on Anthony, how it had picked him out among the thousands of westerners who come to the Soviet Union as tourists every year. It was a safe assumption that all of his letters to his relatives there would have been intercepted and read, but there had to be more to it than that. A little research permitted reconstruction of the probable chronology:

It is routine procedure for the FBI to gather whatever background material is available on any group of Soviets touring the United States; after getting a list of those who have been granted American visas, the Bureau determines whether any of them are known, or possible, operatives of the KGB or the GRU, the Soviet military intelligence organization. In one of the more obvious instances, a group of poets or dancers visiting on a cultural exchange program may be accompanied by one dour man who seems to have no function other than chaperoning; he would almost surely be suspected of being a KGB agent assigned to keep his eye on them, prevent any defections, and, in his spare time, to pick up any useful information he comes across. FBI field offices in or near all the cities on the group's itinerary would be alerted to try to monitor any such agent's activities during the visit. Larger groups, composed mostly of people billed as "tourists," may be more difficult to analyze or monitor, and the intelligence agents in their midst better camouflaged.

As the Bureau experts looked back, they found that one of these groups (the groups are all numbered in Bureau records in chronological order and identified, for example, as "the ninetieth Soviet tourist group") had visited Anthony's hometown some years earlier because several of its members had distant relatives there. During that group's entire tour, the FBI had pegged none of its members as probable agents. But in retrospect, at least one "tourist" surfaced in the reports who had visited no relatives, shunned all sightseeing, and who did not drink any alcoholic beverages. Sure enough, when Anthony was shown the photograph from this man's visa application, he recognized him as someone who had sat in on his interviews and training sessions in the Soviet Union; and one of the names he had been given as a contact seemed to be a variation on the name used on the man's application. When the picture was shown to others in Anthony's émigré community, they vaguely recognized him as someone who had done some aimless prowling around during the earlier tourist visit.

What became apparent was that the Soviet "tourist" had gathered information about Anthony during his visit, and that the information had been stored in Moscow pending any visa application from him (which seemed probable, given his background and predispositions). When he arrived in the Soviet Union, the KGB already had just what it needed to approach him. Further researches on that group of visitors, with the help of the CIA, revealed that it might have had not merely one, but perhaps three, intelligence operatives in its midst after all. But since they had not been pinpointed as such at the time of the visit, no special attention was paid to their activities. Now, in light of Anthony's case, the Bureau had a complicated task: to try to trace the three agents' efforts retroactively in all of the cities their group had visited. Had they targeted other people in situations similar to Anthony's? Had those people since traveled to the Soviet Union and

99

been trained in some aspect of intelligence work? Were some already in place, helping the KGB? Or might some of them be "sleepers," held in reserve until they were appropriately situated to help or to be "activated" on a particular project? Was there a potential for serious espionage out of all this? Was the approach to Anthony just a ruse to divert the Bureau?

These were difficult questions to answer. But the discovery of Anthony, albeit at his own initiative, seemed something of a coup — and an exciting case — for the field office in his city. However, the notion that three Soviet intelligence agents might have run free, doing research and recruiting work under their cover as tourists, could be a troubling indication that the Bureau was negligent. The incident appeared, in any event, to be new confirmation that even in an age of détente and good feeling in foreign policy, old concerns about espionage still had to be taken seriously.

FBI jurisdiction in the counterintelligence and "security" field evolved out of the government's response to crises. A few statutes, such as the Foreign Agents Registration Act, were passed to deal with potential counterintelligence problems; and others, like the Atomic Energy Act, had clauses specifically aimed at espionage threats. But the Bureau's authority to this day rests largely on vaguely formulated executive orders and has never been codified in the statute books.

As Europe moved toward another war in the 1930s and it began to seem that the United States might be drawn into it, disturbing memories of German sabotage and espionage during World War I bred a new vigilance. Franklin Roosevelt was determined to prevent a repetition of that experience. The Bureau had the responsibility to investigate specific allegations of sabotage, treason, or espionage under its broad criminal jurisdiction; but ever since Attorney General Stone and Hoover had abolished the General Intelligence Division in 1924, there had been no general, keep-our-guard-up intelligence patrol. This began to change in 1933, almost by accident.

The German ambassador to Washington wrote to Secretary of State Cordell Hull on March 28, 1933, complaining that he had received a letter from an American threatening the life of German Chancellor Adolf Hitler. The letter went to the FBI for an investigation. The Bureau never did find out the real name of the person who wrote it, but the assignment became an excuse for the Bureau to start on the track of pro- as well as anti-Nazi organizations in the United States. When the investigation was concluded, Hoover submitted a report and saw to it that it reached the President himself. Roosevelt was alarmed, and in May 1934 he convened a White House conference of key officials, including Hoover, which decided to launch what Don Whitehead later described as "an intensive and confidential investigation of the Nazi movement, with emphasis on anti-American activities having any connection with German government officials." It was justified as a limited search for possible violations of the immigration laws.

But two years later, in August 1936, the President restored the Bureau's mandate to engage in general intelligence investigations. In a series of meetings in the President's office, according to Whitehead's authorized version in *The FBI Story*, Roosevelt asked whether there was any way he could get a reliable overview of fascist and communist activities in the United States. The Director pointed out that the Bureau, under its appropriations act, could do anything "when requested to do so by the Secretary of State." Hull was brought in the next day to endorse the Roosevelt plan for ongoing intelligence investigation, and Attorney General Homer Cummings also gave his approval, after Hoover, on September 5, 1936, had already sent a "personal and confidential" letter to his special-agents-in-charge:

The Bureau desires to obtain from all possible sources information concerning subversive activities being conducted in the United States by Communists, Fascists, and representatives or advocates of other organizations or groups advocating the overthrow or replacement of the Government of the United States by illegal methods. No investigation should be initiated into cases of this kind in the absence of specific authorization from the Bureau.

Roosevelt's orders to Hoover and the Director's mobilization of his field personnel were to have implications for both aliens and domestic groups composed of American citizens.

William Bullitt, the U.S. ambassador to France who had previously been assigned to Moscow, warned that Constantine Oumansky, counselor at the new Soviet Embassy in Washington, probably had a subversive intent in his extensive travels around the United States. Bullitt stirred up Hoover when he visited him and Cummings at the Justice Department; as the Director recorded it in a memorandum:

Mr. Bullitt told me that the Communist leaders in Russia make every effort to put spies in all foreign government agencies, and particularly those which are engaged in or charged with the responsibility of knowing about subversive activities. He made this statement in connection with the possibility of Communists entering the employ of the Federal Bureau of Investigation.

It was just that sort of warning which terrified Hoover and put him on his guard not only about prospective FBI agents, but also about people working for any agency of the federal government; it built on his already rabid distrust of Communists. When the Civil Service Commission attempted to restrict Hoover's independence by having the Bureau select new agents from the civil service eligibility lists, he accused it of trying to break down his method of keeping "subversives" out of the Bureau ranks.

Meanwhile a deserter from the U.S. Army and a man who had been dishonorably discharged from the navy were charged with spying for the Germans and Japanese, respectively, and it became clear to Hoover that there was an active threat to national security from various directions. Newspaper publicity about the activities of the German-American Bund eventually got the Bureau concerned about it, too, and Hoover submitted a report to the President in 1938 on that group's efforts to push the country toward a pro-German policy.

By 1939, as prewar tensions built, there was no longer any pretense that the Bureau needed the State Department's authority to conduct intelligence and "subversion" investigations. The FBI and officials of the State Department had clashed over who would coordinate such investigations, and Roosevelt came down firmly on the Bureau's side. In June, acting on his own perception of the executive authority inherent in the Constitution (although he did not say that was the basis), the President accepted Attorney General Frank Murphy's suggestion that jurisdiction over all espionage, counterespionage, and sabotage matters be centralized in the FBI and the military intelligence divisions. Roosevelt issued a confidential directive that other government agencies refer to the Bureau "any data, information or material that may come to their notice bearing directly or indirectly" on these issues. On September 6, 1939, three days after the British and French governments declared war on Germany, Roosevelt issued a public statement, also drafted in the Justice Department, revealing the FBI's urgent new authority. It asked local officials to hand over to the Bureau "any information obtained by them relating to espionage, counterespionage, sabotage, subversive activities and violations of the neutrality laws" — a significant first formal mention of "subversive activities" in presidential directives. A few days later the President authorized the attorney general to increase the size of the FBI to help with "the proper performance of the additional duties imposed upon the Department of Justice in connection with the national emergency." At the Justice Department's request, the September 6, 1939, statement was reiterated in 1943, this time extending the request to "all patriotic organizations and individuals" to report information to the FBI, but leaving out the reference to "subversive activities." (That formulation would later be back, however, when President Truman issued what the Bureau bills as a "restatement" of the FBI role in 1950, after the outbreak of the Korean war.)

Not until June 1940 did Roosevelt divide responsibilities in the foreign intelligence field. After conferences with his chief adviser on intelligence matters, Assistant Secretary of State Adolf A. Berle, Jr.,the President assigned the FBI jurisdiction over the Western Hemisphere, except Panama. The navy had responsibility for the Pacific, and the army for Europe, Africa, and the Canal Zone.*

Hoover plunged right in on the new assignment. Whereas the Bureau had averaged only about thirty-five espionage cases a year between 1933 and 1937, the number increased in Fiscal Year 1938 to two hundred and fifty cases. By January 1940, appearing before the House Appropriations Committee, the Director was predicting that espionage complaints might run as high as seventy thousand a year, most of which would require some degree of investigation. Congressional appropriations for the Bureau's work increased dramatically. Hoover told the subcommittee overseeing the Bureau budget that he had revived the old General Intelligence Division of the Palmer Raid days, renaming it the Security Division.† Under its auspices the Bureau would keep a "general index," alphabetical and geographical, which would permit the immediate location of anyone it wanted to investigate in the name of national security.

The Bureau's first well-publicized venture into its new area smacked more of the Palmer era than of the Roosevelt years. For some time the FBI had investigated those who recruited Americans to go to Spain with the Abraham Lincoln Brigade to fight on the Loyalist side in the Spanish Civil War, but nothing had ever come of the cases. Finally, in February 1940, a federal grand jury in Detroit indicted eleven men and one woman, all with possible communist connections, on charges of raising a foreign army in the United States (even though the Spanish war was by then over, with the forces of Generalissimo Francisco Franco, heavily backed by Hitler and Mussolini, victorious over the Loyalists). The Bureau arrested all of the suspects in simultaneous raids at 5 A.M., although a federal judge would not be avail-

---

* The activities of the Bureau's Special Intelligence Service are discussed in Chapter X.
† It was later termed the Domestic Intelligence Division and today the Intelligence Division, which has jurisdiction over FBI work in both the counterintelligence and internal security fields.

able for their arraignment until 3 P.M. It was later alleged that both in the Detroit arrests and in parallel raids conducted by the FBI in Milwaukee and New York City, agents searched homes and offices without warrants. The Detroit defendants were apparently prevented from telephoning their lawyers, and when the United States marshals took custody of them, they were handcuffed to a long chain for the trip to court.

A wave of criticism broke upon the Bureau for its conduct of the raids. Senators George W. Norris of Nebraska and Burton K. Wheeler of Montana — reverting on this occasion to his old incarnation as a Bureau "enemy" — heaped abuse on Hoover, alleging "third-degree methods" in the questioning of the people arrested in Detroit and denouncing the "spying psychology in this country." *The New Republic,* in a much-quoted editorial, compared the Bureau to the German Gestapo and the Russian OGPU (a predecessor of the KGB) and said the FBI had accumulated "power inconsistent with our conception of democratic institutions." The new attorney general, Robert H. Jackson, quickly dropped the indictments initiated by Murphy, saying he could see no reason to revive "at this late date the animosities of the Spanish conflict," but Jackson cleared the FBI of any wrongdoing. Still, the criticism continued — instigated, as far as Hoover (and later Whitehead, on his behalf) were concerned, by the communists, who were supposedly launching a coordinated "campaign" against the Bureau. But the respectable criticism subsided after Roosevelt, appearing at the annual White House correspondents dinner, made it clear publicly that he was siding with Hoover and the FBI.

But for the flareup over the Abraham Lincoln Brigade, the Bureau's war work seemed to go well and to earn an ever more romantic image for Hoover and his G-men. The FBI adapted enthusiastically to the task of catching spies. One of the more successful ventures involved William Sebold, a German native and naturalized American citizen who, on a trip to visit his family in Europe, had been blackmailed into becoming a German spy. Threatened that if he did not cooperate his relatives would be harmed, Sebold came back equipped with codes, short-wave know-how, and micrographic instructions for other agents already in place. But he went right to the FBI, which urged him to play along. The Bureau built Sebold a short-wave station on Long Island from which he transmitted useless, FBI-cleared messages to a German receiver in Hamburg; it also set him up in a Manhattan office, equipped with one-way mirrors to accommodate watching FBI agents. Into that office came some of the most important

German spies operating in the United States, to pick up instructions and to drop off messages for Sebold's transmission to Germany. Eventually this permitted the Bureau to arrest thirty-three people, including Fritz Duquesne, the espionage ringleader. All were convicted.

The Bureau got onto the trail of other German and Japanese spy rings, succeeding in an unusual number of instances in sending misleading material to the enemy governments via the espionage channels. There was some skepticism about why the FBI never managed to find out and warn the military in advance about the Japanese attack on Pearl Harbor, but government investigating commissions found no reason to fault the Bureau's work.* Hoover made headlines with the arrest and exposure of German saboteurs landed by submarine off Long Island (never bothering to note that some of the saboteurs, frightened and disgusted, had turned themselves in and that incredulous FBI men had at first refused to believe their stories) and of another group that was delivered to Florida. The leader of yet another team, landed off the Maine coast, also turned himself in and led Bureau agents to his colleague; again the Bureau got the credit.

On the less glamorous side of its wartime assignment, the FBI investigated thousands of suspected sabotage cases. One veteran agent, assigned to western Pennsylvania during the war years, told of tedious investigations involving suspicious-seeming industrial accidents in defense plants. Invariably, it would turn out that no sabotage motive could be detected — a workman angry over a labor dispute had thrown carborundum into a machine that was turning out parts for railroad cars; a maintenance man mistakenly left a crowbar inside an electrical generator; or a man at a steel rolling plant, who had had too much to drink at a wedding party the night before, forgot to close a valve and allowed sulfuric acid to escape into Presque Isle Bay, where it damaged steel-bottomed ships. In one case where this agent developed hard evidence that a young workman had deliberately "harmed the war effort" by slowing down production on aircraft engine mounts, the Justice Department decided not to prosecute. In another instance, when a train plunged into a river north of Pittsburgh, the FBI agents thought they had "motivation coming out of our ears," because both U.S. air cadets and some foreign officials had been on the train; but after a long investigation, the Bureau was unable to turn up

---

* In the 1970s, however, Dusko Popov, a Yugoslav who worked for British Intelligence during the war, surfaced to claim that he had tried to warn Hoover in 1941 about the impending attack on Pearl Harbor, but was given the brushoff by the Director. Popov was supposedly the model for Ian Fleming's "James Bond."

any hard evidence of sabotage and wrote the case off as a simple railroad accident.

As Hoover told it in appropriations testimony in 1946, between 1940 and 1946 the FBI investigated 19,587 cases of alleged sabotage. Of them, only 2,447 proved to be actual sabotage, as far as the Bureau was concerned, but there were convictions in a mere 611 cases — "with sentences aggregating 1,637 years and fines of $251,709."

Some agents had bizarre assignments as part of the Bureau's war work. Out of the Butte, Montana, Field Office, for example, they chased Japanese balloons that were sent across the Pacific with incendiary devices and antipersonnel bombs. The balloons were surprisingly effective, injuring campers and starting fires, and the Bureau wanted to prevent that fact from becoming public knowledge while also neutralizing their impact. On some occasions, agents went up in air force B-17s to find the balloons and shoot them down in areas where they would do the minimum damage.

The Bureau, like the country, was now in a shooting war, and its tactics reflected it. As Whitehead put it euphemistically for the Bureau in *The FBI Story:*

Often clandestine methods are necessary to uncover clandestine operations, as for example, obtaining an espionage agent's diary or secret papers. The evidence in the diary may be inadmissible in federal court, but it may contain information which would enable the United States to protect itself at a later date. This is in contrast to a case where legal evidence, admissible in court, has to be obtained to convict the espionage agent of violating the laws of the United States.

Virtually the only way to obtain someone's diary or secret papers without his knowing was through some kind of surreptitious entry or burglary. That the Bureau did with impunity, and sometimes on the basis of only flimsy cause. Hoover, once reluctant, also began to use wiretapping extensively in intelligence cases. Attorney General Jackson initially defended the practice as appropriate "in a limited class of cases" including "espionage, sabotage, and other activities interfering with the national defense"; but later, as controversy brewed in the Senate over the practice, Jackson suspended authority for the FBI to wiretap and declared that the Justice Department would not prosecute cases developed by any government department on the basis of wiretapping. He was only to be reversed by President Roosevelt, who directed in 1940 that the Bureau could wiretap after all, and regulations were drawn up requiring the specific approval of the attorney general in each instance. According to the FBI's interpretation of the Federal Communications Act, which forbade the interception of communications, wiretapping was acceptable so long as the information obtained from it was reported only to people within the government through the appropriate channels. Through such interpretations and relatively loose wartime rules, the Bureau developed a separate standard to govern intelligence cases. It did not expect those cases, let alone that separate standard, to end up in court.

Some of the wartime techniques the Bureau learned through collaboration with Britain's Secret Intelligence Service and its chief operative in New York, William Stephenson. Among other lessons, the British taught Bureau agents the art of "postal espionage," so that they could advance from the fairly primitive technique of purloining letters to more sophisticated methods of opening them and learning what was inside, but then getting them delivered as if nothing had ever happened. In return, the FBI did significant favors for the British, including the planting of "strategic deception material" inside the German Embassy in Washington well before the United States had entered the war. The cooperation apparently cooled somewhat when the Director became jealous of the British agency's American ties and objected to the fact that it was also working with the FBI's new rival, the Office of Strategic Services (OSS), headed by General William J. "Wild Bill" Donovan, with whom Hoover had an old feud.* The OSS, at the request of both American military intelligence and the British, launched an ambitious program of "penetrating" the Washington embassies of neutral countries that were suspected of secret collaboration with the Axis powers. According to a book by Donald Downes, a former undercover operative for British intelligence and the OSS who was involved in considerable wartime burglarizing and safecracking in the Washington embassies, FBI agents were at one point sent to interrupt one of the nocturnal security jobs. Donovan was furious and protested to the White House. But before long, the program had been turned over to the Washington Field Office of the FBI.

Late in the war, when Soviet-American cooperation against the Axis was at its peak, Hoover scored another important point against his rival Donovan. The Director learned of a plan for the OSS and the NKVD (also a forerunner of the KGB) to exchange secret security delegations in Moscow and Washington, supposedly to trade informa-

* The animosity between the two men dated back to the 1920s, when, according to Hoover, Donovan, as an assistant attorney general pursuing a second grand jury investigation of Senator Burton K. Wheeler, used Bureau agents without advising the Director of their whereabouts.

tion about sabotage operations behind German lines. The Director immediately wrote a letter of protest to presidential adviser Harry Hopkins, warning that this would be "a highly dangerous and most undesirable procedure" because everywhere else the Soviet agency operated it had worked to obtain "official secrets" for intelligence purposes. Roosevelt canceled the Donovan plan.

Out of the wartime OSS came the Central Intelligence Agency, with — at the outset — a clear-cut monopoly on foreign intelligence-gathering and operations. At the same time, the FBI was so well entrenched in its counterespionage work, and its success in notorious cases was so celebrated, that even as it was losing the intelligence assignment in Latin America that FDR had given it in the early days of the war, there was little thought within the federal government that it should give up its counterintelligence role within the United States. Indeed, the FBI not only kept that job, but it was also permitted to define its parameters essentially on its own. And in Hoover's hands, those parameters were colored by a heavy dose of the postwar anti-communist hysteria and Cold War ideology. The Bureau, looking at the world from its own parochial standpoint, argued against the expansion of American diplomatic and commercial ties with the communist bloc. It was the purist FBI view that such ties only opened opportunities for espionage and subversion. And the Bureau regarded the establishment of United Nations headquarters in New York as less an achievement than a headache.

In the Red scare era of the late 1940s and early 1950s, the Bureau, egged on and encouraged by the House Un-American Activities Committee, found what it considered vindication for its security worries. One of the first incidents was the *Amerasia* case, involving the publication in an esoteric journal dealing with Far Eastern affairs of material from government documents that were stamped with "top secret" and other security markings. Philip Jaffe, the wealthy editor of *Amerasia*, was followed by the Bureau on visits to the Soviet consulate in New York and to the home of Earl Browder, then chief of the American Communist party. A State Department China specialist and a navy lieutenant with access to sensitive documents, among others, were drawn into the net, and this stirred fear that as a result of the wartime alliance with the Soviet Union, communists and "fellow travelers" had infiltrated the government. But when the case went before a grand jury, it became clear that the FBI had produced no direct proof that the information had actually been passed to the Soviet Union — other than in the quite public pages of *Amerasia* — and the government case was further damaged by the revelation that both the OSS and the FBI had conducted searches without warrants in the early stages of the investigation. The case ended with minor indictments, guilty and no-contest pleas and small fines, but no jail terms. That left powerful political voices denouncing the Truman administration and crying for more forceful action by the Bureau.

Many of the cases that followed grew out of information provided to the Bureau and HUAC by Elizabeth Terril Bentley, a repentant communist who achieved international renown for her elaborate, volunteered tales about alleged Soviet spy rings operating in the United States. She claimed that as a courier for her friend Jacob N. Golos, who operated a travel agency in New York intended to promote American visits to the Soviet Union, she had come to know a number of government officials who were members of the Communist party and who out of that allegiance passed confidential documents and information to the Soviet "enemy" before and during the war. Between them, Miss Bentley and another communist who had recanted, Whittaker Chambers, an editor of *Time* magazine, were responsible for the denunciation of many prominent and lesser-known government employees, including State Department official Alger Hiss, William W. Remington of the War Production Board, and Harry Dexter White, an assistant secretary of the treasury and official of the International Monetary Fund, all of whom Bentley and Chambers said were spies. The Bureau had a heavy stake in the fate of all of these people, and in each instance Hoover seemed to be victorious: Hiss finally went to prison on a perjury conviction, as did Remington (who died after he was attacked in the Lewisburg penitentiary), and White was substantially discredited before he died of a heart attack a few days after testifying before HUAC. But controversy continued for decades over whether they had been wrongly accused or convicted on the basis of twisted testimony and government misconduct, whether they were not the victims of a self-fulfilling postwar prophecy reminiscent of the tactics of nondemocratic governments.*

The Bureau had what seemed like more reliable evidence against

---

* The evidence for and against Hiss, Remington, and White has been reviewed exhaustively in books and articles over the past twenty-five years. Fred J. Cook, in *The FBI Nobody Knows*, points to a number of troubling, still unresolved questions about whether the Bureau and HUAC might have played a role in fabricating evidence and using unconstitutional methods to obtain the indictment and conviction of Hiss and Remington and to ruin White's reputation. Some hope of unraveling the mysteries emerged in 1975, when Attorney General Edward H. Levi, overruling the Bureau, ordered the release to Hiss of microfilms of the "Pumpkin Papers," which were used against him, and of some of the files in the case.

Judith Coplon, a Justice Department analyst arrested by FBI agents in March 1949 while walking in New York with an attaché from the Soviet delegation to the United Nations and carrying memoranda concerning U.S. knowledge of Soviet intelligence activities. But Miss Coplon's convictions in both Washington and New York federal courts were overturned in the appellate courts because the FBI had extensively wiretapped the defendant, destroyed some of the records of that wiretapping, and then sat by as federal prosecutors denied in the trial courts that any electronic surveillance had taken place. Jury verdicts that would otherwise have been upheld were thrown out when appellate courts learned that about thirty agents had listened in on Miss Coplon's home phone, that of her parents in Brooklyn, her office phone at the Justice Department, and the phone she used to consult her lawyer during her first trial. One major legacy of the Coplon case, in the long run, was the embarrassment and abuse the Bureau suffered as a result of the introduction of some of its "raw files" into evidence, which became the impetus for a new Hoover crusade to establish the confidentiality and inviolability of FBI records.

None of those problems emerged for the Bureau in the most dramatic of the postwar cases, the espionage trial of Julius and Ethel Rosenberg, who were accused of helping deliver the secret of the atomic bomb to the Soviet Union. Hoover delighted in the conviction and execution of the Rosenbergs, whom he reviled, and the FBI was proudly confident that it had dealt a major blow to the communist espionage apparatus within the United States; U.S. District Court Judge Irving R. Kaufman seemed to confirm that view as he pronounced sentence:

I consider your crime worse than murder. Plain deliberate contemplated murder is dwarfed in magnitude by comparison with the crime you have committed. . . . I believe your conduct in putting into the hands of the Russians the A-Bomb, years before our best scientists predicted Russia would perfect the bomb, has already caused, in my opinion, the Communist aggression in Korea, with the resultant casualties exceeding 50,000 and who knows but that millions more of innocent people may pay the price of your treason. Indeed, by your betrayal you undoubtedly have altered the course of history to the disadvantage of our country. . . .

Hoover called the initial protests about the Rosenberg case communist-inspired. Some of them may have been, but in later years considerable doubt developed about whether the information passed by the Rosenbergs had actually been so critical; and it was noted that Harry Gold, a member of the spy ring and eventually a key government witness against the Rosenbergs, had been questioned by the Bureau as early as 1947 — after being named by Elizabeth Bentley — and released.*

After the arrest of Colonel Rudolf Ivanovich Abel in 1957 as a Soviet "illegal," it was discovered that he had probably been operating as a spy in the United States for about nine years without detection. And Abel was apparently caught largely on the basis of a tip to the Bureau from one of his subordinates, Reino Hayhanen, who turned himself in to the CIA in Paris while under orders to return to Moscow. Abel was tried and convicted, and he served four years in prison until he was exchanged in 1962 for Francis Gary Powers, the U-2 reconnaisance pilot who had been shot down during a flight over the Soviet Union. But others went completely undetected, such as Conon Molody, also known as Gordon Lonsdale, who claimed to have worked successfully with Abel for five years in the United States before being transferred in 1955 to an assignment in Britain, where he was eventually arrested in 1960. Two others arrested by the British at that time, Peter and Helen Kroger, had previously functioned without difficulty as Soviet spies in the United States under the names Morris and Lona Cohen; they managed to slip out of the country in 1950 after being questioned by the FBI in connection with the Rosenberg case.

On the other hand, the FBI also managed a few spectacular, if relatively unpublicized, victories in the intelligence field. One of the most gripping stories is that of Kaarlo Tuomi, who was recruited by the KGB in the provincial town of Kirov and trained to come to the United States as an "illegal" for the GRU. When he did, at the end of 1958, he was spotted almost immediately by the Bureau — while he was filing for a copy of a birth certificate that would help establish his false identity — and he functioned smoothly for four years, including the period of the Cuban missile crisis, as a double agent under the FBI's control, albeit at an apparently low level in the espionage apparatus. He eventually renounced the Soviet Union, deciding to leave his family behind and remain in the United States. The available details of the Tuomi case, which was never aired in any courtroom or other judicial proceeding, indicate that the Bureau picked him up and tucked him away in a "safe house" before he did any harm to the

---

* In later years, however, many questions were raised about the Bureau's handling of the Rosenberg case. There were allegations that FBI agents influenced the testimony of spy courier Gold in a manner that implicated the Rosenbergs, and that the Bureau may have altered a hotel registration card intended to show that Gold met the Rosenbergs in Albuquerque. Some of the questions surrounding the Rosenberg case may be answered by FBI files that the Justice Department released in 1975 to scholars and to the Rosenbergs' sons, Robert and Michael Meeropol — against the Bureau's wishes but on the order of federal judges.

United States and then meticulously stage-managed his contacts with Moscow. From the variety of message drops and methods of communication available to him, Tuomi seemed to be an independent part of a rather extensive espionage network operating outside the context of, but in communication with, the official Soviet missions in the United States. By monitoring those message drops and carefully analyzing the communications he received, the Bureau was also put on the track of other members of the GRU network. Tuomi's experiences, as eventually recounted to the FBI, revealed extraordinarily thorough and practical facilities in Moscow for the training of potential spies in a simulated American environment, as well as a remarkable research capacity for creating fictitious backgrounds that could be used by Soviet "illegals."

There has been concern on several occasions about whether the Bureau itself might have been penetrated by foreign powers. Suspicion arose during World War II that a few agents who were sympathetic to the Germans may have helped them, and some agents in the New York Field Office were suspected from time to time of becoming too cozy with the Soviets whom they were supposed to be investigating. (One agent there became romantically involved with a waitress from a restaurant near the field office and left some sensitive documents in her apartment; she was thought at one point to have Russian ties, but Bureau investigation failed to document that charge.) Even if such penetration were discovered and documented, however, the preoccupation of Hoover and his lieutenants with questions of image would surely have led the FBI to deal with the matter internally and cover it up, rather than cooperate in a full public airing of the incident.

The Bureau's counterintelligence work today is a complicated, and often confused, side of the FBI mission. It sometimes takes on a Keystone Cop quality: on one occasion a carload of visiting Russian "tourists" went for a casual afternoon ride in the countryside. Their route just happened to go past a military supply base. While taking equipment out of a little black bag to plot the exact coordinates for the location of the arsenal, they discovered that they were being followed by three carloads of FBI agents. But there may also be a quality of deep intrigue; an American businessman, on the verge of signing a lucrative contract with the Soviet government, suddenly discovered an unwritten clause requiring him to submit a piece of esoteric electronic gear as part of the deal. He went ahead and did so out of enthusiasm, only later perceiving that he may have unwittingly helped the Soviets solve a defense-related problem. It was left to the Bureau, when it learned of the incident, to unravel Moscow's intentions.

Other developments on the diplomatic and political fronts notwithstanding, the Soviet Union remains the central preoccupation of the FBI in the counterintelligence field. The basic operating assumption is that the KGB will try to penetrate and subvert the American system in every way possible (just as, it must be said, the CIA, among its other missions, will try to do to the Soviet system). Some of the espionage goals are assumed to be the classic ones: to learn about American defenses and military preparedness, to monitor industrial and technological developments, and to anticipate new Soviet defense needs. But the Bureau sometimes infers subtler Soviet goals, such as efforts to detect ambivalence in American public opinion and to manipulate sentiment, especially within émigré communities, in favor of policies preferred by the Soviet leadership.

Hoover largely failed in his heavy-handed campaigns to discourage expanded consular exchanges, travel, and business between the United States and the Soviet Union; but he had a strong argument that, from an espionage standpoint, the diplomatic openings created one-way benefits for the Soviets. The open societies of the West liberally publicize information and display materials that are kept as tightly guarded secrets in the centrally controlled Soviet state. Whereas Soviet public opinion is generally difficult, if not impossible, to discern, American attitudes and internal differences are seldom hidden from the view of anyone who cares to look. Information which would conceivably be the targets of American espionage within the Soviet Union and other communist countries are readily available, in libraries and the press, to any resident or visitor in the United States. Indeed, some Soviet "tourists" have been observed in drugstores and bookshops buying large-scale county and city maps that show the locations of bridges and railroad lines; and there is nothing illegal about their doing so. A westerner in the Soviet Union would never come by that sort of material so easily.

The Bureau assumes that all other nations with communist governments, including Soviet satellites, the People's Republic of China and its allies, and Cuba,* are also fundamentally hostile to the United States. Their representatives — in consulates, trade missions, and even

---

* After the United States stopped subsidizing and encouraging right-wing refugee-group "invasions" of Cuba, the Bureau was assigned the job of intelligence work to prevent them. Conversely, the Bureau has been on the alert for communist agents coming the other way as "refugees" from Castro.

airline and tourist promotion offices — are watched as possible espionage threats in their own right or, in the case of the Eastern European countries, as potential intermediaries for the Soviets. Even Yugoslavia, which under the leadership of Marshal Tito has had a long and famous feud with Moscow, falls into the net, although the FBI insists that it is careful to coordinate with the State Department in dealing with the citizens of any nation with which the United States is pursuing, or striking up, a friendship. Officially, it is assumed that "friendly countries" would not attempt to spy on the United States. But Bureau officials concede that they became concerned about Portugal, for example, after the Communist party entered the Lisbon government during the 1974 revolution there. And counterintelligence supervisors in the FBI scarcely attempted to conceal their worries and preferences when François Mitterrand, a socialist with communist support, seemed to have a good chance of capturing the French presidency in the elections following the death of Georges Pompidou.

One other category recently added to the Bureau's counterintelligence list is the Arabs — less the official representatives of established governments than the Palestine Liberation Organization and splinter terrorist groups whose actions have been directed at Israel and her allies. The FBI's declared goal has been to prevent terrorist attacks within the United States, and at one point it feared, on the basis of intelligence, that there was a plan afoot for an attack at a major American airport comparable to the massacre at Lod airport in Tel Aviv in 1972. Initially suspect, from the Bureau's point of view, were the thousands of Arab aliens studying and working across the country, especially in small university towns. Some veteran agents had difficulty, however, in their approaches to both these visitors and "ethnic Arabs" who were naturalized American citizens, discovering communication problems based on language and attitude. As one administrator responsible for this area in a major field office put it, "The Arabs tended to get hung up on certain phrases we used, and their description of time periods was difficult for us to understand." As a result, the Research Section of the Bureau's Intelligence Division produced a "psychological study" of Arabs, which included contributions from academic sources and other government agencies, to help agents understand the special methods of approach that might be necessary. Qualified agents were also sent to language school to study Arabic, a language that was not in the Bureau's traditional repertory.

Other languages have been cultivated in the Bureau as routine tools of the trade, and agents show up in some offices with the heaviest counterintelligence load — Washington, New York, Chicago, Los

Angeles, San Francisco — speaking such esoteric tongues as Albanian, Bulgarian, and Serbo-Croatian. The languages are essential both for cultivating contacts at the United Nations and other diplomatic missions and for monitoring the wiretaps and other electronic surveillance routinely placed on every office of a government deemed hostile to the United States.* Those wiretaps generally produce very little of importance, since most of the missions assume themselves to be tapped. Similarly, some of the foreign officials realize that they are subjects of almost constant physical surveillance day and night. Both the electronic and physical surveillance sometimes seem to be a waste of time, manpower, and money, but they are generally justified by the Bureau as preventive harassment that keeps the "legals" of the espionage community from doing anything very bold.

The Bureau plainly worries little about violating the civil liberties and constitutional rights of "someone who is not a citizen and is working to destroy this country," as one official described the foreign operatives. Nonetheless, FBI agents are more circumspect today about counterintelligence methods than they were in the slaphappy days of the 1950s. One agent assigned to a West Coast field office during that period tells adventure stories about posing as a repairman to install bugging devices in the homes of suspected spies. In one instance he made a classic burglar's entry into the home of a man believed to be working for the GRU, but had to run out a side door as the family returned home unexpectedly early. (What would he have done if actually caught in the act and confronted by a member of the family? "I would have done just what a good burglar does — turned and run away as fast as possible.") One widely circulated story has it that a team of agents, frustrated by their inability to neutralize a foreign agent's activity by any other means, in effect kidnapped him and held him incommunicado for several days with the sole intention of raising doubts in his superiors' minds about whether he could any longer be trusted or had gone over to the American side. The scheme was sup-

---

* Such wiretaps are installed without the benefit of a warrant or a court order, on the basis of the attorney general's authorization and approval. Although the Supreme Court rejected the Nixon administration's theory of an executive right to wiretap on "national security" grounds without court order, it has tacitly upheld such non-court-approved wiretaps related to "foreign intelligence." Bureau statistics indicate that 101 such wiretaps were in operation during 1971, and that the number had increased to 190 by 1974; microphone surveillances without court authorization were at 16 in 1971 and 42 in 1974. The number of wiretaps without court warrant seemed sure to decrease somewhat if the Supreme Court upholds a 1975 ruling by the U.S. Court of Appeals in Washington that domestic groups could not be the subject of such taps unless they were the agents of, or were acting in collaboration with, a foreign power.

posedly carried off without causing any diplomatic furor. An agent who served as supervisor of a counterintelligence squad in a midwestern field office tells of an occasion when a local woman, suspected of being a Soviet spy, was persuaded to check into a nearby hotel for three days of intensive questioning. (Eventually the Bureau satisfied itself that she was not an agent and concluded that it had been the victim of some clever KGB "misinformation" and diversionary tactics.)

William C. Sullivan, chief of the Bureau's counterintelligence efforts during the 1960s, complained during his last days in the FBI that Hoover, by suspending special counterintelligence techniques in the late 1960s out of concern over unfavorable publicity, had crippled the agency's ability to deal with spies. The techniques, which included mail covers, handwriting analyses (the Bureau claimed to be able to detect Soviet-taught English handwriting), trash covers, and "black bag jobs" (break-ins) at foreign embassies, were necessary, Sullivan argued at the time, in order to track down the elusive "illegals" who pose the most serious espionage threat.[*] Ever since, and especially after the Director died, the Bureau has been scraping to find new, orginal means of detecting and neutralizing "illegals." The old methods are still employed in special circumstances, however. Agents used a "surreptitious entry" in 1972 to plant a microphone in the home of Dr. Abu Wadi, director of the Arab Information Center in Dallas and the man they believed to be the covert leader of Arab terrorist forces in the United States; while there, they found a folder on his desk containing a "target list" of Jews who might be victims of terrorist attacks and a list of people allegedly reporting to Wadi. The agents simply took the folder with them. (Acting Director L. Patrick Gray III later defended the FBI action on the grounds that it may have saved lives.) And the Bureau on several occasions has persuaded the Immigration and Naturalization Service to intercept Arabs the FBI believes to have terrorist connections as they arrive on international flights and deny them admission to the United States on technical grounds. But for the most part, according to one former agent who worked in the counterintelligence field for several years, "we displayed very little resourcefulness — it was just the opposite of dirty tricks."

Part of the new emphasis has been on "nationalities intelligence," in which agents, speaking the appropriate languages, try to become

---

[*] One recent report had it that Hoover, after being accused of investigating members of Congress, overreacted by ordering Bureau agents not to follow suspected spies to Capitol Hill; supposedly Soviet operatives quickly caught on to this and began meeting there.

well known and trusted in urban ethnic communities that might contain potential "target" individuals who, like Anthony, could be recruited when they travel abroad or when Soviet groups visit the United States. (The debriefing of those who have recently returned from visits to communist nations has sometimes produced positive intelligence, which the Bureau sifts through and theoretically passes on to other concerned agencies.) The Bureau has also instituted extensive coverage of all Soviet ships stopping in American ports, on the suspicion that some of the crew members have other jobs than as merchant seamen; on some occasions it has sent Russian-speaking female informants to parties given for those crews, to see what they can learn and to look for people who could become potential American agents.

It is obviously difficult to evaluate the success or failure of day-to-day Bureau efforts in the counterintelligence field. But both L. Patrick Gray III and Clarence Kelley, on taking over the FBI, became convinced that the Bureau had fallen far behind in Hoover's last years. They were shocked to learn, for example, that a staff aide to a powerful conservative member of Congress, Senator James O. Eastland (D-Mississippi), passed information to the Soviet Union for years before being detected, and that the Soviet Embassy in Washington might have the capacity to monitor conversations on unsecured government telephone lines in the nation's capital, including some at the Bureau itself. There were also signs of Soviet penetration of the American intelligence community, including the arrest of James D. Wood, an agent in the air force's Office of Special Investigations (OSI), in July 1973 during a meeting with a first secretary from the Soviet Embassy in Washington. One of the problems, Gray and Kelley each surmised, was that for years under Hoover counterintelligence work had been largely consigned to unimaginative gumshoe types, in part because it did not produce well-publicized court cases or spectacular statistics that could be fed to Congress and the public. Indeed, the floor of the New York Field Office devoted to counterintelligence was commonly nicknamed "Sleepy Hollow." Some work in this area, such as the procurement and supervision of double agents, is of course far too complex and taxing for many of the men traditionally assigned to it. Younger agents complain that counterintelligence has too often been confused and mixed with internal security investigations and that in the Director's last years it sometimes took a back seat to those more domestic concerns.

With Congress and the press finally investigating these operations, and in the face of arguments that the counterintelligence assignment should be switched to the CIA, the Bureau has sought to sharpen and modernize its efforts. By emphasizing the intellectual challenge of the work rather than the traditional thankless hours of plodding, it is also trying to recruit some of the most intelligent young agents and supervisors into a specialty that is presumed to have a bright future.

VII

Internal Security

*Rome lasted for six hundred years, and we are just coming on to
our two-hundredth. That doesn't mean that we have four hundred
to go. We have to step back and look at ourselves protectively. . . .
How much of this dissent and revolution talk can we really stand in
a healthy country? Revolutions always start in a small way. . . .
Economic conditions are bad; the credibility of government is low.
These are the things that the home-grown revolutionary is monitoring very closely. The FBI's attention must be focused on these
various situations. If it weren't, the Bureau wouldn't be doing its
job for the American people. . . . The American people don't
want to have to fool around with this kind of thing and worry
about it; they don't want to have to worry about the security of
their country. . . . We must be able to find out what stage the
revolution is in.*

                *— Edward S. Miller, for several years assistant
                  director of the FBI in charge of the Intelli-
                  gence Division, later deputy associate di-
                  rector/assistant-to-the-director, in an inter-
                  view shortly before his retirement in 1974*

AT THIRTY-TWO, WITH FASHIONABLY LONG HAIR, a slightly droopy moustache, and a suave and confidential manner, Sam (not his real name)*
seems like a young corporate lawyer — which is what he used to be.
He would just as soon pass for one, actually, because his assignment as
an FBI agent is to a big-city "security squad" that still does not like to

---

* Many of the agents interviewed who work in the "security" area specifically asked
that their true names not be used, and this request was honored.

talk very much about what it does. Sam, being the product of fine universities, probably brings a good deal of subtlety and sophistication to the job, but he still does not sound entirely comfortable with his work, the most controversial — and now, contested — work the Bureau does. He is in the ranks of those who define and then set out to protect the "internal security" of the United States.

Sam did corporate work for a law firm in the South until in the late 1960s, looking for something "glamorous and different," he joined the FBI. At his first office, a small one in the Southwest, he had typical criminal-case assignments, mostly chasing fugitives and bank robbers. Then he was transferred to a large field office and soon entrusted with duty on one of its most sensitive squads. "Security" has all sorts of meanings for the FBI, and the squad at one point chased down some leads in connection with the Watergate case; but mostly it is concerned with "revolutionary groups" which the Bureau considers a threat to the country. Sam's particular assignment is to try to keep track, through informants, of the "urban guerrilla" movement, to learn about the formation of organizations like the Symbionese Liberation Army (SLA), and to figure out ways for the Bureau to penetrate them early on. Everyone on his squad, because they work in a major city that is believed to attract radicals, was theoretically on the alert for the six "left-oriented" members of the FBI's list of the Ten Most Wanted fugitives, sought in connection with crimes or terrorist actions in the name of political causes. Some government officials have long since written off these and other fugitives from the days of violent confrontations in the late 1960s and early 1970s, mostly members of the Weatherman organization, but the FBI still holds out hope of capturing them (two of the six were captured in early 1975). The story is proudly told of an agent who recognized and arrested one woman fugitive while riding next to her on a New York subway train. Sam concedes, however, that in some cases his squad would even be content with "extraterritorial location" — certain knowledge, through intelligence sources, that the fugitive has found sanctuary overseas in a country that will not extradite him or her and that efforts at capture will therefore no longer be fruitful.

"You don't measure success in this area in terms of apprehensions," Sam observes, "but in terms of neutralization." In other words, the inevitable Bureau measure, the statistics, are not that good. The point is to render the investigated groups ineffective, to limit their appeal in any reasonable manner possible. Sam admits to some uncertainty about whether the broad scope of the FBI effort is appropriate, but he feels that some of the abuses of the Hoover era, including the "overabiding interest" in all groups to the left of the John Birch Society, are being corrected. "I think on the field level the direction is proper now," he says; "the rhetoric of the groups we investigate is political, but their real motivation may be different." He cites the SLA — its success in hiding Patricia Hearst, committing other crimes, and exerting public pressures — as evidence of the need for investigative efforts of this nature. Like others in the Bureau, Sam appears to believe that if the SLA had been investigated more aggressively in advance, it might have been prevented from carrying out some of its acts.

Sam recognizes that it is difficult to know where to draw the line between the investigation of actions and of beliefs, and he knows that his own job could be seen as political in nature, but these are issues that he manages to avoid. "I don't attach very much politics to what I do in my work," he says; "I try to divorce the two. I think a lot of agents do."

Richard (not his real name), also a young man who entered the FBI in the late 1960s, works in another large field office, supervising a security squad that deals exclusively with what the Bureau calls "black extremists." He was drawn to law enforcement, despite a promising career in the insurance business, after he helped the police investigate the murder of his father in a holdup. After an initial stint working criminal cases in his first office, he asked to switch to the "security" side and helped investigate local members of the Students for a Democratic Society (SDS). In Richard's second office, when he was bored with his original assignment to draft cases he again requested a change, to an area that few others wanted to work, the Black Panther party. ("They thought I was nuts," he recalls.) His enthusiasm was so great that it had to be restrained at times; at one point the Bureau vetoed Richard's proposal that he move into the same apartment building where one of the prominent local Black Panther leaders lived. (Investigation and surveillance would have been much easier there, he argued at the time, especially with a closed-circuit television system that permitted the residents of any apartment in the building to view the lobby on their own television set.) As a result of retirements and transfers of other agents, Richard became the squad's supervisor.

The Panthers were a particular preoccupation of J. Edgar Hoover (the greatest threat to domestic tranquillity, he called them in 1969), and so even after their influence had subsided, Richard's squad continued to feed material about the organization into an intricate Bureau reporting system. Reports were put together at regular intervals on the finances, organizational and structural changes, ideological debates, weapons, and "fortifications" of each faction of the Panthers, and each field office with any significant contingent in its territory was expected to contribute; the reports were distributed within the FBI hierarchy and to other agencies and congressional committees, even in some instances to the White House. The emphasis on the field level, Richard points out, is "to stop things from happening . . . to maintain sufficient coverage so we know what they're going to do, when and where." One Panther chapter in his area is so well infiltrated by FBI informants that when some of its members once planned to hold up a drugstore, the Bureau was able to get a police patrol there first to await and arrest them in the act. This tactic and others have apparently been so successful in some cities as to put entire Panther chapters out of business.

But the sweep of Richard's squad has expanded considerably as new organizations come along that look to the FBI as if they may be havens for "black extremists." He does not handle the best-organized and -established group, the Black Muslims (for reasons of workload, it is combined on another desk with "white extremists"). But whenever a new group name surfaces during an investigation of others or in a piece of evidence passed along by the police, such as an address book, a ninety-day "preliminary investigation" of it and its members is usually launched. "We try to determine their goals," Richard explains. "If they are just trying to get people jobs, then we drop it. But if it is clear that they want to overthrow the government or encourage crime, then we go in to the Bureau [send a cable to headquarters] and say we are opening a regular investigation." The Intelligence Division normally answers only if it disagrees with the tentative decision to launch a full-scale probe; otherwise the field office goes ahead. Once the investigation is under way, that means attempting to find out how many members are in the group, just who they are and what the racial makeup is, and what their plans are. Each person may become the "subject" of a Bureau "case." "If they start talking more militant, we get closer," Richard adds.

As a supervisor, Richard has found that black agents are far more successful at handling cases involving black groups, but the shortage of minority agents in the Bureau has meant that they are rarely available for that sort of work.* In any event, he has found it "silly and pointless" to send out southern white agents with thick accents to do

---

* The enthusiasm of black agents for "security" work involving "black extremists" varies widely. Among the black agents interviewed, some scoffed at the Bureau's approach and said they would not want to be involved in it, but others said they preferred to handle it themselves rather than leave it to others who would be less sensitive.

security investigations in the black community — especially one agent he inherited on the squad "who was a redneck and still used the word 'nigger.'"

Most of the information needed in preliminary investigations can be obtained from public sources — credit and criminal checks, birth and school records — without any personal interviews or contacts. Whereas the Bureau in earlier days never hesitated to confront anyone directly, Richard insists that the decisions are now taken more carefully, especially on his squad. If there has been no indication of danger and "if it looks like a pretty good home," the agents will directly approach the subject of the investigation, or a neighbor who the agent hopes will provide reliable information. But "when someone gives us a hard time or calls us pigs . . . well, we have learned just to walk away and try a different approach." The information gathered theoretically goes to Washington only if a preliminary investigation produces cause to proceed with something more extensive; but even if headquarters gets only an innocuous "status report" and if the groups and their members appear to be perfectly law-abiding, the material is entered in the indices and files of the field office that gathered it. It is there for reference and consultation until someone makes a decision to remove it.

Many of the cases opened on organizations and their members lead nowhere, Richard concedes. But his philosophy is to err, if at all, in the direction of heavy coverage, including a few "shots in the dark, which sometimes turn up fugitives that we weren't even expecting to find." Some agents, both black and white, he says, suggest frequently that "we are going overboard. They say, 'Why not just open the phone book?'" and choose at random the people to be investigated. But from the supervisor's point of view it is worthwhile deploying all his available manpower; as Richard puts it, "I figure — why not? We're not hurting anybody."

"Security" and "subversion" are words that are virtually impossible to define in either a political or investigative context. What is subversive to one man may, of course, be the height of patriotism to another. And an act or speech intended as the very personification of democratic ideals may be interpreted by others who consider themselves vigilant as a dangerous threat to the nation's internal security. But definitional problems apparently did not loom very large at the start of World War II when President Roosevelt directed the Bureau back to the mission it had given up in 1924 — the investigation of political organizations and affiliations.

No distinction was initially drawn between inquiries involving potential foreign espionage or influence and those involving domestic groups. To look into German and Russian activities in the United States, as Roosevelt asked J. Edgar Hoover to do, meant not only to trace the movements of diplomats and other foreign representatives, but also to investigate organizations like the German-American Bund and the American Communist party (CPUSA). They were, in the main, loyal to other countries, or at least sympathetic enough to arouse suspicion from a national security standpoint during a time of international tension; the FBI covered them very thoroughly indeed. As war approached and the United States became involved, however, vigilance and caution grew into xenophobia and distrust of anyone who veered noticeably from the political mainstream. In the absence of any clear-cut standards Hoover formulated his own, and disagreement with the national policies of the Roosevelt administration, such as lend-lease aid to the European Allies, was enough to attract the Bureau's attention. On the Right, it investigated groups from Father Coughlin's anti-Semitic followers in the Christian Front to the more establishment, isolationist America First Committee. On the Left attention was focused on such groups as the American Youth Congress and the Workers Alliance, which shared members in common with the Communist party and were quickly labeled as "front organizations." As Don Whitehead later described the situation, "Into and through the war years the FBI traced the twists and turns of the Communist Party and the fronts which changed their names as casually as a man changes a suit of clothes"; while the Bureau uncovered only eighty thousand members of the CPUSA at its wartime peak, according to Whitehead it estimated that "almost 1,000,000 people knowingly or unknowingly had been drawn into Communist-front activity. The Communists themselves boasted that for every member of the Party there were ten others who willingly followed the Party 'line.'"

The Communist party was a pushover for the FBI. So riddled was the organization with Bureau informants that Hoover could almost be said to have delegates at all of its official functions during the war. But just in case, agents were also assigned to keep watch from outside. Whitehead recounts with particular relish a secret meeting of the CPUSA's top national leadership in February 1944 in a New York City recording studio, during which debate raged over whether to follow a policy of confrontation or collaboration with the established American political parties. As the theorists debated, every word was picked up on a microphone installed by Bureau agents, who had been tipped off in advance and posed as musicians renting an adjoining studio.

On a local, field office level, individual agents scored smaller but sometimes significant points against the American communists, largely through the use of unofficial counterintelligence techniques like those routinely employed in dealing with suspected foreign agents. Many leaders of union locals in critical war industries, for example, were members of the CPUSA. If that affiliation was concealed, or if the leaders had anything embarrassing in their backgrounds, such as an arrest record, the Bureau would see that full information about them found its way into the local press. The FBI influence reached deep into some of the communists' personal lives, often unknown to them. At one point, the daughter of a Pittsburgh newspaper publisher was engaged to marry a young man named Gus Hall. Rather than "let this occur," recalled an agent who was assigned to the Pittsburgh Field Office at the time, the Bureau "saw to it that her father became aware" that Hall was an up-and-coming member of the Communist party (later its general secretary). That marriage, for whatever the reasons, never came off. When Hall married someone else later, FBI agents attended the wedding as uninvited guests.

The CPUSA would continue to be a Bureau target for decades after the war and long after it had become a paper tiger. FBI tactics, in combination with the changing times, worked to reduce the party's effectiveness and appeal. The last figure published by the Bureau said the organization had about twelve to fourteen thousand members; subsequently all inquirers were told that the membership statistics were "classified." In fact, by the early 1970s, according to the FBI's own private calculations, the CPUSA rolls were down to a pathetic figure of three thousand members, with only about half of them active. Nonetheless, the Bureau continued to investigate.

Having built up a large corps of agents to guard the nation's internal security, Hoover had no intention of giving up the job after the war; nor did anyone take steps to force him to do so. If anything, President Truman's establishment of the Federal Employee Loyalty Program seemed to institutionalize this function still further. With the advent of the "attorney general's list," someone had to determine whether the various suspect political organizations were "subversive" or "loyal." And so the FBI took on the role of a kind of ideological security police, an arbiter of what was inside the boundaries of legitimate political discourse and what outside. It was a role that incensed civil libertarians, who interpreted the Bureau investigations as an interference with freedom of political association and expression. It also made an entire generation of young Americans, coming of age in the late 1940s and early 1950s, feel that they must be cautious about what organizations they joined and people they associated with, lest they tar themselves unknowingly with a radical brush that could affect their job prospects. This function was especially important because of the Bureau's free ticket to define its own terms, to be the traffic policeman who decided which people were "subversive," which were not, and which needed to be checked out at all. The FBI, and especially Hoover, found their own fluctuating justifications for concern — alleged Communist party influence over other groups, international efforts to interfere with American politics, the undermining of the federal bureaucracy, and so on. It was a role, in any event, that formed a significant part of the FBI image in years to come, even though it represented a relatively small percentage of its work.

Professor John Elliff of Brandeis University, a student of the Bureau's evolving intelligence role, has revealed* the nature of the FBI reports in some of its earliest postwar inquiries about organizations — groups scrutinized because, as Attorney General Tom Clark put it at the time, while "presently innocuous," they might later "become the victims of dangerous infiltrating forces." In one instance, a Bronx, New York, child care center was examined; a Justice Department summary prepared from the FBI report noted that although the center was "apparently dominated and run by members of the Communist Party," there was "no indication that the personnel of the organization was all Communist or that the group was used as a device or 'front' for carrying out the program of the Communist Party, except with respect to its avowed purpose of setting up nursery schools and after-school centers." The investigation was suspended because of the group's "localized nature." The Bureau also checked out a group called the League for Fair Play, discovering that it was "formed in 1937, apparently by two ministers and a businessman for the purpose of furthering fair play, tolerance, adherence to the Constitution, democracy, liberty, justice, and understanding and good will among all creeds, races and classes of the United States. The group sought to advance its aims by furnishing speakers to Rotary and Kiwanis Clubs and to schools and colleges."

The FBI submitted reports in 1944 and 1946, according to Elliff, on the Independent Voters of Illinois, a nonpartisan political organization based in Chicago (it became the Illinois chapter of the Americans for Democratic Action), theoretically because it was a typical target of communist infiltration. Like other Bureau documents over the years,

---

* In "The Scope and Basis of FBI Domestic Intelligence Data Collection," a paper prepared for the conference on the FBI sponsored by the Committee for Public Justice and the Woodrow Wilson School of Princeton University in October 1971.

the reports on the IVI have a capacity for making the innocent and the mundane sound sinister. The group, it was noted, was organized in 1944 "for the purpose of developing neighborhood political units to help in the re-election of President Roosevelt and the election of progressive congressmen. Apparently, IVI endorsed or aided Democrats for the most part, although it was stated to be 'independent.'" Later, its goals were described as helping candidates "who would favor fighting inflation, oppose race and class discrimination, favor international cooperation, support a 'full-employment program,' oppose Fascism, etc." and its programs as "supporting the Bretton Woods proposal, the United Nations, placing the atom bomb under U.N. control, and Henry Wallace for Secretary of Commerce." The Bureau reported reassuringly that "IVI never was controlled or dominated by Communists, even though they sought and planned to use it for their own ends and may have tried to gain control." None of the officers were communist, said the Bureau, although the chairman was described as "a very liberal individual" and it was suggested that others in the leadership "may have sought support from some front organizations." Communist involvement was quantified at approximately 10 percent of the IVI membership.

Elliff also cites FBI reports in the postwar period on the Polish American Congress, described by the Bureau as "a right-wing group devoted to the establishment of a Polish Government free from Russian or Communist domination," which was, in the late 1940s, "engaged in raising one million dollars for use in carrying on [its] propaganda activities." The Bureau was aware of PAC telegrams to the State Department demanding "withdrawal of United States recognition of the Warsaw government. . . . PAC did not hesitate to attack the U.S. and the State Department when it believed the Polish question or problems as to displaced persons were not being handled as it desired. . . . PAC brought these matters to the attention of Congress and publicized it [sic] in releases, statements and writings."

Most of the Bureau's concern, however, was unequivocally focused on the left of the political spectrum. Some organizations like the Socialist Workers party were not thought to require review in order to decide whether they should be the subjects of security coverage, but were automatically included in light of their alleged fidelity to some "foreign" ideology. The SWP, for example, was regarded as part of a worldwide Trotskyite movement which could theoretically become a threat to the established order in the United States. The Bureau would investivate on the slightest pretext. When Lori Paton, a high school student in New Jersey, wrote to the Young Socialist Alliance (the youth branch of the Socialist Workers party) for information, as part of a project for her social studies class, agents visited the high school to ask about her. (She eventually won a court ruling that required the FBI to destroy its file on her.) Skeptics pointed out from time to time that the only thing that seemed to keep organizations like the SWP going was the attention and concern of the FBI; just as their appeal would fade, the Bureau would issue a new warning about how dangerous they were and new recruits would flock to the cause.

The FBI took a lot of its cues in the internal security field from the House Un-American Activities Committee, which was still going strong in the 1950s, and, in the executive branch, the Subversive Activities Control Board. Together with those panels and, for a time, Senator Joseph McCarthy's subcommittee investigating Communist influence in government, the Bureau became part of a sort of internal security establishment within the federal government. Lending this establishment a special legitimacy was the new Internal Security Division of the Justice Department, created in 1954 by Attorney General Herbert Brownell to prosecute and supervise developing cases involving "subversives." The division, which existed as a separate entity within Justice for two decades, had its own units to coordinate the flow of intelligence and analysis on radical groups. It became a distinct lobby for vigorous investigative and prosecutive action against those groups. Although the FBI was supposedly an impartial, open-minded agency, it became firmly entrenched with the division, HUAC, and the SACB on the right end of the political spectrum. They whipped the Red scare back into existence, and any person they considered too radical, or even liberal, was liable to be labeled "pink," investigated by the Bureau, and hauled before HUAC, the SACB, or a grand jury. Anyone who agreed with the communists on any issue was suspected. One purpose of the investigations was to develop candidates for the Security Index, which evolved from the special list of potential "subversives" drawn up by the Bureau when its internal security functions were formally revived in 1939. In its more modern form, the Index was intended to be a catalogue of possible wartime saboteurs who would be apprehended under the Emergency Detention Act of 1950 (later repealed) and of persons who might be a threat to the President (whose names, therefore, would be submitted to the Secret Service). In theory, the FBI carefully weighed the activities, associations, and ideas of anyone who was being considered for inclusion in the Index. Once a person was listed in the Index, the Bureau would prepare a standby warrant for his or her arrest, to be executed in time of emergency. The Security Index was officially abolished in 1971, but the FBI still maintains the Administrative Index, or ADEX, a more limited catalogue of about 1,500 people — members of the CPUSA, suspected terrorists and the like — who would come in for intensified investigation and scrutiny during a national emergency.*

The danger in the compilation of any such lists was that often Bureau agents and other operatives of the internal security establishment mistook exposure to radical or "subversive" ideas as indoctrination or belief in them. They undertook to militate against the teaching and lecturing about communist ideas, even in universities. The country could not afford to have its youth "brainwashed."

One result of the Bureau's plunge into internal security work, aside from mountains of files containing irrelevant and often unsubstantiated information, was an angry standoff between the FBI and a significant and influential segment of the population — university professors and students, writers and actors and artists, indeed, most of the liberal intelligentsia. These people were by no means a majority of Americans, but they were "important." They were in positions such that they were often approached by FBI agents conducting background investigations and probes of suspected subversion; and when they were displeased, they had easy access to avenues of communication through which they could complain loudly, sometimes eloquently, about Bureau practices and techniques. The standoff was responsible for a whole new side of the FBI image, that of an agency which stirs fear in the hearts of the people because it seeks to interfere with their political thoughts and associations, and an agency, therefore, which is loathed and occasionally stymied — some would say justifiably so — by those who do not trust it.

Nothing symbolized and dramatized this conflict better than the nasty clash in late 1949 between J. Edgar Hoover and Bernard De Voto, professor, editor, social critic, and historian, and, for twenty years, author of a monthly column in *Harper's* magazine. In his

---

* The Security Index, which at its peak had about 15,000 names, consisted of 5″ × 8″ cards containing "background information, nationalistic tendency, file numbers, and organizational affiliation"; according to the Bureau, most additions and deletions were approved by the Justice Department over the years. Alongside the SI, as it was called, there was a "Reserve Index," composed of the names of people who were considered only slightly less dangerous and would be intensively investigated in time of emergency, but not detained (much like those now on the ADEX). It too was eliminated in 1971. The FBI says that the ADEX "is reviewed continuously," and that once deletions are made, "former lists cannot be reconstructed." Yet the Bureau acknowledged in October 1975 that all of the old cards from the Security Index had been safely tucked aside in 1971, so that it would be theoretically possible to recreate it.

October 1949 column De Voto mocked the way Bureau agents came around and asked people about their neighbors — where they get their money, what they drink, what they talk about, whom they associate with. He reeled off an exaggerated list of typical questions:

Does he play poker or shoot craps? Has he ever been present at a meeting or a party at which anyone who makes bets or plays poker was also present? . . . Does he know any millionaires, or people who own cabin cruisers, or people who have accounts in more than one bank? . . . Does he read the *Wall Street Journal?* Has he ever been present at a cocktail party at which anyone who does read it was present? Is it true that he gave his secretary half a dozen pairs of nylon stockings for Christmas? Could she be fronting or dummying for business deals that are really his? What kind of girl is she? Does she always leave the office at five o'clock?

But De Voto also issued a plea for noncooperation with the Bureau:

I say it has gone too far. We are dividing into the hunted and the hunters. There is loose in the United States today the same evil that once split Salem Village between the bewitched and the accused and stole men's reason quite away. We are informers to the secret police. Honest men are spying on their neighbors for patriotism's sake. We may be sure that for every honest man two dishonest ones are spying for personal advancement today and ten will be spying for pay next year.

. . .

Representatives of the FBI and of other official investigating bodies have questioned me, in the past, about a number of people and I have answered their questions. That's over. From now on any representative of the government, properly identified, can count on a drink and perhaps informed talk about the Red (but non-Communist) Sox at my house. But if he wants information from me about anyone whomsoever, no soap. If it is my duty as a citizen to tell what I know about someone, I will perform that duty under subpoena, in open court, before that person and his attorney. This notice is posted in the court-house square: I will not discuss anyone in private with any government investigator.

Hoover was furious and fought back bitterly, challenging De Voto to furnish proof of his allegations but declining to debate personally with him in any forum. De Voto, for his own part, relished the confrontation; in letters to friends and other correspondents he made ominous overstatements: "Sure, I expect to be roused at 2:00 A.M. and marched to the salt mines." "Anyway I am glad you liked my piece and I will destroy your letter lest the Gestapo find it when they come to ship me to Indiana." "Send an occasional package to my family when I

130

have been put away." Such overstatement, and all the fun and sarcasm it implied, would become characteristic of many of the Bureau's new-found opponents.

But for many, confrontations with the FBI involved less fun than they did humiliation. Robert Crichton, the author, has written of the severe anguish felt by his father, Kyle Crichton (who also wrote leftist tracts during the 1930s, under the name of Robert Forsythe), during repeated interrogations by Bureau men and representatives of HUAC about his attitudes and associations. Many a distinguished American was faced with the choice of "naming names" of others or of being condemned himself — with the possible result of being blacklisted from a decent job. As internal security investigations flourished, almost anyone was liable to undergo the equivalent of a loyalty check. This was a development that left a permanent imprint on the Bureau.

The FBI's authority and jurisdiction for busying itself with "security" were, at best, only casually asserted and explained. There was, of course, the Smith Act, named for Congressman Howard W. Smith of Virginia and passed as a little-noticed rider to the Alien Registration Act in 1940. Modeled after the New York Criminal Anarchy Act of 1902, it made it a crime for anyone "to knowingly or willfully advocate, abet, advise or teach the duty, necessity, desirability or propriety of overthrowing or destroying any government in the United States by force or violence, or by the assassination of any officer of such government"; publication or distribution of printed matter that had the same purposes was also banned. The Smith Act seemed to go further than prior sedition statutes since it applied in peace as well as wartime. In fact, declared the House conference manager during floor debate on its passage, it went about as far as the Constitution would permit to squelch communist and fascist organizations in the United States. The act was used only twice during the Second World War, once against members of the Minneapolis branch of the Socialist Workers party and once against a pro-Nazi group. But later the Justice Department used the Smith Act and enormous legal resources in an effort to destroy the American Communist party. In the Dennis case, which took nine months to try in federal court in 1949, the government prosecuted Eugene Dennis and ten other top leaders of the party; the case resulted in a Supreme Court declaration in 1950 that the Smith Act was a constitutional means for the society to protect itself. Even if the people and organizations prosecuted had little actual prospect of successfully overthrowing the government, the majority ruled, a conspiracy to try to do so could be punished.

The prosecution of fourteen second-string communist leaders under the Smith Act in 1952 was less successful, however; the Supreme Court reversed their conviction in the Yates case (named for Oleta O'Connor Yates) in 1957, complaining that mere advocacy of an abstract doctrine or an "evil intent" could not be punished. Rather, the Court said, the government would have to be able to prove the advocacy of specific action based upon those ideas in order to obtain a conviction. Of one hundred and forty-one persons indicted under the Smith Act, only twenty-nine ever served prison terms. The Yates case effectively weakened the law as a serious instrument for pursuing "subversives," but still the Bureau cited the Smith Act into the 1970s as the basis for many of its internal security investigations.

Shortly after the outbreak of the Korean war, Congress, concerned that the Smith Act did not go far enough, added another weapon to the legal arsenal for fighting the communist movement — the Internal Security Act of 1950, also known as the McCarran Act, after its chief sponsor, Senator Pat McCarran of Nevada.* Passed over President Truman's veto, this law established the Subversive Activities Control Board as a tribunal with which "communist-action organizations" and "communist-front organizations" were required to register. The SACB was authorized to conduct hearings into whether an organization fell within either definition. The registration provisions were stiff, requiring that the name and address of every member of a "communist-action" group, and of every officer of a "communist-front" group, be furnished to the government board, along with an accounting of all money received and spent and a list of printing presses, mimeograph machines, and other duplicating materials. Anyone registering essentially branded himself a traitor, because the McCarran Act declared that those Americans who participated in the communist movement "in effect repudiate their allegiance to the United States, and in effect transfer their allegiance to [a] foreign country"; the purpose of the movement was declared to be to establish a "communist totalitarian dictatorship" throughout the world by "treachery, deceit, infiltration . . . espionage, sabotage, terrorism and any other means deemed necessary." Registered members of communist groups were not permitted to apply for passports, to hold federal government jobs, or to work in a defense facility. No organization that fell under the act was to send any communication through the mails or to broadcast any matter over radio or television to more than two persons, unless it was clearly labeled as coming from a communist organization. The law also in-

* The original draft of the legislation was the work of two Republican congressmen: Karl Mundt of South Dakota and Richard Nixon of California.

cluded a criminal sedition clause, intended to get people whom the Smith Act missed, and the Emergency Detention Act, intended for use in time of national emergencies.*

After eleven years of litigation, the Supreme Court upheld the basic provisions of the Internal Security Act in 1961, while not reaching the question of whether registration with the SACB under the law's provisions would amount to self-incrimination. The Justice Department eventually indicted communist leaders for failing to register, but all of the convictions obtained were ultimately reversed on the ground that the government actions forced the communists into the unconstitutional position of incriminating themselves. Even where isolated orders to register were defied by "communist-front" organizations, efforts to enforce the law never proved successful. Eventually, the SACB died a slow death, as the courts rendered its functions meaningless and Congress denied it money.† Nonetheless, the Bureau clung to the Internal Security Act as one of the justifications for its domestic security investigations.

Other specific statutes have been cited over the years as possibly authorizing FBI investigations in the "security" area. Deputy Assistant Attorney General Kevin T. Maroney — reflecting the Justice Department's latest thinking on the matter — provided an unusually extensive list during his testimony before the House Internal Security Committee (successor to HUAC)‡ on February 20, 1974. He included the laws providing for the protection of foreign officials and official guests of the United States, banning deprivation of civil rights, prohibiting the use of explosives and incendiary devices, forbidding "private correspondence" with foreign governments (the never-enforced Logan Act), requiring respect for American neutrality whenever asserted, and punishing riots and sabotage, as well as the Atomic Energy Act and Section 533 of Title 28 in the federal criminal code, a law generally authorizing the attorney general to order investigations by the FBI, even where no prosecution is contemplated. But whenever the Bureau, if challenged, cannot bring a case into one of those categories, it falls back on the 1939 "directives" (one of them, as noted in Chapter VI,

---

* The Emergency Detention Act was originally offered by liberals as a substitute for the Internal Security Act, on the theory that communists and other "subversives" were a threat only in wartime, but the sponsors of the original bill liked it so much that they tacked it on.

† The attorney general's list of subversive organizations lived on, however, until 1974, when one of its fathers, Richard Nixon, abolished it on the advice of his attorney general, William B. Saxbe, who called it a "vestigial tail" of federal internal security programs.

‡ The House of Representatives abolished HISC in 1975.

133

only a press statement) from President Roosevelt. To base the legiti-macy of much of the FBI's work on such White House orders is to claim that its authorization ultimately lies in the inherent powers of the President to protect the nation under Article II of the Constitution. As Maroney put it in his testimony before the House committee, intend-ing to justify the Bureau's "domestic intelligence-gathering functions":

Without a broad range of intelligence information, the President and the appropriate departments and agencies of the Executive Branch could not properly and adequately protect our nation's security and enforce the numerous statutes pertaining thereto. . . . as the Supreme Court has recog-nized in numerous opinions, the Government has a right, in fact a duty, to protect itself from destruction and to safeguard its institutions from violence and forcible overthrow.

Maroney also cited the Supreme Court's words, in the Dennis case, discussing the meaning of the traditional "clear and present danger" test of when free speech may be abridged: "Obviously, the words cannot mean that before the Government may act, it must wait until the *putsch* is about to be executed, the plans have been laid, and the signal is awaited."

The meaning of "security" can be stretched to extraordinary lengths. The House Internal Security Committee, among its many ad-ventures, undertook to publish a list of people with dangerous ideas — "radical pied pipers" — who were speaking on college campuses. No-where did its report actually say that rights of free speech and associa-tion should be abridged, or that the ideological content of education should be censored, but the implications were strongly there. Senator James O. Eastland's vigilant Subcommittee to Investigate the Adminis-tration of the Internal Security Act and Other Internal Security Laws, fearful over the nation's fate, held a series of hearings on the subject "Marihuana-Hashish Epidemic and Its Impact on United States Secu-rity," in order to "play a role in reversing a trend towards national disaster." With an increasing number of people slipping into a "zombie-like" stupor from the use of marijuana, the subcommittee warned in 1974, the nation might eventually lose its capacity to confront and vanquish its enemies.

For the most part, the Bureau agreed with and encouraged such positions. It certainly wanted to eliminate the campus as a forum for radicals and it militated against any liberalization of drug laws. The FBI never went quite as far in formulating its working premises as did the congressional committees; the latter reaped staff allocations and political capital from the bizarre offshoots of radical movements. Bureau officials preferred to lurk in the background and provide information, sometimes surreptitiously, leaving the dirty work to others. Nonetheless, the FBI read a great deal into the concept of "internal security" during the 1960s and early 1970s. As the country throbbed with social upheavals and crises, with an attempt to readjust racial and economic relationships, with bitter protest against an unpopular Asian war, and with a new protest movement against pollution of the environment, the agents were often dispatched to the ramparts to defend the status quo. In the eyes of the old man for whom only the traditional values had validity, and of a bureaucracy that adopted his attitudes with an almost religious zeal, the winds of change were ominous. He had seen the civil rights sit-ins of the late fifties and early sixties as the work of radicals, surely inspired by communists; what to make now of long hair, beards, blue jeans, and sandals; communes, underground newspapers, and any other expressions of an alternative lifestyle?

The Bureau, even if it was rarely asked for information in some areas, provided it anyway and created an appetite for more. It used its role as gatekeeper of knowledge about what was happening in some areas of society to try to define and focus the attitudes of the federal government and of law enforcement generally. The FBI behaved as if it had an entire way of life to protect.

With what sometimes seemed to be absurd naïveté, the FBI assumed that new organizations and "extremist" ones, like the revolutionary cells of old, would have complete lists with the names, addresses, and phone numbers of card-carrying members. It believed that virtually every urban riot or disturbance was carefully plotted out and organized in advance. It seemed obvious that if only everyone became convinced that, as the Bureau once put it, "there is an FBI Agent behind every mailbox," the level of protest and troublemaking would decline immediately. And so it appeared to long-successful Bureau administrators and supervisors that the situation could be handled with classic tools of the trade, especially surveillance. Bank accounts were monitored, telephone records checked, travel kept track of, and personal social lives intimately charted. The Bureau exhorted its offices to investigate the loosely defined New Left — described by at least one special-agent-in-charge as including "newly formed organizations with leftist or anarchistic connotations" — as distinct from the Old Left, which included "the Communist Party and the various splinter and Trotskyite groups which have been in existence for many years," and from such established protest-action groups as the Women's International League for Peace and Freedom, the Committee for a Sane Nuclear Policy, and the American Friends Service Committee, "which have long been in existence and are now attempting to polarize themselves toward revolting youth. . . ." Some offices went as far as maintaining a New Left Events Calendar.

The FBI revealed relatively little about its investigative efforts in the internal security field during the 1960s, but the descriptions by individuals who left the Bureau and the unauthorized publication of some of its documents have permitted a tentative reconstruction of the character and scope of some of those efforts. Robert Wall, upon leaving the FBI in 1971, told of his work on a security squad in the Washington Field Office — covering such events as a demonstration at the Labor Department to protest alleged racial discrimination at a Bethlehem Steel plant, a teenagers' march on the D.C. City Council chambers to demand restoration of a summer job program, and a protest by high school students against the low quality of food in their school cafeteria. Wall also dealt with "racial matters" and saw the Bureau keeping tabs on a bookshop run by members of the Student Nonviolent Coordinating Committee, monitoring the opening ceremonies of a Smithsonian Institution annex in a black neighborhood of the capital city, and paying special attention to black student unions on college campuses. Until black leader Stokely Carmichael used the term "black power," Wall reported, the investigation of civil rights groups was usually justified on the grounds of possible "communist infiltration" of them; after he coined the term, the heading became "black extremists." Wall also described his attempt to launch an investigation of the Institute for Policy Studies in Washington, which he finally concluded was no more than a "think tank of the Left," sponsor of seminars and research. The case was closed as unpromising, but a year later another, more eager agent reopened it, gathered the institute's telephone and bank records, and tried to penetrate it with student informants. Wall complained that many of his supervisors and colleagues were prepared to read communist influence into anything.

By far the most extensive information on Bureau activities to be released in years resulted from the burglary on March 8, 1971, of the FBI resident agency in Media, Pennsylvania, by a group of unidentified activists calling themselves the Citizens' Commission to Investigate the FBI. Documents taken from the resident agency's files and later selectively leaked to individual journalists included many items showing how the Philadelphia Field Office (of which the Media Resident Agency was a subsidiary) was handling the bustling internal security business, and a few items dealing with overall Bureau policy. While the documents were not necessarily a representative cross section of the office's work,* they revealed preoccupation with domestic intelligence and surveillance of leftists, students, and blacks. One document, for example, showed that a constant wiretap was in operation on the Philadelphia office of the Black Panthers. One day's log of the surveillance included some overheard references to Panther business — money owed for truck rental and telephone bills, scheduling of a breakfast program and a "liberation school," anger with the "pigs" for "saturating" the neighborhood around the office — but also to personal matters — discussion by a woman of when her baby was due and an attempt by one member's mother to talk him into leaving the Panthers. Some of the conversations sounded artificial after they had been summarized in Bureau lingo: "SIMBA requested that he be furnished further information regarding the matter" and two people discuss "student unrest" during a conversation. But given the FBI's desire to weaken the Panthers, the wiretap picked up potentially useful, if trivial, information on their affairs.

One memorandum listed every college and university in the Philadelphia Field Office's territory, from the Pennsylvania State University with 47,520 students to Moravian Theological Seminary in Bethlehem with only 35. Another indicated the existence of twenty separate field office master files in Philadelphia dealing with Students for a Democratic Society, twenty-two dealing generally with the New Left Movement, including some titled "communist influence," "factionalism," "foreign influence (international relations)," and "mental disorders"; and thirty-four on "student agitation" at different colleges and universities. Agents handling "security informants" were alerted to obtain all possible information on a conference of War Resisters International at Haverford, Pennsylvania, "in view of current international situation and the Paris Peace Talks." The Civil Disobedience Unit of the Philadelphia Police Department was revealed to have reported to the Bureau on a peaceful anti–Vietnam war demonstration sponsored by SDS.

In another memo, a secretary to the registrar at Swarthmore College was said to have provided information about a congressman's daughter. A young woman from Scranton, a student at the University of California at Berkeley, according to one document, attended a meet-

---

* In theory at least, complete files are rarely kept in the resident agencies; they are authorized to have only those pieces of paper — individual "serials" — that are relevant to cases being worked on. Compliance with that regulation tends to vary with the closeness in time to the next annual inspection of the office.

ing of the Venceremos Brigade, but was turned down on her application to travel to Cuba for that organization. "During this meeting, there was no discussion of violence or revolution," said the report from the West Coast; "San Francisco source personally conversed with subject and received no indication that she was anything other than the average liberal minded student that is common in the Berkeley area." But the Washington Field Office had earlier described the same woman as "an inveterate Marxist revolutionist, and a type of a person that should be watched as she will probably be very active in revolutionary activities." In yet another item from the Media office, it was revealed that the chief telephone operator at Swarthmore College had promised to report on all long-distance phone calls made or received by a philosophy professor, because he and his wife had been mentioned in a teletype from the Boston Field Office as possible contacts for the New Left fugitives wanted in connection with a bank robbery and police shooting.

The level of some of the observations and surveillance was reflected in a memorandum passing along an informant's report on his attempt to attend a meeting of the Philadelphia Labor Committee. The meeting, it turned out, was canceled; but, said the agent, the informant "was invited to sit and talk awhile with those present."

The report, in part:

All individuals were sitting around discussing the coming Black Panther Party Conference and smoking marijuana.

A meeting of the Women's Liberation group was being held in another room and there appeared to be approximately eight females participating in this meeting including [name omitted], who kept going in and out of the meeting to attend her small child who was in the kitchen. A number of other rather hippie-type individuals were observed coming and going from the upper floors and it would appear that the three-story house is being operated as a commune.

From statements made by [three names omitted], it would appear that they consider themselves "intellectual revolutionaries," but are not organizational types and not personally activists.

The agent's recommendation was to open a case on the commune.

The Media documents showed a variety of investigative efforts directed against blacks and their organizations, what the Bureau called "racial intelligence." During the buildup for the Revolutionary Peoples Constitutional Convention organized by the Panthers in 1970, offices were required to report to headquarters once a week on such details as "mode of travel," "convention security precautions to be observed," and "details concerning available housing." Attention was also focused on the National Black Economic Development Conference and its leader in Philadelphia, Muhammad Kenyatta, with agents obtaining copies of bank statements and monitoring meetings through informants. An informant reporting on the Black/United Liberation Front provided such minute details that the contacting agent was able to say: "The BULF is not going to buy a type setting machine. They are buying an electric typewriter and are supposed to have the use of a type setter the location of which she [the informant] does not know. She said the members are fighting and drinking more than ever." A series of 1968 memoranda, distributed at the peak of concern about urban riots, urged serious efforts to develop "racial informants (ghetto)" — "individuals, white and black, who live and/or work in ghetto type areas and are in a position to advise of activities, rumors, tensions, etc. in those ghettos. More specifically, they may be able to advise of the activities of individual trouble makers and rabble rousers." It was to be a no-holds-barred effort, according to one memorandum:

The Bureau suggests that employees may have friends, relatives or acquaintances who can be of help in gathering racial intelligence. These would include people now residing in other field divisions who could be called to the attention of pertinent offices. Other sources which should be kept in mind are employees and owners of businesses in ghetto areas which might include taverns, liquor stores, drugstores, pawn shops, gun shops, barber shops, janitors of apartment buildings, etc. The Bureau also suggests contacts with persons who frequent ghetto areas on a regular basis such as taxi drivers, salesmen and distributors of newspapers, food and beverages. Installment collectors might also be considered in this regard.

The only organizations at other points on the political spectrum revealed in the Media documents to be under investigation by that office were a Philadelphia-area unit of the Ku Klux Klan and a chapter of the Jewish Defense League.

If the Bureau had clear-cut guidelines for determining who would come under investigation during the expansion of the internal security work, those were never enunciated to the public, if to anyone else. But several dominant themes run through the available documents, and recur in what officials who worked in the field of domestic intelligence during that period have to say. The Bureau was constantly on the lookout for any indication that the American antiwar and other protest movements were controlled by the Communist party or linked to foreign powers, something Hoover always hoped to find. The Director's frenzied concern was easily triggered by any attacks on police as "pigs" or, for that matter, by even the mildest criticism of the FBI itself. The Bureau saw clear and automatic links running from protest to violence, to anarchist agitation to an actual revolution. It took the New Left more seriously than anyone, except the New Left itself. By the time all of these concerns were allowed for and all bases were covered, the Bureau was — as if in a wartime crisis — monitoring almost all forms of political dissent. And it was not alone; a veritable domestic intelligence orgy was on, and the participants included various branches of military intelligence and even the CIA, which until recently was assumed to be officially restricted by its charter from conducting any domestic operations. In fact the CIA began a well-concealed domestic spying operation in the 1960s and intensified it during the Nixon administration. The agency kept dossiers on thousands of American citizens — also motivated in part by suspicion of links between the antiwar movement and other governments.

There were fleeting references in the Media documents, hardly noticed when they first surfaced, to COINTELPRO–New Left. That was the tip, however, which led to discovery of an important evolution in FBI investigative procedures, especially in the internal security area. According to documents eventually released as a result of a lawsuit filed by NBC reporter Carl Stern under the Freedom of Information Act and a report later compiled by the Justice Department, the Bureau, in a series of "counterintelligence programs" (i.e., COINTELPRO) launched over a fifteen-year period — first against Old Left groups like the CPUSA and the Socialist Workers party and later extended to the New Left, "white hate groups," and "black extremists" — moved into officially sanctioned and organized tactics of subterfuge and disruption against groups and individuals that the FBI sought to "neutralize." On the simplest level, the Bureau and other law enforcement agencies (and for that matter, journalists) have long used such techniques to some extent. It is common practice, for example, for agents to make "pretext phone calls" to find out if someone (say, a fugitive whose arrest is imminent) is home, or to approach potential sources of information under false pretenses — claiming to be making a "credit check" when the real goal might be to determine the organizations a person belongs to. But COINTELPRO went much further.

Impressed with the results obtained in the early days of the FBI's program against the CPUSA, Hoover wrote to selected offices on October 12, 1961, to tell of the start of a new "disruption program" against the Socialist Workers party, which, he said, has, over the past several years, been openly espousing its line on a local and national basis through running candidates for public office and strongly directing and/or supporting such causes as Castro's Cuba and integration problems arising in the South. The SWP has also been in frequent contact with international Trotskyite groups stopping short of open and direct contact with these groups. . . . It is felt that a disruption program along similar lines [to COINTELPRO-CPUSA] could be initiated against the SWP on a very selective basis. One of the purposes of this program would be to alert the public to the fact that the SWP is not just another socialist group but follows the revolutionary principles of Marx, Lenin and Engels as interpreted by Leon Trotsky.

It is pointed out, however, that this program is not intended to be a "crash" program. Only carefully thought-out operations with the widest possible effect and benefit to the nation should be submitted. It may be desirable to expand the program after the effects have been evaluated.

Some of the COINTELPRO actions against the SWP — revealed in Bureau documents that were released in 1975 in connection with a lawsuit filed in federal court by the Political Rights Defense Fund — were very inventive indeed. In one instance, the Bureau learned that Walter Elliott, scoutmaster of a Boy Scout troop in Orange, New Jersey, whose wife was a member of the party, had said that he considered the Scouts a better way of influencing young minds than joining the SWP. The Newark Field Office, although its files contained "no public source information of a subversive nature concerning Elliott," reacted by persuading the national headquarters of the Boy Scouts not to renew his troop's charter. In 1965 the Bureau wrote to the president of the Denver School Board, warning that a candidate for the board was a member of the SWP; it signed the letter "a concerned mother."

Years later, after additional — and, from the Bureau's point of view, successful — experience with a similar program directed against the Ku Klux Klan, the Director was much bolder in launching the assault on the New Left and its "key activists" in May 1968. All field offices were now included and urged to assign "an experienced and imaginative special agent" to administer the program. Most of the language in the memorandum prepared in the Intelligence Division to launch COINTELPRO–New Left was identical to that in earlier ones, with only the names of the targets changed. There was, however, some philosophy appended, ostensibly to justify the program and to get it off to a properly energetic start:

The Bureau has been very closely following the activities of the New Left and the Key Activists and is highly concerned that the anarchistic activities of a few can paralyze institutions of learning, induction centers, cripple traffic, and tie the arms of law enforcement officials all to the detriment of our society. The organizations and activists who spout revolution and unlawfully challenge society to obtain their demands must not only be contained, but must be neutralized. Law and order is mandatory for any civilized society to survive. Therefore, you must approach this new endeavor with a forward look, enthusiasm, and interest in order to accomplish our responsibilities. The importance of this new endeavor cannot and will not be overlooked.

Two years later, in 1970, writing to the San Francisco Field Office with ideas for COUNTERINTELLIGENCE AND SPECIAL OPERATIONS against the Black Panthers, FBI headquarters became much more specific:

A wide variety of alleged authentic police or FBI material could be carefully selected or prepared for furnishing to the Panthers. Reports, blind memoranda, LHMs,* and other alleged police or FBI documents could be prepared pinpointing Panthers as police or FBI informants; ridiculing or discrediting Panther leaders through their ineptness or personal escapades; espousing personal philosophies and promoting factionalism among BPP members; indicating electronic coverage where none exists; outlining fictitious plans for police raids or other counteractions; revealing misuse or misappropriation of Panther funds, pointing out instances of political disorientation; etc. The nature of the disruptive material and disinformation "leaked" would only be limited by the collection ability of your sources and the need to insure the protection of their security.

Effective implementation of this proposal could not help but disrupt and confuse Panther activities. Even if they were to suspect FBI or police involvement, they would be unable to ignore factual material brought to their attention through this channel. The operation would afford us a continuing means to furnish the Panther leadership true information which is to our interest that they know and disinformation which, in their interest, they cannot ignore.

The Bureau and the Justice Department, citing national security, have declined to discuss the exact nature of the COINTELPRO activities against "hostile foreign intelligence services, foreign organizations and individuals connected with them." But in a post-Watergate effort to recover its reputation for probity, the Justice Department released a report in November 1974, which, not unlike Nikita Khrushchev's

---

* "Letterhead Memoranda," the summary descriptions of cases, generally purged of the most sensitive material, which are used, among other purposes, for dissemination of information about pending cases outside the Bureau.

famous recanting, acknowledged and apologized for past excesses. The programs directed against domestic groups, according to the report, elicited 3,247 specific "proposals" for action from the field. Of them, 2,370, or about 73 percent, were "approved and implemented." They covered a vast range of actions, some of which, if taken by a private citizen, would have been considered illegal.

The most popular technique was to send anonymous or false materials to organizations or their members in the hope of stirring up dissension over policies and plans and then disrupting those plans. Agents sought out "friendly media representatives" and leaked derogatory public record information — arrests, controversial background — to stimulate bad publicity about the "target." Sometimes the same was done with secret information from the Bureau's files "for the purpose of exposing the nature, aims and membership of the various groups." The Bureau also called any civil or criminal violation by groups or their members, however large or small, to the attention of other local, state, or federal authorities, on the theory that if they could be immobilized with legal problems they would be less active. In some instances, especially with the Old Left, informants were sent into organizations with specific instructions to stir up dissension and exploit internal differences to render the group less effective and coherent. The Bureau also surreptitiously notified "credit bureaus, creditors, employers and prospective employers" about individuals' "illegal, immoral, radical and Communist Party activities in order to affect adversely their credit standing or employment status." Similarly, there were attempts to damage people's "economic interests," especially if they were considered "black extremists" by the FBI, by notifying those with whom they had "economic dealings" about the organizations they belonged to.

On occasion, said the 1974 Justice Department report, the Bureau directly contacted members of organizations "for the purpose of letting [them] know that the FBI was aware of their activity" or in the hope of convincing them to become informants.* Agents also recruited civic and religious leaders "in order to gain their support and to persuade them to exert pressure on state and local governments, employers and landlords to the detriment of the various groups," another technique used especially in relation to blacks under investigation. The Bureau established "sham organizations," which made mailings to groups distrusted by the Bureau for the purpose of disrupting them. Anonymous

---

* This technique was neither unusual nor illegal, and was surely used on many occasions without special permission from headquarters. However, it was listed as one of the special tactics included under the rubric of COINTELPRO.

letters were also sometimes sent to family or friends "advising them of immoral or radical activities on the part of various individuals."

Among the techniques the Justice Department itself conceded were "most troubling" were those related to political and judicial processes — trying to publicize the group affiliations of a candidate for public office, covertly furnishing material to grand juries or court officials, and, for example, "making an anonymous telephone call to a defense attorney, after a federal prosecution had resulted in a mistrial, advising him (apparently falsely) that one of the defendants and another well known group individual were FBI informants." The Bureau also occasionally used the same short-wave frequency as demonstrators on the citizens'-band radio and provided "disinformation" that confused their plans; it tipped parents off or frightened them about the organizations their children belonged to; and it forged business cards and signature stamps. Agents also surreptitiously obtained the tax returns of group members and investigated "the love life of a group leader for dissemination to the press" (an obvious reference to investigations of the late Reverend Martin Luther King, Jr.). The Justice Department report stopped short of admitting the ultimate excess: the Bureau, when it wanted to, could make a target individual's life very difficult — indeed, ruin it. And this without formal charge, prosecution, or trial.

Hoover suspended all COINTELPRO activities in 1971, apparently out of a concern to prevent just the sort of negative publicity and controversy that the FBI later received when details of the program became widely known. But the Bureau insisted that the severe measures had been justified by the "tenor of the times," especially during the late 1960s, when the level of urban riots, attacks on police, and popular protest rose to unprecedented heights. The FBI was frankly frightened of revolution. It was relatively inexperienced at investigating and handling such a situation; this was a struggle to uphold the structure and values of the nation. Even after Hoover ordered the programs suspended in 1971, many of the same activities continued on an informal basis.

With the decline of the New Left in the mid-1970s and the government on the defensive as a result of the Watergate scandals and the disclosures of widespread spying on citizens by military and civilian agencies, the Bureau's internal security role seemed, on the surface, to become less urgent. President Nixon's abolition of the "attorney general's list" of subversive organizations in effect removed one of the major justifications for the domestic intelligence activity, and Director

Clarence M. Kelley continued a policy, instituted after Hoover's death by Acting Director L. Patrick Gray III, of requiring that a formal "legal predicate" be stated in the file of every case opened in the "security" area. That rule was treated as a perfunctory nuisance by many agents, but it may also have prevented some of them from opening frivolous investigations. Growing sensitivity to violations of civil liberties also made it more difficult for the FBI to rely on such traditional "investigative aids" as phone and bank records, as the holders of those records began to demand subpoenas before producing them.

Nonetheless, there were powerful pressures from within the FBI and outside for the agency to maintain its vigilance in the internal security area as a "preventive" measure. In some cases, such as the Wounded Knee incidents involving the American Indian Movement, it was argued persuasively that both criminal and security jurisdiction and techniques of investigation were necessary and appropriate. Militant Indians, in fact, became a whole new category of concern, and special liaison was established with the Bureau of Indian Affairs. There is still a strong tendency in the Bureau to assume that radical or antiestablishment groups are taking their cues from foreign agents, if only because, as one experienced agent put it, "we have to assume that others behave like us. If the CIA has been funding all those groups in foreign countries, the KGB must be doing the same." And an old contention, frequently stated in the 1940s when the Bureau was first expanding in the security field, began to be raised again: that if the FBI did not perform some of these investigations in its own sophisticated and knowledgeable manner, state and local police might take matters in their own hands and do a sloppier and potentially more abusive job at it. Yet in some respects the Bureau seemed as naïve as ever, defining and classifying ideas, organizations, and publications on the basis of old stereotypes; even in 1974, a hefty collection of back issues of a liberal weekly magazine, *The Nation,* sat on the shelf alongside communist-oriented and -produced publications in the New York Field Office's library of "subversive" literature.

Although the custom is gradually changing, the Bureau remains reluctant to assign first-office agents, fresh out of training, to "security" work, even when they have a special interest or pertinent background in it. In the larger field offices, there is still something of a mystique surrounding some of the security squads, and other agents assigned mostly to routine criminal cases will often go out of their way to disclaim any knowledge of what their colleagues do, sometimes out of reverence for the confidential missions and sometimes sounding as if they want to dissociate themselves from that side of the Bureau's work.

Even with some of the old-style dullards removed from those squads, many Bureau officials concede that a powerful bureaucratic impulse still operates to create a "problem" that matches the manpower level and fulfills prophecies of the threat to domestic law and order. The need and desire to stay in business once in business seems to be one of the most important factors motivating the security side of the FBI. At the same time, the grouping of internal security matters with counter-intelligence cases makes evaluation of shifting requirements much more difficult. The two combined, regardless of changing times and conditions, account for a fairly constant 25 percent of the Bureau's time.*

* Another 4 percent of the Bureau's time is occupied by the police training of the National Academy, "foreign police cooperation," and other miscellaneous activities.

Three Different Worlds

VIII

FBI Headquarters:
The "Seat of Government"

They call up and give us orders all the time. . . . Of course, they don't have the foggiest idea of what it's like to go out and do something, because none of them have done anything for years. . . . We've been living in sin with headquarters for too long now. It's time to do something about it.
— *The special-agent-in-charge of a major FBI field office, in an interview*

EVEN RANKING FBI OFFICIALS DO NOT LIKE to venture out onto the floor of the Identification Division around 3:30 in the afternoon. That's when the bell rings and the shifts change, and anyone not firmly anchored in place or tucked away in a corner could risk being swept under by a virtual human tidal wave. It is an awesome sight as one group arrives to take over from the other in working with the Bureau's most impressive resource, its fingerprint files. It is a bewildering, Kafkaesque scene when they dive anonymously into their work, their physical movement reduced to a minimum by efficiency experts, their eyes trained to respond instinctively to the pink or yellow priority slip attached to a fingerprint card, their ears cocked for the loudspeaker announcements that will tell them when the morning and afternoon breaks (ten minutes each) begin and end.

Three thousand three hundred and sixty-nine people work at "Ident," more than lived in all of Partlow, Virginia, hometown of Fletcher D. Thompson, the assistant FBI director in charge of the division. As Thompson once did, in September 1941, many of them have ventured to the capital from small towns and rural areas to sample the exciting city life and to help the FBI fight crime and subversion. They work with a staggering cascade of paper — 22,000 new fingerprint cards a day from about 8,000 active "contributors," about half of them involving criminal cases and half "civil" inquiries; 8,500 "disposition reports" a day, intended to update previously submitted records; 1,600 sets of fingerprints every month that were taken from deceased persons whose identities must, for one reason or another, be confirmed.

Off in a few alcoves highly skilled technicians perform the kind of tests that gave the FBI a reputation for near-magical feats. In the Latent Fingerprint Section, for example, where three thousand cases are handled every month, experts comb over evidence from a St. Louis case involving interstate transportation of stolen property, and they wash thousands of dollars recovered from a Norfolk, Virginia, bank robbery to see if any of it has the same fingerprints as those already found in the getaway car and inside the bank. Others are skilled in use of the "single fingerprint file," which holds the key to the identity of nine thousand individuals especially well known to the Bureau; one print from a crime scene, even a toeprint, could be enough to pin down the responsibility. But most of the employees are involved in far more humdrum pursuits — checking names in vast, motorized circular files; classifying newly received fingerprints according to their loops, arches, and whorls (there are 1,024 different possible classifications); or bending over a magnifying glass to compare new prints with those already in the file. One thousand three hundred "fingerprint technicians" work in one area, searching through Ident's "master criminal file," which extends farther than the human eye can see and contains the fingerprints of some twenty-one million people. The technicians have generally had twelve weeks of special training before being dropped into the midst of the endless row upon row of filing cabinets.

Here is also, the FBI likes to boast, "the largest typing pool in the world." Seven hundred women, an unusually high proportion of them young girls fresh from high school commercial courses in West Virginia, sit at identical desks in a vast hall. There they type rote answers to requests from across the country for fingerprint checks (advising, for example, whether or not the set of prints submitted had appeared previously in the file in connection with a criminal case), add new entries to people's "rap sheets" — criminal records — and disseminate copies of them to the latest fingerprint contributors, and answer other correspondence. The whole operation is repeated, on a far smaller scale, in the "civil" section of the Ident files, where the fingerprints of about forty million people are kept.

Altogether Ident has nearly 169 million fingerprint cards, including many duplicates and an estimated six million that carry the prints of people who are known to be dead. According to the Bureau, which cannot resist toying with such numbers, if all the cards were stacked on top of each other, they would reach a height one hundred and eight times that of the Empire State Building.

The official Ident deadline for processing a routine fingerprint check through the system is three days. But the work requires great precision — on the average, only 3 to 5 percent of the cards submitted in noncriminal matters (for example, in connection with job applications requiring such a check) will match with cards already in the criminal file, although 65 percent of those submitted in criminal cases will match — and if any part of the human machinery is malfunctioning, the speed drops. Just a three-day weekend for a federal holiday or a slight dip in personnel can throw the average processing time off to five days instead of three. Ident is, Thompson confesses, "almost like a factory, an assembly line"; and the major problem is "how to keep the people motivated." Turnover is high among the employees, who may find that working for the FBI is not so glamorous after all, and Ident depends on steady field office recruiting to keep its ranks full. But before long, speed and staffing will be eliminated as problems. The fingerprint files are being computerized and a new "scanner" (whose coinventor now works for the FBI) introduced that will be able to read a print card in six seconds and reduce the average turnaround time on a request from three days to six hours. Already, 1,275,000 arrest records have been stored in a computer (some 3,000 more are added each day), and some of the negative answers (advising that newly submitted prints do not match others in the files) are being automatically handled by computer.* Eventually, two thousand fewer people will be necessary to do the job.

People are already being eliminated by the Files and Communications Division, which has custody of the Bureau's six and a half million investigative files, some consisting of many volumes each, and of its general index with an estimated fifty-eight million cards. The division processes at least ten thousand official documents daily, and, according to authoritative calculations, someone goes to one of its file drawers to remove or consult a record approximately sixty thousand times a day. But messengers are being phased out in favor of an extensive network of pneumatic tubes and a "telelift" system that can automatically

* The Bureau planned to begin converting the actual fingerprints themselves into a computer-readable form in early 1976; the conversion was expected to take several years to complete.

deliver mail and files according to push-button instructions. With an eerie overhead whir, little plastic cars travel along rails in a system of seventy-two stations, installed at a cost of one and a half million dollars, in the new J. Edgar Hoover FBI Building. It is a dramatic change from the old system, which required transport of the files in locked boxes between storage space in the Ident building in Southwest Washington and the main FBI offices in the Justice Department building along Pennsylvania Avenue.

FBI files, the condensation of the agency's vast knowledge and research, are so voluminous that they have been awarded two and a half entire floors in the new building. Every piece of paper in any file — a "serial" — is numbered, and identifiable and retrievable by that number. For every serial in the file at headquarters, there is also an index card with an abstract of its contents, so that questions can be answered quickly without pulling an entire file. In recent years the volume of the files became so enormous that division officials had to ask field offices to submit only what was necessary to have at headquarters, and they went repeatedly to the National Archives to request permission for destruction of some categories of old files. "Intelligence agencies tend to be string-savers," says one ranking official of the division, acknowledging that the Bureau could probably get along perfectly well without much of the information it has stored for years.

So valuable is the resource, however, that the FBI has become concerned about its misuse by those inside, as well as outside, the organization; and anyone seen wandering among the repetitious corridors of filing cabinets without specific authorization is immediately stopped and questioned. As far as the professional old-time record-keepers are concerned, the traditional restriction that Bureau files must remain secret for at least seventy-five years should remain permanently in effect. "People have furnished us with material and information in the past on the basis of the assumption that it will be kept in confidence," says Assistant Director John W. Marshall, chief of the division; "so it must be." His "number one man," Earl McCoy, chimes in that "if the public gets the impression that anything they tell the FBI may become public in fifteen or twenty years, they'll stop talking." As for a new effort to release material to scholars under the terms of the Freedom of Information Act, they have a distinct view: "It's a young program. . . . We would like to see it killed in infancy."

Marshall, an agent since 1949, served two years in the field and then came back to Washington for the rest of his Bureau career. Once a clerk in this division before finishing college, he returned to it in 1964 and "worked my way up to the top through retirements." He is proud of the records over which he has custody and points with amusement to some of their eccentricities, like the fact that there are "several drawers of John Smiths." Marshall is appropriately discreet, however, about the nature of the "special" indices that contain the names of everyone whose voice was ever picked up in an electronic surveillance by the Bureau or who is of "security" interest to the agency.

The first of the files to be computerized were the Bureau's personnel records; with a punch of the appropriate buttons, the computer will within seconds search and display on a cathode-ray-tube monitor the biographical details and a short career summary of anyone who has ever worked for the FBI. It is conceivable that one day all of the Bureau's vast files will be stored in the computer and available for instantaneous consultation on a monitor in every field office. Work is already underway on automating the master index, so that all the regional offices will be able to search a name from a distance, eliminating unnecessary written and telephone communications between Washington and the field.

The Files and Communications Division also supervises and maintains the FBI's secure teletype system, in which all confidential Bureau messages and other traffic is automatically encrypted before it moves over the line between cities. Thus FBI communications are scrambled and theoretically immune from "hostile interception." "We have to assume that attempts would be made" to intercept the traffic, says Marshall; "it's safe to say that all countries are interested in what other countries are doing." To keep all of its wheels turning, the division employs thirteen hundred people.

Only about four hundred and fifty people (fewer than two hundred of them agents) work in the FBI Laboratory, but it too performs specialized services unique to FBI headquarters. Housed for years in musty quarters on the top floor of the Justice Department building, the lab made pioneering tests on bullets, blood, paints, and other substances that held the key to cracking difficult and dramatic criminal cases. But its tasks expanded, as the Bureau grew, to include the examination of such items as secret inks and microdots in wartime and sophisticated analyses of fibers or mysterious particles that turn up in everything from sabotage investigations to routine criminal cases. Among other things, the Laboratory Division now translates foreign documents of "security" value to the FBI, studies voiceprints of people overheard on wiretaps, and compares the bank robbery notes passed to tellers to detect similarities of handwriting and technique. In recent years it has purchased intricate and delicate equipment such as a scanning electron microscope, which took nearly a year to set up and then was of uncertain relevance to the requirements of the lab and beyond the skills of many of its technicians.

Some 75 percent of the lab's work is in Bureau-related cases, including complicated civil suits to which the federal government is a party; but it also provides its services to state and local law enforcement agencies. The agents from the lab who testify in court are permitted to do so only after a rigorous training program, which includes "moot court" rehearsals to prepare them for the tactics of eloquent and experienced defense attorneys and graduate study of forensic science. Once they are experienced, the agents may spend most of their time touring the nation, providing precise and conclusive testimony for the prosecution that impresses juries and sends men and women off to jail. Some agents have appeared in hundreds of cases. "Many defense attorneys will often stipulate to vital information, when they learn that someone from the FBI Lab is about to testify," says Briggs J. White, assistant director for the laboratory; "that is because it has been established throughout the country that we give completely objective testimony and we send out very well qualified people." White, who holds a doctorate in chemistry from the University of Colorado, has been in the FBI Lab since 1940, when he joined as a "junior analytical chemist"; he became an agent a year and a half later, but never served in a field assignment.*

This is the guts of the FBI — the extraordinary fingerprint collection, the massive files, a laboratory that brings science to police and intelligence work, and a fast, secure communications network. Without the backup that they provide, without their much-publicized efficiency, any investigation would obviously be less meaningful and the FBI would be less able to help local authorities fight crime. The fingerprints and the files are among the chief sources of the FBI's influence in the police world and of its power in Washington. They are resources that no other agency could hope to match or imitate.

◆

To manage the Bureau's laboratory work, fingerprints, files, and communications requires thousands of clerical employees — although many of them will soon be eliminated by automation — but relatively few trained and experienced FBI agents. Perhaps a hundred agents

---

* Thompson, Marshall, and White all retired from the FBI between the time they were interviewed and the completion of this book. Director Clarence M. Kelley replaced Marshall and White, who had spent virtually their entire Bureau careers at headquarters in Washington, with men who had greater experience in the field.

are needed to supervise, coordinate, and police these operations; but much of the detail work cannot be done by them, anyway, because as investigators and administrators they do not have the requisite technological know-how. At last count, however, there were seven hundred and twenty-three special agents stationed at FBI headquarters in Washington, almost one for every ten agents in the field. Within the FBI itself, "The Bureau" means headquarters — a powerful force to be reckoned with by those assigned to the field, by other government officials in Washington and the states, and by the public. Apart from those who supervise the FBI's technical functions, they are the policymakers, the managers, the manipulators, and the promoters. They include people whose sole function is to evaluate their colleagues' performance and commend or punish them for it. They are the least typical, but sometimes the most influential, people in the FBI. They earn the most money for the least work, and they make up a distinct subculture within the organization.

It was not always thus. J. Edgar Hoover prided himself in the early years on the small staff he kept at the "seat of government."* The vast majority of agents were assigned to the field, with only a few dozen held behind in Washington to coordinate and organize what the others did. The Director argued persuasively at the time that it was foolish to take men who had been trained as investigators and put them behind desks where they would be doing little more than pushing papers. Hoover himself had never served in the field or actually investigated a case, but he seemed to feel that the field was where the FBI should concentrate its efforts and build its reputation. But as the organization began to grow and take on new responsibilities, its internal bureaucracy seemed to expand in geometric proportion. The basic structure of the Bureau has not changed since Hoover took it over in 1924. Today it consists of thirteen separate divisions,† each headed by an assistant director who can claim some authority over all fifty-nine field offices. Each assistant director has under him at least one inspector, an experienced older agent who serves as his "number one man" and may substitute for him at any meetings or conferences. In most divisions there is additionally a "number two man," also with

---

* The archaic term "seat of government" is still used today among older FBI agents and other employees. A symbol of the FBI's centralized control, it was the official name for the Washington operations of the Bureau until Acting Director L. Patrick Gray III formally introduced the usage "FBI Headquarters" in 1972.

† The thirteen are: Identification, Laboratory, General Investigative, Special Investigative, Files and Communications, Administrative, External Affairs, Office of Legal Counsel, Office of Planning and Evaluation, Computer Systems, Inspection, Training, and Intelligence.

the rank of inspector, who serves as backup for the number one man. Under them are section chiefs, who handle specifically defined areas of responsibility; and under the section chiefs are unit chiefs, who are in charge of still more carefully defined areas. Working for the unit chiefs are agents transferred to headquarters from the field offices, called "supervisors."

The assistant directors for the Identification, Training, Administrative, Files and Communications, Laboratory, External Affairs, and Computer Systems divisions report to an assistant-to-the-director/ deputy associate director for administration. The assistant directors for the Intelligence, General Investigative, and Special Investigative divisions, as well as for the Office of Legal Counsel, report to an assistant-to-the-director/deputy associate director for investigation. The assistants-to-the-director/deputy associate directors, in turn, report to the Bureau's associate director, as do the assistant directors for the Inspection Division and the Office of Planning and Evaluation. It is generally through the associate director, unless he is absent, that anything reaches the director (see organization chart, on endpapers).

These officials, who make up the Bureau's "executive conference" and as a group are advisers to the director on major policy matters, tend to be at least twenty-year veterans of Bureau service and struggles. A few are clearly men of talent and good judgment who would probably have succeeded in other agencies or the private sector, but others fit a particular Bureau stereotype: they climbed through the ranks largely on the basis of sycophancy and plodding work that attracted no unusual degree of attention. While others dropped out of the running as a result of taking chances, they moved ahead slowly but deliberately, content to wait their turn. Once at the top, especially under Hoover, they became as petty and backbiting as the courtiers to any throne. Even today, the assistant directors complain and gossip about each other unrelentingly and compete for the praise and favor of the director. But to the outside world they continue to present a united and loyal front on behalf of the Bureau.

Because jobs at headquarters are generally classified in higher pay grades than those in the field, it has traditionally been regarded as a promotion to be transferred there from one of the field offices. Although they may supervise nothing but pieces of paper, the agents sent to fill the lower-level positions at headquarters all hold the rank of "Bureau supervisor." Theirs can be a dismal existence.

The average Bureau supervisor, who is generally in his thirties or early forties, comes in to work early, perhaps as early as 7 A.M., so that he can put in his compulsory "voluntary overtime" of one hour and forty-nine minutes* and still get home for dinner at a decent hour. If he works in one of the investigative divisions, he is probably responsible for a group of violations ("interstate transportation of stolen motor vehicles" and "crime on Indian and government reservations," for example) or other classifications (such as, in the Intelligence Division, "foreign social conditions," "bombing matters," or "communist groups and individuals") in a cluster of field offices, grouped together either on the basis of geographical proximity or of how busy they are with these violations or classifications. He reviews all the mail and other communications that have come in from the field overnight, from urgent teletypes and less important "nitels" (held and sent during night hours at a lower cable cost) to "airtels" (typed promptly in the field offices, but not urgent or sensitive and therefore sent by regular air mail) and ordinary letters. Any "letterhead memoranda" (LHMs) are disseminated to the appropriate Bureau officials and other concerned agencies. The supervisor checks the "leads" on these cases sent out by the "office of origin" to other offices, and he approves or amends them. If the incoming material seems very important — if it involves a murder, a large amount of money, or otherwise seems likely to stir outside interest and heavy publicity — the supervisor will synopsize it in a "note" on a five-by-eight-inch piece of paper and send it up through the chain of command, with the "note" attached, for informational purposes. Most material is sent straight to the files, with a copy kept behind and a "tickler" attached, so that the supervisor can check in thirty or sixty days whether the field agents are meeting their deadlines. (On most cases, agents are expected to come back with some status report every forty-five days or close the case.) After the clerks come in at 9 A.M. and pull the old "ticklers" from the file, some time is consumed with reviewing them and sending out any necessary messages to the field.

When an urgent case breaks during the work day, particularly a kidnapping, airplane hijacking, or other dramatic incident, the Bureau supervisor concerned will invariably be called directly by the field office and kept informed. But his involvement in the case is usually only vicarious. "We are often more of a nuisance than a help," acknowledged one young supervisor after his first few months at headquarters; "we just ask a lot of questions, and since we are not on the scene, we don't have much to offer." The questions are usually less for the purpose of genuine supervision than to keep the supervisor

* The voluntary overtime is necessary for an agent to qualify to receive the Bureau's "maximum fringe benefits" — $3,536, which is added to his basic annual salary.

covered, so that when his superiors express an interest in the case he will have the essential facts at his command. "At the Bureau, nobody likes to be caught flatfooted," says a supervisor frequently contacted regarding breaking cases in busy field offices; "nobody likes to be caught not knowing. If the attorney general should call the director and ask him a question about the case, he should be able to have the answer immediately." In Hoover's prime, "immediately" meant exactly that, and any supervisor who could not answer a question from the Director on the spot might have hell to pay. More recently, it has been considered acceptable if a supervisor is able to come up with the answer for his superiors in, say, fifteen minutes; but, says the supervisor, "they still get pretty uptight about these things."

From time to time, supervisors find it necessary to send communications out to the field, requesting a clarification concerning a specific case or suggesting a particular course of action. Anyone who has had a measure of independent responsibility in the field before his transfer to headquarters is usually shocked to find that the most trivial matter now under his jurisdiction may require more than a dozen sets of initials and approval from his superiors before it can go out. Even then, so accustomed are some field officials to the need for reading between the lines in communications from headquarters that they may call the Bureau supervisor and ask him, "Now what do you *really* mean by this?" If the supervisor drafts a simple letter to a member of Congress in connection with a case, it may need initials from as many as seventeen people above him, and the supervisor is likely to have phone calls from some of his bosses questioning the use of a particular "and" or "the" in the letter.

Unless they are assigned to an especially busy (and, in a few instances, understaffed) unit, such as those dealing with major kidnapping and extortion cases or with the background investigation of a vice-presidential nominee under the Twenty-fifth Amendment, the supervisors may find that there is simply not enough work to fill their time. In the Intelligence Division particularly, where a personnel buildup occurred during the 1960s because of the Bureau's panic over domestic dissent and black extremism but where the manpower stayed at unnecessarily high levels after the situation calmed, it is said that some supervisors are busy barely a third of the day and are often looking for things to do. Some idle supervisors, accustomed to a frantic pace out in the field, spend their extra time rewriting rules and regulations or dreaming up entries for the Bureau's "Suggestion Program," which, if adopted, could win them money awards. Others draft speeches or policy statements for their assistant directors, or seize every available opportunity to join an in-service training program at the FBI Academy at Quantico.

There is general agreement among many younger agents at Bureau headquarters, and some older ones as well, that the resources there are poorly apportioned and allocated. Officially, the FBI's inspection system monitors such problems and makes the necessary periodic manpower adjustments; but experience has shown that cronyism may be a more important element in those decisions than any rational measurement of workload and performance. Assistant directors tend to regard cuts in their divisional staff as diminishing their position and status, and they can usually prevent them through bureaucratic end runs. Section and unit chiefs, too, like to enhance their own power and authority by advocating the creation of new or larger units within the divisions; if they can end up having more people under their jurisdiction, they may be able to push themselves into a higher pay grade. The impulses and influences against reorganizing the headquarters staff or eliminating duplication, therefore, are very strong.

For agents who did well in the field and looked forward to a meaningful role at headquarters, spirit and morale tend to sag after they get to Washington. They find it demeaning to carry an important title but be trusted with little responsibility. Another category of agents simply feels lost at headquarters; although they were very comfortable and efficient as investigators, they are washouts as administrators. Others, however, enjoy the illusion of supervisory roles and see the headquarters jobs as sinecures; and if they wait patiently and attach themselves to the proper sponsors, they do actually acquire greater authority. Through a combination of inertia and conniving, many of the agents assigned to headquarters over the years managed to avoid ever being sent back into the field again. And although the Bureau's official career development policy called for alternating terms of service at headquarters and in the field en route to the upper ranks, some made the climb without moving far. Nicholas P. Callahan, for example, selected by Clarence Kelley as his associate director, last served in the field in 1945. Within a year and a half of his return to headquarters at that time, he was entrenched in the Administrative Division as its number one man. He then succeeded the powerful John P. Mohr as assistant director in charge of that division in 1959 when Mohr became assistant-to-the-director. William V. Cleveland, assistant director for the Special Investigative Division, came back to Washington from duty in Indianapolis in 1951 and never went out again; twenty years later he took over the division where he had spent most of his time. W. Raymond Wannall, chief of the Intelligence Division, last returned from a field assignment in 1947, and Callahan's successor in the Administrative Division when he became associate director, Eugene W. Walsh, came into that division from the New York Field Office in 1956. Working under these and other men are several layers of officials who last saw field service ten or more years ago. Comfortably settled in the Washington area, content to build a small empire within the larger structure of the FBI, they have tended to avoid controversy and transfer. They see the world through a particular set of headquarters glasses, and their perspective is rarely influenced by the occasional trips they make out into the country. It is difficult to convince them of the need for change.

There has thus grown up within the FBI a dichotomy of "the Bureau" versus "the field." This conflict was officially ignored for decades because under Hoover the FBI was, for better or worse, considered to be the FBI — one Bureau, indivisible. But the standoff played a major part in personal and bureaucratic relations and working conditions within the agency. Headquarters officials sometimes seem to give orders to the field merely for the sake of giving orders, and special-agents-in-charge, especially those with a good record and substantial self-confidence, learn to ignore the instructions. If necessary, to keep headquarters happy, they fudge their reports, tell outright lies, or refrain entirely from reporting unwelcome news. SACs complain that some of the assistant directors and men under them have been gone from the field for so many years that they no longer understand conditions "on the street"; in their comings and goings only to and from the inner sanctum of the FBI, it is argued, the headquarters people have missed whole areas of change and major developments in American society.

The antipathy between headquarters and field emerged as one of the key issues in a series of regional management symposia held by Clarence Kelley in late 1973 and early 1974. At one symposium the assistant director for the Computer Systems Division and one of the special-agents-in-charge from the New York Field Office lapsed into a bitter shouting match that nearly turned into a fistfight. Small-group sessions at the symposia, asked to list the most important problems currently facing the FBI, invariably pointed to the inability of the field and headquarters to understand each other. Later, a confidential survey of all agents conducted by the Office of Planning and Evaluation showed that a substantial majority of field agents considered the "investigative direction" of headquarters less than satisfactory, that all but a few field agents felt their offices seldom needed to look to Washington for "supervisory direction and guidance," and that a vast percentage agreed with the old slogan that "the field operates in spite of FBIHQ."

◆

Within the powerful contingent at FBI headquarters, two groups seem to have noticeably disproportionate authority and influence, men who were once clerks at Bureau headquarters and agents currently or formerly assigned to the Administrative Division.

"Once a clerk, always a clerk" is one of the favorite expressions of those who deride the influence of former clerks within the Bureau. FBI clerks, who have a higher status than messengers and stenographers but a lower one than agents, perform middle-level jobs essential to the ongoing operations of the Bureau. In the field, they manage radio communications with agents out in cars, handle the files, do semi-investigative work by telephone, and coordinate much of the paperwork required by headquarters. At headquarters, they handle some of that same paperwork, give tours, and run errands between divisions; they have a unique exposure to the machinations at high levels, and many, especially those assigned to the Director's office while Hoover was in charge, always played an important unofficial political role. Attentive to conversations they overheard and documents they carried, they often knew about the evolution of policy behind the scenes and tipped off their mentors to things they would want to know. To make their way in the heady world of the FBI, and especially to become an agent, which is what most of them had in mind in the first place, many clerks developed a certain obsequiousness and slyness — a deferential attitude toward anyone with an important title or position and an ability to please them with small details, but at the same time a capacity to look out for oneself. As one cynical veteran agent complained, "The headquarters clerks have always had the 'for reals.' They thought everything was for real. They believed the stuff they said on the tours and that was fed to the old man. They had an inability to see through the veneer to the reality of things." But if they did understand those things, they kept the knowledge to themselves. They were good at finding sponsors who would look out for them.

When a clerk completed the requisite education and applied for a job as an agent, he seemed to have an easier time getting into a class than most other applicants; and once there, because he knew the Bureau, the training seemed easier. Somehow, former clerks often got choice assignments and moved along quickly. Before very long, many of them were back at headquarters as supervisors, and they moved further up the career ladder quickly. Naturally, they accumulated eligibility for retirement more quickly than most agents because their time as a clerk also counted in the calculations. At times these agents seemed unduly preoccupied with petty details and with pleasing people who did not really matter — the sort of attitude that one might expect of . . . well, of a clerk anxious to succeed. But succeed they generally did. Having been a clerk first is nothing that an FBI agent is ashamed of; on the contrary, it is a badge of honor and a ticket to the inside track. At least six of the sixteen members of the FBI executive conference in late 1974 had originally served the Bureau in clerical positions.

It is the Administrative Division, where many former clerks are assigned, that has long held the most awesome power within the Bureau. For many years it had uninhibited control over the FBI budget process, the exclusive channel for the agency's minimal attention to the matter of setting priorities. If a special-agent-in-charge wanted more agents, more cars, or even better carpeting in his field office, he had to be on good terms with the division. Since the federal government's Bureau of the Budget (later the Office of Management and Budget) rarely exercised meaningful supervision over the FBI's financial desires and there was no other external audit of the Bureau's finances, the money managers in the Administrative Division had enviable leeway. The FBI's requests for budget increases were usually justified in terms of a need for new agents or clerical personnel, but the money was often spent in other ways — essentially as Hoover and his top aides desired. Each year when the Director appeared before the House Appropriations Committee, he seemed to have fewer agents on the rolls than had been authorized the previous year; but if any congressman noticed, he never bothered to complain. In the words of one congressman who eventually became interested in asserting control over the Bureau, "There was never any cost analysis, or any examination of their allocation of resources and manpower." With so little executive or legislative supervision, Hoover used the resources where he wanted, and the Administrative Division was the executor of his whims, which often shifted with the temper of the times.

The Administrative Division has other responsibilities ranging from the minuscule to the profound. It prepares agent credentials,*

* Ever eager to save money, the Administrative Division dropped the director's name from the credentials that agents carry when Acting Director L. Patrick Gray III ran into trouble in 1973. It seemed clear then that with the Hoover era over, it might become expensive to keep them current.

sophisticated trial exhibits, and, each year, a booklet carrying the sanitized and edited version of the director's testimony on behalf of the Bureau appropriations, the closest thing to an annual policy statement. It has a typewriter repair shop and does the Bureau's printing. It negotiates contracts for the FBI and handles claims growing out of accidents involving Bureau vehicles. It is in charge of recruiting, including the attempt to bring more representatives of minority groups into the FBI, and, for that matter, all personnel matters. Whenever an agent wanted a transfer or had to take up some personal problem with the Bureau, his request was channeled through the Administrative Division. Until recently, when Kelley established a board to review such matters, the division also controlled the recommendations for and processing of all promotions within FBI ranks. When the director sought to fill a vacancy, the standard procedure was to give him three names to choose from — but all three were people acceptable to the Administrative Division for internal political reasons. Often, those recommended for important jobs came from within the division itself, and thus the Administrative elite placed its own people in key spots in other divisions.

One area that could potentially affect promotion decisions, also in the Administrative Division's bailiwick, is the annual "performance rating" of every agent. Theoretically, it gives a realistic picture of the competence and confidence with which agents handle their cases and other responsibilities. But as one agent in a southern field office put it, "We all know that almost everybody will come out being rated 'excellent.' It's like being in the Boy Scouts." A field supervisor who had been handing out performance ratings for some time admitted that this was generally true, because it takes far less work to give an Excellent rating than an Outstanding, Average, or Unsatisfactory. The Administrative Division did not seem to want those and made them difficult to submit to headquarters. "I rated a guy 'average' once," said the field supervisor, "and I wrote for three weeks until I satisfied them with all the justifications for it. The same thing is true if you want to give an 'outstanding.'"

With such meaningless performance ratings the order of the day, an agent's record is more likely to be based on the quotient of letters of censure and commendation he has in his personnel file. Both may come about on the basis of rather peculiar reasoning. Some agents complain that they have been unfairly censured for sins such as permitting a prisoner to have breakfast with his mother before going to jail, and are confused by some of the compliments. The headquarters attitude may sometimes be difficult to predict; as one special-agent-in-charge put it, "What brought an accolade yesterday may be a grave error today."

The administrative processes that produce letters of censure and commendation, as well as cash incentive awards, consume a great deal of time, energy, and paper. Some supervisors pride themselves on their capacity to wax eloquent for the occasion. One used particularly florid language to recommend two agents for recognition of their efforts in pursuing a "purveyor of smut and salacious activities" on obscenity charges:

In the year since 1968, [the subject] continued his pornographic operations, distributing his libidinous wares in great volume to the voyeur and to the depraved, at their expense, but to his own financial reward. However, as [the subject] became more bold and lascivious, [the agents] became more dauntless in their investigative pursuits to ferret out an Interstate Transportation of Obscene Matter violation. . . . the very nature of this violation is not for the faint-hearted and prudish but rather, it is for those individuals who possess an outstanding character and moral fortitude. . . . As a result of their flawless grand jury presentation [the subject] was indicted. . . . Because of the righteous adversity inflicted upon [him], his pornographic empire collapsed and his financial woes will plague him for years. . . . Thus after five years of continuous and imaginative investigations by [the agents], [the subject's] pornographic operations are removed from the community which he tended to subvert through the prurient interest of young and old alike. The moral fiber of the community has well been served through the efforts of [the agents].

The Bureau's transfer policy, managed by the Administrative Division, has long been a subject of controversy. As early as 1932, Hoover was challenged during the appropriations hearings about why "you do not always permit a man to remain very long at any place" and why the typical agent was "sent away from his home or place where he had established a home." "I am very glad that you brought that up," said the Director with characteristic aplomb as he launched into an explanation:

At one time there were a good many politically minded employees in the bureau. In some cities it was almost impossible to secure fair and impartial investigations if local politicians happened to be involved. That has all been changed now, for I am firmly of the opinion that the Bureau of Investigation should be entirely free from influence, political or otherwise. It is required to make investigations into conditions involving civil, criminal and administrative matters; and the public has a right to expect and demand that this important investigative branch of its Government should function in a judicial manner without regard to influence or favor.

I found it was undesirable to place a man in his home district upon his appointment, because there may be political, personal, or fraternal affiliations which might prove embarrassing to him in the performance of his official duties. We make it a practice to send a new man to some section of the country other than his home district. The statement made, however, that men are never allowed to be stationed at their homes is totally disproved by the facts. Seventy percent of the field personnel of the bureau are stationed at the offices of preference as expressed by them. I think that is an unusually high average in what must of necessity be a basically mobile force. After a man has been in the service a sufficient period of time to enable him to absorb a nonpolitical attitude we endeavor to assign him to his office of preference.

Hoover added that the most important consideration in deciding upon transfers was "the proper training and development of the bureau's personnel." He pointed out that it was thought valuable to have each new agent trained, and judged, by more than one special-agent-in-charge. Some transfers were also necessitated, the Director said, by the fact that "the capabilities of the personnel of any organization may and do improve or deteriorate." Improvement may lead to "greater responsibility and more important work" and deterioration to "an opportunity to rehabilitate himself under different conditions," he said. Hoover also stressed "the fluctuating character of crime conditions" and the Bureau's need for "a certain degree of secrecy" as further rationale for some transfers. He insisted that "no man has ever been transferred for a frivolous reason."

Hoover's reasoning was sound in many respects, and indeed, some of the FBI's early acceptance stemmed from the diverse geographical backgrounds of the agents. It did seem to be easier for a man from one part of the country to conduct an investigation in a distant city than in or near his own home. It was precisely because some people felt that assignments were getting too close to home in later years that the Bureau was sometimes criticized — for example, during the early days of the civil rights movement in the South, when some black leaders contended that too many agents with southern backgrounds were given responsibility for investigations in that section of the country. (The Director rejected the criticism, but at the same time was careful afterwards to assign more northern-born and -educated agents to the South.)

Many agents, however, thought the transfer policy was taken too far. They resented the implication that they could not be trusted wherever they served and complained about their rapid-fire shifts from one city to another, especially in the days when they had to bear most of the moving costs themselves. Traditionally, the first-office assignment was a very short one — almost never more than eighteen months — and the second-office a longer one; in both instances, they had to hope for the luck of the draw because they were unlikely to get their preferences. They knew that by joining the Bureau they had accepted the possibility of being sent almost anywhere; as Hoover put it in his 1932 testimony, "No appointee enters the service of the Bureau without being fully informed as to his inability to be assured of the maintenance of a fixed place of abode in any specific section of the country." An agent was always entitled to list his three "offices of preference," and an effort was presumably made to transfer him to one of the three at the earliest practical time. But the chances for getting there depended largely on the offices wanted; New York and Detroit became such unpopular assignments that the wait for an "OP transfer" to one of them might be very short, only a few months, whereas offices like San Diego and Phoenix had such long lists that an agent might never get there during his career. Salt Lake City was also in that category, because it was a small office greatly desired by the FBI's many Mormon agents. It was also widely known that some offices, like Butte and Oklahoma City, were reserved by headquarters as "disciplinary offices"; even though many agents listed them as offices of preference, it was difficult to be assigned there because many of the spots were saved for people thought to deserve punishment. Some agents' wives caught on early that letters of appropriate praise from them to Hoover could get an unwanted transfer reversed, but the Administrative Division usually intercepted those letters before they reached the Director.

Sometimes, despite Hoover's high-minded demurrers, transfers, even among special-agents-in-charge, seemed plainly frivolous and pointless. So many people were transferred simultaneously at the end of one year in the late 1950s that a legend evolved to explain the situation: the Director, according to the story, slammed his door so hard as he was leaving for his Christmas vacation in Florida that many of the pins fell out of the map on his wall. When Sam Noisette, his office retainer, picked them up, he put them back in the wrong spots. As a result, everyone had to be transferred to the new location of his pin.

Kelley, confronted with the widespread dissatisfaction with transfer policy when he took over the Bureau in 1973, promised to try to ease the agents' plight. Uncertain that it was still necessary for an agent to be broken in by several different special-agents-in-charge, he extended the length of the first-office assignment so that it could be as long as five years and permit an agent's family to settle into a community. The number of offices of preferences to be listed was reduced to one, with the promise that the Bureau, if it could not assign an agent there, would try to send him to another office within five hundred miles, or to his "zone of preference."

The Administrative Division also carried out Hoover's draconian disciplinary policy. Developed and implemented at headquarters with only the rarest input from the field, the policy was based on the premise that whenever something went wrong, somebody — or preferably several people — had to be found to take the blame. The notion of centralized direction and vertical responsibility was so severely interpreted that it was automatically assumed a supervisor bore some responsibility for any subordinate's misdeeds. Thus if a field agent did something sufficiently offensive to the officials at headquarters the entire hierarchy of his field office might be punished. Even in late 1974, for example, the special-agent-in-charge of a desirable field office, Sacramento, was demoted to one of the Bureau's smallest offices, El Paso, after it was discovered that an agent under his command had borrowed money from an informant and ended up in trouble with local loan sharks who were under investigation by the Bureau. The assumption seemed to be that the SAC should have had better control over his staff or should have exerted enough moral influence to prevent such an incident from happening.

Not even the Bureau's most favored and successful agents were immune from harsh and arbitrary disciplinary measures. Robert Kunkel is an example. Once a clerk in the Director's office and a longtime favorite of his executive secretary, Helen Gandy, Kunkel developed a particularly close relationship with the boss. When Hoover worried about the physical security of his plush Northwest Washington home from attack or break-in, it was Kunkel who was sent out to make discreet "security surveys" on the property and recommend precautions that could be taken. Kunkel readily acknowledges that he and the Director shared a "hobby" — an active interest in the stock market — and that they frequently talked about this. When Hoover, whose financial instincts were good, heard a rumor about favorable developments for a particular stock, he would often ask Kunkel to check it out for him. Kunkel's birthday came at about the same time as the anniversary of Hoover's appointment as Director, and they would often celebrate together with a cake. Kunkel, although sometimes intensely disliked by his colleagues and subordinates, prospered. But he made one big mistake with the Director: in December 1959, while assigned as a legal attaché in Japan, Kunkel was notified that he had been selected to come back to headquarters and take up a prestigious position as chief of staff in Hoover's immediate office. Assuming that an inspector who had recently been through Tokyo had reported back to headquarters authorities that Kunkel's newborn child was having medical problems and had to stay under a pediatrician's care in Tokyo for another month or more, Kunkel sent back an itinerary indicating that he would not be able to return to Washington to take up the new post until late January. Immediately a teletype came back, canceling the promotion and ordering Kunkel to report to the Dallas Field Office instead, as an ordinary street agent. Hoover was furious that anyone honored with such an important assignment should for any reason delay his return to start the job. Flustered and heartbroken, Kunkel determined to fly back to Washington at his own expense "to avail myself for questioning" about the family reasons for the intended moving delay. But when he arrived in Seattle, there was a telegram waiting, telling him not to bother, but rather to proceed at once to Dallas. Kunkel went to Washington anyway, but once there he was kept from seeing Hoover or anyone else involved with the decision. If he wanted to remain in the Bureau, he had no recourse but to take up the lowly position in Dallas, where his family joined him in February 1960. Kunkel did penance there for two years and nine months before he was brought back to headquarters as a Bureau supervisor again and started his climb up the career ladder a second time.

Roy K. Moore, one of the best-known special-agents-in-charge in Bureau history, had problems, too. Moore was the chief inspector of the Bureau in 1961, when Hoover sent him to Oklahoma City to look into a conflict between Special-Agent-in-Charge Wesley Grapp and dissident agent William W. Turner, who had alleged serious improprieties by Grapp. Staying only a few days, Moore checked out but half of the allegations against the SAC and returned to Washington with a report that totally exonerated Grapp and found that Turner had been insubordinate. Hoover liked the conclusion, but would have preferred better, more complete evidence to support it, especially since Turner seemed likely to carry the dispute to the Civil Service Commission and the federal courts. In what was intended as a disciplinary transfer, Moore, who at the time was regarded as a sure candidate for an assistant directorship, was instead sent to be special-agent-in-charge of the Little Rock Field Office. It did not help Moore any that he argued with the Director about the Turner case.

Both Kunkel and Moore, of course, snapped back and went on to have prosperous Bureau careers; they would both later praise the Director as if nothing had ever happened.* Sometimes Hoover recognized that his discipline had been too severe, and after a sufficient period of time had passed to let the fact that he was still boss sink in, he would "rehabilitate" the man he had punished. But the FBI's field offices are filled with agents who, having less clout, suffered longer and more ignobly for their supposed sins. There is James P. Hosty, Jr., for example, the man in the Dallas Field Office who was in charge of the security file on one Lee Harvey Oswald at the time of the assassination of President John F. Kennedy. Although Hoover, testifying before the Warren Commission, insisted there had been no reason for the FBI to alert the Secret Service about Oswald as "a dangerous character" at the time of Kennedy's trip to Dallas, he later suspended Hosty without pay for thirty days and transferred him on disciplinary grounds to Kansas City.† Several agents were purged from the Washington Field Office and banished to the provinces when they were caught drinking coffee during a period when Hoover had banned it as an addictive stimulant. One agent was sent to San Antonio against his will because he wrote an article for a magazine for racing-car buffs, under a pseudonym, without advance clearance from the Bureau. The only recourse for such less well known, less conspicuous agents is to lay low and continue their work as uncontroversially as possible until they reach retirement age or the controversy blows over. Some, however, do not have that option; they are fired outright. That is what happened to an agent in Cleveland recently, when a stenographer in the field office there committed suicide and left a long note behind that implicated him in a love affair with her.

A number of people well placed and connected in the Bureau seem to have a remarkable resilience that protects them from reprimand or serious punishment. Special-Agent-in-Charge Kenneth Whit-

---

* Moore said later that he was happier returning to the field anyway. When the Supreme Court eventually refused to consider Turner's appeal of the Bureau's handling of his case, Hoover gave Moore a $300 incentive award. Kunkel, for his part, held important later assignments, including a tour as special-agent-in-charge of the Washington, D.C., Field Office; he had another fall from grace, however, under Acting Director L. Patrick Gray III.
† Years later the name of Oswald would return to haunt the Bureau and to suggest improprieties, or at least negligence, on the FBI's part at the time of the Kennedy assassination. It was revealed, for example, that Hosty's name and phone number were in Oswald's pocket notebook, and there have been rumors that Oswald was receiving $200 a month as an FBI informant at the time of his arrest (a rumor denied by the Bureau). Director Clarence Kelley has acknowledged discovering only in 1975 that shortly before the assassination Oswald, angry that Hosty had interviewed his wife about his Cuban and Soviet contacts, delivered a threatening note to the Dallas Field Office, and that the field office — perhaps on orders from Washington — destroyed the note.

taker of the Miami Field Office, for example, was publicly implicated in two scandals — one involving his private inspection of money from billionaire Howard Hughes that was held by President Nixon's close friend Bebe Rebozo, and the other his son's receipt of a college scholarship intended for indigents from a union official under investigation by a federal grand jury — but emerged relatively unscathed. Finally, however, after a reporter for a Miami television station publicized a memorandum prepared by officials of other law enforcement organizations and complaining of Whittaker's acceptance of free club memberships and flights and his social familiarity with people on the fringes of organized crime, he was transferred to become the SAC in Oklahoma City.

◆

FBI headquarters took pride over the years in the proposition that one of the Bureau's great strengths was its tight centralized control at the "seat of government" over all operations and its minimization of discretion in the field. It liked to compare itself to the military. Under Hoover's guidance, treated as if it had an element of the divine in it, headquarters also developed a world view, a body of dogma that pervaded its decisions and actions. This included some peculiar myths:

Every agent is the same as any other agent, and therefore any member of the FBI is capable of performing any of the Bureau's responsibilities.

The Bureau refused for decades to recognize the need for or value of specialization within the agent force — with the exception of accountants, who were detailed to handle cases requiring their special skills. Despite any variety in educational or social background, all agents were assumed to be competent in all areas by virtue of having participated in the Bureau's brief training program and having accumulated experience in a field office or two. Thus, even if a man had spent years shadowing members of the American Communist party and other alleged subversives, he was presumed capable of walking into a bank just after it had been held up and coordinating the start of an investigation. Similarly, another agent whose specialty was stolen car cases was officially expected to be able to mingle into the audience at a left-wing rally and report back coherently on the significance of what was said. Because agents were required to keep their weight within the strict requirements of a Metropolitan Life Insurance Company table of acceptable limits, they were all assumed to be in top physical condition. With annual renewal of their firearms training, they were also considered to be a good shot in time of crisis.

In reality, of course, many agents had great breadth and versatility, but like any other human beings they tended to have strong points and weak ones. The fact of Hoover's saying they could do something with uniform skill and success did not necessarily make it so. An agent not only tended to enjoy one kind of work more than another, but his individual skills also made him more capable of handling some cases than others. Certain Bureau tasks simply required more sophistication than others. Some men, as they became older, would be terrified by the prospect of being thrust into a dangerous situation that they were no longer really competent to handle, and their younger colleagues hardly wanted their lives to depend on whether or not the old-timers performed according to the ideal. Others, fulfilling responsibilities that essentially confined them to their desks, could not see why it really mattered whether they weighed a few pounds more or less. In many of these areas field personnel thought that headquarters was being hypocritical because, as everyone knew, many people in Washington had not kept themselves in the kind of shape demanded of the field. Ultimately, most agents did develop specialties — and in some of the larger offices, fairly precise ones — because that was the only way to get the job done, in spite of official policy.

A corollary to the headquarters belief about every agent being the same was that *every field office is the same.* Many Bureau headquarters officials claim to this day that the FBI's efforts at standardization have been so thorough and successful that the work in every office, whether it be Denver, Mobile, Anchorage, or Philadelphia, is virtually identical.* It is true, to be sure, that the paperwork and administrative demands put on agents are the same all over (and some would contend that even this should not be so), but any agent or special-agent-in-charge who has worked in a large office and a small one, a northern and a southern one, or any other combination, knows that there is a great variety — that different skills, concepts, and techniques may be necessary in each assignment. And the most successful agents are probably those who came to realize this early on and managed to adapt to the changes necessary with each transfer. There is, of course, a definite hierarchy of field offices, on the basis of size, region, the

* Some headquarters officials say that it would only be necessary to visit one office in order to understand FBI field operations, because "if you've seen one office, you've seen them all." This proved to be far from the truth.

nature of the workload, and its significance to headquarters. A special-agent-in-charge can easily be, and often is, promoted or demoted from one office to another.

The FBI has picked the cream of the crop, and its superb training guarantees that its agents will be the best people in law enforcement.

For most of the time after Hoover became Director in 1924, the Bureau was in the enviable position of having far more applicants for agent positions than it had spots available, and thus, unlike many police departments, it never had to scramble desperately or recruit unselectively in order to keep its ranks full. It had also been an advantage that the FBI rarely chose agents straight out of college, but rather insisted that they have an advanced degree or several years of experience relevant to their probable duties in the Bureau. This increased the likelihood that the agent force would be composed of relatively mature individuals rather than trigger-happy, impulsive ones. The training, especially in the early days, was believed to be the best of its kind available in the country, and it supposedly put a uniformly good polish on men who were already of the highest caliber.

In fact, the intelligence, the motivation, and the competence of FBI agents have always varied widely, as might be expected of any such organization once it grows beyond the small, comfortable size of the Bureau when Hoover was first put in charge. Some seemed to slip through with minimal qualifications while nobody was looking, and others proved themselves to be particularly narrow in outlook and perspective, and therefore unimaginative in the performance of their duties. Inevitably, several people seemed to enter service each year who had no intention of staying on for an extended period of time, but who merely wanted to take advantage of the training and experience and then use the FBI credential to get themselves better-paying jobs on the outside. Many fine agents, after several years of hearing that they were the greatest, and the organization as perfect as any on earth, would wake up one morning and decide suddenly that the advantages did not compensate for some of the routine discipline and petty indignities they were expected to endure. Younger agents, especially of the generation that entered the FBI in the late 1960s and early 1970s, often became disgusted by the Superman image cultivated by headquarters; as one agent in a midwestern field office put it, "we would be better off recognizing, and helping the people understand, our limitations."

Most agents have high praise for the physical conditioning, the firearms instruction, and the courses on legal subjects in FBI training school. But in other areas, some argue, by the time Hoover died Bureau training had fallen way behind the times. There was little attention given, for example, to the subtleties of how to deal with private citizens; as one recently graduated agent put it, "We were essentially taught in training school that when you say 'FBI,' people throw their hands up and start shaking. Well, they don't necessarily do that any more." It was only a few years ago that agents-in-training began to be exposed to sophisticated management concepts and to feel more free to speak their minds in class without worrying about being bounced out for the expression of unorthodox views. Some agents have not really expected to learn very much in training school, but have treated it as an indoctrination — and an initiation rite of sorts — that must be endured before one can get out into the field and do some genuine on-the-job learning. When the new FBI Academy at Quantico was completed in late 1972, there was almost nobody on hand who knew how to operate the sophisticated educational gadgetry that had been installed. Most of it sat unused for months until the instructors began to find their way with it.

Training could be substantially improved, some agents argue, if educational experts from outside the Bureau were brought in to reorganize it and if some of the vast resources and energies now devoted to police training under the aegis of the FBI National Academy were diverted to the FBI's own people. Many feel that agents' training should be substantially longer — the current sixteen weeks is the longest it has ever been — in order to cover in more detail some subjects that are now treated only cursorily. One former New York City policeman who became an agent says that for all the presumed sophistication of FBI training, many of the things he had learned at the police academy in New York about dealing with people and protecting himself had served him better and longer. Another young agent, asked to describe training, said, "It was mostly bullshit. . . . There was no way you could flunk out unless you raped a clerk or were grossly incompetent. One of the most important things we learned over and over again was that 'the Bureau is the greatest.'" He urged that the academic side of agents' training be made far more rigorous.

The older an agent, the wiser and better equipped he is.

Although J. Edgar Hoover took over the Bureau at a remarkably early age, as he became older himself he hesitated to name young men to positions of major responsibility. Eventually the FBI turned into a sort of gerontocracy where anyone with ambitions generally had to wait his turn out for years and years. While young men and women in other federal agencies were often advanced on the basis of performance and promise, seniority counted most within the Bureau. In 1975, the youngest special-agent-in-charge in the country was forty years old, and he was considered a rarity because he had three distinct advantages: he had entered the Bureau when he was very young, he had been a clerk, and he had worked for several years in the Administrative Division at headquarters. Most SACs were in the neighborhood of fifty years old and one was sixty-six. The youngest assistant-special-agent-in-charge was thirty-six. (The oldest ASAC was sixty-one.) That meant that headquarters was heavily stocked with younger men who, having served their terms as Bureau supervisors and having traveled as "aides" on the inspection staff as required for promotion, were theoretically qualified to be assigned as ASACs but were cooling their heels until they became "old enough" to be sent out.

That situation was bound to ease substantially after January 1, 1978, the effective date of a new retirement bill — adopted on July 12, 1974 — that makes retirement from the Bureau compulsory at age fifty-five unless the director grants a special exemption from its terms to any individual; but in the meantime most of the FBI's top echelon at headquarters were well into their fifties and inclined still to favor and trust their own peers rather than younger people coming along the line. The appointment of John A. Mintz as the Bureau's legal counsel at only thirty-eight seemed to establish that risks could be taken with a younger generation, even at headquarters.

The Bureau must preserve the old methods that made it famous and regard all innovations with suspicion.

Hoover long resisted the introduction of computers and other modern technology into Bureau operations, preferring time-tested methods and procedures that he himself had had a hand in developing. To be sure, many FBI cases involve simple, old-fashioned police work, and there is often no substitute for getting out on the street and pounding the pavement in order to follow up leads. But the Bureau never submitted its methods to the kind of scrutiny involved in the research of organizations like the Police Foundation (which found, among other things, that traditional police patrol was not necessarily the best way to prevent crime), and it seldom questioned such fundamental beliefs as the notion that the likelihood of solving a case is directly proportional to the number of agents assigned to it.

Particularly frustrating to some agents was the Bureau's reluctance to bend and adjust some of the old rules to deal with the special problems posed by such crimes as the theft of securities. It was anathema to some of the old guard, for example, to develop a corps of agents who could, among other tasks, serve in an undercover capacity as would-be buyers when an informant led the FBI to a cache of missing securities. Traditionally, agents had seldom worked undercover, and headquarters simply could not see any reason for breaking with the past and running such risks. When a Bureau supervisor in the General Investigative Division finally did launch an authorized program to train qualified agents for such a role, some traditionalists could not believe it would ever get off the ground. Three special-agents-in-charge of relatively large offices were so incredulous, in fact, that they responded to a request that they nominate people to be trained for the program by saying that they could not think of anyone in their offices to send. (Finally, forty agents were selected from among nearly three hundred who were recommended, and they attended special seminars at Quantico.) The Bureau also refused for years to provide the amounts of "show money" necessary to get a thief or a fence into a position where he could be arrested for trying to sell securities or other valuable stolen property that had been transported across state lines. The headquarters officials were apparently not prepared to trust the agents in the field to return the money. In a few instances, SACs took a chance by using the field office's petty cash or money lent by private sources to help their agents or informants lure those holding the stolen materials into an arrest situation. At one point, a Florida field office, unsuccessful in its efforts to get Bureau funds for this purpose, quietly borrowed the money from a state agency instead.

Secrecy is essential in all aspects of FBI work and organization.

The impulse toward confidentiality is sometimes taken to infuriating lengths by FBI headquarters. Although the Bureau has a modern direct-dial telephone system that permits any extension to be called directly from outside, its phone directory remains a top-secret, limited-circulation document. Similarly, the assignment charts that pinpoint the responsibilities within each headquarters division all carry the legend: "This document is for internal use within the FBI, is to be provided appropriate security, and disposed of in confidential trash receptacles when no longer current." If the breakdown of assignments and phone extensions were more readily accessible and widely known, it would undoubtedly help channel outside inquiries and offers of information to the right place more quickly. But the Bureau apparently believes that this advantage would be far outweighed by the prospect that foreign governments conducting intelligence operations against the United States — or even organized crime figures and allegedly subversive organizations — might learn who is responsible for coordinating FBI efforts to deal with them. And so the Bureau keeps virtually all of its organizational detail secret; even ranking officials in the Justice Department are familiar with the structure of only those sections or units in the FBI with which they have regular dealings. Sometimes career lawyers in Justice have no idea whom they should call within the FBI on a particular problem.

The Bureau prefers, in fact, that all headquarters mail be addressed simply to "The Federal Bureau of Investigation, Washington, D.C. 20535" and that all phone calls come through the central switchboard. It has blind faith that its foolproof internal systems will direct every piece of paper and every telephone call to the right place. Even the stationery on which an assistant director responds to an outside query is likely to be either blank white paper or carry his name without any indication of the position he occupies.

Except for a few very well publicized recent exceptions, the Bureau has generally insisted upon keeping all of its files secret, officially to protect both the reputations of those discussed in the files and the confidentiality of the agency's sources. But even the federal or other attorneys prosecuting a case on the basis of an FBI investigation are rarely permitted to see the entire "raw file" on a case. The Bureau provides a case summary and only those "serials" from the files that *it* feels are necessary in court.

Many agents have unlisted telephone numbers and keep their addresses a secret, a policy encouraged by headquarters. Most Bureau vehicles are listed with state registration departments under false names and addresses. All carbon paper and typewriter ribbons are burned after one use so that no one can use them to reconstruct a confidential Bureau communication; a model Bureau secretary leaving her desk at the end of the day can often be seen lifting her ribbon out of her typewriter and throwing it into the confidential trash. The exact agent strength of each field office is officially confidential, as is the breakdown of how many agents are assigned to each kind of work in any particular locality and Bureau-wide. So secret are the names of confidential Bureau informants that they do not appear on any of the files containing the information they provide, but are rather kept in secret indices to which access is controlled.

The Bureau, careful as it has been over the years to monitor and upgrade its own performance, needs no help from the outside.

Hoover believed firmly that the FBI could never trust an outsider as much as its own people, and he insisted that the Bureau do almost everything for itself. Thus, even in specialized areas like the Laboratory and the FBI Academy, no one who was not a special agent or a clerical employee of the FBI was ever given any significant responsibility during the Director's lifetime. Agents were sometimes assigned to the Laboratory on the basis of weak science backgrounds in college, and to the Training Division on the basis of once having taught grammar school; when special expertise was needed, the Director preferred sending his own men to school for the necessary courses rather than hiring a consultant from the outside. It was because of that philosophy that the Laboratory fell years behind the capacity of private industry and even that of some other government departments. Assistant directors in charge of the Laboratory had advanced science degrees, to be sure, but invariably they had been insulated from scientific developments in the outside world for years before they moved into that position.

Central to the Bureau's claim that its operations are being constantly evaluated and improved internally is the inspection system. Established by Hoover as part of his drive to clean up the corrupt bureaucracy he inherited in 1924, it involved a surprise review of the operations of every field office, at first every few months and later once a year. This was a new idea that was widely imitated throughout government; in theory, the Director's men reported back faithfully and candidly on whether the rulebook and his instructions and desires were being followed properly. Initially the system functioned as prescribed and helped keep FBI men on their toes, but its effectiveness was gradually reduced with time. The element of surprise was removed, first as the Bureau grapevine developed sufficiently to alert a special-agent-in-charge that the inspectors would soon be coming, and later when the offices were given a week or two of official notice. The inspections came to be regarded as an instrument of Hoover's control. Some special-agents-in-charge insisted that the inspectors seemed to be arriving with a quota of letters of censure to fill. And as one put it, "There are so many rules and regulations in this outfit that if you're looking for it, you can always find something wrong." In many of the routine annual inspections and some of the special ones occasioned by a crisis in a field office, the inspectors seemed to have been sent out by Hoover with instructions to do a hatchet job on someone who was in disfavor; it was not difficult to carry out such instructions.

Under the current practice, the special-agent-in-charge of a field office about to be inspected receives an advance list of written questions that he will be expected to answer; then he is given an opportunity to reply in writing to any criticisms made by the inspection team after its visit. Even so, the content of the inspection report often seems to depend upon the status of the particular SAC, and in some instances it is the product of delicate negotiation, almost collusion, between him and the chief of the inspection team. This evolving character of the inspections has led some agents to label them a farce and to urge that they be conducted less often.

A federal law is a federal law, and all laws on the books must be enforced with equal vigor.

One of Hoover's favorite expressions was that "the best way to get rid of a bad law is to enforce it vigorously." The Director frequently condemned Congress for passing legislation to deal with a crisis that it did not really want enforced on a continuing basis, and in such a situation he would sometimes, in effect, harass the legislators with unrelenting enforcement. The Bureau resisted stubbornly when the Justice Department tried for years to divert to other matters the FBI resources spent on pursuing cases under the Dyer Act (interstate transportation of a stolen motor vehicle, ITSMV), instituting a new policy of prosecuting only cases involving interstate car-theft rings or organized crime and leaving instances of youthful "joyriding" to state authorities. Whenever the subject came up, Hoover spoke eloquently of the need to "preserve the integrity of interstate commerce." After the FBI finally did accede and began to carry out the new policy, many Bureau officials still privately condemned the policy as "selective law enforcement"; and if irate citizens whose cars had been stolen called headquarters or a field office to complain, the blame was placed squarely on the Justice Department.

What the Bureau position amounted to, of course, was a refusal to set investigative priorities; even with the best of intentions, it would be virtually impossible to enforce fully every federal law in the statute books unless the FBI's manpower were increased tenfold. But whether it always acknowledged it or not, the FBI did make choices, giving its attention first and sometimes foremost to those cases, such as stolen cars, which would be easiest to solve and contribute most to the annual compilation of statistics reflecting investigative accomplishments. Meanwhile the Bureau neglected other important areas where it could have had a substantial impact. Such choices by the Bureau were very important indeed, because most investigations and prosecutions on the federal level that fall within FBI jurisdiction are initiated by the Bureau rather than by the Justice Department. It is only in a minority of cases that the prosecutors come to the FBI with instructions; the more common procedure is for the Bureau to call matters to the attention of the prosecutors.

Everyone outside the Bureau itself, including those who work for other divisions of the Department of Justice, must be regarded with suspicion.

The classic FBI view of the Justice Department was passionately expressed by a retired FBI official who had worked closely with several different attorneys general and their staffs: "Ninety-eight percent of the people are in there for personal aggrandizement. They use their positions in the Justice Department as a stepping-stone to other jobs, and they don't give a damn unless they get involved in a big case that makes headlines. There's no difference between the Democrats and the Republicans in this respect, either. The Department ought to be run the way Mr. Hoover ran the Bureau."

The Bureau both fears and looks down on "the Department." FBI agents often speak of the threat in the post-Hoover era that "the Department" plans to "take over" or somehow "control" the Bureau — as if the FBI had not for nearly seventy years been a part of the Department of Justice, clearly intended by statute to be under its control and jurisdiction. But Hoover's wariness of partisan politicians, dating back to what he had witnessed during the Harding administration, led him never to trust an attorney general fully. He never cut them in on the full scope of FBI activities. It is not clear exactly how many other attorneys general asked to have a look at a copy of the top-secret *FBI Manual* that carries the rules, regulations, and procedures for everything the Bureau does, but it is believed in the Justice Department that Elliot Richardson, who served as attorney general for barely six months in 1973, was the first person in that position ever to see it. It was true, of course, that Bureau officials tended to stay in their jobs much longer than anyone they dealt with in the rest of the Justice Department, and the FBI inevitably worried that Justice people, once they left government service, would betray Bureau confidences. One front on which the Bureau fought a running struggle with the department over the years was that of public relations. The Bureau deeply resented Attorney General Robert F. Kennedy's orders that all FBI press releases be cleared through the Justice Department Public Information Office, and emotions still run high in that area. In the early stages of the bizarre case involving Patricia Hearst, the FBI became so angry with the spontaneous declarations of Attorney General William B. Saxbe that for a time it cut the Justice Department spokesmen off altogether from information about the case.

But some of the most intense internecine warfare engaged in by the FBI involved the Law Enforcement Assistance Administration, established in 1968, also as part of the Justice Department, to help control crime with federal grants to local and state authorities. The Bureau often seemed paranoid about LEAA, and some Bureau officials were convinced for a time that there was a plan afoot to turn over to the new agency the FBI's Identification Division and National Crime Information Center; they did not like it when LEAA invaded areas that were considered exclusive Bureau turf, for example, by doing research and making statements on such subjects as terrorism in the United States. The FBI was particularly suspicious of the plans of Donald E. Santarelli, a young Justice Department political appointee who was named administrator of LEAA by President Nixon in 1973 and who was believed to have ambitious plans for the agency and for himself. After the president of the International Association of Chiefs of Police criticized a speech by Santarelli at a criminal justice conference in Williamsburg, Virginia, in January 1974, the Bureau "went behind" the Santarelli speech in an attempt to discover whether he had deviated from a prepared text and how the audience reacted. Rather than asking LEAA for its tape recording of the speech, the FBI interviewed newspaper reporters about it and embarrassed itself in the process.

In order to stay on the alert about the plans, thoughts, and activities of other agencies that could affect its own activities, FBI headquarters frequently goes beyond and behind public declarations and official conferences. It has an informal network of "friends," not only in other parts of the Justice Department but also in other federal departments and agencies in Washington, and in Congress, who undertake to keep the Bureau informed of matters — sometimes highly sensitive — of special interest to it. That helps the FBI stay a step ahead of everyone else.

Headquarters is the official FBI, the place where everything can be mixed together, put through the paper mill and the meat grinder, and come out as caseloads, categories, percentages, and "interesting case writeups" (the official version of everything, produced in the External Affairs Division and available to anyone who shows an interest in a particular case).

For nearly half a century headquarters was run as J. Edgar Hoover's showpiece, his personal "seat of government" which tended to confuse law enforcement with policymaking. Sometimes consciously and sometimes not, headquarters was the master of the charade. In military fashion, it overstaffed the Bureau's rolls in order to have enough manpower available for when a real crisis occurred. But it never said it was doing that; it justified the overload with artificial "cases" that consisted only of pieces of paper but looked good in the statistics. It created rules to govern everything, rules that were intended more to anticipate and answer criticism than to help the agents with their work. One rule, for example, said that any employee given language training on FBI time must prove regularly that he is using it in his work; an agent once assigned to the Vero Beach, Florida, Resident Agency told of proving he was using his Spanish by "calling Miami once a month and saying '*Cómo está usted?*'" Headquarters developed a corps of FBI bureaucrats who jockeyed for favor with the Director, learning to sense carefully which way the wind was blowing before they took a position on any serious issue. Once a Bureau position was taken, they joined the Director in equating disagreement with dissidence, or even dishonesty. They reevaluated only on command, and they were able to say with a straight face, as one assistant director does, that "the FBI has never done anything that was not entirely in the public interest." They took every one of Hoover's standards seriously, and because they might be seen by him at any time, they always wore the white shirts and conservative clothes that were sometimes scorned in the field. They learned to believe.

Headquarters was the perfect model, as one agent put it, for the "benevolent dictatorship" of the FBI, where reality was whatever the Bureau said it was. Some people had trouble finding the benevolence.

IX

In the Provinces:
The Field Offices
and Resident Agencies

The new agent, fresh out of training school, arrives at his first field office, a large one run by a special-agent-in-charge who has a reputation as a tyrant and is known to be a close friend of Mr. Hoover. With great trepidation and anxiety, he has his first meeting with the SAC, who is stern and harsh and warns him that those who do not perform properly suffer in untold ways. After the interview is concluded, the young agent leaves — or at least he thinks he does. In fact, he goes through the wrong door and finds himself in a closet instead of the hallway. The SAC, preoccupied with a phone call, does not notice the mistake. But the agent, terrified of the consequences should he acknowledge the error, decides he would be better off staying where he is. The boss, as it turns out, does not step out to go to the bathroom, thus giving the agent time to escape, until several hours later. So the agent spends much of his first day on the job in a closet. Nobody notices.

— An FBI legend

FOUR AGENTS, AMONG THE BEST and most accomplished in the Chicago Field Office, head out together at noontime one spring day on important business. Their destination: a nearby bank, one of the city's biggest. They are not investigating any particular bank robbery or securities theft; nor are they lecturing the executives on what to do if one of them should become the victim of an extortion or kidnapping. They have not been called in to look at the circumstances of a suspected embezzlement, a suspicious bankruptcy, or the discovery of some money that was listed among the loot in another unsolved case; and

182

they are not even coming to cash their paychecks. Any of these would ordinarily be a plausible reason for their appearance. But the occasion today is that the bank has opened a new galaxy of private dining rooms and the FBI agents are among the first groups invited to enjoy them, for this is a financial institution with which the field office has a special relationship.

Host for the filet mignon luncheon is a vice-president of the bank, an earthy man who, by his own admission, "could have gone either way." Growing up on the West Side of Chicago in the rough-and-tumble days of Prohibition, he might have had a remunerative career as a bootlegger and racketeer. Many of his childhood friends, in fact, did just that and are now the subjects of ongoing Bureau investigations, some of them making it into the official category of "top hoodlums." But this man chose another path. He had only a grammar school education, but has worked his way toward the top during twenty-eight years of faithful service to the bank. Over the years he has become a particular friend of the Bureau. Since the late 1950s, in fact, certain supervisors in the field office have been able to rely upon him to check bank records "on a confidential basis." He would advise, for example, whether somebody had an account, if there had been unusual activity in it, and who was paying money to or receiving it from an individual under investigation. Then, after getting the confidential information, as one supervisor explained, "We can evaluate whether there is a need to issue a subpoena for the records." The bank official also alerts his contacts at the field office to anything he sees around the bank that seems "suspicious" and to any tips he hears about the widespread underworld activity in Chicago's legitimate business community.

Few, if any, of the vice-president's dealings with the Bureau would be noted in bank records, but as he tells it, "The president of the bank doesn't object to my helping these fellows in any way I can. He knows we can trust them." Indeed, the vice-president is probably nowhere identified in FBI files in connection with the material he passes along, except as "a source who has provided reliable information in the past." And the cooperation pays off handsomely for the bank, buying a kind of informal insurance that is not often available — the extra enthusiasm of the Bureau on cases involving its friends. If this bank reports a robbery or any other problem, it can be sure of an immediate and aggressive response from the field office. When the bank has questions, it need not always go to its lawyers. "We can call up these people and get advice on what is a federal violation and what is not," says the FBI contact. The symbiotic relationship goes even further. If the Bureau needs an office and a cover for an agent working on a stolen securities case, for example, this is one of the places it can turn for help; since a bank official often must serve as the intermediary for the transfer of the stolen stocks or bonds, many arrests are made in just such circumstances, with the fence discovering after he turns over the securities that the man behind the desk is actually an FBI agent posing as a bank employee. The vice-president is quick to explain, however, that the same cooperation is not ordinarily extended to other law enforcement organizations — not to the Internal Revenue Service, which "drags us in when they don't have to," and surely not to the Chicago Police Department, because it is sometimes hard to tell whom an investigating officer is really representing.

The conversation over lunch turns to the subject of police corruption in Chicago and the unusual situation in recent years that has agents from the field office in the position of almost constantly investigating people they would normally expect to work with. One Bureau raid on an illicit gambling house in Cicero, Illinois, once the stronghold of Al Capone, is recalled with particular amusement: not only did the local police officials refuse to help, but they ticketed all the FBI cars on the scene for illegal parking during the raid. One agent tells of the time he saw a shipment of syringes being unloaded from a truck in what seemed likely to be part of an illegal narcotics operation. Having no jurisdiction to step in himself, he called the police. A squad car arrived immediately, but the policeman, sizing up the situation quickly, had a friendly chat with the truck driver and never bothered to ask his name. Another agent remembers gambling raids on the South Side of Chicago when the police called half an hour in advance to say they would be coming; when they arrived, of course, they found nothing incriminating. During one raid in the late 1960s, FBI agents confiscated a list of four hundred and sixty-nine police officers, complete with their badge numbers, who were authorized to take payments in a numbers racket. Eventually, explains one of the agents, "we stopped disseminating information to the police department here, because it just feathered their nest more." Material from the FBI had given corrupt policemen additional information to sell — as a part of their extortion racket, they could offer to protect people from federal investigations.

"That's just the point," says the bank vice-president; "the people have never trusted the police here." They knew that tavern owners were paying kickbacks to cops on the beat in order to keep their liquor licenses, and they realized that it often did no good to call and report a crime involving hoodlums who were in league with the police department. The FBI's advantage developed in part as a matter of contrast. "People began to trust them, mostly because of their reputation. They knew things would not leak out if they talked to the Bureau." And it is only a logical extension of that attitude that makes his bank willing to provide "intelligence-type information" to the agents. "We'll do anything we can," he says proudly.

No particular transactions or exchanges of information occur over lunch. Rather, it is a pleasant ninety minutes of joking, storytelling, and catching up among contacts who have also become friends — a subtle reaffirmation that they can count on each other.

The luncheon in Chicago was a typical event for the FBI in the field. The Bureau has always relied on the business and financial community as one of its strongest sources of support, and banks are a case in point. They have something to gain and something to give. The bankers count on the FBI for prompt and efficient investigation of robberies and other crimes (even though in some areas, by agreement between local and federal prosecutors, all bank robbery cases are automatically turned over to the state for the first try at prosecution), but they also know that their Bureau friends will help in other ways, for example, by not insisting upon immediate release of an estimate of the amount taken. Thus have banks managed for years to conceal other losses, perhaps uninsured, by claiming that more was lost in a robbery than actually was. It is a perfectly safe ploy, because the only witnesses who could reliably contradict the bank are the robbers themselves; invariably the full proceeds from a bank robbery are never recovered anyway. Apart from the confidential and unofficial assistance on investigations that they have long had from banking friends, FBI men have been able to count on banks for hefty rewards to Bureau informants who help break cases. Also, agents rarely have trouble obtaining mortgages or other loans, even in times of tight credit, from financial institutions.

Similarly, airlines often seek to curry the favor of the Bureau, especially during periods when hijackings, cargo thefts, and other federal offenses pose a serious problem for them. At a management symposium of some two dozen key FBI officials from around the country held in San Francisco in early 1974, the regional public relations committee of the U.S. Air Transport Association gave a cocktail party in their honor; the airline representatives offered toasts and speeches saluting the Bureau for the fine job it was doing. When the out-of-town FBI guests arrived in San Francisco for the symposium and checked into their hotel rooms (provided at a reduced rate), they found surprise packages of gifts from local banks, oil companies, and the airlines; additional gifts were given away in a drawing of lots every day — goodwill, a benign form of protection. The printed program for the week-long symposium included a full page of acknowledgments that listed those donors, as well as a local jewelry store, the Napa Wineries, and the Monterey Peninsula Chamber of Commerce, among others. At a similar symposium in Philadelphia, all of the visiting FBI dignitaries and their wives ate one evening at a well-known restaurant at no apparent cost. When another group gathered in Boston, a free lunch was thrown by the Prudential Insurance Company, which strategically placed one or two of its up-and-coming young executives at each table to meet the Bureau people. In these cities and others where symposia were held, the FBI officials were treated as distinguished conventioneers whose goodwill should be courted. It was not that anything was explicitly requested or provided in return, but the idea seemed to be that it might come in handy to have someone within your organization who knows somebody in the FBI, or at least to have a basis for friendly relations.

Well-placed contacts are essential to most Bureau work in the field, of course, and they are often a two-way affair. Some field offices have especially advantageous dealings, for example, with automobile dealers and other merchants who have occasional problems with stolen cars and fraudulent checks from out of state; those relationships may result in privileged-character status and special prices for the agents. The story is told with great relish of the time when an agent in the New York Field Office, known affectionately as "Broadway Joe" MacFarlane (later assistant-special-agent-in-charge of the Administrative Division of that office), came to work with a full rack of trench coats that were available to the agents from a Bureau friend at a particularly attractive price. Fittings were conducted in the middle of a squad room.

In contrast to headquarters, where procedures are invariably formal and the risks of any decisive action minutely calculated and measured, the field is the relaxed side of the FBI, where impulses are regularly acted upon and realism is valued over the rulebook. It is in the field that cases are solved, reputations made, and the Bureau's muscle most dramatically flexed and felt. There are almost eight thousand agents deployed in the field by the FBI — a small contingent by comparison with, say, the twenty-four thousand members of the New York City Police Department and the tens of thousands of military personnel potentially available to the Pentagon, but, as one former assistant director put it, "potentially a powerful force for good or evil,

186

depending on how it is used." The field, insisted one special-agent-in-charge, "is where the, real FBI is. . . . But then I suppose the Roman legions probably felt the same way about Rome."

◆

FBI domestic field operations are spread among fifty-nine distinct offices. The largest — New York, Los Angeles, Chicago, and San Francisco, for example — have hundreds of agents assigned, and the smallest — El Paso, Savannah, Honolulu, and Anchorage — only a few dozen. The geographical distribution of the field offices is based largely on the outlines of federal court districts and therefore, while convenient, is not entirely rational. Both Scottsbluff, Nebraska, and Dubuque, Iowa, for example, are covered out of the Omaha Field Office, although the former is closer to Denver and the latter to Chicago.

The FBI develops the cases that the federal government's prosecutors — the ninety-four U.S. attorneys — then act upon. While some field offices may cover several court districts (Minneapolis, for example, handles North and South Dakota, as well as all of Minnesota) and therefore deal with several United States attorneys, each U.S. attorney is served by only one FBI field office. The lines between field office territories have traditionally been so rigid that agents were forbidden to cross them while investigating cases except with special permission or under very unusual circumstances. Some of the offices, in the biggest cities and most obvious crime centers, have existed for fifty years or more, while others were opened and closed by J. Edgar Hoover as he kept pace with expansions and shifts in the Bureau's budget and responsibilities. The establishment of some field offices as separate entities, while it might not ordinarily be justified by their light caseloads, was based on factors such as their distance from others (San Juan, Anchorage, Honolulu) or the special problems they handle (the border at El Paso and the civil rights cases in southern offices like Jackson, Memphis, and Little Rock). Offices are classified for administrative purposes in four groups, depending on the number of "investigative matters" pending at any given time; Group I offices have at least six thousand open cases and Group IV fewer than two thousand.

Whether located in a federal office building or courthouse or in space leased from private owners, most field offices resemble each other physically. Special-agents-in-charge and assistant-special-agents-in-charge have private suites, generally isolated from everyone else in the office; supervisors and chief clerks have their own cubicles more in the midst of things, and most agents work in large squad rooms where they have little privacy. Every office has a heavily secured gun vault, where rarely used special weapons are kept along with some that are just for display, and an impenetrable steel-walled cable room, where cryptographic and telegraphic equipment are located. Some also have a euphemistically labeled "radio room," where wiretaps and other electronic surveillance can be monitored (although most offices with any significant number of wiretaps also rent outside space — private rooms lined with voice-activated tape recorders that pick up every conversation on the tapped lines). In recent years, separate rooms have also been set aside for the radio consoles used to keep in touch with all agent cars on the street and for the computer terminals that link the field office with the National Crime Information Center at FBI headquarters and with statewide law enforcement information networks. The files on open cases are in rotor cabinets or other units close to the supervisor handling them, but the closed files and alphabetical indices are off in a separate area where the clerks will have ready access to them. In another section is the "steno pool," composed of typists and secretaries recruited locally by the office. Agents dictate all of their paperwork to the stenos, rather than typing it themselves; Hoover always insisted that Bureau documents were to have absolutely no errors.*

The walls of the field offices are generally decorated with FBI seals and Bureau-issued posters extolling the FBI's accomplishments since 1924; every office has a large display board with pictures of the current Ten Most Wanted fugitives. Some of the postings change with the times — recently warning, for example, that thick envelopes posted from abroad may contain letter bombs, or displaying the picture of Patricia Hearst and her companions in the Symbionese Liberation Army. Early in the morning, usually beginning around seven, and late in the afternoon, ending about five, most offices are frenetically active as agents prepare to go out on leads or bring back the result of a day's worth of outside work. After that, the entrances are so tightly secured that a fly could almost set off the burglar alarm,† and but for a few people on night duty, the office is eerily silent and the desks meticulously clear at night because the agents have put their "workboxes,"

---

* The standard seems to have slipped somewhat, as many of the FBI documents released in court cases and otherwise made public in recent years have a startling number of spelling and grammatical errors.
† Security precautions have been substantially increased since the 1971 burglary of the FBI resident agency in Media, Pennsylvania.

containing all the official paper they are handling, in a central, secure location.

Any member of the public visiting the field office arrives at a reception area, typically decorated with maps, trophies, and portraits of the President of the United States, Hoover, and Kelley, sometimes with a rug or tapestry with the FBI seal woven into it, and always stocked with handy pamphlets listing "99 Facts about the FBI," the achievements of the Identification Division, or related subjects. Nearby are interview rooms where complaints or statements can be taken, usually by clerks, without interrupting the normal business of the office or giving anyone an unauthorized glance at it. Agents come and go throughout the day, mostly through back doors and private entrances, required always to note whether they are in or out of the office on their pink "number three cards," kept at a central register or with the secretary to their squad. In most of the newer offices, an internal elevator permits prisoners to be brought in to be fingerprinted and have their pictures taken without seeing any other part of the operations. Somewhere on or near the premises of every office is a facility where the confidential trash is either burned or ground into mushy gray pulp.

In the largest offices, there may be more than one special-agent-in-charge and/or assistant-special-agent-in-charge, sometimes responsible for separate criminal, security, and administrative "divisions." But in most offices there is one of each, and in the smaller offices the SAC and ASAC supervise their own squads, usually the ones handling the biggest, breaking criminal cases ("the cigar squads" they are called in some offices). Every SAC has been an ASAC in at least one office, and every ASAC wants nothing more in life than to become an SAC. Before reaching those positions, they have usually served as street agents, field supervisors, Bureau supervisors, and traveled on the inspection staff, the ASACs for one tour of duty lasting about a year and the SACs usually for two tours lasting about that long. There are exceptional cases, however, of "battlefield promotions," in which an ASAC has been jumped ahead to become the SAC in the office where he is serving without an extra swing as an inspector. Depending on the personality of the SAC, the ASAC may be something of a lackey and personal errand boy or he may serve as a friend-in-court and special confidant for the agents, especially the younger ones.

The field supervisors are in effect the sergeants of the field offices. Some are the personal choices of the SAC and some have been in their jobs so long that no one would think of trying to remove them (still others, in a recent adaptation of the "career development program," are sent out from headquarters as a step toward their assignment as ASACs); they are the real managers of day-to-day field office business. They must initial (and are therefore held responsible for) every piece of paper that originates under their jurisdiction and coordinate the activities of the approximately fifteen to twenty-five agents on their squads. Some supervisors are well known for their ability to inspire agents and keep things moving, others for their tendency to harass them and make their lives miserable. They may contribute real ideas to investigations or be content to settle back and use their "armed and dangerous" rubber stamp.

Officially, all FBI offices are equipped to do all kinds of work. There is invariably a "sound man," who can handle the technical details of a wiretap, a few people with special accounting skills appropriate for sophisticated fraud cases, and somebody who knows the difference between the Communist party USA and the Socialist Workers party (and cares). But the personnel and organization of an office obviously vary with its special needs. In Miami jewel thefts are big, and in Los Angeles two separate squads are required to handle the bank robberies (one for those in the city's jursidiction and the other for those that occur in Los Angeles County). In coastal field offices, agents must be able to develop informants at the waterfront for both criminal and security matters, and in major freight crossroads they have to learn to find out about the loading and unloading of stolen shipments. In any place where organized crime flourishes, some agents are needed who understand the complexities of illegal gambling operations and who can trace "family" loyalties and lines of authority almost with the skill of a genealogist. Language skills, especially Spanish, are essential in some offices. The Bureau has planned future development of a "skills bank" — a computerized record that could immediately tell headquarters where to turn, for example, if someone needs a tall agent under thirty who speaks French and skis well — but in the meantime, assignments to the field offices are based largely on guesswork and rough anticipation of special requirements.

Squads tend to be minutely specialized in the largest offices, with twenty agents handling enforcement of a single statute or investigation of a single organization, yet able to handle a potpourri of assignments in the smallest offices. In Alexandria, Virginia (the fifty-ninth field office to be opened), for example, all security matters and civil rights cases are handled by the same squad, and another takes care of both fugitive (UFAP) cases and applicant matters. Each office has at least one, and usually several, special-weapons-and-tactics (SWAT) teams, recently trained at Quantico to deal with snipers and urban guerrilla situations; a team's members may work on several different squads and come together as a unit only when their special skills are needed. Most offices have an agent or two whose major responsibility is to be "police training coordinator," supervising the selection of law enforcement people from the office's territory who will be sent to the National Academy and sending agents out to lecture and give demonstrations at the request of police departments.

Whenever an office launches an investigation, it becomes the "office of origin" (OO) for that case and will get a copy of every piece of paper produced anywhere in the Bureau in connection with it. If an office was the first to investigate, say, the "Cleaver faction" of the Black Panther party, or the American Nazi party, its OO designation may keep the paper flowing in for years. Similarly, once an agent "has the ticket" on a case, or is responsible for it as "case agent," unless he closes it, retires, dies, or is transferred, he will be held responsible for it indefinitely. The rules and procedures change, of course, whenever a case is designated a "special." Agent reinforcements and perhaps even a particularly well qualified SAC will be brought in from outside, and a special squad room may be set up just to handle developments on that case. Initially at least, people will work on it around the clock. Even if a case goes unsolved for many months or years, like the Piper and Hearst kidnappings, and if it is downgraded to ordinary case status, the voluminous files that have accumulated will be kept together and a few agents will be required to spend a part of every day keeping up with anything remotely related to it. According to FBI tradition, an unsolved case is never officially closed.

If much of the work that must be done every day in the field offices is banal and humdrum, the routine is made to feel even worse by the extraordinary gaggle of paperwork and regulations. Even literate people who have practiced law or written for a newspaper before coming into the Bureau sometimes have trouble learning to master the Bureau's jargon, which calls for a flat, verbose way of describing everything, animate or inanimate. Multiple copies are made where one would serve the purpose, and some documents are retyped over and over again to accommodate minor changes or suggestions of supervisors. The checking of each little lead may require a separate report, and as a result some case files become thousands of pages thick. "We are a paper mill," said one special-agent-in-charge candidly, and many agents complain that their investigative efforts are substantially weakened by the fact that they are slaves to paperwork requirements. Some argue that a heavy price has been paid for the Bureau's strength of being able to produce a documentary record of everything.* The wooden Bureau vocabulary — offices have "complements" of agents, people are always "individuals," and time is invariably "expended" on things — is relieved only by an alternative police-style slang in which agents on the "tamale squad" (handling Cuban matters) persuade a suspect to "open up like a suitcase" (tell his whole story).

There is no question but that many of the rules make work harder. No Bureau car is ever supposed to be used for personal business or to be taken home by an agent, except for the SAC and ASAC. This has meant that in cities with poor public transportation agents must drive from their homes every morning, put their personal cars in a garage, check into the office, take out a Bureau car to do their business, and then reverse the procedure at night — even if their homes are closer to where they have to be in the morning and even if they lose several hours in the process. As a result, the rule has been routinely violated over the years, sometimes with an SAC's knowledge and sometimes without. Agents often do not bother coming to the office first as required, but merely have someone else sign in for them; and they can usually get away with taking a Bureau car home without permission from time to time.† For years, all FBI vehicles had to be black and kept shiny at all times, so they were worthless for surveillances or undercover assignments; that has changed, and now some field offices even have vans and motorcycles in their fleets. Agents are not supposed to keep their copies of the confidential manual of instructions in their desks, for reasons of security; but they generally do, for reference purposes, and just remove them when inspection time comes around. (The inspectors invariably go through everyone's desk at night.) Traditionally Hoover required that agents spend no more than a certain fixed percentage of time in the office because he wanted them out in the street; as a result, supervisors regularly falsified their "time-in-office" statistics rather than force people to comply with an unrealistic standard. (Another way to get around that rule was for agents to take their paperwork to a public library.) There was always a firm stricture against drinking on the job under any circumstances, which of course

* The strength has diminished, however, as Bureau documents have repeatedly been challenged as inaccurate or have taken a long time to locate during recent court proceedings.

† In a new experiment launched by the Office of Planning and Evaluation, agents in several field offices were permitted to take Bureau cars home at night for several months on the theory that the gasoline might cost less than overnight garage expenses. As a result, SACs throughout the country were given the authority to permit individual agents to take cars home whenever it could be shown that this would result in faster performance of duties. Still, it was intended that official cars be taken home only occasionally.

made it impossible for agents to conduct a surveillance in a bar; they either waited outside or ignored the rule and had a drink. The Bureau has generally refused to provide any false identification cards that could be used on undercover assignments, and so some agents have obtained counterfeit driver's licenses for that purpose through their informants for twenty-five dollars or more, out of their own pockets. In the days when only agents were permitted to go out on surveillances and there were no women agents, some men, if they thought it would make things more believable, simply took their wives along. Agents also routinely allow their informants far more latitude than provided for in the official rules — for example, by agreeing not to pass along everything the informants have told them, for the informants' personal safety, or by letting the informants hold on to stolen property they have shown to the agents.

One former agent, who participated for years in the system of defying the rules and faking details of reports and statistics, asks the troubling question, "How does a guy learn to cheat and lie on a daily basis regarding administrative matters, but then become perfectly honest on the witness stand?"

Although there sometimes seems to be plenty of fat in the budget at headquarters, the field can be a laboratory of the FBI's tightness and parsimony. It was years after most other government agencies did so that the Bureau got any air-conditioned cars for agents, and they often bought their own guns because they found the ones issued by the Bureau to be cheap and impractical. Agents have no soft expense accounts, and if they take a source out for lunch or dinner there are almost no circumstances under which the Bureau is willing to pay. There is no cost-of-living allowance except in the Anchorage, San Juan, and Honolulu offices, and those traveling on official business for the Bureau receive a fixed per diem allowance regardless of how much their food and lodging cost. If an agent loses money in selling a house or on other transactions connected with a transfer, that is his own problem to handle. It was only a relatively few years ago that the Bureau began paying moving costs at all, and prospective agents are still required to pay their own way to Quantico for training.

One headquarters attitude that carries over into the field is that of keeping other, potentially competing law enforcement agencies at arm's length. This includes not only local and state police departments, particularly those suspected of corruption, but also other federal agencies like the Drug Enforcement Administration and the Immigration and Naturalization Service. Bureau agents tend to feel — sometimes quite correctly — that they are better trained, more highly motivated, and more trustworthy than the others. Yet there is an initial tendency to sympathize with the position of any lawman under attack. But prodded by U.S. Attorney James R. Thompson of the Northern District of Illinois, the Chicago Field Office plunged in vigorously on police corruption cases in the early 1970s; and agents sent in from the Kansas City Field Office to investigate the actions of federal and state narcotics officers during raids in Collinsville, Illinois, did not hold back, but produced the evidence on the basis of which the officers were indicted.

The official headquarters attitude toward the press usually does not prevail in the field. Reporters and street agents regularly provide each other with mutually helpful information, especially in small towns, and most SACs are on sufficiently friendly terms with local editors to be able to persuade them to hold off on the publication of stories considered undesirable or untimely by the FBI for whatever the reasons. The field relationships between the Bureau and the press are generally governed by a mutual measurement and balance of self-interests, and each side realizes that the other will use whatever tactics it must to further those interests. One special-agent-in-charge, known for his especially good relationship with the press, takes great delight in telling about the time he ordered agents simply to block the passage of press cars that were trying to follow the Bureau to a critical rendezvous in a kidnapping case. By the next week, though, he was back on friendly terms and giving his reporter friends information that would never be authorized for release by headquarters.*

In most ways the New York Field Office, where almost 12 percent of all field agents are stationed, is a special case. As in most offices, some agents have been there for years and would not trade what they consider the Bureau's "best work" for easier working conditions. But most agents, especially those with families, consider New York a hardship post. To get along there on the same salary they would be paid in Jacksonville or Portland, they must strain much harder and, in many instances, live much farther away from the office than they would anywhere else. Reacting to the widespread dissatisfaction on this issue, Kelley adopted a policy that any agent who wanted it would be able to get a transfer away from New York after five years. A task force appointed by Kelley, and including young agents, also recommended that a significant percentage of personnel assigned to the New York office be moved out to "satellite offices" in Brooklyn, Queens, and other outlying areas, rather than all moving together to a new office in a

* The largest field offices now have agents assigned to be press liaison officers.

federal building under construction in Lower Manhattan. (The old field office, in a converted warehouse on the Upper East Side, had the advantage of being just around the corner from one of its prime targets, the Soviet Mission to the United Nations — SMUN, in Bureauese — so the task force also suggested that some security squad agents stay in that neighborhood.) At the same time, however, pilot studies are also under way in some field offices to evaluate the practicality of consolidating large and small offices into regional units that would no longer pay such careful attention to the boundaries between states and federal court districts.

It is in the field that most agents feel they get their real training. Often it comes at the hands of an experienced older agent who is delegated by the SAC to take new arrivals under his wing. (Some veterans are particularly proud of their role in breaking new people in and give their trainees a key chain fashioned from a bullet shell or some other memento of the experience.) What the agents learn in the field is generally invaluable and makes the official course at Quantico look mostly like a combination of elementary civics, indoctrination, and institutional self-glorification. They come to realize, for example, that certain categories of agents are the most uniformly respected: those who have shot someone in the line of duty or been wounded themselves, those who get their job done with minimum harassment from their superiors and the least preoccupation with the rulebook, and those who get what they want within the Bureau without becoming unduly obsequious toward the people in a position to give it to them.

Agents pick up a skeptical view of United States attorneys as political appointees, and they resent young assistant United States attorneys who get excellent practical training with the Bureau's assistance and then leave to use that training to their own advantage and enrichment as defense attorneys in private practice. They try to cultivate an attitude of hard-nosed singleness of purpose that will permit them to put human considerations aside and, if called upon to do so, arrest a deserter from the military at his father's funeral or his sister's wedding. They tend to develop a kind of martyred sense that the FBI, try though it might, is doomed to be unappreciated by politicians and misunderstood by the public. And they come to see the other institutions of the criminal system — the courts, the prisons, parole and probation officers, the bar — as working at cross-purposes with the Bureau, undoing with leniency and a "bleeding heart" attitude the good that manages to get done by the FBI. They also learn to loathe many of the people at Bureau headquarters. Some yield only partially to this set of beliefs and remain open to honest discussion of competing views and attitudes; others adopt them, but shed them as they gain more self-confidence and develop independent ideas about their work — but almost everyone is significantly affected by these principles as he starts out in the field.

Every field office, to be sure, has its share of drones who shuffle through without doing very much of anything; usually they are assigned to security squads where they can keep uninteresting cases on individuals open for years or to applicant work that will never require an original thought. Most offices also have a number of older agents who came in as office-of-preference transfers because they want to retire in the area and see an opportunity for the Bureau to pay the moving expenses. This is particularly true in certain southern and West Coast cities that are attractive as retirement havens. Long on stories about the good old days but short on energy and ambition, these agents tend not to carry their share of the workload and to avoid any controversial cases where they would be liable to rock the boat and lose the dream of a lifetime. These drones make a sharp contrast with the hard core of bright enthusiastic agents who are dedicated to their jobs and often make considerable sacrifices to do them properly. Most big-city offices also have one or two agents who are wheeler-dealers and who know their way around the community; they may serve as right-hand men for the SAC, especially when he is new, and coordinate the special arrangements for a distinguished visitor like the director.

Certain offices take on a unique character because of their location, their leadership, and the people assigned there. Tampa, for many years, was regarded as one of the best training offices. Detroit — "a place of nonpreference in the Bureau," as Special-Agent-in-Charge Neil J. Welch euphemistically puts it — is considered a grueling office, but as a result also an exceptionally young office where ambitious people may move quickly. (Welch caused a sensation recently by appointing two supervisors who were under thirty.) Paradoxically, Kansas City is regarded as an especially good assignment by some of its agents even though many of them arrived as the result of disciplinary action, a fact that seems to have fostered a healthy degree of irreverence toward established authority, inside the Bureau and out. Minneapolis became a lively and especially young office recently, because so many of the agents sent on special duty during the Wounded Knee occupation of 1973 were then permanently assigned to that office to help handle the follow-through on the cases growing out of it. New York is an office where the streetwise seem to congregate. They accept little abuse from their superiors because, as one put it, "There is no way you can threaten a New York agent with a transfer . . . most would consider it a reward." Chicago, an office despised by some and much sought after by others, attracts and produces many of the Bureau's most competent agents because it always had a heavy load of exciting criminal cases. Agents assigned to the Washington Field Office, on the other hand, tend to be preoccupied with presumed threats of espionage and subversion. Those who have served the Bureau well in an important place at a special moment often carry that success with them for the rest of their careers as a special qualification. The alumni of the FBI's involvement in civil rights cases in the Deep South during the mid-1960s, for example, have tended to do exceptionally well ever since; some of them are now running field offices.

One of the most basic decisions that every agent in the field must make is whether he wants to be considered for "administrative advancement" in the Bureau. If he does, the first step is to volunteer as a "relief supervisor" for his squad, filling in during a supervisor's absence at no extra pay. With any luck, he will soon be spotted by an inspector or recommended by his SAC as a good prospect to be brought to headquarters as a Bureau supervisor. Eventually, after appropriate tours of duty behind a desk in Washington and on the inspection staff, if he does not do anything wrong, he may become an ASAC and SAC (or advance within the hierarchy at headquarters). But traditionally that climb has taken most people almost twenty years, and it involves significant sacrifices: as soon as he starts the progression, an agent effectively and probably permanently removes himself from availability for doing any practical investigative work, the most exciting part of being in the Bureau; and he may be in for frequent moves from one end of the country to the other, not to mention long periods of time away from his family while on inspections or handling "special" cases. Many of the FBI's most talented agents, in fact, decline the opportunity and prefer to stay "on the street" and avoid frequent transfers, even though that means they can never go beyond a certain salary level. Others opt to go no further than service as a field supervisor, preferring to stay in a city they know well and work there on a particular FBI problem about which they have gained expertise.

The most successful field agents are pragmatists and risktakers in the extreme. In the old days they rarely hesitated to do some free-lance wiretapping and bugging to find out what they wanted to know. (One agent tells of having installed two separate microphones in a hall where a suspected Communist group was to meet, so that agents were able to listen in stereo.) The source of the information was usually well concealed from headquarters, although the subject of rumors in the field office, and only agent friends who helped each other install unauthorized bugs and taps after office hours might know exactly what was going on. Most of the circumstances in which such informal electronic surveillance was used would not have met the standards for formal approval by the Director, even in the days when those standards were fairly loose and permissive. The more modern and somewhat less risky version of the procedure was to have the dirty work done by friends in the intelligence unit of the local police department, who were generally less carefully supervised; then the agent could cite a "police source" for the information and still be telling the truth. The police rarely objected because they were probably interested in having the information themselves, and the agent could always do a favor in return, such as slipping the cooperative policeman a copy of something he wanted from the Bureau files. Even that less audacious technique has, according to most accounts, all but faded because of the fear of being found out by superiors.

Yet many agents say they would still use forbidden procedures "if necessary to get the job done." One young agent, discussing the revelations about the Bureau's COINTELPRO activities between 1956 and 1971, said, "These things were great for getting at groups like the Klan and SLA [Symbionese Liberation Army]. You have to break their balls any way you can. . . . Kelley said it won't be done anymore, but I can assure you that it will, informally if not in an official program." Many agents in security work, he said, would not hesitate to try to have the subjects of their investigations fired from their jobs or evicted from their homes, as was sometimes arranged under COINTELPRO. He added that "if I, as a case agent, have an extremist, I would probably do anything I can to put him in jail. If I have to buy information or read his mail sometimes in order to accomplish that, I would do it. I would conduct a neighborhood investigation just to discredit him, and tell his neighbors about the groups he was affiliated with." This kind of unofficial activity, he explained, might be widely known within a field office where it goes on, but would rarely be documented on paper and therefore could not be proved from the Bureau files. He concluded reassuringly with a smile, however, that "I'm not going to do something illegal without a very significant reason."

While most people probably would not go as far as that agent would, new recruits learn in the field that they have an extraordinary, unexpected amount of discretion. Many federal crimes tend not to be clear-cut or obvious, and, in Bureau jargon, a violation must be "developed" — i.e., activities are monitored with a view toward spotting

something that will be prosecutable. The agents, sometimes in conjunction with prosecutors but often before a U.S. attorney has even
been brought into the matter, have a choice then of pursuing that
individual or trying to turn him into an informant who can help make
cases against others. In consultation with his supervisors, an agent may
decide to make such an informant available to the prosecutors as a
grand jury witness or to conceal his identity entirely.

Service in the field also has its early disillusionments. Agents
quickly come to realize that many of the calls and approaches to the
field office by the public are utter nonsense that will just waste their
time if taken too seriously (yet it is difficult to find a formula for
sorting out the crackpot calls from those that have merit). People
sometimes turn to the FBI to solve their personal problems. A woman
whose husband had left her ten years earlier called the Tampa office
recently, asking that the Bureau find him. There are constant re-
minders that the system does not function smoothly — for example,
when an agent, looking for a man reported to the Bureau as a deserter
from the army, goes to the man's parents and is greeted with tears
because, unknown to the agent, their son was killed on active duty a
few months earlier. Agents tend to be skeptical of those outside the
Bureau who seek to befriend them; as often as not, these people may
have an ulterior motive for wanting to get to know someone in the
FBI. Most agents, in fact, are distrustful of outsiders and are inclined
to stick together, finding their friends mostly among their colleagues.

The best job in the FBI, in the view of most veterans, is that of
the special-agent-in-charge. Many aspire to it and spend twenty or
twenty-five years of their Bureau career trying to reach that point;
once they have attained it, they may hold on doggedly and resist all
pressures and temptations to return to headquarters even as an assistant director. Those who yield to that pressure and give up a comfortable spot in the field to join the rat race at headquarters may live to
regret it, or even request transfer back to the field.

The SAC is ruler in his own realm. Even within the context of the
countless rules and regulations prevailing at any given time, he can
shape a field office according to his own style and his perceptions of
how its workload can best be organized and handled. He may choose
to be a tyrant or a teacher, frightening his agents into submission and
efficiency or training them to perform intelligently, or some of each,
but the choice is largely his. He can leave his door open or closed,
encouraging agents and clerks to bring their ideas and gripes directly
to him for discussion or requiring them to work through their super-

visors at all times. There may have to be adjustments from time to time to satisfy headquarters or the inspectors, but he can decide for himself where to put his most effective manpower. Through the use of his discretionary fund, he is free to determine which informants will be cultivated most aggressively. "I'm the one who actually controls people and priorities," said one special-agent-in-charge known for his strong-headedness, even defiance; "we don't neglect anything. They can cry back at headquarters, but we must interpret those cries." The old Bureau view that every field office is the same and must be run in a standard manner is "a lot of crap," he says. "You must have a necessary degree of uniformity, of course, but individuality and individualism are a source of strength for the Bureau." As for headquarters, "I never call them; I let them call me." The SAC may also encourage individuality among his agents, or he may supplement the Bureau-wide regulations with his own — banning agents, as one SAC does, from sitting on top of their desks or, as others do, from congregating in certain bars and night spots near the office after work. He may establish an atmosphere of joviality and looseness in the office, or he may insist upon sobriety and seriousness; he may know many of the agents well, especially in a small office, or hardly at all. He may see himself as a camp counselor, an administrator, or an activist, or as a combination of them all. But he is very much in charge, and except in a few cases there is little ambiguity about his authority over day-to-day operations.

At the same time, the special-agent-in-charge is a symbol, the supercop, the official embodiment of an organization that is widely considered to be the elite of law enforcement. To this day he is required, whenever possible, to lead all raids in search of someone on the Ten Most Wanted list and to be present during any other highly dangerous situation (a rule designed by Hoover to prevent SACs from arbitrarily sending their men into circumstances where they would not themselves be willing to venture). He must be able to negotiate, perhaps by loudspeaker and perhaps on live television, with an escaped prisoner who has taken a family hostage or with an airplane hijacker threatening to blow up all his captives. He must have the capacity to take command in a crisis and work well not only with his own lieges, but also with members of other agencies who are on the scene; in such situations, he must not control matters to the point of offending others, yet he has to be able to convince the Bureau that he was in charge, not some lowly chief of police. He should be able in his statements to sound a credible alarm about crime locally and nationally and be convincing about the FBI's commitment to do something about it.

He is also a public relations man and promoter who is supposed to be able to talk about the FBI and its responsibilities to everyone from the city fathers to grammar school children. Headquarters expects the special-agent-in-charge to keep his field office well wired with the local political establishment, whoever is in power, and to build proper contacts in the commercial, professional, and educational communities. Among the other people the SAC may cultivate are newspaper editors and reporters, hotel managers, sports stars and entrepreneurs, real estate developers, and religious leaders. He must have appropriate ties or access also to the social and cultural aristocracy, members of whose families may be kidnapped or whose help may be sought at unpredictable moments. Depending upon the size of the city, his own social obligations may be considerable, requiring him to be welcome at exclusive clubs and to attend some of the best-publicized community functions. Almost in a parallel to the American diplomatic corps, this once meant that an SAC, in order to travel in the necessary circles, either had to be wealthy in his own right (some still are) or to accept quite a few "freebies" — free tickets, memberships, meals; special discounts on merchandise; gifts; and other attentions that seemed fitting for men of their esteemed rank and station. Although the salaries have improved considerably over the years — SACs were frozen at a top salary of $36,000 for several years, but then were included in a cost-of-living pay increase voted by Congress in 1975 for the highest-ranking federal employees — the custom of accepting favors to ease the way lingered on, and the Bureau, despite its myriad rules, has apparently never issued policy guidelines for the special-agents-in-charge to follow. It is considered imperative, in any event, that the SAC establish himself as an important person in the community, someone not to be trifled with and someone to be trusted.

This combination of roles has traditionally made it possible, especially in smaller or medium-sized communities, for any special-agent-in-charge to retire in his last city of assignment and find an excellent job. His experience is considered relevant to almost any executive function, and he can move on to banks, airlines, and other important businesses. Except that he is no longer required to report to Washington, his life-style may change hardly at all.

◆

Among the people who have come and gone as special-agents-in-charge over the years, some stand out as exemplary leaders and others as ruthless and difficult despots. Still another category includes the bizarre characters who, by chance or with the help of champions, work their way into special niches where they are not so much forces for good or bad as sources of amusement.

Two SACs of recent years who are frequently included on lists of the most unpopular among the agent force are Wesley G. Grapp and Joseph F. Santoiana, Jr., both now retired. Grapp was the classic example of the regional empire-builder who gained great authority and independence under Hoover over the years. According to those who worked closely with him, he believed that no one but the Director had the right to give him orders or even suggestions; he was known to tell off assistant directors on the telephone whenever they tried. One of the reasons Grapp, who wound up in charge of the prestigious Los Angeles Field Office, did so well with Hoover was apparently that he took seriously as one of the responsibilities of the SAC the duty to send the Director a steady supply of juicy gossip about politicians and other prominent citizens. A federal judge recalls sitting next to Grapp at a judicial conference dinner in Portland, Oregon, and mentioning in the course of conversation that he felt sorry for the state's governor because his son had a drug problem; Grapp's reaction was to take out his notebook, write down what he considered a tip, and say, "We'll have to look into that." Grapp was a merciless disciplinarian of agents. One told of being punished for taking his suit coat off at a field office dance and refusing to put it back on at Grapp's suggestion. Agents in the Los Angeles Field Office who grew moustaches while Grapp was in charge were helped to mend their ways by being sent on long road trips into desert territory in the summertime in cars with no air-conditioning. There were frequent allegations of improprieties on Grapp's part — the acceptance of very large favors and special deals from people who might have occasion to want something specific from the Bureau in return — but these were usually brushed off as inconsequential — until he was found to be taking out unsecured loans in Los Angeles on the strength of his title and position, which upset headquarters. When Grapp installed special electronic equipment in his personal office to record his conversations with agents and others, his luck ran out. Acting Director L. Patrick Gray III first ordered him demoted from SAC in Los Angeles to El Paso, and then he magnified the punishment to make him a street agent in Minneapolis. Grapp resigned rather than accept the humiliation.

When Joseph Santoiana retired at the end of June 1973, after thirty-three years in the Bureau, he had been a special-agent-in-charge of various offices from one end of the country to the other for twenty-three years, the last thirteen of them in a new office he was responsible for opening, Tampa. Santoiana, all work and no play, was a stickler for detail and the kind of administrator who tried to make it a point to be familiar with the intricacies of every single case under his jurisdiction. Because of his thoroughness and his demanding nature, Tampa came to be regarded as a good place to break in. To be the son of an assistant director sent to Santoiana for first-office training, as many were, was one thing; but to go as just any agent was quite another. As some of the veterans of his reign in Tampa tell it, he treated ordinary agents as slaves, and on at least one notorious occasion, as the time for the annual inspection approached, he required some idle agents to wash the office walls. Santoiana also apparently developed an intricate network of unofficial informants within the office, who would report to him regularly on what the agents were saying and doing; he was not one to tolerate disrespect or insubordination. He enforced such rules as the one that required every agent to call in and advise the field office of his whereabouts every two hours, even on weekends and when off duty. "I believe in a certain amount of discipline," Santoiana acknowledged in an interview after his retirement at the office of a Tampa real estate development corporation for which he had become director of security; "but then I grew up under Mr. Hoover, and I also had firm discipline at home."

One of the legendary characters of recent FBI and SAC history is John Francis Malone. Once a fraud investigator for the Scranton regional office of the Pennsylvania Department of Public Assistance, he worked his way up to become head of the Bureau's largest field office and its chief spokesman in New York. Malone believes fervently in the FBI, its merits and its mission. An early experience convinced him that it was better than most places to work. At the start of World War II he tried desperately to find a good job that would permit him to wear a uniform. Answering an advertisement in the *New York Times* seeking men with interviewing experience to help the navy debrief pilots returning from bombing missions, he easily passed the test; but then because the job required that one be commissioned as an officer, he was told that the "facts of life" were that he would have to "know somebody" in order to get the position. Discouraged, he returned to Scranton and contacted a friend in the FBI who had been encouraging him to apply; he found that the Bureau was willing to consider him purely on the basis of his credentials, including the fact that he spoke several foreign languages. Despite his worry that it might look as if he were trying to evade the draft, he became a G-man and very much acted the part. Brash of manner and loud of voice, Malone never was noted for the calm and deliberate calculation of alternatives. He barged in, gun drawn, and always emerged the master of the situation.

His colleagues, and eventually his subordinates, nicknamed him "Cementhead," but he won one commendation after another.

Malone freely admits that his rapid progress through the ranks — SAC in San Diego, Louisville, Chicago, Los Angeles, assistant-director-in-charge of the Training and Inspection Division, and then assistant-director-in-charge of the New York Field Office — was related to his personal closeness to Hoover, whom he cultivated especially during the Director's visits to the West Coast.* At the Director's behest, while in Los Angeles, Malone developed a friendship with bandleader Lawrence Welk. Malone firmly believes that Hoover had powers of foresight and that "things always worked out the way he predicted." He was a determined and unquestioning enforcer of any policy established or whim dictated by the Director, and that loyalty was rewarded by Malone's service as an honorary pallbearer at Hoover's funeral, which was held on the very day when the Director had been scheduled personally to present Malone with his thirty-year service pin. When Malone retired in early 1975, Clarence Kelley attended a dinner in New York honoring him.

Malone never had an easy time with names, and that problem became even more complicated when he took over the New York office. It has nearly a thousand agents, and they learned to answer to any name he called them. But Malone kept an index with the photographs and backgrounds of all the agents who ever served under him in the New York Field Office and from time to time he studied those of the people he expected to be seeing. The agents respected him for trying and for still getting down on the firing line with them despite his lofty position. ("I never missed a hijacking," boasts Malone.) Still, he was often suspicious of agents' motives and instincts and acted, as one veteran of service under Malone put it, "like a schoolmaster of a school for bad boys." One of Malone's admirers asserts that "the best thing about him was that he did not become a sophisticated New Yorker. He still had plenty of rough edges, and that's good."

Another special-agent-in-charge who owed his success more to his closeness with Hoover and Associate Director Clyde Tolson than to

* There is, however, another explanation for Malone's success. One story has it that while ASAC of the Cleveland office, Malone paid a routine courtesy call on Hoover and after the session the Director wrote on his file, "Why is this man still an ASAC?" Hoover meant that Malone should be demoted, according to the story, but the Administrative Division misunderstood and immediately promoted him to SAC. Also, while Malone's dispatch to New York as an assistant director in 1962 was billed as a great compliment (reviving a job title that had been retired when the man holding it died in a plane crash on a secret mission in World War II), some contend that it was really meant as a way to get Malone out of Washington without hurting his feelings.

any demonstrated competence was Paul Young, who declares in the first few moments with a visitor that "Mr. Hoover was the greatest living American of our time." Young's climb up the administrative ladder was not all that fast. As a nonoutdoorsman he was miserable during a three-and-a-half-year stint as assistant-special-agent-in-charge in Butte, where, as he tells it, his wife used to pray for a transfer. Finally he got out, after suggesting to the Director that he was "being overtrained in a small office." (Later he told Hoover that he supposed his wife had "prayed to the wrong guy" and the Director apparently enjoyed the joke.) But then Young spent nearly three years traveling as an inspector, which is believed to be something of a record for the modern Bureau, before being assigned his own office as SAC. After several years in Omaha, he was transferred to Kansas City, where his management method included a warning to agents that he did not want to be bothered with the details of most cases. Under Young, agents often seemed to get away with violating the rules because of his loose control, but he did expect them to perform certain personal services for him. Some agents, for example, were required to spend weekends transporting large rocks to his home, where he built a Japanese garden in the backyard, which was later featured in *The Investigator*.

Young behaved clumsily when Clarence M. Kelley was named FBI director while serving as chief of the Kansas City Police Department. Kelley was a former SAC himself, and thus would ordinarily have been entitled to special courtesies from the Bureau, but Young did not like him and treated him unpleasantly and sometimes abusively. At a dinner attended by Kelley shortly after his appointment, Young came right out and said during a toast that "never in my wildest dreams did I imagine" that the police chief would become his new boss. A constant thorn in Kelley's side whenever the new director returned home to Kansas City, Young was finally transferred to the Sacramento office in early 1975.

Some SACS who are not well liked or respected may become the brunt of nasty practical jokes by agents. Frank V. Hitt, for example, was especially unpopular while assigned to the Atlanta and New York offices. Agents sometimes ordered pizzas delivered to him and referred to his telephone extension at the office or his home phone many of the "nut calls," including the old reliables from people who claimed they were intercepting enemy messages through the fillings in their teeth.

The special-agents-in-charge most universally preferred and admired by the agents who worked under them in recent years were Charles Bates, Richard Held, and Roy K. Moore. (Bates served in

The SACs: Agents often point to three men as the prototypes of the special-agent-in-charge of an FBI field office — Richard Held, Roy K. Moore, and Charles W. Bates.

FBI

F

Richard Held

Roy K. Moore

Held, who at sixty-six was the oldest SAC in the Bureau in 1975, served for years in Minneapolis and then was transferred to Chicago; a longtime friend of Clarence M. Kelley, he was credited with presenting the new director with the views and attitudes of the average street agent. Moore had his ups and downs with Hoover, but was given the sensitive task in 1964 of reopening the FBI's Jackson, Mississippi, Field Office in the midst of the civil rights crisis; he investigated both

Charles W. Bates

the Ku Klux Klan and civil rights groups with vigor and eventually came to be respected in Mississippi. Bates was one of Hoover's favorites and spent several years as the chief FBI attaché in London; after a string of SAC assignments he served as assistant director for the General Investigative Division, but became something of a hero for requesting reassignment to the field in the midst of the Watergate affair.

Omaha, Cleveland, Chicago, and San Francisco; Held in Minneapolis and Chicago; Moore in Little Rock, Jackson, and Chicago.) They were favored by Hoover, yet did not become total sycophants. All were praised as "stand-up guys" who defended agents rather than making them scapegoats when something went wrong or when an inspector appeared to be harassing them. They resisted unreasonable orders and interference in cases from headquarters, and looked the other way if agents had to violate some minor rules in order to get a particular job done. They also saw to it that their agents got letters of commendation and incentive awards when they performed well. Agents who worked for them or come with their recommendation are likely to be better received and given better assignments than others when they are transferred to a new office. Each of the three SACs managed to build up some of the best outside contacts in the Bureau without making agents feel that they were neglecting day-to-day operations in the office. Held became close to the Democratic political establishment in Minnesota headed by Senator Hubert Humphrey, and in Chicago he managed a delicate liaison with Mayor Richard J. Daley despite Bureau investigations of the mayor's closest aides. Bates, something of a hero for asking to return to San Francisco after serving as assistant director for the General Investigative Division, was admired by many for his blunt remarks both within the Bureau and outside it and for his willingness to hear out any agent or clerk who wanted to see him. To have worked with Moore on one of many "specials" he managed around the country before his retirement at the end of 1974 is considered a badge of honor by most agents. Held, one of the tallest men ever to serve in the FBI, is an accomplished raconteur who can make any audience laugh, and Bates and Moore were in demand as public speakers; all had superb contacts in the press.

But the average special-agent-in-charge is neither a fool nor a genius nor a unique character. He has gotten where he is through some combination of unspectacular plodding and careful plotting, moving his family without protest wherever the Bureau wanted to send him. He has learned over the years to be careful about committing himself too quickly on any subject, lest it become an unpopular position, and he participates in a sort of underground communication network among SACs, who feel they have to defend themselves against the schemes and machinations at headquarters. After a time, many seem to abandon the pretense of great accomplishments and just try to avoid rocking the boat until they can retire comfortably. The Bureau's "career development program" has a certain homogenizing effect, and those who rise to the top, even in the field, are often the least controversial rather than the best people available. Kelley, upon taking over the FBI, appears to have been disappointed by the number of generally competent, but essentially lackluster, SACs he inherited, but it takes several years, perhaps a decade, for any significant change to occur in their ranks. Those he named himself were almost impossible to tell apart from the men they succeeded; they were, for the most part, unexceptional. Chances are that competition for the position of SAC will increase, however, for they are bound to gain even more independence when the Bureau reforms itself.

The fifty-nine field offices are in effect the Bureau's state or regional capitals. Scattered between them, and under their jurisdiction, are 516 smaller subsidiary offices, called resident agencies (RAs), where a total of 2,243 agents are assigned. J. Edgar Hoover was suspicious and distrustful of the resident agencies, which he referred to as "a necessary evil" — necessary because most field offices' geographical territories were too large to be covered out of a single location, but evil because they were too far out of headquarters' reach, too difficult to control and supervise reliably. That is apparently why he required daily time reports on which every agent assigned to an RA was expected to list exactly how he spent every hour (a requirement that was abolished shortly after the Director's death). But the characteristics that Hoover considered disadvantages are the same ones that have long attracted some of the most dedicated agents in the Bureau to seek assignment to a resident agency, and then to stay there as long as possible.

From Bangor, Maine, to Key West, Florida, and Fairbanks, Alaska, to Brownsville, Texas, the resident agencies are generally relaxed offices where agents come and go as they please or as their workload dictates. The largest RA, in Oakland, California, is staffed by about thirty-five agents; many are staffed by only one agent. They do not worry particularly about what they are wearing at any given moment, where their Bureau car is parked (in many RAs agents are allowed to take the cars home without special permission), or exactly how much time they take off for lunch. They may have more contact and communication with local law enforcement officers and community leaders than with Bureau officials and, especially in small towns, it is likely that the agents themselves, rather than people with titles back in Washington, will shape the image and reputation of the FBI among the majority of the local people. Within the framework of assignments from

209

the field office to which they report, resident agents are largely able to set their own investigative priorities and to use whatever techniques they have found to be most successful.

The assignment of agents to the resident agencies is in the hands of the special-agent-in-charge of each field office, although any appointment must be officially confirmed by the Administrative Division at headquarters. The philosophy of the assignments differs from one office to another; whereas some SACs assign the maximum possible number of young agents to resident agencies on the theory that it is the best training experience possible, many also reserve certain less desirable RA posts as a means for sending agents who are out of favor into exile. In any event, older agents who are happy with their resident agency slots and have been there for years (a few as long as thirty years) seem to be able to hold on to them under one SAC after another, perhaps through friends back at headquarters. Some are so well entrenched after decades in the same place that it would be foolish, from the Bureau's point of view, to move them.

The resident agency map (see endpapers) shows that the distribution of these offices corresponds roughly to the density of the population across the country. Every state capital that does not have a full-fledged field office has an RA for federal-state law enforcement liaison purposes, and there are also offices strung along the busy international borders and coastal areas. Field offices that cover vast empty spaces, like Las Vegas, El Paso, and Salt Lake City, have only a few resident agencies and make up for any lack of geographical coverage with old-fashioned agent "road trips," in which agents cover accumulated leads on various cases in one town and then move on to the next. Other offices have the majority of their agent force dispersed in the RAs. Some, like Minneapolis and Kansas City, have to rely on complicated relay systems for radio contact with their farthest resident agencies, which may be hundreds of miles away. A number of resident agencies — in Eureka, California; Naples, Florida; Culpeper, Virginia; and Bemidji, Minnesota, among others — have remained or become one-man operations where the agent must recruit a local sheriff's deputy or policeman to come along on any arrest; several of the one-man RAs are run out of the agent's home rather than from any actual office space. A few RAs, on the other hand, such as the one in Oakland, have become as large as the smallest field offices. There is now a resident agency at or near most major airports in the country, but Hoover, in a classic overreaction, closed 103 small offices after the 1971 raid on the RA in Media, Pennsylvania. (Some of these were closed for other reasons, and many later reopened.)

Each agent assigned to a resident agency reports officially to a squad in the parent field office, and it is from that squad that he gets his formal case assignments. Theoretically, then, everyone in an RA may be responsible to a different person back in the "headquarters city" of the "field division." In practice, however, there is a good deal of shuffling around of assignments, and any urgent matter is likely to be handled by whoever is available in the resident agency at the moment it arises; thus, most agents end up working for several different squads and supervisors — an advantage for newer agents who have not yet had occasion to develop a specialty. The senior resident agent (SRA)* has no formal authority over the others assigned to the office, only responsibility for matters of administration and coordination. Depending upon his experience and personality, however, he may be regarded as a sort of "boss" and exert considerable influence over the others. In recent years, the senior agent in any resident agency with more than eight agents has been entitled to a higher pay grade than the others and he is responsible for supervising the clerical personnel recently assigned to the RAs.

The first thing that usually strikes a visitor to a resident agency is the pervasive atmosphere of informality. When a witness to a crime comes in to file a complaint or discuss a case, rather than being hustled off to a small interview room and dealt with hastily and perfunctorily, he may be ushered into the midst of the office, made comfortable with a cup of coffee, and encouraged to tell his story to a small audience of interested listeners, all of the agents who happen to be in the office at the time. On a typical day in a small southern resident agency, the cashier from a neighborhood grocery store that had been robbed of money orders† came in to be shown photographs of suspects in the case. The agent handling the matter gave the woman plenty of time to talk about how scared she had been during the robbery and then, to the woman's relief, told her that the person whose photograph she had identified had been arrested in Birmingham, Alabama, after trying to spend some of the stolen money orders. The agent laughed along while the woman described being teased about getting a phone message from the FBI and then listened with fascination as she told an old wives' tale that had it that her birthmarks resulted from the fact that her mother had been frightened while pregnant with her. With no one

* The position of SRA is based solely on length of service in the Bureau, so that a new man may arrive in a resident agency but still have seniority over someone already there.
† The theft of the money orders, which came from out of state, rendered an ordinary robbery into a federal case, classified by the Bureau as interstate transportation of stolen property (ITSP) or theft from an interstate shipment (TFIS).

looking over their shoulders or second-guessing them, the agents assigned to RAs have time for that kind of casualness.

But it is the comfortableness and acceptance in a community that seem to appeal most to many of the devotees of resident agencies. One agent, working as a Bureau supervisor in Washington, spoke wistfully of his years as "Mr. Law Enforcement" in the small resident agency in Gallup, New Mexico. "You may be twenty-eight or twenty-nine when you get an assignment like that," he said, "but suddenly you find law enforcement officers with fifteen years' experience asking your advice about important matters. . . . They may ask about local arrest problems, where the FBI has no jurisdiction at all, but they expect you to help, and you do." He also recalled some of the unofficial gestures resident agents find themselves performing, such as giving money for food to the wife and children of a man arrested and jailed for taking a stolen car across state lines (only to have the wife spit in his face later out of anger over her husband's arrest). It was an exciting, if exhausting, responsibility, he said, to be called to the scene of small-town emergencies in the middle of the night and to be making decisions as the only federal officer around. After being so seemingly important in Gallup, he pointed out, it was "a very humbling experience"— although an official promotion — to be called back to headquarters as one of hundreds of agents shuffling papers.

Another agent, assigned for several years to the resident agency in Santa Maria, California, fondly remembered his work there, which involved a great deal of driving around San Luis Obispo County in search of fugitives, parole violators, deserters, and Selective Service defaulters. There was an advantage, he explained, to the fact that one agent, himself, was regularly in contact with "my sheriff, my Selective Service girl, and my magistrate" — so that they came to know each other well and to work closely together. They apparently respected his performance and fully cooperated with him. The agent also came to know the people of "his" county, and the longer he stayed, the more that helped him on cases. He became a master at reassuring parents that it was the best thing for their sons who had deserted to be returned to the military and at not taking their anger personally. In both the deserter and draft cases, he said, "you had to be sensitive in handling the situation; you have to sell yourself. . . . You can generally be logical with the father. He understands. . . . You have to explain to the people what's going to happen, help them understand the procedure and that their son won't even necessarily spend the night in jail." It was with some regret that he accepted his transfer to the parent field office in Los Angeles, but he felt he could now do a better job all around as a result of his experience in the resident agency.

Even in larger cities with resident agencies, agents may become particularly well known and entrenched. After Bradner Riggs had served in Rockford, Illinois (now that state's second largest city), for sixteen years, the fact of his retirement from the Bureau and his acceptance of a job as a prosecutor in the state's attorney's office was a major news item in the local newspaper and on two television stations. When he walked along the main streets of town, he was stopped by well-wishers from the local business and professional communities. Riggs had had mixed feelings about his transfer from the Chicago Field Office to the Rockford Resident Agency when he went there in 1958. He got to see his young children far more often than he had before because his hours were better and more flexible; but at the same time he switched from handling assignments on the "major case squad," which dealt with "some of the best thieves in the country," to being preoccupied with matters of such import as "a seventeen-year-old kid who stole a car and took it across the state line to Beloit," Wisconsin. After a few years, however, when the Chicago Field Office suddenly became aware of the existence of a Mafia "family" in Rockford, Riggs was authorized to spend all of his time investigating its members. That he did for ten years, with considerable success, until he retired at age fifty.

Why would a man from New Jersey who had traveled widely in the Bureau decide to retire and settle in northern Illinois and start up a new job there? Because, as a resident agent, "I made more friends here than anywhere else at any time. It is home for my kids." Riggs became involved as a leader for a local Boy Scout troop and joined the county bar association, serving on its civil rights and federal courts committees. He helped write the constitution for the new parish council of St. Peter's Catholic Church and his son became a basketball star at a local high school. There were a few awkward moments, such as when some of the people he was investigating also turned up helping with the Boy Scout troop and his wife found herself serving at a church dinner after the funeral of a Mafioso. But with Riggs's contacts, together with those of the other agents assigned to the office, the Rockford Resident Agency had an enviable range of sources of information. In an RA, it is particularly easy to get confidential material from friends and never have to explain to higher authorities in the Bureau exactly where it came from.

The Rockford office is definitely more effective as a result of the longevity of service, insisted one of Riggs's colleagues, Jerome Nolan, who has been in the RA and the Bureau even longer than Riggs and has been senior resident agent in Rockford for almost the whole time. "We have better sources. People tend to trust you more when you have been around for a long time," he says. As for how he had manged to stay in Rockford for seventeen of his twenty-three years in the FBI, Nolan said, "I was lucky, just plain lucky. I was fortunate not to have stubbed my toes or made any booboos that would have had me transferred away." That was more than could be said for Nolan's predecessor as senior resident agent, who once lost his FBI credentials and, out of fear, failed to report that fact to the Bureau until substantial time had passed; he was severely punished. Unlike many people in the FBI, Nolan had no desire to travel or advance. "The oldest of our five children was nine when we came here. It was nice to buy a house and settle down; you like to claim some place as home. Chicago has been my office of preference since 1953." Riggs, for his part, had only listed Chicago recently; he had a long-standing desire to be assigned to the FBI office in London. But the special-agent-in-charge in Chicago advised him at one point that he simply did not "have enough clout back at the Bureau" to get that post.

In smaller towns, the FBI contingent is often watched by the community for the trends it sets or the attitudes it signals. Progressive white parents in Greenville, Mississippi, for example, who were struggling to show that their public schools could be successfully integrated, were angered when the senior resident agent there took his children out of the public school and sent them to a segregated private academy. Greenville is one resident agency among many where the several agents assigned are not especially close friends; they have perfectly cordial relations in the office but see each other only seldom otherwise. But there are RAs where closeness and fellowship are cited as one of the most important advantages, where those who are assigned together form a bond that lasts throughout their Bureau careers. In Lakeland, Florida, for example, where most of the agents are within a close age span, they gather socially at each other's homes; the working relationships and friendships both seem to be very strong.

The resident agency in Barstow, California, is a particularly graphic example of a small office that is busy, successful, and extraordinarily well entrenched in the community. Located at the junction of two major interstate highways and old U.S. Route 66, Barstow is a dreary desert town of 18,000 people about one hundred and fifty miles northeast of Los Angeles. As Senior Resident Agent Mal Wessel puts it, "If you're going to steal anything in St. Louis, Las Vegas or Denver and head to southern California with it, you're going to come through

Barstow." That distinction means there is an unusually large contingent of the California Highway Patrol and an important substation of the San Bernardino County Sheriff's Office in the vicinity — poised to pick up stolen cars, often driven by fugitives from justice, like butterflies in a net. The official policy change deemphasizing the prosecution of individual stolen car cases under the Dyer Act may be fully implemented in other FBI offices, but in Barstow that would be like a shopkeeper sending away customers. Each time a possible stolen car is located in the area (often after being stopped on a routine speeding or other traffic violation), the resident agency is alerted. If a search of the car reveals anything suspicious, or a check with the National Crime Information Center computer indicates that the car, its occupants, and any weapons or merchandise found in it are involved in some other pending out-of-state case, one or two of the three agents assigned to Barstow will participate in the questioning of the people and the investigation. Predictably, many pending cases from around the country are solved that way — with only minimal exertion by the agents, although admittedly at all hours — and the statistics credited to the Barstow Resident Agency are among the best in the Bureau.

Mal Wessel is a small, frantic man with a strong personality, who takes his role as the senior agent in the office very seriously indeed. He is also a veteran of resident agencies. Having served in Billings, Montana (out of the Butte Field Office), and Wausau, Wisconsin (out of the Milwaukee Field Office), previously, when he was transferred to Los Angeles in the early 1960s, he looked around immediately for a small RA with an opening. Barstow filled the bill. "I wanted to bring the kids to a small town and let them have the advantage of that atmosphere," he explains; "besides, the desert is an intriguing place. . . . It is also noted for its educational system; the teachers are paid well to come here, and they are good." The two younger men assigned here with him, Al McElwain and Tom Farris, have also come and stayed by choice. McElwain, who would choose to leave Barstow only for Montana, Utah, or the Pacific Northwest, explains that after an earlier assignment in St. Louis he was delighted to "get away from the turmoil of big cities." Farris, for his part, was pleased to get the RA slot after two years working on bank robbery cases in "the crush and the smog" of Los Angeles.

All three men are involved in the community, attending high school football and basketball games ("We don't get to see the Los Angeles Rams very often, but we are big on the Barstow Riffians") and working on church councils and parent-teacher associations. They are much in demand as luncheon speakers to Rotary and other service clubs in the area and participate in "career day" at the high school, as well as lecturing occasionally at a nearby junior college. Like most resident agents, they may be called upon to become instant experts on some subject under Bureau jurisdiction and teach a class about it to the local police department. "Every time we get a chance to go out and talk about the FBI, we do it," says Wessel; "it makes you known. . . . When we are involved in the booster club for a school team that hasn't won a game, that's good, too. It may make new friends for the FBI — and for law enforcement in general. You have to let them know that you're just human."

Because of this community involvement and recognition, cases tend to fall into the RA's lap. "People just call up and say they want to talk to you about something important," says Wessel. One man, for example, reported that his son had stolen a pair of expensive binoculars from a nearby marine base (an FBI case because it is "crime on a military reservation"). The resident agency was able to "help" the man, Wessel says, by "getting his son convicted, put on probation, and back in school, having him go to a mental health clinic and getting him involved in church activities." The agents recommended probation for a local Selective Service violator and then helped him apply for a job with VISTA; his grateful mother sent them a Christmas card. In another case, a woman came to the agents complaining that her husband had a drug problem and was stealing materials from a local government installation where he had a security clearance. He lost that clearance, but not the job, after being convicted and sentenced to probation; the agents found psychological counseling for both husband and wife and credit themselves with helping "put a family back together." As Wessel puts it, "You just can't help solving some personal and community problems in the course of your work."

Relations with local law enforcement groups are exemplary in Barstow. The FBI rotates with other agencies from the area as the host for a monthly "law enforcement breakfast"; the resident agency has also thrown picnics and barbeques, at the agents' personal expense, for the police officers they work with, sometimes luring one of the executives out from the Los Angeles Field Office for the day. If something important happens while the agents are out of their office, they can usually count on the Highway Patrol or Sheriff's Office to track them down — a task made easier by the fact that both agencies' radio channels are monitored in the Bureau cars, which is standard procedure in most offices. Even when just going out to lunch (perhaps at the local restaurant where Wessel's daughter works part-time), they will report their whereabouts to the Highway Patrol or Sheriff's Office. Wessel insists that "there is never a problem here over who gets the credit" for solving a case; "we always say that it was a classic example of cooperation between local and federal officers."

But perhaps the most important ties of the resident agency are with the part-time U.S. magistrate in Barstow, Conrad Mahlum. Also serving as city attorney and counsel for the local housing redevelopment authority, as well as handling his own cases in a private civil law practice, Mahlum owns the building — just behind his own offices — where the U.S. General Services Administration rents the second-floor office space for the resident agency. (In fact, the offices were designed to FBI specifications under Wessel's predecessor as senior resident agent.) Mahlum is empowered to handle the preliminary proceedings of all cases and the full trial of misdemeanors. After more than ten years in his position, he has established a fairly reliable pattern: most cases are brought in as or reduced to misdemeanors, and most of them are resolved with guilty pleas, fines, and short or suspended jail sentences. Defense attorneys are appointed in rotation from a list of about half a dozen local lawyers, but the prosecution is usually represented only by the Bureau, on the authority of the U.S. attorney's office in Los Angeles (unless the charge is a fairly serious one, in which event all but the preliminaries will be delayed until an assistant United States attorney makes a trip out from Los Angeles to handle several cases at once). All formal proceedings before Mahlum are recorded on sophisticated sound equipment and are officially subject to review by the judges of the U.S. District Court in Los Angeles; but in practice he is very much on his own in dispensing desert justice.

The magistrate and the resident agents have nothing but praise for each other. Mahlum, noting that he has been a close personal friend of three consecutive senior resident agents, says, "You betcha I have respect for the work of the Bureau — not only me, but everybody else here. They do a terrific job. . . . These agents know everyone in town. They are very well respected and received, absorbed into the community." He was especially impressed when his office was fire-bombed and it took the FBI "about twenty minutes" to solve the case by arresting a man who was disgruntled over a divorce settlement. Wessel, for his part, says of Mahlum that "he'll do anything I ask," including driving to Needles, a desert town on the California-Arizona border which in the summertime is often the hottest spot in the United States, to arraign a defendant who had been injured. Mahlum finds the work interesting and important enough to do that, or even to hold court in Barstow at night, if it suits the agents' schedule. "You really get some lulus coming down the highway," says the magistrate; "we arraign them as fast as we can." Even though Mahlum sometimes lowers defendants' bail further than Wessel thinks he should, the agent approves of the magistrate's performance, including his preference for fines rather than jail sentences in many cases. "He feels the way to hurt a person is financially," says Wessel. Some court officials in Los Angeles have expressed concern over Mahlum's unusual role as land- lord, friend, and judicial officer for the FBI, but from the Bureau there have been no complaints.

All of the resident agency's work in Barstow does not involve following up on car thieves who happened to be driving ten miles over the speed limit at the wrong moment. The three men assigned there are actually responsible for a vast territory of fifteen thousand square miles, one of the largest RA jurisdictions in the continental United States (it was larger still until a piece of its territory was broken off when a new resident agency was established in Victorville), and al- though its population is only eighty thousand people, including mili- tary personnel at five separate bases, there is a wide range of crimes that invoke some of the more obscure areas of Bureau jurisdiction. They do not have to worry about bank robberies — Wessel could re- member only one in four years, in which the robber simulated a gun with a dill pickle — but they may have to hop into the RA's jeep to track down some fugitives thought to be holed up in a desert shack. Occasionally they arrest vagabonds sleeping under the wing of a dis- carded airplane and charge them with trespassing on a military reser- vation — less because that crime is taken seriously than to head off the possibility of damage suits against the federal government for negli- gence, in the event that they are shot and injured or killed by others wandering the desert. Some people have been arrested for scavenging and hoarding the thousands of brass shells to be found in the desert after target practice (theft of government property). In one instance, the air force built a full bridge in the middle of the desert for bombing practice, and overnight it was stolen and melted down; the agents tracked the culprits to a smelter at the other end of the Mojave Desert.

Some of the tiny communities in the area, where jobs are always available, have been used by fugitives seeking to pick up a new iden- tity, but the Bureau sometimes gets a tip as to their true names from a friend or relative who passes through and recognizes them or receives a letter. The town of Baker "hates to see us coming," says agent Tom Farris, "because nearly every time we take someone away with us." On occasion that has included the cook in one of Baker's few restaurants. The resident agency is also called in by the Interior Department's Bureau of Land Management whenever the ancient Indian petro-

glyphs and burial grounds along the Colorado River, officially preserved and protected by the federal government, are damaged. The
agents look for tire tracks or other evidence and, if anything was
stolen, check the art dealers in the area to see if any new suspicious-
looking material has been received. "This kind of stuff is important to
just as many people as a bank robbery," Wessel asserts. For variety,
the agents also find themselves traveling to distant cities to testify
against fugitives who were captured in connection with the stolen car
cases that make up about 25 percent of their workload.

Barstow has also had its share of dramatic incidents, including the
safe recovery of a child who had been kidnapped in New Orleans and
a bus accident that required the services of the FBI Disaster Squad to
identify some of the victims. (As it turned out, a federal fugitive on
the bus rescued some of the injured and became the hero of the day.)
And there have even been leads to follow up as part of the FBI
background investigation of important presidential appointees.

Inevitably, in a town as small as Barstow, FBI agents find themselves investigating people with whom they have had other dealings,
and even the relatives of their children's friends. "I arrested one guy a
while back," says Al McElwain, "and I got a notice the other day that
he's now my insurance agent." A leader in one local church turned out
to be involved in a veterans' fraud and was placed on probation provided he make restitution of the money. A prominent restaurant owner
was found to be buying stolen meat, and the son of a local banker,
neighbor of one of the agents, was charged with interstate theft. The
resident agents also investigated three members of the local police
force with whom they had worked, including the assistant chief, for
accepting money from a federal grant for classes they never attended.
But the agents insist that they are not troubled by such circumstances,
that they are able to do their job well even when they have had other
connections with the offenders. As Wessel puts it, "the three hardest
words to say in the English language are 'You're under arrest' — no
matter who you have to say them to."

The three agents assigned to Barstow have occasion to make the
trip to the field office in Los Angeles only about once a month each, for
the purpose of reviewing files and dictating memoranda in connection
with pending cases. They feel even more distant than their hundred
and fifty miles from the hustle and excitement and corporate-style
organization of the office; the longer they stay in Barstow, the fewer
people they know at the field office and the less they seem to care
about the office grapevine gossip. Occasionally a member of an inspection team reviewing the Los Angeles office will come out for a look at

the RA, or one of the special-agents-in-charge will drop in (especially if he is en route to a weekend in Las Vegas), and the office will be polished up for the event. But the actual supervision from the field office is minimal, especially in a resident agency like Barstow where at least one of the agents has been on the scene for a long time and is a particular expert on the RA's special needs and responsibilities. The only trouble Wessel could recall during the reign of the unpopular Wesley Grapp as SAC in Los Angeles was that, after one visit, Grapp left a note saying the office needed a new toilet seat.

Similarly, the resident agents in Barstow feel far removed from the influence and demands of FBI headquarters in Washington, even more so than in field offices, which, however many miles away they may be, still have regular daily contact with "the Bureau." They avidly read *The Investigator*, the monthly publication of the FBI Recreation Association, to catch up on news about friends, retirements, and other offices. Each enjoys getting a letter from the director on a happy occasion such as the birth of a child. But they say that they do not even know the names of the Bureau's assistant directors at any given time, and they insist that the shifts and changes at headquarters after Hoover's death, the turmoil over Watergate and the resignation of Acting Director L. Patrick Gray III, had absolutely no effect at their level. The local image and reputation of the FBI is based more on their own actions than on any people or events in Washington, they contend, and they believe that will remain true almost no matter who is running the Bureau. Wessel, in fact, says that but for a few administrative matters like the abandonment of the required daily time report, his work has not really changed since he first went to work in the resident agency in Billings, Montana, in Hoover's heyday. As for things like the liberalization of dress regulations, he says he has always worn what was appropriate and customary in the area where he worked, "remembering that when I walk into a room, I represent the FBI."

Like field offices in general, the resident agencies have over the years developed particular specialties that vary with their location. The agents assigned to the Berkeley, California, RA, for example, have spent almost all of their time investigating leftist political organizations, while those in Troy, Michigan, after the school bus bombing in nearby Pontiac, have become experts on the Ku Klux Klan. Certain resident agencies in Ohio are preoccupied with organized crime investigations, and in West Virginia they spend a great deal of time recruiting and investigating young clerks for FBI headquarters. Occasionally, though, even a potentially major espionage case will be worked out of a small, obscure resident agency, especially if a person suspected of being a spy lives in one of the towns it covers.

For each agent who is as happy with the resident agency life as those assigned to Rockford and Barstow, there seems to be another who suffers in the obscurity and quietude of working in a small-town RA. One young agent, a native of a large city in the Northeast, described feeling trapped in the small southern town where he was assigned. "Sometimes you feel like you're wasting your life here," he said, and as a result, he has weighed the possibility of doing something drastic — requesting a transfer to New York, which he would be almost sure to get. Responsible for covering two rural counties, he finds them "empty" and unexciting, and he thinks that he has a "puny" caseload of largely insignificant cases. After a while the agent finally joined a country club and made some friends outside the resident agency, but still he felt like a fish out of water. What makes the situation more difficult is that all but one of the other people in this resident agency feel the same way and are serving there against their will. The one who does not is the senior resident agent, for whom the others have developed a profound dislike.

In most of the resident agencies visited, however, the agents professed to be happy with their assignments and felt that they had a crack at some of the Bureau's best work with a minimum preoccupation with bureaucratic annoyances and harassment. If anything, the problem, only recently recognized, is to get them to move. There is now some concern in the Bureau that when a man has served as long as thirty or more years in one place, such as Jefferson City, Missouri, or Oakland, California, his perspective on the FBI's needs may become severely distorted and he may identify more with the community and its leaders than is healthy in a sensitive federal law enforcement position.

Officially, field office and resident agency — and even individual agent — performance is measured by that most pervasive of Bureau standards, statistics. When a fugitive is captured, a stolen car located, or a bank robbery solved, the appropriate offices and people are "credited" on the books with the accomplishment. At the same time, headquarters and the traveling inspectors also attempt to evaluate an office's intangible achievements, such as the quality of its local contacts and sources and the image that a special-agent-in-charge has cultivated.

To some extent, the offices compete with each other in these areas, and every agent has some field of endeavor in which he can claim that his office is the best or the most worthy in the Bureau. But for most, the pride takes the form of a more general feeling — a sense that an FBI field office is the best place that one could ever hope to work. One supervisor in a large field office made the point by throwing his wallet on his desk and saying, "I could leave that here overnight, even for a week or a month, and know that when I next came in, it would be sitting right there, with nothing missing."

X

The FBI Overseas

Collecting intelligence information is not our real goal overseas, it is not actually our mission . . . but we have done it for a long time now. We feel we are part of the United States government, and we want to make a contribution. . . . Why, sometime back in the fifties, our man in Rio picked up information about a coup that was coming someplace in Latin America. He sent it back to Washington, and it turned out to be the first information our government had on the subject.
— *An FBI official, discussing the Bureau's role in gathering "incidental intelligence" overseas*

THE BUILDING, ONE OF SEVERAL ANNEXES to the United States embassy, is set back about a hundred feet from a busy Paris street at the end of a courtyard behind a bank. At one suite of offices on an upper floor, people come and go frequently. The secretaries speak English with charmingly thick French accents and the rooms are brightly decorated. The agents — there are about eight of them — seem like streetwise, jovial types, not particularly self-conscious about where they are seen and what they are doing. Because of a protocol in effect for several years, they often go on joint operations with their French counterparts. The main door to the office is wide open, and anyone who has made it past the marine guard downstairs is free to wander in and out as he chooses. It is a busy and lively place, the regional headquarters for Europe and North Africa of the U.S. Drug Enforcement Administration (DEA).

A rather different situation prevails in the suite around the corner on the same floor, the office of the embassy's legal attaché. "Legal attaché" — "Legat" — is the euphemism for a representative of the Federal Bureau of Investigation. There are three sturdy locks on the entrance door, and anyone who does not have a key must be buzzed in electronically. Only two agents work here, along with three female clerical assistants; the assistants' accents are pure American because they are career employees of the FBI, specially selected and cleared for overseas service. Everything seems to have been shipped over from the States, down to the special little plastic wastebaskets with the word BURN in bright red letters. The decorations, aside from a few personal mementoes, are stark, consisting mainly of the FBI seal, pictures of Bureau facilities, and large portrait photographs of J. Edgar Hoover and Clarence M. Kelley. Except that it is so small and somber, it could be an FBI office anywhere. It is, above all, a private place, so much so that when an assistant U.S. attorney general who is passing through Paris wanders in one morning, he is not trusted to sit alone unobserved in the senior agent's office or to use the office in the agent's absence to chat privately with a visitor. For that purpose, the assistant attorney general — one who, incidentally, has a fair amount of discretion over the FBI budget — must stroll into the DEA office or down to a café in the street below.

The Legats are a peculiar and unique part of the FBI, a legacy of past bureaucratic feuds, and of dramatic wartime — and Cold War — exploits. They are expensive but efficient, no longer secret yet still somewhat mysterious, and only seldom noticed or talked about. Assignment to be one is variously regarded within the Bureau as a step up the career ladder or a soft touch, depending on whom you talk to; a means of achieving recognition or of escaping from the rat race at headquarters or in the field. In the Legats perhaps more than anywhere else in the FBI, the special agent is a combination of investigator, bureaucrat, diplomat, gumshoe, gossip, and public relations man. They number only thirty-four, assisted by forty clerks, assigned to fifteen cities — Bern, Bonn, Brasilia, Buenos Aires, Caracas, Hong Kong, London, Madrid, Manila, Mexico City, Ottawa, Paris, Rome, Tel Aviv, and Tokyo — but they play an important role. They have no authority to make an arrest overseas, only to serve as "liaison" with foreign government agencies. Whether they have the authority is questionable, but they also collect intelligence.

Many FBI agents, although they were officially exempt from the draft, took leave to join the military during World War II. But some who stayed behind did a special kind of war work, after President

Roosevelt decided in 1940 to assign jurisdiction over nonmilitary intelligence in the Western Hemisphere to the FBI. There was a large German émigré community in South America believed to be loyal to the Hitler regime, and a number of Latin American leaders were prepared, when confronted with a choice, to work diligently against American interests. The Director quickly organized a supersecret Special Intelligence Service (SIS), which he built up to a force of three hundred and sixty agents, mostly concentrated in strategically important nations like Mexico, Argentina, and Brazil.

Some of the American wartime intelligence efforts were marred by infighting with the Office of Strategic Services (OSS) headed by Hoover's enemy, William J. Donovan; at one point, Hoover and his bureaucratic ally, Assistant Secretary of State Adolph Berle, tried to require that any information passed along to the OSS by British Intelligence first be cleared through the FBI's SIS, an initiative rejected on the basis of British objections. But what the Bureau did by itself it did well, and although it never got the degree of publicity that OSS eventually did, the SIS operation enjoyed some extraordinary successes.

SIS agents usually went into Latin American countries in undercover roles, pretending to be salesmen, stockbrokers, or journalists. They tracked down secret German radio transmitters and operators, pursued illicit platinum smugglers, and planted double agents inside the Nazi courier system. Sometimes they used classic counterintelligence tricks of harassment and disruption, for example, planting useless materials in place of strategic goods that German operatives were trying to smuggle home. The SIS men became so involved with and trusted by leaders friendly to the United States that the FBI was in a position to draft decrees and other formal documents for signature by foreign governments to help punish spies and smugglers. In Argentina, which was on the brink of joining the Axis powers, they developed a virtual underground railroad to slip themselves and their helpers out of the country and across the Rio de la Plata to safer ground in Uruguay. Working with British colleagues, SIS also intervened in time to foil plans for a coup d'état intended to put a pro-Axis government into power in Bolivia.

When the war ended and President Harry S Truman established what would become the Central Intelligence Agency, Hoover lost his bid to expand his Western Hemisphere intelligence operation into one that would cover the whole world in peacetime; not even an avalanche of mail from the Bureau's friends in Latin America, undoubtedly well orchestrated, could turn the decision around. Many of the SIS agents with language and undercover skills went over to work for the CIA.

Hoover accepted his demise in the foreign intelligence field reluctantly. He did not bring everyone home, but rather kept a few people on as "liaison" officers with foreign governments, and even assigned some new ones. In addition to those in Latin America, the SIS contact men who had been assigned to London during the war stayed on, as did others in Ottawa. At General Douglas MacArthur's request, some were assigned to help the American occupation forces in Japan in 1945. It was easy enough to keep the agents busy with the complications growing out of the war and the establishment of new governments. Some of the liaison men became highly regarded members of American overseas missions, almost fixtures, whose local connections were impeccable.

There was another way in which FBI agents came to work outside the country over the years — by informally crossing the Canadian and Mexican borders. In fact, the first FBI agent officially assigned to duty outside the United States had been the special-agent-in-charge of the El Paso Field Office, sent across the Rio Grande in 1939 for intelligence purposes. Later peacetime operations there and in Canada were governed by strict guidelines hammered out to prevent the appearance of American interference with Canadian or Mexican sovereignty. The rule in the Seattle Field Office, for example, was that agents could make working trips over the border only to consult with their counterparts on cases that had Canadian ramifications, and that each visit was to last a maximum of seventy-two hours. But William W. Turner, an agent who was later forced out of the Bureau under protest and wrote a book harshly critical of Hoover and the FBI, claims that when he was assigned to Seattle, he and others in the field office were fully operational during frequent excursions into Canada. For the price of lunch, he says, it was easy to get constables from the Royal Canadian Mounted Police (RCMP), the Canadian equivalent of the FBI, or Vancouver city police officers to go along on a search for a fugitive, especially as the approach of the seventy-two-hour deadline made the agent nervous for results. On at least one occasion, Turner has alleged, the RCMP picked up a man the FBI was looking for and unofficially and unceremoniously "kicked him across the border" into the arms of waiting Bureau agents.

Another agent, still in the FBI, who worked for several years in an office near the Mexican border, says that along that frontier "you had to break the rules to do your job." The rules included strictures that an agent was not supposed to take his gun along on a trip into Mexico and he was not permitted to be present during the arrest of an American fugitive by the Mexican police. There was a firm limit of twenty-five miles south of the border on most excursions, except for certain standard exceptions like cities farther away that were known to attract fugitives. "You would try your best to respect the mileage limit," the agent recalls; as for the gun — "You put it in the trunk of the car until you got across . . . but then you would keep it close by while you watched the arrest. The Mexican officer might have maybe one bullet in his gun, and the gun might be corroded. You had to protect your-self." But he insists that "the Mexicans looked up to the Bureau. They knew that on important matters, we honestly would respect their sovereignty."

The development of easier international commercial air travel after the war made the mobility of criminals greater than ever before. That fact and the Bureau's continuing preoccupation with "security" matters dictated the need for some more formal arrangements. When the International Criminal Police Organization, popularly known as Interpol, was revived in 1946, it seemed the logical mechanism for some of the work. With Interpol building up a central data bank of criminal information at its headquarters in Paris to which tens of nations would contribute, it promised to be a valuable resource for the FBI. Initially Hoover was an enthusiastic supporter of Interpol, and he especially enjoyed the opportunity for the Bureau to contribute the tales of its most famous and successful cases to the *International Criminal Police Review*. But before long, mutual suspicions developed between the FBI and European police officials. Hoover worried that some nations, especially the communist-controlled ones that became Interpol members, would not abide by its charter's exclusion "of all matters having a political, religious or racial character"; the Europeans, for their own part, were skeptical of the Bureau's renewed postwar preoccupation with the Red menace and other antisubversive work, which in their view was "political." What is more, some American officials distrusted the French civil service, which was filling many of the administrative posts at Interpol headquarters, as corrupt, and they were concerned that the integrity of confidential information trans-mitted from Bureau files might be compromised in the Interpol net-work. Hoover abruptly withdrew the FBI from Interpol in 1950 when Czechoslovakia demanded that the organization's resources be em-ployed to hunt down ten refugees who had fled that country for West Germany on political grounds. It was the Director's evaluation, prob-ably correct at the time, that the Bureau had less to gain from Interpol than it had to give.

As other nations recognized that fact, they repeatedly appealed to the Director in the years that followed to forgive and forget the Czech incident and to rejoin the international organization. But as with most decisions he made, Hoover was adamant, and it was only in 1958 that he would even give his blessings to a plan for the Treasury Department to become an official U.S. participant in Interpol, for the benefit of its enforcement agencies, including the Secret Service; the Bureau of Customs; the Bureau of Alcohol, Tobacco and Firearms; the Internal Revenue Service; and the Federal Bureau of Narcotics, then still under Treasury's jurisdiction. (As the only American representative, Treasury would refer the requests of other agencies to Interpol.) For the rest of his days, the Director seemed to resent Interpol, especially after it held its annual meeting in Washington in 1960 and became the subject of a laudatory series on American television. On one occasion, when he met the Washington representative of Interpol at a social gathering, Hoover seemed unpredictably eager to engage him in conversation. "Where are you located?" the Director asked in a friendly tone. When the Interpol man replied that his office was in the basement of the Treasury Department, Hoover snorted, "Well, that's where you belong," and walked away.

For the Bureau's own needs, Hoover turned to the network of agents he had posted overseas, not just in Latin America, but by the end of World War II in Europe and Asia as well, with their offices in American embassies. It was an arrangement that the State Department accepted willingly, in part because it expected the Bureau to be able to take some of the less exciting and desirable work off its hands, such as dealing with American citizens arrested in foreign countries and with the families of those who died abroad. FBI officials can cite no date when the Legat system was formally launched. They say that it evolved from existing overseas offices and new interests that developed in the late 1940s and early 1950s. The title "legal attaché" had been accepted during the war, by both the State Department and some countries where agents were assigned, as an appropriate "cover," and so it was extended to the new overseas offices as a good way to keep the Bureau presence from becoming widely known. It was, after all, true that many of the agents had legal training and that they dealt with legal affairs.* At most of the foreign posts, the FBI representatives, unlike those of some law enforcement agencies, such as the

---

* The title "legal attaché" is still used for all FBI agents overseas, except in Bern, Switzerland (where the agent is merely listed as an "attaché" of the embassy), in Hong Kong (where they are called "legal liaison" officers), and in the three sub-offices in Monterrey, Hermasillo, and Guadalajara, Mexico (where they are designated "special assistant to the consul general"). The Bureau's shorthand term for all the agents and the offices where they work, however, is "Legats."

Internal Revenue Service, would have all the privileges, responsibilities, and contacts of anyone else on the Diplomatic List in that city.

Apart from those left over from their wartime duty with the SIS, the early appointees to Legat positions tended to be those who had somewhere along the line curried favor with the Director, especially if they had previously spent a year or two abroad as a student or a soldier, or had even been there on a brief special assignment, and could claim some acquaintance with the countries where they were to serve. Eventually, a strong personal relationship with Hoover became both a prerequisite and a result of Legat duty. They were special folk. Charles W. Bates, for example, later special-agent-in-charge in San Francisco, did postwar surveys for the FBI in England, Switzerland, Belgium, the Netherlands, and Norway to determine whether those nations' security systems were adequate to meet the standards for the United States to share information with them under the Atomic Energy Act; as a supervisor at Bureau headquarters handling liaison with the Atomic Energy Commission, Bates submitted his reports in this critical area directly to Hoover and impressed the Director with his qualities. He became a Legat in London. Another was Robert Kunkel, who had served as a clerk in the Director's office before he ever went into agent's training and whose standing in Hoover's eyes was later to fluctuate so abruptly. He served in England with the military during World War II and during that time studied briefly at several British universities. Some years later Kunkel landed a Legat spot in Tokyo. That was a fairly unusual assignment, since Kunkel did not speak a word of Japanese when he first arrived, and only a few at the end of his twenty-seven-month tour.

For the most part though, the Bureau eventually made it a point to assign people to the Legats who had a high proficiency in the appropriate language. In some instances they have been among the most proficient people in the embassy. Vadja V. Kolombatovic, for example, the son of a member of the old royal Yugoslav diplomatic service, passed the Bureau's fluency test in six languages besides English and was considered particularly well qualified linguistically for his assignments as a Legat in Madrid and Paris. Toby Harding, a former Mormon missionary assigned to the Bonn Legat, was comfortable enough in German to address a convention of police officers in Aachen in their own language. Once settled in overseas, most of the Legats could stay as long as they pleased, especially if they brought appropriate gifts when they came back for home leave and their special personal conferences with the Director — although there is a story about one Legat whose New England accent Hoover mistook for a British one during the man's visit from London. "Bring him back; he's gone native," the Director reportedly wrote in the agent's file.

The Legat system was initially a low-key, discreet operation. The CIA agents overseas, who often have a haughty attitude toward the Bureau anyway, were not terribly happy at first to have FBI agents on the scene, but they adjusted after a while. Besides, the FBI presence was generally quite small and frugal compared with the large staff and expenditures of what is usually called "the other agency." The two arrived at a division of responsibility abroad that was roughly parallel to the distinctions in their general mandates as government agencies. While the CIA dealt with matters of positive foreign intelligence (and, it would turn out, covert operations in other countries), the FBI was theoretically to restrict itself to criminal cases involving Americans or others resident in the United States; counterintelligence; matters concerning the internal security of the United States; and other tasks specifically assigned to it. "Our respective roles are clearly defined," says one CIA official; "there is no confusion about who does what. . . . The American citizen is not our target, our concern, or our responsibility." He adds with a smile that "our business overseas is liaison with foreign intelligence communities on information relating to foreign affairs." That distinction, of course, has been substantially blurred, especially since the CIA opened offices in several major cities within the United States. One difference is clear, however: while the CIA offices abroad have continued to conceal their agents' identities and to hide behind their cover as "special assistants to the ambassador" or members of the embassy's "political section," the designation "legal attaché" has remained a cover in name only. The FBI has given up trying to conceal or obscure its overseas presence and has, if anything, gone public.

◆

Except that he does all of his work in English, Alden C. McCray is probably a typical Legat. In London for the FBI since 1958 (after briefer stints as an agent in Cleveland, New York, and at Bureau headquarters), he has become the senior American, in years of service, in the entire United States mission to Great Britain. He owns a home in London and may know the city as well as any foreigner; his expertise is recognized both within the embassy and among British police and security officials. As John S. Wilson, deputy assistant commissioner of Scotland Yard in charge of its Criminal Investigation Department (CID), puts it, "Mack is an old hand. [The police in] every

county, every city in Britain know who he is, they are aware of him.
. . . He's got so many friends in this country that he can arrange
everything himself now; he needn't even go through the Yard." Wilson
is a particular partisan of the FBI. Whenever he has made a trip to the
United States, whether to attend a conference or to look at technical
equipment like computers, the Bureau has helped arrange his itinerary
and set up appointments with the appropriate people for him. He, in
turn, has been a prime contact for McCray and other Legats who have
admiringly watched Wilson climb through the ranks from being a
Special Branch detective on the street to becoming one of the chief
administrators of Scotland Yard. This has all contributed to what Wilson calls "a first-class relationship" between Scotland Yard and the
FBI.

McCray is a paunchy, jovial man who has made the most of an
ability to be at ease with everyone from the constable on the beat to
the guests at the queen's annual garden party. He waited for years to
become the man in charge of the London office (another agent, who
was skipped ahead of McCray early in his tenure, also stayed on for
many years and eventually died in London), but this did not dilute his
undying loyalty to the Bureau and his frenzied devotion to his assignment.

In an average week, McCray and the other agent who works with
him will be on the phone with "the Yard" several times a day, exchanging requests for positive identifications and criminal records of individuals who have been arrested in one country or the other, discussing
fugitives believed to be hiding on each other's soil, or asking their
opposite numbers to conduct interviews or searches in connection with
ongoing investigations. According to Bureau statistics, such trades of
information on criminal cases through the Legats helped the FBI
"locate" overseas 1,141 federal fugitives and 72 wanted by state and
local authorities during Fiscal Year 1974. Presumably there was a similar impact in the other direction, although American criminals seem to
be wealthier and therefore more mobile than those from most other
nations. (Extradition of those "located" is another, far more complicated matter; because of differences in law and court procedures and
the technicalities of treaties, only a fraction of those found abroad are
generally returned to the United States for trial. But once they are
found, they no longer occupy agent time in domestic field offices.)

When McCray wants to call someone at Scotland Yard, he need
not worry about switchboard delays and operators because he has a
direct line to the Yard on his desk. Next to it is another telephone that
connects him directly to the British Security Service (also known,

dating back to wartime, as MI-5); that line has a "scrambler" device that, when the appropriate button is pushed at both ends, supposedly makes a conversation impossible to intercept anywhere in between. The Scotland Yard phone was installed after a tabulation of the volume of "traffic" between the two; the MI-5 line, however, grew out of an incident in which a man with an American accent was known to be requesting asylum at the Soviet embassy in London and British security officers were unable to get through to the FBI because its embassy lines were busy. McCray also deals occasionally with the Intelligence Service (MI-6), the British equivalent of the CIA, and is in on the well-kept secret of who runs both it and MI-5.

During a recent visit to the London Legat on a typical day, a wide variety of calls and requests poured in. A warning from MI-5 that leftist groups in Italy have attacked installations owned by the American-based conglomerate, the International Telephone and Telegraph Corporation, and might try the same elsewhere, especially in London during protest demonstrations commemorating the overthrow of Chilean President Salvador Allende and condemning clandestine actions against his regime by ITT and the CIA. (McCray decides to discuss the matter with CIA representatives and to alert the embassy's security officer and weekend duty officer, but not to bother passing any details on to FBI headquarters.) A suggestion from the Bureau that McCray go out to Heathrow Airport early one morning to meet an elderly dentist arriving from Washington, who happened to be a good friend of "Mr. Hoover" and may need help getting through Customs. (He goes and helps.) Advance notice about some appointments that Associate Director Nicholas P. Callahan would like to have when he passes through London two weeks later. (He sets them up.) An introductory call from the head of a new department at Scotland Yard that will have responsibility for protecting foreign missions and their personnel in the London area. (He arranges a meeting for him with the embassy security officer.) Discussion with a British colleague about helping get a U.S. visa for an undercover informant working on efforts to control international arms smuggling. (He will have to take it up with headquarters and with the embassy's consular section.) A request to check on a bizarre story, told by a man in prison, about stealing a suitcase full of money from the brother of the late President Lyndon B. Johnson. (He asks headquarters to consult the Secret Service and local police departments.)

During one two-day period, McCray drives to the north of England on business. He consults with a police department in Lancashire County to ask that it follow up on leads in several pending cases.

(Upon his return to London he gets a call saying that one of those cases has been solved, following the arrest of an Englishman who allegedly made extortion threats over the telephone during a visit to Florida.) He meets with a professor of criminology at Manchester University, who had a reputation of being "pro-police and appreciative of police problems," to discuss the possibility of the professor writing an article about crime statistics for the *FBI Law Enforcement Bulletin*. He also attends the closing banquet of a detective training course in Preston to which he had lectured earlier in the year. McCray's appearances at such affairs are much in demand, especially because of his enjoyment in telling old Bureau stories and his knack for imitating a variety of English provincial accents.

The Legat in Copenhagen was recently closed, after American participation in the Vietnam war wound down and the flow of military deserters and draft resisters to Scandinavian countries diminished, and so jurisdiction over FBI affairs in that area has been returned to London. McCray, as a result, will soon make a "road trip" to Oslo and Copenhagen, and later his colleague will go to Stockholm and Helsinki. (Finland, however, is one country where the Bureau is especially careful about what information it shares with the police, because of its concern about leaks to the Soviet Union.) In Copenhagen, for example, McCray will make three main stops. At the American embassy he will get a list of Americans recently arrested in Denmark; he will "open a case" on any that seem particularly interesting or were the subject of special inquiries by the Danish police. The consular section will also give him a record of all Danes who were granted a "waiver" when they applied for a U.S. visa, despite their membership in a communist or other leftist organization or their conviction for "crimes of moral turpitude," such as prostitution. That list and any supporting information will be tucked away at Bureau headquarters for consultation should any of the people come to FBI attention during their stay in the United States. He will discuss routine criminal cases with contacts at the Danish National Police Service headquarters. And at the Danish Security Service, he will get requests for background investigations of Americans marrying Danish government employees, and will swap the latest information on controversial matters like newly discovered types of terrorist bombs and other explosive devices. (What McCray learns will be sent back to the National Bomb Data Center maintained at FBI headquarters.) McCray will also be brought up to date on "persons of security interest to the Bureau" — generally Americans who are members of organizations being watched by the FBI — who have recently worked, studied, or traveled in Denmark.

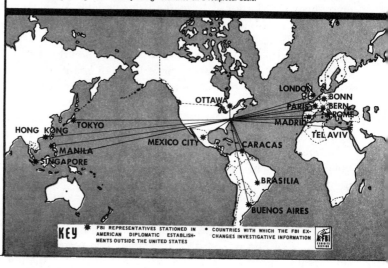

NUMBER OF FBI PERSONNEL STATIONED ABROAD		
	SPECIAL AGENTS	CLERKS
BERN Switzerland	1	1
BONN Germany	2	3
BRASILIA Brazil	1	1
BUENOS AIRES Argentina	1	2
CARACAS Venezuela	2	2
HONG KONG British Crown Colony	2	3
LONDON England	2	3
MADRID Spain	1	1
MANILA Philippines	1	1
MEXICO CITY Mexico	12	13
OTTAWA Canada	2	4
PARIS France	2	3
ROME Italy	2	2
SINGAPORE Republic of Singapore	1	1
TEL AVIV Israel	1	2
TOKYO Japan	2	2
TOTALS	35 Special Agents	44 Clerks

TOTAL PERSONNEL 79

FEBRUARY 27, 1975

FEDERAL BUREAU OF INVESTIGATION
UNITED STATES DEPARTMENT OF JUSTICE

FBI FOREIGN LIAISON OPERATIONS

The FBI maintains liaison posts abroad in 16 countries. These offices function in a liaison capacity in connection with criminal and security matters involving the Bureau's domestic responsibilities. In addition, the Bureau belongs to one international security committee and corresponds with police agencies all over the world except in countries controlled by the communists. In addition to the activities of its representatives abroad, the Bureau exchanges certain types of information with, and where warranted, arranges to have investigations conducted in the U. S. for, law enforcement and intelligence agencies in many foreign countries on a reciprocal basis.

KEY ✳ FBI REPRESENTATIVES STATIONED IN AMERICAN DIPLOMATIC ESTABLISHMENTS OUTSIDE THE UNITED STATES ● COUNTRIES WITH WHICH THE FBI EXCHANGES INVESTIGATIVE INFORMATION

Although the Bureau claims that its overseas "legal attachés" are engaged purely in liaison relationships with foreign police agencies, they also collect intelligence. In 1970, during a period of intense rivalry with the CIA, J. Edgar Hoover persuaded President Nixon to authorize a considerable expansion of the Legats, and thus the FBI ended up with representatives in bizarre locations like Singapore.

As in most overseas offices, the FBI relationship with British police and intelligence officials is described by both sides as a "professional" one that is not affected by changes in the leadership or the politics of either government. Regardless of who is Prime Minister or President at any given time, for example, if Scotland Yard's Special Branch found two or three Americans playing a significant role in a rally at Trafalgar Square, it would probably ask the Bureau for background information about them, and it would get a prompt answer. As Deputy Assistant Commissioner Wilson explains it, Scotland Yard prefers dealing with the FBI over all other United States agencies, including the American representatives of Interpol in the Treasury Department. Whereas many local police officers, reporting through Interpol, "might try to gild the lily for reasons of personal advantage," Wilson suggests, the FBI can be depended upon not only for "speed and accuracy" but also for "a high quality of reporting and an even level of reporting. There is a uniformity of language, style and assessment. Four agents in the East, West, North and South would probably evaluate an informant in the same way. . . . The response is of an even calibre, whether it comes from Los Angeles, San Francisco, Chicago or wherever." As a result, 90 percent of Scotland Yard's queries on American matters go through the FBI.

McCray has enjoyed his long tenure in London and his opportunity to work on some exciting and well-publicized cases like the cracking of an international art smuggling ring with the help of Scotland Yard's Art and Antique Squad, and the capture at Heathrow Airport in 1968 of James Earl Ray, who was imprisoned for the assassination of Martin Luther King, Jr.* He insists that in spirit as well as miles, he is no farther from Washington than is the FBI field office in Los Angeles. Continuity, McCray says, is important to the Europeans and has helped make him more effective in his job. But the Bureau nevertheless pulled him out in the fall of 1975, after seventeen years, and assigned him to the Intelligence Division at headquarters.

◆

As the Legats have gone more public over the years, one area where they have increased their efforts, and thereby won new recruits to the

---

* The manhunt for Ray is another case in which the Bureau claimed the lion's share of credit, which, according to some observers, it did not really deserve. They say the crucial work was done by the Royal Canadian Mounted Police, which pored through two hundred and fifty thousand passport applications until they discovered the alias under which Ray was traveling, Ramon George Sneyd.

fold of FBI friends, is "foreign police cooperation." Hoover opened the National Academy police training classes to foreign officers in the early 1960s, on the basis of a suggestion made to him by President John F. Kennedy in a casual conversation. (Those chosen to attend the academy from less affluent countries would have their transportation and incidental costs paid by grants through the State Department's Agency for International Development.) The Legats have been responsible for selecting the foreign officers who will be invited to attend the academy and then for having background checks run on the officers by the security agencies in their own countries.

The Bureau has gone still further in some instances to train foreign police units in its own image. After the massacre of Israeli athletes by Palestinian Arab commandos at the 1972 Olympic Games in Munich, Legat John C. F. Morris in Bonn was instrumental in arranging sophisticated assistance for a new unit of the West German Bundesgrenzschutz (federal border control), set up to deal with terrorism and hijacking and to protect foreign visitors. The commander of the special unit, a politically well connected officer named Lieutenant Colonel Ulrich Wegener, was invited to Quantico along with two other officers for three weeks of special-weapons-and-tactics (SWAT) training. (In the same class were officers of another West German police agency, the Iranian army, and the Canadian RCMP.) In addition, the Legat in Bonn provided copies of training manuals and American reports on the suppression of terrorists that could be readily translated into German and used by Wegener's group. FBI advice also influenced the choice of weapons and other equipment for the new unit. Wegener has nothing but praise for the Bureau training and assistance, which he says helped on everything from simple matters like police roadblock technique — approaching a car from behind instead of the front, especially if it is believed to contain an armed fugitive — to more complex ones like the disposal of bombs. "The FBI has experience in the fight against criminal gangs and organizations that can teach us a great deal," says Wegener, adding that he hopes to send more officers to the United States for SWAT training and to shop for new crime-fighting equipment there. His FBI shooting cap is displayed proudly in his office. *

Most Legat time and attention, however, is still spent on traditional FBI functions, with the constant stricture that the Bureau re-

* The Bureau has long had a similarly close — some say manipulative — connection with the police forces of the Bahamas. That contact, however, is handled out of the Miami Field Office.

main a "nonoperational" liaison force overseas, lest it provoke an embarrassing controversy. (So reluctant have some agents been to appear to violate that rule that they have shunned virtually all appearances "in the streets," even meetings in cafés with their contacts. On some occasions, when criminal informants from the United States have traveled abroad and required "handholding," the Bureau has asked the CIA to take over that babysitting job.) By contrast, the Legats have not hesitated to be in the thick of things within foreign police circles, and sometimes, in cases of critical interest to the Bureau, agents have lurked nearby in the station and have been kept informed minute by minute while the local police question a suspect.

A classic example of FBI consultation in a criminal case was its efforts to trace the origins of an American-manufactured hand grenade thrown into a busy Paris shop in September 1974. Intelligence information transmitted through the Legats in Beirut and Rome helped the Bureau reach two of three bombs planted by Arab terrorists at Israeli offices in New York before they exploded. (A third bomb went off but was too weak to do serious damage. In Bureau lingo, this is known as the TRIBOMB case.) If someone like American black activist leader Angela Davis goes on a European speaking tour, the Legats will keep tabs on it, but primarily through newspaper clippings. They would also monitor stops in East Germany and other communist states by figures like American Communist party leader Gus Hall, largely by using their intelligence agency connections in countries with FBI representatives.

Monthly statistics compiled in the Intelligence Division, which has administrative jurisdiction over the Legats at FBI headquarters, indicate that the main burden of their work may be shifting gradually from criminal matters to areas the Bureau classifies as security concerns. In one month, although not necessarily a typical one, the Mexico City office logged 35 percent of its agent time as being in the security field; London, 34 percent; Singapore, 51 percent; Paris, 52 percent; and Bonn, 58 percent. The Bonn figure is explained by that office's preoccupation with espionage that may be conducted across the long border between West and East Germany — especially in light of the revelation that Gunter Guillaume, a close aide to former West German Chancellor Willy Brandt, was spying for the communist regime in the East — and its representation of the FBI on the North Atlantic Treaty Organization's "special committee" of counterintelligence officials. The Hong Kong Legat had its origins in Hoover's desire to have his own listening and watching post on China. The FBI is also unwilling to leave certain specific concerns to others, such as the threat to American nationals from urban guerrillas and other terrorists in Latin America* and the prospects that the Soviet Union may develop a new method for smuggling KGB operatives out to the West by camouflaging them among Jewish émigrés traveling to Israel.

But there has also been an increase in the reporting by the Legats of "incidental intelligence" that comes to their attention — matters not clearly within FBI jurisdiction, such as information on trade deals between Western nations and the communist world, or details of public demonstrations and disorders that do not necessarily directly involve American interests. As Legat Morris in Bonn put it, "Sometimes it dawns on you: 'I may be the only one who knows this, I'm an American, and I work in the embassy.' . . . You're not parochial. Of course, you report it." Theoretically, any important intelligence matters are promptly relayed to the CIA or other interested agencies when they are received in Washington. Toward the end of Hoover's days, apparently at his personal urging, some Legats began reporting routine "political intelligence" — rumors about when new elections would be held, shifts within the leadership of political parties, parliamentary debates and such — often duplicating the work of political officers in the embassies and even of journalists. It was as if Hoover were operating his own private State Department. Unless it involved some startling development that was not already well known in American government circles, most of this material just went down the drain in Washington, since the Bureau has no evaluators trained to make assessments of the effect that such political developments could have on the United States.

It is in these areas of intelligence that the Bureau sometimes has difficulties of communication with its foreign counterparts. Several non-American police officials in Western Europe who were interviewed said they could not identify with the FBI's interest in local Communist parties, for example, insisting that their own police agencies generally would become concerned about political groups only in the event that they became involved in overt criminal acts. The police officials also pointed out that there is a fairly clear separation in their countries between ordinary criminal police functions and the intelligence-gathering, counterintelligence, and analysis done by such units as MI-5 or the French Direction de la Surveillance du Territoire (DST).

* That concern and the growth of terrorism in Argentina led to a move at FBI headquarters to shift the Buenos Aires Legat to Montevideo (a shift opposed by the U.S. Embassy in Buenos Aires, which saw the Bureau as additional protection in a dangerous situation).

Invariably the Legats get involved in some bizarre cases, such as that of an Englishman living in Los Angeles who mailed a live snake to the late President Georges Pompidou of France and then found himself charged with the American crime of threatening a head of state. ("There is always a danger," said Gilbert Raguideau, a senior official of the French Police Judiciaire who handles foreign liaison matters; "the next time, it could have been an explosive.") And there are many of the same humdrum tasks as in any FBI office, such as obtaining copies of monthly Dutch government statistics, which are the equivalent of the FBI's *Uniform Crime Reports.* ("I don't know who gets them or what they do with them back there," says Bonn Legat John Morris, who also covers the Netherlands, "but they complain if one month's issue is a few days late.")

Whatever the work, the Legats take themselves very seriously indeed and treat their assignments as secret and sensitive. All communications with Washington are encrypted and sent over a secure teletype line that cannot be read even by the State Department. Files are kept to a minimum so that, as one Legat put it, "they can be burned quickly in the event of a coup or some other emergency." Doors and vaults are double- and triple-locked, and one Legat was observed scouring his office on hands and knees before leaving at night to make sure that no confidential materials had inadvertently slipped onto the floor. Although they do not ordinarily carry their guns ("Diplomats don't do that sort of thing," says Alden McCray), they generally keep them in embassy vaults, also in the event of an emergency or a need to defend the building against attack. ("It's like having a fire extinguisher in your kitchen," says John Morris.) With the CIA and others from each embassy, the Legats serve on a committee that drafts contingency plans that would apply if the ambassador or one of his aides were kidnapped or otherwise threatened.

The Legats' relations with the rest of the embassy personnel and the American communities in foreign capitals are generally good. (In Bonn, among other places, the agents live in an American residential compound that sometimes has the effect of cutting them off from exposure to local color and customs.) Largely because of Hoover's prestige and influence some Legats, especially those that have been open for many years, occupy some of the most choice and ample office space in the embassy. There have been only rare moments when the Bureau clashed openly with others in the diplomatic mission. One was in Tel Aviv in the early 1970s, when the deputy chief of mission sought to have all Bureau message traffic back to Washington approved by his office and routed through State Department channels, apparently out of concern over the kinds of intelligence information the Legat might be sending. That conflict was resolved in the Bureau's favor, as most are, and relations improved again once a new ambassador and deputy arrived. On at least two other occasions, of which the FBI is not proud, the Bureau's channels in Bern and Beirut were used by former Attorney General John N. Mitchell to transmit secret interventions on behalf of financier Robert Vesco, a major contributor to President Nixon's campaigns and the subject of a Securities and Exchange Commission investigation.

Relations with the CIA are, of course, a special matter. Overseas personnel from both agencies insist that whatever bickering went on in Washington, their relations in the field have been excellent — despite orders from Hoover to the Legats, about the time that he was breaking off Washington relations with the CIA, that they were not to have any communication with CIA employees. The Legats have been pleased to let the CIA, with its greater resources, handle such jobs as investigations of the background of visa applicants who have aroused the suspicions of an embassy's consular section. (Only if a waiver of some exclusion is granted and a visa is issued does the FBI then become involved.) One CIA official in Europe noted in an interview that, during the Hoover era, "it was especially important to cover yourself by reporting back home, whenever you talked with the Bureau people. Otherwise, it might be distorted by them." But he stressed his profound respect for Legats who had been in their overseas posts for many years: "They are very well plugged in. They can explain what they want clearly and get results, in both the criminal and security areas." As for the popular old dichotomy that has portrayed the CIA as the intelligentsia and the FBI as glorified policemen in the intelligence field, the CIA representative added, "This is an easy trap to fall into. Agency people tend to think of the Bureau, and other law enforcement people for that matter, as cops. The concern is that we [of the CIA] sure aren't cops and we always want to make that clear. . . . Sure, they sound like the CIC [Counter Intelligence Corps] in the army, they use police language, and some of their stuff reads strangely. They use the same language on intelligence matters as in criminal cases. . . . But they're not thugs."

The CIA men were not so happy when they learned — if they did — about some of the FBI's clumsier adventures into foreign intelligence collection. From time to time over the years the Bureau has encouraged, or even sponsored, overseas trips by its domestic "security" informants, especially for the purpose of reporting back on the activities of other Americans traveling abroad, but also on anything else of interest that they might see. The FBI pulled off a particular coup by having a young woman informant among one of the first groups of American leftists to visit China when Sino-American relations began to improve in the early 1970s; she filed a report on the trip with her agent contacts.

It was one President's reliance on the old assumption that the Bureau can do anything, and do it well, that led to the first widespread public awareness of the FBI performing a role overseas. In May 1965, President Lyndon B. Johnson sent twenty-five special agents to the Dominican Republic to join the twenty-five thousand American troops who had been dispatched to see that that country chose a government to American liking. The agents' mission, incredibly, was to do security checks on potential members of the provisional government the United States was installing in power, to ascertain whether there were not too many communists or other leftists. Skeptics suggested that perhaps the real purpose of sending in the Bureau was Johnson's desire to have some data, even after the fact, that would justify his controversial decision to put the military into Santo Domingo, because the CIA had let him down on this score. In any event, the FBI agents (not Legats, but men dispatched from domestic field offices) — wearing standard dark suits in the tropical climate, black shoes and socks, and sporting uniformly close haircuts — were absurdly out of place. Reporters there said that the Bureau and CIA contingents, for lack of anything more constructive to do, had resorted to watching each other.

Perhaps the Dominican mission, reminiscent as it was for him of the grand old days of World War II or of the Legat the Bureau had once had in Havana, went to Hoover's head, because there were widespread reports soon afterward that the Bureau planned a significant expansion of its Latin American work and would open several additional posts to serve as an "independent new source of intelligence data" for the nation. The expansion never happened then, but it did about five years later when Hoover, claiming the specific endorsement of President Nixon and overriding the strenuous objections of his intelligence chief, William C. Sullivan, decided to double the Legat system to include twenty offices instead of ten. (The number had fluctuated over the years, as some Legats were opened and closed depending on political conditions and Bureau finances.) The justifications for the increase included reference to the growing number of draft resisters and deserters overseas, the tendency of black extremist fugitives to seek refuge abroad, the general growth of terrorism and airplane hijacking, a desire to find some international origins and financing of the American student protest movement, and an interest in the expanding international narcotics traffic. Some government officials believed that Hoover had simply sold Nixon a bill of goods about the FBI's ability to gather better intelligence than the CIA. Former White House chief of staff H. R. Haldeman said in his broadcast interview with CBS that the Director pushed for expansion of the Legat system every time he saw Nixon. While some of the ten new locations for Legats opened over a two-year period were logical enough, including Beirut, Brasilia, Tel Aviv, and Caracas, others were rather curious choices — Managua, Nicaragua; La Paz, Bolivia; and Singapore. Sullivan fought relentlessly within the Bureau's executive conference for a reversal of the decision to expand the Legats, insisting that it was a waste of money and that the more appropriate decision might be to close some of the existing overseas offices and improve relations with other intelligence agencies. The intelligence chief lost the battle, however, and this was one of the factors that precipitated his forced retirement from the Bureau.*

The 1970 expansion of the Legats was given the code name of the HILEV program, for the "high level" intelligence that Bureau representatives were now meant to be sending back to Washington; when they submitted material they considered to be significant, they tagged it with the HILEV designation, so that it would get immediate attention. Within the FBI, Hoover claimed the highest authority for, and interest in, the program — Nixon himself. Indeed, many HILEV reports went directly to the White House or to Secretary of State Henry Kissinger, albeit undigested and uncoordinated with the material available through other government agencies.

Asked about the selection of La Paz, Managua, and Singapore as new Legats, one Bureau official close to the Legat operation suggested that "somebody must have been smoking pot in the Director's office." The man assigned to open the La Paz office in January 1971 because of his fluency in Spanish, Nick F. Stames (later special-agent-in-charge of the Tampa and Washington field offices), was at a loss to explain the choice of that capital high in the Andes, where he spent eighteen months. "I have often asked that question," he said, "but never had it answered. It is true that it was in an area where we had no Bureau representation, and that Peru was of interest; it kicked out the Peace Corps while I was in La Paz." But he could think of no other reasons. Some Bureau men, speculating retroactively on what Hoover's motives

---

* The vehemence of Sullivan's protests, coming from a man who had long championed the value of the Legats, took many other Bureau executives by surprise and has remained an enigma. Some FBI colleagues still believe this was part of Sullivan's alleged secret conniving with the Nixon administration to put himself in a position to replace the faltering Hoover, an allegation that he has denied.

might have been, suggest that he was drawn in part by the fact that Cuban guerrilla leader Ché Guevara had operated in Bolivia and was killed there, and that the Director thus thought La Paz might be a good place to study terrorism. Stames, however, did no such thing. Shortly after he arrived, there was a right-wing military coup, which rendered Bolivia a rather uninteresting place politically and made the Legat's work surprisingly difficult. Stames apparently found little to do beyond routine liaison calls on Bolivian and Peruvian law enforcement agencies. He had "very little contact" with other agencies' representatives in the American embassy and generally found "a lack of activity" in La Paz. In a word, he says, "it was hell"; and he was delighted to be transferred to the Bureau's inspection staff after what seemed like a year and a half in exile.

The La Paz office was closed after three years and after Hoover's death. So was Managua (although the Intelligence Division later considered establishing a new one in a better Central American location to ease the heavy workload on the Mexico City Legat, which is staffed with eleven agents and twelve clerks). Not so Singapore, but for a special reason. It is not that the one agent assigned to that distant outpost in the spring of 1972 was kept extremely busy. In an average month he had a total of only 54 cases pending (as compared with 455 for the two agents in London), and his overabundant response to memos from headquarters about minute issues seemed to indicate that he had time on his hands. But in order to accommodate the Legat in the first place, $25,000 was spent to add a room onto the U.S. embassy in Singapore, and so it was considered prudent in Washington to give that office an extended trial period. The Singapore office was finally closed quietly in June 1975. Beirut, too, lost its Legat in February 1975, when the Bureau decided that it was not justifying itself on a cost-benefit basis.

Such chaotic developments in the Legat system are accountable in part to the manner in which many Bureau policy decisions were made during Hoover's last years — on the sole basis of his whims and desires. One agent suggested, for example, that it would have been fully consistent with the Director's style merely to decide that he wanted ten new overseas offices and then to order his subordinates to pick out, almost at random, ten appropriately spaced points on a map of the world as homes for them. One former Bureau official said it was always a mystery why Hoover wanted an office in Bern, apart from the fact that many of his wealthy friends visited Switzerland and sometimes asked for FBI help with their arrangements. The people directly responsible for supervising the Legats' work have generally never even seen the offices or learned firsthand about their problems unless they happened to be on an inspection team that came through at some point.

L. Patrick Gray III, during his tenure as acting director, brought to headquarters a man with administrative and supervisory experience in the security field in the New York Field Office, Homer Boynton, to become chief of the domestic and foreign liaison section in the Intelligence Division — with a mandate to supervise and study the Legat system and, among other things, to help reestablish the Bureau's relationship with the CIA, which had been completely ruptured by Hoover. Among the matters to be evaluated was whether the Legats, without regard to their prestige for the FBI, justify their expense. (A one-agent operation costs the Bureau about $100,000 a year; one with four agents, about $350,000.) There have also been suggestions that duplication could be avoided if the Legats' routines were coordinated more thoroughly with those of the foreign liaison officials — generally members of security agencies like MI-5 — based in Washington, at the embassies of Canada, Britain, Australia, Japan, France, and several other countries. As things stand, the counterparts often compete with each other. After Clarence Kelley's accession to the directorship, the question was asked whether the unusually long service overseas of some Legats, for all its advantages, had created a small subculture of agents who fell out of touch with Bureau trends, let alone political and social developments in the United States. A new policy was adopted that set a rough maximum of four years on any agent's assignment to a single overseas office. The qualifications and credentials considered appropriate for foreign assignment were to be standardized, and agents coming off Legat duty were to be rotated through positions in the Intelligence Division before being sent overseas again.

But any review of the Legats inevitably leads also to reconsideration of the Bureau's antipathy toward Interpol. In the early years of the Nixon administration, Eugene T. Rossides, an assistant secretary of the treasury for enforcement, tariff and trade affairs, and operations, substantially beefed up the American connection with Interpol; after Hoover died, the FBI began showing cautious interest in the organization it had spurned two decades earlier.

For the first time in years, the 1974 annual conference of Interpol, this time in Cannes on the French Riviera, was attended and observed by a Bureau official with a rank higher than the Legats, Associate Director Nicholas Callahan. He was impressed and heard the arguments of many foreign officials that the FBI, with its unequaled contacts with police forces across the United States, should resume its original role as the agency that handles Interpol channels in the United States. Such changes still come slowly in the FBI, however, and one plan was to accomplish a gradual transition by first bringing Interpol jurisdiction back into the Justice Department, where most people feel it logically belongs, but assigning it to the Drug Enforcement Administration (which often uses its facilities) while the FBI reconsiders its position. Some department lawyers worried that privacy legislation developing in Congress might legally preclude the Bureau from permitting the Interpol network to draw freely on its extensive files and Washington data banks. And many in the FBI still wonder about the advisability of full participation in an organization that includes as members such communist-governed states as Romania and Yugoslavia.

The FBI People

XI

The King

FBI Director Clarence M. Kelley came to the office of Senator James O. Eastland (D-Mississippi), chairman of the Senate Judiciary Committee, one day in June 1974 for a little ceremony in which Eastland presented Kelley with the first copy of a handsome black volume in memory of J. Edgar Hoover, containing Memorial Tributes in the Congress of the United States and Various Articles and Editorials Relating to His Life and Work. The following exchange occurred, as Kelley sought to turn a rather stiff and formal occasion into a relaxed and social one:

> Kelley: "Senator, there's an awful lot about J. Edgar Hoover in this book."
> Eastland: "Chief Kelley, there's an awful lot about J. Edgar Hoover that ain't in this book."

THERE IS A TREASURY OF JOKES about J. Edgar Hoover in FBI folklore, stories that agents tell each other during long, uneventful surveillances while they wait for things to happen and that assistant directors use to cheer each other up in moments of exasperation. In one, the Director is at the beach with his constant companion, Clyde Tolson. Tolson agitatedly scans the shoreline back and forth and finally says with a sigh of relief, "Okay, Boss. The coast is clear. Now you can practice walking on the water." Another tale has it that Hoover and Tolson, as they became older, decided to check into the cost and availability of cemetery plots. When Tolson reported back to him on the high price, Hoover, a notorious cheapskate, was outraged. "Never mind, Clyde,"

249

he declared. "You buy yours. But I'll just rent a crypt. I don't plan to be there for more than a few days anyway." Yet another related that whenever Tolson became depressed or dispirited, which was apparently often, the Director would seek to cheer him up by saying, "Clyde, why don't you tranfer somebody?" If that didn't do the trick, Hoover would escalate the suggestion: "Go ahead, fire someone." And if Tolson still complained that this didn't help, the Director would add, "Fire him with prejudice" — a device that made it nearly impossible for the victim to find another job. Only then, went the story, did Tolson feel better.

Such bizarre fantasies conjure up the image of a man who regarded himself as infallible and godlike and who exercised arbitrary and sometimes inexplicable control over thousands of lives. J. Edgar Hoover had a degree of authority and prerogative seldom seen in democratic governments. The longer he stayed in power, the greater those prerogatives became and the more inconceivable it became that he might ever be removed; the phenomenon seemed at times to grow out of the medieval notion of the divine right of kings. Indeed, some suggested that, in times of trouble, the elevation of Hoover was just what the country needed, and his friend, Senator Joseph McCarthy of Wisconsin, tried more than once in the 1950s to launch Hoover-for-President boomlets.

But Hoover disavowed any such ambition. He was content to stay where he was, ruling over a limited but significant realm — an agency that he had salvaged from the depths of scandal and raised to the heights of honor and influence. The Director turned away other job offers — to become national baseball commissioner or head of the Thoroughbred Racing Association. Hoover put his own distinct imprint on the FBI and then turned himself into an institution. It became a tradition — and a necessity for those who sought to advance through the ranks — to say what the Director wanted to hear. By definition, it was right. It also became a tradition, as one FBI official put it, "that you do what the Director says without really agreeing with him." Hoover's words and acts were converted into legends, and some of them came out sounding as stiff and unreal or as difficult to believe as those of such other authoritarian leaders as Chairman Mao Tse-tung of the Chinese Communist party. If an attorney general or a President made him angry, the Director could just threaten to resign, and that was usually enough to bring the offender back into line. No President could afford to lose him.

Reflecting on the reverence that came to be accorded Hoover, Clarence Kelley, his successor, says, "His most casual remark [to a member of the FBI leadership] would be turned into a point of philosophy. They would even go out and document it and build it up, so it could aid them at a future time."

This treatment could be taken to laughable extremes. Once asked how he got along so well with the Director, Sam Noisette, Hoover's black retainer who was an "honorary agent," replied, "It's easy. . . . If it's snowing and blowing outside and the Director comes in and says it's a beautiful, sunny day, it's a beautiful, sunny day. That's all there is to it."

John Edgar Hoover — he abbreviated his name when he learned of a namesake who had large debts — was born the third child of an obscure family of civil servants in Washington on the first day of 1895. His father, like his father before him, worked for the Coast and Geodetic Survey, and his brother, Dickerson N. Hoover, Jr., became inspector general of the Steamboat Inspection Service in the Department of Commerce. In high school Hoover distinguished himself as a good student, a debater (overcoming an early childhood stutter and arguing, on occasion, in favor of American annexation of Cuba and against women's suffrage), and a member of the cadet corps. He had to work for anything he obtained after his high school graduation in 1913, and while studying law at night at George Washington University he had a daytime job, for thirty dollars a month, as an indexer at the Library of Congress.

After obtaining two degrees, a bachelor's and a master's of law, and passing the District of Columbia bar exam, he went to work in 1917 as a law clerk in the Justice Department. As Jack Alexander noted in a unique and intimate 1937 profile of Hoover in *The New Yorker*, from his earliest days in the Department,

certain things marked Hoover apart from scores of other young law clerks. He dressed better than most, and a bit on the dandyish side. He had an exceptional capacity for detail work, and he handled small chores with enthusiasm and thoroughness. He constantly sought new responsibilities to shoulder and welcomed chances to work overtime. When he was in conference with an official of his department, his manner was that of a young man who confidently expected to rise. His superiors were duly impressed, and so important did they consider his services that they persuaded him to spend the period of the [First] World War at his desk.

Rise he did. By 1919, at the age of twenty-four, Hoover became a special assistant attorney general in charge of the General Intelligence Division of the Bureau of Investigation. In that position, he was re-

sponsible for assessing the threat to the United States from communists and other revolutionaries, and the information he developed
became essential background for the "Red raids" conducted by Attorney General A. Mitchell Palmer in 1920. Few of the ten thousand
persons arrested and detained in the raids were ever convicted under
the wartime Sedition Act, but Hoover was successful in his personal
efforts before a Labor Department tribunal to have at least three well-
known figures deported: radicals Emma Goldman and Alexander
Berkman as well as Ludwig Martens, the unofficial representative in
the United States of the new Soviet government. Hoover became an
assistant director of the Bureau of Investigation under Director William J. Burns during the presidency of Warren G. Harding; but his
patience and freedom from association with the Harding scandals were
rewarded when after his exchange with Coolidge's new attorney general, Harlan Stone, about the need to keep politics out of the Bureau,
Stone named Hoover its Acting Director at age twenty-nine.

Before and after he took over the troubled Bureau of Investigation in 1924, Hoover was something of a mystery man in Washington.
He kept very much to himself, living in the house where he was born
and caring for his mother, the descendant of Swiss mercenary soldiers
and a strong disciplinarian, until her death in 1938. But although he
remained close to her, Hoover apparently shunned the rest of his family. His sister Lillian fell upon hard times, but got no help from him.
"J.E. was always accessible if we wanted to see him, but he didn't
initiate contacts with his family," said Margaret Fennell, his niece, to
interviewer Ovid Demaris. Indeed, even Hoover's most persistent
admirers and defenders within the FBI complained occasionally that
the absence of any family devotion on his own part contributed to his
lack of compassion toward or understanding of strong family men who
worked for him. "Hoover couldn't have a family-type feeling toward
anyone," observed one agent long stationed in New York; "a man who
has never been a father cannot think like a father." The wife of a
former assistant director of the FBI said that "the man just had no
feeling at all for families." There was a certain paradox to this attitude,
as Hoover expected his married agents to be loyal family men.

Hoover's coldness to his own family could not be readily explained by a busy schedule of other commitments and associations. For
a time, especially in the 1930s, he was seen frequently with well-known
writers and other friends on the New York nightclub circuit; and sometimes he went with bachelor friends to baseball games and other
sports events (he was occasionally joined on excursions to watch the
Washington Senators in the 1950s by then Vice-President Richard M.

Nixon); but Hoover generally turned away all other social engagements, unless they involved official business at the Justice Department. There was little socializing in the top ranks of the Bureau itself, and relations between Hoover and his associates were intentionally kept on a businesslike level. The only woman in the Director's life, it was often said, was Shirley Temple, his favorite actress and then a child. His most frequent and celebrated diversion, especially as he became older, was horse races, where he generally placed small, losing bets and sometimes presented trophies in the winner's circle.

The replacement for family, and eventually for everyone else, in Hoover's celibate life was Clyde A. Tolson, a native of Missouri who came to Washington at the age of eighteen to work as a clerk in the War Department. He eventually became confidential secretary to Secretary of War Newton D. Baker and two successors, but after getting a law degree in night school at George Washington University, he joined the Bureau in 1928. He originally planned to move on to practice law in Cedar Rapids, Iowa, where he once attended business college for a year. But for reasons that were never entirely clear, Tolson rose quickly and was soon working at the Director's side. Hoover and Tolson became so close that, as Don Whitehead put it in his history, "They have even reached the point where they think alike." They also came to spend a great deal of time together, including, on most days, lunch at a restaurant and dinner at one or another's home. When Hoover appeared at an official function, Tolson was invariably a few steps behind and to the right of him, almost like a courtier carrying a king's cloak. As associate director, a title Hoover finally gave him in 1947, Tolson was in effect the Director's chief of staff and his mouthpiece. He chaired the Bureau's executive conference of assistant directors. Many of Hoover's attitudes and opinions, his wrath or his satisfaction, were transmitted through Tolson, who, as the years went on, seemed to do very little thinking or acting on his own. Tolson would invariably write his comments on a memorandum in pencil rather than pen, so that he could change them to conform with the Director's point of view if necessary. If the executive conference voted unanimously on a matter but Hoover was later found to disagree,* Tolson would take it upon himself to solicit unanimity for the "correct" position, and he usually got it. Longtime Bureau officials, asked to list Tolson's contributions and innovations to the service, are generally unable to come up with any. And even to those who worked for years near his office, he remained an enigma. Efforts to fraternize with him

---

* The Director's famous euphemism was to say, "I approve the minority view."

were turned away abruptly, and any other Bureau executive presumptuous enough to try to join him and the Director for their ritual daily lunch at Harvey's Restaurant or the Mayflower Hotel risked disciplinary action or some more subtle punishment.

Tolson's only known diversion was to dream up obscure inventions, and he actually obtained patents on a few, including a mechanism to open and close windows automatically. Hoover usually agreed to try out Tolson's inventions, either in the Bureau or at home.

According to the persistent gossip in Washington for decades, Hoover and Tolson were homosexuals; and — according to this interpretation — their attempt to repress and conceal their relationship helped explain the Bureau's vigilant, even hysterical bias against men of that sexual orientation. In fact, any such relationship between the two was never acknowledged or discovered. As one former ranking official put it, "If it was true, they were never caught. And you know how we feel in the Bureau: you are innocent until proven guilty." Another debunked the rumors about their relationship on the basis of the fact that Hoover "liked to crack jokes about sex."

Tolson was always the more sickly of the two men, and whenever he fell ill, he would move into Hoover's home to be nursed back to health by the Director's servants. When Hoover died suddenly in May 1972 Tolson was grief-stricken, and after going through the formality of being acting director of the FBI for about twenty-four hours, he announced his retirement. But for a few token items and sums of money willed to others, Hoover left all of his worldly possessions — an estate valued at half a million dollars — to Clyde Tolson. Tolson, increasingly ill, closed himself up in Hoover's home and declined to talk with anyone, even most of his former Bureau colleagues. He died on April 14, 1975, at the age of seventy-four, passing most of the fortune on to other loyal Bureau folk.

From all accounts, of those who knew Hoover and those who studied him, the Director was a cold and self-indulgent man. His expressions of warmth were few and far between and private — friendship with neighborhood youths whom he invited into his house; a gift of a beagle pup to replace one that died which had belonged to his neighbors in the 1950s, Senator and Mrs. Lyndon B. Johnson; offers to pay a hospital bill for one of the children of Assistant Director Cartha D. DeLoach. But according to one official who was sometimes the beneficiary of such largess from Hoover, "He extracted a pound of flesh for every ounce of generosity," especially from those who worked for him. From them he expected repayment in the form of intensified loyalty and utter obeisance. From someone like Johnson he wanted political capital; from other neighbors he seemed to require only respect and deference. Seldom did his gestures seem to be motivated simply by unselfishness or humanitarian concern toward others.

Hoover moved only once in his life — after his mother's death in 1938, from the family home in Seward Square on Capitol Hill to a large red-brick house that he bought on 30th Place in Northwest Washington, near Rock Creek Park. There he built a huge collection of antiques, art objects, and pictures, mostly of himself with other famous people. According to his neighbors, the position of each item, once settled upon, remained the same year after year. Each time a new President was elected, Hoover would move a photograph of himself with that President into a place of particular prominence in the entrance hall. Some of the art objects were fine and valuable, but others, it was discovered when they were auctioned after his death, were peculiar items like an eight-sided basket made of Popsicle sticks; a wooden stork from the old Stork Club, one of the Director's favorite New York nightclubs; a salt shaker with a nude woman on the side; and other assorted bric-a-brac. Hoover's house was impeccably well kept (he had a fear of insects and germs and kept an ultraviolet light in the bathroom) and his Kentucky bluegrass front lawn was the pride of the neighborhood until it was replaced with artificial Astro Turf shortly before his death.

He was a man of habit, leaving the house and returning at precisely the same hour every day. He always ate cottage cheese and grapefruit for lunch. If he ever had serious health problems, beyond an ulcer condition, they were a carefully guarded secret; and he did not even like it to be known that in his later years he took a nap in the office for about two hours each afternoon. Hoover did not smoke, and he took only an occasional drink of bourbon, preferably Jack Daniels, with water.

His life was the FBI and there were few diversions from it. The Director did have pretenses of being a religious man. (As a high school student he sang in a Presbyterian church choir and taught a Sunday school class, and at one point, according to his biographers, he considered becoming a minister.) But one man who worked closely with Hoover for many years claimed in an interview that the Bible on his desk was really just "a prop" and that the Director exploited organized religion and famous preachers and evangelists for his own and the FBI's selfish purposes. Despite his extraordinary power and exposure, in the eyes of most of his associates Hoover seemed to remain a man of small dimensions who never became sophisticated or graceful. He was prejudiced and narrow-minded, overtly biased against black people ("As long as I am Director, there will never be a Negro special agent of the FBI," he was often heard to say in the years before Attorney General Robert F. Kennedy exerted pressure on him to change that policy), distrustful of other minority groups, and intolerant of women in any but subservient positions. Always somewhat defensive and insecure about his own education, Hoover had a notorious distrust of people who had gone to Harvard and other Ivy League universities; he claimed that they had little knowledge of the real world. He was embarrassingly susceptible to manipulation through flattery or fulsome praise and sometimes hopelessly out of touch with the realities of changing times. He was, above all, a lonely man.

When Hoover first took over the Bureau, he was little known and seldom noticed. When he was appointed to the job, *Time* magazine remarked only that he was distinguished by "an unusually accurate and comprehensive memory," but most of the press merely ignored him. It was almost five years, in fact, before he ever achieved a distinction symbolic to Washington bureaucrats, mention in the *Congressional Record*. A Democratic congressman from Texas, Thomas L. Blanton, took the floor of the House of Representatives in early 1929 to compliment Hoover for "the high character of the splendid work they are doing" at the Bureau. Four years later, during a budget debate, Congressman John McCormack (D-Massachusetts) — later Speaker of the House and always one of Hoover's staunchest supporters — praised the Bureau as "a credit to the Federal Government" and the Director as "a brilliant young man . . . one of the finest public officials in the service of the Federal Government."

But before long, once he had consolidated power and genuinely improved the agency, Hoover determined to go public, to build a reputation for the Bureau and to construct what came to be a cult around himself. This took the form initially of an anticrime "crusade," a zealous effort to awaken the citizenry to the threat and the consequences of lawlessness and to the need to cooperate with the authorities. The wisdom and invincibility of the "G-men" (a name that gangster George "Machine-Gun" Kelly allegedly gave the Bureau agents, who had previously been known mostly as "the Feds") were trumpeted in comic strips; children wore G-man pajamas to bed and took G-man machine guns out to play. Alongside the easy, mass-appeal aspects of the crusade, however, there was also a loftier pitch for the federal police efforts, the development of a philosophy that gave the Bureau coherence and lasting importance. The Director came to have the image of an expert, a sage, almost of a saint come to deliver the nation from the forces of evil — even if he had never been out on the street working a case.

Hoover was hardly a scholar, nor was he a particularly literate man. He had made an early effort to "understand" the radical forces in the country, holding long arguments in his Justice Department office, for example, with Emma Goldman and others he had deported during the Palmer Raid era. But he soon abandoned any such dialogue and effort to understand and turned to the attack. Apart from the most important reports crossing his desk, he was said to read very little, and one of the best stories about the Director was that not only had he not written the books published under his name, but he hadn't even bothered to read them. His letters often bordered on incoherence, especially in his last years, and sometimes what semblance of logic and rationality they had came from "corrections" mercifully made by close aides like Louis Nichols and Cartha DeLoach or Hoover's lifelong secretary, Helen Gandy. The Director was notorious for his mispronunciation of words that he used often, such as communist ("cominist") and pseudo ("swaydo"), a term he generally put in front of "intellectual" or "liberal" as an expression of contempt; but it was taboo for anyone who intended to have a bright future in the Bureau to correct him on such matters.

Most of Hoover's vocabulary was graphic and quotable, and some of it was crude. Criminals were generally "rats" of one form or another and those who failed to keep them in jail were "yammerheads." One of the greatest threats to the nation came from "venal politicians." Those who criticized him might be diagnosed, as columnist Westbrook Pegler was, as suffering from "mental halitosis." The press, for that matter, was full of "jackals." In a speech before the Washington, D.C., chapter of the Society of Former Special Agents of the FBI in 1971, he attacked the "few journalistic prostitutes" who could not appreciate the FBI; in that same appearance, one of his last major public addresses, he insisted that the FBI had no intention of compromising its standards "to accommodate kooks, misfits, drunks and slobs." "It is time we stopped coddling the hoodlums and the hippies who are causing so much serious trouble these days," he declared; "let us treat them like the vicious enemies of society that they really are regardless of their age."

Whatever the level of the discourse, Hoover found respectable forums and outlets for his ghostwritten elegies on law and order. He appeared regularly, for example, in the *Syracuse Law Review*. His treatise there on juvenile delinquency in 1953, replete with footnotes, advised the reader:

Of primary importance in the child's early environment is a wholesome family life. A happy home which glows with morality provides a healthy atmosphere for the growing child. During the years of accelerated character development, the child quickly learns from observing his parents. As the language of his parents becomes his language, so the cleanliness of body and soul displayed by them exerts early influence on him. The child who is confronted with parental strife, immorality, and unhappiness in the home must look beyond the family circle if he is to develop orderly, wholesome ideals. Too often the child does not find proper guidance when it is not provided in the home.

The same article advised that it was a bad idea for both parents in a family to be employed, that poolrooms and other "hangouts" bred juvenile delinquency, and warned that "law enforcement agencies in various parts of the United States are required to adhere to restrictions which hamper police efficiency. . . . the tendency to discount juvenile crime and to assume an overly protective attitude toward the juvenile offender is dangerous." And there were generally a few words on behalf of the old virtues:

Truthfulness is one of the strongest characteristics of good citizenship. All criminals are liars; their lives are patterned after the deceit which they reflect in both word and deed. Certainly each parent must insist of his children that they be truthful in their every word. A child should be disciplined more severely when he attempts to hide his misconduct behind a lie than when he is guilty of misconduct alone. That truthfulness can best be learned in the everyday association between the child and his parent is self-evident. Likewise the father who is caught in a lie hardly can demand the truth from his child.

Eleven years later, he was back in the same law review on the same subject, with some rather strident warnings:

There is a growing possibility that Nikita Khrushchev will never be forced to make good his boast of burying us — we may save him the trouble by doing it ourselves through the dissipation of the youth of our country. . . . The moral deterioration in our people is another basic cause for the large juvenile involvement in criminal activity. . . . Either we solve the problem or we may well go down!

In his prime, Hoover gave frequent speeches, and he had something to say about nearly everything:

• *Corruption.* "One of the worst degenerative forces in American life during the past fifty years has been corruption in public office.

Corrupt politicians make venal politics, and right-thinking citizens know there is but one answer and one remedy. Corruption must be eradicated. . . . Few communities in the land are free from contamination of the syndicated leeches who masquerade behind the flattering term — 'politician.'" (National Fifty Years in Business Club, Nashville, May 20, 1939.)

• *American home life.* "When the home totters, a nation weakens. Every day it is my task to review the histories of scores who obey only the laws of their own choosing. Always the one thing that stands out is a lack of moral responsibility and any feeling of religious conviction. . . . While we fight for religious freedom, we must also fight the license sought by the atheist and those who ridicule, scoff and belittle others who would seek spiritual strength." (Commencement exercises, St. John's University Law School, Brooklyn, June 11, 1942.)

• *Loyalty.* "In our vaunted tolerance for all peoples the Communist has found our 'Achilles' heel.' The American Legion represents a force which holds within its power the ability to expose the hypocrisy and ruthlessness of this foreign 'ism' which has crept into our national life — an 'ism' built and supported by dishonor, deceit, tyranny and a deliberate policy of falsehood. . . . We are rapidly reaching the time when loyal Americans must be willing to stand up and be counted. The American Communist Party . . . has for its purpose the shackling of America and its conversion to the Godless, Communist way of life." (Annual convention of the American Legion, San Francisco, September 30, 1946.)

Hoover was even sought out by *Parents' Magazine* in 1940 for remarks on "The Man I Want My Son to Be." His answer:

I would want him to be intelligent, not necessarily possessed of learning derived from reading, but equipped to face the world with a self-reliant resourcefulness that would enable him to solve, in the majority of instances, the problems of human existence. . . . I would want him to realize that nothing in life can be truly gained without paying the equivalent price and that hard, intensive work is necessary.

There were subjects, perhaps, that Hoover, with his accumulation of influence and credibility, could have profitably addressed himself to, but did not. For example, he never wrote or spoke about the need to control the distribution of handguns. Instead, in sensationalized accounts written for *American Magazine* under his byline by Courtney Ryley Cooper, with titles like "Gun-Crazy," he seemed to lend some romanticism to such groups as the "Brady gang," "the gun-craziest gang of desperadoes ever to fall to the lot of the Federal Bureau of Investigation to blast into extinction."

The Director did not hesitate to pronounce his views on other issues of national controversy. He bitterly opposed the visit to this country of Nikita Khrushchev in 1959 (although he would later endorse President Nixon's voyages to Moscow and Peking). He frequently spoke out against the parole system, which he felt was administered by "sob sisters" with irresponsible leniency. "It is time that we approached the parole problem with a little more common sense," Hoover proclaimed in 1939; "it is time that sound practical business-like methods supersede the whims of the gushing, well-wishing, mawkish sentimentalist. . . . The guiding principle, the basic requirement, the sole consideration in judging each and every individual case in which parole may be administered, should be the protection of the public."

Hoover often made decisions about people and chose his friends on the basis of their conformity with his own ideological attitudes. He was delighted, for example, when federal Judge Irving Kaufman in New York gave death sentences to Julius and Ethel Rosenberg, who were convicted of espionage in his courtroom for the alleged leak of U.S. atomic secrets to the Soviet Union. Kaufman and Hoover became fast friends. Whenever the judge went to visit his son at college in Oklahoma, he was chauffeured by agents from the Oklahoma City Field Office; and even into the 1970s, after Hoover was gone, the FBI did special favors for Kaufman, by then chief judge of the U.S. Court of Appeals for the Second Circuit. Just a phone call from the judge to the New York Field Office, complaining about a group that was demonstrating outside his courthouse, was enough to launch a preliminary Bureau investigation of the group.

With the help of his publicity-conscious lieutenants, Hoover cultivated his own image as the fearless enemy of every criminal, so effective in his job as to be loathed by them all. The Director always behaved as if there were an imminent danger to his life. He would put his hat on one side of the rear-window ledge in his chauffeured limousine and then sink down in the corner on the other side, on the assumption that any would-be assassin would fire at the hat first. He and Tolson always sat against the wall in a restaurant so they could see anyone approaching them. And whenever Hoover traveled out of town, he invariably had a large retinue of agents from the nearest field office on duty to protect him. On one occasion, Hoover became alarmed over the origin of suspicious stains that appeared on the floor of his limousine. He ordered the FBI Lab to do tests on the carpet. The conclusion: the stains came from a package of bones that he had taken home from a banquet for his dog. As former agent Joseph L. Schott has reported in his lighthearted memoir of life in the Bureau, *No Left Turns*, after an incident in California during which Hoover was jostled uncomfortably during a left-hand turn of his car, he issued a strict order of procedure: there would henceforth be no left turns. His drivers would have to learn to chart their routes accordingly.

Occasionally the Director was criticized — for example, by Senator Kenneth McKellar of Tennessee in 1936 — for having little, if any, experience himself in the investigation and detection of crime and for never having made an arrest. As one sympathetic Hoover biographer, Ralph de Toledano, puts it, after McKellar's criticism "Hoover was boiling mad. He felt that his manhood had been impugned." In response, he staged a dramatic trip to New Orleans and supposedly led the raiding party to capture a member of the "Barker gang," Alvin Karpis. Later, thanks to arrangements made by his friend, columnist Walter Winchell, he repeated the performance in New York for the capture of rackets boss Louis "Lepke" Buchalter. Such gestures grabbed headlines and calmed his critics. It was only years later that it became known that Hoover strolled into both situations after all danger was past and that he had played a purely symbolic role.

Many of those who worked closely with the Director privately resented his comfortable daily schedule. While he took an interest in all the important matters before the Bureau, says one longtime aide, he "never lost sleep" — neither from working around the clock nor from worrying about the progress on cases. While his agents logged the required "voluntary overtime," he usually left the office on schedule at 4:45 P.M. There was a standing order not to call him at home after 9 P.M. He handled Bureau affairs in a routine and businesslike manner, apparently leaving most of the stresses and strains to others. Nonetheless, Hoover showed unusual leadership abilities and maintained the undying loyalty of almost everyone in the FBI for nearly half a century. He managed to persuade underlings that he cared deeply about their careers, and there are thousands of people still in the FBI who, like Special-Agent-in-Charge Arnold C. Larson of Los Angeles, attribute their success in life to such inspirational personal advice from Hoover as "Set your goals high. Go to college. Better yourself. Don't remain a clerk forever." Anyone in the Bureau who ever had a personal audience with the Director remembers it in intimate detail, even if it consisted merely, as it often did, of listening to a Hoover monologue on the evils of communism or the misdeeds of politicians. There was competition among some people to the very end to offer proof of their closeness to the Director; one ex-Bureau official, John P. Mohr, asserts that he was the first to be notified of Hoover's death, and John J. Rooney, the New York congressman who supervised the FBI budget for many years, boasted that he was the only member of Congress at the gravesite after Hoover's funeral.

Hoover was often arbitrary and unreasonable, especially with those jockeying for his favor, but they seldom resisted his way of doing things. "There was a constant desire on your part to please him," explained one man who worked at it for some thirty years. "You wanted to obtain that praise from him, that letter of commendation, that incentive award. When you did, you had a great sense of pride in it. It gave you a feeling of exhilaration; you had accomplished something. He had an ability to keep you at arm's length, yet make you want to work your guts out for him. . . . I rebelled at the idea of working through fear, but I did it anyway. This was my niche. I have always wondered whether the fear was necessary, whether it might have been better to rule on the basis of mutual respect. But it is hard to fight success."

Working for the FBI and for Hoover meant, above all, submitting to discipline and regimentation that sometimes exceeded the military in its severity and lack of compassion. During the Prohibition era, taking a single alcoholic drink was grounds for being fired, if it were discovered. Hoover assumed the right to set standards for his agents' personal lives, and the sexual taboos, for example, were absolute. Not only would young unmarried male and female clerks be dismissed if it were learned that they had had illicit sexual relations, but the same punishment would be dealt to a fellow clerk who knew about any such indiscretion and failed to report it. The rules persisted, at least for agents, well after Hoover's death, and as late as mid-1974 Director Clarence Kelley approved the transfer and demotion to street-agent status for the special-agent-in-charge of the Salt Lake City Field Office because of his alleged amorous adventures.

Cars had to be kept bright and shiny, and agents were to wear conservative suits and white shirts — even though such uniform characteristics often gave them away and made them less effective at their work. Coffee-drinking on the job was forbidden, especially at FBI headquarters, and some veterans still tell of "Black Friday," in the 1950s, when a large number of agents were caught drinking coffee in the Justice Department cafeteria after the deadline hour of 9 A.M. and severely punished. The official justification for such harsh standards was that Hoover wanted all his men to have "an unblemished reputa-

J. Edgar Hoover kept his distance from most FBI employees and permitted few of them to develop a close personal or social relationship with him. The most notable exception was Clyde Tolson, who joined the Bureau in 1928 and soon began working closely with the Director; from 1947 until Hoover's death, he had the title of associate director. Tolson became the Director's surrogate, his alter ego, and his constant companion — at lunch, dinner, meetings, ceremonies, and at occasional recreational outings to the racetrack and other sports events; above, they are shown attending the Joe Louis–Jack Sharkey fight on August 18, 1936. Louis B. Nichols, who joined the Bureau during the dramatic days of the 1930s and later launched its aggressive public relations policy, won his way into the Director's heart by naming his first-born son for him; below, Hoover posed on July 14, 1939, with Nichols, his wife and young John Edgar Nichols.

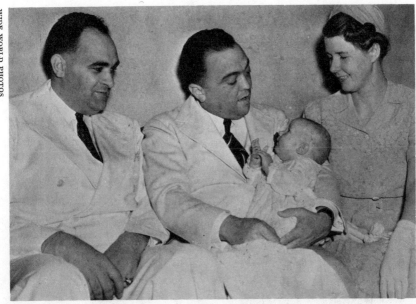

There were not very many women in J. Edgar Hoover's life. He lived with his mother until her death in 1938 and seldom accepted invitations to Washington cocktail parties and other social events. But he did have a soft spot for some female celebrities, and here are two of them: above, Shirley Temple, the child actress, who toured the FBI and examined some of its exhibits on June 24, 1938; below, Martha Mitchell, the outspoken wife of Richard Nixon's attorney general, John N. Mitchell, and guest of honor at a dinner given by the American Newspaper Women's Club on May 24, 1971. Hoover was in rare form at the dinner for Mrs. Mitchell; asked whether he had ever received one of her famous late-night telephone calls, he said, "I stay up at night waiting for it." Mrs. Mitchell, for her own part, joked about Hoover's longevity by saying that "if you've seen one FBI director, you've seen them all."

tion." As one official explained it, "The FBI name was to be so good that whenever an agent went before a jury, he would be believed."

Sometimes Hoover was simply mean; when he discovered that one agent's wife had an alcohol problem and his son was in trouble with drugs, he exiled the family to a small resident agency far away, apparently out of concern that the Bureau would be embarrassed if the agent remained where he was stationed. The Director was so angered when he heard that another agent had indiscreetly said he was willing to serve "anywhere but New York or Detroit" that he made a personal effort to guarantee that the man's entire career was spent in those two cities. The no-mistake concept that Hoover constantly preached caused the Bureau to lose some valuable people to other agencies. William V. Broe, for example, was an up-and-coming supervisor when one minor error in a report that came to the Director's attention brought him a cut in pay and a transfer. Broe decided he could not afford to accept the punishment and instead resigned and went to the Central Intelligence Agency, where he rose to one of its top positions.

One of the most-publicized disciplinary excesses involved agent Jack Shaw of the New York Field Office, who was taking graduate courses at the John Jay College of Criminal Justice under FBI auspices. Shaw wrote a letter to one of his professors, in part defending the Bureau but also criticizing Hoover for concentrating on "dime-a-dozen" bank robbers and neglecting organized crime, and for a "sledgehammer" approach to public relations, among other matters; foolishly, Shaw had the letter typed in the office secretarial pool and its contents became widely known. Hoover, when the matter reached him, sent Shaw a telegram accusing him of "atrocious judgment" and transferring him to the Butte, Montana, Field Office, despite the fact that his wife was dying of cancer. When Hoover learned that the Shaw letter had been stimulated in the first place by remarks critical of the Bureau by one of Shaw's professors, he also ordered that no more agents were to attend the John Jay College or any other educational institution where the FBI was not held in appropriate esteem. Shaw sued for reinstatement, and on behalf of agents' freedom of speech, but ultimately dropped his efforts to return to the Bureau and settled for damages of $13,000. He eventually came back into the Justice Department after Hoover died, first working for the Office of National Narcotics Intelligence, then the Drug Enforcement Administration, and eventually the department's Office of Management and Finance.*

* The Bureau can bear a long grudge on its late Director's behalf, however. When it issued passes in 1975 authorizing access to the new FBI building for certain Justice Department personnel, it excluded Shaw.

Hoover had some extraordinary fetishes. His dislike for sweaty or moist palms was rumored to be so extreme that some desperate agents with hands that tended to perspire were nearly driven to seek medical or psychiatric assistance in advance of an occasion when they were expected to shake hands with the Director. Jay Robert Nash, in *Citizen Hoover,* tells of an incident in which Hoover, meeting with a new agents class, stared repeatedly at one man in the group who had a sallow complexion. The reason was that the man had been wounded in the face during wartime combat, and plastic surgery had been only partially successful; but Hoover didn't like his men to look that way, and so the prospective new agent, who had previously done well during the training course, was told that he had failed a critical examination. The Director also instituted a stringent "weight-control program" which followed a life insurance company chart and went well beyond the actual restrictions within which men would be able to perform their jobs effectively. But resourceful individuals sometimes found their way around the rules, and on occasion the nation's number one G-man was easily fooled. Kenneth Whittaker, for example, later special-agent-in-charge of the Miami Field Office, once found himself overweight in advance of a scheduled interview with Hoover. He solved the problem by buying a suit and shirt that were too big for him — to create the impression that he had lost weight, rather than gained it — and personally thanked the Director for "saving my life" with the weight requirements. In another instance a man slated to be assigned to one of the Bureau's overseas offices was hesitant to keep an appointment with the Director because he had gone bald since their last meeting and Hoover did not like to promote bald men. Thinking ahead, and with the help of some clever colleagues, the man wrote to Hoover saying he felt that it would be selfish and unfair to take up the Director's precious time just before his annual appearance before the House Appropriations Committee. Hoover agreed and appreciated the man's sacrifice. When the agent later had to visit Hoover on his return from the overseas post, he brought the Director a gift large enough to distract his attention from his offensive hairless scalp.

Gifts to Hoover — and sometimes to Tolson — were the clue to many dramatic promotions and rapid advances within the FBI ranks. One up-and-coming man had especially good luck after giving the Director a custom-made Persian rug with the initials JEH woven into the center. After a time, major gifts to Hoover from the top leadership were, in effect, informally required on such occasions as his birthday and the yearly anniversary of his appointment as Director. Each time his choice, usually things for the home, would be communicated through Tolson, and then the assistant directors would chip in the appropriate amount of money to try to find the item wholesale through Bureau contacts. On Hoover's last Bureau anniversary before his death, his forty-seventh on May 10, 1971, his aides spent almost two hundred dollars on a trash compacter obtained through an FBI friend at the RCA Whirlpool Corporation. Sometimes, if Hoover was not particularly fond of a gift, he would not hesitate to give it to someone else in the Bureau, even though the recipient might have seen it the first time around. It saved him money. On one occasion, office assistant Sam Noisette was surprised and pleased to receive an expensive pair of cuff links from his boss; then he discovered that they were engraved with JEH on the back.

In order to believe that he looked good himself, the Director often needed to hear that others looked bad. Some of his men played up to that need. In an FBI memorandum that became available to Justice Department officials during a court case in the 1960s, an assistant director, James H. Gale, described to Hoover a meeting with the attorney general, in this case Nicholas deB. Katzenbach — Gale wrote that the attorney general "squirmed" in his chair and "turned pale" during the discussion; when they later shook hands, the assistant director said, the attorney general's hand was "cold and clammy." On another occasion, Hoover returned from a meeting at the White House with President Truman and was furious — the Director had quoted a passage from the Bible and Truman had insisted he was misquoting and had corrected him. Back at the Bureau, Hoover wanted the matter researched. As it turned out, the Director was wrong; but his aides twisted the context and presented their findings to Hoover so that it was the President who seemed foolish.

Others found different routes to favor with the Director. One, Robert Kunkel, spent years as a clerk under the tutelage of Hoover's influential secretary Helen Gandy; she was generally considered to be responsible for his becoming an agent and, eventually, a special-agent-in-charge (although he also gained some leverage by giving good stock market tips to the Director). John F. Malone, long the special-agent-in-charge in Los Angeles and later the assistant-director-in-charge in New York, is another Bureau executive who became close to Hoover, in part because of the friendship he developed with bandleader Lawrence Welk, whose television program was one of the Director's favorites.

Even those who admired Hoover's style and tolerated some of his excesses had difficulty with his more irrational and extreme acts. He tended, for example, to go overboard in trying to correct abuses or avoid controversy. After the Central Intelligence Agency was exposed in the late 1960s for having funded the National Student Association and other university groups, the Director for a time withdrew authorization for anyone in the FBI to contact anyone on any campus, a ruling that made it difficult for agents to handle some routine inquiries. Eventually he relented. When Hoover declared in 1969 that agents were forbidden to fly on Trans World Airlines, because a TWA pilot had criticized the FBI's handling of a hijacking crisis, agents simply ignored the order because, as aides had tried to point out to Hoover, there were some air routes covered only by TWA. (In connection with the same incident, Hoover wrote to the president of the airline and, apparently drawing upon confidential files, told of the pilot's earlier "difficulties in the Air Force.") When Hoover was dissatisfied with the cooperation of the Xerox Corporation in the investigation that followed the theft and distribution of documents from the Bureau's Media, Pennsylvania, Resident Agency, he sought to have all Xerox photocopying machines removed from all FBI offices and replaced with another brand; that plan was canceled only when assistant directors persuaded him that the change would be cumbersome, time-consuming, and expensive.

It required considerable Bureau resources to build and nourish the desired public interest in Hoover. A "correspondence section" handled the replies to incoming mail that sought personal information about the Director, ranging from his favorite recipe for apple turnovers to how he ate his steak and what color neckties he preferred. Sometimes the correspondence was handled in a laughable, almost cynical way. Once, for example, a two-page letter was drafted explaining why Hoover's favorite hymn was "When the Roll Is Called up Yonder." When the Director saw the draft, he changed his mind and ordered up a new one giving his choice as "Rock of Ages." The correspondence section merely substituted the name of one hymn for the other and sent the letter out, with the explanation for the choice left the same.

One of the major occasions for pronouncements of wisdom from the Director was his annual trip to Capitol Hill to justify the Bureau's budget request before the House Appropriations Committee. (He testified only occasionally before the parallel Senate committee.) The transcripts of these sessions read smoothly and show Hoover first giving an eloquent statement and then responding with impressive clarity to every question posed by his congressional interrogators. Bureau officials familiar with the closed-door committee meetings, however, say that quite a lot of work went into sprucing up the public version of the transcripts; one told it this way: "There would be serious mistakes every time he appeared, especially before the House committee. The Director would recite the facts concerning particular cases, and he might have them all wrong, even providing false information about individuals. Sometimes he would be completely off base, especially when he attempted to answer the congressmen's questions. . . . So we would always get the record back the next day, and we would work almost around the clock for three or four days to straighten it out. The job was controlled by John Mohr in the Administrative Division. We would take out the garrulous crap and replace it with perfect language and grammar. When the record came out [publicly], it would be beautiful; it had to be, because Hoover would issue it to everyone on the FBI mailing list. . . . The congressmen were proud to be part of it all, and most of them probably didn't even notice the difference."

But some of the Hoover statements were impossible to take out or doctor up, especially if some of the legislators had immediately latched on to them for their own purposes. The story is told of the occasion in the late 1940s when the Director was asked how much crime cost the country each year and he answered, off the top of his head, twenty-two billion dollars. Back at headquarters later, in trying to justify the figure, the best anyone could come up with was eleven billion. But the public record was left to stand, of course, since Hoover's word was assumed to be gospel. That figure was used blindly for years until finally someone wrote in and asked why, in light of the increase in crime, its cost to the nation never changed. From that time on, the Bureau began raising the estimate slightly each year.

These slips and quirks were not publicly known, however, and even had they been revealed, they would have posed no serious threat to Hoover's position. He had himself locked securely in place and employed foolproof techniques for keeping himself there. One was to let it be widely known, or at least believed, that his men in the field were collecting juicy tidbits about political figures, unrelated to pending cases but submitted for Hoover's personal interest and, if necessary, his use. Francis Biddle, one of President Franklin Roosevelt's attorneys general with whom Hoover got along well, wrote in his memoirs that the Director, in private sessions with him, displayed an "extraordinarily broad knowledge of the intimate details of what my associates in the Cabinet did and said, of their likes, their weaknesses and their associations." Such information was stored in special locked file cabinets in Hoover's inner office. Access was permitted to only about ten Hoover lieutenants through Miss Gandy. The Director's personal files included some political dynamite — allegations about the extramarital affairs of President Roosevelt and his wife Eleanor, the inside story about an undersecretary of state believed to be a homo-sexual and his alleged attempt to seduce a porter during a train ride to Tennessee, incidents from Richard Nixon's years as Vice-President, and the early escapades of John F. Kennedy. The files grew thicker and more significant all the time, because whenever someone entered the running for President, Hoover would have any records on him in the Bureau's general files pulled out, updated, and transferred to his office. What use Hoover made of any particular file is a matter of speculation; but what is now clear is that the implicit threat to use them was always there. It was one way of instilling in politicians a special kind of loyalty toward the FBI: fear of what Hoover might have on them and could choose to reveal. What became of each of Hoover's controversial private files after his death is still a subject of some mystery and concern. Miss Gandy and Tolson are each believed to have taken some with them when they left the Bureau, and others were moved into the office of W. Mark Felt, who became acting asso-ciate director under Acting Director L. Patrick Gray III, and were later inherited by Associate Director Nicholas Callahan. Many of the files are unaccounted for and were probably shredded before Hoover died or shortly after.

Attorney General Edward H. Levi, testifying before the House Judiciary Subcommittee on Civil Rights and Constitutional Rights on February 27, 1975, announced an inventory of the 164 files that had been made available to him from the associate director's office. Classi-fied as Official and Confidential material or marked OC, they included "many routine, mundane and totally innocuous materials," Levi said; but he also acknowledged that at least forty-eight of the folders con-tained "derogatory information concerning individuals," including members of Congress. It seemed clear that some of the most important OC files were missing — and that there was probably another entire set of delicate Hoover files, perhaps labeled Personal and Confidential, that were missing and were never made available to the attorney gen-eral at all. Miss Gandy later admitted destroying the "personal" files.

Another of Hoover's successful techniques was to calculate care-fully his relationships with those in power. As one former associate noted, the Director had "many of the attributes of a genius. He could identify people's foibles and weaknesses and play upon them cleverly." He was not particularly fond of the Kennedy brothers, but the brother he liked least was Robert, who sought to assert unprecedented control over the FBI when he became his brother's attorney general. (One irritant, according to those in the Justice Department in the early 1960s, was Kennedy's personal comportment; Hoover felt that he desecrated the hallowed halls of the Justice Department by strolling around in his shirtsleeves and by bringing his dog to the office.) Hoover knew of, and exploited, Lyndon Johnson's distrust of Robert Kennedy, and immediately after John Kennedy's assassination the Director virtually suspended communication with the attorney general. He replaced a Kennedy intimate, Courtney Evans, as White House liaison with a Johnson favorite, Cartha D. DeLoach. Hoover's antennae were excellent and helped him move quickly to keep up with any realignment of power.

Whatever the complaints about Hoover, most observers generally praised him for keeping the Bureau honest and above the temptation of corruption to which so many other law enforcement agencies succumbed. But it has become clear that the Director himself did not measure up to the rigorous standards of honesty and avoidance of conflict of interest that he set for others. In an agency where a man could be severely disciplined for taking an office car home overnight without special permission, it was a little difficult to reconcile and justify the fact that the Director had five bulletproof limousines, each worth about $30,000, at his service — two in Washington and one each in Los Angeles, New York, and Miami — and that he regularly used them for personal business, like trips to the racetrack or on his vacations with Tolson. The vacations, in Florida or southern California, were never officially called vacations but "inspection trips" — meaning that Hoover would drop in at a field office or two each time and shake hands. That was enough for him to charge the whole trip to the government.

In Miami Hoover stayed free at a hotel owned by Meyer Schine, who admitted in congressional testimony that he also had ties with big-name bookmakers. (Schine's son, G. David, was counsel to Senator Joseph McCarthy's investigating subcommittee, along with Roy Cohn.) In La Jolla, California, his stays at the Hotel Del Charro were at no cost, courtesy of the owners, millionaire Texas businessmen Clint Murchison and Sid Richardson. Sometimes they had elaborate parties in La Jolla in Hoover's honor, flying in specially prepared chili from Texas for the occasion; the bills that were never presented to Hoover and Tolson ran into the thousands of dollars. Murchison and Richardson gained control of a nearby racetrack that Hoover frequented; some of the profits from it were supposed to be channeled to a newly established charitable foundation, but prominent members of the foundation board soon quit when they found that this was not happening. Both of these Hoover friends came under investigation in the mid-1950s in connection with a controversial proxy fight to win control of the New York

Central Railroad, and it was learned years later that Richardson, who had extensive oil holdings, made payments to Robert Anderson while Anderson was serving as President Eisenhower's secretary of the treasury and was in a position to influence national oil policy. By means that were never publicly known, Hoover himself amassed substantial oil, gas, and mineral leases in Texas and Louisiana — they were valued at $125,000 at the time of his death — alongside his other valuable investments. All the while the Director was growing rich, he never hesitated to accept free accommodations wherever he traveled.

His annual visit to the West Coast became one of the most important events on Hoover's calendar. If the invitation to stay at the Del Charro did not arrive on schedule, the SAC in San Diego was asked to nudge it along. One year the field office there was sent into a frenzy because it had neglected to stock the hotel's freezer with the Director's favorite ice cream. When he asked for it upon arrival, the SAC had to call the ice cream manufacturer to open his plant at night in order to satisfy Hoover's needs. A stenographer from the field office was then dressed up as a waitress and dispatched to the Del Charro to serve the ice cream to Hoover and Tolson.

The Director eagerly used the extensive and sometimes expert facilities of the Bureau for his own personal whim and benefit. He was reluctant, ostensibly for security reasons, to permit outside workmen in or near his home, so it was the FBI Laboratory that performed such duties as building a porch or installing new appliances. The Lab was sent in on one occasion because Hoover was impatient with how long it took his television set to start up. The problem was solved by rigging the unit so that it was always on; he just had to turn it up to get the picture. Unknown to Hoover, this just meant that the tubes burned out and had to be changed often — at government expense. Sometimes the Lab's assignments nearly resulted in disaster, as on the occasion Hoover decided that he wanted a new toilet installed. But the Director did not like the new one, because it was too low, and he demanded the old one back. Fortunately, the technicians were able to reclaim it from a junk heap after a search.

In his earliest days at the Bureau, Hoover had steadfastly and emphatically declined to profit from the G-man boom, turning back the honoraria when he gave speeches and declining to endorse cigarettes or other commercial products. But as time passed he became avaricious. When the Freedoms Foundation, a conservative organization based in Valley Forge, Pennsylvania, twice gave him its gold medal and five-thousand-dollar award, it called ahead to the Director's aides, pointing out that it was customary for the recipient of the award to donate the money back to the foundation. Both times Hoover refused and said he intended to keep the money for himself. Perhaps the most profitable transactions, however, involved the books published under Hoover's name, especially the enormously successful *Masters of Deceit,* subtitled *The Story of Communism in America and How to Fight It.* The book was written primarily by agent Fern Stuken-broeker, a Bureau researcher on subversive groups, but the substantial royalties were divided five ways — one-fifth each to Hoover; Tolson; Assistant-to-the-Director Louis B. Nichols; William I. Nichols (no relation to Louis), editor and publisher of *This Week* magazine, who helped to market the book; and the FBI Recreation Association — which permitted the Director to contend that the profits were going to the hard-working FBI personnel. Hoover aides urged that Stuken-broeker be rewarded for his efforts with an incentive award. Hoover balked, but agreed after a dispute; however, he knocked the amount down from five hundred dollars to two hundred and fifty. Later, when Warner Brothers wanted to launch a television series about the FBI, Hoover's condition was that the film studio purchase the movie rights to *Masters of Deceit.* His price was seventy-five thousand dollars. As the deal was being closed, the Director suddenly got cold feet and worried whether he would be subjecting himself to criticism. He sent Cartha DeLoach to President Johnson to discuss the situation, and Johnson gave his confidential approval. The television series, with Efrem Zimbalist, Jr., as the star, got off to a successful start. Hoover pocketed the money and later left it to Clyde Tolson.

When J. Edgar Hoover died suddenly on May 2, 1972, the news was initially kept from the agents for about three hours; the day began like any other in the Bureau, early and busily. When the word finally came out, it was greeted with a combination of shock and relief. Some felt comfort, for Hoover's sake, that he had died painlessly and in the job rather than suffering the indignity of replacement after forty-eight years; others looked ahead to the opportunity, at last, for a review and reconsideration of the FBI and its roles. Many were oblivious to the turmoil Hoover was leaving behind, and few sensed the trouble ahead.

That night, hundreds of agents and former agents, some traveling from far away, gathered at a funeral home in Washington to pay their respects to the Director. One who came from out of town later recalled the scene this way: "They had washed his hair, and all the dye had come out. His eyebrows, too. He looked like a wispy, gray-haired, tired little man. There, in the coffin, all the front, all the power and the color had been taken away."

The next day his body lay in state in the rotunda of the United States Capitol and Hoover was eulogized by Chief Justice Warren E. Burger as "a man who epitomized the American dream of patriotism, dedication to duty and successful attainment." A day later, in the National Presbyterian Church, President Nixon added his own tribute: "He was one of those individuals who, by all odds, was the best man for a vitally important job. His powerful leadership by example helped to keep steel in America's backbone and the flame of freedom in America's soul." He was buried not at Arlington National Cemetery but, in accordance with his instructions, at the Congressional Cemetery in the Capitol Hill section of Washington, with members of his family.

On the first anniversary of Hoover's death — a day that one can imagine Hoover would have wanted to be elaborately noted — there was no ceremony because the FBI was in disarray. On the second anniversary, Director Clarence M. Kelley led the assistant directors in a solemn, private wreath-laying ceremony at the Director's grave. For the faithful, that made things seem a little better again.

XII

The Dukes

DeLoach was a capable and loyal administrator while in the Bureau and he has still maintained that loyalty since he left the Bureau. I know of several instances in which he upon his initiative came to the defense of the Bureau, one being in talking particularly with Congressman Boggs, the old drunk from Louisiana. As for Sullivan, your comments concerning him were certainly true. I only wish that I had been able to spot his instability long before I did. When the crisis finally came, I moved swiftly and forced him into retirement. . . . I personally think that I have been blessed with an exceptionally outstanding staff of executives through my administration of the Bureau with the exception of Sullivan. You certainly were tops when you were in the Bureau and I have never questioned your loyalty since you left it.

— From a letter from J. Edgar Hoover to Louis B. Nichols, January 7, 1972

ONCE J. EDGAR HOOVER BECAME ENTRENCHED in his position, it was heresy for anyone high up in the Bureau to express a desire to succeed him. As far as he was concerned, no one could ever really take his place, and so he made absolutely no preparations for any such eventuality. It was never clear whether Hoover actually had dreams of immortality or merely wanted to die in office, but Clyde Tolson was heard to say on many occasions that "I don't think Mr. Hoover will ever leave this job." Even to be the subject of rumors about the directorship, or to discuss it with anyone, was a sin. When an FBI man came up with an unpopular idea, or disagreed with Hoover, he was, as likely as not, accused of aspiring to become director. "I used to think,

'What the hell's wrong with wanting to be director?'" says John P. Mohr, for many years a close assistant to Hoover on the administrative side. "Does the President get mad at every kid that wants to be President? . . . I never said that to Hoover, though." Mohr knew better than to commit such an indiscretion.

Heresy or not, there were many key FBI men who dreamed over the years of taking charge of one of the most powerful agencies of the American government and of stepping into the most prominent job in the world of law enforcement. It was never clear, however, just how a successor to Hoover might be selected, since there was no precedent and, until 1968, no precise legal machinery to govern the exercise.* In order to enter the unofficial running, anyone who aspired to the position had to fulfill several unwritten requirements. He had to:

- show unremitting devotion to his work, putting in days of perhaps sixteen to eighteen hours, sometimes merely weeding through stacks of paperwork, often at the expense of family life and even personal health;
- display unrelenting fealty to Hoover, supporting him on the most insignificant of issues and reporting faithfully on his opponents;
- get transferred back to FBI headquarters in Washington at the earliest possible moment in a Bureau career and stay there, learning the protocol and power structure, and practicing how to control the field offices;
- exhibit a healthy respect for the old values, a strong religious faith or a pretense of same, and an awe for the titans of big business and others who hold private power;
- gain some powerful political allies in both houses of Congress as well as a few major cities; and
- build a durable constituency or two outside the FBI, preferably elsewhere in the Executive Branch of government and among private organizations such as the American Legion.

As Hoover's reign progressed, a few people rose to the very top through a combination of cunning and luck, plus skill — in bureau-

---

* As an amendment to the Omnibus Crime Control and Safe Streets Act of 1968, Congress adopted a measure, sponsored by Senator Harry F. Byrd, Jr. (D-Virginia), and George Murphy (R-California), requiring Senate confirmation of any future directors of the FBI. As Senator Murphy put it during debate on the amendment, Hoover "will regrettably not be with us forever."

cratic politics as well as in the performance of official FBI duties. They were generally in the right place at the right time, somehow caught Hoover's attention and moved quickly; and they did not rock the boat. Insofar as the public was concerned, they remained anonymous and gave their best for the endless glorification of the Director. They were friendly with each other, but cautiously so.

One man long assumed to be a prime candidate for the succession was Louis B. Nichols. He spent many of his twenty-three years in the FBI bureaucratically and personally close to Hoover, and, until his retirement in 1957, he may have been the last person inside the Bureau capable of getting Hoover to change his mind or reverse a decision. (Nichols and his wife named a son John Edgar Nichols, after Hoover.) In his early agent days, Nichols was involved in manhunts for notorious gangsters like Alvin Karpis, but by 1935 he had moved to FBI headquarters to stay. Nichols developed the Bureau's aggressive approach to public relations, from early wartime puff-stories to co-operation in the production in the 1950s of a phenomenally successful authorized biography of the Bureau by onetime Associated Press and *New York Herald Tribune* reporter Don Whitehead, *The FBI Story*. Nichols had reporters eating from the palm of his hand, and one Associated Press news analyst wrote on the occasion of his retirement:

This country loses one of its best and most dedicated public servants. . . . the FBI can thank him for much of the enormous goodwill it enjoys. . . . he was, in this writer's opinion, the best public relations man any government agency has had in our time. His technique was simple: You could call him with a question. If he could answer, he would immediately; if he couldn't, he'd say so. He was utterly reliable. If it was possible, without revealing FBI secrets, to talk off the record for background, he'd do that, too. Through all these years the public has had a picture — justly deserved — of the FBI as an extraordinarily [sic] government agency. It was Nichols who for years presented that picture.

It was also Nichols who got the American press accustomed to the idea that the FBI knew best what should or should not be printed about itself.

When Hoover and Tolson were away together, Nichols served as acting director, and in that capacity he handled a number of major cases in Hoover's name. During the early 1950s he took under his wing a young Capitol Hill staff lawyer named Roy Cohn, giving him a great deal of guidance — and, it was often alleged, documents and other

information — during the controversial Red-hunting hearings conducted by Cohn's boss, Senator Joseph McCarthy.*

Nichols's public position was always that he did "not want to be in
the Bureau the day after Mr. Hoover leaves it." But many who worked
with Nichols, and learned from him, had the distinct impression that
he would not mind returning after Hoover had left, as director, to
carry on the tradition. Some said that the new position he took after
leaving the FBI, as executive vice-president of Schenley Industries in
New York, was a way for Nichols to make a great deal of money and
keep in touch with things until a propitious moment arose — such as
the election of his close friend Richard Nixon as President. In 1965
Nichols persuaded his boss at Schenley, liquor industry magnate Louis
S. Rosenstiel, to establish and endow the J. Edgar Hoover Foundation.
A lawyer, he became active and influential in American Bar Association
affairs, and sometimes when he was in Washington to lobby for Schen-
ley's interests, Nichols also made a few discreet pitches on Capitol
Hill on matters of special concern to his alma mater, the FBI.

But by the time Nixon was elected in 1968, it was more inconceivable than ever that a President would take the political risk of replacing Hoover, and Nichols, sixty-two, was about to retire from Schenley.
If he had ever had designs on the FBI directorship, he had by then
abandoned them. Nichols advised the new President to reject the advice of those who might become impatient with the Director and to
leave Hoover in the job as long as he was able to function. He also
implored the President to name Hoover's successor, when the time for
that came, from within the FBI. Nichols was furious, and told Nixon
so, when the President made L. Patrick Gray III acting director of the
Bureau to succeed Hoover in 1972. "This is doom," he warned the
President.

Other Bureau men got within reaching distance of the top.
Edward A. Tamm, who had shared some of the exciting early gang-
busting days with Hoover, moved out of contention when named to a
federal judgeship in Washington by President Harry S Truman in
1948. His brother, Quinn Tamm, stayed on and was considered a man
to watch, but he departed in 1961, after a dispute with the Director, to
become head of the International Association of Chiefs of Police. Men

---

* The Nichols-Cohn relationship was a lasting one. Years later, after Nichols had
left the Bureau, he intervened to obtain punitive transfers for three agents in the
New York Field Office, assigned to work with then U.S. Attorney Robert Morgen-
thau, who Cohn complained were "harassing" him in connection with a federal
investigation of his business dealings. When the agents complained that they had
been unfairly treated, their deadline to move was shortened.

who were later, if only briefly, considered candidates included W. Mark Felt, who had wide field experience and was one of Hoover's favorites in his last years, and Mohr, the efficient and powerful assistant-to-the-director for administrative matters, who was said to retain substantial influence within the FBI even beyond his retirement a month after Hoover died. Mohr was abrasive in tone and rough in his manner — he is one of the few men in FBI history who got away with contradicting or talking back to the Director — and this may have hurt his chances; he seemed content, in any event, to manipulate things from behind the scenes without actually aspiring to the directorship. Although second in command to Hoover, the one man who was never really considered as a possible successor was Clyde Tolson, whose interest was only in helping the Director; indeed, as Tolson's health failed over the years, some Bureau officials were amazed that he was still able to do even that.

But as the FBI grew to maturity in the mid-twentieth century, during the years when reasonable men dared to believe that Hoover might one day retire, fade, or be unseated, two Bureau figures emerged who seemed at times to be jockeying for the succession and trying to make themselves available. They stood out from the rest. They were the dukes of the FBI, Cartha Dekle DeLoach and William Cornelius Sullivan.

◆

"There's something about a man from a country town in Georgia," President Lyndon B. Johnson used to say in an attempt to explain his reliance upon people from that state, including Secretary of State Dean Rusk, White House aide Tom Johnson — and "Deke" DeLoach, who became as close to Johnson as any FBI man below the rank of Director ever became to any President in the Bureau's history. Perhaps closer.

DeLoach's "something" included speaking softly, moving gently, and oozing humility; only an occasional twitch of the cheek hinted at anything less than total control of himself and his surroundings. He was the kind of man who inspired confidence, who could be sent on delicate missions and be counted upon to perform occasional unsavory tasks. Sometimes he sounded like a fundamentalist, punctuating his conversations with thanks to the Lord for the most minute of favors. He was smooth. Because of Johnson's faith in him, and Hoover's unprecedented degree of trust, DeLoach sometimes had to walk a tightrope; but he exercised extraordinary prerogatives as Hoover's surrogate, and occasionally as Johnson's, so that during the 1960s he became a very powerful man in Washington. To the public, DeLoach was little known, but his could be the kiss of life for a newsman who sought favor with the FBI, or the kiss of death for a congressman who offended or defied the Director. He could be gracious or mean, whichever seemed necessary for the good of the service.

The country town in Georgia was Claxton, west of Savannah, where he was born into the poorest of families. His father died when Deke was eight years old, and his mother ran a boardinghouse. While growing up, he delivered newspapers and picked pecans and cotton to earn money. His mother wanted him to stay in Claxton after high school, but he won a football scholarship to Gordon Military College and then, after a year, to South Georgia College, where he stayed for two years before going on to the Stetson College of Law in Florida. DeLoach was determined to stand on his own two feet. He washed dishes and sold jewelry to earn spending money; he often told the story that once, when his mother sent him a check for eighteen dollars, he sent it back (in part, he confessed, because he thought she wouldn't have enough money to cover it in her bank account).

DeLoach was enrolled in law school in 1942 when he heard a radio announcement about the FBI's capture of saboteurs from Nazi Germany who had been landed on Long Island after crossing the Atlantic in a submarine. (What the announcement did not say was that one of the saboteurs wanted to throw in the towel and put the FBI onto the case with several phone calls upon arrival.) Excited by that romantic image, as so many others were at the time, the twenty-year-old DeLoach applied immediately to the Bureau; but the assistant director who interviewed him in Washington found him "baby-faced." So he was required to spend time as a messenger on the midnight shift before being admitted to agents' training class. Although his FBI career got off to a good start when some of his early work as a street agent in Norfolk, Virginia, came to the admiring attention of supervisors at headquarters, DeLoach soon found himself ringing doorbells in Toledo and Akron, Ohio, investigating members of the Communist party. Bored by this, he applied for military leave, joined the navy, and spent most of his service time teaching boxing and other sports in Norman, Oklahoma. He never did finish law school.

After the war the FBI assigned him back to Ohio, but within a year DeLoach was one of many young agents called to Washington and assigned to help coordinate the flood of work gathered by the Bureau's new responsibility for background investigations of people who were required to have security clearances under the Atomic Energy Act. This work was rather dull; however, because it grew out of the FBI's security role in World War II and seemed such an important part of the new Cold War era, the atomic energy section had a certain appeal, and some of the people assigned to it were quickly marked for more prestigious duties. DeLoach, for example, was transferred to the group that handled liaison with the Central Intelligence Agency and the Office of Naval Intelligence — sensitive duty because of Hoover's deep and abiding resentment of any agency with which the Bureau shared jurisdiction in the intelligence field. In his new capacity, DeLoach was assigned to attend an international conference on intelligence matters in Europe and to write a report about it for Hoover.

That was in 1951, and when Hoover called the young man in for a discussion about his report, "an immediate spark," as DeLoach would later describe it, was struck between them. The Director apparently decided to take DeLoach under his tutelage as he had done with only a few agents over the years. As their relationship became closer, many FBI colleagues observed that DeLoach seemed to fulfill the role of a son to Hoover; others thought it was more like that of a hatchet man.

Hoover gave DeLoach sensitive special assignments, mostly involving investigations of men in the field who had violated FBI rules. Within months the Director's new whiz kid had been skip-promoted to the rank of inspector. DeLoach's arrival in a field office was not exactly welcomed, because he was known to be the enforcer of the Director's harsh and impersonal disciplinary policies. The yardstick for determining severity of punishment usually involved subjective factors such as "extent of embarrassment to the Bureau" or "damage to Mr. Hoover's position with the American public." One DeLoach mission, for example, took him to Honolulu, where two agents had been unwittingly tape-recorded while they interviewed members of the American Communist party and tried to persuade them to become FBI informants. When the incident was widely publicized, Hoover became furious about the way it made the Bureau look. DeLoach recommended that the two agents be placed on probation and suffer a thousand-dollar cut in pay; Hoover agreed, but then added to the punishment a thirty-day suspension without pay and transfer to different field offices.

Sometimes DeLoach was considered fair by his colleagues in the ranks, as when he urged that two agents in the New York Field Office not be punished for their failure to convince a spy to become a double agent. But Hoover was outraged by that recommendation; he not only punished the unsuccessful New York agents but also censured De-

Loach for his unsatisfactory advice. On other occasions DeLoach was involved in the punishment or dismissal of FBI agents for sexual infidelity to their wives.

Before long DeLoach tired of the travel and the amount of time he was spending away from his family, so he asked Hoover for reassignment. Many people would have suffered for such impertinence, but DeLoach again landed on his feet, this time as a special assistant in Clyde Tolson's office. There he remained at Hoover's beck and call.

In 1953, Hoover called upon DeLoach to help with "the American Legion problem." The Director had long enjoyed enthusiastic, unrestrained support from the Legion, but there had been moments when the Legion's fervor had become embarrassing. In 1940, for example, as American involvement in World War II approached, there was a move to establish an investigative corps within the Legion to look into alleged subversive activities that legionnaires felt were a threat to the national security. It would have been a vigilante squad, like the American Protective League of an earlier time. Hoover calmed the organization by proposing that Legion post commanders maintain liaison with the special-agents-in-charge of FBI field offices and hold discussions of "national defense" issues. The Legion could call the Bureau's attention to problems, but would not actually investigate. Now in the midst of the McCarthy era, the American Legion, as Hoover put it, was "causing trouble" — demanding FBI investigations of specific liberals and left-wing figures. Hoover did not object to the spirit of the Legion's interest, but he liked to set the ground rules and choose the targets himself. The Director also felt that the antics and horseplay at Legion conventions reflected poorly on the mutual cause.

Hoover wanted DeLoach to join the Legion and try to straighten it out. DeLoach took the job seriously. His FBI credentials served him well inside the organization, and he became a post commander, department vice-commander, department commander, and eventually national vice-commander. At one point he was urged to run for the position of national commander, but Hoover vetoed that as "too political" a job for one of his FBI men to hold. Instead, DeLoach became chairman of the Legion's national public relations commission in 1958. In that position and in his other Legion offices over the years, he exercised a great deal of influence over the organization's internal policies as well as its public positions. The American Legion remained a strong supporter — some might even say a servant — of the FBI. It was a substantial resource that could be mobilized behind Hoover and his views in moments of controversy, and a good vehicle for honoring and saluting officials and friends of the Bureau. Occasionally there were accusations, from legionnaires and FBI men, that DeLoach sought to take unfair advantage of his position in the Legion and that he ran roughshod over his opposition; but for the most part his role in keeping the organization he helped lead in line with the government agency he worked for was seldom questioned.

Back at the Bureau, DeLoach moved from Tolson's office into what was euphemistically called the Crime Records Division, which was responsible for FBI public relations and the Bureau's dealings with Congress. There he worked for Lou Nichols, who sought to mold DeLoach in his own image. In 1959, two years after Nichols left to join Schenley, DeLoach took over Nichols's job of assistant director for Crime Records. Six years later, DeLoach moved up to the rank of assistant-to-the-director in general charge of all investigative activities, and also retained jurisdiction over Crime Records as well as handling other special jobs for Hoover. These included liaison with LBJ's White House.

DeLoach's rapid advance provoked both admiration and resentment among his colleagues. He cultivated a good image for himself that was bound to rub off on others and on the FBI as an institution — young, dynamic, personable, a conservative but spiffy dresser whose FBI cuff links gave off just the right amount of sparkle. He was an organization man, ever loyal to Hoover. He lunched almost every day with Alex Rosen, an older man, assistant director for the General Investigative Division. But even some of DeLoach's friends in the Bureau were quick to call him a wheeler-dealer; they were not quite willing to trust him. Everything Deke DeLoach did seemed to have been well thought out in advance.

Sometimes there were several Deke DeLoaches. One was a public speaker who could outdo some of the archest right-wing ideologues with his invective and sloganeering. In an address to the American Farm Bureau Federation, DeLoach assessed the social movements that were sweeping the country in the mid-1960s as a "malignant disease." Reflecting the Hoover line but seeming to go well beyond it, he declared:

. . . growing numbers of citizens — racketeers, Communists, narcotics peddlers, filth merchants and others of their ilk — hold themselves above the law. . . . Look, for example, at the "celebrity status" which has often been accorded those morally and emotionally immature misfits who have cast a shadow of disgrace across the streets of many American communities and the campuses of some of our educational institutions. I refer to the lawless demonstrators, the draft-card burners, the raucous exalters of the four-letter word. I refer to the arrogant nonconformists, including some so-called educators, who have mounted the platform at public gatherings to urge "civil disobedience" and defiance of authority. And I refer also to those members of the self-proclaimed "smart set" who consider it a sign of "sophistication" to ridicule decency, patriotism, respectability and duty.

Later, talking to the Association of County Commissioners in Georgia, he said that those who commit civil disobedience in the name of a cause used "infantile reasoning" and were dedicated criminals who "don't give a tinker's dam about the rights of others." He called for "a new impatience" in dealing with such tactics.

Some of DeLoach's speeches, in the early days, were written for him by an expert, William C. Sullivan, a man eight years older who was making his way through the Bureau ranks at the same time. They were friends for many years, exchanging gifts and favors, living similarly one-dimensional lives that had them driving in from the Washington suburbs early in the morning and returning late at night. Often Sullivan, an expert in the field of subversion and espionage, would recommend books for DeLoach to read. DeLoach seemed preoccupied with more mundane concerns, borrowing money occasionally to keep up the front that he thought was necessary for a man in his position in the FBI. Over time, the friendship faded, especially as DeLoach advanced more quickly than Sullivan. DeLoach eventually accused Sullivan of being obsessed with his specialty, of exaggerating the importance of some security work for the purpose of his own self-aggrandizement within the Bureau hierarchy, while Sullivan would charge that DeLoach had no principles and was a vicious, brutal, political creature.

Another DeLoach was a discreet operator who, like Nichols before him, labored behind the scenes to sustain a Bureau image to the Director's liking. Every press release was required to begin with Hoover's name and to include at least two other mentions of him; the Director's name also had to appear twice in every script approved by the Bureau for the weekly program about the FBI on NBC radio's weekend "Monitor" program. Part of the press policy also involved cooperating only with certified FBI "friends," and cutting off all contact with reporters, editors, and organizations perceived to be "enemies."

As chief spokesman for the Bureau, DeLoach kept a stable of trusted journalists well supplied with information — people such as Hoover's close friend Walter Trohan of the *Chicago Tribune*, labor columnist Victor Riesel, Jeremiah O'Leary of the *Washington Evening*

Star, Sandy Smith of *Time* and *Life* magazines, and syndicated columnist Jack Anderson, who was later classified as a bona fide enemy. Like many other government agencies in Washington, the Bureau profited from selectively leaking material to its friends that it wanted to see in print or on the air. Several influential journalists, not all of them close FBI friends, revealed at one point that DeLoach had privately played tapes of some of the indiscretions of Martin Luther King, Jr., for them, warning the journalists that if he were revealed as the source he would deny having done so. (They kept his secret for years before revealing it.)

One man who profited from this system was conservative newscaster Paul Harvey, whom Nichols spotted early as someone who would go far. (He did; Harvey's morning broadcast from Chicago eventually became the country's top-rated network radio program.) Harvey got into serious trouble in 1951, when he was caught late one night scaling the fence of the Argonne National Laboratory to prove that security was lax at the center for the development of nuclear reactors. Investigations by the FBI and a federal grand jury led nowhere, except that Harvey was quietly invited to Bureau headquarters for a chat with Nichols, who urged the broadcaster to pursue his concern over security by subtler means and offered to help. Harvey and the Bureau emerged good friends, and on several occasions DeLoach arranged appointments with Hoover for Harvey. Harvey's broadcasts, which frequently extolled the FBI, reached millions of Americans, especially in small towns. (In 1965, Harvey was presented the Fourth Estate Award for Distinguished Public Service in the Field of Communications by the American Legion, and his plaque was signed by, among others, public relations chairman Deke DeLoach. When Hoover died in 1972, Harvey requested and received a souvenir from the Director's desk.)

DeLoach's job also required getting things done on Capitol Hill. It was standard operating procedure for the FBI to draft letters for friendly members of Congress to use in making statements important to the Bureau or in prying loose documents from other parts of the government; sometimes this was even a useful tactic in intramural disputes with the Justice Department — particularly during the tense period when Robert Kennedy was attorney general in President Johnson's cabinet and his feuds with both Johnson and Hoover were coming to a head. It was an intricate game, in which DeLoach played a role not unlike that of an outside lobbyist. He kept his tracks carefully covered. One former Bureau official who worked with him on Capitol Hill says that DeLoach was especially good at "tooting his own horn" in his memos to Hoover about congressional contacts, boasting, for example, about having brandy with Senator Eastland and always reporting things in a manner that would enhance his own prospects and power within the FBI.

In dealing with Congress, DeLoach drew upon the Bureau's elaborate indexing system, which catalogued every reference in FBI files to a member of Congress, whether it was part of a criminal or background investigation, unsolicited and unsubstantiated material transmitted by members of the public, or information submitted by the field offices to satisfy Hoover's taste for gossip. If there were enough individual items, they would be gathered together in a separate file on the congressman. In addition, under a system begun by Nichols in the early 1950s, the Bureau's Congressional Services Office kept a sheaf of clippings and other background material on each congressman, enough to indicate whether he could be counted as a Bureau "friend."

Former Congressman Cornelius Gallagher (D–New Jersey) charged on the House floor in 1972 that in 1966 DeLoach had prepared a letter for Gallagher's signature to then Attorney General Nicholas deB. Katzenbach, asking for copies of the authorizations once signed by Robert F. Kennedy as attorney general for electronic surveillance of Martin Luther King and of casinos in Las Vegas. Hoover was then in the midst of a feud with Kennedy who, as a senator from New York, was criticizing the Bureau's wiretapping and bugging. Gallagher claimed that the draft of the letter had been phoned to his congressional office by New York attorney Roy Cohn, the former aide to Senator Joseph McCarthy and a mutual friend of the FBI and Gallagher. The congressman, then chairman of the Special Subcommittee on Invasion of Privacy of the House Government Operations Committee, was conducting an inquiry into government wiretapping. According to Gallagher, Cohn said the FBI would consider the New Jersey congressman a good friend if he would obtain the Kennedy authorizations and make them public, to help Hoover. Gallagher apparently never sent the letter, and in his 1972 speech he contended that many of his future problems — extensive articles in *Life* magazine, seemingly based on leaked FBI files, that were damaging to his career and reputation, and his indictment by a federal grand jury for tax evasion — were the punishment for his defiance of the Bureau. DeLoach denied Gallagher's allegations, and Gallagher was later convicted and went to jail. But whatever the fact about his own activities, Gallagher's story about being approached by the FBI to run its errand rang true to others who had been similarly contacted by the Bureau in DeLoach's day. In fact, the FBI finally brought the authorizations signed by

Kennedy for surveillance of King into the public domain by writing both sides of a correspondence between Congressman H. R. Gross (R-Iowa) and Hoover and getting Gross to insert the correspondence in the *Congressional Record*. Other members of Congress have vivid — and unhappy — memories of the angry and sometimes abusive letters they would get from DeLoach, on plain white paper, whenever they said something publicly that displeased the FBI.

DeLoach was one of the few Bureau officials who appeared to believe in cordial diplomatic relations with some of the more political and partisan appointees in the Justice Department, usually the objects of FBI scorn. At one point, he even offered to include some of Attorney General Robert Kennedy's aides in a typical Bureau "deal," an arrangement whereby top FBI personnel bought their meat from a Washington supplier at wholesale prices. DeLoach was also a friend of Ramsey Clark, who was a guest in DeLoach's home the night after he was named attorney general by President Johnson. (The two men had an irreparable falling out, however, when the FBI announced the solution of the Martin Luther King assassination case in the midst of Robert Kennedy's funeral, without first notifying Clark. Nonetheless, DeLoach, like Hoover, remained friendly with Ramsey's father, Tom Clark.)

But by far the most important role DeLoach played was in his assignment as liaison with President Johnson, almost from the moment Johnson succeeded to the office. He developed a degree of involvement and intimacy with the nation's First Family that was previously unheard of in the FBI. Other FBI agents had had close relationships with presidents — Ralph Roach was a confidant of President Truman, for example, and Orrin Bartlett sometimes traveled with President Eisenhower — but it was perhaps Johnson's own personality, and his tendency to suck people into his inner circle, that made DeLoach's situation unique. During the Johnson administration, White House communication with the Bureau not only circumvented the attorney general, which was often the case under other presidents, but it sometimes even bypassed Hoover. DeLoach and his family were invited to White House social functions (although not to the weddings of the Johnson daughters) and spent an Easter weekend with the Johnson family at Camp David, the presidential retreat in the Maryland mountains. Lady Bird Johnson would seek out DeLoach's official and private advice from time to time on whether it was safe for her to make certain public appearances. DeLoach was the only Bureau official ever to have a White House phone extension in his home. Johnson ordered it installed — in the master bedroom — in a fit of temper one Saturday night when he was unable to get through because DeLoach's teenage daughter was on the family telephone. He would call DeLoach at home for information about demonstrations and riots, to check on the progress of FBI background investigations of presidential appointees, to make informal requests for help, or just to chat about his problems as President.

Johnson had met DeLoach when they were senator from Texas and Hoover's representative on Capitol Hill respectively. During the 1950s, when word was passed by Tolson that it would be a nice thing to do, DeLoach worked with Johnson and Senator Styles Bridges (R–New Hampshire) on legislation that would maintain payment of Hoover's full salary even if he retired as FBI director. As Democratic Senate majority leader and as Vice-President, Johnson enjoyed De-Loach's cooperation and extended his own in return. When Johnson became President, and feared for his life, he wanted protection by the FBI. Although there was no specific statutory authority for the FBI to do so — the job is officially assigned to the Secret Service — DeLoach established a procedure whereby an FBI agent would ride with John-son on the presidential aircraft, *Air Force One,* on virtually every trip he took as Chief Executive. DeLoach selected the agents who would go along, and the Bureau field office at Johnson's destination was often pressed into service. Frequently DeLoach himself was invited to travel on the plane, but he generally refused.

There was little surprise to anyone familiar with the relationship when Johnson asked Hoover to send a team of about twelve FBI agents to the Democratic National Convention in Atlantic City in the summer of 1964 and the Director selected DeLoach to lead the team. The official reason for sending the special detachment was to deter-mine the seriousness of any "danger" or "threats" to the President. The convention task force also supervised another operation, the ongoing electronic surveillance of Martin Luther King, Jr., and other civil rights leaders whom the Bureau was then insisting were under the influence of the American Communist party. It would later be charged, how-ever, by Sullivan and others, that the information gathered by De-Loach's team at the convention was purely political in nature, and that the only "danger" in question was Johnson's worry about whether Kennedy loyalists — not least of all King — would work among dele-gates to interfere with the President's control and manipulation of the convention that was to nominate the Johnson-Humphrey ticket. Years later, in a statement to the Senate Watergate Committee, Leo T. Clark, who was senior resident agent in Atlantic City at the time of the 1964 convention, said that DeLoach had told him the special convention surveillance of "threats" to LBJ was not to be revealed to the Secret Service and especially not to Hoover's nominal superior, Attorney General Robert Kennedy.

That fall, when White House aide Walter Jenkins was arrested on a homosexuality charge, Johnson, who was campaigning in New York, called DeLoach at home. The President ordered him to pick up Mrs. Johnson at the White House and to get a statement from Jenkins in the hospital room to which he had been taken so that the President could decide whether to fire Jenkins. DeLoach never did reach the hospital that night; he got as far as the White House, however, where he met with Mrs. Johnson and presidential confidants Clark Clifford and Abe Fortas in Jenkins's office. DeLoach ultimately kept watch over the investigation of the incident conducted by the FBI's Special Investigative Division, said to be one of the most extensive in Bureau history. The man with whom Jenkins was arrested in the basement of the YMCA in Washington was interviewed with the goal of determining whether — as Johnson wanted to believe — he was part of a Republican plot. After more than five hundred people had been questioned in the investigation, Johnson requested that several good friends of Jenkins be added to the roster of those interviewed, and he asked DeLoach if the Bureau would put into its report some statements about Jenkins's good character and hard work. DeLoach, who had himself been a close friend of Jenkins, tried, but Hoover apparently refused to go along. (The Director had already been embarrassed by publicity over the fact that he had sent Jenkins flowers in the hospital, as a friendly gesture.)

After the Jenkins incident, Johnson brought DeLoach into the White House for two weeks to do a survey of the files and determine how such a problem could be avoided in the future. One revelation was that the Secret Service, in a routine check of Johnson's White House staff, had not looked into a prior Jenkins arrest in 1959 for "disturbing the peace," as the FBI would ordinarily have done. (The 1959 arrest, also on a homosexuality charge, was dismissed for lack of evidence.) One result was to institute FBI background investigations for future members of the White House staff, a procedure that had been followed under Presidents Eisenhower and Kennedy, but not Johnson.

DeLoach has repeatedly denied the allegation that the FBI conducted electronic surveillance of the 1964 Republican presidential campaign of Senator Barry Goldwater at Johnson's request, as has

The Dukes: Cartha D. "Deke" DeLoach, a smooth talker from Georgia, was the FBI man most trusted by Lyndon Johnson; he became so close to the President as Bureau liaison that a White House phone extension was installed in the bedroom of his home. William C. Sullivan, a New Englander through and through, was the Bureau's expert on communism and subversion, a tireless advocate of vigilance on the domestic front; here he is shown giving a speech (as he often did) on July 23, 1970. Once friends, the two men became bitter rivals and were very different from each other in manner and style. But they had important things in common: both hoped to succeed Hoover and became engaged in intricate machinations toward that end; both failed. DeLoach retired at age fifty and took a lucrative job with the Pepsico conglomerate. Sullivan was forced out by Hoover after a nasty dispute over policies and personalities.

been frequently charged.* Four years later DeLoach was the intermediary for a request from Johnson that a check be made of telephone calls from the campaign plane of then vice-presidential candidate Spiro T. Agnew to determine whether Agnew and the Chinese-born Republican socialite, Anna Chennault, were in touch with South Vietnamese officials in Washington in an effort to sabotage the Paris Vietnam peace talks launched by Johnson. It was widely believed in American intelligence agencies that the Republicans were trying to keep the South Vietnamese away from the Paris talks — the National Security Agency routinely intercepted a cable from the South Vietnamese Embassy in Washington to Saigon, advising delay in the hope that the South Vietnamese would get a better deal if the Republican ticket were elected. Johnson, fuming with anger, initially called DeLoach at home at 11:00 P.M. and demanded an immediate investigation, but DeLoach did nothing before discussing the matter with Hoover the next morning. Then he had the Albuquerque Field Office check the record of toll calls made from a portable telephone that had been plugged into the Agnew campaign plane during a stop there a few days earlier. The investigation also included a wiretap and physical surveillance of Mrs. Chennault, but the FBI never conclusively connected Agnew or her to the maneuvering with the South Vietnamese. DeLoach and Johnson discussed this incident by telephone in 1973, just after it had surfaced in the press and shortly before the former President died.

Some of DeLoach's prestige with the Johnson administration had obvious advantages for the Bureau. For example, DeLoach was the FBI representative on Johnson's National Crime Commission, and thus he was in a position to defend the agency in another important forum.

After a time during the Johnson presidency, it became clear that DeLoach was emerging as an heir apparent to Hoover. The Director began to show his irritation and his jealousy of DeLoach's closeness with the President — by pouting and making sarcastic remarks — and DeLoach worried that his position might become analogous to that of Courtney Evans, who became so close to Attorney General Robert Kennedy as FBI liaison that he felt he had to leave the Bureau as soon as Kennedy left the Justice Department.† Sensitive to the delicate bal-

* A review of FBI practices by Attorney General Edward H. Levi later revealed, however, that Bureau files and other resources had been used to run "checks" on Goldwater's staff for Johnson.
† Evans, no friend of DeLoach, had become a pawn in Hoover's paranoia about holding on to his job. In 1963, before the assassination of President Kennedy, rumors circulated that if Kennedy were reelected in 1964, he would request the Director's retirement at seventy and replace him with a younger man. As someone

ance he had to strike between his relationship with the Director and his warm personal friendship with the Johnsons, DeLoach several times specifically asked the President to make things easier for everyone concerned by occasionally calling Hoover himself with requests rather than always going around him to DeLoach. Johnson usually replied that although he had once revered Hoover, and although he and Mrs. Johnson had gotten along with him back in the years when they were neighbors in Washington, he now had difficulty understanding him because the Director talked too fast. The President complained, further, that he was no longer sure he could believe everything that Hoover told him. Johnson promised to try to change his habits, but generally he slipped right back into the routine of calling DeLoach, and sometimes DeLoach was in the difficult position of having to take the calls while in Hoover's office.

Rumors frequently swept the Bureau (sometimes helped along by Sullivan) that Johnson was ready to urge Hoover to retire and to replace him with the younger man he trusted so much more. Hoover acted to make that difficult to do, using as his delegate, of course, DeLoach, just the man he thought might present a threat. The word filtered down, through Tolson as usual, that it would be a good idea if President Johnson were to waive the mandatory federal retirement age of seventy in order to permit Hoover to stay on indefinitely in the Director's chair. DeLoach dutifully went to Johnson with the request, and the two men had a soul-searching discussion in which the President warned, "Deke, I hope you know what you're getting into" — the probability that DeLoach would never become director. Neither man was prepared, however, to risk Hoover's wrath, and so the waiver was promptly granted, phrased in such a way that it sounded like something Johnson had thought up for the good of the country. Johnson's action made it even less likely that any future President would take the political gamble of trying to separate Hoover from his FBI during his lifetime.

After Nixon's inauguration in January 1969, DeLoach was noticeably less in the swing of things at the White House, despite the efforts of his mentor Lou Nichols, a Republican who was active in the 1968 campaign and was thought to be headed for an administration job, to commend DeLoach to Nixon. The White House phone was taken out of his home ten days after Nixon took office. At the Justice Depart-

---

who was close to and trusted by the Kennedys, Evans was a logical candidate for the slot, and so Hoover began to freeze him out. Once the President was dead and the attorney general had left to run for the Senate, Evans found it impossible to stay on.

ment, however, DeLoach was seen as an ideological ally of the new hard-line officials, and he became a close friend of Deputy Attorney General Richard G. Kleindienst. Despite what was thought to be a close affinity between Hoover and the Nixon administration, Attorney General John N. Mitchell disliked dealing with the Director, and after a short time he adopted the policy of waiting until Hoover had left for the day and then calling DeLoach with any direct requests of the Bureau. DeLoach was a practical man, some would say a chameleon. But one consistent factor, convenient for both Johnson and Nixon, was his role as an adversary of the Kennedy clan; thus it was only logical for him to be at Mitchell's side throughout the furor surrounding the incident at Chappaquiddick Island off Martha's Vineyard in July 1969, when a young woman riding in Senator Edward M. Kennedy's car, Mary Jo Kopechne, drowned — an incident on which the Nixon administration hoped to capitalize.

With Johnson gone, DeLoach was close once again to Hoover. But at their best moments the relations between Hoover and his favorite young lieutenant were peculiar and ambivalent. DeLoach would be trusted with the most sensitive of assignments — including the task of taking signed statements on two occasions from people who accused Hoover and Tolson of having a homosexual relationship. And yet, as someone who was thought to be playing the part of Hoover's son, DeLoach was invited to Hoover's home only three times in his entire FBI career, and Hoover accepted invitations to DeLoach's home only twice, although he often gave Christmas presents to the DeLoach children. At one point the Director offered to pay the $1,700 hospital bill of one of DeLoach's sons, but DeLoach declined the gift and borrowed instead. Never did the Director look in on his trusted young protégé; if Hoover wanted to talk with him, DeLoach, like everyone else, was summoned to the Director's office. When DeLoach showed even mild disagreement with Hoover, or when stories appeared in the press suggesting that he might be a logical successor, the Director would invariably react like an angry child and sulk for weeks.

One of DeLoach's most extravagant and successful gimmicks as the FBI's public relations chief was a party for newsmen that he gave for many years in conjunction with the annual convention of the American Society of Newspaper Editors; Hoover always praised him for it, but one year he saw some of the editors giving gifts to DeLoach rather than to him. The Director promptly ordered his aide never to hold such a party again.

At certain crucial times Hoover rejected DeLoach's advice and got into situations that resulted in ridicule of the FBI. One was the famous

1964 press conference in Hoover's office, for selected women reporters only, in which the Director twice blurted out the remark that Martin Luther King was "the most notorious liar in the country." DeLoach slipped Hoover a note, asking him to make it clear that this comment was off the record, but the Director sent the note back. When asked by one of the reporters for clarification, Hoover said his remark about King was definitely for attribution. DeLoach tried two more notes, but the advice was rejected, and finally Hoover said aloud, "I will not. . . . DeLoach is trying to tell me to take that off the record, but I will not." Hoover's words about King were, of course, widely reported and served to aggravate the FBI's already mixed reputation among black people.

By mid-1970, as he approached his fiftieth birthday, DeLoach had resigned himself to the fact that Hoover would probably never step aside voluntarily, and he had decided that he was not willing to chance the controversy that might come from being Hoover's replacement if the old man were forced out. Donald Kendall, chairman of the board of Pepsico, Inc., a prominent Republican and a friend of President Nixon, had offered DeLoach a job previously, and DeLoach had said that if Hoover were still Director when he turned fifty, he would accept. Now he decided that he was no longer willing to stay at a salary of $38,000 a year with seven children to support and considerable debts to pay.

DeLoach broke the news to Hoover six weeks before his birthday and was greeted with utter disbelief. "I thought you were one who would never leave me," said the Director in a conference that DeLoach clocked at two hours and forty-seven minutes. Unable to persuade DeLoach to change his mind, Hoover reacted characteristically, cutting him off for a couple of weeks, refusing to talk with him or send him mail. He eventually relented, however, and gave DeLoach a warm sendoff, including a gift of a set of gold buttons. Later he would tell DeLoach he was welcome to return to the fold anytime.

There is another theory of DeLoach's retirement — that he had come very close to some brushes with scandal and wanted to keep them from surfacing. It is not that he was ever formally under investigation or that there was any incriminating proof against him, but the rumor mill was kept especially busy in 1970 with tales about DeLoach. From his earliest days in the FBI, he had been hard up for money. People who rode in car pools with him in Washington back when DeLoach was liaison with the Pentagon say that he was sometimes caught claiming for mileage reimbursement even when he drove there in someone else's car; and later it was claimed that he double-billed the Bureau and the American Legion for some of his travels. At one point, a wealthy Florida builder was reported to be picking up some of the mortgage payments on DeLoach's home; but he said this was merely a "low-interest loan" from a friend. DeLoach came under the scrutiny of a federal grand jury in Baltimore early in 1970, after it was discovered that he had frequent social contact with Victor Frenkil, a contractor under investigation for alleged efforts to bring pressure on the Architect of the Capitol to make extra payments to him for construction of an underground garage for Congress. (The grand jury said later in a presentment that it had wanted to indict Frenkil for conspiracy to defraud the United States, but Attorney General John Mitchell forbade U.S. Attorney Stephen H. Sachs, a holdover Democrat from the Johnson administration, to sign the indictment.) According to a memorandum that DeLoach submitted to the federal prosecutors in Baltimore to explain his relations with Frenkil, the contractor had pestered him relentlessly as part of his efforts to win new friends in Washington; some of their contacts were also apparently related to Frenkil's commission to construct the new FBI Academy at Quantico. (When an agent from the Baltimore Field Office attempted to interview Frenkil in connection with an earlier case, his SAC had a phone call from DeLoach's office within an hour asking why.) An article detailing some of these controversies concerning DeLoach was written for the *Los Angeles Times* in mid-1970, but it did not run, presumably on the grounds that he was about to leave government and start a new life in the business world.

Before DeLoach left, he did one last important favor for Hoover: he persuaded Attorney General John Mitchell to endorse the Director's opposition to a new domestic intelligence program that was being pushed by the White House and by Assistant FBI Director William C. Sullivan. Then Hoover named Sullivan to replace DeLoach as the number three man in the FBI, just behind Tolson.

◆

Bill Sullivan was as rough as Deke DeLoach was smooth. Or so it seemed. Although his personal appearance had been questioned in some of his earliest field office assignments, Sullivan had managed to climb up through the Bureau ranks without paying any of the attention that most of Hoover's top men did to being neat and fastidious. His ties were often spotted, his shirt collars curled, and his suits sometimes looked as if he had slept in them overnight. His personal style of management and organization was chaotic; he moved frenetically and could easily misplace things or, in the midst of a conversation, lose his train of thought. He had a habit of coming in to his office on the weekends and typing his own letters; they were unmistakable for the smudges and dropped words or transposed letters. His temper was unrivaled. Sullivan became legendary for calling up colleagues in the Bureau leadership on the special telephone circuit that circumvented their secretaries, shouting a tirade into the receiver about something that had annoyed him and then hanging up without giving even a moment for a reply. Whatever Sullivan said, fast or slow, came out in a coarse New England country accent that years of travel and experience had never flattened.

But there was another side to Sullivan. While many of the other ranking FBI officials associated mostly with one another and often knew surprisingly little of what was going on in the outside world, Sullivan had a wide circle of acquaintances — wealthy businessmen, philanthropists, and even some of the intellectuals whom Hoover despised. Sullivan impressed them with his knowledge of communism and espionage and his assessments of the country's internal security. He mixed at dinner parties with people like Henry Kissinger, then a Harvard professor. While others in the Bureau hierarchy would give no credence to someone like liberal historian Arthur M. Schlesinger, Jr., who was on the FBI's "no-contact list" (because of an article he had written for *Life* magazine that had displeased Hoover), Sullivan voraciously read and annotated books by Schlesinger and writers ranging from Will and Ariel Durant and Aleksandr Solzhenitsyn to religious philosophers. In his early years as a Bureau supervisor, while others gossiped or stared idly on their way to work, he was likely to be buried in a book they had never heard of. A lifelong Democrat, he had a way of letting conservatives believe he was a conservative and liberals believe he was a liberal.

"Crazy Billy," as he was sometimes affectionately known by friends and detractors alike, did some things none of his Bureau peers would have dared. For example, he went out of his way to befriend former members of the Communist party of the U.S.A. who had left the organization in disgust and undergone conversion to anticommunism. Among them were Jay Lovestone, who had been ousted in 1929, and John Gates, once the editor of *The Daily Worker*, whom Sullivan personally investigated as a veteran of the Abraham Lincoln Brigade in the Spanish Civil War. With other former communists he corresponded or carried on communications through intermediaries. At one point, uncertain about the quality of information the Bureau would get on a peace march between Baltimore and Washington, Sullivan simply marched along himself and wrote his own report. In 1968, Sullivan filed a surprise request with Hoover for military leave, asserting that he wanted to go to Vietnam and see if he could help save American lives by using counterintelligence techniques that had worked against the communists and other groups within the United States. (Hoover denied the request.) He never hesitated to leap personally into the fray; during the 1971 Mayday antiwar demonstrations in Washington, for example, he personally tackled and arrested a protester who was spray-painting a slogan on a wall of the Justice Department.

When people made unflattering references to Sullivan's disheveled appearance, he liked to reply that he "grew up in overalls" in a farm community where that sort of thing did not matter much. Indeed, Sullivan was raised on a farm on the outskirts of Bolton, Massachusetts, and even when he went to high school in nearby Hudson, the "city boys" there poked fun at him as a scrawny country bumpkin. In high school, where he excelled in athletics, he had some of the same teachers and advisers as had his childhood hero Burton K. Wheeler. Wheeler had graduated from the school thirty years earlier, headed west, and became a United States senator from Montana — and, as recounted in Chapter III, first a powerful Bureau "enemy" and later a friend. Decades later, Sullivan got to know Wheeler personally for the first time and would take him on nostalgic automobile trips to the Massachusetts countryside.

Sullivan obtained a degree in education from American University in Washington and returned to New England, first teaching school in Bolton, then earning a master's degree and working for the Internal Revenue Service in Boston. As the Second World War approached, he applied for a position with army intelligence, but a college friend who was working for the FBI urged Sullivan to try there. The Bureau was building up its manpower because of new internal security responsibilities given it by President Roosevelt, and the thought was that Sullivan, with his background in education, could teach in the Training Division. He had a choice between the army and the FBI, and picked the FBI. Like most other new agents of the era, after he entered on duty in August 1941, Sullivan was rapidly transferred from one field assignment to another — Milwaukee, Albuquerque, Philadelphia, Baltimore, and San Antonio. Those were the days when the FBI was not so heavily regimented and regulated as it would later be, and as resident agent in Brownsville, Texas, Sullivan regularly made impromptu excursions into Mexico to look for fugitives. He paid a fixed dollar amount to the Mexican police for each head they helped him hunt. Sullivan came to believe then that the best investigative techniques were the ones that worked.

During the war, Sullivan joined the Bureau's Special Intelligence Service and was sent on a "confidential mission" to Spain, which was being used by the Germans for the transit of espionage agents. Sullivan's assignment was to calculate how the Bureau could intercept the agents. While in Spain he became ill, apparently because of his hectic pace, and he had to come back home early. On his return, he became a supervisor in the security field at FBI headquarters in Washington; there he spent the rest of his FBI career.

"Security" was big business for the FBI in the postwar years, and there was no better place to be, from the standpoint of having your work appreciated by Hoover, than in the research section of the Domestic Intelligence Division. Sullivan moved steadily up in the hierarchy, from supervisor to unit chief to section chief to inspector to chief inspector, and finally, in 1961, to the rank of assistant director of the FBI in charge of the Domestic Intelligence Division. Along the way he achieved the reputation of being the house intellectual and its foremost anticommunist, who was invariably buried in a scholarly analysis of espionage techniques or subversive literature. (He eventually had a personal library of three thousand books in this field, many of which he kept at his office so that his associates could use them. At one point he willed the entire collection to the FBI, but later he changed his will.)

Sullivan could be an ingratiating personality. He made all the fawning gestures toward Hoover that were necessary for advancement, not the least of which, in his case, involved feeding the Director's obsession for derogatory information about the CPUSA and warnings about the danger it presented to the country. He wrote the obligatory admiring letters to Hoover as others did. Sullivan liked to compare the Director to German Chancellor Konrad Adenauer and French President Charles de Gaulle and urged him to follow their example by remaining in office until a ripe old age. He was one of the few assistant directors close enough to Hoover to be addressed by his last name only — as in "Dear Sullivan" — for Hoover, a more familiar and respectful form of address than the first name alone.

Only rarely did Sullivan challenge the biases and predilections of Hoover's closest aides, as he did when he disputed Lou Nichols's contention in the early 1950s that the newly established Fund for the Republic was a dangerous radical organization. (Nichols succeeded in getting Hoover to attack the fund, which later became the Center for the Study of Democratic Institutions in Santa Barbara, California. The Bureau labored in vain for years to have the organization's tax exemption revoked by the Internal Revenue Service.)

Sullivan was exceedingly skillful at the FBI's peculiar variety of bureaucratic politics. He knew, for example, that if Hoover and Tolson were going to a cocktail party at a foreign embassy in Washington, they did not like to discover any of their subordinates there; so he would check carefully before accepting any such invitation, and go only when he would not run into Hoover and Tolson. He also realized that they could be equally upset if one of their assistant directors gave a speech that was widely praised or attacked. Sullivan tried to stay in the noncontroversial middle range. He also made it a point to quote Hoover at least once in every speech, even if that meant quoting something he had himself previously ghostwritten for the Director.

In the heyday of Cold War concern about the CPUSA, and even after those days, Sullivan was much in demand as a lecturer. He spoke three years running in the early 1960s at the Harvard Graduate School of Business Administration, and those addresses were later published, in a pamphlet called "Freedom Is the Exception," by the Standing Committee on Education Against Communism of the American Bar Association. They include strident warnings of the sustained communist assault on capitalism, descriptions of how communists had managed to infiltrate and take over American labor unions, and explanations of why "with few exceptions, the leaders of the emerging nations look to Lincoln, not to Lenin." He appealed to the future businessmen to remember that "every citizen should report facts regarding communism to the FBI," and he sounded a theme that he would take up more strongly in later years:

No realistic approach toward combatting communism can be achieved until reasonably specific areas of action are delineated. These areas are primarily those of Government and of individual action. If experience in dealing with communism has taught us anything, it is that there are certain types of communist activity which can be countered effectively only by the employment of highly trained, professional intelligence services. For the most part, communist intelligence, espionage and underground operations, as well as some aspects of Communist Party activities, are conducted by professionals. To deal effectively with these communist operations, we must resort to professionals of our own — trained investigators and experienced counterintelligence personnel. Today, counterintelligence activities stress skills and training which depend upon complex scientific aids. This is no area for amateur anticommunists. Rather, it is the province of experts.

Sullivan got along well with the Kennedy administration and its Justice Department under the President's brother. During the Johnson administration, by contrast, Sullivan was at times somewhat out of the mainstream, and beginning in 1964, he began to warn Hoover and Tolson that Deke DeLoach was involved in political dealings with the White House that could "subtly undermine" the Director's position.

Although Sullivan repeatedly followed a Hoover dogma alleging communist infiltration of the civil rights movement — insisting, for example, that the 1963 March on Washington had included some two hundred CPUSA members trying to exploit the occasion for their own purposes — he also took the position that the Ku Klux Klan was hurting the nation and urged that the FBI use its substantial resources against that organization, something Hoover had always seemed reluctant to do. Sullivan's father had spoken out against the Klan in Massachusetts and as a child he had once been frightened by a cross-burning in Bolton, and so he was now upset by reports from the South that blacks were being beaten and synagogues attacked without any significant police response.

After a characteristic dispute among assistant directors, responsibility for the Klan was transferred at Sullivan's request from the General Investigative Division to his Domestic Intelligence Division. Sullivan soon convened a conference in Atlanta, where he invited veteran agents who had spent most of their careers in the South to talk about how the Bureau might fight the Klan. According to one participant in that meeting, "They really told the truth," as they had apparently never done in their reports to headquarters. "They talked about what goes on, the problems they had with sheriffs, police departments and hostile communities." Out of the conference came a bold decision — and what would turn out to be a major precedent: to use against a purely domestic organization techniques that had previously been reserved primarily for espionage cases, foreign intelligence matters, and the CPUSA and other old-line leftist political groups with alleged foreign connections; to set up a full-fledged "counterintelligence program," in Bureauese a COINTELPRO, against the Ku Klux Klan.

"The purpose of this program," said a memorandum that went out from headquarters to Atlanta and other southern field offices on September 2, 1964, "is to expose, disrupt and otherwise neutralize the activities of the various Klans and hate organizations, their leadership and adherents." The memorandum continued:

The devious maneuvers and duplicity of these groups must be exposed to public scrutiny through the cooperation of reliable news media sources, both locally and at the Seat of Government. We must frustrate any effort of the groups to consolidate their forces or to recruit new or youthful adherents. In every instance, consideration should be given to disrupting the organized activity of these groups and no opportunity should be missed to capitalize upon organizational and personal conflicts of their leadership. . . . All Special Agent personnel responsible for the investigation of Klan-type and hate organizations and their membership should be alerted to our counterintelligence plans relating to these groups. Counterintelligence action directed at these groups is intended to complement and stimulate our accelerated intelligence investigations. . . . You are cautioned that the nature of this new endeavor is such that under no circumstances should the existence of the program be made known outside the Bureau and appropriate withinoffice security should be afforded this sensitive operation. . . . To insure our success in this new endeavor, the Agent to whom the program is assigned in each office must have a detailed knowledge of the activities of the racist groups in the territory and that knowledge must be coupled with interest, initiative and imagination. The Agent must be alert for information which has a disruptive potential. The information will not come to him — he must look for it.

A victory for Sullivan, the COINTELPRO — Disruption of White Hate Groups led to a broad expansion of such techniques in the domestic intelligence field. Eventually he proposed, and obtained Hoover's approval for, other similar COINTELPROs against "black extremists" and the constellation of groups that the FBI helped to label as the New Left. Sullivan glowed with satisfaction as FBI agents made phone calls under false pretenses, faked documents, and otherwise gummed up the works of organizations they were "investigating."

But while Hoover endorsed some of Sullivan's ambitious programs, he irritated his domestic intelligence chief in other ways. In 1966, without much explanation or discussion, the Director suspended the use of a number of traditional FBI tactics, including the "black bag job," generally used to break into foreign embassies and consulates to obtain cryptographic information, and legal "mail covers," in which the post office cooperated with the FBI by recording the names and addresses of the people who corresponded with the subject of an investigation, as well as illegal mail covers, which involved opening mail addressed to certain overseas destinations by suspected spies.* With no apparent motive except to avoid embarrassment of himself and the Bureau, Hoover also cut back substantially on the use of wiretaps and other forms of electronic eavesdropping. Those restrictions chafed

* Director Clarence Kelley has acknowledged that there were nonetheless "a few" break-ins at foreign embassies after 1966.

Sullivan, who felt they would make it more difficult for the FBI to combat the espionage conducted by "illegals" from the Soviet Union and other communist countries.

Sullivan had other problems. He was increasingly involved in petty internal quarrels that seemed to divert energy from the substance of the Bureau's work. He and DeLoach sparred often; they quarreled over DeLoach's alleged leak to selected reporters of information from the Domestic Intelligence Division. (Sullivan's evidence at the time was that a reporter had inadvertently left some of the material in a phone booth on Capitol Hill.) Now Sullivan complained bitterly and often to Hoover about the way DeLoach handled FBI liaison with the Johnson White House, and he was thought to be the source of repeated rumors — albeit indirect ones, in best counterintelligence style — that DeLoach was conspiring with President Johnson to become Hoover's replacement as Director. (So strong was Hoover's paranoia on this point that he would sometimes assign agents to investigate the rumors, and would direct that signed, sworn statements be taken from the FBI aides who figured in them.) Sullivan's insistence that the Johnson administration was making improper political use of the FBI usually fell on deaf ears, except that it seemed particularly to aggravate one of DeLoach's original patrons, Clyde Tolson. That would usually result in tiffs with Tolson over such issues as whether Sullivan properly initialed all the mail that came across his desk. The skirmishes would generally conclude with Sullivan writing a properly contrite letter to Hoover, like one in November 1969, in which he quoted a speech by President Theodore Roosevelt in Paris in 1910 and had these musings to share with the Director:

No person knows better than yourself that life is never simple and human relations are not always tranquil. This is a world of tension, struggle, strife and turmoil. It has always been so. We may not understand it fully in all instances but irrespective of this we have no choice but to accept it as it is — understood or not. Hence, the wisdom in the old saying: Change that which can and ought to be changed. Accept that which cannot be changed. Learn to distinguish between the two.

It is this learning "to distinguish between the two" where I have on occasions failed in life and sometimes seriously.

Sullivan complained that agents borrowed from his division for special duty in the Dominican Republic during the American intervention in 1965 were being kept on there too long. He lost on that point, and the agents stayed. He also lost when he tried to have his division moved back into the main Justice Department building from its temporary quarters more than a mile away in downtown Washington; Hoover ordered a special study of the issue by the Inspection Division, which concluded it would be foolish to move out two other divisions just to bring Sullivan's back in. Instead, the Domestic Intelligence Division moved into a nearby private office building, but it still remained outside headquarters, a symbolic separation that bothered Sullivan.

When Sullivan had difficulties, they were often compounded by W. Mark Felt, a ranking official in the Inspection Division and eventually its assistant director. Felt, an uncannily handsome, white-haired man who looked about ten years younger than his actual age, could be as smooth, if not as clever, as DeLoach, and he became one of the Director's favorites in his declining years. It was Felt who had the responsibility of policing the Hoover-ordered cutbacks in wiretapping and who blew the whistle when he discovered orders coming out of the Domestic Intelligence Division to about twenty field offices to open an investigative file on every resident of every commune in their territory. He also opposed in executive conference a proposal to open a file on every member of Students for a Democratic Society.

Sometimes Sullivan just did what he thought was necessary without getting advance approval or without notifying those above him after the fact. At the 1968 Democratic National Convention in Chicago, for example, he directly contravened Hoover's instructions by assigning several agents from the field office there to dress appropriately and penetrate the ranks of the antiwar protesters who were threatening to disrupt the convention. The agents fed substantial information to the Chicago Police Department, information that may have had an effect on the violent confrontations that ensued.

Although he apparently voted for Democratic candidate Hubert Humphrey in the 1968 presidential election, Sullivan was delighted with the policies and performance of the administration of President Richard M. Nixon. He welcomed the arrival of a get-tough attorney general, John N. Mitchell, and of a White House staff that was willing and eager to pursue the sources of alleged security leaks from the government, a job that Hoover regarded with reluctance since he felt that each federal department should police itself. Sullivan was the key middleman when, beginning in May 1969, President Nixon and his then national security adviser, Henry Kissinger, launched a "special program" of wiretaps on thirteen government officials and four newsmen in an attempt to determine how information was getting out about secret American military operations in Southeast Asia and the strategic arms limitation talks (SALT) with the Soviet Union. Sullivan

303

was responsible for reporting to Kissinger and his deputy, Alexander M. Haig, and later to presidential chief of staff H. R. Haldeman, whenever the taps produced something of interest. Two of the taps were kept in operation, on Morton H. Halperin and Anthony Lake, after they had left the National Security Council staff and had gone to work for Democratic presidential aspirant Edmund S. Muskie, a senator from Maine. Sullivan kept the logs and reports of all these wiretaps in his own office, rather than in the Bureau's general files, with Hoover's knowledge and approval.

Hoover also selected Sullivan in June 1969 for a confidential mission to Paris, where Sullivan arranged with French authorities to have electronic surveillance placed on syndicated columnist Joseph Kraft, who was interviewing communist representatives to the Vietnam peace talks and was then planning to proceed to the Soviet Union on a reporting trip. Sullivan instituted full coverage of Kraft, in his hotel room and elsewhere, and later the FBI's "legal attaché" at the American Embassy in Paris shipped the tapes back to Washington in the diplomatic pouch.

One development that pleased Sullivan was the appointment of a kindred spirit, Robert C. Mardian, as assistant attorney general in charge of the Justice Department's long-dormant Internal Security Division. Mardian was a hard-liner and, like Sullivan, seemed to have an almost pathological concern about student protest and the growth of the Black Panther party and other black militant groups. Mardian's office, like Sullivan's, was in the Federal Triangle Building, a short walk from the main building that was Justice Department and FBI headquarters. The two men spoke often, initially at arm's length — they argued about politics, with Sullivan suspicious of Mardian for having worked in Senator Barry M. Goldwater's 1964 Republican presidential campaign organization — but later more intimately. Mardian let Sullivan in on what the assistant attorney general said was a developing Nixon administration plan to dump Hoover and name a new director.

Relations between Hoover and Nixon were officially cheerful, but several of the President's closest advisers were impatient with the aging Director, and they saw Sullivan as an ally on that front. In meetings of the U.S. Intelligence Board, Sullivan, as the FBI representative, complained openly that restrictions imposed by Hoover were preventing the Bureau from coping adequately with the espionage threat.

The standoff was dramatized in the summer of 1970, when Nixon convened a meeting with Hoover and the directors of the Central

Intelligence Agency, the Defense Intelligence Agency, and the National Security Agency to discuss what they perceived as a need for better domestic intelligence operations in light of the antiwar upheaval and other civil disturbances across the country. Sullivan was Hoover's delegate to, and therefore the effective chairman of, the working group of intelligence agency representatives that came up with a proposal for reinstituting the surreptitious entries, mail interception, and other programs suspended by Hoover in the mid-1960s. Although the recommendation was signed by White House aide Tom Charles Huston, many parts of it were revised and typed in the FBI's Domestic Intelligence Division, where Sullivan and some of his aides were ready to expand operations. Hoover balked again when he saw the final proposal. Although he approved resumption of a few of the tactics — such as "trash covers," which involved rummaging through a suspect's garbage looking for potential intelligence or character information — and backed down on his opposition to some others — including the recruitment of college-age informants who would be able to spy on radical groups more effectively than older ones — he vetoed most of the plan. Whether some parts of the plan were instituted unofficially anyway has never been clear, but President Nixon later claimed Hoover's veto was the reason he found it necessary to establish the Special Investigations Unit, better known as the "plumbers," in the White House. Similarly, the CIA, and both its friends and critics, cite the Director's recalcitrance, and resulting feuds with other agencies and with the White House, as an important cause of that agency's escalation of its already controversial domestic intelligence activities in the early Nixon years.

As strained as relations were becoming between Hoover and Sullivan, in June 1970, the Director nonetheless named his rebellious intelligence chief to replace DeLoach as assistant-to-the-director for all investigative activities, the number three job in the Bureau. Cynics entertained two theories about the appointment: either Hoover was trying to appease the Nixon administration by advancing one of its favorites; or he was trying to hurt DeLoach, who had been so disloyal as to retire, by replacing him with his archenemy.

Tensions only increased. Although Sullivan was assumed by the outside world, and even by some in the Justice Department, to be a close and trusted associate of Hoover, his colleagues in the Bureau leadership kept him at a distance. In his resistance to the Hoover-Tolson world view and to their long-established system of doing things — he even refused to accept gifts on his thirtieth anniversary as an FBI agent — Sullivan was saying what a lot of other people were thinking but felt should not be said. Although they might have complained privately about Hoover for years, they did not approve of Sullivan's insulting the Director so blatantly. A few discreetly egged Sullivan on, but most of his associates opposed him. The FBI became as polarized internally as it had ever been since Hoover took control in 1924; within the Crime Records Division, there were even informal spokesmen for the two factions.

On October 12, 1970, Sullivan gave a well-publicized address to the United Press International Editors and Publishers Conference in Williamsburg, Virginia, in which he warned that radical organizations, including the Weatherman faction of Students for a Democratic Society, were turning to a strategy of "urban guerrilla warfare" and might try to kidnap campaigning politicians or foreign heads of state attending the twenty-fifth anniversary celebration of the founding of the United Nations. He also complained that the Black Panthers were in "the vanguard of black extremism," were responsible for increasing numbers of attacks on police officers, and were visiting Arab nations for training in terrorist tactics.

The speech was perfectly consistent with Bureau policy, as far as it went, but it was Sullivan's answers to questions that attracted most of the attention back at headquarters. Sullivan flatly declared that there were no direct links between the communists and the student radicals, and that the American Communist party no longer represented a significant threat to national security, answers he knew to be accurate on the basis of his experience in the Domestic Intelligence Division. But that was a challenge to the Director's credo; and as soon as Hoover and Tolson heard about it, they called Sullivan on the carpet for "downgrading" the Communist party. They fumed for months. Sullivan refused to recant, however, privately or publicly. He also quarreled with Hoover and Tolson on another matter of Bureau orthodoxy: whether communists and other Marxists had infiltrated the Protestant clergy in the United States. The Director claimed that they had, but Sullivan, who had friends in the National Council of Churches, insisted they had not. (For this stand, Sullivan was denounced in print by the right-wing Church League of America, as he was from time to time in *Fiery Cross*, the magazine of the United Klans of America.)

Sullivan criticized the Director for breaking off liaison with the Central Intelligence Agency over a minor dispute. He opposed Hoover's move to expand the number of "legal attachés" representing the Bureau in American embassies overseas and accused him of using that proposal in an effort to paper over the FBI's failings at home. He spoke up against some severe examples of the Director's disciplinary policies. He was one of the FBI officials who were enraged when, in an appearance before the Senate Appropriations Committee in November 1970, Hoover revealed an investigation of Reverends Daniel and Philip Berrigan and other militant antiwar Catholics. Hoover all but declared that the Berrigans were guilty of conspiring to kidnap presidential adviser Kissinger; and his prejudicial remarks, which he insisted upon releasing publicly, gave the Bureau and the Justice Department serious trouble as the investigation and eventual prosecution of the Berrigan case evolved.

In June 1971, when the *New York Times,* the *Washington Post,* and other newspapers published the top-secret Pentagon Papers, Hoover was initially reluctant to launch a major investigation, preferring to treat it as a "leak case" that was the primary responsibility of the department where the leak had occurred. Once Daniel Ellsberg, a former researcher for the Defense Department and the Rand Corporation, had been identified as the probable source of the documents, Sullivan and his protégé C. D. Brennan, then heading the Domestic Intelligence Division, prepared a recommendation that Hoover permit agents in New York to interview Ellsberg's father-in-law, millionaire toy manufacturer Louis Marx. Special permission was necessary because Hoover and Marx were casual acquaintances and often at Christmastime Marx sent the Director a large shipment of free toys to distribute to the children of friends and to his favorite charities. Through a communications mishap, the interview with Marx was already completed by the time Hoover's reply denying permission came through. The Director, characteristically, became furious; he demoted Brennan and ordered his immediate transfer to Cleveland. Sullivan went straight to his friends in the Nixon Justice Department and got Mitchell to rescind Brennan's transfer. But the demotion stuck, and for months Brennan was virtually in solitary confinement, permitted to work only on the Ellsberg case.

By the next month, July 1971, Hoover had apparently resolved to squeeze Sullivan out and gave him a powerful hint to that effect by promoting a Sullivan opponent, Mark Felt, into a newly created number three position of deputy associate director, between Tolson and Sullivan.* What Sullivan did not realize or anticipate was that Hoover, in an exercise of classic bureaucratic good form, had gone to Mitchell

---

* Felt's promotion also affected the authority of John Mohr, Sullivan's counterpart on the administrative side, with whom Hoover had also become somewhat disenchanted.

and obtained official endorsement of his intentions for Sullivan. Mardian exhorted Sullivan not to press the dispute, but it was already too late.

Sullivan's bravado only intensified, and he deliberately provoked further confrontations with the Director. He went to his office on Saturday morning, August 28, 1971, and wrote Hoover a bitter letter outlining broad criticisms of the Director's policies and management. "It is regretted by me that this letter is necessary. What I will set forth below is being said for your own good and for the FBI as a whole of which I am very fond," he wrote and then went on to challenge allegations that he had been "disloyal" to Hoover:

I wish to direct your attention to my 30 year record in the FBI. It is well documented and I don't need to present it to you here with its letters of commendation and awards given by you. You have access to all this. If this record of three decades is not conclusive evidence of loyalty, what is? You have said that I consistently put the work of the Bureau above personal considerations. My family certainly will attest to this for they have year in and year out suffered from my neglect. This I now realize was a mistake on my part. . . .

. . . during the past year in particular you have made it evident to me that you do not want me to disagree with you on anything. . . . you claim you do not want "yes men" but you become furious at any employee who says "no" to you. . . . If you are going to equate loyalty with "yes men," "rubber stamps," "apple polishers," flatterers, self-promoters and timid, cringing, frightened sycophants you are not only departing from the meaning of loyalty you are in addition harming yourself and the organization. There is no substitute for incisive, independent, free, probing, original, creative thinking. I have brought up my children to believe and act upon this truth. They disagree with me regularly. But, they are not disloyal to me. In fact I think their loyalty is more deep, strong and lasting because of this kind of thinking. . . .

. . . you are incensed because I have disagreed with you on opening new foreign liaison offices around the world and adding more men to those already in existence. It seems to me you should welcome different viewpoints. On this subject I want to say this here. I grew up in a farming community where all people in a family had to literally work from the darkness of the morning to the darkness of the night in order to make a living and pay their taxes. It could be that this is what causes me to be so sensitive about how the taxpayers' money is spent. Hence, I want to say once more that I regard it to be a serious waste of taxpayers' money to keep increasing the number of these offices, to continue with all that we now have and to be adding more and more manpower to these offices. . . . You keep telling me that President Nixon has ordered you to do it and therefore you must carry out his orders. I am positive that if President Nixon knew the limitations of our foreign liaison operations and was given all the facts relative to intelligence matters he would reverse these orders if such have been clearly given. A few liaison offices can be justified but this expansion program cannot be no matter what kind of "reports" your inspectors bring back to you. Do you think many (if any) will disagree with you? What would happen if they did? . . .

. . . you have refused to give Assistant Director C. D. Brennan and myself any more annual leave. The reason you give is not valid and you know it. All it amounts to is this: you dislike us and you intend to use your absolute power in this manner as a form of "punishment." I am hardened to all this and can take it. But my family cannot. My oldest son is registering for college in New Hampshire this coming Tuesday. Naturally he wanted me to be with him and is extremely disappointed that I cannot be. Of course, I want to be with him and find out what kind of a roommate he has, talk to his professors, etc. My wife, in addition to respiratory trouble is now ill. . . . Surely, I don't need to explain to you why my wife and three children regard you, to put it mildly, as a very strange man. . . .

. . . what I have said here is not designed to irritate or anger you but it probably will. What I am trying to get across to you in my blunt, tactless way is that a number of your decisions this year have not been good ones; that you should take a good, cold, impartial inventory of your ideas, policies, etc. You will not believe this but it is true: I do not want to see your reputation built up over these many years destroyed by your own decisions and actions. When you elect to retire I want to see you go out in a blaze of glory with full recognition from all those concerned. I do not want to see this FBI organization which I have gladly given 30 years of my life to along with untold numbers of other men fall apart or become tainted in any manner. We have a fine group of men in the FBI and we need to think of every one of them also.

. . . When you are angered you can take some mighty drastic action. You have absolute power in the FBI (I hope the man who one day takes over your position will not have such absolute power for we humans are simply not saintly enough to possess and handle it properly in every instance). . . . you can fire me, or do away with my position . . . or transfer me or in some other way work out your displeasure with me. So be it. I am fond of the FBI and I have told you exactly what I think about certain matters affecting you and this Bureau and as you know I have always been willing to accept the consequences of my ideas and actions.*

Three days later, Hoover excoriated Sullivan during a long, angry session in the Director's office, called to discuss the contents of Sullivan's letter.

Hoover relented on the matter of vacation, but that was all. The

* The complete text of Sullivan's letter to Hoover of August 28, 1971, appears in the Appendix.

Director wrote back on September 3 — by now calling his assistant "Mr. Sullivan," a clear indication of his fall from grace — as follows:

> I have given, as you know, very careful attention to your letter of August 28, followed by a lengthy conference with you concerning it's [*sic*] contents.
>
> It has been apparent to me that your views concerning my administration and policies in the Bureau do not meet with your approval or satisfaction [*sic*], and has brought about a situation which, though I regret, is intolerable for the best functioning of the Bureau.
>
> Therefore I suggest that you submit your application for retirement to take effect at the close of business after you have had such leave to which you are entitled.

Sullivan left Washington for his family's new home in New Hampshire (bought a few years earlier because of his wife's respiratory ailment) on September 13, but first he contacted Mardian to warn that the end of his FBI career was in sight. Sullivan said that unless something was done with the logs and other materials he had been keeping that related to the seventeen special, secret wiretaps, Hoover "might use the records in some manner" to blackmail Nixon into letting him remain as Director. Mardian flew to the Nixon estate in San Clemente, California, for an urgent conference with the President, who directed that the wiretap information be removed from the FBI offices. Sullivan gave the material to Mardian, at the assistant attorney general's request, and was apparently unaware of what would then be done with it. (Six months later, Sullivan wrote to Mardian, saying that "no other person should have possession of it except yourself.") But as it later became clear, Mardian immediately transferred the wiretap records to the White House. There are conflicting versions as to whether the material was turned over to John Ehrlichman, then Nixon's chief domestic adviser, or to the President himself; but with Sullivan's cooperation it was safely out of Bureau files where it could have been found and submitted, as required, in federal criminal trials of people who had been overheard, including Ellsberg.

By the time the recalcitrant Sullivan had returned to Washington from New Hampshire, Hoover had named as his successor, in what was now the number four position in the Bureau, Alex Rosen of the General Investigative Division. Sullivan still resisted, so Hoover wrote again on September 30:

> Since you have not as yet responded to my suggestion in my letter of September 3, 1971, you are hereby being relieved of all duties as Assistant

to the Director at once and placed on annual leave pending your submission of application for retirement.

I deeply regret the occasion to take action such as this after so many years of close association, but I believe it necessary in the public interest. Your recently demonstrated and continuing unwillingness to reconcile yourself to, and officially accept, final administrative decision on problems concerning which you and other Bureau officials so often present me with a variety of conflicting views has resulted in an incompatability [*sic*] so fundamental that it is detrimental to the harmonious and efficient performance of our public duties.

While Sullivan took a day of "sick leave" the next day, Hoover had the lock changed on his office door and his name removed. Five days later, on October 6, 1971, after first considering an appeal through his friends Mardian and Mitchell, Sullivan relented and submitted his retirement after more than thirty years of service — but not before sending Hoover a final, even longer, written blast tracing the same ground, which was never answered.* Hoover called DeLoach at Pepsico to discuss the situation; they talked for forty-seven minutes.

◆

DeLoach settled into the lap of luxury as a corporate vice-president at Pepsico's world headquarters on an estate in Purchase, New York. Board chairman Kendall assigned him important projects — including working up plans for a Nixon Library — and he moved to Greenwich, Connecticut, to live the life of abundance he had always dreamed of. When the Director died in May 1972, people from all over the country called DeLoach — to express their sympathies and to discuss the implications of Hoover's passing — and he was in the front ranks of the mourners who gathered in Washington. DeLoach had visited with Hoover at a banquet in New York City just a week before the old man's death, so he had had new and affectionate blessings from the Director.

Sullivan, for his part, went into exile in Westport, Connecticut, where he worked briefly for the Insurance Crime Prevention Institute, run by James F. Ahern, former police chief of New Haven. He too had an unprecedentedly comfortable income, but he nevertheless longed for vindication and dreamed of eventual reattachment to — or at least reacceptance by — the Bureau.

Barely a month after Hoover's death, Sullivan received a call from

* Excerpts from Sullivan's last letter to the Director appear in the Appendix.

311

Attorney General Richard G. Kleindienst, inviting him to return to Washington and help establish an Office of National Narcotics Intelligence (ONNI) within the Justice Department, which would theoretically serve as a clearinghouse for intelligence information gathered by various agencies about the nation's drug problems. Sullivan accepted and by August, less than a year after he had left Washington in disgrace, he was back in an ambiguous status. He was assigned a suite of offices in the Federal Triangle Building, just a few floors away from his old colleagues in the FBI's Domestic Intelligence Division. His presence stirred up considerable tension, especially when he hired individuals who had left the FBI under fire from Hoover, including Jack Shaw.

Once back in Washington, Sullivan had a kind of government-in-exile at ONNI. Men who had once worked with him in the Domestic Intelligence Division, now going out on assignment as special-agents-in-charge or assistant-special-agents-in-charge, would pay discreet, diplomatic calls on him — to say good-bye, to seek his advice, and to hedge their bets just in case the wily Sullivan should come back into power in the Bureau.

If the Nixon administration concealed any ulterior motives it might have had in bringing Sullivan back, he was perfectly open about his own motives for returning: he wanted to be close by to "help" the Bureau, to provide his ideas for reorganizing and restructuring it. Some accused him of trying to weaken the position of the new acting director named by Nixon to replace Hoover, L. Patrick Gray III, and capture the job for himself, but Sullivan insisted that he could stay in Washington only until September 1973, when he had to be back in New Hampshire to care for his wife after their youngest son went off to college.

Sullivan made several approaches to Gray, offering his advice. But Gray, who had named Mark Felt his acting associate director, kept his distance from Sullivan and met with him discreetly only a few times. As if to strike the appropriate balance, Gray, at the suggestion of Kleindienst, also called DeLoach to Washington for consultations. Eventually Sullivan made a move that seemed predictable on the basis of an old, unsettled score: he asked Kleindienst to move ONNI into the main Justice Department building, to office space occupied by the Bureau. Gray opposed the request, and he and Sullivan had a bitter fight in Kleindienst's office. Sullivan won. When he moved ONNI into its new suite of offices, he had plush wood paneling and soundproofing installed.

With Gray giving him the cold shoulder and with rumors spreading that Gray might not be able to hold on to his job, Sullivan turned elsewhere. Robert Mardian was now an official of the Committee for the Re-election of the President, someone who would presumably have some influence after November 1972, and Sullivan besieged him with letters about the FBI at his home address. He sent Mardian commentaries on the FBI's budget, its structure, its management, and on myriad other topics. Mardian encouraged the letters, but never replied to them on paper. Sullivan also wrote a number of rambling letters about the Bureau to Kleindienst, offering proposals for changing it.

There were mysterious events in early 1973 involving the dukes: John Mitchell, no longer holding any office and increasingly under suspicion in connection with the Watergate scandals, met with Deke DeLoach in New York City and apparently said he was authorized by President Nixon to offer him the permanent directorship of the FBI. DeLoach, after discussing it with his wife and Kendall of Pepsico, came back to Mitchell and said no. Gray was thereupon nominated for the job, a nomination that was never confirmed by the U.S. Senate.

DeLoach still had his own people at the Bureau, however, in the manner of a duke who never really leaves the royal family. One agent in the External Affairs Division (successor to Crime Records) at headquarters, a particular protégé of DeLoach, occasionally did "name checks" for him, to see if there was anything in the Bureau files on people of interest to Pepsico. When DeLoach came to Washington, the agent would take time off from work to greet him at the airport and drive him to his appointments. In return, whenever it came time for an American Legion convention, DeLoach would have his private Pepsico plane stop in Washington to pick up the agent — who was also De-Loach's successor as liaison with the Legion — and take him along in style.

While Gray's nomination was in trouble before the Senate and there were charges that he had abused the FBI for political purposes, White House counsel John W. Dean III was in touch with Sullivan. Dean and Sullivan had had occasional contact while Sullivan was still in the Bureau, and on at least one occasion the White House counsel phoned Sullivan to ask for an FBI check on a woman Dean was dating. Now Dean asked the former FBI official about the seventeen secret wiretaps, about how he thought the White House should handle the Watergate scandal, and about previous political exploitation of the FBI. On the latter point, Sullivan said he knew of voluminous examples and offered to testify publicly about them. Dean, in conversations with Nixon that were tape-recorded and later released by the White House, said Sullivan would cooperate in exchange for a job as head of a new domestic security agency. (Sullivan denied that interpretation and said he never sought or was offered any such job.) There were also suggestions in the White House tapes that if DeLoach did not cooperate in detailing political uses of the FBI under other presidents, the White House would have Kendall fire him from Pepsico.

The Office of National Narcotics Intelligence was dissolved — before it had done anything of substance — and merged into a new Drug Enforcement Administration within the Justice Department. Sullivan was one of several candidates considered for the post of administrator of the new agency, but he was never formally offered the job.

Gray resigned, under fire for destroying documents connected with the Watergate investigation. William Ruckelshaus, as interim acting FBI director, hunted down the records of the secret wiretaps (which led in part to dismissal of all charges against Daniel Ellsberg in the Pentagon Papers case). Even after Sullivan's role in conducting and concealing those wiretaps had become known, he was considered by the White House as a possible permanent director of the Bureau. According to some sources, he came close to being named. Instead, Clarence M. Kelley was selected.

One theory had it that Sullivan blew any chances he had left for an important government position by doing the unthinkable — giving an on-the-record interview to the *Los Angeles Times* in which he spoke his mind openly about Hoover, calling him a "master blackmailer" and declaring that in his last days the Director had been senile and unable to function. (The interview provoked an angry letter to the editor from Clyde Tolson, who dismissed Sullivan as "a disgruntled former employee" of the FBI.)

Sullivan returned to New Hampshire. He did some consulting work on security problems for the Atomic Energy Commission, suffered a severe heart attack, and considered a teaching position at a small college in New Hampshire. He sent a paper to a conference sponsored by the Roscoe Pound–American Trial Lawyers Foundation on "Privacy in a Free Society," in which he allowed as how "the FBI as it is now structured is a potential threat to our civil liberties." DeLoach stayed at Pepsico. Sullivan lived humbly ever after, and DeLoach, graciously. Each was called to testify before the Senate committee and grand juries investigating the Watergate affair. Both men's names surfaced often in controversy concerning the Bureau and in recycled news stories about the inter- and intra-agency intrigues of the 1960s and 1970s. Both offered their cooperation to Kelley.

Each man wondered whether, had he done things differently, he might have become director of the FBI.

XIII

The Agents

It was a good combination of people, brought together with a great deal of enthusiasm and idealism, most of them with stars in their eyes. . . . It gives you a pretty good feeling to be able to walk into any bank, show your credentials and get a check cashed. . . . The children of agents have great prestige among their friends, too, just because of what their fathers do.
— A former, high-ranking Bureau official, discussing the appeal of becoming an FBI agent

FOR JOHN BASSETT, THE FBI IS SOMETHING of a dream come true, the victory of his ambition and ability over his adventurousness and aimlessness. A high school dropout in Burlington, Vermont, he began boxing professionally under the name of "Sparky Bassett" at age fifteen, well below the legal limit, and then went off to spend two years in the Coast Guard; by 1946 he was in New York City, appearing in fights at Madison Square Garden and Yankee Stadium, among other places. But a close friend, a regional official with the Veterans' Administration, pleaded with him to get out of the boxing world and into something more respectable. He took Bassett for lunch with the president of Seton Hall University in New Jersey. One thing led to another, and because he had completed high school equivalency courses at the University of Vermont, Bassett was immediately admitted as a college student. The VA official also helped Bassett find a system for paying his own way: for four years he attended classes by day and had a job as a policeman in East Orange, New Jersey, from midnight until 8 A.M.

Working as a cop in those days, one tended to meet FBI agents, and when Bassett graduated from Seton Hall in 1954, a friend in the Bureau encouraged him to apply; it was a period when police experience was being accepted as an especially relevant qualification for becoming an agent. Imagining the New York fight managers and other characters who might be interviewed during his background investigation, Bassett never expected to be chosen; but he was, and, he says unabashedly today, "It was wonderful." Assigned to Buffalo and Charlotte, he quickly became something of a Bureau legend – a guy who might take off in the wrong direction after a bank robber, but who would invariably come up with his man anyway. In Chicago since 1961, he has served as a sort of man Friday, a facilitator and arranger, for one special-agent-in-charge after another. He is the perfect airport greeter and guide for visiting Bureau firemen and a natural investigator on organized crime cases to boot.

Bassett spent his twentieth anniversary as an agent at Quantico, where he served as a "counselor" to a group of fifty policemen attending the National Academy. They threw a surprise party for him on the occasion, saluting him as the best and most down-to-earth sort of fellow the Bureau has to offer.

Tony Christy, a casual man with a degree in finance from Ohio State University, was quite content with his job as an auditor at the Mead Corporation in Dayton. In fact, he was about to be promoted in 1970 when his mind began to wander.

One Sunday night he and his wife were watching an episode in *The FBI* television series with Efrem Zimbalist, Jr. He thought it was silly and glossy and probably unrealistic, but still he wondered: what would it be like? Christy had no background in law enforcement or any prior inclination toward it, but somehow at that moment the idea of the FBI struck his fancy. "So why don't you find out about it and apply?" his wife suggested. "Just as a lark," he insists, he dropped in at the Dayton Resident Agency later that week and filled out some forms. Before long he had a phone call on a Saturday night, asking him to report to the Cincinnati Field Office the next morning – Sunday – for an interview. The Bureau had an appropriation to hire a thousand new agents, it seemed, and the push was on. The Christys drove to Cincinnati as requested, and Cheryl Christy sat freezing in the parking lot for what seemed like hours while her husband was grilled upstairs. By the time he was finished, he felt even more intrigued by the idea. Very soon thereafter he had a telegram offering him the new job and giving him a date to report to Quantico. He never even hesitated.

Christy bought five white shirts for training because he had none; he hasn't worn them since, finding them unnecessary in the Atlanta, New York, and Jackson field offices, except during occasional court appearances on behalf of the Bureau.

When Edward Allen Tamm graduated from the Georgetown University Law School in Washington in the depths of the Depression, he did not have the twenty-five dollars it cost to take the bar exam. But because his father had worked for the Milwaukee Line, he did have a railroad pass that would take him as far as Chicago. There he went, and as he tells it, he "worked the Loop — every floor of every building" looking for a job; the best he could come up with was a salary of five dollars a month.

It was out of desperation and because he was still "single, free and easy" that he finally applied instead to the FBI. He was under the age limit, but the combination of his law degree, his earlier college study of accounting, and his strong performance on the entrance examination made him an exception to the rule. Tamm came in to a cozy little Bureau, where there were fewer than three hundred agents and the starting salary was $2,900 a year; and he reached some of his earliest assignments in Texas traveling in the caboose of freight trains. As a bright young man, he rose quickly, and by 1934, during the buildup of the Bureau under the Roosevelt administration's new federal crime legislation — it went from 353 agents in 1933 to 609 in 1936 — Tamm was already an assistant director. During World War II, as assistant-to-the-director, he served on an interdepartmental committee that met secretly at 1 A.M. three times a week to discuss intelligence-gathering and policy questions such as whether the writ of habeas corpus should be suspended for the duration of the wartime crisis.

But in 1948, after eighteen years of Bureau service and at the peak of his authority, Tamm accepted an appointment from President Truman to become, at forty-one, the youngest federal district judge in the nation. He says now that he made the decision largely for financial reasons; at a time when he had two children arriving at college age, the $15,000 judicial salary looked a great deal better than the $10,000 he was making at the Bureau — "I had to admit that I had an obligation to someone other than the FBI." Later Tamm would become an influential federal appellate judge in Washington and a leader of committees concerned with judicial ethics. He always disqualified himself from cases involving the Bureau, in part because he knew that he felt a particular "loyalty" toward J. Edgar Hoover ("I could never forget that he gave me a job in 1930"), even during the Director's long public quarrel with the judge's brother, Quinn Tamm, who left the FBI to run the International Association of Chiefs of Police. Only a few days before Hoover died, in fact, Tamm lectured to the National Academy and then spent an hour in the Director's office, finding him "as alert and vigorous as he was in the early thirties."

After seven years as a member of the New York City Police Department, J. P. Morgan, the son of a New York police detective, recalls, "I had to make a decision whether to go corrupt." One choice, made by some of his colleagues, would have been to accept payoffs and get into crooked operations that could have raised his annual unofficial income to about two hundred thousand dollars; another was to "go straight." "In the back of my mind," says Morgan, "I guess I always wanted to be an FBI agent. That seemed like the ultimate in cops. But I felt it was out of my reach, and I was always told that 'if the FBI wants you, they'll come look for you.'"

Despite this pessimism, the fact that at thirty-two he was older than the average applicant (and color-blind) and that he had a couple of police-brutality complaints pending against him, Morgan was accepted in 1964. He took a cut in pay, and he and his wife moved out of their recently purchased "dream house" to be sent by the Bureau to the Charlotte, North Carolina, Field Office. "It was the greatest thing that ever happened to me," he now feels; "I had thought the world ended at the other side of the George Washington Bridge. It was wonderful to get a chance to travel. A whole new world opened up to me." On Morgan's first case, a man he was attempting to arrest told him, "I used to eat guys like you for breakfast," and physically attacked him, a situation that required summoning reinforcements from the field office. But it was all uphill from there — single-handed capture of a Most Wanted fugitive; work in important civil rights cases elsewhere in the South; six months at the Defense Language Institute in Monterey, California; assignment to Miami; and then transfer to headquarters to help establish a "management unit" in the Training Division. But although Morgan had intended to make the Bureau a career, he was lured away in 1969 by the offer of a professorship at the University of Georgia, "an opportunity to preach what I had been practicing." Later he served as police chief of St. Petersburg, Florida, and as a consultant for the Police Foundation. His was a short Bureau career, but one that opened great new vistas to him.

"I am what used to be called a patriot, in the good sense of the word," says John C. F. Morris; "but I never dreamed that I would have the opportunity to do anything more for my country than volunteer for the army and serve three years." In 1951, however, he got the chance to do more.

Out of the service after World War II, he went back to Nebraska, where he had grown up "in grinding poverty" on a farm during the Depression, but he soon migrated to Texas, where he had a married sister who helped him finish college. Morris seems almost pained as he recalls the circumstances in the country and his feelings during that immediate postwar period. "I had always been politically aware, I read *Time* magazine and noticed things that were going on," he says, "but then for the first time, I noticed an outward manifestation of a desire, on the part of some people, to affiliate themselves with political organizations that . . . were not primarily interested in the welfare of the United States, like the Communist party." Hard as it is now for him to "recreate the frame of mind" of those times, he recalls being appalled when he saw people signing petitions that seemed to him unpatriotic or downright subversive. He decided to try to do something about it. Although he did not think he had the necessary qualifications, he signed up for an interview with the FBI recruiter who was coming through Austin. The fact that he spoke fluent German helped make him a strong candidate. The interview went well, as did the written and physical examinations, and on July 2, 1951, Morris became a special agent of the FBI.

It is a calling, an identification and a commitment that has meant a great deal to him. "I took that oath very seriously," says Morris; "I haven't forgotten what I swore to faithfully defend and uphold."

It was just as Wason G. Campbell was getting out of the Army Security Agency in 1947 that he saw a clipping from *This Week* magazine that posed the question: "How many people who apply for the FBI are accepted?" The answer that appeared in print was "one in a thousand." That was a gross exaggeration (although the kind of myth that the Bureau did not mind encouraging), but enough to pique the thirty-year-old soldier's curiosity. His background was appealing to the Bureau and he was snapped right up for agent's training.

"The low moment" in his Bureau career, it turned out, came immediately. Assigned to San Francisco as his first office, Campbell found the postwar housing market depressingly tight, and he and his wife, along with a number of other new agent families, by Thanksgiving found themselves living in almost barracks-style in a converted shipyard. Soon, however, he was transferred to Los Angeles and that began a series of better days — fourteen years there, including six on an espionage squad; several years as a Bureau supervisor in the General Investigative Division; a tour as assistant-special-agent-in-charge of the Buffalo Field Office; and then several other important jobs at headquarters, including a stint directly under Mark Felt, when Felt was serving as acting associate director with Pat Gray. But after only a year as assistant director for the new Computer Systems Division, Campbell decided to exercise his option to retire. A rather nervous man, he had tired of taking the heat from congressmen, civil libertarians, and newspapers about the possible threats to individual privacy from the National Crime Information Center and other computerized Bureau records. There seemed no prospect for an early lifting of the $36,000 pay ceiling on his and most other Bureau executives' salaries, so the difference between salary and pension was small. And he finally decided, at fifty-six, that the time had come to return to his hometown of Greenfield, in the northwestern corner of Tennessee, population three thousand, where he still owned property. There he would build a house, doing some of the work with his own hands, and try to live a quiet life.

"I don't want to sound corny," says Esteban Uriarte when asked how he happened to become an FBI agent, "but I wanted to pay this country back." The United States, as he puts it, "opened its arms to me" in 1960, when he left Cuba with only the clothes on his back and five dollars in his pocket. His parents, who had originally left Spain in the 1930s during the Civil War, followed three years later. Eventually, through refugee aid programs, he attended Louisiana State University, graduating with an accounting degree in 1972.

But already in 1971, as soon as he became an American citizen, Uriarte had applied to the Bureau for employment. Shifting uncomfortably as he talks, he explains that "I saw what went on in Cuba — the shooting and all that. You couldn't go to church or a movie without a bomb going off. . . . I saw the need for law enforcement, and the FBI is the strongest law enforcement organization in the country. I wanted to do something to help this country defend itself, and the FBI seemed the best way to do that." When he first got his degree, there was a freeze on the hiring of new agents; but with his skills in accounting and the Bureau's most-needed language, Spanish — not to mention his resentment toward the Castro regime in Cuba — Uriarte was a natural, and in May 1973 he got a letter inviting him to training. After breaking in on general criminal cases, he was quickly shifted to a squad where his accounting knowledge would be helpful — but he was also used for surveillance work on other cases, since his Latin look distinguished him from the usual FBI agent.

"The more I get into it," he said after a few months in the field, "it's incredible how much crime there is . . . and how the public doesn't know what's going on. So much money is taken from the public; you could work twenty-four hours a day and never get through."

Joe David Jamieson would just as soon have gone home to Trinity, Texas, in 1941, when he graduated from Baylor Law School, and hung out a shingle. "But the trouble was," as he recalls it now, "they already had a couple of lawyers in town, so who wanted another one?" Besides, he was only twenty-two.

From a farming family, Jamieson had never known his father and he was ready to strike out in the world. "I was looking for a job, frankly, where I could make a little money," he says. Just about that time he heard that starting FBI agents were making a yearly salary of $3,200, which was "more money than I had ever seen"; and word had it that one of his former law professors and other people he knew who had joined the Bureau were "happy and enthusiastic." When Jamieson took the plunge himself, he was not disappointed. "Back in those days, in the war years, your whole life was the Bureau," he remembers with some pride; "you worked until ten o'clock at night, most of Saturday, and even Sunday. There weren't a helluva lot of us to do the work." When he went to the Los Angeles Field Office as his second assignment, it had about eighty agents; some of the same men were still there thirty years later when he returned as assistant-director-in-charge of the office. He had been almost everywhere in the meantime — Phoenix, Little Rock, Houston, Albany, Denver, Knoxville, Savannah, Philadelphia — but remained remarkably cool and well preserved through it all.

Later, in charge of the Training Division at Quantico, Jamieson seemed a bit restless, but aware that "maybe I was getting too old for the field." He derived some inspiration, though, from being in a position to watch the new people coming into the Bureau from up close: "Some are born poor and some rich, some have sophisticated college educations. There are seminary graduates, schoolteachers, army officers, people from all walks of life and faiths." His one great regret is that none of his three sons became an agent.

The winner of the Heisman Trophy for the best college football player of 1973, John Cappelletti of Penn State University, interviewed by sportswriters in his moment of glory, was asked about his career plans. Without hesitation, he replied that what he would most like to do eventually is to become a special agent of the Federal Bureau of Investigation. It is difficult to calculate the reinforcing effect that may have had on tens of thousands of grammar school and high school students who already thought that football players and FBI agents were two of the best things in the world that one could ever be. But it was probably very gratifying indeed to the 8,600 FBI agents that even as they were going through some of the most difficult times in the agency's history, their job was still one aspired to by people in other glamorous roles. For it is often the matter of image that has recruited men into the FBI and their image — of themselves and in others' eyes — that has kept them there. As one agent in Los Angeles put it, "I never really knew what it was like to be on top of the heap until I came into the FBI."

In practical terms, "the top of the heap" has usually meant that doors open to them that would not open to others, that one is respected in the community and among one's peers, and that daily life has an overlay of theoretical, if not actual, excitement and romance to it — and those factors cannot help but make a man feel good. Initially, the image was sustained in large part by the general esteem in which J. Edgar Hoover was held; it seemed to rub off on the men who worked for him. "I felt when I came in the Bureau that Mr. Hoover had hired me," said the Los Angeles agent; "I felt proud to be one of his men." Hoover was such an important part of the image that many agents displayed a portrait of the Director on the wall in their homes. (A few still do.) After some years, however, the image and the pride began to sustain themselves. FBI agents, filled with the Bureau's own propaganda but also casting a realistic look around themselves, came to feel that they really were better than almost everyone else with a job remotely similar to theirs.

It is demonstrably true that FBI agents probably are of a higher caliber generally than anyone else in American law enforcement, but not exactly in the way that many people think. For years the Bureau got away with the myth and the reputation that every agent is either a fully trained lawyer or accountant; it did not actually state unequivocally that this was the case, but it allowed, even led, people to believe it. In fact, that has never been so. During Hoover's first years running the Bureau, he hired mostly lawyers — less on the basis of any abstract principle, it seems, than of the fact that he himself had a law degree — until the percentage of agents with legal training had dramatically increased. There was also a corps of accountants, who were considered to be in a category apart from the other agents and who worked only on cases requiring their special skills; as those cases increased in quantity, more accountants were recruited. Before very long, however, the Director saw that it was neither necessary nor desirable to insist on those qualifications for every agent hired. Gradually others were added and substituted: college graduates "with a major in a physical science for which the Bureau has a current need," "with fluency in a language for which the Bureau has a current need," or with "three years of professional, executive, complex investigative or other specialized experience." That meant that while lawyers and accountants were still welcomed, and in some periods given preference, there was also room for, among others, high school teachers and coaches, military veterans (especially marines), policemen, stockbrokers, insurance men, bank officers, geologists, journalists, and, of course, Bureau clerks. The official circular on agent jobs also points out that "the FBI reserves the right to waive a qualification not bearing on character and integrity when found necessary to obtain an employee with demonstrated ability in some particular skill that is unique or unusual, and for which a need exists." In other words, the rules leave room enough for the Bureau to take anyone it wants, and without the constraints and regulations of the Civil Service Commission. Today, in fact, only 14 percent of the agents are lawyers and 8 percent accountants. About 23 percent of the agents are former FBI clerks, and some 64 percent are former members of the military who qualify for veterans' preference.

Most of the other qualifications are standard — good vision and hearing and an otherwise "excellent physical condition," as well as a driver's license. For more than thirty years applicants also had to be at least five feet seven inches tall, but the height restriction was abolished in June 1975 — in part because it was thought to discriminate against the women newly competing for agent positions. The college degree requirement and the age restriction, now twenty-three to thirty-six at the time of application, have assured that FBI standards remain much higher than those of most police departments and other law enforcement agencies; many agents enter the Bureau with master's degrees or even doctorates (or work on them nights and weekends while on duty). Completing the application for Bureau employment alone requires a certain level of stamina and literacy. It is an exhaustive ten-page form, with spaces for such matters as biographical details of "wives (including maiden names) and husbands of brothers and sisters," of "brothers and sisters of your husband or wife" and "name and present location of ex-spouse." (Divorce is not a disqualification, as is, say, homosexuality.) The application becomes the basis for an extensive field investigation of every prospective agent, which theoretically weeds out anyone of questionable background, character, or "loyalty." The Bureau refuses to make a sample of its written examination available for any outside inspection, but insists that it is a rigorous test of aptitude, judgment, and legal-style reasoning.

Another characteristic that puts the FBI well above most other police-type agencies, not to say government agencies in general, is the absence of large-scale corruption, or even the appearance of corruption, among agents. As noted elsewhere, the contacts and connections of FBI officials have often brought them favors and special considerations, but there are remarkably few documented instances of agents accepting payoffs or kickbacks, making personal use of evidence seized in connection with cases, or peddling their influence — practices that are notoriously common among many local and state police forces. The Immigration and Naturalization Service, Bureau of Customs, and federal narcotics enforcement agencies, for example, have all been hit by well-publicized scandals concerning the financial improprieties of their field personnel. But colleagues consider FBI agents straight arrows by comparison. And despite some investigative abuses under the COINTELPRO rubric and on the initiative of individual agents, the Bureau has not often been tainted by such illegal and abusive tactics as those associated with agents of the Drug Enforcement Administration — knocking down doors in midnight raids on the wrong house, selling hard drugs themselves on the side, and the like. Whatever else it might do, a knock on the door from the FBI does not send most citizens cowering in a corner in fear for their lives and possessions.*

The FBI also profits from its reputation for continuity. Bureau agents tend to stay in their jobs longer than most, and the turnover figures are astonishingly low. Even with new federal incentives for

---

* The Bureau's reputation for clean, unintimidating tactics suffered somewhat during its frustrating nineteen-month-long search for Patricia Hearst. Several people who had the misfortune of vaguely resembling her complained that agents mistreated them out of enthusiasm for the big capture. But the worst complaints concerned a March 15, 1975, raid on an Alexandria, Virginia, apartment where an anonymous telephone tipster claimed Hearst was hiding. When the women in the apartment refused to open their door without first seeing the agents' credentials, the FBI men and the police detectives accompanying them broke down the door, only to discover that Hearst was not there at all. Clarence Kelley later defended the agents on the grounds that they feared the people in the apartment might be armed and suicidal; but he acknowledged that "the leisure of later reflection and the luxury of subsequently available facts may indicate the wisdom of a different course of action."

early retirement, the Bureau lost only 419 agents in 1972 and 358 in 1973, 4.9 and 4.1 percent respectively. In 1974, the number leaving, including those who died or retired without taking another job, was down to 258, or only 3 percent of the agent force. (Some Bureau officials suggest that the higher than usual figure for 1972 may have been a result, at least in part, of the Director's death; a number of agents simply no longer wanted to serve after he was gone.)* The unofficial agreement is that any person graduated from agent's training will stay a minimum of three years, but the average agent now stays much longer than that — sixteen years and three months. Once he does stay beyond the three-year mark, the odds are that he will last for twenty years or more and then retire with a very attractive pension. The transfer policy and other bureaucratic factors mean that the continuity will not necessarily carry over to individual citizens' dealings with the Bureau; they may be approached by different people on the same case from one time to another. But the same paperwork and standardization of style that so annoys some agents also assures that one can usually pick up where another has left off. Similarly, reports from different parts of the country will invariably be prepared with uniform language and format. Although FBI agents have recently been harassed and embarrassed on the witness stand in some federal court trials for errors and inconsistencies in their reporting, they are considered far more reliable than those from other agencies.

Who are these agents who present themselves as being so proud and sure of themselves, the self-styled elite of law enforcement? The Bureau insists that it does not compile and computerize official biographical statistics, but an unscientific composite profile is relatively easy to construct on the basis of observation of, and conversation with, a substantial number of agents. They are overwhelmingly white males of an average age somewhat older than the Bureau would like to acknowledge, for what is called a "young man's profession." There is a high representation in Bureau ranks of Catholics,† especially of Irish origin, many of whom attended church-run or -supported colleges and universities, especially in the northeastern part of the United States. (If the CIA prototype is a Yale man, his FBI counterpart likely went to Fordham or Notre Dame.) Agents tend to be churchgoers, but not to live overly restrained personal and social lives. (A striking number

---

* The turnover among clerical personnel is much higher, sometimes reaching more than 20 percent a year. But in 1974 it was only 15.7 percent, a full eight percentage points lower than the turnover among federal government employees generally that year.
† Since the Bureau began stressing language skills, there are also many Mormons, who have developed language proficiency during their overseas "missions."

have relatives in the clergy, and there is irony in the fact that some of those relatives showed up on the other side of cases involving radical protesters during the Vietnam war.) Most are married and have children; if they were not married when they entered the Bureau, the chances are good that they will meet and marry an FBI stenographer or other clerical employee. They are robust, but not as rough-and-tumble as the 1930s gangbusters types. Quick-tempered, they can be rather easily provoked into arguments. They usually want to be assigned as close to their original hometown as possible.

Becoming an FBI agent is, for many people, a matter of upward mobility, an achievement of social status and recognition that is difficult to equal. They have seen their parents struggle to put them through school, or, especially in the case of former Bureau clerks, they have worked at one or two jobs to put themselves through. They are rarely wealthy, but usually able to afford most of the comforts of life, and they are solidly planted in the middle class. Quite a few agents are the sons of policemen, and they see their career decision as a natural progression, a step upward that is still in the same great tradition of law enforcement. Their fathers are proud of them and their mothers, although they should be accustomed to this sort of thing by now, worry about their safety on the firing line. Interestingly, there is a subtle, residual bias within the Bureau against agents who are themselves former policemen. It is sometimes suggested by agents with other backgrounds and qualifications that these ex-cops slipped in while the standards were lowered to expand the agent force; and former policemen rarely make it into the highest-ranking Bureau positions. (The former policemen, for their own part, are proud of their ability to defend themselves physically better than most.)

At the same time, there is a growing number of father-and-son agent families in the Bureau. Jerome T. Nolan, of the Detroit Field Office, whose father is senior resident agent in Rockford, Illinois, says that he wanted to follow in his father's footsteps from the time he was ten years old. He did it the hard way, though, getting married and going to Washington after only one year of college; there he worked for the Bureau in various clerical capacities, including as a tour guide, for five years while completing his college degree. Nolan says that the strongest sanction in his home while he was growing up was in favor of telling the truth; as he recalls it, his father used to say, "I have to deal with liars [criminal suspects] every day of my life. I don't want to come home and deal with them!"

The Bureau has always prided itself on good geographical distribution, drawing agents from every section of the country and, in keeping with Hoover's original policy, generally sending them to another area for their first assignments. But one striking aspect of the average field office for many years was the number of agents who originally came from small towns. The reasons for the attractiveness of an FBI career to rural and small-town boys have long been the subject of speculation — is it that they are less cynical and more idealistic about the notion of government service; that the image of policemen has been held in more awe in small communities than in big cities; or just that background checks on agent applicants are less likely to turn up derogatory information or other problems if the person has spent most of his life in sparsely populated, clean-living areas? Whatever the reasons, the effect, especially among old-timers in the FBI, was to carry over small-town values and principles to the Bureau. That meant an uncommon degree of openness and friendliness, but also a sense of horror about what goes on in the big cities where most of these agents ended up working. Younger agents have complained that the small-town mentality in the FBI also led to a certain narrow-mindedness and intolerance, an unspoken insistence that all agents should conform to the same set of personal standards and ideas. Inevitably that meant that some agents would judge the people they investigated by those standards as well. The small-town influence seems to have diminished considerably in recent years, however.

Homogeneity can obviously be an advantage in an investigative force that requires discipline and high standards of conduct. But it can be taken too far. Most Bureau officials now concede that the FBI lost some of its effectiveness and created occasional problems for itself over the years by failing to diversify and open the agent ranks. For years there were very few Jewish agents or members of other minority ethnic groups, and only a smattering of American Indians or Spanish-surnamed agents. The only blacks were people dubbed "honorary agents," who were really assigned as personal servants, retainers, chauffeurs, or office boys to the Director, and of course there were no women agents at all.

Part of the reason for this uniformity of race and background was the personal prejudices of J. Edgar Hoover and Clyde Tolson. They wanted to be surrounded by average, all-American types, and not to allow too much variety to be mixed in. In fact there were Jews among the men who worked closely at Hoover's side over the years, including Harold "Pop" Nathan in the 1920s and 1930s and Alex Rosen from World War II until the Director's death, but it was always assumed that law enforcement was not a very popular profession or a status career choice among the Jewish population. One former agent who worked on a security squad in New York recalls that Jews were not expected to be particular friends of the FBI, and that one way to list somebody — and in the process, manage to skip interviewing him — was to describe him with the telling epithet, "a Jewish academician of known liberal persuasion." But the paucity of Jewish agents also meant that there were few people considered eligible, for example, to conduct investigations among Orthodox Jewish communities in Brooklyn or at the Catskill Mountain resorts of upstate New York in the summertime. Similarly, the Bureau had very few agents it could confidently send into Mexican-American or Puerto Rican communities, onto Indian Reservations or into black ghettos, so it often had to rely instead on informant coverage or help from the police, who were themselves sometimes not very welcome in those communities.

There is little question that Hoover simply had an old-fashioned, narrow-minded southern — old Washington, D.C. — attitude toward blacks. When Robert Kennedy became attorney general in 1961 and said that every branch of the Justice Department, including the FBI, would have to increase its minority recruiting and hiring, the Director made an enormous fuss over the fact that he was not going to "lower standards" just to integrate the Bureau. It turned out that the FBI, like so many other employers, did not really have to lower its standards, but just had to develop some new recruiting techniques and make blacks feel they would have an equal shot at advancement in the Bureau. When Hoover did yield, he did so slowly and painfully. Fifteen years later, after other black recruiting pushes and the establishment of an equal employment opportunity office within the Administrative Division, there are still only about a hundred black FBI agents out of the total eighty-six hundred, and only a handful of them are in supervisory positions. One problem, according to Bureau officials, is that there is a higher turnover among black agents than among agents in general; once trained by the Bureau, they are inevitably offered other, perhaps better-paying jobs with private industry, and some leave to take those jobs. (One black agent maintains that it is Bureau policy to discourage black agents already on duty from seeking law degrees because of a concern that once they have them, they will immediately leave for greener pastures.) As for Chicanos, of whom there are also very few in the Bureau, FBI officials have been heard on Capitol Hill to offer their own pop-sociological explanation: "They don't like to leave their families or take the chance of being sent far away from home."

Once in the Bureau, black agents, because they are so few in number, tend to have particularly good experiences, the closest thing to the flying-squad image of fictionalized television programs. They were urgently rushed in, for example, to work on the recent murder cases in the Virgin Islands, and have been similarly deployed when and where their skin color would be an obvious investigative advantage. "I have already had experiences," said one black agent after five years of service, "that some guys don't get in twenty years." Another young black agent confirms that his role poses special problems because he tends to have somewhat different values from his fellow agents, but he is also regarded with suspicion in the black community. Unlike many white middle-class agents for whom the Bureau is the most important identification, he said, "I'm a man first, and second I'm a black man — FBI agent ranks way down on the totem pole. That's hard for some people to swallow." At the same time, he has found that skeptical young blacks, especially in the big cities, tend to regard a black agent as being "the big supernigger. The kid on the street only reads about the Bureau's harassment of the Black Panther party. He's forgotten about Selma [Alabama] and the Bureau's role in protecting the right of blacks to vote." Most blacks in the FBI are opposed, but thus far quietly, to the Bureau's easy tendency to label black people "extremists" and investigate them indiscriminately; they suggest that when their representation in the Bureau ranks is greater, as inevitably it must become, and there are blacks in special-agent-in-charge and assistant-special-agent-in-charge positions, these hangovers from the past will change dramatically.

The FBI's overall minority-hiring record compares favorably with that of many other federal agencies, but the complaint is that relatively few of the minority employees hold the prestigious position of agent. In August 1975 the Bureau statistics showed 104 black agents, 107 with "Spanish surnames," 19 "Asian-Americans," and 13 American Indians.

The world of FBI agents would be fertile ground for a social anthropologist interested in analyzing the evolution of customs, attitudes, and values. In many respects, it is a closed subculture that was frozen for years at an early stage of development because it was hermetically sealed off from the changes in the rest of society, but that suddenly broke open and began to lurch forward clumsily.

The world view of agents generally includes a heavy component of political conservatism. They tend to favor a strong American military presence around the world and to long for a good old-fashioned anticommunist foreign policy. They believe that too many people are on welfare and receive food stamps and that something should be done to put them to work. "Socialist" is a dirty word that gets pinned on a lot of liberals, who are held responsible for the deplorable softness of the judicial and corrections systems. One legacy of Bureau policy and investigations of the early twentieth century is a relatively strong bias against organized labor accompanied by an admiration for and identification with big business. Federal legislation and regulations to help members of minority groups are viewed with considerable skepticism, since agents feel that others should have to work their way to the top the way their own ancestors did, with blood, sweat, and tears. They were pleased by the election of Richard Nixon in 1968 and by his appointment of John N. Mitchell as a tough law-and-order attorney general (and felt betrayed, after the Watergate scandals) and considered Senator George McGovern, the Democratic presidential candidate, a threat to the nation's security and stability in 1972. Most of them, for reasons of family background and tradition, are registered Democrats, but are inclined to believe that the Democratic party has gone off the deep end of radicalism. They consider Daniel Ellsberg a traitor for disclosing the Pentagon Papers, and they viewed antiwar demonstrations as unpatriotic. Above all, they feel a tremendous world-weariness, which leads them to distrust many people with whom they have contact, especially politicians and newsmen.

Not every agent shares these views on his arrival in the Bureau, but the organization has a powerful conservative influence on new recruits. Although the FBI is officially a nonpolitical agency, one relatively new agent said he was surprised to find that "everybody feels obligated to take a stand on every political issue, and after a while you realize that this is a right-of-center organization." Several agents insisted that being in the Bureau for a few years is enough to make almost anybody feel "up against it." Another young agent, assigned to a midwestern field office, speculated that much of the conservative mindset derives from the law-and-order issue and the Bureau's constant frustration with the courts. "I can't stand seeing these bad guys released from prison," he said mournfully; "I haven't yet seen people turn around and follow the straight and narrow path. . . . I'm twenty-eight years old, but feel forty-eight sometimes. I get very upset and cannot sleep some nights — at the expense of the taxpayers, agents are risking their lives to capture people, and then those people are just turned out on the streets again." But increasingly, one agent posted in the South claimed, young recruits to the Bureau are taking the chance of expressing more liberal, progressive attitudes in conversation with their older colleagues — especially on issues like the environment, defense spending, and unfair tax laws. They remain distinctly minority viewpoints, however.

The life-style of FBI agents is usually in keeping with their image as solid citizens. They tend to buy their own homes, preferably in the distant, newly developed suburbs, and to send their children to public or parochial schools. Except in cities like Miami, where the norm is different, they generally dress conservatively, notwithstanding the repeal of Hoover's old white-shirt-and-black-shoes rules. Their hair is still relatively short, and anyone who starts growing a moustache will likely be teased as a "hippie" for a while before it is ultimately accepted. There are only a few rebels here, who, in contrast to the many in the military, feel tempted to make themselves a test case by growing a beard. (It remains the official Bureau view that a beard and other manifestations of nonconformity are outside the average citizen's reasonable expectations of an FBI agent. But it is not absolutely forbidden, and there are probably about a dozen bearded agents these days — but usually because of special undercover assignments.) These external characteristics are also often important to agents in their judgments of others, including those they investigate. One agent who worked on the investigation of the National Guardsmen who fired into a crowd and killed four students during the May 1970 antiwar demonstrations at Kent State University in Ohio acknowledged frankly that "what those kids looked like" and their obscene gestures at the guardsmen had affected his ability to feel sympathy for them — "and they didn't look like the nice high school graduation pictures that ran in the newspapers."

Agents have a strong yearning for normality and stability; one young agent said that he would not under any circumstances want to work with a colleague who had been seeing a psychiatrist. "I could never be sure whether I could rely on him," he said. It was scandalous enough when an agent assigned to the Louisville Field Office committed suicide,* but considered even more so when it was learned that he had been seeing a psychiatrist without the Bureau's knowledge; that is something he was, according to the rules, required to tell the appropriate FBI authorities about. The story that circulated about this agent in the field was that he was depressed over the prospect of

---

* There have been a number of agent suicides over the years, some in small-town resident agencies, but they have usually been hushed up and papered over, rather than studied, by the Bureau.

331

transfer to FBI headquarters in Washington. It is a basic assumption that Bureau agents simply do not have the sort of emotional problems and needs that affect other people.

An FBI agent has a number of choices in how he views himself and his role, and as new, freer-thinking people come into the Bureau there is some degree of tension among the various roles. Some older agents, especially those who have previously been FBI clerks, think it is important to "know their place" and be appropriately subservient and obsequious toward those of higher rank or greater power. Thus, if called upon to be part of the detail protecting the attorney general of the United States during a reception at a U.S. senator's home, they will take it upon themselves to park the cars of the guests and perform other menial tasks; if invited to join the party (which, after all, might be the most effective way of handling the duty), they will invariably decline and remain on the fringes. Other agents, however, especially young ones, feel quite comfortable in a social situation of that sort — quite able to converse with an attorney general or a senator — and say that it is demeaning to relegate themselves to being parking lot attendants or elevator door holders. One agent interviewed suggested the dichotomy that everyone in the Bureau sees himself as either "a glorified policeman," in which event he especially enjoys stolen car and fugitive cases above all else, or as "a sophisticated investigator" who warms to the challenge of complicated investigations of organized crime or espionage cases. Given the variety inherent in the FBI's mandate, some of each are obviously needed; but the wave of the future would appear to be an emphasis on the creative and innovative agent over the old-fashioned gumshoe type. Some agents can obviously take too far their perception of themselves as heirs to Sherlock Holmes and have to be brought down to earth from time to time; but others must be encouraged to broaden their horizons to include more ambitious notions of what they and the FBI can do.

Virtually every FBI agent can cite the exact date when he entered on duty. In the typical instance, it was a major event in his life which meant important changes in his routine and perhaps even in his personality. It made him part of an organization that is sustained on an extraordinarily high level of spirit and enthusiasm. The mere fact of acceptance into the hallowed ranks brings with it a fellowship, an automatic feeling of empathy and understanding of one agent for the other. As one veteran agent based on the East Coast put it, "If I were to need to go from here to anyplace in the country tonight, there are things I could count on. . . . If I called the RA in Wichita, for example, even though I don't know him, if I just identify myself, I would get automatic and immediate help. He would probably pick me up at the airport, or arrange for a complimentary Hertz rental car for me. . . . And I would do the same for somebody else in the Bureau." Just being an agent, having the credential, provides a magic password.

It is a while before full membership in this brotherhood takes effect. An agent must make an arrest or otherwise prove his mettle on the firing line before he is really accepted as an equal by his immediate peers and colleagues. And traditionally, as long as he is still in his first-office assignment, he has been regarded as an apprentice and a neo-phyte; by the irrational, unofficial rules of the game, an agent who has been in the Bureau only seven months but is in his second office might be trusted with more independent responsibility than one who has been on duty twice as long but is still in his first assignment. Two first-office agents, in fact, are not supposed to make an arrest together.* Second-office agents somehow have always exuded more self-confidence, perhaps because they feel that if they have made it that far, they will be fine (unless they have flubbed and the transfer was for disciplinary reasons).

Once an agent has been through initiation and is accepted as a full-fledged member of the happy few, his job will invariably give him a profound feeling of security, in more than the ordinary sense. The FBI is unique for the extent to which agents, particularly in the field, will bail each other out of crises. If an agent is ill but has used up all of his sick leave, it is standard procedure for his colleagues to chip in and make up his paycheck every week; if his wife or other family members have problems, or if he otherwise falls into a desperate financial situation, the same thing would be done. The widow of an agent who dies suddenly, on or off duty, can count on unofficial help of every sort as long as she wants it, and sometimes even longer. In the midst of disasters, colleagues are always available to help. When the resident agent in Wilkes-Barre, Pennsylvania, was a victim of the floods caused by Hurricane Agnes in the summer of 1972, for example, a whole crew from the Philadelphia Field Office, to which he reports, drove up and spent a weekend helping him dig out. If an agent is suspended or docked a month's pay as a result of what seems to his colleagues an unfair disciplinary action, they will generally all sacrifice a little themselves to help him get along (although, interestingly, they will probably not protest to higher Bureau authorities in his behalf).

But let an agent renounce the Bureau or otherwise defy the unwritten code of conduct, and his colleagues may immediately turn

---

* The new policy of Clarence Kelley to try to leave agents in their first assignment for an average of five years should have an interesting effect on these traditions.

against him. When the chips are down and the lines of battle drawn, the instinct is to defend the Bureau as an institution against all attackers, even from within. Disenchanted former agents like William Turner and others may have been saying publicly nothing more extreme than what hundreds of agents had said privately for years, but the fact of their saying it publicly and becoming "enemies" of the FBI disqualifies them entirely for support. Agents still complain privately that agent Jack Shaw was poorly and unfairly handled when he was drummed out of the Bureau — and once the Director had died, most of the Bureau hierarchy admitted that they too agreed — but few gave him solace at the time, and for the most part all have remained unwilling to go on the record with that view. One does not challenge the tenets of the founder of the realm, even after they have been shown to be outrageous.

So strong is the pull and the security of the Bureau that some agents who leave eventually come back into the fold; with few exceptions, depending on the current needs of the Bureau at any given time, they are welcomed back in good standing. Hunter Helgeson is an example. After his graduation from the University of Minnesota Law School in 1952, he spent his first three years as an agent assigned to Philadelphia and Newark, but then he quit to go to work for a business firm back in Minnesota. "I was a country boy," he explains, "and this had been my first experience in a congested area. I thought I would enjoy getting back to the open spaces." Almost immediately, however, "I realized I had made a mistake. I missed my associations with people in the Bureau and felt less stimulated by the people in business." Within six months, "I asked Mr. Hoover if I could come back. It was clearer in my mind from then on that I wanted to be an agent." Helgeson returned at the same level at which he had left, and he went on to have a successful FBI career, working as a field supervisor in Jackson during the Bureau's involvement in the civil rights fights of the 1960s, later serving in the Domestic Intelligence Division at headquarters, and going on to become assistant-special-agent-in-charge of the Chicago Field Office and an inspector.

Mort Nichell had a similar experience. A native of Ashland, Kentucky, he had an urge to go back there and practice law after a period of time as an agent assigned to field offices in Illinois and Virginia. It was not that he was dissatisfied with the FBI, but that "I just had an itch to see whether I would enjoy the practice of law; you never know unless you try." In his case it took two years to discover that he was "missing something" after he had left the Bureau. "It is difficult to describe what I missed," he says, "but I think it was the rapport with the agents. The closest thing to it is probably a fraternity in college, a situation where you are not worried about somebody supporting you when you need them. . . . Hardships draw agents together. There is not even the same spirit in the army as in the FBI." Nichell went to the field office in Louisville to reapply, and after a new interview, physical examination, and a background investigation to cover his two-year absence he was back. Assigned to Detroit, he had no trouble recapturing the closeness he had felt with other agents and gained great satisfaction from his work on the bank robbery squad there.

Those who do leave the FBI under friendly circumstances generally remain profoundly loyal to it and reap considerable personal advantage from that association. Their Bureau training and experience is thought to qualify them for employment with the security or public affairs divisions of major corporations or small businesses, as a prosecutor or a lawyer with a private criminal law practice, as police chief in a small town or a big city (depending on how long they have been in the Bureau and how far up the line they have advanced), or even as a candidate for public office in communities where they have been assigned as agents. Many of these former agents achieve powerful positions from which they are able to show their gratitude to the FBI, whether by surreptitiously providing information to agents, speaking on the Bureau's behalf in moments of controversy, or helping it gain subtle and sometimes undetected influence on the political scene. But the relationship has dividends in the other direction, too. People who have left the Bureau are often able to call upon their former colleagues quietly to check matters for them in FBI files and to do them other occasional favors. It is an exchange that goes on all the time.

Most former agents are united in a gigantic fraternity called the Society of Former Special Agents of the Federal Bureau of Investigation. Headquartered in New York, the organization serves primarily to facilitate contacts among former agents, and in mid-1975, 6,387 of them were members. It publishes a confidential directory so that people can readily locate old associates but also find new ones, in an area where they have a need, who share an important bit of common background and therefore will probably be predisposed to help. There is a monthly publication called *The Grapevine,* which consists largely of gossip about the Bureau and its alumni, and an annual convention, strictly off limits to the press and the public.* The director is always invited to address the annual meeting, and although Hoover stopped

* The author requested the society to make an exception to its rules and permit him to attend one of its conventions in order to explore the spirit felt by former agents; the Board of Directors considered but rejected the request.

doing so in his last years, L. Patrick Gray III and Clarence Kelley after him seized upon the opportunity to cultivate an important source of support outside the government. The ex-agents' association often serves as a powerful lobby for the Bureau's interests, both with Congress and local governments. Regional chapters may throw their weight around in one direction or another, asking the Bureau to do something for their city or paving the way for a change the Bureau would like to make. In one recent example, the organization's Oklahoma chapter directly intervened and asked Kelley to cancel plans to send a man to Oklahoma City as special-agent-in-charge who had received bad publicity for his conduct elsewhere. At first the director honored the request and changed the assignment, but he later decided that was taking things too far.

Among the agent population of the FBI, there are several clearly definable generations of recruits who came in under circumstances that were different each from the others. Those circumstances often affect the way they do their work, view the Bureau's mission and its relationships with the outside world, and look toward the future. Not everyone fits into one of these groups, obviously, because the FBI is always hiring some agents; but the generations correspond, for the most part, to particular waves during which the Bureau expanded.

One generation entered the FBI just as World War II was beginning and the Bureau had only recently been assigned by President Roosevelt to make a major effort to combat espionage and subversion. The war was a dominant influence in their lives, and they saw the FBI as an extension of — in fact, it was an alternative to — military service; they considered it a great privilege to be part of the war effort and to shape the Bureau to the needs of the time. Among the recruits of the era were Clarence Kelley, William Sullivan, Cartha DeLoach, Roy K. Moore, and others who would later become powerful special-agents-in-charge or otherwise very important in Bureau history. To them, a war was a war, be it in Europe, Korea, or Vietnam, and one did not question national policy in such a time of emergency. But at the same time, these people tended to have a more flexible sense than Hoover did of what the FBI should be doing, and they considered it only logical that such an institution should shift gears and change emphasis (to civil rights, organized crime, terrorism, or whatever) with the temper and the needs of the times; they saw that to do so enhanced the Bureau's importance in the life of the nation and in law enforcement circles. If Hoover had stepped aside ten years or so before he died, and if this generation had had an opportunity to shape the

Bureau at the peak of their careers, it might have become an agency that was uniquely relevant and responsive to the changing times, if not greatly innovative about techniques.

Another group flocked into the Bureau as the Korean war broke out, heating up the Cold War. Hoover, by then taking his security mandate very seriously and permanently indeed, asked for and obtained substantial increases in the appropriations for hiring agents. The people who came in, for the most part, had served in World War II and they perceived their country to be going down the drain in its aftermath. With the McCarthy era in full swing, they were frightened by Soviet moves abroad and saw possible domestic parallels in the offing; they were sympathetic, and sometimes publicly so, with the witch-hunts of the senator from Wisconsin and the House Un-American Activities Committee. These agents were perhaps the most stridently and enduringly conservative people ever to enter the FBI. They did not merely believe in the importance of the Bureau's internal security work, but favored its considerable expansion. Many of them serve today as special-agents-in-charge or assistant directors, and in a relaxed moment they will pine for the good old days when the Bureau could call someone a "commie" and not have to worry about the consequences. They are the most adoring of Hoover, unable usually even to joke about his foibles and mistakes, and especially wary of any significant changes within the FBI. Until more of them have retired — a time that the new retirement bill will hasten — those changes cannot occur smoothly.

A third generation is made up of the children of the 1950s and 1960s, who came of age during a period of great upheaval in American society, culture, and government. They too entered the FBI in wartime, during the latter stages of the conflict in Vietnam in the later 1960s and early 1970s; but that was, of course, a different kind of war, which had declining support among the people. This group includes one contingent known by some as "The Berrigan 1000," the extra agents specially authorized by Congress after Hoover's dramatic testimony in 1970 about the alleged "incipient plot" of Fathers Daniel and Philip Berrigan and other militant Catholic activists to kidnap government officials, blow up buildings, and throw Washington into havoc; according to the terms of the Director's request, they were to help the FBI with its increased workload in covering organized crime, airplane hijackings, and the New Left. Under the circumstances of their hasty recruitment, one might have expected these new agents to be especially right-wing characters, yearning for the scalps of student demonstrators and angry over the decline in public esteem for the Bureau.

But whether by the force of history or by some accident, what the FBI got was people who were especially loose and free-thinking, who did not necessarily react to events on the basis of knee-jerk instincts. In contrast to the cozy Bureau the World War II generation of agents entered, these young people came into an impersonal and growing bureaucracy. They did not automatically yearn for involvement in security work, and indeed, some shunned it as outmoded and over-done; they were more interested in organized crime investigations and other areas of the FBI's criminal jurisdiction.

Most Bureau officials did not appear to realize it at first — in part because it is not their wont to find out what ordinary agents think — but this new breed of agents, even if they were military veterans, tended to see the Vietnam war in some perspective. Many of them were vaguely troubled by the idea of looking for Selective Service violators and deserters who were possibly of their own age and similar backgrounds. They were less dogmatic about some of the Bureau's political and social attitudes and less likely to overreact to the appearance of a liberal organization in an applicant-type investigation. Some, shock of all shocks, chose to let their hair grow longer even before L. Patrick Gray III gave agents permission to do so, and they tried to draw older colleagues out on the subject of why young people's hair and clothes should be matters of such emotional contention in the FBI, why "hippies" provoked such wrath and hate. There is always a chance that these agents, like other generations before them, will become crusty and narrow-minded with the passage of time, but they insist — still quietly — that if and when their time comes, they will help bring reform to the Bureau.

XIV

The G-Women

There are two things you tell your wife — when you get a transfer, and when you get a cut in pay.
> *— A veteran Bureau agent, quoting his first special-agent-in-charge on the subject of how much a good FBI man should tell his wife about his work*

CLARENCE KELLEY IS HOLDING A PRESS CONFERENCE at the Sheraton Boston Hotel as the highpoint of one of his eight regional symposia for the top management of the FBI. He has been in office only a few months, and the symposia and press conferences are still quite a novelty. An even greater novelty lies in the fact that the Bureau executives have been encouraged to bring their wives along on the trip. Most of them have, and the presence of the women at the public meetings, social functions, and even at some of their husbands' late-night bull sessions is one of those little changes that seem revolutionary when viewed from inside an organization that has long considered change to be an enemy. Kelley, very much a family man himself, is proud of having the wives there, and this is something he feels like boasting about. Toward the end of the press conference, after discussing such weighty matters as wiretapping, organized crime, and police corruption, the director takes public notice of the wives; in fact, Kelley has them stand up and asks his audience, "Aren't they lovely ladies?" No one knows quite how to react. It is a rather uncomfortable moment for everyone, but the tension is finally relieved when some FBI officials applaud and the press conference breaks up. The wives then line up along one wall of

339

the room to take their turns meeting the director who has honored them by inviting them.

The FBI has always been a man's organization, in both work and play. Hoover would never have it otherwise. The Bureau's responsibilities were assumed to be too taxing, too physically demanding, too complicated and serious for women, except insofar as they could help out in menial or subservient roles. To the extent that the FBI was a social and fraternal organization outside of office hours, women could never really belong to the club; they were always on the perimeter. Female clerks, even those performing critical and sensitive tasks in the field offices, although they might be officially on a par with their male counterparts, always had a lower unofficial status, not to mention far less promising opportunities for promotion.

The traditional lot of the Bureau wife was a simple one that told a great deal about the FBI's attitude toward women. She, like her children, was expected to be seen occasionally — usually on the command of the Bureau — but not often heard. Her political and social attitudes were assumed to be those of her husband, which is to say those of the FBI, and she was expected to join enthusiastically the crowd of staunch and outspoken defenders of J. Edgar Hoover. This was especially true of any wife (there were many) who had herself come from the ranks of Bureau employees, where she served time as a clerk or stenographer until meeting an agent–prince charming through whom she could live vicariously. The typical Bureau wife became an expert at rolling with the punches, including an arbitrary disciplinary action that reduced her husband's salary or a sudden transfer that meant uprooting the family in the middle of a school year. If she worked, she often had to be careful that her job would create no conflict of interest with her husband's sensitive position; and she had to realize that the Bureau would never consider her career a factor in what her husband did or where he worked. The life of an FBI agent's family revolved around his occupation; it provided excitement, status, restrictions, and occasional intrigue. Any resentment of the Bureau usually remained private. When the wives from a field office gathered for an evening, as they often did, their talk about the Bureau was restrained and respectful. They knew their place.

This system was accepted by most Bureau wives without challenge for decades. As the wife of one assistant-special-agent-in-charge, who had endured an unusual number of transfers during her husband's twenty-year FBI career, put it, "You learn to take these things in stride. . . . At one point, you just have to decide — either the Bureau is worth the trouble or it isn't." One agent notes that those who advance along the FBI career ladder often have family trouble — wives with emotional difficulties, children with drug problems or especially poor academic performance in school, severe alienation between parents and children — but this is a subject that has never been considered proper for Bureau study and analysis, not to say attempts at remedy. Although no reliable statistics exist, the divorce rate among agents is believed to be higher than in most comparable professions.

Wives of young agents who have recently joined the FBI tend to be more outspoken and less accepting of the traditional Bureau order. The wife of one man posted to a southern office, who is embarked on a professional career of her own, says she is frankly "bored" with the wives of her husband's colleagues, most of whom, she finds, do nothing creative with their time and "won't express an opinion about anything." Therefore she avoids the demure gatherings of field office wives. Another young agent's wife explains that during "my first six months as a Bureau wife, I was scared to death to open my mouth about anything. I was warned not to be politically active, as I had been before." Eventually, however, she mustered the nerve to write letters to congressmen on issues that she felt strongly about. Among some of her counterparts, that branded her as a troublemaker. "A lot of wives really hate the Bureau," she says; "they especially hate the inspectors, and they quiver every year when they come around, because they know what those people can do to their husbands' salary with a censure over some picayune thing." If it were not for the FBI's extraordinarily good retirement benefits, according to this wife, many women would pressure their husbands to leave the Bureau after only a few years. "What you come to learn very quickly," she says, "is that the Bureau doesn't care a damn about wives and families — until they cause trouble."

It was inevitable that as soon as Hoover died, and Clyde Tolson left the Bureau, the FBI's institutionalized misogyny would diminish. Society's ideas about and attitudes toward women were changing, and even the Bureau had to be affected eventually. It was a shock to the average special-agent-in-charge that when Acting Director L. Patrick Gray III announced he would be visiting any field office, he encouraged the SAC to have his wife in the office that day as well, for Mrs. Gray would also be coming along. The appearance of the outgoing, gregarious Beatrice Gray in the field offices, shaking hands, drinking tea, and chatting, was a major breakthrough. Whatever agents later thought about Gray in connection with other issues, they tended to admire him for including his wife on his field office tours. It set a precedent that was occasionally imitated in the field — women began to be invited to more field office functions — and it was taken as a signal that women might now be accepted as something more than junior members of the FBI world. Kelley, who often cited his involvement in family life as a major difference between himself and Hoover, built upon what Gray had started. He invited wives to his symposia and other Bureau events and insisted that agents' families would become more of a Bureau concern. Some were so pleased as to thank him directly. For those families that had grown up in the aura of the old Bureau, it was nothing less than culture shock; said the wife of one assistant director to her husband, "Imagine — talking and caring about 'the director's wife.' "

But the most dramatic change in the traditional FBI attitude toward women, of course, came with Gray's decision that the Bureau would accept female agents into its ranks.* That was the clearest possible chink in the all-male armor that Hoover had spent so many years fashioning.

◆

When Maria Eugenia "Peggy" Parga walked into the El Paso Field Office of the FBI in the summer of 1972 and said that she was looking for a job, the first reaction of the agent who interviewed her was to ask whether she could type and take shorthand. She quickly pointed out that she had something else in mind, that she had heard the Bureau was looking for new agents, including women. Suddenly the agent recognized the responsibility in his hands. "Don't move," he said, as he ran off to find out just how to handle the situation — horrified by the notion of female agents but at the same time excited over the prospect that he might win an incentive award for signing up one of the first. At about the same time, on the other side of Texas, another young woman visited the resident agency in Corpus Christi after reading that Acting Director Gray was interested in recruiting female agents. The baffled man who greeted her immediately called the applicant supervisor in the Houston Field Office. "There's a broad here who wants to be an agent," he said; "how do I handle this?"

It was not easy for the men of the Bureau to adapt to the idea of sharing their work with women, and the decision to accept female applicants for the position of special agent was initially greeted with

---

* For a discussion of Gray's method in making the decision, and of the resentment it stirred, see Chapter XXI.

confusion and puzzlement. No one seemed to have any clear idea of how the women would be absorbed into the ranks and what they would do. Some Bureau traditionalists obviously hoped that the change would be like the time when Hoover created black "agents" by giving an oath and a badge, but nothing else, to his office boys and chauffeurs.

With some flourish, Gray announced that the first two women were in a class that began agent's training at Quantico on July 17, 1972. They were Susan Lynn Roley, twenty-five, a three-year veteran of the Marine Corps, and Joanne E. Pierce, thirty-one, who had been a Catholic nun for eleven years and had worked for the two years since leaving her convent as a clerk for the FBI in Washington. The announcement provoked considerable annoyance within the Bureau because the names and entry into training of individual male agents were never announced publicly. But Gray insisted that in every significant respect the women would be treated no differently from any other FBI agent; he simply wanted to make it clear that the policy change had taken practical effect, he said.

In fact, the publicity about the first two women entering agent's training brought dozens of additional applications. Some, like Roley (who later gained a Bureau-wide reputation for toughness after roadblock duty during the American Indian Movement's occupation of Wounded Knee, South Dakota), were of the classic, tough policewoman stereotype. Others, like Parga, were young college graduates who spoke Spanish as well as English and sought some more original way to use their language skills than in teaching. There were nurses looking for something new and more adventurous, guidance counselors with a particular knack for interviewing, and bright young women lawyers who were not inspired by the traditional options available on leaving law school. Carol Leininger was in charge of the commercial department of a high school in Springfield, Illinois, and worked as a sales clerk on the side; when an agent came to recruit potential Bureau stenographers from a class that she taught, she became more interested in his job than in the ones he was talking to her students about. One woman, Linda Durbin, was married and had a child; she had previously worked for the Social Security Administration and went looking for a job again while her husband, an automobile factory worker, was out on strike against General Motors. Another, Christine Hansen, a newspaper reporter in Des Moines with a law degree, was fed up with the second-rate job opportunities for women in journalism and in most government agencies. She became particularly aroused when she was reporting a newspaper story about a woman in Des Moines who wanted to be a policewoman but was only permitted to apply for the secondary job of "matron." Hansen says she finally chose the FBI among several new jobs open to her "for the same reasons a man would — for one thing, it paid more than anything else available at the time."

Most women agents describe their Bureau training as a difficult, sometimes depressing experience. Initially, FBI officials went to an extreme to prove that they were not making things any easier for the women than for men, and the physical part of the training, designed for men and their particular physical capabilities, was a special problem. As one of the first female recruits puts it, "I had never tried to do a man's pushup, and nobody bothered teaching us how. . . . The first time they said, 'Hit the deck,' we just stood there and didn't know what to do." Sheila Horan, who trained in late 1973 and early 1974, says it became demoralizing for some women to be put on the "weak squad" after failing to achieve the required number of points for physical fitness within four weeks. That meant they had to go for an extra hour of work in the gymnasium at Quantico every day. About ten members of Horan's class, male and female, were in that category for a time, but all of the others eventually made the grade and "towards the end, I hung in there alone." A few weeks before graduation, however, she qualified. Many women who had no previous experience with guns also went through the same difficulty in firearms training — some got frostbite trying to learn to load a revolver quickly in the cold — finally qualifying after extensive special tutoring by the Bureau instructors. Some, excellent in the classroom, were washed out when they could not measure up in the gym or on the firing range.

But the psychological strain of training — the isolation and the anxiety over not measuring up in the male subculture of the FBI — was far worse than the physical difficulties, according to some of the women agents. This was especially true for anyone who came through as the only woman in a training class. "It was heartbreaking at first," says Linda Durbin, who had left her husband and son behind in Cincinnati when she went off to Quantico; "I was quite ready to leave by the second day." Later, however, she found that "the fellows adopted me. . . . When I had trouble running, two guys grabbed my hands and dragged me along." For others the trauma lasted longer. Kayleen Drissell, for example, also the only woman in her class, says she became "really isolated and stuck" at Quantico; for her the three and a half months of training "felt like a very long time." For another woman, even though there were several others in her class, "it came to

344

be a very negative experience. . . . I spent every weekend I could staying with a friend in Washington." Peggy Parga also had three female classmates, but still felt "very homesick" during training.

One reason for the strain was the teasing and hazing, at first gentle but sometimes fairly vicious. It was more severe from the younger agents than from the older men, one female agent on the West Coast remembers: "I finally became convinced that they felt threatened by us," she says. But worst of all was the harassment from the local and state policemen attending the classes of the FBI National Academy, some of whom already resented male Bureau agents and seemed to feel even more strongly about female recruits. One woman agent recalls being asked once too often by policemen attending the academy whether she had joined the Bureau "to look for a husband." Another says that several of the local law enforcement people went out of their way to tell her that they would never consent to take a woman along on an arrest, be she an FBI agent or anyone else. Even with women police officers joining the National Academy classes, it did not let up.

Some of that bias, of course, extended to the field, both in relationships within the Bureau and in contacts with the outside world. Some male agents have remained reluctant to bring a female counterpart along on a dangerous or difficult assignment unless another man is also present, and one woman agent noticed after a few months in her first field office that she was being sent out primarily to interview other women — bank tellers, the mothers of military deserters, and the like. (A gentle protest led her supervisor to alter the pattern somewhat.) Another woman agent found that she faced a special challenge because "many informants simply don't want to be interviewed by a female . . . especially not truck drivers or hoods. The Mafia people have their own sense of a woman: she is somebody who stays home and cooks pasta." The attitude is scarcely any better among some of the women whom agents must approach. When the same female agent went along with two men for what was to be her first arrest, the mother of the young man named in the arrest warrant — as if fulfilling the new agent's worst fears — turned to one of the men and asked, "Is this your wife you brought along?"

Some women agents, of course, have found their sex to be a distinct advantage in performing their duties. There is no particular stereotype of a "G-woman," as there was for years of the typical conservatively dressed, short-haired FBI man. Although the female recruits initially had to meet the same minimum height standard as the men (five feet seven inches) and were therefore taller than the aver-

345

age American woman, they did not particularly stand out in the crowd. The Bureau has refrained, wisely and mercifully, from instituting any strict dress or grooming regulations for women agents; and so some have short hair and some long, some go to work in dresses or skirts and some in slacks. It would require a well-trained eye to spot the "Bureau purse" issued from Washington, a heavy-duty one with a special inside pocket to hold a gun,* but not all of the female agents use it anyway. The unpredictability of appearance and the unusualness of women agents enhance their effectiveness, according to Carol Leininger. "The element of surprise really helps," she says; "I can go into a bar with a man on assignment, and there is nothing suspicious about it." A number of women agents say that on some occasions, even when a male subject suspected that he had spotted a typical Bureau car, he decided against fleeing or hiding after seeing a woman at the steering wheel.

On occasion, women agents have drawn special assignments that make their male counterparts envious, if not angry — converging in a single location from various field offices, for example, to conduct a gambling raid on an organized crime syndicate operation when a number of women were expected to be present. Christine Hansen, assigned to Los Angeles, posed as a "lady in white" from the Israeli consulate there during the Bureau investigation of an extortion threat on the consulate. Several letters received by the Israeli officials had promised that a payoff of $30,000 would buy a list of the possible targets for Arab terrorists and prevent the attacks. As demanded in the notes, Hansen, supposedly an employee of the consulate, appeared at a series of phone booths in Los Angeles to receive calls and then, on instruction, drove out along the Pasadena Freeway (with a male agent in the trunk of the car) to drop the payoff money at a specified spot. The man behind the scheme, who proved to know nothing about Arab terrorist plans, was arrested when he came to pick up the money. Hansen received a letter of commendation from the director and a $150 incentive award for her work on the case.

The approximately thirty female agents† are assigned to FBI field

---

* Initially, the women were issued revolvers with two-inch barrels — "A silly little gun," one called it — as compared with the four-inch-barrel model that is standard for male agents. Later the Bureau switched to one with a two-and-a-half-inch barrel, but still insisted that the female agents should carry a smaller, more easily concealed weapon than the men.

† The ranks of women agents numbered only thirty-two in the summer of 1975. One woman, assigned to the detail that guarded Attorney General William B. Saxbe and his wife, died in an airplane crash near Washington in December 1974, and at least one other resigned when her husband was transferred away from the city where she was assigned. The Bureau says it does not know exactly how many

offices in all parts of the country, and in a few instances two are assigned to the same office. A major breakthrough was made when Mary Lou Mertens, after six months in the Tampa Field Office, was sent to Lakeland, Florida, as the first woman assigned to a resident agency. A graduate of the University of Texas Law School, she suddenly found herself interviewing Klansmen and tracking down deserters in the countryside. Having once joked with the other woman agent in Tampa about the desperate social situation of a single male agent who was assigned to Lakeland, a small town where there are few amusements or diversions, Mertens was at first very upset when she was designated to replace him. Because there were only six agents assigned to the busy resident agency, she could not even count on being free to spend most weekends in Tampa with her friends from the field office; when she did go to Tampa, she sometimes missed out on some of the most exciting cases in Lakeland. Before long, however, Mertens was well ensconced, enjoying the relaxed and informal environment of the RA, taking tap-dancing lessons, going out on nighttime raids with the five male agents ("We pulled three loaded rifles out from under a bed one time"), and socializing regularly with them and their families. Mertens took the Florida bar exam, stirring rumors that she was planning to leave the Bureau; but she insists that "right now, there is nothing else I want to do [other than being an agent]. . . . I wouldn't even want to be a supervisor. . . . I like going out and talking to people."

As if to fulfill the Old Guard's most dire predictions about women agents, some of them married their male counterparts. Officially the Bureau made no promises about assignments and transfers, but it was clear that it would have to mount a special effort to accommodate the married couples or it would be losing some of its best new agents. Margaret Lewis, a former schoolteacher and the young widow of an American soldier killed in Vietnam, was in a class of agents who completed their training in April 1973. While at Quantico, she met John Epke, a navy veteran who was at first a bureau clerk working in the gymnasium (he helped her train to meet the physical requirements) and then a member of the agents class that started about a month after hers. Toward the end of her training, they were married in the chapel at the Quantico Marine Base. Initially she drew an attractive and rare first-office assignment to Phoenix; but after they were married and

---

women have applied to become agents — field offices need not keep track of those applications that are never forwarded to headquarters — but it is clear that interest fell off sharply after the initial excitement. Even the dropping of the height requirement for agents produced no substantial increase in candidates.

required assignment together, both were sent to Detroit, she a month ahead of him. Once settled in, the Epkes were attached to different squads in the field office, with Margaret investigating organized crime cases and John tracking down fugitives; as a result, they saw each other at work very seldom and had lunch together on only about three workdays during their first year in Detroit. There were a few complications, such as when they drove in to work together from the suburbs in the morning and then had different schedules and finished at different hours. (They worked on the same case together only once, when a male and a female agent were needed to "pose" as the married friends of a prominent citizen who had received an extortion threat.) John Epke says that he has probably endured more teasing from his colleagues than his wife, especially because she is considered to have "more energy than I do"; it helps, he says, "not to be a jealous person."

Margaret Epke, for her part, is one of the female agents who found life in the Burau lonely, even with her husband working in the same field office. Being the only woman agent in an office can be a solitary situation, she complains, and she favors the grouping of several women in a single office — perhaps three or four, "so that you can at least have a peer group." Like others in her position, she rarely had the free time to make friends outside the FBI. Indeed, some women agents have felt cautious about making outside contacts, preferring to be discreet about revealing their jobs until they come to know people well; one even swore her landlord to secrecy, out of fear she would be getting phone calls, for help or harassment, in the middle of the night. The typical female agent has found that it is difficult just to become "one of the girls in the office," as one put it, when all of the others work at a lower level. Most of the women agents have made a stab at developing friendships with the clerks and secretaries in their field offices, but they invariably find barriers — differences in education, incompatible interests, and sometimes resentment over the women agents' status. One of Margaret Epke's solutions to the dilemma was to attend some of the meetings of the Detroit office's "wives' club"; at one meeting, she was herself the guest speaker, telling of how she came to be an agent and of the experiences she had had in the job. She found her contact with her colleagues' wives successful and smooth: "To most of them, I was just another wife. . . . I made a definite effort not to alienate them."

In that regard, Margaret Epke was luckier than most, for many Bureau wives are free to say that they are not enthusiastic about women agents having joined their husbands' ranks. They do not express their feelings so much in terms of jealousy or suspicion of infidelity, but rather fear. "What I am concerned about is the backup capability," says the wife of a young male agent; "I wonder how safe my husband will be, walking into a dangerous situation with only a girl along? I just don't believe that she provides the same protection for him as he does for her." Inevitably that kind of attitude is greeted with sharp rejoinders from the strong feminists among the women agents. "I have found nothing in the Bureau's work that cannot be done by a woman as well as, or perhaps better than, a man," said one after a year's service in the field; "sure, maybe I couldn't tackle a two-hundred-and-fifty-pound man, but a lot of male agents couldn't either." Another point of resentment among the wives of agents is that the women have already benefited from a kind of favoritism in transfers. One young wife, displeased with the city where her husband was assigned and yearning for a transfer, watched with unconcealed envy as a woman agent assigned to the same city was easily transferred away to an office where her husband-to-be, also an agent, was working; the same is generally done for women agents marrying people not in the FBI. It is a simple truth that a male agent would not have such an easy time being tranferred to a location convenient for his wife's career.

Some of the female agents say that they are indifferent to the number of women admitted to agent's training, and a few even advocate keeping the number small. "Personally, I hope we don't get too many women in the Bureau," says one assigned to a midwestern field office; "maybe it's an ego thing . . . but we were the first ones, and I think we should have a chance to prove ourselves before the number grows." But most of the women are dissatisfied with the slow pace of recruitment in the first three years, and urge that the number of female agents be dramatically increased if they are to have any meaningful impact within the FBI. "Maybe it needn't be fifty-fifty," says one woman agent, "but I do think there should be hundreds of women agents in the FBI." The women have an active underground communications network, and some keep maps with the up-to-date locations of all the female agents in the Bureau; several groups, especially those who were in the same training class together, have held informal reunions to discuss the way they are treated by this male-oriented and -directed organization. There are already stirrings about joining blacks and others among the tiny minority of FBI agents who are not white males in agitating for better promotion opportunities.*

At the same time, most women agents are less certain than male

* Since few people advance within the Bureau until they have been an agent for at least five years, however, it is too soon for them to know if there will be discrimination in promotion policies.

recruits of their intention to make a career of the FBI. A few say they are convinced enough already to make a decision to stay on indefinitely, but most echo the words of a woman assigned to an office on the West Coast: "It's a great job. I like it. . . . But I'll have to see how things go." Some women wonder how willing the Bureau will be to give extended maternity leaves to agents, and they have their doubts about whether they would be able to raise young children on an unpredictable FBI schedule. For the married agent couples, there are special questions about just how much the Bureau will cooperate with their needs. As Margaret Epke put it, "If one of us got assigned to Sacramento and the other to New Haven, that would obviously be the end of one career — and frankly, it would probably be mine." That issue was never really tested by the Epkes, however, because when they had a baby, she decided to resign from the FBI.

What the Bureau Does
—and Doesn't—Do

XV

Winning Friends and Influencing People on Capitol Hill

MR. ROONEY. *The Committee will please come to order.*

This morning, gentlemen, we shall consider the request for appropriation for the Federal Bureau of Investigation for the coming fiscal year, to wit, fiscal year 1967.

In this connection we are pleased to have with us again the distinguished Director, the distinguished and indestructible Director of the Federal Bureau of Investigation, the Honorable J. Edgar Hoover.

. . .

MR. FLYNT. *Mr. Director, it is always gratifying to have you appear before us as a witness, someone who is as forthright as you are.*

MR. HOOVER. *Thank you.*

MR. FLYNT. *At the same time, someone who has the most comprehensive grasp of the statements that you make to us of any witness with whom I have any knowledge or with whom I have had any experience.*

MR. HOOVER. *I appreciate that.*

MR. FLYNT. *I would like to ask you if you are training your associate director, and your assistant directors, in this fine art which you have mastered, to develop the sense of communication with Members of Congress, members of this committee, and with the public generally in such a way as to naturally instill the confidence that you seem to?*

. . .

MR. ROONEY. *Mr. Director, on behalf of the committee, I wish to thank you for a highly interesting and informative three-hour session. It was well worthwhile and I express, on behalf of all*

members of the committee, our thanks to you for your fine and
efficient administration of the Federal Bureau of Investigation.
MR. HOOVER. *Thank you.*

> *— From the transcript of hearings on February 10,*
> *1966, before the House Appropriations Subcom-*
> *mittee on Departments of State, Justice, and*
> *Commerce, the Judiciary and Related Agencies*

J. EDGAR HOOVER QUICKLY PERCEIVED, when he took over the Bureau in 1924, that the most important place for a Washington bureaucrat to cultivate friends and admirers is on Capitol Hill. With an enthusiastic constituency there, an agency head is bound to feel secure in his job, capable of resisting pressures within the executive branch from everyone up to and including the President, and likely to be treated more tenderly by the courts when cases reach them. No one understood this fact of life better than the Director, and no one was more successful than he at manipulating it to his own best advantage.

Hoover began early collecting congressional friends, and his instincts and antennae led him toward people who accumulated considerable seniority and gained enormous power — Emmanuel Celler of New York, John McClellan of Arkansas, Lyndon Johnson of Texas, John McCormack of Massachusetts, James Eastland of Mississippi, and Thomas Dodd of Connecticut, among many others. Hoover did not necessarily know all of these legislators well, but they came to share a commonality of concerns that served both sides of the relationship. Eastland and Hoover, for example, had totally different personalities, and therefore never spent much time together; but they could always count on each other politically and bureaucratically when it mattered. Such friends and other names great and small, including the many ex-agents in Congress,* became the clients of the FBI's Congressional Services Office, whose main responsibility over the years was to swap favors and hold hands on Capitol Hill. If a friendly congressman needed to find his son or daughter traveling in Europe, the Bureau,

---

* The Ninety-third Congress included eight former special agents of the FBI: Democratic Representatives Omar Burleson of Texas, George E. Danielson of California, Frank E. Denholm of South Dakota, and Don Edwards of California; and Republican Representatives Samuel L. Devine of Ohio, Lawrence J. Hogan of Maryland, Wiley Mayne of Iowa, and Wendell Wyatt of Oregon. It also included three former Bureau clerks: Republican Garry Brown of Michigan, and Democrats Harold L. Runnels of New Mexico and Robert O. Tiernan of Rhode Island. Five of these eleven men (Denholm, Hogan, Mayne, Wyatt, and Tiernan) retired or were defeated in 1974 and no other former Bureau employees were elected to the Ninety-fourth Congress.

through its overseas contacts, could often do the job. If he showed special interest in a pending case, the Bureau put in extra effort and gave him regular reports on its progress. When he was arguing a tough law-and-order position in legislative debate and was dissatisfied with the background material provided by his own staff or the Library of Congress, the FBI Research Section might be able to come through with something more persuasive. Such favors tended, of course, to build up the obligations to the Bureau in Congress. This system, developed and refined by the master Bureau spokesman and promoter, Louis B. Nichols, was nearly foolproof.

To keep the machinery operating smoothly, the FBI gathered a certain amount of background information that enabled it to pick and choose among its potential friends in Congress and to maintain an alert against potential enemies. Beginning in the early 1950s, the Crime Records Division asked field offices to submit to headquarters "pertinent background information and data from office files on major nonincumbent candidates" for Congress after local primary elections were held. FBI files at headquarters included a "memorandum prepared for the information of Bureau officials" on each member of Congress, and the current data gathered by agents in the field were used to update those memoranda or, in the event an incumbent was defeated, to replace them. As justified in a memorandum from then Assistant Director Thomas E. Bishop to Acting Director L. Patrick Gray III on October 26, 1972, the procedure permitted the FBI to gain "some knowledge of the background of these individuals" that would make a Bureau investigation more effective if any sitting or elected member of Congress should become the target of assassination, kidnapping, or assault (jurisdiction over such a crime was given to the FBI early in 1971). But Bishop, head of Crime Records, trying to convince Gray of the value of the program, went on to explain that it was invaluable in helping the Bureau find its friends:

[I]t provides information needed to determine whether or not we should initiate a contact with the newly elected Congressman or Senator to explain our operations and offer our services where appropriate. If such a contact is made, the information enables the person making the contact to channel the conversation into areas of known interest and certainly enhances our possibilities of establishing a friendly relationship with the new member.

In the same memorandum, Bishop explained:

Basically, what we are interested in is biographical information; any background indicating interest in law enforcement, either pro or con; any prior contacts between the candidate and the FBI; and any information which would indicate a friendly or hostile attitude toward the FBI or law enforcement in general.

On paper, unless the candidate was under investigation in connection with an alleged federal violation or was the subject of a background check for an executive or judicial appointment, the information was to come only from "public source material readily available to the office." But of course anything in the field office files that might tend to incriminate, embarrass, or compromise the candidate, even if unsubstantiated, was usually included. "Under *no* circumstances should you make outside inquiries such as checks of credit bureaus or newspaper morgues" warned the routing slip that made the standard annual request of the field offices in 1972; "these matters must always be handled *with extreme discretion* to avoid the implication that we are checking on candidates."

The compilation of the supposedly innocuous memoranda on congressmen first came to public attention in the fall of 1972, when a young agent assigned to the FBI resident agency in Lorain County, Ohio, apparently believing he was following Bureau instructions, made open inquiries about a local Democratic congressional candidate, setting off newspaper publicity about the "investigation" and a furor that led Gray to suspend the program. One revealing aspect of the incident was that it was handled with a classic, instinctive cover-up. Rather than explain that the intended purpose was to provide "briefing material" for the Bureau on potential congressmen, both the resident agent and his superior, the special-agent-in-charge of the Cleveland Field Office, claimed that the reason for the inquiries was merely that the agent was an "interested new voter" in the area. (The disciplinary ax fell heavily after the incident: the special-agent-in-charge was transferred by Gray from Cleveland to a smaller office in Albany. The resident agent was suspended without pay for a time and then put on probation for an extended period; he eventually resigned from the FBI.) Bishop, for his part, urged in his memorandum that "we should continue to handle this program, but . . . eliminate any written instructions emanating from the Bureau pertaining to it. This will avoid the possibility of Bureau instructions reaching the hands of newsmen under any circumstances." Although responsible for the FBI's press and congressional relations at the time, as head of the Crime Records Division, Bishop opposed Gray's issuance of a press release explaining the program and announcing its cancellation. But Gray, feeling he had been deceived earlier when he asked about files on congressmen, insisted that the announcement be made.

Despite frequent rumors and allegations about FBI files on congressmen, members were uncertain whether they were really the subjects of such systematic FBI records until the misdirected inquiries in Ohio. Some of them knew that when the Bureau did hold compromising information about a congressman, it was standard procedure to confront him with that knowledge and then promise to be discreet. The Bureau notified one member of the House, for example, that it was aware he had been arrested on a homosexuality charge and had been the victim of blackmail, but it agreed to help him keep his secret. The man had not been a particularly close friend of the FBI, but it was clear after that communication that he would not want to risk becoming an enemy.

Reviewing the situation in February 1975, shortly after he had become attorney general, Edward H. Levi said that "the FBI maintains the same kinds of files on members of Congress as it does on other American citizens." Altogether, Levi said, there were at that time 1,605 Bureau files relating to members of Congress, 883 on senators and 722 on congressmen. Most of the senators' files involved instances when they were the victims of criminal activity, including extortion demands or assassination threats, and half of those on members of the House concerned correspondence with or about them, including letters making unsubstantiated allegations about their personal lives; some of the others related to background investigations when the legislators were considered for executive branch or other appointments. Only a tiny percentage of the files — perhaps 2 percent — concerned "possible violations of the security laws" by members of Congress, Levi said. As with other Bureau files, most of this material is stored indefinitely by the FBI.

Only occasionally did any of the powers in Congress dare to lock horns with Hoover and the Bureau. One time was in April 1971, when the late Congressman Hale Boggs of Louisiana, then the Democratic majority leader, took the floor and contended that the FBI was conducting wholesale wiretaps and other eavesdropping on senators and congressmen. He demanded that Hoover resign. Although he promised proof, Boggs never produced it, except to cite the well-known case of Congressman John Dowdy (D-Texas), the subject of a federal investigation on bribery, conspiracy, and perjury charges. (Some of the evidence against Dowdy had been obtained by strapping a tape recorder to the back of the government informer in the case.) Boggs was bitter over the fact that some time earlier he had himself figured in an FBI investigation of a friend, a Baltimore contractor who remodeled Boggs's garage at a bargain price while seeking the congressman's help with a claim against the government in connection with a garage he had built on Capitol Hill. Hoover tried to make peace with the influential congressman by sending Robert Kunkel, then special-agent-in-charge of the Washington, D.C., Field Office, to discuss the matter with him, but Boggs refused to meet with Kunkel. In the end, Boggs's criticism, although it rang true to some people, was just the kind of unsubstantiated attack that produced a backlash and tended to strengthen Hoover's position with Congress (and Boggs's position in the dispute was not helped by the fact that he was known to be drinking heavily at that time). Less powerful members of Congress, usually people the Bureau considered "enemies," came to attack the FBI frequently during the late 1960s and early 1970s — as the Bureau's immunity from criticism began to run out — but this usually had little effect except to reinforce the opinions of those already favorable to or critical of the FBI. Hoover and his allies always felt the Director was strengthened, for example, by intemperate attacks on him from such liberals as Democratic Senators George McGovern of South Dakota and William Proxmire of Wisconsin; their attacks generally sent milder critics of Hoover rushing to his defense.

A significant example of the Bureau's cashing in on its reservoir of favors owed on Capitol Hill came in the late 1950s, when it became alarmed over the Supreme Court's reversal of the conviction of Clinton Jencks, a union official from New Mexico who was charged with perjury for signing a noncommunist affidavit. Dividing 7 to 1, the high court declared that it had been unfair to deny the Jencks defense access to the original accusations against him by a government informer; it said that a defendant had a right to see all prior statements that dealt with the testimony against him by a government witness. The one justice in the minority, former Attorney General Tom C. Clark, warned that the decision could create "fishing expeditions" into the Bureau's files, and Hoover, ostensibly concerned about protecting the sanctity of FBI documents, took up the battle cry. Within a few months votes had been mobilized in Congress — among other methods, by hinting darkly that the espionage case against a Soviet spy, Colonel Rudolph Abel, might be damaged by the decision — and a bill was rushed through that sharply cut back on the effects of the Jencks decision. FBI lobbyists were victorious and grateful, and by 1959 the Supreme Court, apparently reading the election returns, endorsed the new law, thus settling things essentially the way the Bureau preferred them to be. The law left several loopholes that permitted prosecutors and agents to keep pretrial statements out of court.

Other Bureau interventions were more surreptitious and less successful. Hoover wrote discreet letters to influential senators, for example, urging them to vote against President Johnson's consular treaty with the Soviet Union because it would create more diplomatic positions that could be used as cover for communist spies in the United States. But the treaty was nonetheless adopted.

The story of the FBI's extended love affair with Congress — and of its growth as an agency — is perhaps best traced through the record of the Bureau's budget hearings before the House Appropriations Committee, where Hoover annually gave his most enthusiastic description of the Bureau's work and found his most avid and admiring listeners. Even when he was making few other appearances toward the end of his life, the Director always testified personally before the House subcommittee that considered the Justice Department budget. His appearance was a major event on Capitol Hill. Although some of the subcommittee members were often absent during other budget presentations — even for the testimony of Supreme Court justices — they invariably all returned to the hearing room in time for Hoover's performance. And quite a performance it was, because the Director spent days, even weeks, preparing for it, committing his formal statement to memory and, in the later years, having elaborate accompanying charts done up in the FBI Exhibits Section. He occasionally testified before Senate appropriations hearings as well, but the House sessions, which came first, had a special importance for him.

From Hoover's earliest visits to the Hill, he sought to establish that the Bureau was clearly worth more to the country than it cost. His single device was to tabulate the total, in all cases touched by the Bureau, of fines (amounts levied against those convicted of crimes or losing civil suits to the government), savings (how much the government received or avoided having to pay in the course of winning civil cases), and recoveries (not only in cash, as from bank robberies, but also in the value of recovered cars and other stolen property, with the value often assigned on the high side). One trick built in was that the totals involved every case on which the Bureau had opened a file, even if its investigative efforts involved only a phone call to discover that the local police had solved the case. These were the kinds of statistics that could not go anywhere but up.*

* See Chapter V, page 95.

Hoover's appropriations testimony was crucial to the establishment of the FBI's reputation for efficiency, doggedness, and parsimony. His familiarity with extraordinarily minute details and the Bureau's precision bookkeeping could not fail to impress. In the early days, it was all very modest, but then it grew dramatically. In 1926, Hoover requested an increase in the Bureau's budget of exactly $95,720, to cover the increase in the per diem allowances for government employees from four dollars to six. He reported that field personnel, including agents, accountants, stenographers, and clerks, numbered four hundred and forty-two and that at the "seat of government" there were but one hundred and fifteen, among them only eight agents. "No man can move in the field without there being a record here in Washington as to when and where he has moved," he boasted. "I have in my office in the department a map of the United States, and on that map each man is represented by a tag. As a man moves, his tag is changed, and each field office has to wire in the whereabouts of every agent when he moves." Questioned by subcommittee members about the increase in crime and the possibility of a "crime wave," the Director could not answer with precision. But he saw the opening for an intriguing proposal: "When I was at Chicago last summer, at the meeting of the chiefs of police, this question came up; that there is no place today, in the United States, to which one may turn to find out exactly what the situation is as to crime. There are no crime statistics. There are several crime commissions in New York, Cleveland, Chicago, etc., but there is no central place to assemble your facts and to study those facts, upon which to predicate your laws and preventive measures; and the suggestion was there made that the Identification Division of the Department of Justice [part of the FBI] might be a very logical place in which to assemble statistics on crime, because all fingerprints taken in connection with felonies in the United States are sent to us."

During his testimony in 1928, to discuss the budget for Fiscal Year 1930, Hoover reported that the Bureau would be returning to the Treasury as unused from the last appropriation the sum of $57,998.12. By the next year, however, with the Bureau's work growing, the Director was reporting a deficit of $262,545.92. He assured Congressman George Holden Tinkham of Massachusetts that "we have a very definite rule in the bureau that any employee engaging in wiretapping will be dismissed from the service of the bureau. . . . While it may not be illegal, I think it is unethical, and it is not permitted under the regulations by the Attorney General." By 1930, the Director was able to describe the Bureau's new job, finally authorized by Congress, of compiling crime statistics. "Another subject that would be interesting in connection with crime statistics," Hoover noted in an enlightened aside that would have been considered close to heresy by the FBI ten or twenty years later, "is the relation to crime of unemployment, of disease, and of the various items which make up the economic life of a country."

By the 1933 hearings, when Hoover was accompanied by Attorney General Homer Cummings to Capitol Hill, the Director was beginning to draw the fulsome praise that became characteristic of his appearances. Congressman Thomas S. McMillan of South Carolina, a relatively new member of the audience, pronounced himself "thrilled" with Hoover's statement. "The committee in the past has always been impressed with the informing and thorough statement which Mr. Hoover presents. He is always so thoroughly familiar with the work of his Bureau that he is prepared to answer any question relating thereto with definite information," purred the subcommittee chairman, William B. Oliver of Alabama.

Hoover's statement in 1934 was highlighted by boasts about major criminals recently killed or captured and expressions of the prospects for success under the Roosevelt administration's crime bills. The Director promised to pursue the "shyster criminal lawyers" who were helping major gangsters, explained that every branch of government except the navy was submitting fingerprints for the Bureau files, and complained of lenient parole systems in the states and local communities. "I do not want it believed or felt that we are trying to develop a group of so-called 'trigger men,'" Hoover assured the subcommittee as he discussed the killing of "desperadoes" like John Dillinger, "Baby Face" Nelson, and "Pretty Boy" Floyd in the previous year; "those men were killed, each one of them, either actually engaged in gunfire with us or drawing a gun to fire. We have never killed a single one of those men until he has drawn his gun to shoot at one of our agents. I think that is perfectly justifiable action upon our part." So good was his reputation that no one thought to challenge or investigate the truth of the Director's claims; there was no source for evaluation of the Bureau's performance other than the Bureau itself.

In 1936, testifying on behalf of a budget increase request for Fiscal Year 1937, Hoover cited the Bureau's legendary "voluntary overtime" — 56,050 hours in 1935 — necessary, he said, in order to handle the growing workload.* The Director noted with satisfaction that

---

* Later, of course, that voluntary overtime would in effect become compulsory for all agents, so that Hoover would be able to continue to impress the Appropriations Committee with the total number of extra hours worked every year by his

"there has been a great change in public opinion toward law enforcement in the last three years. I receive many letters from young boys asking what they can study to become 'G-men.' They are now beginning to want to emulate the law enforcement officer instead of a gangster. . . . You have seen the change, also, in motion pictures. It has been a change toward a glorifying of the law enforcement officer instead of the gangster, and that has been reflected all through the country." One device Hoover used was to list a large number of "unassigned cases" that could not be handled with the existing manpower, but required an increase in authorized personnel. Such precise statistics were kept of the Bureau's work that the Director was able to tell the subcommittee in April 1939 that betewen Fiscal Years 1937 and 1938 the volume of outgoing mail had increased from 2,169,945 pieces to 2,907,578, a change of 34 percent.

With the Appropriations Committee so accustomed to measuring the FBI's accomplishments in terms of statistics, the Bureau continued to spew them out after Hoover died. Clarence Kelley reported in his first appropriations testimony, on March 6, 1974, for example, that in Fiscal Year 1973 "a record 14,465 convictions were recorded in FBI-investigated cases as compared to 13,822 in the previous fiscal year." He also noted that the number of fugitives located reached "a new high" of 37,543. Kelley had to acknowledge, however, that "fines, savings and recoveries" were down to $474,542,568 from the previous year's high of $547,361,685, "principally due to a change in the internal procedure for reporting recoveries of stolen automobiles" (meaning that after years of pressure to make the change, the Bureau had finally agreed to count only the value of those cars actually recovered by its own agents, rather than of all cars recovered, including by other law enforcement agencies, in "Bureau-investigated cases"). Nonetheless, the FBI was still able to calculate that "the fines, savings and recoveries in the 1973 fiscal year averaged out to $1.32 for every $1 of direct funds appropriated to the FBI for the year."

The graphic language of Hoover's annual appropriations testimony made it all the more titillating to the admiring congressmen. Some fugitives were labeled "mad dogs," others plainly declared "public enemies." Wartime work, both at home and overseas, increased the Bureau's prestige; as Hoover explained the FBI's conduct of "national

---

men. Sometimes Hoover amused his special-agents-in-charge with orders that "everyone in the office must be above the office average" in overtime — a statistical impossibility. In 1975, agents at FBI headquarters and in the field were generally expected to put in at least one hour and forty-nine minutes of overtime per day, whether or not they had any work to fill that time with.

defense training schools" for police during his 1943 testimony, sub-committee chairman Louis C. Rabaut of Michigan cut in to observe that "your Bureau has always had a very good place in our regard. It has always been regarded very highly by the people of the country. And I should say that from my own observation I think that if you ever were [at] a high, you are at [a] high right now. It is the proper place to be at [a] high with an organization of this kind in the times in which we are living. So I think that you should be highly compli-mented."

Hoover was encouraged by the subcommittee from time to time to speculate on the causes of such problems as the general increase in crime, and his answers played into the hands of congressmen who lamented the passing of the good old days. "You cannot disregard the home and the church in the building of a nation," the Director said in a colloquy with Representative Butler B. Hare of South Carolina on February 18, 1943; "it cannot be done, and never has been done in the world. And the thing that we need today, I think is a return to the old-fashioned method of life so far as the home and the church are concerned."

And so it went. Rabaut on one occasion expressed himself as being so satisfied with Hoover's "splendid work" that he told the Di-rector, "We hope that the Lord will preserve you in health and protect you." Hoover began taking the congressmen into his confidence on security-related matters, and the transcripts of the hearings were in-creasingly peppered with references to "off-the-record" discussions of unspecified subjects. If the Bureau of the Budget cut the FBI's appro-priations request before submitting the annual overall budget to Con-gress, the subcommittee invariably sided with its favorite agency and restored the money. The Director's examples of the Bureau's work, including the accomplishments of the Identification Division, cleverly kept pace with the temper of the times; in the early 1950s, for example, he was likely to cite instances where the fingerprint files had helped the United States keep out aliens suspected of being communists or those whose entry was sponsored by Americans with communist ties. The preoccupation with communism grew during the McCarthy era, until Hoover began devoting large sections of his presentation to the subcommittee to that subject. Even after the Smith Act trials, in February 1953, Hoover was telling the congressmen that the Com-munist party of the United States represented a serious threat: "The communists enter in every field of activity — civil rights, youth groups, veterans' groups, press and radio and television, motion picture, politi-cal organizations of every kind whereby they can proselyte and spread

363

their beliefs and doctrines." The communist menace also became a new way to justify budget increases; whereas one agent had been sufficient "for proper coverage of a Nazi," Hoover testified at one point, "We have to use as many as ten in connection with the covering of communist subversives by reason of their intensive revolutionary training for years. Surveillances have to be conducted more frequently and require greater expenditure of investigative personnel."

The chairman of the subcommittee from January 1949 until his retirement from the House in 1974, with the exception of two years when Congress was controlled by the Republicans, was Democratic Representative John J. Rooney of Brooklyn, New York.* Rooney, an artful politician of the old school, became the guardian angel of the FBI. While he would rail about the inefficiency and poor performance of other agencies that came to him for money, such as the United States Information Agency (he called it the "U.S. Inflammation Agency"), he was almost always happy with the Bureau. "USIA would come up to the Hill with dozens of people; they needed a truck to deliver their briefcases," Rooney complained with characteristic hyperbole in an interview after his retirement. "One would pass a question to the other, and you would never get an answer. The information might be submitted later for the record, but then you lost your opportunity to cross-examine. . . . But the FB & I — they brought three witnesses, Hoover, Tolson and the man in charge of the budget [during most of Rooney's era, John P. Mohr]. You could ask them any question and you got a ready answer. If you wanted to know how many cars they had in the Chicago office, you would find out immediately — with the mileage on each."

"That's for the birds, that empire business," said Rooney whenever confronted with the allegation that the Director was an empire-builder; "everyone knows that a small, tight operation gives you better control. Hoover was nobody's fool; he fully realized this." It was Rooney's view that responsibility for the FBI's growth lay squarely on Capitol Hill, where his colleagues "kept thinking up new things for the FBI to do, giving them additional responsibilities under the laws we passed." But once any responsibilities were added to the FBI's mandate, Rooney saw to it that the Bureau received what he and the Director considered adequate financing to handle them. For good

* It is worth noting that one aspect of the Hoover-LBJ relationship was that Rooney's counterpart on the Senate side — the chairman of the Senate Appropriations Subcommittee dealing with the State and Justice departments and the Judiciary — was, in the late 1950s, one Lyndon B. Johnson of Texas.

measure, it happened that the staff assistant to his subcommittee was a former agent.

Rooney played the foil to the Director, tossing him predictable open-ended questions about communism or farcical ones like "Do you have any agents who are members of the Mattachine Society [a homosexual organization]?" The chairman invited Hoover's verbal forays into diverse subject areas — one year eliciting criticism of the University of Maryland, for example, for inviting a civil rights leader to speak on campus who had once pleaded guilty to a sodomy charge. "I thought J. Edgar Hoover was the greatest man in the United States government," Rooney said later. "He could do more than anyone with the money invested in his agency. I never knew him to exaggerate or tell an untruth. He never lied, and I found plenty of other people in government who did. . . . Toward the end there were too many people who were trying to tear him down; but they never laid a finger on him."

The relationship between Hoover and Rooney was informal and close enough that when the Director sought some official sanction for his more ambitious projects, between annual appropriations hearings, he would consult Rooney privately, either on the telephone or in person. Sometimes the subcommittee chairman would let the ranking Republican of the subcommittee in on the conversations, but often he evaluated the matters alone. Rooney was told about some of the Bureau's controversial counterintelligence programs (COINTELPROs) during the 1950s and 1960s, and his approval was taken inside the Bureau to be tantamount to a congressional authorization. If Rooney asked that something be done, the Bureau also took the request as a formal congressional mandate. There was little potential for petty disagreements or policy conflict. As Rooney would say in retirement, "I don't believe in being taken for a sleigh ride by any commies . . . I get sick and tired of being sold down the drain . . . so, I just think like J. Edgar Hoover."

Other committees of Congress were content to leave all scrutiny of the FBI to Rooney and his subcommittee, a situation unique in the federal establishment. William D. Ruckelshaus, who served as acting FBI director for seventy-five days during the Bureau's troubled times in 1973, was astonished to find that not once during that period was he summoned to Capitol Hill, or even telephoned, by a congressional committee to explain some aspect of Bureau operations or policy. (Rooney would have called him only when the time came for annual appropriations hearings — by which time Ruckelshaus was out.) In his previous role as head of the Environmental Protection Agency, Ruckelshaus had been called upon frequently to answer questions.

As Rooney became older and his Brooklyn district changed in character, he was repeatedly challenged in the Democratic primary by younger, more liberal candidates. Two of them, Peter G. Eikenberry and Allard K. Lowenstein, Rooney's primary opponents in 1970 and 1972 respectively, later filed lawsuits with the support of the American Civil Liberties Union, charging that the FBI, eager to keep a friend in office, had investigated them and secretly turned the result of the investigations over to Rooney for use in his campaigns. According to the lawsuits, Bureau agents poked into the personal lives of Rooney's opponents and also tipped the congressman off in advance about their schedules, activities, and political operations. But both Rooney and the FBI denied any such liaison. (Rooney died late in 1975.)

Beyond the Bureau's coziness with the subcommittee that examined its budget, it also maintained the closest of ties with the parent House Appropriations Committee. Beginning in 1943, at the request of the committee chairman, Congressman Clarence Cannon of Missouri, the FBI began lending its agents to the Appropriations Committee to help conduct bipartisan "surveys, studies and investigations" of new programs for which various federal agencies were seeking funding each year.* Initially only two agents worked on the Hill, but that number would grow. While the committee later also borrowed investigators from other agencies, especially those with defense-related assignments, it was the FBI agents who came to serve as "executives" of the special appropriations research staff. Today assigned to the committee for an average of about three years, the agents may travel widely, examining whether budget requests are justified, for example, for a new veterans' hospital, Indian school, or weapons system. The reports that grow out of these trips are intended as briefs that congressmen may use in preparation for hearings, but sometimes a negative report may kill a program before it ever reaches the appropriations hearing stage. On one occasion, after six weeks of study in Germany, a committee investi-

---

* Professor John Elliff of Brandeis University has reported that he found a 1943 memorandum among the Roosevelt papers at Hyde Park, New York, from Attorney General Francis Biddle to the President, in which Biddle said he was "strongly opposed to the plan" for the FBI to assist the House Appropriations Committee, because "it would put the Department of Justice in the impossible position of investigating other departments, including the Army and Navy, and passing on their needs." According to Elliff, Roosevelt noted, "You are absolutely right," and vetoed the plan. Still, the Bureau says it began the special work for the committee in 1943.

gating unit led by FBI agents put the kiss of death on a $24 billion proposal to develop and manufacture a new tank for the American military.

The agents assigned to the Appropriations Committee are generally well along in their Bureau careers and destined for important positions in the hierarchy. (The first one so assigned, in fact, was Hugh Clegg, who later became a powerful assistant director.) In late 1974 there were thirty-one agents on loan as committee investigators "on a reimbursable basis" (the committee paying the equivalent of their salaries into Bureau funds) and three others serving as the "executives" (temporarily severed from FBI rolls and paid directly by the committee). The rule is that what the agents do for the committee never reaches the Bureau, but it is clear from experience that the program gives future FBI leaders an intimate acquaintance with and extensive contacts in other government agencies, not to mention an additional foothold on Capitol Hill for the Bureau. The agents were also a convenient source of the gossip that Hoover liked to have on members of Congress. There are obvious advantages to the Appropriations Committee of having trained FBI investigative personnel do its legwork, and the gratitude of senior members for their devoted service is always clear when the committee takes up the Bureau's appropriations each year. It is rare, of course, for any such study team of agents to take part in an evaluation of FBI budget requests. The House committee has always felt that they need no such special scrutiny.

In the past, one element notably absent from the FBI's relationship with Congress was any cooperative review of substantive policy relating to the Bureau's responsibilities, and to law enforcement generally. The FBI generally waited for legislation to evolve. Then it tried to change it to its own liking through influence-trading and behind-the-scenes pressure. It preferred not to make its considerable research and resources openly available to Justice Department policymakers and legislative draftsmen on Capitol Hill during the earlier stages of the process. It was only after the arrival of Clarence Kelley as director that the Bureau, beleaguered by congressional pressure on such issues as privacy, established in its Office of Legal Counsel a unit responsible for helping develop legislation mutually acceptable to the White House, Congress, outside groups, and the FBI and other divisions of the Department of Justice. At the same time, the Bureau was confronted by the reality that Congress might finally seek to exercise meaningful oversight of FBI operations rather than continuing mere rubber-stamp approval of the status quo through the appropriations process.

XVI

Building a Public Image

I knew nothing about the FBI before the series began; it was just a magic word to me. . . . But I certainly did learn to identify with the Bureau. I was very devoted to Mr. Hoover. I felt very keenly all that he was going through, and the Bureau with him. . . . I met him in connection with the series, when I went to Washington for a week of indoctrination and familiarization. I will never forget that interview with him: I was taken into his office by Deke DeLoach. There was no time for the amenities. Mr. Hoover began to talk, and he talked at machine-gun speed — about Hollywood, Washington society, Shirley Temple and his great range of interests. It lasted two hours and four minutes. . . . When I got home, there was a letter from him. It began "Dear Efrem" and was signed "Edgar." I was deeply fond of him. . . . It became one of the richest friendships I ever had. . . . When I travel, I always try to visit the field offices.

        — *Efrem Zimbalist, Jr., "Inspector Louis Erskine"*
        of The FBI *television series, in an interview*
        during the filming of one of the last episodes
        before the series was canceled by ABC

EFREM ZIMBALIST WAS JUST WHAT every FBI agent would like to be — quick-witted, dashing, respected by everyone he met except the nasty criminals (sometimes even by them, too), and able to summon a helicopter at the snap of a finger. In his role as Inspector Louis Erskine, he had loyal, devoted, and efficient helpers, and he never failed to crack a difficult case. The people he caught invariably went off to jail or paid stiff fines, and if they did not, the implication was that it was the fault of soft-headed judges or mushy-minded liberals in charge of some other part of the criminal justice system. Zimbalist got only the best cases, where the FBI jurisdiction was clear and unambiguous and when local law enforcement officials were content to take a back seat and serve as support personnel for the Bureau.

The romantic image of Inspector Erskine was a typical television glamorization of a lawman's role — and a successful one at that. *The FBI* ran for nine years in prime time on ABC with the prestige sponsorship of the Ford Motor Company and other major corporations (and then attracted substantial royalties for domestic and foreign sale of the reruns after the series was canceled by the network in 1974). Many matters depicted on the program had little basis in reality. The Bureau does not own a single helicopter, although it may occasionally borrow one from local police or the military.* Its cases rarely go as smoothly and spectacularly as Erskine's. And although one or two special-agents-in-charge of field offices have been regularly used in recent years to supervise the investigations of major cases ("specials"), it has been some time since the Bureau had a roving inspector the likes of Erskine of the television program, who was dramatically dispatched to save the day. (One such agent, Earl J. Connelley, raced from one crisis to another for years until he retired in 1954. Another, Joseph A. Sullivan, performed the job somewhat less flamboyantly between 1963 and 1971, coordinating long and difficult investigations in various parts of the country.) Zimbalist, in fact, while officially revered by the Bureau and even invited to speak at the FBI Academy in Quantico, was the laughingstock of many agents in the field — they thought the television characterization pictured Erskine's job as soft and glamorous; they knew their own one was tough and often thankless. In lighter moments the agents joked about the series and how unrealistic it was, but sometimes they complained that because of the image it portrayed it actually made their work more difficult. Bureau officials in Washington, however, insisted that the series, for all its lack of realism, helped the FBI, both in recruiting people to join the agency and in persuading members of the public that they should cooperate with agents whenever approached by them. At its peak of popularity, the show attracted almost forty million viewers weekly, and letters addressed to "Inspector Erskine" were often received at Bureau headquarters in Washington.

What some agents and most of the public did not realize was that

---

* The FBI did recently buy two airplanes, however — light fixed-wing propeller craft that had been declared surplus by the military, for use primarily by California field offices.

the FBI image portrayed by Zimbalist, including much of its gloss, was developed with the avid cooperation and effective control of the Bureau. From the outset, the FBI worked with producer Quinn Martin* (having selected him over others who vied for the lucrative opportunity) and gave its official approval to the series; indeed, permission was even granted for use of the Bureau seal on the television screen. As the routine evolved, the Bureau submitted memoranda on "interesting cases" to Martin, who farmed them out to Hollywood screenwriters to come up with scripts that could be used for each season's more than thirty episodes. Every script was first funneled through the Los Angeles Field Office and sent to Washington for suggested changes and final approval in the Crime Records Division (later known as the External Affairs Division) at headquarters. If the Bureau officials vetoed anything, such as scenes that read as if they would be excessively violent or that made the FBI look weak, their opinion was final. As a result, of course, unlike the situation in other police-related television programs, the agents in *The FBI* series never lost their patience or temper and they lived exemplary lives. According to screenwriter David W. Rintels, in testimony before the Senate Subcommittee on Constitutional Rights, the FBI and the sponsors also ordered that the plots avoid sensitive political subjects like civil rights.

Hoover handpicked Zimbalist from a list of candidates as the man he wanted to play "Inspector Erskine" in the series. The actor was a wise choice from the Bureau's point of view. He not only performed handsomely on the screen but also took on the responsibility of helping defend the FBI publicly in moments of controversy. At a time when Hoover was under fire, Zimbalist helped form an organization called Friends of the FBI, which produced and distributed reports favorable to the Bureau. Zimbalist, once identified with an entirely different kind of character in *77 Sunset Strip*, became the epitome of the FBI agent for a whole generation of young Americans and their parents, who watched him faithfully. His private life, unlike that of some other Hollywood stars, gave the Bureau no particular cause for concern or embarrassment, and he had the additional qualification of having ex-

---

* Martin had previously produced the highly successful television series *The Untouchables*, starring Robert Stack as Elliott Ness, a Treasury agent who was the scourge of the underworld in the 1920s and early 1930s. The Senate Juvenile Delinquency Subcommittee in 1962 obtained and released a memorandum from Martin to his subordinates in that production company, pleading for "a different device than running the man down with a car, as we have done this now in three different shows. I like the idea of the sadism, but I hope we can come up with another approach for it."

pressed political views so right-wing that they became a liability to Senator Barry Goldwater's 1964 Republican presidential campaign.

To keep the television image in line with Bureau requirements, the Director ordered that the Los Angeles Field Office maintain careful liaison with, if not supervision over, the Hollywood team producing *The FBI*. For most of the program's nine-year life, that job fell to a man chosen by Hoover to be its technical adviser, Special Agent Dick Doucé. Doucé had been an announcer on radio and television before he ever joined the Bureau, and he looked and acted the part of a Hollywood liaison man — silver-gray hair, well-preserved soft features, a graceful soothing voice, and a smoothness that inspired confidence rather than suspicion. When he moved through the production company during the work on an episode — he or his relief man attended the filming of every part of each week's installment — adjusting Zimbalist's gun so that his suit jacket would not get caught on it, urging changes in the questions asked a suspect, or suggesting that in real life the agent would be driving more slowly, an outsider never would have suspected that Doucé was an agent rather than a professional director. He made certain that the FBI employees depicted on television did not smoke or chew gum, held their weapons properly, and were always polite to the citizenry.

As Doucé saw it, the goals of the series were to "educate the public about the problems that law enforcement faces . . . to educate, inform and entertain at the same time. . . . Despite fierce competition for the ratings, we want to get across Mr. Hoover's values. . . . They [the production company] would like to do gangbusters sometimes, but we want to feel that good taste prevails. Mr. Hoover admonished me, 'Make sure that it's appropriate for a family audience. There should be no unnecessary brutality and violence.' The producers may have been disappointed . . . but I always knew that Mr. Hoover was watching every week." Along with his responsibilities for the television series, Doucé coordinated all FBI contacts with the motion picture industry; he spoke the language of the movie people, and he was a good agent to send out, say, to interview a cameraman about a nephew wanted for bank robbery on the East Coast.

In some instances, Doucé intervened during the filming of an *FBI* episode to point out that the writer was drawing a potentially wrong conclusion from the evidence available at that stage of the story, or that enough information had not yet been presented in the episode to justify the issuance of a warrant for the villain's arrest (in which case an additional expository scene might be necessary). During one segment he found it implausible that Bureau headquarters was calling a special-agent-in-charge of a field office to be briefed on a car theft ring because under ordinary circumstances officials at headquarters would have already had adequate information available to them in the regular reports required from the field. In one of the final episodes of the series, he helped an actress who had never before held a gun carry out a scene in which she was supposed to be a new woman agent undergoing firearms training at Quantico. Despite the Bureau's care there were occasional mistakes — such as a palm tree in Pittsburgh — in the final cuts of *The FBI* as shown on television, but the series was remarkable for the amount of help it got from a government agency.

The television series was only the latest in a tradition of romantic broadcast portrayals of the Bureau. Earlier entries, in the heyday of radio, were "The FBI in Peace and War," based on the book by Frederick L. Collins, and "This Is Your FBI," which produced four hundred and two half-hour programs between 1945 and 1953. "This Is Your FBI" had official Bureau cooperation. "The FBI in Peace and War" did not, but Collins had been substantially guided in his book research by Hoover. The FBI had no hand in *I Led Three Lives,* the early television series based on the adventures of FBI counterspy Herbert Philbrick, but it had earlier helped Philbrick with his book and was very favorably portrayed on that program. The cancellation of the series starring Zimbalist after its ratings began to slip seemed to mark the end of an era, but soon thereafter the Bureau's favorite producer, Quinn Martin, came up with a new plan for at least four full-length feature films for television based on important moments in FBI history, to be broadcast as part of the CBS *Thursday Night at the Movies* series. Director Clarence Kelley gave his go-ahead and once again the Bureau approved and improved scripts that dealt with cases ranging from the career and capture of gangster Alvin Karpis in the 1930s to the FBI's solution of the 1964 murder of three civil rights workers in Philadelphia, Mississippi. (The Bureau pressed Martin to focus more on recent accomplishments than on the gangster era.) The movies were somewhat less heavy-handed and one-sided than *The FBI,* but still reflected a substantial injection of what the Bureau wanted the public to see and think of the FBI. The dramatization of the Karpis case, for example, went out of its way to assert that Hoover had long planned to arrest the fugitive personally (in fact, he apparently did so only in direct reaction to congressional criticism), and the two-part film about the Mississippi murders, based on Don Whitehead's Bureau-approved version of events, simply ignored a number of unresolved controversies surrounding the Bureau's role in the case.

There have been other, more modest efforts to promote the Bureau through the broadcast media. For years the NBC radio "Monitor" program ran a five-minute segment every weekend on some aspect of FBI operations; when it was dropped in 1964, the idea was picked up by ABC as "FBI Washington." The program continues today with a five-minute interview, broadcast every Sunday morning, with the assistant director in charge of the External Affairs Division. Field offices have been encouraged to emulate these projects in their local areas, and similar radio and television interviews have been arranged by the Bureau in Chicago and Columbia, South Carolina, among other places. In the 1940s and early 1950s the Bureau also participated — even supplying agents as actors — in a number of commercial films glorifying its exploits, including *The House on 92nd Street*, *Walk a Crooked Mile*, and *Walk East on Beacon*.

It was not only in broadcasting and movies that the Bureau pitched in to help what it had reason to expect would be favorable portrayals. Over the years the FBI also cooperated enthusiastically with several authors, on the condition that the Bureau would have the final right of approval over what they wrote. The prime example and crowning accomplishment of that policy was *The FBI Story* by the double Pulitzer Prize–winning reporter Don Whitehead. Washington bureau chief of the *New York Herald Tribune* at the time, Whitehead was notified in 1955 that if he renewed an earlier request for help with a history of the Bureau, it would be agreed to. For the next year Whitehead was spoon-fed by the Crime Records Division, with Assistant-to-the-Director Louis B. Nichols carefully supervising the project. Whitehead saw exactly what the Bureau wanted him to see and only that, notwithstanding the Director's claim, in his foreword to the book, that "we felt it was our duty to provide him with full facts so that he could form his own independent judgement on our policies, procedures and performance." As Nichols put it in an interview years later, "Whitehead made a few mistakes, but by going over the manuscript we were able to put him back on the right track. . . . We corrected a few of his facts, but we never interfered with his conclusions."

Whitehead produced a book that is an extraordinary document and a fascinating period piece. He was able to include many stories that had never before been told, including details of the FBI's Special Intelligence Service work during World War II, and he had access to private Hoover memoranda recording some of the Director's recollections of confidential prewar conversations with President Roosevelt. The book reports the official FBI version of events surrounding its

373

birth and development; it speaks in intricate detail of the Bureau's successes and accomplishments. But it also suffers from being packed with self-serving minutiae provided to Whitehead by the FBI about itself, down to the dollars-and-cents terms of pension funds and the premium for government group life insurance. Its "you are there" style dialogues recounting important moments in Hoover's career are difficult to believe because they are so stilted and one-sided. The chapters dealing with the postwar era take a straight Bureau line on the Red-hunting controversies of that period and are not balanced with more skeptical views. Whitehead actually states near the end of his book that the Bureau "isn't perfect," but nowhere in the preceding chapters can one find evidence to support that proposition. The book's dust jacket carries the FBI seal, and the foreword, signed by the Director, endorses Whitehead's effort over other accounts about the Bureau that had been "distorted" or "figments of the imagination."

The FBI Story was a best-seller, thanks in part to Bureau promotional efforts on its behalf. The FBI Recreation Association's (FBIRA's) purchase of copies helped to boost sales and distribution. The popular film version of the book starred James Stewart as an agent, and Hoover wept with joy at its premiere. From the time of its publication new recruits for the position of special agent were required to read, and practically to memorize, Whitehead's book in training school. It was offered as an example of perfect "objectivity" about the Bureau. At least one prospective agent found himself in trouble in the late 1960s when he did a "book report" during training critical of *The FBI Story*, in which he suggested that the Bureau's true interests were not served by such fawning, unobjective material. The rumor spread that this trainee was merely infiltrating the agency for the purposes of writing his own book, and before he graduated and was sent to his first field office, FBI officials scrutinized law review articles he had written during law school before applying to the Bureau. (They finally decided he was safe and let him proceed.) Even in the mid-1970s the Bureau still had a stock of copies on hand, and on July 30, 1975, a new shipment of 98 copies was put on the shelves of the library at Quantico, making a total of 148 there. By contrast, there were 6 copies of other books, critical of the FBI, on the shelves.

Whitehead became one of the special, favored Bureau "friends" for whom Hoover ordered extra attention, and when he retired, first to Tennessee and then to Florida, he was looked after by the Knoxville and Miami field offices. When he traveled — for example to Texas, for the funeral of a member of his family — the nearest office would dispatch an agent to meet him at the airport and drive him wherever he needed to go. The Bureau also used its international connections to pave the way for another Whitehead book about interesting criminal cases around the world, and years later material was made selectively available once again so that he could write *Attack on Terror: The FBI Against the Ku Klux Klan in Mississippi,* published in 1970. But there were others, too. The FBI contributed assistance and a Hoover introduction to a picture book about the Bureau produced in 1947 by the editors of *Look* magazine. It retold favorite old FBI tales in simple language and used both genuine and staged photographs to illustrate them. The text also recited key elements of the Hooverian philosophy:

FBI records reveal that the home is the most important factor in the prevention of juvenile delinquency. It must be closely supported by the churches, schools, law enforcement agencies, civic and fraternal groups. It has been found that the amount of crime in a given locality may be inversely compared with the efficiency of the municipal government and its interest in the development of good citizenship.

One of Hoover's long-time journalist friends, Andrew Tully, had access to individual Bureau files for his 1965 book, *The FBI's Most Famous Cases,* including "Machine Gun" Kelly's involvement in the Urschel kidnapping, the Rosenberg atomic espionage case, the exploits of bank robbers Bobby Wilcoxson and Albert Nussbaum, and the 1963 kidnapping of Frank Sinatra, Jr. Tully's book, also promoted by the FBI and purchased in quantity by the FBIRA, included a characteristic introduction by Hoover, a fresh quotation from him to begin each chapter (such as "Dillinger was a cheap, boastful, selfish, tightfisted pug-ugly, who thought only of himself" and "We are courting disaster if we do not soon take some positive action against the growing moral deterioration in this land"), and an afterword with the Director's advice on how citizens may avoid crime. Another book assisted and promoted by the Bureau (some field offices distributed copies to local civic groups and schools) was *The FBI in Our Open Society,* by the husband-and-wife team of Harry and Bonaro Overstreet. Published in 1969, it is largely a compilation of Bureau responses to and refutations of criticisms by other writers and commentators, in some instances pointing out genuine unfairness but in others merely nitpicking on minor points.

The Overstreets, in taking to task writers who had criticized the Bureau — Max Lowenthal, William Turner, and Fred Cook, among others — were doing no more than the FBI itself, which tried to discredit any "negative" book or article that it thought would hurt its public image. Once the Bureau had finished its job of discrediting Max Lowenthal's *The Federal Bureau of Investigation,* which originally appeared in 1950, it became difficult to find copies of the book on bookstore shelves; articles appeared in a number of newspapers dealing with Lowenthal's statements in terms remarkably similar to official Bureau responses. The Lowenthal book contained some revealing material on the Bureau's early days, but it primarily used selective quotation from and reference to debates, hearings, and reports in order to build what one reviewer called an "unrelieved condemnation of the Bureau." It was an admittedly unsympathetic work, a case against the FBI. But in the politically charged days when it appeared, it was characterized as a vicious and unpatriotic attack on the Director, and Lowenthal's eventual reward, incredibly, was a subpoena from the House Un-American Activities Committee. Much of Lowenthal's technique, and some of his material, was incorporated by Fred Cook into *The FBI Nobody Knows,* published in 1964, and as a result he too was severely dealt with by the Overstreets and by reporters who had help with their research from friends inside the Bureau's Crime Records Division.

William Turner, a former agent who had carried his personal fight with Hoover to the Supreme Court and lost, published his book, *Hoover's FBI: The Men and the Myth,* in 1970. When Turner appeared on radio and television shows to promote the book, he kept finding that unexpected guests were there to debate with him, or that the program host was unusually well equipped with hostile questions to ask. Similar steps were taken against another, less well circulated book, *Inside the FBI,* by Norman Ollestad, who had served as an agent for a short time. The technique was also used, although more subtly, in an effort to discredit a novel, *Don't Embarrass the Bureau,* written by ex-agent Bernard Connors. The Bureau's resources and contacts were so considerable, and unauthorized books about it or their authors so likely to have some flaws, that the FBI would almost always succeed in some measure in weakening such opposition. The Bureau's efforts were usually subtle and surreptitious enough to avoid public controversy of the sort later stirred up when the CIA went to court to try to prevent publication of once-confidential material from its files or derogatory comments by former employees. The FBI was invariably well equipped for any refutations it wanted to make; it had remarkable success in obtaining advance copies of manuscripts or articles about it, sometimes by appealing to the patriotic motives of someone who worked for the publisher, and it kept thorough files of the "negative" articles that had appeared under anyone's by-line, sometimes sup-

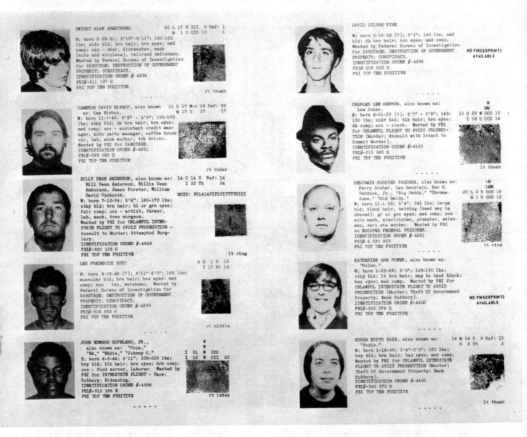

One of the best gimmicks the FBI ever developed was its list of the Ten Most Wanted fugitives. Displayed in post offices and other public places, the list invariably led to the capture of dangerous criminals and garnered the Bureau large doses of the publicity it loved so well. But when, as in this edition of the Top Ten from early 1975, it included six young adherents of the New Left, wanted for bombings and other politically inspired crimes, the Bureau record fell off sharply. They managed to live underground and evade detection for years; in March 1975, however, two of them, Susan Saxe and Cameron Bishop, were captured.

Each symbol and color in the FBI seal has special significance. The dominant blue field of the seal and the scales on the shield represent justice. The endless circle of 13 stars denotes unity of purpose as exemplified by the 13 original states. The laurel leaf has, since early civilization, symbolized academic honors, distinction and fame. There are exactly 46 leaves in the two branches, since there were 46 states in the Union when the FBI was founded in 1908. The significance of the red and white parallel stripes lies in their colors. Red traditionally stands for courage, valor and strength, while white conveys cleanliness, light, truth and peace. As in the American Flag, the red bars exceed the white by one. The motto, "Fidelity, Bravery, Integrity," succinctly describes the motivating force behind the men and women of the FBI. The peaked bevelled edge which circumscribes the seal symbolizes the severe challenges confronting the FBI and the ruggedness of the organization. The gold color in the seal conveys its overall value.

The Bureau mythologized every little thing about itself, as in this "heraldry" of its much-displayed seal. When the U.S. Mint struck a special medal in Hoover's memory, with the seal on the reverse side, the FBI rejected the first drawing for it because the seal did not have the proper number of leaves on the branches.

plemented with personal material about the author. When Ovid Demaris, for example, who was writing a book about Hoover, went to interview Attorney General William Saxbe about the FBI, the Bureau sent in a file of "background material" about the author in advance.

Left to Hoover, any counterattack against criticism of the Bureau risked suffering from severe overkill. As early as 1940, when the FBI had been criticized, the Director said in a radio talk that "your FBI is respected by the good citizens of America as much as it is feared, hated and vilified by the scum of the underworld, conspiring Communists and goose-stepping bundsmen, their fellow travelers, mouthpieces and stooges." He seemed unable to accept the notion that critics of the Bureau or others who analyzed its work in a less than adoring fashion could possibly be motivated by good intentions. Sixteen years later, in his foreword to *The FBI Story*, Hoover wrote:

In recent years, a campaign of falsehood and vilification has been directed against the FBI by some ignorant and some subversive elements. In the world-wide struggle of free peoples, the truth is still one of our most potent weapons. And the record of the FBI speaks for itself. It is the best answer to the falsehoods, half-truths and rumors spread by Communists, their stooges and defenders.

On other occasions he would tell offending newsmen or publications that their critiques of the FBI were "the sort of material I might expect to find on the front page of *The Daily Worker* or *Pravda*."

The Bureau's usual manner of dealing with individual reporters or writers they felt had wronged the FBI was not to approach these people directly, but rather to go to their editors or other superiors with a complaint, on the assumption that everyone had a "policy" toward the Bureau. That practice continued under Hoover's successors. Many of the Bureau's calls or visits to the editors, or their outcome, never became known, but two of them did in 1974. When syndicated columnist Lowell Ponte wrote an article expressing concern about the FBI's computer network, the publisher of one newspaper that ran the column, the Anaheim, California, *Bulletin*, had a visit from two agents who said they wanted to explain "what the FBI computer system was really like." Similarly, agents visited the office that syndicates Andrew Greeley's column from the *Chicago Tribune* after he wrote a piece critical of the way the Bureau handled the case of the disappearance of newspaper heiress Patricia Hearst. The philosophy behind such visits seemed to be that if a newspaper or syndication executive, just like the head of any bureaucracy, could be persuaded to see the light, he would then automatically bring around the recalcitrant writer or at least heavily edit his copy in the future to reflect a view more sympathetic to the FBI. That technique may have worked at one time, especially in the heyday of the Crime Records Division, but in these instances it backfired dramatically. The principals in the California incident told *The New Republic* what had happened, and the magazine ran a piece about it that made the FBI look silly. Greeley's syndicate immediately reported to him about the visit from the agents, and he wrote yet another column critical of the Bureau, this time taking up both the Hearst case and the Bureau reaction to the first column. He followed later with other pieces about the FBI that were none too favorable.

Seldom did the FBI react as severely and angrily to "negative" material as it did to a 1970 article by reporter Jack Nelson of the *Los Angeles Times*. Nelson, once a favorite of southern field offices for his stories on the Bureau's role in civil rights cases, wrote a lengthy piece contending that the FBI had directly provoked a Mississippi firebombing incident involving the Ku Klux Klan and unnecessarily caused the death of some of the Klan members involved. Hoover tried everything to get Nelson fired, including visits by FBI emissaries to editors and executives of the newspaper and the spreading of allegations about Nelson's character and personal life.

One crucial element in the Bureau's image-building was the material turned out over the years under the Director's name. Apart from the endless flow of magazine and law review articles, there were the Hoover books. The most successful and widely circulated was *Masters of Deceit: The Story of Communism in America and How to Fight It*, a would-be scholarly treatment that ran to almost four hundred pages. In 1958, when it was published, vehement anticommunism was still a major element of the popular support the Bureau enjoyed. The book, produced in Crime Records, traced the early origins of communism, the lives of Marx, Lenin, and Stalin, and then discussed the "basic, everyday facts of communism which will be of maximum help to the people of our country in recognizing and fighting the enemy in our midst." It recounted the internal squabbles of the first American communists; explained the significance of "fellow travelers," "sympathizers," "dupes," and "opportunists" in the growth of the party; and drew attention to the "five false claims of communism": "Communists are not liberals." "Communists are not progressives." "Communists are not social reformers." "The communists do not believe in democracy." "Communists are not American." It told how some American communists had become disillusioned by the atrocities under Stalin and related instances where party discipline had split up families. With classic overstatement, the book purported to "translate" communist slogans for the reader:

"*Repeal the draft law*" and "*peace*" mean curtailing our national defense effort and allowing Russia to become militarily stronger than the United States. "*Increase trade with the Soviet bloc*" means selling materials that could be used by the communist nations for armaments. "*Restore academic freedom*" means to communists that we should permit the official teaching of communist doctrine in all schools and that we should allow communists to infiltrate teaching staffs. If the communists had their way, America would be rendered helpless to protect herself.

It portrayed communism as the enemy of Jews, blacks, and other minorities, and as the violator of the rules of society that the FBI was devoted to upholding:

Sexual immorality is also abetted. In one instance an organizer, leaving his wife and children, lived in Chicago with another woman. In an Eastern city, a woman whose husband was underground carried on an affair with another man. In still another instance a wife kept company with a man while her husband was forbidden by the Party's underground leaders to see her.

The book outlined the importance of the FBI in fighting communism, complained of communist attacks on the Bureau, and pleaded with the public to report to the FBI "any information about espionage, sabotage, and subversive activities." In shrill tones it warned, "Be alert. America's best defense lies in the alertness of its patriotic citizens."

While epics like *Masters of Deceit* were an important part of the Bureau's long-range efforts, the FBI was always good at grabbing daily headlines, too. In 1940 Hoover himself called New York reporters to the field office there to reveal the discovery of a "plot" in which seventeen members of a "Christian Front" organization — including some part-time soldiers, a telephone mechanic, a baker, a tailor, a chauffeur, and others — were allegedly planning to wipe out the New York police and all of the nation's Jews, seize the gold stocks, take over all public utilities, and set up a dictatorship. "We have evidence to substantiate every claim we have made," Hoover declared, sounding his familiar theme that "it took only twenty-three men to overthrow Russia." A minor scandal resulted over the fact that three weeks passed between the men's arrest and their indictment, and little ever came of the case.* But the alarmist style took hold and seemed to convince people that the Bureau was always on the job. That style and thirst for publicity prevailed whenever the FBI got onto what it considered an important case, from the "arrest" of the World War II German saboteurs who were landed off Long Island to the early announcement by Hoover of the alleged plot of the Berrigan brothers and other militant antiwar Catholics in 1970 to kidnap presidential adviser Henry Kissinger and blow up public buildings in Washington. Some skeptics suggested that Hoover's well-publicized alarm over the national well-being emerged most emphatically whenever he was asking Congress for a big jump in appropriations, but it was probably not as calculated as that. The Director undoubtedly believed — and he seemed to be right — that the public had an insatiable appetite for news about their G-men. To be certain that appetite was responsibly satisfied, the Crime Records Division also turned out the routine articles about the Bureau for the *World Book* and other encyclopedias.

One of the most brilliant publicity innovations, launched in 1950, was the FBI's list of the Ten Most Wanted criminals in the United States. Started with the cooperation of International News Service (INS), the "top ten" gimmick was an instant success, an adjustable honor roll of the fugitives the Bureau and local authorities most wanted to nab. Almost every newspaper in the country, at the start, was sure to run the photographs of all ten from time to time and certain to feature anyone added to, or caught and therefore removed from, the list. Often the criminals were picked up on the basis of a tip from someone who saw their pictures in newspapers, magazines, or post offices. In one 1953 issue, *The Saturday Evening Post* ran a feature story about the FBI list, with the fugitives' pictures, and alerted its readers to "call the nearest office of the FBI if you see one of these men"; as a direct result of calls from people who read the *Post* article, the Bureau promptly arrested three of the ten.

It was an expensive matter to put someone new on the Ten Most Wanted list, because the appropriate inserts had to be sent out for the display boards in every FBI field office and other prominent locations. (Officially, each fugitive on the list has an agent assigned to look out for him or her in every field division.) But Bureau officials felt that it paid off and cited instances where captured criminals said, "As soon as I opened up the newspaper and found out I was on the Top Ten, I knew my days were numbered." Altogether, three hundred persons on

---

* Nine of the defendants were acquitted, and a mistrial was declared in the case against five others. The charges were dismissed against two, and one committed suicide.

the list were "located" during the first twenty-four years of its existence.* For most of them, there was a federal warrant for unlawful flight to avoid prosecution or confinement growing out of state charges. If legal process was dismissed against a fugitive because the statute of limitations had made it impossible to try him, he was dropped. One member of the original top ten from 1950 was finally removed from the list only in 1964, after the FBI became convinced that his body was somewhere in the concrete beneath the New Jersey Turnpike, and the case against him was dropped. The average length of time a person has remained on the list before being found is, as calculated by the Bureau, 153.63 days. The figure went that high because of six New Left underground fugitives, wanted in connection with bombings and bank robberies, who eluded the authorities for years. At one point the list was expanded to sixteen to accommodate that group, but eventually it returned to ten by attrition. As the radical fugitives were found by the Bureau or police, they were replaced on the list by more conventional criminals, presumably easier to catch.

The Crime Records Division (abolished under Gray but later reconstituted by Kelley as the External Affairs Division) was never openly acknowledged as the Bureau's public relations and image-building arm, but that is what it was. It never operated as a typical public information office, but rather as a part of the bureaucracy responsible for calculating, and acting aggressively upon, the Bureau's best interest at any moment. Its budget for Fiscal Year 1975 was $2,868,000.† Even when it was spending far less in the early days of its image buildup, critics like Senator George Norris of Nebraska denounced Hoover as "the greatest publicity hound on the American continent today." However, the Bureau's answer was always that for a law enforcement agency to be effective, it had to be widely known and respected. Measured in those terms, the aggressive public relations

* There was a trick in the Bureau's use of the word "locate." It included fugitives apprehended by other authorities or discovered to be dead or otherwise beyond the FBI's reach. It could be legitimately argued, at the same time, that the publicity attendant to the Ten Most Wanted list was a crucial factor in any such arrest or identification by the local police.

† The Bureau, in explaining this large budget, says that it is spent "employing all communications media to increase public awareness of the responsibilities and services of the FBI, and to alert the public to the criminal and subversive dangers threatening society, thereby encouraging citizen cooperation in combatting these elements, which constitute critical and costly problems to each member of society." The External Affairs Division also routinely responds to the vast quantity of mail received by the FBI and conducts tours of Bureau headquarters that draw tens of thousands of tourists every year.

approach worked; public opinion polls consistently showed that the Bureau had high recognition and admiration among the citizens.

Agents assigned to the division would freely acknowledge that they are motivated less by any lofty notions of "the public's right to know" than by concern for "how the FBI can be helped through publicity to fulfill its investigative responsibilities"; they would be less likely to admit their almost pathological attempts to make the Bureau look flawless and faultless in any and all circumstances. These preoccupations, and the fact that few agents in the division ever had any practical experience with or as members of the press, explain its penchant for classifying all newsmen as either Bureau "friends" or "enemies." The representatives of certain chains — including Hearst, Copley, and Scripps-Howard — or any newspaper or magazine with a staunchly conservative editorial policy were for years bound to get better treatment than their competitors. One former staff member for the *New York Daily News,* long a Bureau favorite, tells of rocking the boat when he was first assigned to the newspaper's Washington bureau by writing a story that upset the FBI. The reporter located in Brussels a man the Bureau had been unable to find, and he failed to alert the FBI in advance that his article was coming. He was scolded by both Crime Records and his own superiors for breaking the rules of their relationship. Amends were quickly made, however, and he was soon enjoying the special FBI tips and leaks to which the *Daily News* was accustomed. During the 1967 antiwar march on the Pentagon, for example, when the Bureau was turning a cold shoulder to other newsmen, the *News* man practically had an open line to Crime Records; his contact there inundated him with facts and figures promptly on schedule for each new edition deadline.

The Bureau's particular relationship with people it classified as "friendly media representatives" involved routine and frequent violations of the "attorney general's guidelines" that officially restricted what the FBI could release about any pending or sensitive case. But most of the leaks would have been difficult to trace, because there was nothing on paper to indicate the source of the information and Bureau officials usually covered their tracks carefully. The Bureau's well-developed art of leaking was probably one reason for Hoover's long-standing reluctance (not always successful) to get the FBI involved in investigations of leaks of documents and information from within government departments. He took the position that this was the internal housekeeping business of each department, and that the only meaningful punishment for such infractions was administrative discipline. To take a different position would have been hypocritical, given the FBI leaks, and some of the investigations, if vigorous, could have been very embarrassing to the Bureau.

Serious problems sometimes arose for the Bureau when two of its closest friends would quarrel with one another. One instance of that came when Drew Pearson wrote in his "Washington Merry-Go-Round" column in the 1960s about the financial wheelings and dealings of Senator Thomas Dodd of Connecticut, including Dodd's double billings for some of his trips. Dodd, a former agent himself, was one of the FBI's and Hoover's staunchest defenders in Congress, a Democrat who took a tough law-and-order line and also saw eye to eye with the Bureau about the threat of communism; his Juvenile Delinquency Subcommittee of the Senate Judiciary Committee explored problems of youthful criminality and sounded themes that were dear to the Director's heart. The Bureau hated to see Dodd weakened, especially by Pearson. For despite the public antipathy between Pearson and the FBI on a few subjects, the powerful columnist had long been a friend of Hoover and had gotten many tips and leaks from the Bureau over the years.* Eventually, of course, as things looked worse for Dodd and he was censured by the Senate, the Bureau had to abandon him; the support of a man who is shown to have done wrong is an embarrassment to the Bureau. Pearson's successor, Jack Anderson, also maintained excellent relations with the FBI for a time. He has said publicly that he had an arrangement with Hoover that permitted him to look directly at confidential FBI files of interest to him. Later, Anderson and the Director had a well-publicized break. The Bureau, in a leak investigation, sent agents out to rummage through Anderson's trash. Anderson reciprocated by sending his assistants out to do the same, and proceeded to write a column about what could be learned from the Director's trash. Hoover developed an enthusiasm when it came to leak investigations related to Anderson's column; the FBI repeatedly obtained the telephone records of Anderson and his associates.

One reason that some newsmen found out so much from the FBI was that they also provided the Bureau with information, sometimes filling in details of situations where reporters could move more easily than government investigators. For years it was standard operating procedure for reporters to tip their FBI contacts off about people or situations they knew were of interest. In the days before reporters became acutely sensitive to incursions on their First Amendment rights, they cooperated with agents without particularly worrying whether they would be identified as the source of the material in FBI

* Pearson's published *Diaries* include many confidences entrusted in him by Hoover over the years, including references to the Director's dislike for President Truman.

385

reports. Trading favors with the FBI inevitably helped a reporter's career. But as concern about freedom of the press developed, some of those ground rules changed. James Mone, a photographer for the Associated Press in Minneapolis, for example, was suspended in April 1974 after he acknowledged under oath that he had given information to FBI agents more than a year earlier about the conditions prevailing inside the village of Wounded Knee during its occupation by the American Indian Movement. The Bureau was troubled by Mone's suspension because of the implication that he had done something wrong; in the FBI's view anyone interested in saving lives or protecting the national interest should be willing to cooperate and not be punished by his employers for doing so.

The Crime Records Division became an especially important outpost of the Hoover empire, and some of the people who ran it were permitted to be close with the Director. One of the most recent examples was George Quinn, a fast-talking, hard-driving New Yorker who wrote many of Hoover's last speeches. Quinn was even trusted enough to straighten the Director's tie and mix his drinks.

Apart from its liaison, public and confidential, with Bureau "friends," the FBI's public relations department devoted much of its energy over the years to two high-visibility projects that contributed substantially to building the image: the *FBI Law Enforcement Bulletin* and the *Uniform Crime Reports.** The *Bulletin,* first published by the Bureau in September 1932, initially served as one of the only means available to police departments to alert their counterparts around the country about the fugitives they were looking for. The precursor, in a sense, of both the Ten Most Wanted list and the computerized National Crime Information Center, the monthly *Bulletin,* as described by Hoover during congressional testimony in 1936, contained "the name, description, fingerprint classification, and one finger impression of all wanted fugitives who have committed crimes of a serious character." The Director cited various examples of successful apprehensions traceable to the FBI publication. One, from Pennsylvania, went like this: "The bulletin was received by the sheriff in the morning who arrested a couple of tramps coming through about noon on a railroad train, and he looked into the bulletin and found both were wanted for murder in Ohio." Distributed free to thousands of police departments (some of whom, the Bureau said, requested thirty or forty copies for precinct commanders or officers on the street), the

* Responsibility for the *Uniform Crime Reports* was later transferred to the Bureau's Computer Systems Division.

Bulletin was gradually expanded into a sort of law enforcement magazine, with articles on such subjects as fingerprints, explosives, and the collection and preservation of evidence. (The function of listing hundreds of fugitives obviously became outmoded.)

As it grew older and circulated more widely, the *Law Enforcement Bulletin* also became more slick and sophisticated. Recent issues, using the latest in graphics, have color covers with photographs showing policemen helping a lost child, using modern camera equipment to detect evidence on a car involved in a hit-and-run accident, and explaining regulations on snowmobile trails. A typical issue included a centennial tribute to the Royal Canadian Mounted Police and articles on "A Judge's Views on Law Enforcement Education and Training," by a district judge in Montana; "The Personal Patrol Car Program," by a police chief and sergeant from the Maryland suburbs of Washington; "An Automated Field Interview System," by Los Angeles Police Chief Edward M. Davis; and "Film: What Should It Accomplish in Your Training Program," by the chairman of the police science department at a community college in Florida. There was also an explanation of recent court decisions on obscenity by the head of the Bureau's Office of Legal Counsel, a report on the latest graduation ceremonies of the FBI National Academy, and a "Crimescope" of curious and intriguing developments in law enforcement. The last page of the *Bulletin* was a Wanted flier for a woman schoolteacher sought in connection with an alleged conspiracy to bomb New York City buildings in 1969, and the inside back cover carried pictures showing how the Louisville police had discovered that the armrest of a luxury automobile could be used to conceal a gun. At the front of every issue is a "Message from the Director to All Law Enforcement Officials," a space used by Hoover and his successors to talk about issues like the need to fight police corruption and the inappropriateness, in the Bureau's view, of the concept of "victimless crime." On the back cover each month is a single fingerprint with an explanation of its "interesting" or "questionable" pattern and details on how it might be searched in fingerprint files.

As early as 1932, Hoover was boasting in his congressional testimony about the value and usefulness of the *Uniform Crime Reports*, launched in 1930 to meet the demand for national crime statistics and compiled from figures submitted by local police departments. The purpose, the Director said, was "to determine whether there is or is not a crime wave and whether crime is on the increase or decrease." From that time on, it was invariably on the increase, and the FBI took it upon itself to chart the degree and nature of the increase, any geographical variations in the rise, and other significant trends that seemed to emerge. For years, in an effort to make the statistics more meaningful, the Bureau tried to persuade local police departments to adopt a uniform system of classifying and reporting offenses listed on the FBI Crime Index; its success depended largely on the good faith and honesty of the reporting departments.

In their current form, the crime statistics include quarterly reports on the incidence of crime (the categories are murder and nonnegligent manslaughter, forcible rape, robbery, aggravated assault, burglary and breaking and entering, larceny, and auto theft) in more than one hundred and fifty cities with a population of over a hundred thousand. But the main showpiece is an annual booklet, *Crime in the United States,* running to almost three hundred pages, based upon material submitted by nearly eleven thousand city, county, and state law enforcement agencies in the United States. It includes rather alarming "crime clocks," which indicated that in 1973, for example, there were 16 serious crimes every minute, an auto theft every 34 seconds, a forcible rape every 10 minutes, and a murder every 27 minutes. Various charts and graphs indicated that 77 percent of the people identified in connection with the killing of law enforcement officers were "offenders with a prior arrest on a criminal charge," that larceny goes up in the summer and robbery in the winter, and that the robbery of grocery stores had skyrocketed while gas stations were becoming more secure from such incidents. A note on "crime factors" at the beginning of the volume cautioned that various conditions, including "economic status and mores of the population" and "standards of appointments to the local police force," made it inappropriate to compare crime in individual communities strictly on the basis of their population. But a glance at the tables for "standard metropolitan statistical areas" showed, for example, that the crime rate per 100,000 inhabitants was apparently higher in the New York area than in the Philadelphia area.

It was just that kind of conclusion, virtually leaping out from the crime reports, which helped establish the FBI's image as the nation's leading authority on crime trends — a useful reputation for an agency that seeks appropriations to fight crime. The image was substantially weakened, and the Bureau's methods and reliance on local statistics called into question, however, in early 1974, when the U.S. Law Enforcement Assistance Administration (LEAA) released the results of a study conducted by it and the federal Census Bureau of crime "victimization." It showed that most categories of serious crime went grossly underreported and that the relative dangers of major American cities had been substantially misestimated over the years. Detroit, Denver, and Philadelphia, for example, were shown to have crime rates far higher than (in fact almost double) that of New York. In Philadelphia, the ratio of unreported crime to reported crime was estimated at more than five to one. The LEAA/Census Bureau study showed that sophisticated survey techniques might be necessary for a true understanding of the shape of crime in the United States and led some experts to urge that the Bureau reform its statistics collection and crime evaluation techniques. With victimization shown to be consistently high, the study stimulated serious questions about the sudden nationwide drop in crime reported by the Bureau during the months leading up to the presidential election of 1972. (The suspicion was that someplace along the line — perhaps in some local police departments — the figures had been tampered with to help the law-and-order reputation of the Nixon administration.)

In late 1974, after discovering the substantial interest in its original statistical study, LEAA announced that it would continue the research on crime victimization indefinitely and thus challenge the Bureau's claims to exclusive knowledge about crime rates. LEAA's national survey revealed that most serious crime was about three times higher in the first six months of 1973 than reported to police and that in one category, larceny, it was probably five times higher. The revelation indicated a low level of citizen confidence in the police — since they felt there was no value in reporting some crime — and led to further suspicion that the figures available through the FBI might not be honest. Some police, LEAA suggested, might keep their crime incidence rate down in order to be able to claim a higher solution rate.

LEAA, aware that the FBI's tender feelings can turn nasty when something the Bureau has considered a public service is criticized, was deferential to the *Uniform Crime Reports* in announcing its own continuing, competitive program. It stressed that the traditional statistics would still be useful as "workload measures" and "tactical information," urging that the two be consulted "in conjunction with one another to attack crime." The Bureau, for its part, took formal notice of the LEAA survey in the foreword to its volume of *Crime in the United States* covering 1973. "These first efforts in connection with victimization studies have encountered problems," the foreword said; "however, one by one the problem areas will be resolved and these studies will undoubtedly develop more useful information relating to the causes and nature of crime." In the meantime, "every effort is made on a continuing basis to improve the overall quality of the information collected in connection with the Uniform Crime Reporting Program." When the Bureau's crime statistics shot up in early 1975, some cynics suggested that it and the local police reporting the figures were merely trying to "catch up" with the victimization figures. (Still, new LEAA victimization studies released in 1975 showed that in many other cities — including Boston, Houston, San Francisco, and Washington — crime was underreported.)

The Bureau did seem to become more sensitive to the drawbacks of some of its annual calculations and observations about crime nationally. After Hans Zeisel, a professor of law and sociology at the University of Chicago, had made a persuasive argument that the FBI's annual tables on "Careers in Crime" — a section of the Uniform Crime Reports dealing with recidivism and implying criticism of the courts and penal system — were based on a seriously biased and incomplete statistical sample, those tables disappeared from the 1973 and subsequent editions.

XVII

Arriving Late
at the Scene of the Crime

*Robert F. Kennedy, while attorney general, occasionally visited the
New York Field Office of the FBI, among others, for briefings on
matters of special interest to him. The story is told that during one
visit, the following conversation took place between Kennedy and
John Francis Malone, assistant director of the FBI in charge of the
New York office:*

> *Kennedy: "Mr. Malone, could you please bring me up to date
> on what's been happening with organized crime?"*
> *Malone: "To tell you the truth, Mr. Attorney General, I'm
> sorry, but I can't, because we've been having a newspaper
> strike here."*

BECAUSE J. EDGAR HOOVER EXERCISED almost single-handed authority
to pick and choose where the FBI would concentrate its resources, the
Bureau's focus was sometimes hopelessly misdirected or, at best, out of
date. To many, the stereotype of the FBI agent was someone who kept
looking for those stolen cars and deserters while more complex, organized violations of the law passed under his nose. In part, the Director
was simply clever enough to steer clear of the toughest problems —
the ones that were less likely to produce prompt and stunning results,
that might test conflicts of loyalty among agents, or that would require
them to be exposed to the seamier side of life (and, as with many
policemen, tempt them into corruption).

But Hoover's deftness at winning his own game by keeping it
controllable is not the whole story. The Bureau itself had just not kept
up with the times, whether by design, by default, because it did not

have the necessary grants of statutory authority, or, as is closest to the truth, through some combination of those factors. At critical moments it became obvious that the FBI was playing virtually no role in connection with three of the most important issues in law enforcement: organized crime, civil rights, and narcotics abuse. The story of how the Bureau hesitated but then plunged into the first two, and stayed out of the third, provides some revealing insights into its development as a crime-fighting police institution and as a bureaucracy.

Organized Crime

When a sergeant in the New York State Police discovered dozens of gangland figures meeting at the home of Joseph Barbara in the upstate town of Apalachin on November 14, 1957, it became a major news event across the country. Here was a conclave of shadowy merchants of private power, summoned from every corner of the nation for the purpose of discussing their illegal rackets and adjudicating disputes, their pockets stuffed with hundreds of thousands of dollars in cash as they did so. The crime convention, it turned out, was as much news to the Federal Bureau of Investigation as to anyone who picked up a newspaper the next day.

There had been similar gatherings before, as early as 1928 in Cleveland and the next year in Atlantic City, where the kingpins of the informal nationwide organization known in common parlance as the "syndicate," the "mob," or the "outfit" divided up territories and jurisdictions, planned the execution of unruly subordinates and competitors, and charted the corruption of public officials. But J. Edgar Hoover, for all his willingness to perceive gangsters behind every national problem, repeatedly asserted that no such crime confederation existed. As he said at one point, "No single individual or coalition of racketeers dominates organized crime across the nation." Neither the investigation of Murder Incorporated in Brooklyn in the early 1940s, nor the work in the 1950s of New York District Attorney Frank S. Hogan and the Federal Bureau of Narcotics, nor the inquiry conducted by Senator Estes Kefauver of Tennessee could persuade the Director to say otherwise. Various theories have been advanced to explain Hoover's stubbornness on the issue. One was that he did not want to cause trouble for powerful FBI friends on Capitol Hill or in city halls or statehouses who were themselves cozy with mobsters.

Another was that some of the Director's own wealthy friends were involved in dealings with the underworld. But the most plausible thesis is that he was unable to acknowledge that the Bureau had performed a task inadequately; if the FBI had not found something, then by definition that something did not exist.* Some organized criminal activities, Hoover argued, involved *local* rather than *federal* crime, and so he scoffed at the idea of creating a national crime commission or any other central group that would coordinate investigative efforts in various parts of the country. He warned, as usual, that such a policy might lead to a "national police force."

But the Apalachin meeting, with the publicity and controversy it attracted, led President Dwight Eisenhower's Justice Department to act without quite the usual deference to Hoover's views. Attorney General William P. Rogers soon established a Special Group on Organized Crime, with regional offices, that was directed to conduct an inquiry into events leading up to Apalachin and to launch a national attack through the courts on what later came to be known as the Mafia. The group lasted two years and enjoyed limited success; several of its leaders complained, however, that it had been stymied by the jealousy of the FBI. Richard B. Ogilvie, head of the group's midwestern office and later sheriff of Cook County (Chicago) and governor of Illinois, alleged that "Hoover was very cool to the whole idea. . . . He ordered the FBI files, containing the very information we needed on organized crime, closed to us. . . . The FBI is still organized to fight a crime pattern of the twenties and thirties. It is not set up to do battle with the criminal syndicate — the organized conspiracy that drains $22 billion a year from the United States." Hoover, for his part, used appropriations testimony on Capitol Hill to suggest in reply that the Special Group on Organized Crime had been largely concerned with "nest-feathering publicity" and had sought to waste the time of Bureau agents by assigning them to "fishing expeditions" and "speculative ventures."

The point was that Hoover, as on so many other occasions, wanted to do things his own way. He immediately launched the FBI's Top Hoodlum Program in November 1957, which required that every field office, large or small, draw up a list of the ten (no more, no less) most

---

* Apparently an FBI report produced in the fall of 1958 did acknowledge the existence of an organized criminal network, but it was quickly taken out of circulation by Hoover, who called it "baloney." The Director's usual approach to future disclosures about organized crime by other agencies and the press was to say, or at least to hint, that the Bureau was already *au courant*, and to suggest that if others were not careful about what they said publicly they might hinder investigative efforts.

suspicious underworld characters in its jurisdiction; they would be investigated and watched in an attempt to ferret out any significant organized criminal activity. From places like Little Rock and Butte came lists that included small-time operators hardly worth the attention; but the largest offices, once they looked into the matter, had to resolve competition among possible nominees for the list. Indications at the time were that the Bureau thought it had a six- or eight-month special assignment on its hands, and that once it had put a few tough guys in jail the clamor would subside. But that is not how it was to be; the Top Hoodlum Program exists even today in major field offices.

One office that had no trouble at all coming up with a list of ten hoodlums was Chicago, where there had been an attempt in the late 1940s to reactivate the gang once led by Al Capone. A group of young, energetic agents — bored with the security cases they had been working — was assigned the job, and by checking back into the old files and with friendly newspaper reporters who had followed the gangs more consistently than the FBI, they came up with prominent names like Anthony Accardo and Sam Giancana. So glad were the agents to have the new assignment that they plunged in more enthusiastically than Hoover and his lieutenants had ever intended. On the basis of a tip they began to watch a fancy custom tailor's shop over a restaurant on the "Magnificent Mile" of Chicago's North Michigan Avenue; from a lookout post in a high-rise building across the street they saw an unusual number of people coming and going, enough to permit the conclusion that the shop was serving as headquarters for some of the people they had singled out as "top hoodlums." In midsummer 1959 the young agents advanced a radical proposal: to apply an old security method to the criminal field by installing a microphone that would permit electronic eavesdropping on events at the tailor's shop. No information obtained by that method would be usable in court, but the prospect was for a steady flow of intelligence on the plans of the Chicago group. Hoover gave his approval, and in a series of what were in effect burglaries, usually in the early hours of Sunday morning, the agents installed a fairly primitive, large microphone in a radiator in the tailor's shop and strung the wires down the elevator shaft and out of the building so that conversations could be monitored and taped back at the field office. Some of the installation work was so sloppy that it caused the ceiling of the popular restaurant below to sag, but the agents got away unnoticed.

The bug at the shop lasted five years without detection or compromise. It became the precedent for others, in Chicago and elsewhere, and was a veritable fount of information; it may have played an historic role in wrenching the FBI around on the issue of organized crime. One morning early in 1960, when the agents on the special squad came into the Chicago Field Office and picked up their earphones to tune in on the day's events, Giancana, just back from an eastern trip, was asked by one of his associates to name the current members of "the commission." While the tape whirred away silently, he reeled off about a dozen names in different cities across the country. The Chicago agents shot an urgent communication off to headquarters and to the FBI offices in the cities named, recommending immediate investigations that could crack the national syndicate. Invariably, the other field offices, after checking a name with their usual sources, including the local police, replied that there must be some mistake, that the person in question was a retired gentleman of considerable stature in the community. As a result, headquarters became skeptical and demanded the original tape; but after hearing it, ranking Bureau officials agreed that more serious investigations were warranted in several locations. Many offices began to emulate Chicago's method in the early 1960s and used electronic surveillance as their chief tool; as Bill Roemer, one of the agents who worked the original case at the tailor's shop, puts it, "This was the only way. One microphone was worth a thousand agents."

Use of the microphones, in each case specifically approved by Hoover but not necessarily passed upon individually by the attorney general or any other Justice Department official, continued into the time when Robert F. Kennedy became the nation's chief law enforcement official.* As former counsel to the rackets investigating committee run by Senator John McClellan (D-Arkansas) (of which his brother John, the President, had been a member), Kennedy pressed for an all-out fight against organized crime. With Hoover still resisting the establishment of any kind of national unit outside the structure of the FBI, Kennedy instead enlarged the Organized Crime and Racketeering Section of the Criminal Division at Justice to coordinate investigations and handle intensified prosecutions, and he set up field offices for the section around the country. The Director and the at-

---

* There has been a long, ugly, and rather tiresome dispute over whether Kennedy actually approved of the bugging, a dispute that is exhaustively detailed in Victor S. Navasky's *Kennedy Justice*. To the end, Kennedy claimed he was not aware of the source of some of the FBI's intimate information, but many Bureau agents insist that they sat at the same table with him as he listened to tapes from the microphones, clearly identified as such. (One theory is that Kennedy thought the tapes were made by local police.) Navasky concludes that Kennedy should have known, if he didn't; the Bureau for its part believes that he not only knew but approved, and then misrepresented his role later.

torney general clashed on many issues and procedures, but Hoover appeared willing, for the first time in decades, to make the Bureau responsive to pressures from above. One move was the separating out of organized crime matters (along with a few other things, including "applicant work") from the General Investigative Division into a newly created Special Investigative Division, headed by veteran agent Courtney Evans, previously number one man under Alex Rosen in General Investigative and, as a Kennedy friend, the most logical Bureau official to be liaison with the new attorney general. Now there would be more people, at least at headquarters, whose primary function it was to concentrate on organized crime.* The Director resented the Kennedy move, however, to get the Internal Revenue Service involved in developing vigorous tax cases against individuals singled out for their links with organized crime, and he opposed the decision to surface Mafia informant Joseph Valachi for public — and televised — testimony before the McClellan committee about the intricacies and intrigues of La Cosa Nostra.

But whatever later disputes developed between the Director and Robert Kennedy as his nominal boss, and then between the FBI and Robert Kennedy as senator from New York, for the agent in the street and even some at headquarters Robert Kennedy the attorney general was a hero. As they saw it, he encouraged bugging, wiretapping, and any other techniques necessary to get a job done. In fact, he did press for new legislation to permit legal wiretapping and bugging. It was during his tenure that a new language was added to the repertory that agents might study during temporary assignments to the Defense Language Institute in Monterey, California — Sicilian, which helped immeasurably when listening in on an electronic surveillance of the Mafia. Kennedy visited field offices for briefings on organized crime, and when special-agents-in-charge and their assistants tried to hog the show, he insisted that the men actually doing the work on the firing line also be included in the conferences. Young agents frankly had an easier time identifying with the charismatic Bobby Kennedy than with Hoover, who was beginning to show his age and his staleness.

Kennedy encouraged the philosophy that any available law should be used to disable mobsters, and thus Louis Gallo and his father were prosecuted for making false statements on a Veterans' Administration loan application and Joseph Aiuppa was taken to court under the

---

* Skeptics in the FBI insist to this day that the drive against organized crime was an incidental part of the decision to create the Special Investigative Division. The real reasons, they say, were Hoover's desire to placate the Kennedys by advancing Courtney Evans and to punish Alex Rosen for some minor transgression.

Migratory Bird Act for having possession of more than the legal limit of mourning doves. In 1961 Kennedy also sought, and in record time obtained, new legislation that the Bureau considered essential in the fight against criminal syndicates. It made federal crimes of interstate travel or transportation in aid of racketeering (the Bureau classification became ITAR) such as gambling, bribery, or extortion; interstate transportation of gambling paraphernalia; and the interstate transmission of gambling information by wire.* Agents now felt they had specific "violations" they could aim to pin on gangland figures. One Bureau agent, a supervisor at headquarters in the Kennedy days at the Justice Department and later a special-agent-in-charge, says that the FBI rank and file was inspired by "the sight of rolled-up sleeves" among the Kennedy people. Whereas the Justice Department had previously been "a sleepy place," Robert Kennedy was an attorney general who "would even come in on Saturdays, a time when you used to find only Bureau people. There was a great sense of momentum, mission, purpose and cause. He really put the Department, and therefore the Bureau, on the attack against organized crime." In a sense, the FBI had its own little corner of Camelot.

After the assassination of his brother in November 1963, however, Robert Kennedy apparently lost some of his interest in the drive against organized crime and Hoover found excuses to slack off somewhat in an area that was disappointing to him statistically anyway. There was also a growing sensitivity to the questionable legality of the Bureau's electronic surveillances. In July 1965, after some FBI bugging devices had been discovered in a Las Vegas hotel and Senator Edward V. Long (D-Missouri) (himself the subject of investigations of possible links to organized crime) had launched a crusade against the practice, President Johnson declared that all federal agencies must stop electronic eavesdropping except in cases clearly involving national security. (Regarding the policies and personal convictions of LBJ and RFK on the subject, it became hard to follow the plot, for at various points each claimed he believed the other was pursuing their famous feud by electronic means.) "We pulled all the wires," recalls Ralph Hill, a veteran agent assigned to organized crime investigations; "it was like being in a cave and cutting off the lights."

Insofar as it was inclined to continue what was at best a frustrating mission — and there were still relatively few agents assigned to organized crime cases — the Bureau had to find some new methods.

---

* The 1961 law, perhaps by oversight, did not cover loansharking activities. They came clearly under FBI jurisdiction only in 1968, with passage of the federal Truth-in-Lending law.

One was to cultivate informants within the syndicates (always difficult, because most underlings feared reprisals if they broke the code of silence and talked) and to pay steeply for information; another was to increase the manpower assigned to organized crime and create some productive, if not very cost-effective, investigations. Attorney General Ramsey Clark, and the Nixon administration after him, thought that one clever approach was to set up regional "strike forces" with representatives of several federal investigative agencies, each looking out for the kind of information that fell within his expertise and jurisdiction but all pooling their knowledge to maximize the chances for prosecution and conviction. Hoover declined, however, to permit Bureau agents to participate in the strike forces. He did not want them responsible to anyone outside the Bureau's chain of command, and he simply did not trust the other agencies involved, to whom he feared the FBI agents might be surrendering control over the information they gathered. Even at the expense of letting others get the credit for some sensational cases, he stayed at arm's length and merely had SACs assign individual agents to handle "liaison" with the strike forces. The Bureau would do odd jobs for them when asked and occasionally it would even volunteer information to the interagency strike forces, but it would not get involved in any joint operations.

In some instances agents built up enormous frustration and resentment when, through electronic surveillances or informants, they heard about crimes — tortures, executions, extortions, and briberies — but could not pull together enough evidence to construct a case that would stand up in court. Some admit that they occasionally entertained the idea of using disruptive tactics and planting false rumors in order to have some of the most unsavory characters done in by their jealous rivals, but they insist that they never yielded to that temptation. "We used to sit around and talk about what we could do," says one agent who worked major Mafia cases. "We would say, 'We'll get them to knock off someone, and then we'll arrest them.'"

Several field offices did resort to strong tactics, however. In Chicago, for example, where there was an unusual concentration of agents interested in the organized crime problem, it was decided in the late 1960s that the only way to neutralize some of the illegal activities of mob boss Sam Giancana would be to "lockstep" him. Giancana was put under a constant twenty-four-hour-a-day surveillance so that he could no longer even hope to meet privately with his associates. "It drove him crazy," remembers one agent who was part of the surveillance; "we kept hoping that he'd take a punch at one of us" — thus laying the groundwork for prosecution on charges of assaulting a federal officer. At one point Giancana changed what had been his lifestyle and began going to church and playing golf. But the agents were inevitably there, too, sitting in the pew next to him or playing one hole behind him on the golf course (and trying to hit him with a ball). Instead of taking a punch, Giancana finally filed a lawsuit in federal court alleging that he was being harassed; to support his case, he submitted photographs of the agents who were constantly on his tail. Marlin Johnson, special-agent-in-charge of the Chicago Field Office at the time, was held in contempt of court at one stage of the litigation for refusing to provide for identification purposes the official photographs of the agents assigned to Giancana. The surveillance was ultimately suspended, but Giancana himself went to jail for a year on contempt charges for his failure to testify before a federal grand jury under a grant of immunity, which achieved the Bureau's goal of getting Giancana off the street. As soon as he got out, he took off to Mexico for an eight-year vacation. The moment he arrived back in Chicago, the FBI was on Giancana's tail again, seeking to question him about syndicate activities, both privately and before grand juries. In the summer of 1975, however, Giancana was suddenly murdered in gangland fashion at his suburban Chicago home. One theory had it that some of his rivals struck because they feared that he had implicated them during secret testimony; another, that Giancana, scheduled to testify before the select Senate committee investigating the intelligence community, would finger others in his tale of the bizarre links between the Mafia and the CIA during the 1960s.

Those links, apparently based on the CIA's belief that the Mafia could provide the perfect hit-men to carry out the agency's dream of assassinating Fidel Castro, led to some curious discoveries by the FBI agents. "We looked on them [the CIA] as a bunch of idiots," remembers one Bureau man — especially after discovering that the CIA was doing some extracurricular wiretapping at a Las Vegas hotel as a favor to Giancana, who wanted to find out if his girlfriend, singer Phyllis McGuire, was involved with other men. Hoover bitterly protested the CIA's role, but the Bureau agents involved in the investigations of Giancana and his friends insist to this day that it did not really impede their work. In fact, they say, once they heard that the CIA was involved with Giancana, "we redoubled our efforts."

Part of the key to getting the Bureau deeply involved in the fight against organized crime was a matter of definition. Many cases that the FBI had usually treated as isolated incidents — especially involving interstate transportation of stolen property (ITSP) and theft from an interstate shipment (TFIS) — turned out to be Mob-related; when they were treated in that context, one investigation could lead directly to another. There were also old statutes such as the Hobbs Act, banning any interference with interstate commerce, which could be dusted off and used against organized crime. But to cries that still more new laws were needed to fight the menace of organized crime, the Nixon administration responded by getting Congress to pass the Organized Crime Control Act of 1970. Among other things, that law made it easier to force people to testify under a grant of immunity from prosecution. It inaugurated an immunity of a new form — "use immunity," which guaranteed only that an individual would not be prosecuted on the basis of his own testimony about an illegal act, but left open the possibility that he could be pursued on the basis of testimony from others about the same "transaction." (The old variety, "transactional immunity," much disliked by prosecutors, prevented any prosecution at all of an individual who had admitted his complicity in illegal activity.) The act also provided for the empaneling of special grand juries, and extended Bureau jurisdiction to cover major local gambling enterprises and underworld infiltration of legitimate businesses. Already, under Title III of the Omnibus Crime Control and Safe Streets Act of 1968, Congress had provided a procedure for obtaining a warrant from a federal court to permit wiretapping on the basis of probable cause, a procedure that was deemed especially useful in gambling and narcotics cases.* The Bureau appreciated the new legal wiretap capacity, but often complained about clauses in the law that limited the length of each intercept (unless an extension were sought in federal court) and required that the subject of the investigation be informed afterward that he has been overheard.

But now the Director was warming to the fight against organized crime, for — discovery! — in this area too, it became clear at last, it was possible to compile impressive statistics. Both headquarters and individual field offices began to churn out fact sheets and summaries of accomplishments for journalistic and popular consumption (sometimes on plain white paper that would not be traceable to the Bureau). One,

---

* In another Justice Department–FBI conflict, Attorney General Ramsey Clark declined to use the wiretap authority; the Nixon administration, on the other hand, to the Bureau's delight, made broad and frequent use of it. In 1974, however, the Supreme Court ruled that the evidence obtained in many Title III wiretaps had been tainted when Attorney General John N. Mitchell, failing to follow precisely the procedures outlined in the 1968 law, improperly delegated his authority to process telephone-intercept applications before they were submitted to the courts.

prepared by the Chicago office in 1971, boasted that of one hundred and sixty-four "active LCN [La Cosa Nostra] members" in its territory, thirty-seven had been convicted as the result of Bureau efforts. It also said that over an eight-year period extending back through the 1960s, local law enforcement officials in the Chicago area, using warrants obtained by the FBI or information disseminated by the Bureau, had obtained nearly a thousand convictions and confiscated or destroyed almost a million dollars' worth of "gambling paraphernalia." There were many instances, of course, where the Bureau found no federal violations and therefore could take no action on its own. On some occasions, one field supervisor says, when there was no federal jurisdiction but the agents did not feel they could trust the local police with advance information, "we would take the police by the hand, not even tell them where we were going, but when we got there let them conduct the raid." Sometimes a field office, even in cases that had to go through the local courts, would actually type up the local warrants and then "shop around for an honest judge and a police unit that we could trust."

A document produced at headquatrers in early 1974 claimed that "FBI investigations in the organized crime area during 1973 led to more than 1,250 convictions of hoodlums, gambling and vice figures," up from 1,026 the previous year. It detailed, month by month, FBI successes from Jacksonville, Florida, to the Finger Lakes of New York and the state of Wyoming. Once reluctant to share its knowledge, the FBI now pointed proudly to its "prompt dissemination" of information as "a major factor in the government's nationwide drive against the organized underworld." As one example, it claimed that the Bureau had during 1973 shared "approximately 17,000 items of criminal intelligence data relating to narcotics offenses"; it also took credit for the fact that information provided by the Bureau was "utilized by the Internal Revenue Service in confiscating, or assessing liens against, $14,861,000 worth of property in the States of Connecticut, Florida, Georgia, Massachusetts, Michigan and Washington" during the year, all presumably in connection with organized crime syndicates.

Despite the impressive string of statistical achievements that the Bureau is now able to cite, much of its work against organized crime has been of a more informal *ad hoc* nature that does not usually get recorded on paper. The frustration of not always being able to build tight cases on specific violations that will stand up in court leads field offices and individual agents to take action against well-known mobsters that the agents themselves sometimes concede is merely harassment.

Some of the harassment is mild and amusing, at worst an annoyance to its victims. In one large city, for example, agents learned that mobsters, using the cover of a "saddle and gun club," had rented the entire dining room of a major hotel for a dinner and get-together that they wanted to keep secret. There was nothing illegal about the session, of course, but the agents, wanting to sabotage the good time, quietly notified all of the local newspapers. When their photographers arrived to take pictures, the festive evening broke up early. On another occasion the harassment was costly: the field office learned that the daughter of a powerful Mafioso was about to be married and that the wedding reception would be held in a suburban restaurant known to be controlled and frequented by underworld figures. The restaurant had apparently paid off the local fire chief to ignore safety violations, so the Bureau tipped off the state fire marshal's office. The result was that the restaurant was closed down and $25,000 worth of repairs were required before it could reopen in time for the wedding.

In Rockford, Illinois, which was considered the "still" for Chicago during Prohibition, the Bureau found an independent offshoot of a Chicago Mafia family operating in the mid-1960s. The resident agents there began driving by mobsters' homes whenever possible, sometimes going around the block time after time, even if working on other cases. Such cruising around, even when no specific investigation is under way — "piking" is the name for it in Bureau lingo — "may stir up their wives. They'll probably call up their husbands each time and get them worried about what we are doing," said one of the agents. The tactic also permitted agents to learn about an important signal at the home of one local Mafia leader: when it was considered "safe" for his associates to come in and meet with him, his statue of the Virgin Mary would be in a particular position on the front lawn.

One agent told of a long, tedious Friday-night surveillance of a major crime figure while he was assigned to the New York Field Office. After a time, the subject picked up two women in a bar and appeared to be heading for a motel; under ordinary circumstances, the agents would be expected to follow him there. But the agents were tired and wanted to go home, so to end the night's work and keep the gangster where he was, they simply let the air out of his tires and left. In another case, when a member of the "Colombo family" was sought on a warrant for unlawful flight to avoid prosecution, agents from the New York office used the opportunity to "put the press on" all of his family, friends, and associates, visiting and questioning them almost daily in an effort to develop useful intelligence information.*

In Youngstown, Ohio, a major center of organized criminal activity, the resident agency at one point overheard a conversation on a wiretap concerning a Mafia plan to score a "hit" on an FBI agent whom the leaders particularly disliked. "How many hit men do we have in town?" asked the local leader. "Three," replied his subordinate, and a plan was established for them to meet the next evening. An urgent message went to headquarters and even to Hoover, who responded that he wanted a "message" delivered to the mobsters. As a result, about twenty of the meanest- and toughest-looking agents available in nearby offices were immediately dispatched to Youngstown. They went to the Mafia leader's penthouse and barged in, dropping lit matches on the carpeting, tipping over vases, and doing other damage; they told their unwilling host that "you may have three hit men, but Mr. Hoover has thousands." The agent thought to be the object of the Mafia plot was never bothered. "That was the way some of this stuff had to be done," said one former agent who worked on organized crime matters; "there are so many situations where the only way to fight fire is with fire."

The Special Investigative Division at FBI headquarters coordinates a Top Echelon Criminal Informant Program, and Bureau officials concede that the development of good informants in the organized crime area requires special skills and techniques that not every agent is capable of. "Frankly, the agents who work in this area are pretty good con men," said one old-timer responsible for coordinating their work; "some of them won't even describe their methods to their own supervisors." Generally, the agents now selected to cultivate organized crime informants have a particular ability to talk with underworld characters in their own language, to persuade them to do things that do not initially seem to be in their best interest. In order to deal from a position of strength, the agents usually investigate the prospective informants as if they were themselves the subjects of major cases (sometimes they are); the hope is to find a weak point in their background, such as a mistress, that may become a factor in their decision to help the FBI. An agent may work for a year or more on trying to bring around a potential informant and then use code names and secret

* Joe Colombo struck back with his own harassment in 1970, when his Italian-American Civil Rights League put a picket line around the FBI field office in New York. The league's agitation was responsible for orders from the Justice Department that the terms "Mafia" and "Cosa Nostra" should not be used anymore.

hideaways for all dealings with him. In some instances, FBI agents unknown to an organized crime informant will follow him on the day he is scheduled to meet with his contact, to determine whether the local police or Mafia enforcers may also be after him that day. In major cities like New York special care is required, because the Mafia has been known to turn some dirty tricks around against the Bureau, for example by sending women into bars to try to pick up agents and compromise them.

In these and many other respects, Bureau officials have become convinced, organized crime work may have more in common with sophisticated security investigations than with most of the FBI's traditional criminal jurisdiction. The difficult cases invariably require heavy manpower commitments and a great deal of patience, for they develop slowly. With organized crime as powerful and ubiquitous as it is in the New York area, the field office there created a separate division with some two hundred agents to handle it. Entire squads within this division concentrate on individual Mafia families in order to understand their rivalries with others and to try to anticipate their activities. (Other offices have had to adapt differently. Miami, for example, is considered by the agents to be a "wide open" city, where members of various Mafia families come and go without any particular pattern.) Investigations may produce a steady flow of intelligence, but no court case that will add to the Bureau's statistics or the agent's self-esteem. To be effective, some of the agents must work undercover and learn to blend in unobtrusively among the people they are investigating. ("You can't go to a formal in a jock strap. For too many years, though, the Bureau tried," said one field official responsible for organized crime cases.) There is a premium on inventiveness and sophistication rather than plodding, especially as agents attempt to trace gangster money and control in what is ordinarily expected to be legitimate business activity.

As field offices — under pressure from headquarters to provide hard, marketable evidence of the Bureau's success in fighting organized crime — turned from gathering intelligence to developing prosecutions, a major part of their focus has been on gambling cases. From minor numbers rackets to major complicated rings that control millions of dollars' worth of activity, they tend to be the easiest cases to construct, especially with the help of court-authorized wiretaps. The conviction rate is high, but the gambling cases usually provide another source of frustration for the agents — the reluctance of judges to hand out heavy jail sentences or stiff fines for what are essentially white-collar crimes. Some agents complain, too, that headquarters is more interested in easy cases against small-time gamblers than in devoting the manpower necessary to get major figures. In another area that is lucrative for organized crime, loansharking, the Bureau has been somewhat less successful, in part because of the fear and reluctance of victims to talk with police officials. (Once they do and if they testify, they often have to be given new identities and helped to relocate in cities distant from their original homes.)

"You're probably never going to do away with organized crime completely," says one young agent assigned to a squad that concentrates on it in a major field office, "but there is no question about the fact that the Bureau suffered from not getting into this area soon enough. They all knew that there was something there, but they could never really put their finger on it." In Hoover's last years, he began to carry on about organized crime as if he had personally discovered it. But it is probably true that until the Director died, the Bureau could not make a full commitment to fighting it. Clarence M. Kelley signaled a real change in emphasis when he led off the FBI's annual report for the 1974 fiscal year with a whole page devoted to accomplishments in the area of organized crime. The record, when pulled together, had become impressive, and some field offices insisted they had all but crippled the power structure of organized crime in their territories. Other offices, however, were still crying for more manpower to deal with a problem whose surface, some SACs feel, has barely been scratched.

Civil Rights

In honor of the American Bar Association convention held in Washington in the late summer of 1960, the FBI submitted an article to the *ABA Journal* signed by J. Edgar Hoover, "The Federal Bureau of Investigation: The Protector of Civil Liberties." Drawing a contrast with the evil communist system of "terror and brutality," the Director wrote of the Bureau's dedication "to preserving the liberties which form the fabric of our constitutional government" and of its work "around the clock to protect [the American people's] rights, lives and property." While conducting its investigations into criminal and security matters, Hoover promised, the FBI "scrupulously protects the liberties of the individual. The criminal and the subversive must be defeated, yet the historic rights of the individual must be held inviolate."

With only a few known exceptions since Hoover became Director in 1924, the Bureau had shown a regard for the rights of those it arrested that was unusual among law enforcement agencies. In fact, the Supreme Court decision in the landmark case of *Miranda* v. *Arizona,* which became a cause célèbre in the late 1960s, had virtually no effect on the work of the FBI; for about twenty years agents had already been advising an arrested person of his rights before questioning him. On that front, the Bureau was way ahead of virtually every other police agency in the nation, and the "advice of rights" formula used by the FBI since 1948 was widely adopted by others after the *Miranda* decision. Charges of mistreatment by Bureau agents are still uncommon and rarely substantiated.

The nature of the FBI's mission — to enforce all federal criminal statutes not specifically assigned to another agency — is such, however, that the Bureau is responsible for monitoring the extent to which others in law enforcement respect the civil rights of the citizenry. Two laws passed during the post–Civil War Reconstruction period, codified in the 1947 revision as Sections 241 and 242 of Title 18 in the federal criminal code, made it illegal for two or more private persons to "conspire to injure, oppress, threaten, or intimidate any citizen in the free exercise or enjoyment of any right or privilege secured to him by the Constitution or laws of the United States," and for anyone "under color of law" to deprive persons of their "rights, privileges or immunities" or to subject them to "different punishments, pains, or penalties" because of their color, race, or status as an alien. For decades a legal debate raged over just how the federal government could employ these statutes, and the FBI generally came down against using them to investigate state officials' conduct. According to a report published by the U.S. Commission on Civil Rights in 1961, only a year after the Director's article appeared in the *ABA Journal,* Hoover's boasts about protecting individual rights were not justified. The Bureau, said the commission, "has little enthusiasm for its task of investigating complaints of police brutality. . . . The Director has used the strongest possible language to stress the need for cooperation between the Bureau and law enforcement officials at all levels." It continued:

The policy of notifying the heads of law enforcement agencies whenever one of their officers is under investigation for alleged acts of brutality presents [a] problem. . . . [It] can jeopardize a . . . case. Police force supervisors may adopt an unduly protective attitude toward their officers. They may share the racial prejudices of their subordinates and of their communities. These men cannot always be counted upon to cooperate in cases in which the victim is a member of a racial minority.

Still another difficulty may arise from the cooperative relationship between the FBI and local policemen. . . . there is evidence that some victims and witnesses, especially Negroes in the Deep South, are afraid to bring information to the Bureau's field offices. . . . Some of their fears appear to be based upon the fact that agents and local policemen often work closely together, and that officials somehow soon learn the names of complainants.

. . . the fact remains that at the present time the constitutional rights of a significant number of American citizens are being invaded by acts of police brutality. Their rights are not being secured and protected. This problem is not being adequately handled by State and local officials. A Federal statute makes such action a crime; yet the number of prosecutions under this statute is small. The number of convictions, smaller yet.

The Civil Rights Commission report was also critical of the Civil Rights Division of the Justice Department for failing to be sufficiently aggressive in initiating court cases. Another report, in 1965, indicated that the situation had improved, but that federal civil rights enforcement still did not meet the needs.

Historically, federal prosecutive action based on the Reconstruction laws was infrequent and seldom successful; when it occurred, it was liable to draw protests from the states that their own authority was being abused. After the Bureau looked into a 1952 incident in a Pennsylvania state reform school in which a young black died under circumstances suggesting brutality, that state's governor, John S. Fine, complained about a federal invasion of the state's police power. At a national governors' conference, he was joined by the governor of Virginia, among others; Governor Thomas E. Dewey of New York, fearing agents would "swarm" into his state to investigate inmate complaints, demanded repeal of the Reconstruction laws.

Ironically, it was just as social currents were beginning to stir in the South, just as demonstrations and protests were being launched to test the federal guarantees of civil rights in the 1950s, that the Justice Department and FBI seemed to rein in and put new procedural restrictions on their enforcement activities, which had been gradually expanding. Attorney General Herbert Brownell seemed to favor that expansion. In the aftermath of the 1954 and 1955 Supreme Court school desegregation decisions, he proposed a legislative program that would establish the Civil Rights Commission, give the old Civil Rights Section in the Justice Department's Criminal Division full status as a separate division, and empower it to file civil suits in federal court in defense of voting rights and on other constitutional issues.

Brownell pressed the program at a March 1956 cabinet meeting, but he was accompanied to the session by Hoover, who delivered an extraordinary report on "Racial Tensions and Civil Rights." The Director's presentation blamed the Supreme Court decisions for creating problems in the South, and he lined himself up with the bitter southern resistance. He complained of "a lack of objectivity and balance in the treatment of race relations by the press" and said "the South is in a state of explosive resentment over what they consider as unfair portrayal of their way of life, and what they consider as intermeddling." Behind the tension over "mixed education," said the Director, revealing one of his own most deeply felt prejudices, "stalks the specter of racial intermarriages." As for "the crusade for integration," Hoover stated derisively that its leaders had "learned the techniques of mobilization, pressure, and propaganda to build momentum for their cause." He warned that communists were seeking to infiltrate the National Association for the Advancement of Colored People (NAACP) and that other groups active in the integration fight were preaching "racial hatred" and otherwise acting in an un-American manner; by contrast, he said, the new Citizens Councils formed to oppose desegregation included "bankers, lawyers, doctors, state legislators and industrialists. . . . some of the leading citizens in the South." The Ku Klux Klan, Hoover told the cabinet, was "pretty much defunct."

The Director's report, bigoted and narrow-minded as it might seem in retrospect, had a powerful impact. It was probably a major factor in President Eisenhower's decision not to push for the Brownell civil rights program. (The attorney general, in an unusual display of independence and defiance, pressed for its adoption anyway, and he was partially successful in 1957.) Hoover skillfully resisted efforts to put the Bureau into an information-gathering role in cases involving, for example, the Interstate Commerce Commission's ruling that public transportation facilities must be integrated. When William P. Rogers (later secretary of state in the Nixon administration) succeeded Brownell as Eisenhower's attorney general, he bowed in the extreme to Hoover's preferences and predispositions on the matter of civil rights. Criminal enforcement under the Reconstruction laws was virtually dropped, and the first chiefs of the new Civil Rights Division declared that the department would do nothing in civil rights cases if there was any prospect at all that the state was launching its own investigation of a complaint. Initial inquiries by the Civil Rights Commission showed that the Bureau was conducting hardly any investigations in the civil rights field in the late 1950s. Rogers established a policy that U.S. attorneys and other Justice Department lawyers were not to record any complaints about the FBI in writing, and an FBI man close to the

Director was assigned to the Civil Rights Division to "help" it formulate any requests it made of the Bureau.

Bureau attitudes toward civil rights enforcement, so powerful in influencing Justice Department policy, were the logical outcome of its practices and folkways, not to mention the Director's own strong feelings. The FBI, from the earliest days of the Hoover reign, had worked closely with local police and depended on their help. Police manpower, much greater than the Bureau's comparatively meager force, was often the key to solving cases, both routine and difficult. Thus, when confronted with allegations of police brutality, FBI agents preferred to look the other way rather than point an accusatory finger at people who were their friends, associates, and helpers; even if the agents recognized the brutality, the chances were that they were sympathetic with the position the policemen had been in, and felt they might have acted similarly themselves under the circumstances.

When the fledgling civil rights movement launched its sustained assault on southern practices and attitudes, even though federal law and constitutional principles were usually on its side, this posed special problems, practical and psychological, for the Bureau. Apart from its genuine efforts (at least in some categories) to draw a rational distinction between local and federal crimes, the FBI had an instinctive respect for and strong relationship with the established legal and social order in every part of the country. A special-agent-in-charge or senior resident agent was expected to be on excellent terms with local police chiefs, sheriffs, and mayors; he was hardly accustomed to treating them as possible subjects of criminal investigations. The SAC was required to attend important community events, and in the South that often meant segregated, restricted events. Agent's training taught the men on the street how to interview sympathetically people who shared their values, their backgrounds, and their skin color; experience in the field gave them an automatic distrust of disturbers of the peace. There was only a handful of black agents in the Bureau at the time, and few agents in the South knew or associated with any blacks, who were the complainants in the vast majority of proposed civil rights cases. Agents generally felt uncomfortable and uneasy, not to say ill-equipped, interviewing the blacks and others they considered "troublemakers," people who dressed differently and challenged many of the old ideals and principles.

Hoover, for his own part, did not want to upset the southern congressmen who were the providers of his generous appropriations, the granters of his every legislative wish, and, in many cases, his personal friends. These people, including powerful figures like Senator James O. Eastland of Mississippi, were stirred to a frenzy by the Supreme Court and other government rulings, and they fed grist to the Bureau mill that churned out warnings about alleged communist involvement in and intentions for the civil rights movement. Even without such a practical motive, however, Hoover probably would have reacted the same way. A product of the gracious old southern style in Washington, D.C., the Director could not understand or sympathize with the equal rights drive. The only blacks he liked were those who "knew their place"; if they knew it and stayed in it, he could patronize them quite well.

Campaign rhetoric and confidence in liberal intellectuals led civil rights advocates to expect that all this would change after John F. Kennedy became president and his brother Robert was installed as attorney general. They counted on an aggressive, interventionist civil rights policy by the Justice Department, and they asserted that constitutional principles and guarantees dictated that the Bureau and other federal enforcement agencies be employed to *protect*, rather than to investigate, those challenging the established order in the South. But the civil rights movement was to be deeply disappointed. Burke Marshall, the scholar and antitrust lawyer whom Robert Kennedy selected to head the Civil Rights Division, was more interested initially in slow-going civil cases than in criminal investigations that would send a clear message to public officials in the South who were ignoring, or even encouraging, violence against blacks. Marshall and others who worked with him bought the Hoover argument that using the Bureau in a protective role would raise that ever-present threat of turning the FBI into a "national police force" available for deployment in any crisis by those in power. They had confidence that the system would work to correct injustice if only given enough time.

That attitude, so frustrating to the civil rights activists, lent a kind of official imprimatur to the Bureau's own persistent noninterventionist policy, which in turn sometimes infuriated the Kennedy men. FBI agents stood by and took notes, for example, when John Seigenthaler, a journalist who served as special assistant to Robert Kennedy, was knocked unconscious by a mob in Montgomery, Alabama, where he was serving as the President's representative during the "freedom rides" of 1961 intended to test and defy segregation in the public buses and bus terminals of the South. Similarly, two Justice Department lawyers joined four FBI agents in watching passively from a distance when state troopers and the local sheriff arrested three blacks who showed up at the courthouse in Selma, Alabama, in 1963 to register to vote. Indeed, when there were violent confrontations in the course of civil rights efforts in the South during the early 1960s, it was usually not the FBI that was sent in to preserve order, but federal marshals and representatives of the Immigration and Naturalization Service, the Alcohol, Tobacco and Firearms unit of the Treasury Department, and even the Border Patrol.

When Kennedy's Civil Rights Division did choose criminal cases to pursue, it ignored many instances where civil rights demonstrators had been brutalized by whites. But it did, by contrast, prosecute on charges of obstructing justice nine blacks who picketed the grocery store of a white man in Albany, Georgia, who had sat on a jury that acquitted a local white sheriff charged with shooting a black prisoner. The demonstrators claimed they were picketing the store, in a black neighborhood, because of the owner's discriminatory policies, but they were accused of interfering with the jury process. Once the Justice Department decided to go ahead with the case, tens of FBI agents flooded into town to investigate. The sight was disillusioning to those who had seen the department and the Bureau avoid well-documented instances of civil rights violations against blacks in the same community.

The tide finally did begin to turn — and dramatically at that — in the summer of 1964. Northern students who flocked South to fight for civil rights encountered violence and terror, especially in Mississippi. In Washington, Congress passed a major civil rights bill that, among other things, forbade discrimination in the access to and use of public accommodations. One force for change was the new President, Lyndon Johnson, a man of the South who over the years came to believe in civil rights perhaps more passionately than his predecessor John Kennedy, but also a man of Capitol Hill, whose pragmatism worked better and faster than Kennedy's exhortations to get things done.

But there was also a crucial, bloody event that had a catalytic effect: the disappearance in late June of three civil rights workers, Michael Schwerner and Andrew Goodman, both whites from New York, and James Chaney, a black from Meridian, Mississippi. They had been arrested for allegedly speeding in Philadelphia, the county seat of Neshoba County, an area where they were looking into the burning of a Negro church. As national concern developed over their disappearance and it seemed apparent that the local Mississippi authorities were making no serious effort to find the three missing youths, Robert Kennedy declared that the Justice Department would enter the case and treat it as a kidnapping. The FBI had only a meager presence

in the state, with the few resident agents in the northern half reporting to the Memphis Field Office and those in the southern half to New Orleans, and so substantial reinforcements were needed from outside.*
After the young men's burned-out car was found in a swamp, Hoover dispatched his long-time aide Alex Rosen, assistant director for the General Investigative Division (who had conducted liaison with the Civil Rights Division on other matters while Kennedy was attorney general), to take charge of the search. Sailors from a nearby Naval Air Station were also brought out to help the agents dig in the swamp.†
Eventually the Bureau began trying to identify and interview every member of the White Knights of the Ku Klux Klan of Mississippi until they found a man who, for a steep price (rumored to be as high as $30,000), was prepared to tell what he knew about the murder of Schwerner, Goodman, and Chaney. Finally, on August 4, the three bodies were dug up by FBI agents from a farm dam near Philadelphia, Mississippi. It ultimately became clear that the Klan's Imperial Wizard, Sam Bowers, had ordered their execution, which was carried out by a vigilante squad that included the deputy sheriff of Neshoba County, Cecil Ray Price. After long and complicated legal maneuvering, Bowers, Price, and five others were convicted in federal court on charges of conspiring to violate the three men's civil rights.

In the early stages of the investigation of the Philadelphia murders, President Johnson sent the retired director of the Central Intelligence Agency, Allen Dulles, to Mississippi to survey the tense situation. After meeting with Governor Paul Johnson and other officials, Dulles concluded that the situation there was genuinely explosive. His suggestions coincided with recommendations that had already been urged on the President by Kennedy's Justice Department: that action had to be taken to control the Klan and other white terrorist organizations, and that the federal law enforcement presence in Mississippi should be increased. There was an FBI field office in the state capital

---

* There was and is feeling — shared by the victims' parents, and some of the young men's colleagues — that the Bureau could have moved sooner, and that if it had, Schwerner, Goodman, and Chaney might have been saved.
† At one point during the search, President Johnson mistakenly told a press conference that two hundred marines were helping. (He had apparently misunderstood when Hoover told him about the sailors.) When the Director told him he was wrong, the President said the Bureau had better bring the marines in. So it was that the order went from Hoover to Assistant FBI Director William C. Sullivan to Defense Secretary Robert McNamara to send exactly two hundred marines to Mississippi — a rather unusual chain of command for the call-up of troops. The press conference caused such an immediate stir among Mississippi politicians, however, who feared that their state was being invaded by the military, that Johnson reversed the order just after the first marine helicopter had taken off for the state.

of Jackson during World War II, but it had been closed in 1946; President Johnson now wanted it reopened. The President ordered Hoover to get the job done as quickly as possible and said he would provide a presidential aircraft to take the Director there to officiate personally at a formal opening ceremony. The White House thought that the presence of a man so widely respected in the South, but who was hardly a radical civil rights advocate, could help calm the situation; the move also seemed likely to please northern voters in an election year.

Hoover assigned the task of opening the field office to Roy K. Moore, then fifty years old, a successful and well-known agent who had solved a number of dramatic cases in the past and had had experience elsewhere in the South. Once special-agent-in-charge in Charlotte, North Carolina, he was now SAC in Little Rock, Arkansas. Moore had little knowledge of Mississippi, but one of his earlier special assignments for the Director had been on a bombing case in Birmingham, Alabama, and he knew how delicate it could be to work with a power structure that did not want the Bureau around. He was a take-charge type who also believed that the FBI often had to depart from the rulebook to be successful, and that the appearance of control over a tense situation could be as important as actual control. The Director sent Moore into Jackson on July 5, 1964, and gave him only five days to have a field office ready for opening.

Moore quickly determined that the FBI office space in the federal building, occupied by the six-man Jackson Resident Agency reporting to the New Orleans Field Office, was inadequate. The next day he discovered that an old friend from Charlotte was now vice-president of a bank in Jackson and that the top three floors of the bank's new office building were vacant. Under such pressure, he recalls, "money was no object." It was impossible, of course, to do the necessary adaptation of the three floors in the time remaining, and so Moore devised a plan to throw together a dummy office — a sort of false-front Potemkin village — just opposite the elevators on the top floor. With carpenters working around the clock, three rooms were contructed, walls, ceilings, rugs, and all. Moore borrowed furniture from a local store, had a single telephone line installed, put pictures on the flimsy walls, and brought in two stenographers from New Orleans to act as receptionists. "We had to be sure everyone came and went through the front door," Moore said later, because the rest of the floor was just a shell, a construction site. When Hoover arrived with Associate Director Clyde Tolson and held a press conference on July 10, the office was convincing enough to fool some reporters, who wrote of the Bureau's "plush"

413

new quarters in Jackson. It was never clear whether Hoover himself thought Moore had actually set up a full-fledged office in such a short time; "he never asked, and I never told," Moore says. After the Director left, the dummy office was torn down and construction of the real one began.

The Director was shielded from some of the grim realities of the situation in Mississippi. He was talked out of his plan to drop in at the scene of the investigation of the Philadelphia murders, which was being run out of the Meridian Resident Agency. Deke DeLoach, who arrived in Mississippi a day ahead of Hoover, intercepted the threatening calls that came to the Jackson motel where Hoover and Tolson were staying. The Director did visit with Governor Paul Johnson and the state attorney general, as well as with other Mississippi officials, to assure them that the Bureau was by no means invading the state, or arriving in a mood of hostility. Part of the deal struck between the FBI and the state government was that the Highway Patrol would be professionalized: Hoover gave Governor Johnson a list of patrolmen who, according to Bureau investigation, were members of the Klan, and the governor promised they would be given an ultimatum to quit one or the other. In exchange, the Director agreed that room would be made in several upcoming classes of the FBI National Academy for members of the Highway Patrol, and the Bureau also promised to lobby in Washington for federal money to help upgrade Mississippi's own state police training academy. Hoover made it clear, both in his press conference and in private statements, that the FBI would not be offering protection to the out-of-state civil rights workers. (It was obvious that the Director himself disapproved of the workers, their attitudes and goals, and their life-style; he was much more comfortable with even the most fiery segregationist local officials.) The civil rights movement was not very pleased with these remarks of Hoover, but its leaders realized that the movement of FBI agents into the state in force had to have the effect of making their work somewhat safer.

With the eyes of headquarters, the Justice Department, the White House, and, to a degree, the entire nation focused on the new Jackson Field Office, Moore lost no time. Initially Jackson was a "voluntary office," because of the possible danger of the work there, the inevitable long hours, and the uncomfortable position that agents would be in. Many aggressive young agents who were tired of what they were doing elsewhere gladly came to Mississippi (a number jumped at the opportunity to be transferred out of New York); some others who were assigned to Jackson against their wishes resigned from the Bureau rather than go. One agent later told of crawling under a grocery

414

store in Canton to look for a bomb on his first night in Mississippi, and many others had similar baptisms under fire. The field office became an action- and information-central, where hundreds of reporters checked in on their arrival in Mississippi, in part because they feared for their own safety and in part because it was a good place to trade information with the garrulous, if bombastic, Roy Moore and his aides.

Moore's approach — both to satisfy Hoover and the Mississippi authorities and because he believed it would make sense in the long run — was to investigate on both sides of the civil rights crisis. Hoover, who only a few years earlier had declared the Klan to be dead, now said publicly that "there are four hundred and eighty Klansmen in Mississippi. . . . I had our agents interview every member of the Klan there, just to let them know we know who they are." Indeed, Moore had always believed in the blanket approach to investigations, and he was relentless in his efforts to infiltrate the Klan and create internal confusion and suspicion. Helped along by the framework of William Sullivan's new COINTELPRO — Disruption of White Hate Groups, agents from the Jackson Field Office spread rumors, true and false, about Klansmen, exposing their financial manipulations and personal foibles. Some of the unofficial actions against members of the Klan were more extreme even than anything permitted under COIN-TELPRO and were never recorded on paper; rumors still circulate that on one occasion, in order to solve a case involving the firebombing of a black family's home, agents in effect kidnapped a Klansman and ex-tracted a confession from him. Moore encouraged his men to use those techniques that worked, and once the field office was in high gear it scored a number of dramatic solutions to difficult cases.

The solutions inevitably had a deterrent effect, and a statistical chart prepared by the Jackson Field Office shows that while there were 175 "acts of violence" (civil rights–connected shootings, beatings, bombings, and burnings) in Mississippi in the last seven months of 1964 and 294 during calender year 1966, there were only 70 in the twelve months ending in September 1970. Moore took it upon himself to try to persuade Mississippi police that brutality got them nothing but trouble: "I would go down and interview policemen who had been brutal and explain to them what was within the law and what was not. . . . I felt that the FBI was just like a father coming in and straightening them out."

But at the same time, Moore used his blanket technique to investigate the civil rights workers, many of whose motives the Bureau suspected. He had a file opened on every resident of every "COFO house" set up by the Council of Federated Organizations, the umbrella group that sponsored the influx of civil rights workers from the North, about a thousand people in all. After a basic check of criminal and credit records and the Bureau's indices in Washington revealed that more than half the people were of further interest to the Bureau, the agents looked more deeply into their backgrounds and activities. In some instances, the field office drew up a study of individual houses to find the "strong personality" dominating each one and to predict whether the residents might be violence-prone or have "selfish motives." One house, for example, was found to include a Catholic nun, a former FBI agent, the son-in-law of a prominent northern newspaper publisher, the daughter of a member of the Communist party in a midwestern city, a reporter from a small newspaper in the West, and someone the investigators concluded was "an oversexed Vassar girl." Some of the people originally investigated in the "Mississippi summer" of 1964 were then watched for years more by the FBI. In effect, some of the Bureau's civil rights work turned into classic "internal security" investigations.

The Bureau's sense of righteousness about what it was doing led it into some extraordinary actions that look in retrospect like outright violations of civil rights and human decency. Under the rubric of COINTELPRO, for example, agents proposed, invented and, in April 1969, sent a threatening letter to civil rights activist Donald W. Jackson, also known as Muhammad Kenyatta, accusing him of "various criminal activities in and near Tougaloo College" and warning him to leave that town. It was signed by the fictitious Tougaloo College Defense Committee. The letter apparently worked and was a major factor in getting him to return to Pennsylvania.

Interestingly, the Bureau used very little electronic surveillance in the new wave of investigations in the South. Agents found it easy to learn about the civil rights workers' plans by other means, and they discovered that Klan members were too paranoid ever to discuss their activities except among themselves in secret meetings. (Some Klansmen were apparently so convinced that hidden agents and cameras were being used to read their lips that they sometimes covered their mouths with their hands while walking along the street.) More commonly, the Bureau broke cases through the use of well-paid informants; one of its men, Gary Thomas Rowe, was in the car, for example, with the nightriders who shot and killed Viola Liuzzo, a white woman who ferried marchers between Selma and Montgomery, Alabama, during the demonstrations of 1965.

There were allegations that the Bureau went too far in almost every direction. Jack Nelson, of the *Los Angeles Times*, revealed in 1970, for example, that two years earlier the FBI had paid two Klan informants — brothers who were involved in the mob that killed Schwerner, Goodman, and Chaney in 1964 — and an intermediary a total of $38,500 to give the Bureau information about a plan to bomb the home of a Jewish businessman in Meridian. The money, it turned out, had been raised in the Jewish community, with the assistance of the Anti-Defamation League of B'nai B'rith, as part of an effort to work with the Bureau and other authorities to halt a wave of terror bombings against the Jews of Meridian and Jackson. At the last moment a schoolteacher who was a secret Klanswoman filled in for one of the men who had been scheduled to plant the bomb at the businessman's home; she was killed when the waiting policemen opened fire (only after they had been fired at, the policemen said). The FBI insisted that the money had merely been used to pay its informants for their advance warning that the bombing was coming, but Nelson's sources said it had really served to provoke the event, that the bombers were lured into their action by the paid informant. The one bomber who was wounded and sent to prison in connection with the incident, Thomas A. Tarrants III, at first seemed to support the Nelson version of events, but he later gave the FBI a signed statement from prison saying that he had acted on his own. Some Bureau officials argued that whatever role the informants had played, and notwithstanding the death of the woman, the Bureau-arranged police trap that caught her and Tarrants ended the wave of anti-Semitic bombings and further weakened the Klan. That, after all, was the goal, they said.

But in the view of Kenneth Dean, a social activist who has been involved in many Mississippi reformations of recent years — including the establishment of a biracial television station in Jackson — the Meridian bombing case was a dramatization of how the Bureau had moved, improperly, "from a law enforcement organization to an agent of social change. . . . It wanted to promote social change, but also to contain it." For him, the Meridian case is no different from the murder of the civil rights workers in Neshoba County: "Men of the law acting outside the law."

Both Mississippi blacks and out-of-state white civil rights workers alleged that FBI agents, both before and after the opening of the Jackson office, often questioned them in an accusatory and skeptical manner when they filed civil rights complaints while they treated the policemen and other officials who were the subjects of the complaints with deference and respect. With exceptions, the agents did not like, or approve of, the civil rights workers; and they were disinclined to risk a deterioration of their good working relationship with local police.

In a few instances the FBI coziness with local police who were under investigation reached the level of scandal, especially in areas of the South other than Mississippi, where the Bureau was not so carefully and routinely scrutinized. One example, also exposed by Jack Nelson in the *Los Angeles Times* and a few other newsmen, involved the federal probe of the shooting of unarmed black student demonstrators at South Carolina State College in Orangeburg on February 8, 1968, when three students died and twenty-eight were wounded. No sooner had the FBI begun its investigation than the locally based agent who was supervising it was found to be sharing a motel room with an old friend, the top state police official involved at Orangeburg, himself a subject of the investigation. Also, two of the three agents who had been on the scene during the gunfire initially told the Civil Rights Division of the Justice Department that they had not been there, apparently because they did not want to get involved in testifying about their friends from the state police.

After the Orangeburg case, Bureau officials became somewhat more sensitive to the conflict of interest that some agents might feel in investigating lawmen with whom they ordinarily work closely. But it was only after Hoover died that Acting Director L. Patrick Gray III established a policy (later reaffirmed by Clarence M. Kelley) that in any such difficult cases, agents from a distant field office — sometimes even including an outside special-agent-in-charge — would be brought in to conduct and coordinate the investigation. There might still be a pro–law enforcement bias, but at least not a close daily working relationship between the investigators and the investigated. The rule was so stringently applied in some southern field offices, including Jackson, that when an agent was assigned jurisdiction over a particular county, he usually handled all cases there except those involving civil rights, which were generally given to an agent less well known by the local authorities.

From the earliest days of the Kennedy administration there have been running disputes between the Bureau and the Civil Rights Division of the Justice Department. Sometimes, rather than hassle with an unenthusiastic Bureau, the division sent its own lawyers to the South to conduct investigations that would ordinarily be the responsibility of the FBI. There were times when the constituencies of the two groups were so obviously disparate that the department lawyers would interview the blacks involved with a case while the Bureau agents would interview the whites. One young attorney who worked in the Civil Rights Division in the early 1970s said that even then the division was so intimidated by and disinclined to risk disputes with the FBI, that it measured carefully which southern cases it sent over to the Bureau. This became a particular problem, he explained, in the spring, budget review time on Capitol Hill, when all divisions of the Justice Department seek to close as many old cases as possible to avoid trouble from inquisitive congressional committees. "The Bureau didn't like cases that were more than sixty days old," the lawyer said, even if all that a case involved was having someone check whether a commercial establishment had remained segregated or whether it was still even in business. So rather than take the chance of being "dumped on" by the FBI, the Civil Rights Division would pay the air fare and other travel expenses of an attorney who flew out from Washington to look into just such minor matters. "We would usually end up closing the file anyway," he said; "this way, it would just be more expensive, but easier."

Despite the dramatic reversal in the attitudes of some blacks toward the FBI after the change in its performance in Mississippi that began in 1964, many will never forgive the almost pathological pursuit of the Reverend Martin Luther King, Jr., by Hoover and his men — even though much of the electronic surveillance of King was authorized by Robert Kennedy. To this day, because the FBI has never released proof to substantiate its allegations that King was for a time in touch with "foreign principals," the extensive wiretapping and bugging conducted on the black leader seem incomprehensible except in terms of the domestic counterintelligence programs of the 1960s, which were extended to cover King and other nonviolent black leaders as targets. That the Bureau persisted in trying to link the civil rights movement to subversive elements or foreign powers indicates to some observers a basic hostility of the FBI toward blacks, or at the very least an insensitivity to the human and social factors that led to their new struggle for equal rights — an insensitivity, it must be acknowledged, that was pervasive at many levels of the government and the society.

Inevitably the issue of the Bureau's minority hiring practices is linked to its civil rights stance. Although its equal-employment record has slowly improved, especially at the clerical level, it still lags behind in the South. Perhaps because field offices tend to be molded in the image of their host communities, one sees relatively few black faces in the average southern FBI office. Even in the Jackson office, trailblazer that it was, the first black agent to be permanently assigned (as distinguished from special short-term duty) came only in 1974; less than a year later, he was transferred away to a larger city as the size of the force in Jackson was trimmed back. However, the chief night clerk, who in effect runs the office after closing time, was since 1968 a black man whom Moore encouraged to get a college degree and to apply for agent's training.

As tensions subsided in Mississippi, the Jackson Field Office settled into somewhat more normal operations. But there were still some areas that remained sensitive, with Mississippi's powerful members of Congress always keeping their eyes on the operation. On one occasion in the early 1970s, Senator John Stennis complained in Washington about the way a civil rights investigation of a Jackson city policeman had been handled, and that was enough to bring an inspector on an unannounced visit. (He decided that the agents had acted properly.) But after a decade the FBI was so well entrenched in Mississippi that it was considered to be something of a model for other states; with the Klan subdued and blacks making substantive gains by peaceful means, the Bureau seemed to have the respect of blacks and whites alike. Whereas agents were once the targets of abuse when they walked down the street, they were now greeted warmly. Roy Moore (who remained SAC in Jackson until his retirement in December 1974, with only a year away during which he was assigned to Chicago) became something of a state legend, and an agent was liable to be greeted as "one of Mr. Moore's boys." Moore was invited to participate in a Mississippi Oral History Project, and some said that he could have been elected to statewide office had he chosen to run.

Civil rights cases came to be treated as a rather routine annoyance by some agents. As one young agent put it, "Every black in town knows the civil rights laws by heart, and if he just gets into an argument with a cop, he'll come straight up and file a complaint. Without any right to be selective and screen out the ones that obviously have no merit, we are expected to go and investigate every one of these cases, even though we know they will hardly ever result in a prosecution." At Parchman State Penitentiary, a primitive institution that is the object of almost constant private and federal lawsuits, agents laboriously go about investigating civil rights complaints filed by individual inmates against individual guards, and sometimes vice versa — "with the full knowledge," said one agent assigned nearby, "that it is one person's word against another's, and nothing will be provable in court."

With the racial situation calmer and in view of the unusualness in Mississippi of bank robberies and some of the other crimes that are the bread and butter of FBI jurisdiction, agents in the state came to have a smaller workload than most of their colleagues elsewhere. The Jackson office became gradually smaller. In fact, when Donald Sullivan succeeded Moore as head of the office, he followed a traditional SAC's instinct and urged the agents to "get your caseloads up" (meaning that many of them would probably open files that obviously had no merit, only to close them again after a short time). There was talk of closing or consolidating Jackson and other small southern offices, but most Bureau officials and agents assigned there opposed that idea because of the symbolic importance the offices had come to have.

Narcotics Abuse

"I am against, and have been for years, the growth of the FBI," said J. Edgar Hoover. "I think we are entirely too big today, bigger than we should be. I would have liked to see the FBI remain small; but that has been impossible because Congress has yearly enacted legislation expanding the investigative jurisdiction of the Bureau."

The Director talked that way often even though, as many of his former aides acknowledge, he did not always mean it, especially when he was in one of his aggressive empire-building phases. But on this occasion, an appropriations hearing in early 1964, Hoover spoke with particular vehemence after his friend, Congressman John J. Rooney of New York, raised the fact that many people were proposing that the Department of Justice take over "the enforcement of the narcotics laws." In a classic dose of his faint praise for others, Hoover insisted that "the Narcotics Bureau [then part of the Treasury Department] has done a very good job under very great difficulties."

The Federal Bureau of Narcotics (FBN), in fact, had not done such a wonderful job, and that was exactly why officials were upset and were urging a change in the administrative framework. Just at a time when drug abuse was being recognized as a major national problem, federal agencies with overlapping jurisdictions were competing with and stumbling into each other. No one on the national level seemed to have a clear grasp of the situation, and the few breakthroughs in the field were scored mostly by local police, whose own efforts were hampered by the problem of corruption. The congressional reaction was invariably to create another bureaucracy or to spread the jurisdiction around still more thinly, a remedy that predictably aggravated the problem. So from time to time someone would come up with the standard idea: "Let the FBI do it."

If the FBI had come to be regarded as the elite of federal law enforcement, the FBN was looked upon as its lowest common denominator. There had been glamorous earlier days when its chief, Harry Anslinger — a man who exhibited some of the same regal characteristics and pretensions of grandeur as Hoover, who considered Anslinger a rival — boldly led the agency into headline-catching adventures. The Bureau of Narcotics, actually, had been the first on the federal level to recognize the existence of the Mafia, and after the mobsters' Atlantic City convention of 1929, the FBN had sketched out what would prove to be a fairly accurate impression of the national crime syndicate's informal bylaws. If anything, Anslinger posed the opposite problem from that of Hoover; he tended to go too far and see the Mafia behind everything. Some of the nation's most notorious gangsters, including Louis Buchalter, were originally sought on warrants sworn out by the federal narcotics agents. But by the mid-century years their reputations and performance had paled by comparison with the FBI's G-men. Although they performed dangerous, sometimes delicate tasks, the narcotics agents started out much lower on the federal pay scale than the FBI men, generally earning about a third less. This meant that the FBN often had to settle for recruits with less education and fewer professional qualifications. Sometimes that had its advantages: they were willing and prepared to get their hands dirty and tended to be earthy, streetwise characters who could blend in well with the people they had to investigate. But it also meant that they were more vulnerable to corruption. When the Bureau of Narcotics was merged in 1968 with the Bureau of Drug Abuse Control (a small new agency that had been established as part of the Food and Drug Administration in 1965) to form the Federal Bureau of Narcotics and Dangerous Drugs (BNDD), some fifty agents were fired on the spot for their seamy dealings and more than a dozen were indicted on charges of selling narcotics themselves or accepting bribes.

That was just the kind of situation that played into Hoover's hands. After working so hard for decades to build the FBI into a paragon of honesty and expert performance, he argued publicly and privately, he could not be expected to absorb into the Bureau's ranks what he considered a motley crew of questionable character. And from an administrative point of view, he insisted, it was unworkable to try to incorporate one separate agency within another. One experiment with that — when the Bureau of Prohibition was merged, in its dying days, into the Bureau of Investigation of the early 1930s — had failed, and Hoover had no desire to repeat the experience. What the Director did not say publicly, but what other Bureau officials stressed quietly in their lobbying on Capitol Hill and discussions with newsmen, was that FBI agents simply were not trained in the kind of undercover skills and special techniques necessary for narcotics work if they were to do it themselves (as they would inevitably have to do, if jurisdiction over the drug laws were subsumed into the Bureau's responsibilities). The point was also frequently made that it would be inappropriate to mix the regulatory function of drug agencies with the FBI's focus on investigative and enforcement duties. There were other arguments in the FBI arsenal: that narcotics agents often had to be very selective about which cases to pursue, a notion that was anathema to the even-handed Bureau agents; that narcotics enforcement involved international operations outside the scope of the FBI's foreign liaison setup. And then there was Hoover's bromide that if new responsibilities were heaped onto the Bureau, it risked becoming a "national police force."

As in most other areas, Hoover repeatedly won his struggle to fend off the task of enforcing the narcotics laws. The compromise reached when BNDD was created in 1968, however, brought the agency over into the Justice Department from Treasury, on the theory that it would be wise to have it close at hand to, and under the coordination of, federal prosecutors. Hoover obviously did not like the idea, but it was easier to swallow with the BNDD offices actually located a mile or more from department and Bureau headquarters in another part of Washington. Other agencies outside Justice, such as the Bureau of Customs (part of Treasury), continued to share responsibility for narcotics enforcement. And the Nixon administration, trying to do something dramatic and vote-catching about a major crime issue, created still others, including the Office of Drug Abuse Law Enforcement (ODALE) and the Office of National Narcotics Intelligence (ONNI); intended to be a kind of CIA of the drug field, ONNI became William C. Sullivan's vehicle for getting back into the Justice Department.

When Hoover died, the agitation started up again almost immediately for the FBI to take over responsibility for narcotics matters. Senator Abraham Ribicoff (D-Connecticut) drew up a bill to accomplish just that goal. The point was persuasively made that there was already a good deal of overlap between Bureau investigations and those of the drug agencies, especially as the FBI became more involved with combating organized crime, which controlled much of the nation's illicit narcotics traffic. The same people were often the subjects of several simultaneous inquiries, which could be efficiently consolidated under a single agency's authority. Still the Bureau was hesitant; but it was no coincidence that in August of 1972 the Special Investigative Division, which handled organized crime matters, set up a new desk at headquarters to handle intelligence information concerning narcotics. Every field office was directed to name an agent as the local narcotics coordinator, who would collate all of the information relating to drug traffic that came through the office and be sure that it was passed along promptly to the concerned agencies, local, state, or federal. Some insiders interpreted that development as an effort by the FBI to show that it could help out without being handed the entire job; others as a step in the direction of taking over narcotics responsibilities.

The latter course was clearly what L. Patrick Gray III, the new acting FBI director, hoped for. He had been persuaded to that view by Attorney General Richard G. Kleindienst, who felt that only with the resources and field network of the Bureau applied to it could the nation hope to beat its worsening drug problem. Hoover's philosophy, Kleindienst argued, was that "if you always want to be a winner, then you don't take on the tough situations"; but Kleindienst insisted that this had worked harm, and that the people would understand if the FBI had to feel its way for a while in the narcotics field before registering any dramatic accomplishments. Although the FBI bureaucracy expressed strong resistance (a poll showed the vast majority of special-agents-in-charge were opposed), Gray, who was becoming more and more attached to his new job at that point, was delighted with the idea of having more authority and another few thousand people responsible to him.

The White House convened a committee in late 1972 to study the alternatives for reorganization of the federal narcotics enforcement effort, including representatives of the Treasury Department, the Office of Management and Budget (OMB), the Justice Department, and the Domestic Council, then run by presidential adviser John D. Ehrlichman. The Justice Department representative on the committee was Donald E. Santarelli, then associate deputy attorney general and head of the Office of Criminal Justice (and later administrator of the Law Enforcement Assistance Administration). During a series of private hearings in late 1972 and early 1973, where representatives of the various agencies with narcotics work testified, it became clear that Santarelli strenuously opposed the Kleindienst-Gray position. He argued that the issue of drug enforcement was so critical and so different from most other types of criminal investigation that a single agency should be created to deal with the problem as its sole responsibility. Also opposed to the Bureau takeover, each for his own reasons, were John Ingersoll, director of BNDD and an ambitious man in his own right, and William Sullivan. George Shultz, then secretary of the treasury, argued, perhaps to keep his own underlings happy, that the whole job should be turned over to the Bureau of Customs; eventually, however, he voted with the representatives of OMB and the White House in favor of establishing a new agency. Only the Justice Department, overruling Santarelli, dissented.

As a result, President Nixon threw together all of the competing agencies in the drug field, including BNDD and ODALE, whose employees loathed each other, into a new Drug Enforcement Administration, with a status in the Justice Department theoretically parallel to that of the FBI, the Federal Bureau of Prisons, and the Immigration and Naturalization Service. In his reorganization message to Congress, Nixon stressed that the FBI would be expected to make a special effort to turn up narcotics-related information during its researches and investigations into organized crime.

Kleindienst and Gray felt they had lost a battle. But the heirs of the Director — the people who made up the *real* FBI — knew they had won one, albeit through a quirky set of circumstances and with unaccustomed allies. There were some career Bureau men who wished that Mr. Hoover could have been there to celebrate.

XVIII

Leading the Law Enforcement Community

I personally hope that in a few years we may have in every city, every town, every community of this country, at least one man who has come to Washington to spend three months with us and learned what he could learn from our work and our training. Then that man can go back and in turn be a real missionary of good will in that community in the field of law enforcement. He can not only serve as a liaison officer between the local officers and our representatives in that district, but he can also help to educate the other members of his police department. If that is done, there will spread — there is bound to spread — a great development of the recognition of the need of education and need of training in law enforcement.

> — J. Edgar Hoover, in an address before the second
> session of the FBI National Police Academy in
> Washington, January 6, 1936

J. EDGAR HOOVER MAY HAVE SOUNDED THE ALARM about a "national police force" rather more frequently than necessary, but the fear was a real one that emerged often in American law enforcement policy debate in the early years of the twentieth century. The theme was taken up by the friends and foes alike of federal agencies. Testifying before the House Judiciary Committee in 1924 in favor of legislation to establish a new criminal identification bureau, but against putting it in the Justice Department, Richard E. Enright — then police commissioner of New York City, representing a rump group of police officials in the International Police Conference, who had broken from the International Association of Chiefs of Police (IACP) — warned against "nationalizing the police." "We rather object to becoming an annex to the Department of Justice," said Enright, who urged that the identification operation be lodged anywhere else, even in the Department of Interior, War, or Treasury, but not Justice. (On that point, of course, he lost; a month after Enright testified, Hoover was named to take over the Bureau of Investigation at Justice and he soon incorporated into it the previously scattered criminal identification work.)

Other politicians and statesmen insisted that the decentralization of police functions was an important characteristic of the federal system and helped to prevent erosion of fundamental constitutional and human rights. Invariably they invoked as specters the powerful national police agencies that developed in czarist Russia, the Soviet Union, and Nazi Germany. It was not only Gestapo tactics that were feared, but also a Gestapo-style organization of the various police forces in the nation — the formation of any central bureaucracy with access to all investigative and intelligence information whose elite force could step in and take any case it wanted. The fear was so strong at times that it interfered with limited and legitimate efforts at regional cooperation among local and state police agencies.

But at the same time, while almost everyone opposed the idea of a national police, it became increasingly clear that some kind of national initiative and role was desirable to help improve the quality and capacity of the poorly trained local police. In sorry contrast to many other nations, such as Britain, police work in the United States could hardly be called a profession in the early years of the century; it was something a man did when he could find no other job. Many officers, scarcely educated to begin with, were simply handed a gun and sent out on the street. The National Commission on Law Observance and Law Enforcement, headed by former Attorney General Wickersham, reported in 1931, after surveying and studying police forces, that "no pains are taken, so far as we can learn from these studies, to educate, train and discipline for a year or two the prospective patrolmen and to eliminate from their number such as are shown to be incompetent for their prospective duties." In some small towns, the Wickersham Commission found, a prospective policeman was never asked whether he knew how to handle a weapon, and many police forces "sent the man out on duty with no instruction and even without the aid and advice of an experienced man."

Young Hoover, settling into his job, saw in the problem an opening for the Bureau: in discussions at home and correspondence with knowledgeable Europeans, he explored the idea of trying to take a leading role in the training and professionalization of police. Once the federal crime bills of 1934 had established broader national responsibilities for the Bureau, this became a more acceptable idea; with the authority of Congress and the Justice Department, the support of the IACP and an advisory committee of police chiefs drawn from its membership, the Director established the FBI Police Training School in 1935.* It was initially a humble affair, with twenty-three students from different police agencies completing a twelve-week course. But eventually it became a major part of the FBI's business and budget, turning out thousands of people annually who had been trained by, and felt a special relationship with, the Bureau. (The FBI's appropriation request for Fiscal Year 1975 included nearly $15.5 million for all of its training activities — of agents and police.) The role soon grew to include the instruction of police by FBI field offices in their own territory and the convening of special seminars and conferences to discuss the latest issues in law enforcement. The National Academy and the other free teaching services became a means for Hoover to say that the Bureau was upgrading the police, fighting the various crime waves, and spreading goodwill, all the while, he said, avoiding the dangers of a "national police force." The usual justification for an ever-growing Bureau involvement was that if the standards of local police agencies could be improved, then there would probably be fewer and less frequent demands for federal action and expansion in troublesome areas of law enforcement. But the police training was also a method for the FBI to establish an extraordinary network of willing friends and valuable contacts, to extend its influence and its example to the grass roots; and some officials close to Hoover did not hesitate to justify it in those less idealistic terms. That was exactly what led critics to assert that the Bureau was taking on some of the characteristics of just the kind of national police force it had so stridently warned against.

Hoover quickly came to presume, and for that matter to declare, that the Bureau was the leader of the American law enforcement community. This became one of those self-fulfilling truths that the FBI worked hard at propagating, and it was accepted rather easily. As the Bureau's stature grew, so did that of the National Academy. It was the sort of institution whose "graduations" were addressed by presidents and attorneys general, not to mention the television G-man Efrem Zimbalist, and sometimes even used for major policy declarations in

---

* A year later, the name was changed to the more grandiose-sounding FBI National Police Academy, and in 1945 simply to the FBI National Academy.

the law enforcement field. Although he would often skip the graduation of a class of new agents (and toward the end of his tenure no longer even bothered meeting them all), the Director and his successors invariably attended the NA graduation ceremonies, presented diplomas, and had their picture taken with each policeman. When Lyndon Johnson's administration and a Democratic-controlled Congress were groping for ways to find new solutions to the problem of crime, a clause was written into the Omnibus Crime Control and Safe Streets Act of 1968 increasing by a factor of ten (from two hundred to two thousand) the number of American police officers authorized to be invited for training at the academy each year and providing federal funds to pay for all their transportation expenses. The mystique was more important than the substance. No one seriously imagined that twelve weeks of study under the benign guidance of the Bureau would transform a policeman into a wizard, but anyone who attended the National Academy was assumed to have been touched by the magic wand of the G-man. He (or, after Hoover's death, she) inevitably returned home to prestige and excellent prospects for promotion. According to the latest Bureau figures, about one in every five of the NA graduates who are still in law enforcement jobs is "the executive head of his agency." The implication is that somehow the FBI made the difference.

Once an officer has been to the academy, he is automatically thought, by the FBI and usually by himself and others, to be a member of the select (although larger all the time) fraternity of Bureau men among the nation's estimated four hundred thousand law enforcement personnel. If he is in a big city where there are many of his breed, he is invited to special events by the local FBI field office. In a small town, he is the first person consulted by a Bureau agent who is a stranger and has come looking for information. Wherever, he is somebody the FBI will approach whether openly or surreptitiously, seeking assistance or offering a tip about somebody the Bureau wants arrested or investigated on any available charge. Visiting Bureau inspectors call on him to see if his police department is satisfied with its relationship to the Bureau and to test impressions of the image built for the FBI by the local field office. He is invited to regional "retraining" sessions where Bureau agents dispatched from Washington lecture on a current problem in law enforcement and present the FBI's ideas for a solution. And he is almost sure to become a member of the FBI National Academy Associates, a sort of alumni association complete with blazer patches, coasters, and festive reunions and conventions. Except for a few who, especially during World War II and again in recent years, are later accepted for agent's training, he remains an outsider, but he is let inside just enough to have a taste of the Bureau spirit.

Because of the status and honor attached to the National Academy, local police departments and officers within them often compete to be chosen. Selections are made within the restrictions of a geographical quota system (the Tampa and Jacksonville field offices, for example, can each pick three people from their territory to attend the quarterly sessions in Quantico, and Miami is allocated four every time), but over a period of time a single police force can build up a corps of a dozen or more officers who have attended the NA, usually including the chief. If that department was not on especially close terms with the nearest field office before its people went to the academy, it probably has become friendlier as they have returned. National Academy attendance is in a category with examinations of evidence performed by the FBI Laboratory or help provided by the Identification Division to match fingerprints with known criminals, in that it creates a sense of obligation to the Bureau on the part of the "locals." Ed Campbell, the number one man of the Training Division, acknowledges as much when he says that "the Academy earns the FBI a great deal of good will with local police departments. It improves their rapport with us." Theoretically that means an even-handed and consistent exchange of information, but according to one southern county sheriff, who is considered an especially close friend of the Bureau, "The FBI has always been on the receiving end in its dealings with local people. . . . They ask for a lot, but they don't give out much information at all. . . . So, even though they don't always realize it, everybody holds back a little bit with them sometimes." That is especially true whenever a field office reverts to the old Bureau style and claims primary credit for solving a case that it could not have handled without the help of local police and other agencies.

FBI relations with local police are, at best, a very complicated matter. It would probably be impossible ever to establish a genuinely fair and equal trade of information, because in most instances the policemen tend to have far more that the agents need in the field than vice versa. Most of the truly effective cooperation probably takes place on an informal level of trading favors, favors that cannot necessarily be charted or quantified. This kind of cooperation sometimes becomes a liability, of course, especially when the Bureau is called upon to investigate a police department that has been a valuable source of information. Agents have not only been reluctant to work on civil rights cases for this reason, but they have also sometimes held back on probes of police corruption until they are prodded along by an aggressive U.S. attorney or by a special-agent-in-charge who is willing to sacrifice some of the field office's good contacts with the local establishment if necessary. Such investigations may cause police-Bureau ruptures that take a long time to repair.

What the Bureau is willing to do to help a local police department, on a practical investigative level, varies widely. Some SACs, sticklers for the rulebook, may decline to assist in emergencies unless some probable cause to believe that a federal violation has occurred can be shown. (One local chief complained that the FBI used to take a cold, detached attitude even when a child was thought to have been kidnapped — until some interstate aspect was established, when it would plunge in as if there were nobody else around to do the job.) On the other hand, in a few parts of the country, such as Mississippi, where local law enforcement tends to be very weak or Bureau cooperation developed under special circumstances, agents spend a good deal of their time helping out on local murder cases and others where the federal government has no jurisdiction at all; that kind of help would probably never be officially reported to headquarters.

The prospects for a good relationship are obviously maximized whenever a Bureau man — a former agent or an NA graduate, someone perceived to feel a sense of loyalty to the FBI — is in charge. Some, like Sheriff Peter Pitchess of Los Angeles County, became well known for this connection and are considered important Bureau conduits. When the Bureau feels it has a good friend in an important position, as it did for years with Edmund L. McNamara as police commissioner in Boston, it will often intervene to try to talk him out of any plans to retire, or make subtle efforts through the political process to try to head off his replacement by a more independent type. (Both Pitchess and McNamara were once FBI agents.)

It is the selfish Bureau attitudes — expecting police to repay for any help they get and taking credit where it is not necessarily due — that have led some police departments to keep their distance from the FBI and the National Academy. Others had the distance kept for them by the Bureau. The late William H. Parker, for example, who was chief of the Los Angeles Police Department for seventeen years until he died in 1968, often offended Hoover with his independent attitudes; part of his punishment was that there was never any room for members of his department to attend the National Academy. In some of the Director's more irrational moments, if a National Academy graduate did something considered sufficiently offensive to the Bureau, he might be dropped from the roster of alumni, as if he had suddenly died or become a nonperson.

But the common syndrome is for the local police to go along and accept a kind of junior G-men status next to the Bureau. Whatever grumbling the men on the beat may do about the agents they have contact with, many police departments have an official policy of trying to emulate the FBI. (If they can get public compliments from the Bureau in the bargain, that may mean better appropriations and other assistance from the city council or other local governing bodies.) Indeed, many an intelligence division, or "Red Squad," of a big-city police department has taken its cues from, and sometimes done odd jobs for, the Bureau. When the Bureau is big on pursuing Black Panthers or the Students for a Democratic Society, the locals will invariably follow suit, often with less sophistication and slyness, and then share the results with the FBI. A number of state governments have established their own "bureau of investigation," capitalizing on the similarity to the FBI's name and hoping the good image will follow automatically. In many instances, though, the state agencies hire cast-offs from other police groups who are clumsy and not so well trained or disciplined. They often end up being the subjects of scandal themselves. The Illinois Bureau of Investigation, for example, has been the target of a probe for extensive, seemingly illegal wiretapping, some of it done with equipment privately purchased for it by a state legislator whose car had been bombed and who wanted everything possible done to solve the case.

Every field office now has a "police training coordinator" who chooses the regional contingent for each session of the National Academy and arranges the classes and other formal instructional help given by the Bureau to local police in the field. Hoover's initial hope was that those who attended the National Academy would then go home and teach what they had learned to their colleagues, but by 1937 the Bureau was formally preparing some agents in every field office to serve as part-time "police instructors" in addition to their investigative duties. They were expected periodically to conduct "police schools," in which they lectured to officers, perhaps from several departments gathered in one central location, on the latest developments and concepts in law enforcement. By 1951 the Bureau counted more than seven hundred and fifty agents in this category, and they would teach not only on topics where the FBI had experience to share, such as the collection and preservation of evidence, but also on issues in which the Bureau was rarely involved directly but had some strong opinions, such as riot control. (Some states eventually came around to passing laws that required all police departments to have a minimum amount of initial training and retraining. Especially in smaller departments that did not have their own training facilities or access to others, the FBI's classes became a convenient, cost-free way to meet the requirements.) In the average field office, the police training coordinator's room is stocked with hundreds of pamphlets and reprints published by the Bureau — on subjects from fingerprints to terrorism and, inevitably, on why the FBI is so wonderful and how it got that way — which the instructors take along with them when they lecture. In some offices the police training coordinator may be a young, gung-ho agent, perhaps a former coach or schoolteacher, who likes to get out to a shooting range and teach advanced FBI firearms methods to rookie policemen or to talk about the dangers of corruption; but in others the job is a sinecure for an agent close to retirement age, who rarely budges from his desk and does most of his work on the telephone.

After prodding from President Kennedy, Hoover opened up the National Academy to foreign policemen, with their transportation costs sometimes paid by grants from the State Department's Agency for International Development. And the Bureau made some discreet, tentative steps in the direction of technical advice and training assistance to police outside the United States — notably in the Bahamas, where the FBI needed plenty of favors, as the islands became a haven for U.S. gangsters escaping the authorities. The motive was invariably proclaimed to be altruistic, but as Kenneth E. Joseph, an agent who became an instructor at Quantico, put it in his doctoral thesis on the Bureau's role in police training,* the overseas graduates of the National Academy "have been of valuable assistance on many occasions."

As in most other areas, Hoover encouraged measuring the FBI's police training accomplishments in terms of statistics, and those statistics had to improve every year. The Bureau's annual report for Fiscal Year 1974 noted that in its first ninety-seven sessions held over thirty-nine years, the National Academy had graduated 8,173 policemen. It

* The Bureau has discouraged any outside assessment or evaluation of its police training programs over the years. Joseph's 1970 thesis, "A Study of the Federal Bureau of Investigation's Contribution to Law Enforcement Training and Education in the United States," submitted to the College of Education at Michigan State University, provides some useful factual detail but suffers from some of the obvious problems of an FBI evaluator trying to study objectively a Bureau program during the late Hoover era, when no criticism was tolerated, whatever the source. It was apparently those constraints that caused Joseph to use words like "inspirational" in describing the Bureau's performance, and to print the entire long, rambling, self-serving answers that the Director gave to seven questions Joseph had submitted in writing.

also said that instructors sent out from Washington had "conducted more than 155 specialized field schools for law enforcement administrators and command personnel in such areas as hostage negotiations, crisis intervention and executive development." But the truly overwhelming statistic was that agents in the field had "provided 102,739 hours of instruction while participating in 11,013 law enforcement schools attended by 343,104 criminal justice personnel." Each special-agent-in-charge is able to open his desk drawer and read to a visitor from a data sheet that tells exactly how much of that teaching activity took place under his own field office's jurisdiction. But one former agent who was involved with police training work insists that such statistics are farcical. Often, he said, the field office will record, and report to the Training Division, the number of policemen who had been "expected" to attend a training course or a lecture, but conveniently never bother to update it later with the actual attendance figure. He recalled one occasion when two agents were dispatched to Juneau, Alaska, to teach a specialized management course to twenty-five people, only to find that all but seven were absent. "The phonying of these statistics really used to gall me, because I saw no need for it," he said; "if a police department borrowed a training film from the FBI and the only time we spent on it was dropping it off at the station, then we counted the number of people who were expected to watch it as having been instructed by the Bureau that night."

There were occasions when the Director and some of his minions seemed eager to convert the FBI's preeminence in the field of law enforcement administration and training into a form of control. Any other organization that became involved, governmental or private, including at different times the IACP, LEAA, the Police Foundation, and even the Central Intelligence Agency,* was viewed as a competitor or a spoiler. Cooperation was only possible if the FBI were in charge. Sometimes the bids to centralize police training in the Bureau were bold and brazen, as when Hoover's men on Capitol Hill lobbied behind the scenes to have a measure adopted that would have required an FBI role in the training of any police department's personnel before that department could obtain funds from the FBI's rival, LEAA. The measure, opposed by Attorney General Ramsey Clark and

---

* The CIA for a time helped to train fourteen officers of the Intelligence Division of the New York City Police Department in "the analysis and handling of large amounts of information," and the agency was believed to be involved in discreet training efforts with other departments, including the Metropolitan Police of Washington, D.C.

IACP Executive Director Quinn Tamm, among others, failed. The point was made that if any single agency or group were to gain such control or influence over most police training in the United States, it could begin to dictate priorities, standards, and philosophy, which would otherwise logically vary from place to place and time to time.

Some of Hoover's most dramatic public feuds were with Tamm. The brother of Edward Allen Tamm, the Hoover aide who retired from the Bureau in 1948 to accept a federal judgeship, Quinn Tamm had risen quickly to be one of the Bureau's brightest stars. In 1938, at the age of twenty-eight, he had become the youngest agent ever to hold the rank of inspector, and for seventeen years he ran the Identification Division. Later, he was in charge of the combined Training and Inspection Division, and then the FBI Laboratory. Because of his long responsibility for FBI fingerprint matters and then training, Tamm served for years as the Bureau's liaison with the IACP. As he later told it, that translated to mean that he dominated the police organization on Hoover's behalf. Tamm had participated behind the scenes in the Bureau's selection of a National Academy graduate, the retired chief from Endicott, New York, as the IACP's executive director in the late 1950s. "We used to control the election of officers" of the IACP, Tamm said; "we had a helluva lot of friends around, and we would control the nominating committee." If that system failed, the Bureau sometimes had other methods; in 1959, for example, when the well-known Chief Parker of Los Angeles, whom Hoover detested, was slated to become a vice-president of the IACP (and therefore would automatically move up to the presidency later on), FBI lobbying on the floor resulted in the opposing nomination, and overwhelming election, of a relatively unknown chief from Newton, Massachusetts, who was also an NA alumnus.

But when the hand-picked executive director had a stroke and the job of running the IACP fell vacant in early 1961, it was offered to Tamm, and he accepted. Although Tamm had already had some differences with Hoover and some of his most loyal lieutenants, the Director apparently believed that as a career FBI man, Tamm would keep the IACP in the Bureau's pocket as a lobbying and pressure group that could be depended upon to support the Hoover world view in all the various policy discussions and petty quarrels that arose in the law enforcement community. Hoover began to be suspicious of his former protégé as the IACP started growing — it took over the sponsorship of a program that had been run at the Northwestern University Law School in Chicago to place trained lawyers as legal advisers to police departments — and developing its own independent positions.

Tamm came right out and said that he felt the IACP, rather than the Bureau, should be the spokesman for the nation's police. But Tamm's big break with Hoover came a few years later, when he publicly opposed a bill pending in Congress that would have given the Bureau an unusually powerful role in all police training nationwide. The Director, who could not tolerate what he saw as insubordination, tried and failed to have Tamm fired. From then on the FBI considered the IACP an "enemy" and unilaterally suspended all relations. Later, when one of the Director's unquestioned supporters was serving as the elected president of the IACP, Hoover tried, through Deke DeLoach and others, to have the organization's annual convention transfer most of the executive director's powers to the president, but again he failed.

Several years later, President Nixon convened an urgent session at the White House to discuss the problem of the killing and wounding of police officers in street attacks; Hoover, predictably enough, made up the invitation list. Conspicuously excluded were Tamm and Patrick V. Murphy, police commissioner of New York City. Murphy was one of the most important people to have at the meeting, because about a dozen of his officers had been killed during the previous year. But Murphy too was on Hoover's enemies list because of differences in philosophy and the Director's distaste for the reform-minded New Yorker's liberal pronouncements on the issue of crime. The publicity surrounding Hoover's petty insult overshadowed any good that came out of the White House conference.*

There was a time, to be sure, when the FBI was a significant innovator in the field of police training. It was the first organization, for example, to attempt the systematic exposure of cops on the beat to simplified explanations of the important legal points in major Supreme Court decisions. (The Bureau's Office of Legal Counsel still distributes widely its own explanations and interpretations of cases that are expected to have an impact for law enforcement personnel.) The monthly *FBI Law Enforcement Bulletin* often contains articles advising the police of the latest technical and sociological developments in the field. Even in subject areas where the Bureau had its own problems, such as civil rights, when the topic became a burning issue agents undertook to lecture on the subject to local police officers. In

---

* Tamm and Murphy, two highly respected and influential men in police circles, were rehabilitated by the Bureau only after the Director died. Tamm was not only invited as a guest of honor for the swearing in of Clarence M. Kelley as director in Kansas City in July 1973, but he flew there in a government plane with Attorney General Elliot L. Richardson. Murphy, as head of the Police Foundation, was later invited by Kelley to speak to top-ranking FBI officials at regional management symposia partly financed by the foundation.

1956 alone, according to the FBI, agents in the field taught four hundred and sixty "specialized police schools" on civil rights. Meanwhile the more traditional areas of instruction, such as traffic and juvenile delinquency, were being phased out. In 1967, the Training Division took a major step forward by introducing courses, at the National Academy and in the field, on management principles and human relations as they apply to police work, subjects previously considered irrelevant. But still the Bureau was mired in traditionalism while some of the most innovative thinking in law enforcement came from other organizations. It was not the FBI that came up with the concept of "assessment centers" to evaluate the various candidates for a job as police chief, but the IACP. It was that uppity newcomer in the federal bureaucracy, LEAA, not the Bureau, that studied and reevaluated the traditional methods of compiling crime statistics and funded research to develop new possible crime reduction programs through environmental design. Funded by private philanthropic money, the Police Foundation reviewed traditional law enforcement concepts like neighborhood patrol and found they were not necessarily effective in cutting down crime; it also studied the role of women in police work. Any or all of these were areas where the FBI, with its manpower, facilities, resources, and research capacity, could have made a contribution but did not. It stood by its old way of doing things, designed and blessed by Hoover, as the only true way.

Clarence Kelley did come up with an innovation in 1975, when, with the encouragement of — and a $25,000 grant from — the Police Foundation, he launched a "crime resistance program" designed to promote federal-local cooperation as well as citizen involvement in fighting crime. Under its provisions, two FBI agents were assigned to work with four different local police departments, each on a different problem — traffic in stolen property in Birmingham, Alabama; crimes against youth in DeKalb County, Georgia; crimes against the elderly in Wilmington, Delaware; and crimes against women in Norfolk, Virginia. (On this occasion, the Bureau received widespread praise for launching the effort, rather than criticism for trying to meddle in local police affairs.)

"A university for law enforcement" was the Bureau's own characterization of its new modern academy complex on a seventy-nine-acre enclave, woodsy and isolated, within the U.S. Marine Corps Base at Quantico, Virginia. Opened a month after Hoover's death, the academy — its detractors within the Bureau call the achitectural style "penitentiary modern" — was outfitted with all the latest educational technology and such special features as a simulated crime scene laboratory and indoor firing range. Its dormitories have enough space for more than seven hundred people to stay overnight at a time, and its gymnasium would be adequate for training professional athletes. With a cafeteria that serves three meals every day, a Marine Corps commissary, a barber shop, a bar, an auditorium where a different movie is shown every night, and other recreational facilities, it is like a self-contained village. Once the hermetically sealed passageways between all the buildings are completed, it would be possible to exist there for months without ever going outside.

The academy is used for training new agents (three hundred and twenty-seven in Fiscal Year 1974, but only eighty-three in 1975 because of budget restrictions) and for in-service training of agents already on duty (almost 2,800 agents, or a third of the Bureau's manpower, came back at one time or another during Fiscal 1974 to attend short training sessions in everything from Special Weapons and Tactics [SWAT] to photography and white-collar crime investigations). But many of the agents and trainees feel like strangers because most of the multimillion-dollar facility is devoted to fulfilling J. Edgar Hoover's private dream of training the nation's police — a dream at odds with his frequent public invocation of the specter of a "national police force." In addition to short-term special seminars and programs for police, about a thousand officers attend the National Academy each year, in four three-month groups of two hundred and fifty each (still only half the number authorized in the Omnibus Crime Control and Safe Streets Act of 1968).

Officially the classes are said to be composed of the most promising police officers the FBI can find, but in reality they are preselected by their own chiefs. The police training coordinator in one field office, responsible for processing applications to the National Academy, acknowledged that the NA background investigations are the most cursory the Bureau does and that unless something like a criminal record is turned up, the recommendations and judgments of their superiors are almost always accepted (meaning that not too many mavericks make it to Quantico). The only condition of acceptance is that the officer remain in a law enforcement job for several years after graduation from the training course. The average class is a heterogeneous group from virtually every corner of the United States as well as military police departments, plus several people from overseas. One recent class included officers from the American Samoa Police Department in Pago Pago, the "Internal Security Forces" of Lebanon, the "National Bureau of Investigation" of the Philippines, the "National

Security Bureau" of the Republic of China (Taiwan), and the police department in Hobart, Tasmania.*

For many policemen, the NA is one of the most significant experiences of their career, and perhaps the only advanced education. Some of the students have academic problems (although rarely does anyone fail to pass the courses); others become frustrated by their isolation in the countryside an hour's drive from Washington. A few invariably get annoyed with some of the summer camp regime of the National Academy, such as nightly curfew and a weekly "birthday table" in the middle of the dining hall. To handle these and other potential problems, the Bureau selects five of the most personable agents in the FBI as "counselors" to the policemen at each session.

Since the new facility opened, the National Academy's academic pretensions have grown considerably. There is a well-equipped library — although it is one where few points of view not authorized by the Bureau, and not many books critical of the FBI, can be found. And as a result of a new agreement, the School of Continuing Education of the University of Virginia gives academic credit, graduate or undergraduate, for most of the courses. The minimum requirement for students in the standard police-training program is fourteen semester hours of classes, two in Forensic Science and three each in Education and Communication Arts, Management Science, Behavioral Science, and Law. Among the courses that can be taken to satisfy the requirements are those on "Socio-Psychological Aspects of Community Behavior" ("Basic tenets of sociology, psychology, and political science are applied to the present day problems of community relations and crime"), "Police Problems in the Urban Environment" (treating "minority recruitment, community control, response to family disputes and civil disobedience"), and a basic review of "The Criminal Law," which features study of the Constitution and Bill of Rights plus "a detailed examination of laws governing investigative techniques including arrest, search and seizure, confessions, evidence and theories of proof, electronic surveillance, eyewitness identification, entrapment, civil liability, and the system of juvenile justice." The elective offerings include studies of "Police Unions," "Budgeting for Law Enforcement," "Problem Solving and Decision Making," and "Electronic Data Proc-

---

* The focus on recruiting young officers from internal security agencies has led some to wonder whether the National Academy, like the International Police Academy run by AID, has taken on a quasi-political role of the sort dramatized in the film *State of Siege*. But although three months at Quantico expose a foreign visitor to plenty of good old-fashioned FBI anticommunism and other traditional ideology, there seems to be no "counterinsurgency" training of the sort depicted in *State of Siege*.

essing for Law Enforcement." In addition to the formal academic requirements, the policemen are expected to do several semester hours
of noncredit work in Law Enforcement Arts, defined as "firearms,
defensive tactics, and physical education training, as well as related
duties necessary to complete the performance ability of the law enforcement officer."

Some of the courses include guest lectures by outsiders, including
distinguished professors from major universities (Felix Frankfurter,
while a law professor at Harvard, lectured to one of the earliest NA
sessions on "The Law Enforcement Officer and the Prosecutor"), but
most of the teachers and all of the administrators at the National
Academy are fully qualified street agents who went back to school,
some for their doctorates, in order to become part of the Quantico
faculty. They are assigned there full-time. Hoover insisted that all FBI
programs remain in the hands of inside people, and his successors have
generally turned away proposals that they find professional educators
to run the training programs. The Bureau has also insisted that the
new complex in Quantico must be used only for FBI-designed and
-supervised activities, not for any other federal enforcement agencies.
That position led to suggestions that the Justice Department should
perhaps take over the academy at Quantico and use it more generously
to upgrade the training of such people as agents of the Drug Enforcement Administration, if necessary cutting back on or suspending the
instruction of local police representatives until the professional qualifications and standards of other federal forces have been raised to equal
those of the FBI.

One policeman from a city of nearly half a million people, who
recently graduated from the National Academy and was promoted to
training responsibilities in his own police department, complained that
the program had suffered from its effort to find the lowest common
denominator in the diverse student body. So much time was spent on
elementary forensic science–type issues — such as examination of evidence and testimony in judicial proceedings — he said, that more
sophisticated material dealing with management problems and other
issues relevant to the top echelons of police departments tended to be
shortchanged. He urged that the Bureau do away with the fiction that
everyone attending the National Academy comes with the same basic
police background and instead adjust the program to meet the particular needs of officers at various levels. The NA alumnus also said he had
been astonished "by the way they throw money around down there" —
on the firing range, for example. But "one of the best things" about his

three months at Quantico, he noted, "was the feeling of companionship and camaraderie" among the policemen themselves, if not with the Bureau. "You find out that your problems are not so far out in left field, that other people and departments have the same difficulties. Now that's encouraging."

XIX

Gathering Information

The main reason that crime does not pay, if it does not, is that criminals talk so much about what they have done . . . so they get caught.

— *"Jack," an FBI informant*

THE MOST IMPORTANT SINGLE RESOURCE of the FBI, the ticket that often makes it succeed where others might fail, is its vast store of information, catalogued and classified, filed and refiled, retrievable more quickly all the time. Whether the information is right or wrong (and the Bureau is finally able to acknowledge that some percentage of its unevaluated and unconfirmed information is bound to be incorrect), this resource has been the basis for accusations, investigations, recriminations, prosecutions, and convictions, and for just plain knowledge of criminal and security matters.

A belief developed over the years that the FBI had somehow found unique and wondrous ways of gathering information, that its bag was full of extraordinary tricks, that its cloak and dagger were enough to foil the cleverest malefactor. The reality is, of course, that the Bureau's means of finding out most of what it knows are undeniably and disappointingly prosaic. To be sure, there are a few gimmicks. When an agent carries a briefcase instead of the usual, simple under-the-arm padded clipboard, the briefcase may well prove to have a microphone hidden in its handle and a tape recorder inside. If he seems to use lip balm with unusual frequency, the little container he puts to his lips may actually be a radio microphone he is using to transmit messages to a distant point. And on certain occasions, an agent or another person actively cooperating with the Bureau may be wearing a concealed "body recorder" capable of taping all events and dialogue in a room for later reference. Some agents carry with them, or have tucked away somewhere, a little set of classic burglars' tools, but most could not use them in a pinch if they had to. And although more sophisticated electronic listening equipment is available all the time because of technological advances, legal trends and bureaucratic caution have generally pushed it aside in favor of old-fashioned investigative techniques. The Bureau is an inveterate clipper of newspapers, collector of photographs, and requester of transcripts; as a result its favorite reference is its own files. Agents are generally anything but surreptitious as they go about their rounds.

Ironically, it was during the early days of Hoover's directorship, when the reputation of the Bureau was gaining dramatically, that many successes were scored through the use of tactics that are widely feared and suspected today, yet are for the most part being abandoned. In the 1920s and 1930s, when the technology of wiretapping was at a relatively primitive stage and the risks of detection high, it was used promiscuously by many FBI men. In the words of one retired agent who entered the FBI ranks during the early 1930s, "When we were doing investigations under the White Slave Traffic Act, there was one dependable way to find out information about call girls — by wiretapping. And we didn't hesitate a bit." According to this man, both field supervisors and officials back at Bureau headquarters were fully aware of the electronic surveillance — which also came to include the placement of hidden microphones, or "bugs" — but probably kept the knowledge away from the Director, whose official position at the time was that he strictly opposed such tactics.

As Don Whitehead puts it in *The FBI Story*, "Hoover regarded wiretapping as a lazy man's way of obtaining information and he believed that its uncontrolled use was a handicap in the 'development of ethical, scientific and sound investigative technique.'" Whitehead insists that even though Justice Department regulations were changed in 1931 to permit wiretapping whenever it was specifically authorized by the FBI director, Hoover did not exercise that authority until the next year, when the Bureau became concerned about the national wave of kidnappings, and even then he did so reluctantly. Seven years later, in 1939, the Supreme Court in effect banned the new investigative tool by declaring that evidence obtained through wiretaps was not admissible in federal court. But a novel theory was developed, in reaction to the court decision, that the illegality of a wiretap came not from the actual interception, but only from any disclosure of the information that was picked up during the interception. Attorney General Robert Jackson took this position after President Roosevelt sent him a memorandum on May 21, 1940, as war approached, in which the President expressed his confidence "that the Supreme Court never intended any dictum in [the 1939 case] to apply to grave matters affecting the defense of this nation." The President continued:

You are therefore authorized and directed in such cases as you may approve, after investigation of the need in each case, to authorize the necessary investigating agents that they are at liberty to secure the information by listening devices directed to the conversation or other communications of persons suspected of subversive activity against the Government of the United States, including suspected spies. You are requested furthermore to limit these investigations so conducted to a minimum and to limit them in so far as possible to aliens.

Hoover's "liberty" under that directive was very broad indeed, and the Director, somehow converted on the issue, now took ample advantage of it. In theory, the telephone interceptions were to be used only to collect intelligence information and not, as prohibited by the Supreme Court, to gather evidence for use in court. The line between the two can be a fine one, and sometimes the Bureau was caught stepping over, under, and around it.

Every attorney general from Jackson on through Nicholas deB. Katzenbach, who served in the mid-1960s, asked Congress to pass legislation that would formalize the wiretapping authority — "The existing situation," complained Robert Kennedy as attorney general, "is chaotic" — but each one failed. Each attorney general then went ahead anyway and approved the FBI's conduct of the telephone intercepts on the basis of the Roosevelt memorandum.* The presidential authorization was not exactly secret, but neither was it public; at best, it was unclear and needed to be updated.

Bugging, or the use of concealed microphones, was also favored by the Bureau as a means of gathering information; it had all the advantages of wiretapping with few of the disadvantages (since it did not necessarily use telephone lines) — such as early court decisions restricting its use and federal regulation of interstate communications networks. Some argued that bugging was a far more productive means

---

* There was some irony in the fact that the first attorney general to get explicit congressional endorsement of wiretapping, Ramsey Clark, was the first one who didn't seek it.

444

of gathering information than wiretapping, because people were more likely to talk freely in what they thought was a private conversation than on a telephone line. The Director insisted upon approving each individual installation of a microphone, but the attorney general usually was not cut in on this confidential FBI technique. Instead, the Bureau encouraged an aura of wonderment and mystery about how it managed to learn so many intimate details about some of the people it had under investigation. On the rare occasions when he was challenged on the subject, Hoover invariably referred to the Roosevelt memorandum on wiretapping. Later, he would draw a distinction between the two techniques and cite a confidential memorandum he had received from Attorney General Herbert Brownell on May 20, 1954, also in the aftermath of a court decision — this one invalidating the use of microphone surveillance by city police in a gambling case. Brownell found the case distinguishable from most of the circumstances that confronted the Bureau and he outlined a permissive standard for Hoover:

It is clear that in some instances the use of microphone surveillance is the only possible way of uncovering the activities of espionage agents, possible saboteurs, and subversive persons. In such instances I am of the opinion that the national interest requires [that] microphone surveillance be utilized by the Federal Bureau of Investigation. This use need not be limited to the development of evidence for prosecution. The FBI has an intelligence function in connection with internal security matters equally as important as the duty of developing evidence for presentation to the courts and the national security requires that the FBI be able to use microphone surveillance for the proper discharge of both of such functions. The Department of Justice approves the use of microphone surveillance by the FBI under these circumstances and for these purposes.

. . . [The Supreme Court's] action is a clear indication of the need for discretion and intelligent restraint in the use of microphones by the FBI in all cases, including internal security matters. Obviously, the installation of a microphone in a bedroom or some comparably intimate location should be avoided wherever possible. . . .

. . . It is realized that not infrequently the question of trespass arises in connection with the installation of a microphone. . . . The Department in resolving the problems which may arise in connection with the use of microphone surveillance will review the circumstances of each case in the light of the practical necessities of investigation and of the national interest which must be protected. It is my opinion that the Department should adopt that interpretation which will permit microphone coverage by the FBI in a manner most conducive to our national interest. I recognize that for the FBI to fulfill its important intelligence function, considerations of national security and the national safety are paramount, and therefore, may compel the unrestricted use of the technique in the national interest.

In the FBI's hands, the "national interest" encompassed a great deal, and after the Brownell memorandum the Bureau continued to do essentially what it had done before — even more so when it began earnestly to pursue organized crime investigations and to eavesdrop on such people as Martin Luther King. But now it claimed to have durable authority, which was cited time and again whenever questions were raised within the Justice Department about the FBI's bugging practices.

The new orders issued by President Johnson on June 30, 1965, in a memorandum to the heads of executive departments and agencies, involved a more restrictive definition of "national security" and resulted in the disconnection of many of the Bureau's microphones. Wiretapping had by then become a matter of growing public controversy, and Johnson also declared himself "strongly opposed to the interception of telephone conversations as a general investigative technique." The wiretap was still widely used, however, for "investigations related to the national security," although Johnson's last attorney general, Ramsey Clark, has testified that he devised a strict standard for evaluating Bureau requests to wiretap and bug. Clark says he cut the number of security-related electronic surveillances from one hundred and seven in November 1966 to forty-three in the last days of 1968. He declined to use the new procedure for court-authorized wiretapping contained in the Omnibus Crime Control and Safe Streets Act of 1968 and, by his own account, he rejected FBI requests to tap Israeli Foreign Minister Abba Eban, the Organization of Arab Students in the United States, and the Tanzanian Mission to the United Nations, among others, including a number of domestic protest organizations and black leaders. Even while attorney general, in 1967, Clark testified that "nothing so mocks privacy as the wiretap and electronic surveillance. They are incompatible with a free society and justified only when that society must protect itself from those who seek to destroy it." Later, in 1974, Clark told a Senate hearing that as attorney general he had "doubted [the] real value" of wiretapping, even for national security purposes; he called upon Congress to "evaluate the information obtained" from wiretaps and to "decide the practice is not worth the price we pay in public morality."

Between those two congressional appearances by Ramsey Clark, however, wiretapping experienced a major, albeit brief, revival as one of the FBI's major investigative techniques. When President Nixon's first attorney general, John N. Mitchell, arrived at the Justice Department in 1969, the Bureau was set loose to wiretap more extensively in the name of defending the "national security." With the justification provided by William H. Rehnquist, the assistant attorney general for the Justice Department's Office of Legal Counsel, the Nixon administration claimed an "inherent right" under the Constitution to gather information by this means in order to protect the country. Taps and, in some instances, microphones were used widely to gather intelligence on radical organizations and other groups under investigation by the Bureau, especially during the panic over demonstrations against American involvement in the Vietnam war. But by 1972 the Supreme Court on which Rehnquist was then sitting (but not participating in the case) rejected the Nixon-Mitchell position and said that government agencies could not wiretap without court approval on "national security" grounds. The immediate effect was to force the Bureau to disconnect only four taps, but a number of others were switched over to justification under the rubric of investigating matters related to "foreign intelligence" rather than domestic activity. Under that decision and subsequent Supreme Court cases, wiretaps with a foreign connection were considered implicitly legal without court approval.

Although a limited number of "warrantless" telephone interceptions and electronic eavesdrops were still permitted — the Bureau's latest figures show that in April 1975 it had a maximum of eighty-two such wiretaps and sixteen microphones without court order in operation, all purportedly connected with investigations of foreign intelligence — the sequence of legal and bureaucratic events meant that the FBI had to give up some of its silent and impersonal information- and intelligence-gathering, and other pending cases and legislation could bring further restrictions. If the Bureau is to be believed on this score, it has all but abandoned the surreptitious methods in favor of more open and direct ones.

That does not mean, of course, that electronic devices are rarely used. "Consensual monitoring," or the monitoring of a conversation with the consent of one of the participants in it, is not only accepted, but even encouraged and expected, on the part of the FBI and other federal investigative agencies. In the typical case, one party to a personal face-to-face conversation is either cooperating with the government or is a government agent himself, and he is carrying a concealed recording device. The federal courts have placed few restrictions on the practice, but it has been formally supervised and controlled administratively by the Justice Department since 1965. Ordinarily, the head of a federal department or agency is expected to obtain advance

447

approval from the assistant attorney general for the Justice Department's Criminal Division before using any mechanical device to overhear, transmit, or record private conversations without the consent of everyone participating. Records compiled by the Justice Department indicate, however, that approaches from agencies are seldom turned down. Between the start of 1969 and mid-1974, 3,664 requests were granted and only 13 denied. (The figures include other agencies as well as the FBI, but it is safe to assume that a majority comes from the Bureau.) The rules do not extend to telephone conversations, which can be monitored with the permission of one party merely on the initiative of an agency head. Nor do they cover emergency situations, defined as occasions when there is a possibility of "imminent loss of essential evidence or a threat to the immediate safety of an agent or an informant"; in those circumstances, the head of an agency may act on his own authority but must later report the event to the Justice Department anyway* — hardly a serious form of "control." According to the Justice Department statistics for the period from 1969 through mid-1974, 1,945 instances of such emergency monitoring were reported. Doubtless there were many other unreported instances.

It was the unreported and undocumented electronic surveillance that began to cause the most concern in the early 1970s. There was a growing body of evidence that big-city police departments, with the avid cooperation of telephone company officials (many of them former FBI agents) and the tacit endorsement — indeed, the encouragement — of the Bureau, were indiscriminately wiretapping the subjects of both criminal and security investigations. The information obtained, in many instances, was passed along to various interested federal agencies, including the FBI, which would simply indicate in the records that it came from a "police source" or a "concealed source." Two cases received particular attention, in Richmond and Houston; in both places, the local FBI field office knew about police wiretapping that violated federal law, but failed to confiscate the listening devices or to initiate or follow through on interception-of-communications (IOC) investigations. Anthony J. P. Farris, the former United States attorney for the Southern District of Texas, testified before the House Select Committee on Intelligence that he tried repeatedly, but in vain, to persuade successive SACs of the Houston Field Office to probe vigorously the out-of-channels FBI–police–phone company arrange-

---

* Hoover refused to delegate his discretion to any subordinate, even on nights and weekends, and so during his last years it became virtually impossible for FBI agents to obtain emergency permission for body recorders and other "consensual monitoring" except before 4:45 P.M. on weekdays.

ment. According to Anthony V. Zavala, a former narcotics officer with the Houston police who was himself convicted on wiretapping and narcotics charges, there were perhaps a thousand illegal taps conducted by the department's narcotics division alone between 1968 and 1972, with the results often shared widely. But a similar situation has existed in other major cities, including Baltimore, Chicago, and Washington, for years.

One young agent says that he and most of his colleagues would find it "extremely difficult" to launch an IOC investigation against a police department with whom they had worked closely. "Our living depends in a lot of cities on police cooperation," he explains, "because they simply have more guys on the street. They can really hurt us if they don't want to help." Usually, he insists, agents are quite capable of telling when the original source of information they obtain from the police is an electronic surveillance: "When they tell you that [a subject] is going to be someplace at eight o'clock tonight . . . after they tell you that kind of thing ten or fifteen times . . . you realize there's only one way they could know." But most agents will avoid rocking the boat, and will bend over backward to avoid having "guilty knowledge" of an illegal source. Thus, the illegal wiretapping at the local level continues, in part because the only people with a mandate to investigate it are instead sharing in its fruits.

Because the internal FBI and Justice Department procedures for obtaining approval of a Title III legal wiretap are so complex, some agents, before they actually go ahead with one, may make an illegal, unauthorized interception on the line first — to be certain that the people under investigation are still using the same phone.

Another variety of unofficial, unspoken interception of communications by the Bureau that went on for decades involved the routine pickup by agents of copies of all international cable traffic transmitted from Washington on the channels of Western Union, RCA, ITT, and the like; the cables were perused for any material of security interest to the FBI and other intelligence agencies. The practice was suspended in 1975, however — less out of any feeling that it was improper than out of confidence that the same information could now be obtained more efficiently by electronic means by the National Security Agency (which also monitors, records, and stores for future retrieval all international telephone calls to and from the United States, as well as some domestic ones).

FBI reports and other documents are often sprinkled with phrases that seem to indicate exotic sources of information — such as a "confi-

449

dential source who has provided reliable information in the past" or mysterious combinations of letters and numbers, symbols that mean nothing to an outsider. Often the actual sources represented by the codes are delicate, perhaps a public official, bank officer, or newsman who does not want to be identified on the record. On some occasions, the source is the transcript of a wiretap or other recording. But there have also been many times when the Bureau used the symbols to make an investigation look more sophisticated and complicated than it really was; when a prosecutor or administrator outside the FBI had a rare opportunity to examine the underlying documentation and explanation of symbols, he might find that some of the "sources" were credit reports, published journals, and other fairly commonplace items. Thus the codes are used to prevent the investigating agents from being embarrassed about how predictably they went about their work.

Increasingly, however, FBI information has been "live," provided by individuals who, for one reason or another, have decided to cooperate with the Bureau. They are known by the FBI as "informants,"* and because of the Bureau's traditional reluctance to assign its own agents to work undercover, they have played a very important role indeed. Some critics contend that the FBI relies heavily on informants because it wants to keep its agents' hands clean, both literally and figuratively; but Bureau officials insist that it is just that their way is far more efficient and productive. As the importance of informants has grown in recent years, with other methods of investigation closed off, the confidential funds in the Bureau budget that are designated to pay sources have grown substantially larger, into the millions. Some people have found that it is almost possible to make a living largely on the basis of "working" for the FBI. Only a few provide their services without cost to the Bureau.

Every new agent, whatever his particular assignment, is impressed from the start by his supervisors with the need and requirement to develop dependable informants. Some agents feel extreme pressure in this area and find that the recruitment of their own sources comes only with difficulty. Many have been known to fudge in their reports, making a standard resource such as newspaper files look like a live and exclusive one. But most agents find that with ingenuity they are able to come up with a few people, not yet discovered by anyone else in the

---

* The more common usage is to call such a person an "informer"; the word "informant" usually designates someone who provides material to scholars, such as anthropologists studying a culture. But the Bureau, like some other police organizations, prefers the term "informant," perhaps because of the derogatory connotations of "informer." Invariably, if the person testifies in court, the prosecution will call him an "informant" and the defense, an "informer."

Bureau, who, for patriotic or other motives, are willing to provide information to the FBI from time to time. One agent in a midwestern field office told of dressing up in particularly "mod" clothes on Friday night every six weeks or so and prowling around the city's cheap nightclub district, "just to see what's happening." Some of the best sources, especially for his assignment to a fugitive squad, turned out to be people hanging around in bars, including the bartenders, who have always learned a great deal from the snatches of conversation that regularly take place in front of them. The best informants are often people who are themselves involved in, or on the periphery of, criminal activity — and inclined to talk, even boast, about it.

Some people fall almost unwittingly into the role of informant after getting to know an agent in a casual, social way; he may ask them questions often, and they may find it difficult not to respond. But most good informants have to be fairly skillfully cultivated, and agents have become experts at exploiting the flaws and weaknesses in a person's character in order to persuade him or her to become a friend and helper of the FBI. Perhaps the most common stimulus to become an informant, says a veteran resident agent with a particular talent in this area, is that "they think they owe you a favor. . . . You know about something they have done, but they are not getting prosecuted. . . . As likely as not, the U.S. attorney has declined prosecution, but they don't realize this and you don't have to tell them. You let them believe that you have taken care of it for them." A minority of informants seem to be motivated primarily by the desire to make a great deal of money; they are best, says the agent, in situations that are low risks for them, such as "turning" (identifying) fugitives after seeing their photographs; they will probably balk at requests that they help the Bureau recover stolen property, or take part in any other situation in which others might have to be drawn in. There are also many informants among fences, the people who dispose of stolen goods, because, according to the agent, "they like to cut down on the competition by exposing their rivals." And one of the most common motives for an informant is apparently the desire to seek revenge against someone he feels has wronged him. Some informants have provided so much useful material to the Bureau that they have been employed to help the FBI solve cases in several different cities. The Bureau pays for them to travel wherever they have good contacts in the underworld.

Generally, informants' pay is meant to be commensurate with the time they spend and the success they have in breaking cases. One agent in every field office is assigned to keep track of the local informants' "productivity" and to evaluate whether they are really earning

Boys and Girls
COLOR THE PICTURE AND MEMORIZE THE RULES

FOR YOUR PROTECTION, REMEMBER TO:

- Turn down gifts from strangers
- Refuse rides offered by strangers
- Avoid dark and lonely streets
- Know your local policeman

Director, Federal Bureau of Investigation

With J. Edgar Hoover's guidance, the FBI tried to make itself essential to the lives of most Americans. It sought to set moral standards for them, it influenced them on political matters, and, as in this poster distributed to thousands of schoolchildren, it frightened and reassured them at the same time. The Bureau seemed to be saying that it would always be vigilant on behalf of the people.

what they are being paid. There is always a risk, says one field supervisor in a big-city FBI office, that an informant will "hype it up to earn more money. He may try to set us up" by exciting interest in something that turns out not to be of great concern or relevance to the Bureau. On some occasions, the FBI has discovered that a person who was thought to be an exclusive informant is also working for other agencies, perhaps including the local or state police and, depending on the nature of his contacts, the Drug Enforcement Administration, the Central Intelligence Agency, or the Secret Service. That is strictly against an old Bureau policy that requires that an informant choose his loyalties and stand by them. "Our rule," said the field supervisor, "is that he works only for us, and we will take care of any dissemination to others that seems appropriate. We have to be controlling the informant, or he may be useless to us."

Whether working in the criminal or security field,* informants are usually expected to provide the Bureau with ongoing intelligence information as well as helping to solve specific pending cases. But to keep that sort of relationship going, the FBI must sometimes look in the other direction while its informants continue with what may be their own lives of crime. One well-publicized example was that of Herbert Itkin, a New York lawyer who was apparently involved in passing bribes and payoffs and other illegal activities while serving for five years as a Bureau informant. The FBI would pursue the people Itkin told about in his regular gatherings with an agent contact, but it would never bother him about his own part in the schemes, nor would it pass the information along to local authorities. As with many other informants, the Bureau's tolerance of Itkin paid off: when one of his accomplices, New York City Water Commissioner James Marcus, was ready to turn himself in and tell his story of corruption, Itkin guided him by the hand to the Bureau rather than to local prosecutors who were already investigating his activities.

Jack (not his real name) is a well-dressed, middle-aged man who, although short on education, is well spoken. He has a way of drawing people into his engaging narratives and would make a perfect companion on a long train ride; he is warm and, in his own unpolished style, gentle. Jack is also a crook. Though he prefers the term "thief," he would not dispute that characterization. He has held a real job, in a factory, for only one of the last twenty years and instead has made his living mostly by gambling. When gambling goes poorly, he steals —

* For a discussion of FBI informants in the internal security area, especially as their role evolved in the 1960s, see Chapter XX.

not so much from people as from institutions. Some years back, Jack got into a jam and, as he puts it, "made the decision to go with the Bureau." In FBI parlance, he is an "informant," but he prefers to think of himself as a "source." Whatever the title for the relationship, it has been a mutually beneficial one: he has helped the Bureau solve some sticky criminal cases, has made some money, and has stayed out of jail.*

Born into a family that once had money but lost it, Jack was exposed early on to the rougher side of life. Beginning when he was only fourteen years old, he worked in a card parlor, dealing cards and running errands, and it never occurred to him to leave that milieu. By a year later, he "had an okay" to telephone the biggest bookmaker in his home state and place bets of up to ten thousand dollars on credit. His early goal in life was to find a way "to make money without having to go to prison"; the dream that danced often in his head was to come away from a racetrack with a twenty-thousand-dollar profit from a single day's effort. He became a true professional, wise enough to teach others — learning such tricks as keeping the odds favorable on a particular horse by betting as much as possible away from the track rather than at the window (but also learning that "if you win too much from one bookie, it may become cheaper for him to have you killed than to pay off the bets").

If Jack ran short of money to place his bets or to pay his family's debts, he borrowed, usually from one of the many loansharks he knows. "I could have gone to a bank," he says, "but I usually had a car financed already and a few small loans, and a shark is quicker. . . . This is a way of life with me, and I've always done it that way. . . . You become shocked when you realize that it's not the same for everyone." A few years ago, an acquaintance helped Jack out of his mounting financial difficulties by lending him some stolen securities against which he could borrow cash. But that, of course, created a special obligation to the man, who reminded Jack often that "a dime [for a phone call] puts you outta business." Through that connection and his other ties, Jack became involved in some new and sophisticated rackets involving esoteric and elaborate frauds in connection with sporting events. When some of these endeavors failed, he began to "pyramid — borrowing all over the place" to finance new ones. Special family problems created a need for even more money. On the

---

* Through arrangements made by an intermediary, the author met with Jack at an airport in the eastern half of the country to learn about his life and work on the perimeter of the law. He spoke freely and frankly, asking only that certain details be omitted or left vague in order to protect his identity.

very day when one of his schemes seemed about to pay off, Jack was approached at a sporting event by an FBI agent who wanted to ask about his peripheral involvement in a case at the other end of the country. His potential dream world seemed to be collapsing.

Jack did not want to talk about that racketeering case, at least not before a grand jury, because he feared it could put his life in danger. "So I figured that I might as well make my best deal" — trading information about it and other matters for a promise that he would not have to testify and would not become involved in the court proceedings. He and the FBI agent with whom he opened negotiations hit it off well, and they both realized that ongoing communication between them might be a good idea. Although the Bureau did not explicitly say so, it tended to ignore Jack's private wheelings and dealings. Meanwhile, he kept his eyes and ears open for situations that might interest the FBI. Jack was hardly a power in the Mafia, but he had excellent contacts and he was sometimes offered a chance by mobsters to bid on available supplies of stolen merchandise, such as antique coins, art objects, money orders, traveler's checks, and securities, or to look for another buyer. He knew how easy it was for organized crime to corrupt someone inside a brokerage house or at the high levels of a bank, and he could help the Bureau sort out some intricate deals into which it was looking.

In some of these situations Jack was playing with fire, and he knew it. If word had gotten out that he was an informer for the FBI, he would have been in deep trouble. "I always figured it would only cost about a thousand dollars for somebody to have me killed," he says; "if I'm lucky, it would be a personal friend who did the job. At least he'd let the body be found so my family could collect on some pretty good insurance policies I have."

But when his role worked, it usually worked beautifully. If Jack arranged a "buy" of stolen securities, the buyer might somehow turn out to be a slick FBI agent working undercover who, by flashing a simple sign like the lighting of a cigarette, called in reinforcements to arrest the sellers. Sometimes, to maintain his credibility, Jack had to be arrested himself and spend some time in jail, only to be let out later and to have the charges dropped after a safe interval of time. In the process, however, he helped the Bureau make some significant recoveries. If the "score" was large enough, he would be paid by the FBI; but on some occasions there would be a direct reward from a bank or an insurance company, perhaps a fixed percentage of the value of the items recovered, and Jack learned quickly that they "pay much better than the Bureau."

455

Sometimes Jack worked faster than the FBI. He would come up with the numbers from, or a sample of, stolen securities that had not yet even been reported as missing or stolen; the Bureau's rules were so strict that it did not move to make a recovery under those circumstances, even though an informant of known reliability was confirming that they were stolen. That meant that Jack either had to hold on to the stolen materials (which could be dangerous), decline the opportunity to obtain them, or just give them back to be sold elsewhere. (In some instances, he says, he burned the samples rather than run the risk of being caught with them.) In his earliest days as an informant, Jack clashed with a few agents who said they were not willing to "protect" him without reservation when he showed up with stolen goods, but might turn him in for arrest if he became too demanding. (Sometimes he took a particular risk by crossing state lines with stolen securities; if the Bureau had wanted to turn against him, that would have been the perfect pretext.) This made him turn cautious and led him to insist on dealing with a few agents for whom he feels special trust. As that trust has evolved, he can now call one of those agents with the number from a security, and the agent will discreetly check whether it has been reported stolen or not without making any formal record of the inquiry. Jack swears that he has never taken advantage of that trust by cashing in a security that does not yet show up in FBI records as a "hot" rather than a "good" one. (But he has been tempted.)

"To be honest with you, I don't believe in violence," Jack said. "I'm not against stealing, but I'm against using a gun to do it." As a result, he developed his own "beat," a nonviolent if common way to steal from banks. Using false identification papers, he opened bank accounts in two cities that are in different Federal Reserve districts, so that checks written on one and deposited in the other took at least a week to clear; sometimes he made fraudulent deposits, using stolen checks from a distant city or counterfeit ones based on nonexistent bank accounts. Then he cashed in quickly — writing large checks on the phony balances, or buying a large gift certificate at a department store and after using it for a small amount of merchandise taking the balance of its value in cash. He could usually stay ahead of most bookkeeping systems. Once Jack had the money he needed to get along on for a while, the mythical persons who opened the bank accounts dropped out of sight. As for the effect of such schemes, Jack says, "Mostly it doesn't matter. You're not hurting anybody. . . . Maybe you're hurting an institution by taking some money out, but that's it." Never having been convicted of a crime, Jack's rule-of-thumb was "never to do anything so serious that I couldn't get probation the first time." But his bank tricks became sloppy, and sure enough, he was caught short one day. He was convicted and did get sentenced to probation. That sentence, and the fact that the FBI was watching him more closely, convinced him that he should be more careful, that he should not get involved with anything too risky. Even so, Jack had frequent opportunities, such as a request to help fence the proceeds of a diamond robbery in a city where he had good contacts in the business world. He acknowledged that he couldn't help handling a few "small scores" from time to time — "some checks, gold coins and watches." But for the most part he determined to "play the other side," to try to help solve cases for a while rather than become involved as the subject of them.

Jack says he is unsure himself sometimes why he got involved informing for the Bureau. He insists that he does not feel he is "playing Robin Hood. . . . I don't think I'm doing any great service." His initial motivation, it seems clear, was one that the FBI counts on in many of the thieves it approaches: to stay out of jail. When Jack needed money quickly to take care of some family hardships, the option of informing influenced him, although, he says, "there isn't that much in it," because his arrangement with the Bureau involves payment only when the information he provides leads directly to a recovery or arrest. Another motive, after he participated in a number of "sitdowns that were just like in the movies" and frightened him, was his feeling that "there are some people who really should be locked up so they can't hurt others. . . . They are creeps, crumbs . . . they kill people. They should be off the street." But there is also a trace of patriotism about his decision: "It's funny, but I'm sort of a believer in the FBI . . . and I like this country, I think it's the best country."

That belief in the Bureau has been severely tested, however, and Jack admits to mixed feelings toward the organization that has become his patron. The FBI, he insists, loses out because it tends to follow strict guidelines rather than adjusting to varying circumstances. "They have to have everything concrete, they can't stay flexible," he says; "they say, 'We want you to work for us, but you can't do this, you can't do that, and you're not getting paid unless you do something else.' . . . They talk and talk and talk, and meanwhile people are out on the street stealing." Jack is convinced that the Bureau hasn't made a meaningful commitment to fight the Mafia: "They don't really go at it. They're not aware of what's going on and who's running what. They don't put people in the middle the way they should." On occasion Jack has had one of his agent contacts search in the FBI indices for names — the names of people he knew to be mobsters — only to find that they weren't listed at all. And he insists that he has known personally of organized crime payoffs to judges and prosecutors. What is needed, he feels, is for the Bureau to pursue the Mafia "like it used to go after the Communist party." His own unsolicited advice is that the Bureau should let many more agents work undercover in order to accomplish this.

But the FBI's traditional commitment to war against the American communists and leftist groups fits right in with Jack's own personal political philosophy. He was a staunch supporter of President Nixon, especially because of his foreign policy. ("If I was Nixon, I would never have let anyone know about those tapes. He should have paid someone off to take the blame for Watergate right at the start.") If one reason for the Bureau's inadequacies in fighting organized crime is that it feels internal security comes first, that is perfectly understandable to Jack. After all, he says, "the Mafia's not gonna overthrow the government. All they're doing is making money."

For all his complaints, he has enough confidence in the FBI to believe that "if they really tried, they could probably put organized crime out of business in five years. They are smarter than the Mafia. . . . Whenever they want to take the wraps off of something, they can get the job done." He identifies sufficiently with the Bureau to have taken a position (against) on the appointment of L. Patrick Gray III as its acting director in 1972. But he feels strongly that he would never be able to work full-time or on a retainer arrangement with the Bureau. "If I were to do that, I would have to be able to move in a certain way," Jack says; "I would have to be able to pick up people's dinner checks and things like that. . . . I think it would frustrate the Bureau, because they wouldn't know how to evaluate the product of each dinner. . . . Besides, I spend more money than I should already. I'm not sure they would permit me to maintain the same standard. And the Bureau might abuse the privilege of using me."

Jack has dreams of making a fast buck that would enable him to give up both parts of his dual personality as thief and informant. "If I won thirty or forty thousand dollars tomorrow," he says, "I would move out of the mainstream, I would not stay around these same people." In the meantime, his exposure to things from the other side of the law, the FBI's side, has added a trace of moral outrage to his repertoire of bravado: "One of the great mysteries to me is why so many people steal, when they make such good money" in their legitimate jobs.

The Near Collapse and
the Great Crisis

XX

J. Edgar Hoover's Decline
and Refusal to Fall

*It's a question of failing to adjust to the times. . . . We had a revo-
lution in values in this country in the 1960s that would bring most
countries to their heels. There was a questioning of institutions,
religious, governmental and all others. Why, it was a cultural
revolution of sorts. . . . I think we have to admit now that some
people in the Bureau went overboard and failed to take account of
this. After all, Mr. Hoover's interests lay in that area. . . . This
may be true of the government in general, but the Bureau has
always been slow to adapt to change.*
> — *The supervisor of a "security" squad in a major
> FBI field office, discussing the Bureau's role
> in the 1960s during an interview in 1974*

IF THE ERA OF STUDENT PROTEST IN AMERICA BEGAN with the Free
Speech Movement at the University of California at Berkeley in 1964,
then that is perhaps also when the Bureau's misunderstanding and
misperception of recent history began. J. Edgar Hoover's view was
probably set in place from the moment he learned that Bettina
Aptheker, daughter of longtime American Communist party theoretician Herbert Aptheker and herself a member of the party, had been a
"leading organizer" of the Berkeley demonstrations. That meant to the
Director that the protests were communist-inspired and -dominated,
and inasmuch as later campus uprisings were heirs to the events at
Berkeley, so subversive motivation and influence were assumed to extend to them. This was a position taken by the Bureau less out of
malice than out of ignorance — the product of hasty conclusions and
prejudiced assumptions — and faithfully repeated and propagated by

461

the dogged lieutenants at FBI headquarters who sought to please their boss. Most of them had not been on a college campus in years and had made no real effort to understand the forces at work in the growing discontent, but they purported to know exactly what was happening there and, more importantly, why.

As Hoover put it in his testimony before the National Commission on the Causes and Prevention of Violence, chaired by Milton S. Eisenhower, in September 1968, "Communists are in the forefront of civil rights, antiwar, and student demonstrations, many of which ultimately become disorderly and erupt into violence." The commission itself recognized that attitude as simplistic, but stressed that the point of view, coming from that source, would have to be reckoned with: "Mr. Hoover's statement is significant not only because he is our nation's highest and most renowned law enforcement official, but also because his views are reflected and disseminated throughout the nation — by publicity in the local media and by FBI seminars, briefings, and training for local policemen." Circulation of that attitude, the commission added, encouraged police to "view students, the antiwar protesters, and blacks as a danger to our political system"; and the circumstances had special significance for blacks because "racial prejudice pervades the police attitudes and actions."

The FBI's shocked reaction to the counterculture of the 1960s was hardly surprising. But Bureau men were not just scandalized Middle Americans feeling that their values were being insulted and threatened by such aspects of "movement" life-style as drugs, communal living, and abundant hair. They were the nation's elite law enforcement force; their very work was, in a real sense, the maintenance of a national law and order. For the typical FBI man, a personal sense of disgust fed professional concern; the result was too often absurd overstatement of the dangers posed by new organizations and individual activists. And polarization. And, with the growth of the groups and escalation of their protests, some of them openly violent, a Bureau that became ever more frightened and confused until it saw itself as a bulwark against the lawlessness and disintegration of the American way of life. The FBI felt it had a mission to set things right again, and if that meant its own escalation of tactics and some desperate measures in the name of the law, so be it.

At the center of the crisis was the war in Vietnam, a military involvement quite unlike any other in American history for the extent to which it was despised and distrusted among the generation and the class that was expected to fight it. But to the Bureau, run by men many of whom were veterans of World War II or Korea, wartime was purely and simply wartime, and there was no further understanding to be done. According to the code of patriotism and good citizenship decreed by Hoover and rarely questioned by his associates, one did not go about weakening the home front by questioning the government's policy while it was engaged in an actual battle overseas. Few people in the FBI examined in any detail the issues that were being raised by the protesters. (One exception, ironically, was Assistant Director William C. Sullivan, who would chart some of the Bureau's toughest reactions. Sullivan studied, and tried to refute, the arguments.) One thing was certain: there were communists on the other side, and that counted a great deal; if one opposed fighting them, perhaps one was being influenced by them. An influx into Bureau ranks of young veterans of the early stages of the Vietnam war, back when it was still easy to support it, only served to reinforce attitudes within the FBI — "Why should some dirty, draft-dodging, left-wing kid, probably a queer to boot, get away with making all this trouble, when these other guys have done their duty for their country?" The belief developed that the protesters were, among other things, simply bad Americans.

Meanwhile, the civil rights movement became the Black Power movement and took to the streets of the big cities of the North. The Bureau saw itself confronted by yet another grave challenge. Tolerance of one form of violence had led, and would obviously continue to lead, to other forms, as the FBI interpreted it all, and something had to be done. The police were under verbal and physical assault and the Bureau, which saw itself as the leader of the nation's police forces, tried to help formulate an appropriate response. Efforts like the Community Relations Service, launched under the terms of the Civil Rights Act of 1964 as a peaceful means of resolving interracial crises, faded into the background in favor of more conventional methods of reaction. As the violence commission headed by Milton Eisenhower noted, the nation's police were emerging as an "independent political power" that "rivals even duly elected officials in influence." Studying the police forces of five major cities, the commission found them to be "coming to see themselves as the political force by which radicalism, student demonstrations, and black power can be blocked." Policemen were becoming "increasingly frustrated, alienated, and angry" and their "response to mass protest has resulted in steady escalation of conflict, hostility and violence." The mounting toll of police officers killed on duty served to magnify the crisis. The FBI, rather than acting as a calming influence, was ready to join the police on a crusade that had a growing ideological twist to it.

Conveniently for Hoover, who liked to be able to get an easy handle on things, the various new objects of FBI concern came in neat packages. The "black extremists," for example, besides individuals with ominous-sounding names like Stokely Carmichael and H. "Rap" Brown, included the growing and ever more noticeable Black Panther party. Talking a revolutionary line, openly espousing violent methods, and stockpiling guns, the Panthers stirred fear across the country, among black people as well as white. Their ability to recruit donations and moral support from the liberal intelligentsia was fuel on old fires for J. Edgar Hoover.

As early as 1967 Hoover began complaining about the Black Power movement and the fact that it was "tailor-made" for alleged communist efforts to stir up unrest in the United States. He berated its supporters as foolish. But it was only in mid-1968 that the Bureau began paying close attention to the Panthers, its interest stirred in part by widely circulated newspaper reports that the group had specifically rejected moderate, conciliatory tactics and was arming for "protection" of black communities from the police. Almost as if to fulfill Hoover's prophecy, the Panthers' rhetoric began to include Marxist denunciations of capitalism and invocations of the need for a class struggle. The Panthers' membership figures were a secret, but groups calling themselves by that name seemed to be cropping up in almost every major city in the country.

The Director went on one of his old-fashioned offensives, pouring enormous resources into investigating the Panthers and calling them every name in the book. They were the "most dangerous and violence-prone of all extremist groups"; they stirred "intense hatred of and vindictive hysteria against local police"; they were a band of "hoodlum-type revolutionaries." Hoover suggested that Arab guerrillas were "heavily subsidizing" and perhaps training the Panthers, and he warned that members of the group might try to "ape Arab tactics" by hijacking airplanes in an effort to obtain the release of others from prison. Whenever a policeman was killed and no one else was clearly to blame, the death was considered another notch in the Panthers' gunbelt.* Every field office that had a Panther contingent within investigative range put a special squad on the job, and alarming reports poured in to Hoover's office until he went so far as to say that the Black Panthers were "the greatest threat to the internal security of the country." "Now I admit that was probably going too far," says one agent who was at headquarters supervising black extremist investiga-

---

* On the other side, there would also be exaggerated claims of the number of Black Panthers allegedly killed, or "assassinated," by the police, as pointed out by Edward Jay Epstein in *The New Yorker.*

tions in the late 1960s, "but when you read that stuff every day it's very reinforcing. . . . I can see how, reading the reports he was getting, he could say something like that."

When John Mitchell became attorney general in 1969, he acceded to the Director's request that the Panthers be classified as a threat to "national security," which under the Nixon administration's doctrine made the group eligible for extensive wiretapping and other electronic surveillance without court approval. The Justice Department also found a pretext for convening a federal grand jury in San Francisco to investigate the Panthers after one of the party's leaders, David Hilliard, allegedly threatened President Nixon's life during an antiwar demonstration there in November 1969. That grand jury created a major freedom of the press controversy when it subpoenaed Earl Caldwell, a *New York Times* correspondent who had done much of the original and exclusive reporting about the Panthers, to testify and to surrender for inspection any notes and tapes from his interviewing sessions with Panther members and staff. (Caldwell eventually lost the fight when the Supreme Court ruled against his challenge to the subpoena in 1972, but by then the grand jury investigation had been abandoned. Officials from the Justice Department and the FBI had meanwhile privately spread the rumor that the reporter was himself a member of the Panthers.) Members of the organization, perceived as "cop-killers," fomenters of a new urban revolution, and heirs to the street gangsters the FBI had fought decades earlier, were put in a squeeze by federal officials, and local law enforcement officers were encouraged to do the same.

There were shootouts between Panthers and local police in several major cities, but the most dramatic and widely publicized incident occurred in Chicago on December 4, 1969, when city policemen assigned to the office of State's Attorney Edward V. Hanrahan conducted a predawn raid on a house occupied by the Panthers on the city's West Side, supposedly looking for a cache of weapons. Killed during the raid, under circumstances that have never been fully clarified, were two prominent members of the party, Fred Hampton, Panther chairman for Illinois, and Mark Clark, a member of the Peoria chapter. The claims of Hanrahan and the policemen that the raiding party fired shots into the apartment only after some had been fired out seemed to be contradicted by the physical evidence found at the scene and the fact that Hampton was killed in his bed.

Only four years later was it learned, during proceedings on a lawsuit filed in federal court by Hampton's family, that the man serving at the time of the raid as Hampton's bodyguard and chief of security for the Chicago Panthers, William M. O'Neal, Jr., had also been an FBI informant who provided information crucial to the raid, including a map of the apartment. According to a sworn deposition given by O'Neal's agent contact, Roy M. Mitchell, the Bureau originally gave the floor plan of the apartment to members of the Gang Intelligence Unit of the Chicago Police Department who were planning a raid, but when that unit backed down, the FBI passed it on to State's Attorney Hanrahan's office. It is fair to say that the FBI was shopping around for a law enforcement unit that was willing to conduct a raid that it, the Bureau, wanted to see carried out, but had no legal pretext for staging on its own. After the raid, agents installed a "national security" wiretap on the telephones used by its survivors to talk with their lawyers. In the trial of another case in which O'Neal figured, there was testimony that O'Neal boasted to others that he had drugged Hampton and Clark before the December 4 raid. And other reports, including one in *New Times* magazine, had it that federal authorities, the state's attorney, and Chicago police may have believed, mistakenly, that Hampton and Clark were responsible for killing a Chicago policeman a week before the raid. Taken together, the indications were that the Bureau might have tacitly encouraged the unprovoked killing of two Black Panthers at a time when there was no legal way of pursuing them otherwise.

Initially the FBI seemed to approach the New Left with some degree of moderation, but as the Director saw that he was on to an issue that was stirring considerable emotion in the country, he embarked on a veritable crusade against the groups. The buildup was gradual, but very noticeable outside the Bureau. Once an organization or activist, such as Students for a Democratic Society (SDS) and its leaders, had been put into the category of a threat, they were pursued with a vengeance almost unknown in FBI annals. Their phones were tapped, their associations and philosophies traced, their meetings infiltrated, their every movement watched in the hope that some basis could be found for charging them with a local or federal crime. The manpower assigned to such domestic intelligence and surveillance responsibilities was sometimes doubled, tripled, or quadrupled — even at the expense of the Bureau's responsibilities for genuine counterintelligence efforts against foreign espionage — as the FBI pursued the Director's new public enemy number one. The goal was never entirely clear: whether to establish some evidence that the demonstrations were inspired or financed from overseas, to help government officials reach some understanding of the magnitude and motivation of the protest, or to try to make them go away altogether.

But whatever the goal, the Bureau was omnipresent, watching and listening on every possible occasion. Agents even covered the 1970 Earth Day rally in Washington that launched a new militant environmental protection movement.* Particular attention was paid to the epic antiwar rallies that drew hundreds of thousands of people to the nation's capital for the "moratorium" and "mobilization" in late 1969 and the protest against the U.S. incursion into Cambodia in May 1970. When Martha Mitchell, the attorney general's wife, said that the sight of demonstrators in the streets in the fall of 1969 made her think of the Russian Revolution, it was probably not without some prompting from her good friend J. Edgar Hoover. The FBI could not see these protests as mere expressions of dissenting political views or as the frustrated outcry of people who felt the political and social system was being unresponsive, but rather interpreted them as evidence of a new subversion abroad in the land. The Nixon administration was perfectly prepared to accept that interpretation. As with the Panthers, the reports coming in to Hoover served to reinforce his own narrow, by now relatively uninformed, views, and so the orders that came back out from FBI headquarters invariably escalated the investigative response. At times there was no stopping the investigators, let alone the demonstrators.

With the FBI's customary method of confronting and interviewing people not practical under the circumstances and with wiretaps and other forms of surveillance not always available as a recourse, the Bureau came to depend heavily in this area, too, on informants and infiltrators. Much in the way that it had once sent people in to report on the American Communist party, the FBI sought to penetrate the core of the student protest movement. Some who were selected for this honor early on, and stayed for a while, were virtually tutored in politics by the Bureau; they were manufactured student activists. As one of the longtime informants, William T. Divale, who was recruited in 1965 and later played a key role in the revelation that UCLA philosophy instructor Angela Davis was a communist, wrote in his book, *I Lived Inside the Campus Revolution:*

In time, perhaps correctly, the FBI would come to list me among its "most valuable" student informers. I had filed nearly eight hundred under-

---

* The Bureau's report on Earth Day was meticulous, down to the words of the songs that were sung, the slogans on the signs, and the speeches of politicians who attended. The justification for the coverage was that members of radical groups had attended and that the environmental movement, like others, was threatened with takeover by dangerous elements.

cover FBI reports, 602 of them written or recorded transcripts, the rest verbal — in telephone contacts with Bureau agents in the half-dozen cities (New York, Chicago, Washington, Montreal, San Francisco) I had visited as a student activist and during secret once-a-week meetings with my FBI handlers in Los Angeles.

My undercover file for the Bureau ran to thousands of pages, documenting day by day, meeting to meeting and over a perspective of years, the campus' evolution from social democracy to radicalism and on to revolution. I had named names — the names of perhaps four thousand activists with whom, from one end of the nation to the other, and across international borders, I had worked or had become acquainted. My value to the Bureau lay in the increasingly active role I played within the student "revolution." I was a leader, not merely a follower. My perspective was that of an "insider" — from the top of the pyramid of dissidence rather than from its more populous base.

In many ways I was a product of the Federal Bureau of Investigation. The Bureau had "recruited" (solicited) me when I was a political virgin. At the time I had no politics of my own and little of anyone else's. It was the FBI that pointed me toward membership in the Communist Party, urged me to penetrate the W. E. B. Du Bois clubs and to infiltrate SDS (Students for a Democratic Society). It had molded me to political consciousness. Once that consciousness was fully matured, I had "turned" — "soured," the Bureau was to say. I came to see the Bureau not as the defender of "democracy," but as the keeper of the status quo — not as an instrument of orderly change, but as the handmaiden of reaction and the tool of entrenchment. My break with the FBI was inevitable.

In a sense, Divale proved a key point for the Bureau by entering the student protest movement by the route of (and also at the urging of) the Communist party. And he concluded his association with the FBI dramatically, by surfacing at a Los Angeles hearing of the Subversive Activities Control Board in 1969 to expose and denounce some of his friends as communists. The Bureau would cite people like Divale as evidence for its argument that the antiwar movement, indeed the entire New Left, was filled with and controlled by communists.

Just about the time Bill Divale was ending his association with the FBI, Thomas E. Mosher was beginning his. Mosher was a veteran of service in the southern civil rights struggles of the mid-1960s, later participated in the activities of SDS, and traveled to Cuba at a time when the United States government was still getting very upset about unauthorized trips there by groups of Americans sympathetic to Fidel Castro's regime. After moving to California and enrolling at Stanford University, as he later told the Senate Internal Security Subcommittee, Mosher "established my relationship with the FBI" and, although white, "insinuated myself into a relationship with the national office of the Black Panther Party" in Oakland. Mosher became well known in protest circles in the San Francisco Bay Area and, according to his testimony, played a role in forging links between the Panthers, SDS, and other leftist groups, including the Revolutionary Union. He described participating in target practice and training sessions with explosives at a hideaway in the Santa Cruz Mountains of northern California where violence-prone groups stored ammunition, and he gained an intimate knowledge of violent sabotage activities conducted by various organizations and individuals — all apparently while he was reporting regularly to the Bureau.

Critics of the FBI would later suggest that Mosher and other FBI informants like him, recruited during the advanced stages of the New Left's development, had become classic *agents provocateurs*, who entered the protest movements at the government's urging and helped stimulate violent incidents that could be used to justify a severe, perhaps repressive, police response. In a film prepared for the Public Broadcasting Service in 1971, journalist Paul Jacobs interviewed three men who insisted that their agent contacts had encouraged them to join in bombings and burnings, or to propose that the groups they had infiltrated commit criminal acts. As one of the men put it to Jacobs, "The FBI agent . . . told me to burn the buildings . . . so that the state troopers could have an excuse to come on campus and crush . . . the rebellion on campus." Invariably the Bureau denied any such allegations, and so long as the informants could produce no written or documentary evidence it was difficult to establish whether or not these people who were paid by law enforcement men had carried out some of the most violent acts of the protest period.*

If informing did lap over into the zone of provocation with alarming frequency, especially with the Black Panthers, student groups, and the New Left organizations, the practice may have been encouraged, if not especially authorized, by the existence of the "counterintelligence programs" (COINTELPROs) developed in the Domestic Intelligence Division at FBI headquarters. COINTELPRO–New Left put the Bureau's considerable resources to work disrupting, confusing, and unnerving the groups and individuals who had put together such an overwhelming protest movement. A field supervisor explained that one

---

* One new factor that the Bureau had to cope with was the likelihood that informants in the internal security area, from Divale to Mosher to more extreme types, would eventually "sour" and recant, often out of feelings of embarrassment and guilt. In contrast to the criminal field, there was rarely any danger to them if they surfaced; on the contrary, they could become folk heroes for seeing the error of their ways.

reason why the FBI came to think that disruption was the only viable course of action was that it had become impossible for the Bureau to conduct "a normal investigation" in a campus setting. "They had a freedom, a maneuverability, a sanctuary . . . which they would not have had out among the general population," he said; "and we did not have what we usually count upon — the cooperation and participation [in an investigation] of the local citizens. Some of the educational people were torn about what was right and what was wrong." The Bureau, believing it should try to contain violence, became frustrated, the supervisor recalled, when "we couldn't find out their next move, because they didn't know it themselves." Therefore, the FBI sometimes chose to help the organizations make their plans — through bogus communications or through informants and infiltrators who took a very active role — the better to counteract them. COINTELPRO also wreaked havoc with some people's personal lives in a manner that probably never would have been tolerated had it been publicly known at the time. Morris Starsky, for example, an associate professor of philosophy at Arizona State University between 1964 and 1970, was the organizer of antiwar teach-ins and rallies and a member of left-wing organizations. The FBI sent an anonymous letter about him to a committee of professors who were reviewing his faculty appointment, accusing Starsky of involvement in activities on a par with those of the Nazi or Soviet secret police. In what appeared to be a direct result, Starsky lost his teaching job and was unable to find another one elsewhere.

Confronted with such examples now, Bureau officials acknowledge that they were sometimes tactics of desperation. Pleading the need to understand the tenor of those troubled times, the FBI men insist that some things were justified then which, in retrospect, look shameful or, as Attorney General William Saxbe put it in 1974, "abhorrent." This is how Clarence Kelley cautiously justified the situation when official documents describing COINTELPRO were released in December 1973:

In the late 1960s, a hard-core revolutionary movement which came to be known as the "New Left" set out, in its own words, to bring the Government to its knees through the use of force and violence.

What started as New Leftist movement chanting of Marxist-Leninist slogans in the early years of their "revolution" developed into violent contempt, not only for Government and Government officials, but for every responsible American citizen.

During these years, there were over 300 arsons or attempted arsons, 14

470

destructive bombings, 9 persons killed, and almost 600 injured on our college campuses alone. In the school year 1968–69, damage on college campuses exceeded 3 million dollars and in the next year mounted to an excess of 9.5 million.

In this atmosphere of lawlessness in the cities mobs overturned vehicles, set fires, and damaged public and private property. There were threats to sabotage power plants, to disrupt transportation and communications facilities. Intelligence sources informed the FBI of plans that were discussed to poison public water supplies.

At this time of national crisis, the Government would have been derelict in its duty had it not taken measures to protect the fabric of our society. The FBI has the responsibility of investigating allegations of criminal violations and gathering intelligence regarding threats to the country's security. Because of the violent actions of the leadership of the New Left, FBI officials concluded that some additional effort must be made to neutralize and disrupt this revolutionary movement. . . .

While there is no way to measure the effect of the FBI's attempt at counter-subversion, I believe that it did have some impact on the crisis at that time.

What Kelley did not, and could not, speculate about is whether some of the violence ever would have developed if the earlier, peaceful stages of protest had been treated as legitimate dissent rather than dangerous subversion. And he did not calculate the effects of the Bureau's own failure to understand the various strains of dissidence.

Ambitious as the Bureau's efforts may have been to save the nation from ruin at the hands of students, blacks, and radicals, they were not enough for some people, most notably the Nixon White House. Top presidential aides frequently heard, and themselves made, the complaint within government circles that between restrictions on FBI tactics instituted by Attorney General Ramsey Clark in the mid-1960s and those imposed by Hoover, the Bureau was simply not performing up to expectations on its task of protecting the country's internal security. As Tom Charles Huston, "coordinator of security affairs" on the Nixon staff, put it in a memorandum to chief of staff H. R. Haldeman in July 1970,

Domestic intelligence information coming into the White House has been fragmentary and unevaluated. We have not had, for example, a community-wide estimate of what we might expect short or long-term in the cities or on the campuses or within the military establishment. . . . I believe that we will be making a major contribution to the security of the country if we can work out an arrangement which provides for institutionalized coordination within the intelligence community and effective leadership from the White House.

Huston, then twenty-nine years old and a former leader in Indiana of the arch-conservative student organization Young Americans for Freedom, had participated throughout June of that year in the meetings of "a working group consisting of the top domestic intelligence officials" of the FBI, CIA, Defense Intelligence Agency, National Security Agency, and the three military services. The agencies had been brought together by the President — but apparently at Huston's own initiative — to discuss what was perceived as a major threat to the stability of the government and how to cope with it.* Hoover could not help but notice, and nor could anyone else for that matter, that as the deliberations proceeded, there were both explicit and implicit criticisms from his colleagues in the intelligence community of how the Bureau had been doing its job, not only in the area of internal security but also in combating the threat of foreign intelligence. As eventually formulated by Huston† and approved by everyone involved but the Director, the committee's recommendations were extensive:

• Broadened coverage by the NSA "of the communications of U.S. citizens using international facilities." The action would involve "no appreciable risk," Huston said, but he noted that "it would be to our disadvantage to allow the FBI to determine what NSA should do in this area."

• A substantial increase in "electronic surveillance and penetra-

---

* The twenty-three-page "assessment of the existing internal security threat," which formed a part of the committee's report, painted a grave portrait of the danger. Huston, in a 1973 interview with a reporter for *Rolling Stone* magazine, explained how he had felt three years earlier:

> You had bombs going off everywhere in 1969 and 1970. . . . I never was worried that these guys were going to overthrow the government of the United States by force and violence. . . . Rennie Davis in his greatest heyday wasn't going to mobilize enough people to march on Washington to overthrow the government. But the way governments have historically been overthrown in the 20th Century is . . . by small groups of dedicated people postulating the revolutionary theory. Through random acts of terror and violence you generate, first of all, widespread insecurity and fear, which is then followed by demands upon the state to take . . . some kind of action to stop it. I wasn't concerned about gathering lots of evidence to prosecute on conspiracy charges and that sort of thing. I just wanted to get the thing stopped.

† The White House aide is believed to have had critical drafting assistance from William C. Sullivan, the Bureau's representative in the working group, who was assistant FBI director for the Domestic Intelligence Division when it began its deliberations and was promoted to be assistant-to-the-director before they were finished.

tions" of both "individuals and groups in the United States who pose a major threat to the internal security" and "foreign nationals and diplomatic establishments in the United States of interest to the intelligence community." Huston commented:

> Mr. Hoover's statement that the FBI would not oppose other agencies seeking approval for the operating electronic surveillances [*sic*] is gratuitous since no other agencies have the capability.
>
> Everyone knowledgeable in the field, with the exception of Mr. Hoover, concurs that existing coverage is grossly inadequate. CIA and NSA note that this is particularly true of diplomatic establishments, and we have learned at the White House that it is also true of New Left groups.

• The removal of all restrictions on "legal mail covers" (in which the post office merely notes return addresses of those corresponding with a person under investigation) and relaxation of restrictions against "covert mail covers" (in which mail is opened illegally for the purpose of investigation). "There is no valid argument against use of legal mail covers," said Huston, "except Mr. Hoover's concern that the civil liberties people may become upset. This risk is surely an acceptable one and hardly serious enough to justify denying ourselves a valuable and legal intelligence tool."*

• Lifting restrictions against "surreptitious entry," or burglary, to obtain "vitally needed foreign cryptographic material" and to "turn up information about identities, methods of operation, and other invaluable investigative information which is not otherwise obtainable" from "urgent security targets." The device would be "particularly helpful," Huston suggested, against the Weatherman faction of SDS and the Black Panthers. "The FBI, in Mr. Hoover's younger days, used to conduct such operations with great success and with no exposure," Huston pointed out; the deployment of the new Executive Protective Service to guard foreign missions in Washington might make the job a bit more difficult, he allowed, but "it is the belief of all except Mr. Hoover that the technique can still be successfully used on a selective basis."

• An expansion of the coverage of "violence-prone and student-related groups" through the active recruitment of informants on col-

---

* One FBI mail-intercept program, conducted between the 1940s and 1966 at Kennedy airport in New York, involved intercepting and opening letters going to certain European addresses considered "maildrops" for Soviet intelligence; Bureau sources say that program helped expose several important "illegals." Other mail-opening programs, carried out by the Bureau in a number of cities without the authorization of any attorney general, were suspended by Hoover in 1966 out of concern for the FBI image.

lege campuses. Noting that the Director had banned the use of campus sources under twenty-one, Huston complained that a change would be necessary "in order to forestall widespread violence." The White House aide argued:

> . . . Mr. Hoover is afraid of a young student surfacing in the press as an FBI source, although the reaction in the past to such events has been minimal. After all, everyone assumes the FBI has such sources.
>
> The campus is the battleground of the revolutionary protest movement. It is impossible to gather effective intelligence about the movement unless we have campus sources. The risk of exposure is minimal, and where exposure occurs the adverse publicity is moderate and short-lived. It is a price we must be willing to pay for effective coverage of the campus scene.

Hoover opposed all of the recommendations, and at his insistence his attitudes were prominently cited in footnotes to the report. From the very start, he had apparently attempted to sidetrack the committee's mission to be the compilation of a historical study and analysis of domestic intelligence collection. Once the actual review was under way, the Director made it clear that he did not feel anyone else was entitled to evaluate or comment upon the way the Bureau had performed its intelligence responsibilities. Hoover was, in Huston's words, "the only stumbling block" to successful completion of the assignment, and as the aide summarized the Hoover position to Haldeman: ". . . he is perfectly satisfied with current procedures and is opposed to any changes whatsoever. As you will note from the report, his objections are generally inconsistent and frivolous — most express concern about possible embarrassment to the intelligence community (i.e., Hoover) from public disclosure of clandestine operations."

But the proposal that apparently bothered the Director most was the one that would institutionalize the study panel in the form of a standing "Interagency Group on Domestic Intelligence and Internal Security," composed of representatives of the various intelligence agencies with Huston sitting in on behalf of the President. Remedying the "need for increased coordination, joint estimates and responsiveness to the White House," the group, as outlined by Huston, would "define the specific requirements of member agencies of the intelligence community"; "effect close, direct coordination between member agencies"; "provide regular evaluations of domestic intelligence"; "review policies governing operations in the field of domestic intelligence and develop recommendations"; and "prepare periodic domestic intelligence estimates which incorporate the results of the combined efforts of the intelligence community."

One reason for that recommendation was the break in diplomatic relations between the Bureau and virtually all other agencies of government, especially those that gathered intelligence. In early 1970, Hoover had become furious with the CIA over an incident involving the disappearance in 1969 of Thomas Riha, a Czech-born professor of modern Russian history at the University of Colorado and a man deeply involved in international intrigues. Riha had vanished mysteriously, but the FBI — which apparently dealt with him as an informant and knew his whereabouts — would not reassure the president of the university or the police in Denver and Boulder about the professor's well-being, lest this jeopardize its confidential sources. An agent in the Bureau's field office, however, passed on information about the man to a representative of the CIA in Denver, because that agency was also vitally interested in Riha (some say it employed him as a secret agent); the CIA man, in turn, briefed the university, local police officials, and the district attorney. When Hoover got wind of this breach of FBI security, he demanded that the CIA reveal which FBI agent had broken the code of obedience. But the CIA agent in Denver said he had a code of conduct too, and declined to violate the confidentiality of his own sources. The Director's overreaction, despite frantic counsel to the contrary by his subordinates, was to order that all personal liaison between Bureau employees and CIA personnel be suspended, and that contacts be conducted only by correspondence. CIA Director Richard Helms wrote a conciliatory letter to Hoover, expressing his hope that the Riha affair "not impair our mutual efforts in making certain that we have not overlooked factors possibly having a significant bearing on U.S. intelligence and internal security interests . . . it is necessary that we continue to conduct our business in an atmosphere of mutual respect." But the Director was livid. "Helms forgets it is a two-way street," he scribbled in the margin of the letter from the CIA. "This is not satisfactory. I want our Denver office to have absolutely no contacts with CIA. I want direct liaison here with CIA to be terminated & any contact with CIA in the future to be by letter only." Some Bureau agents, at their own peril, violated the rule; but appeals to Hoover — even warning that correspondence was too clumsy and slow, that there were not enough secure phone lines to transact all the necessary interagency business, and that some important espionage cases might be endangered — were denied. While others shook their heads in amazement and anger, the Director stood on principle.

To the argument that he was discriminating against the CIA in favor of other agencies with which the Bureau maintained regular personal communication, Hoover responded by eliminating the seven-man liaison section at headquarters that kept in contact with the Defense Intelligence Agency, the National Security Agency, the Office of Naval Intelligence, Army Intelligence, the Air Force Office of Special Investigations, the State Department, the U.S. Information Agency, the Post Office Department, the Department of Health, Education and Welfare, the Bureau of Customs, and even the Immigration and Naturalization Service within the Justice Department. With those government offices as well, the agents were supposed to discuss matters only in letters and phone calls. Only the White House remained favored with authorized personal FBI contact.

Now the "Huston plan," as it later came to be called, would seek not only to force the FBI back into a regular working relationship with the CIA, which Hoover had never liked or trusted anyway, but it would also interpose a new standing committee above the Bureau to supervise and coordinate its intelligence-gathering functions. It had always seemed inconvenient enough to the Director to have to bother with an attorney general and a formal Justice Department structure — and often he did not — but as far as he was concerned, this was taking things one intolerably giant step further.

Huston thought he had his brainchild all wired for acceptance and implementation. He presumed that Hoover would be pacified by his designation as chairman of the proposed "Interagency Group on Domestic Intelligence and Internal Security," the supersecret high council whose very existence would be guarded on a strict "need to know" basis. Acknowledging that it still might be difficult to get the Director to accept what amounted to a major diminution of his prerogatives, Huston advised Haldeman on strategy for Nixon to follow:

Mr. Hoover should be called in privately for a stroking session at which the President explains the decision he has made, thanks Mr. Hoover for his candid advice and past cooperation, and indicates he is counting on Edgar's cooperation in implementing the new decisions.

Following this Hoover session, the same individuals who were present at the initial session in the Oval Office [the heads of the intelligence agencies] should be invited back to meet with the President. At that time, the President should thank them for the report, announce his decisions, indicate his desires for future activity, and present each with an autographed copy of the photo of the first meeting. . . .

I hate to suggest a further imposition on the President's time, but think these steps will be necessary to pave over some of the obvious problems which may arise if the President decides, as I hope he will, to overrule Mr. Hoover's objections to many of the proposals made in this report. Having seen the President in action with Mr. Hoover, I am confident that he can handle this situation in such a way that we can get what we want without putting Edgar's nose out of joint. At the same time, we can capitalize on the goodwill the President has built up with the other principals and minimize the risk that they may feel they are being forced to take a back seat to Mr. Hoover.

. . .

I might add, in conclusion, that it is my personal opinion that Mr. Hoover will not hesitate to accede to any decision which the President makes, and the President should not, therefore, be reluctant to overrule Mr. Hoover's objections. Mr. Hoover is set in his ways and can be bull-headed as hell, but he is a loyal trooper. Twenty years ago he would never have raised the type of objection he has here, but he's getting old and worried about his legend. He makes life tough in this area, but not impossible — for he'll respond to direction by the President and that is all we need to set the domestic intelligence house in order.

But it was not twenty years earlier, and the Director was raising very powerful objections indeed. As with the situation thirty years before, when he opposed the incarceration of Japanese Americans on the West Coast, Hoover was making points that sounded as if they might be motivated by concern for civil liberties and constitutional rights, but in fact had more to do with pragmatic, bureaucratic considerations. In this instance, he was not about to agree to a system in which a committee decided which homes and embassies ought to be burglarized and then sent FBI agents in to run all the risks themselves. And it was true that Hoover was almost pathologically concerned about issues like image and embarrassment. He had spent forty-six years building the Bureau the way some people raise a child, and there were certain chances he no longer wanted to take, surely not when they were being bulldozed over him by a bunch of his rivals from other agencies, a smart-alecky theoretician from Indiana who was not even born until Hoover had been running the FBI for seventeen years, and other members of a White House staff of whom he was mistrustful.

Huston's "decision memo," in the President's name but apparently without his signature, went out in late July — the actual committee to supervise domestic intelligence operations was to come into being on August 1, with each agency to report on its implementation of the new program by September 1 — and Hoover exploded the moment he saw it. Deke DeLoach had already primed Attorney General John Mitchell on the issue before retiring from the Bureau, and Mitchell now endorsed the Director's outrage. Hoover and Mitchell apparently persuaded Haldeman within a few days to recall the memo and announce to the other agencies that the intelligence plan was dead. Part of the spoils taken by the victorious Hoover was the head and humiliation of Tom Charles Huston. At the Director's insistence, he was removed from his job as coordinator of security affairs (which were reassigned to the man just settling in as White House counsel, John W. Dean III), and before long Huston went home to join a law firm in Indianapolis.

There has been considerable debate over whether parts of the Huston plan nevertheless went into effect. It seems likely, for example, that by means of some other directive the NSA expanded its communications intelligence to include American citizens using international channels. And there is solid evidence that Hoover, in his own good time and manner and on the basis of internal FBI pressure, loosened up some of his strictures against legal mail covers and the recruitment of campus informants under twenty-one, among other tactics. The Bureau's already fervid investigative activities against the protest movement were intensified and the various COINTELPRO operations were allowed to grow more ambitious — until they were all abruptly canceled in April 1971. According to testimony given the Senate Watergate Committee on May 7, 1974, by J. Fred Buzhardt, then White House counsel to President Nixon, the FBI carried out a number of burglaries while Nixon was in office. Various left-wing groups and their lawyers have repeatedly contended, since the Watergate scandals broke open, that the Bureau or another intelligence agency must have been responsible for mysterious break-ins at their offices or homes, crimes that have never been solved by the local police.

But in the end, no new executive committee was created to coordinate and oversee the activities of the various intelligence agencies in the domestic sphere. Some years later (after Hoover had died and could not challenge him) an embattled Richard M. Nixon, caught in the midst of the Watergate scandals, claimed publicly that the Director's veto of the special 1970 domestic intelligence charter and his reluctance to expand operations were among the factors that led to the President's establishment a year later, in June 1971, of a Special Investigations Unit in the White House. That unit, commonly known as the "plumbers" for its mission to plug leaks of classified information, played a key role in events leading to the ultimate "responsiveness" of the intelligence-gathering process to the White House: the bugging of the Democratic National Committee headquarters as part of Nixon's reelection efforts.

Another important development seems to have grown out of the

478

furor over the Huston plan. One paragraph in the original confidential recommendations, as listed by Huston, the only paragraph that criticized an agency other than the FBI, reads as follows: "CIA claims there are not existing restraints on its coverage of overseas activities of U.S. nationals. However, this coverage has been grossly inadequate since 1965 and an explicit directive to increase coverage is required." Whether the directive, if any, that followed was written or oral, or whether the CIA took that paragraph as a pretext, is not clear, but the agency appears to have done its part to please a White House that wanted more domestic intelligence. The CIA had set up a Domestic Operations Division in the early 1960s, with headquarters near the White House, despite the statement in the National Security Act of 1947, which created the CIA, that "the agency shall have no police, subpoena, law enforcement powers, or internal security functions." A network of offices was established at that time in other major cities, supposedly for the purpose of CIA recruiting and for the convenience of work within the United States that is related to "foreign intelligence sources"; in reality, the offices were also used for the agency's questionable domestic work. Begun under President Kennedy, that work continued, virtually unchallenged, under President Johnson. But it was after the collapse of the special 1970 intelligence plan, when the Nixon administration still wanted more buggings, break-ins, and mail covers, that CIA Director Richard Helms apparently agreed to increase his agency's espionage on the home front — "Operation Chaos."

The exact scope of the CIA activities, which supposedly ended after the agency's complicity in the Watergate affair was revealed, may never be fully known. But it is clear that CIA operatives were in the street, infiltrating radical groups and demonstrators, perhaps pulling COINTELPRO-type stunts,* and keeping extensive files on American citizens. Reports went directly to the White House and, in effect, competed with the material being provided by the FBI. (Hoover was not supposed to know what the CIA was doing, but it is probably more than coincidence that at the same time "the agency" was getting deeper into domestic affairs, the Director, to the chagrin of the CIA, was setting out to expand the Bureau's overseas liaison offices.) Much of the CIA's effort originated at the White House and was justified by the old goal, by then Nixon's too, of establishing the elusive link of the domestic antiwar protest movement and other militant groups to for-

---

* The CIA has admitted providing technical assistance in 1971 to its former employee, E. Howard Hunt, when he led the White House "plumbers" in a burglary of the Beverly Hills, California, office of a psychoanalyst who had once treated Daniel Ellsberg, the man who disclosed the Pentagon Papers. The agency also provided the White House with a "psychological profile" of Ellsberg.

eign nations. But for a few isolated incidents and connections, it is a link that was never found. Another attempt was to identify and isolate the small subversive conspiracy of individuals who were assumed to be fomenting most of the civil disorder and campus unrest; that too proved to be an impossible mission to accomplish. The CIA, like the Bureau, was disinclined if not incapable of facing and stating the fact that the widespread protests came, in large part, from profound dissatisfaction over conditions in the United States and the policies of the government regarding Southeast Asia.

The domestic intelligence field, if uncoordinated as Tom Charles Huston and the White House complained, was also crowded. The Bureau had further competition from a vast network of surveillance activity conducted by the military, particularly the intelligence units of the army. Those efforts grew out of the call-up of troops during some of the urban riots and mass demonstrations of the mid-1960s, but for a time took hold as standard operating procedure. By 1967, scattered army commands and offices were, on their own initiative and without central direction, collecting huge quantities of information on domestic groups and individuals. As the Senate Subcommittee on Constitutional Rights later put it in a report:

> The chief subjects of the surveillance were protest groups and demonstrators whose activities the Army attempted to relate to its civil disturbance mission. Little distinction was made between peaceful and non-peaceful groups. Protests and demonstrations of a peaceful, non-violent nature, which have come to be recognized as significant parts of this country's legitimate political process, were all targets for the Army's agents. More traditional forms of political activity were similarly monitored if they involved dissident groups or individuals. . . .
> . . . What began as a limited intelligence activity by individual commands responding to the military's limited need for information for use during civil disturbances mushroomed into an elaborate, nationwide system with the potential to monitor any and all political expression. No person or organization was too insignificant to monitor; no activity or incident too irrelevant to record.

Indeed, under the laissez-faire approach that seemed to govern the army's intelligence collection, some units kept a watch on legal union activities while others monitored politicians, at one point including Senator Adlai E. Stevenson III and Representative Abner Mikva, both Democrats of Illinois.

But the Bureau knew about the military intelligence activity and apparently did not object strongly. The findings may have been unsophisticated on occasion — some reports listed a person as having a "Red background" or noted he had been "reported to be a psycho"— but they were voluminous. They sometimes filled in holes for the FBI; the army could call on the resources of many available young blacks in its ranks, for example, to infiltrate and report on some groups to which the overwhelmingly white Bureau had little access. The FBI accepted material from military intelligence and gave some in return; they generally integrated it into their respective data banks.*

Local police departments also got into the act. One man who went public in 1973 and claimed to have been an informant first for the Metropolitan Police in Washington, D.C., and later for the Bureau, said that at one time or another he had learned of surveillance on an extraordinary range of groups, including the American Civil Liberties Union; *The Advocate,* a publication of the National Law Center at George Washington University; the Catholic Peace Fellowship; Common Cause; the D.C. Statehood party; the Gay Activist Alliance; the National Organization for Reform of the Marijuana Laws; and RAP, a local Washington drug rehabilitation program.

At the same time the Justice Department, especially under Attorney General John Mitchell, increased its own capacity to accept and make use of domestic intelligence information. Mitchell's predecessor, Ramsey Clark, had established an Interdivisional Information Unit (IDIU) in 1967, primarily for the purposes of summarizing and evaluating urban demonstrations, providing early-warning "incident reports," and of attempting to monitor the activities of black militants who were thought to be inciting riots in the cities. The idea was to pool information from various sources. Under Mitchell, IDIU's name was changed to Interdivisional Intelligence Unit and its budget by the spring of 1970 was increased to $274,000. Twelve intelligence analysts evaluated the material coming in, and they eventually also took on the role of collating evidence that might be used in criminal prosecution of those who organized mass protest demonstrations against the Vietnam war. The IDIU, under the terms of an agreement between the Departments of Justice and Defense in 1969, became part of a "civil disturbance group" that came under the authority of the deputy attorney

---

* The extensive hearings into military surveillance of civilians conducted by the Senate Constitutional Rights Subcommittee under chairman Sam J. Ervin, Jr. (D-North Carolina), led to pressures for an end to the activities, considered in most quarters to be irrelevant to the military's mission. After several false starts in that direction, the Defense Department issued regulations in 1971 prohibiting future surveillance of civilians and requiring that past records of it be destroyed; but in 1975 it was revealed that many of the files had merely been shifted from one office to another.

general's office. In addition, at White House urging, Mitchell created an Intelligence Evaluation Committee, headed by a former FBI agent, a unit shrouded in secrecy, which was also expected to evaluate reports coming in from various government agencies and put them together into studies of the potential for violence on particular occasions. Nixon, in a statement in May 1973, claimed that the IEC, which had representatives sitting on it from a number of different agencies, including the National Security Agency, the Secret Service, and the army, was one of the steps taken to "help remedy" the situation created when Hoover broke off liaison with the various other governmental groups.

Apparently neither the IDIU nor the IEC* engaged in any operations of its own, but they digested and redigested the domestic intelligence information available from the FBI and others. Eventually housed in the Justice Department's Internal Security Division, the relic of the 1950s that was revivified by Mitchell and put under the command of Assistant Attorney General Robert C. Mardian, the evaluation units obviously made a contribution to the Nixon administration's crusade against radicals, which sometimes reached fanatical proportions.

With most of the burden carried by Guy Goodwin, a former county prosecutor from Wichita, Kansas, who had become chief of the Special Litigation Section in the Internal Security Division, the Justice Department also convened federal grand juries in every corner of the country — sometimes in out of the way places like Tucson — to investigate the leaders and followers of the antiwar movement. In most cases the grand juries were initially convened to look into a particular bombing or other incident, but their mandate quickly expanded into a general probe of the relationships among various organizations and individuals. Legal critics, noting that some of the panels asked witnesses questions about their sex lives and other private matters, and that they often continued to collect evidence for use at trial after an indictment had already been handed up, charged the Justice Department with an exploitation and perversion of the historic role of the grand jury system to protect the accused. In many cases, the grand juries were used to send young radicals to jail for months because they refused to testify about their friends under grants of immunity. Eventually regional United States attorneys, who generally tried to have nothing to do with Goodwin, themselves charged that the grand jury system was being abused in the crusade against dissent and disorder.

---

* It is still unclear why the Intelligence Evaluation Committee, as a nonoperational unit, had to be kept such a secret. Most ranking officials in the Justice Department did not even know of its existence.

Some leading Justice Department officials, in their own sort of unconcealed COINTELPRO-type operation, often leaked tidbits of information that had been collected by the grand juries; one took particular delight in telling newsmen that he had proof that some of the best-known antiwar leaders were "a bunch of fags."

These specially convened grand juries were, of course, the idea and the tool of the Justice Department. But most of the information they got — and many of the witnesses who testified before them and at the eventual trials on the indictments — came from the FBI. The Bureau, in fact, because of its visibility, was held responsible by the public and the press for many of the deeds of the other agencies that were involved in domestic intelligence and surveillance work. Years of self-promotion and image-building had conditioned most people to believe that whenever the FBI got involved in something, it was the first, the foremost, and the leader. Hoover, of course, did not decline the credit, because he felt that, the times being what they were, there was something to be gained from it, politically and bureaucratically. But the situation also produced some Bureau enemies — genuine, self-proclaimed enemies, for once.

The tensions and confrontations between the angry government and its persistent critics reached a crescendo in the spring of 1971. The Justice Department announced the indictment of the Reverend Philip Berrigan and other militant Catholic antiwar activists for their alleged scheme to blow up Washington and kidnap Henry Kissinger in the name of their cause, the crime of which Hoover had already proclaimed them guilty months earlier. That indictment provided a new impetus for scattered demonstrations and organizing efforts by the "movement" and it led to another in the series of expensive, embarrassing, and, from the government's point of view, unsuccessful politically oriented trials, this one in Harrisburg, Pennsylvania. The Vietnam Veterans Against the War (VVAW) came to Washington and camped on the Mall in front of the Capitol in April; they were followed by the grandiose finale of the major antiwar protests, the Mayday series, during which thousands of people were arrested for their efforts to grind the federal government to a halt, or simply for being in the wrong place during those efforts.* In June, a Vietnam war–related crisis of a different nature was unleashed when the *New York Times*, the *Washington Post*, and other newspapers published the Pentagon Papers,

---

* Federal courts would later rule that many of the Mayday demonstrators had been unlawfully denied their rights of free speech and assembly by the police deployed by the angry, frightened Nixon administration.

provided to them through the courtesy of a reformed architect of the war, Daniel Ellsberg. Eventually the VVAW and Ellsberg were also dragged into federal court for long trials in which the government was the loser.

But the watershed event for the FBI — perhaps the real beginning of a significant decline — occurred on the night of March 8, 1971. The attention of many millions of Americans was riveted that night on the heavyweight championship boxing match between Muhammed Ali and Joe Frazier. But on the protest calendar this was International Women's Day, and in the quiet Philadelphia suburb of Media, a small band of antiwar activists, perhaps three or four, celebrated the occasion stealthily and dramatically. Working according to a plan that had been drawn up well in advance, the group entered a four-story Delaware County building and easily knocked down the door of the FBI resident agency on the second floor. There was no alarm system and no lock on the filing cabinets (one report had it that the door was not even locked), so the burglars spent about half an hour in the small office suite, sorting through the papers they found; they decided to take hundreds of items with them. Early the next morning, a Philadelphia journalist received an anonymous phone call advising him that the raid in Media had been the work of a Citizens' Commission to Investigate the FBI.

Antiwar raids on draft board offices, in which records were stolen, destroyed, or defaced, had become commonplace around the country, and the FBI had become expert at investigating such cases. But for the Bureau itself to be the target was a new twist, one that caught Hoover and the Justice Department off guard. According to sources familiar with the Media break-in, the action was the work of about twenty people, most but not all of them from the Philadelphia area. On the model of modern revolutionary groups in Latin America, however, the knowledge of each participant about the others was kept as limited as possible.

Among the participants, there were three separate groups: the thieves, who actually broke into the resident agency and removed the documents; the sorters, who determined which of the papers were worth circulating; and the distributors, who duplicated them and chose the reporters and organizations they thought would be appropriate recipients. The initial operation went smoothly, except that a personal crisis caused the person who was supposed to provide storage space the first night to withdraw his offer, and new arrangements had to be made hastily. The sorting took place in New York and Boston, as well as in Philadelphia. Some documents dealing with internal FBI administrative matters were burned; others relating to foreign matters were tucked away, lest they divert attention from the raiders' major purpose, to expose the nature and degree of the FBI's domestic surveillance.

Those that remained were photocopied in random batches at various locations over a period of weeks and the copies were posted from mailboxes around the country. (In some instances, an unsuspecting friend would be given an envelope and asked to drop it in a mailbox while away on a trip.) The silence that followed the raid was broken after two weeks, on Monday, March 22, when Senator George S. McGovern of South Dakota and Congressman Parren J. Mitchell of Maryland, both Democrats who had criticized the Bureau, received packages containing copies of some of the stolen files. Both turned the copies over to the FBI. "I refuse to be associated with this illegal action by a private group," McGovern said. "Illegal actions of this nature only serve to undermine reasonable and constructive efforts to secure appropriate public review of . . . the FBI." Mitchell also declined to condone the burglary, but he said that his look at the files persuaded him that Bureau agents were guilty of illegal surveillance of private citizens and groups. But the same week — after rejecting the argument by Attorney General John Mitchell that disclosure of some of the documents "could endanger the lives or cause other serious harm to persons engaged in investigative activities on behalf of the United States" — the *Washington Post* published an article describing materials taken in the Media raid that had been sent to reporter Betty Medsger. Initially, the *Post* was cautious about quoting from the stolen material or publishing the names that appeared in the documents, but as time went on the *New York Times* and other publications also received copies and printed substantial segments of the files. (The most complete compendium eventually appeared a year later in *WIN*, a magazine published by the War Resisters League.)

The Media documents, which became the first FBI files ever read widely by the general public without authorization, gave an extraordinary picture of some of the Bureau's domestic intelligence activities. They were by no means a cross section of FBI files, nor were they necessarily representative of the materials to be found in the average FBI office. Media was in the midst of a university area where there was a great deal of antiwar and other protest activity that the Bureau was following, and there were copies of materials from elsewhere, some of them several years old. But, judged by any standard, the documents did show an almost incredible preoccupation with the activities of black organizations and leaders, both on campuses and in the cities. The efforts to keep track of leftists and peace groups sounded even more perfervid than had been widely suspected, and in one document (entitled "New Left Notes") an agent acknowledged the Bureau's desire to encourage paranoia among the people it was inclined to investigate. There was an obvious naïveté, almost comical in some of the Bureau reports, about forces and ideas foreign to the FBI, such as the Women's Liberation movement. Routine memoranda from Special-Agent-in-Charge Joe D. Jamieson of the Philadelphia Field Office revealed the FBI's efforts to maintain contact and "liaison" with virtually every bank, airline, brokerage firm, trucking company, big business, and government agency operating in the office's territory. It was clear that the telephone company, for all its usual denials, had a special relationship with the FBI and, for example, provided the Bureau with unlisted numbers. The Bureau was revealed to have tried to infiltrate a conference of War Resisters International, among others. Through established sources like switchboard operators and clerks, it was keeping track of college professors it regarded suspiciously. Some documents indicated that the FBI was checking up on every car or visitor observed at the Soviet Embassy in Washington, and that even a group of Explorer Scouts who sought to make a trip to the Soviet Union had been of special interest to the Bureau.

Explanations could be offered for some of the items that had been "liberated" from the Media Resident Agency. The reason for watching a particular professor at Swarthmore College, the Bureau said, was that two New Left women fugitives held responsible for a Boston bank robbery were expected to be in touch with him. And liaison was maintained with so many organizations in eastern Pennsylvania just so the Bureau could make sure that all violations under its jurisdiction would be reported appropriately. But the overall impact of the documents could not be denied or explained away. They seemed to show a government agency, once the object of almost universal respect and awe, reaching out with tentacles to get a grasp on, or a lead into, virtually every part of American society. They confirmed the widespread notion that, where any leftist or protest group was concerned, the Bureau was almost certainly listening or watching or both. They justified and intensified the hostility toward the FBI felt by students and blacks.

These impressions were reinforced by the careful strategy of the group responsible for the burglary. They chose the items to be released each time in order to make a specific point of protest about the Bureau's activities; to assure ongoing in-depth coverage, they sent only a few documents at a time to each favored newspaper reporter. In addition, some of the files were individually released to the organizations that were the subject of them; the organization would then usually call a press conference to protest the FBI surveillance, and there would be still further coverage, especially in the Philadelphia press, where the Media incident became a major running story.

With the Media raid so much in the news and many of the documents so readily available to the public, this protest had a much greater impact than a run-of-the-mill draft board raid or antiwar march. Critics were now able to argue against the Bureau, and against the government's reaction to antiwar protest, on the basis of some new, authoritative exhibits. People both in and out of government who had thought of the FBI as a generally benign presence began to reconsider. Here was evidence, after all, of wiretaps that picked up every manner of personal details that could not possibly be relevant to the solution of a crime or the gathering of evidence on a matter vital to the national security, and proof of the enormous expenditure of manpower required just to keep track of the expression of dissenting views on major national issues. After the Media burglary, the Bureau was more vulnerable to serious criticism than it had been since its partisan political incarnation in the early 1920s. Without condoning the method by which the documents had become public, people could accept them as a new window on part of the FBI's operations. Members of Congress could complain that perhaps their appropriations committees had not kept such careful track of the nation's most powerful law enforcement agency after all.

The significance of the event was not lost on the Bureau. Hoover was enraged and, in FBI tradition, somebody had to be found to serve as the scapegoat. The fact that Thomas F. Lewis, who was in charge of the Media Resident Agency, had long since requested secure, locking file cabinets for the office was ignored. Lewis, declared culpable for the raid, was suspended for a month without pay and handed a punitive transfer to the Atlanta Field Office.* His punishment leaked to the press. In a move that must have been particularly annoying to the Bureau and embarrassing to Lewis, the Citizens' Commission to Investigate the FBI issued a statement on the occasion of a farewell testimonial dinner in Lewis's honor:

We have read in the newspapers of your month's suspension without pay by the FBI and of their ordering you to move to Atlanta. We regret this

---

* Lewis stayed there until after Hoover died; Acting Director L. Patrick Gray III later granted his request to return to Philadelphia.

disruption of your and your family's life and hope that you will consider finding constructive work here so that you can stay in your own community, rather than continue the alienating work of the FBI.

We invite you now, just as we did in our public statement of early March, "to join with us in building a peaceful, just, and open society."

In a typical bit of overreaction, the Director had within four months ordered the closing of 103 of the Bureau's 538 resident agencies, lest more of them become the targets of nocturnal antiwar adventures. The rules governing what papers and files could be kept in the resident agencies — only those absolutely necessary for pending investigations — were tightened and more strictly enforced. And for those RAs that were not in well-guarded and well-secured buildings, intricate burglar alarm systems were installed, with the alarm connected to the local police station and sometimes even to the distant field office supervising the resident agency. One Bureau hope was obviously that the same band would try again on another FBI office and be captured, but that prospect never materialized. (At one point, the leaders of the People's Coalition for Peace and Justice, which organized the Mayday demonstrations, received a telegram signed by the Citizens' Commission, announcing a plan for the Media burglars to surface and seek sanctuary in a Washington church, but the plan was canceled at the last moment.)

As for the investigation of the Media burglary itself, the Bureau classified it as a "major special" — MEDBURG by name — and Hoover sent one of his all-stars in to run it, Roy K. Moore, of Jackson, Mississippi, fame. This was one case about which the boss cared very much indeed, and no effort was to be spared. Agents came from other cities to help in Philadelphia, and other field offices were immediately drawn into the national manhunt. Almost anyone who had been active in the antiwar movement was initially suspect.

A court document filed by the Justice Department later in connection with a lawsuit described the Bureau's approach to the investigation and hinted at the frustration that evolved:

Philadelphia by teletype March 9, 1971, instructed other FBI offices to concentrate investigation on individuals previously involved in draft board and industrial break-ins. . . . These capable or probably disposed to such action as the Media break-in were to receive concentrated investigation and their whereabouts during the pertinent period were to be established. . . .

. . . Headquarters instructed that thorough investigations were to be conducted prior to considering a person as having been eliminated as a suspect. . . .

. . . Philadelphia instructed other offices that persons developed as suspects were expected to be hostile and were to be informed of the extremely serious nature of the crime, including the felony charge of theft of government property, possible espionage and misprison [sic] of felony, obstruction of justice, accessory before and after the fact, and conspiracy.

. . . FBI headquarters teletyped instructions that all the manpower necessary was to be used in each office to include or exclude persons from the suspect list.

Philadelphia instructed other offices by teletype on April 1, 1971, that investigation of this crime was to be given top priority and that results were to be reported immediately.

. . . Offices were instructed to use such techniques as physical surveillance, check of telephone tolls, informant penetration, securing of handwriting and handprinting of suspects, securing of specimens from suspect typewriters, and the obtaining of fingerprints of suspects.

Offices were instructed that a suspect could not be eliminated merely on the basis that he or she was not in Media, Pa., on the night of the crime. Offices were told that the nature of the crime indicated pre-planning, later analysis, duplication of stolen material, and various related support activities extending beyond the individuals who could be charged as the actual burglars. Offices were instructed that the location and identification of an analysis and duplication center through investigation of individual suspects was central to the solution of the case. Offices were told that interview of suspects would be an important elimination step.

. . . writings and reproduced speeches and the like of each of the prime suspects were to be collected and submitted to the FBI Laboratory for composition comparisons with a view to establishing the author or authors of the original press release of the "Citizens' Commission to Investigate the FBI.". . .

On May 19, 1971, Philadelphia instructed accelerated investigation in order to exclude peripheral persons as suspects. Investigation was ordered concentrated on prime suspects in order to resolve their status vis-à-vis the Media burglary as soon as possible. Each office was to furnish Headquarters and Philadelphia a daily teletype of their progress in excluding persons from the suspect list.

Within Philadelphia itself, investigative attention focused on Powelton Village, a section near the campus of the University of Pennsylvania where many members of peace groups, antiwar activists, and other young people lived in communes. Large contingents of agents, some of them sporting newly sprouted beards and suddenly lengthened hair styles, appeared in the neighborhood, watching people, interviewing them, photographing them, and sometimes searching their apartments or houses. In a lawsuit later filed in federal court in Philadelphia, the American Friends Service Committee, an antiwar organization called "Philadelphia Resistance," members and employees of those organizations, and others charged "continuous and malicious harassment" and invasion of their constitutional rights by FBI agents apparently investigating the Media burglary. One plaintiff claimed that people riding in a Bureau car had tried to run him down while he was riding his bicycle; another said that agents with a search warrant had broken into her apartment, read her personal letters, and seized notes and materials she had used in preparing a book that dealt in part with the FBI, all because she had a few "third-generation" photocopies of some Media documents. A newspaper reporter complained that agents had taken pictures of her talking with activist friends on the front steps of her home. A doctor who lent his Cape Cod home to members of the Resistance organization for a vacation said that both it and his Philadelphia residence had become the objects of Bureau surveillance. Others said they were being constantly pursued and asked by agents to discuss their political views and associations.

In one of the documents the Justice Department was later required to file in connection with the lawsuit, it acknowledged that agents had spent hours on end, sometimes entire days, on an almost daily basis, watching the comings and goings at the office of the Resistance organization and at the commune where many of its workers lived. The Bureau also admitted taking the photograph of some people six or seven times and revealed that it had repeatedly overheard several of the plaintiffs in the lawsuit on "warrantless national security electronic surveillances" even before the Media burglary had occurred. The image was of an angry agency responding to the insult of the Media burglary with the same kind of tactics revealed in the documents that were the product of that burglary.

But the Bureau, for its own part, would contend that it was the agents who were subjected to unprecedented and systematic harassment by the residents of Powelton Village and others who were validly under investigation. A court filing by the Justice Department noted that one plaintiff in the lawsuit against the FBI had himself been in "a group of individuals who verbally abused two agents" and that he later "sprayed a liquid on the agent's car." Members of the Resistance would sometimes stand near the agents with signs reading THIS IS YOUR FRIENDLY FBI AT WORK, and one person often rode along the streets on his bicycle at 6 P.M., sounding a foghorn and shouting, "The FBI is changing shifts." Others made a concerted effort to photograph the agents whenever they could — some took pictures of the agents taking pictures — and blowups of those photographs, some converted into jigsaw puzzles, were featured at a street fair held by the youthful residents of Powelton Village in June. To taunt the Bureau, the organizers of the fair posted photocopies of the stolen Media documents on trees and poles, along with pleas to the FBI agents to "turn in" their guns. If nothing else, the antiwar activists in Philadelphia succeeded in making the Bureau even angrier.

Tireless, thorough, and unrelenting though it might have been, the FBI's investigation of the Media burglary was unsuccessful. With the help of the Xerox Corporation, the Bureau did manage to detect that some copies of the documents which were distributed had been reproduced on that company's model 660. Publicity surrounding that fact, however, led the group distributing the Media documents to switch to other photocopying machines. Still the Bureau could not locate the originals. Eventually Moore and those assisting him in Philadelphia concluded that they had identified most of the participants in the break-in and related events, and sources on the other side of the case confirm that the FBI actually confronted and interviewed some of the people who were involved. But the Bureau, an organization not often inclined to underestimate the quality of the evidence it has gathered, still never felt certain that it had information reliable enough to take before a federal grand jury or to obtain arrest warrants in connection with the burglary. And, the times being what they were, this put the Bureau in line for criticism from another direction — the law-and-order types who wanted the federal government to take a harder and more effective line against protesters.

Insisting upon results, Hoover denied Moore's requests to return to his home in Jackson, Mississippi, and required him to keep working out of Philadelphia on redeeming the FBI's name. Those whom Moore's crew felt they had identified as implicated in the burglary were primarily affiliated with the Catholic Left, ironically including the sister of one agent assigned to Philadelphia and the priest brother of another. (The latter agent invited his brother to the field office and pleaded with him to "help us solve a crime." The priest refused, and the agent reported back to his superiors that "I can no longer understand my brother.") When Robert Hardy came to the FBI in the summer of 1971 to tell what he knew about a plan for a raid on the Selective Service office in Camden, New Jersey, across the Delaware River from Philadelphia, some of the names he provided of potential participants were among the people suspected by the FBI in the Media case, and it was apparently with that in mind that the Bureau urged Hardy to play an active role in helping set up the action in Camden. When the raid occurred in August 1971, the authorities were waiting, and one man who arrived shortly after the arrests, and called the raiders by their nicknames, was none other than Guy Goodwin, the radical-chasing Justice Department attorney. Moore and his weary colleagues in Philadelphia told the Director that that was as close as the Bureau would ever come to solving the Media mystery.

Almost two years after the Camden raid, in another insult to the Bureau (spared Hoover only because he had died), the defendants in that case were acquitted and went free. Officially the Media burglary was still an open case that would not be forgiven or forgotten. But almost everybody in the FBI who thought about it knew that the Bureau had lost — to a group of antiwar protesters — and that the damage was done.

Almost overnight, the FBI seemed to have given up some of its charm, its special immunity from criticism and scrutiny. On Capitol Hill, the Bureau's old supporters were on the defensive, and there were questions that they refused to confront and answer; the routine statements of endorsement for Hoover and his every gesture began to sound forced and obligatory rather than sincere.

The attacks came in cascades: Senator George McGovern of South Dakota, an early contender for the 1972 Democratic presidential nomination, released an anonymous letter, purportedly from ten FBI agents, complaining that the Director padded the Bureau's conviction statistics, concentrated on the arrest of minority group members on charges often too insignificant to attract the attention of the local police, and required agents to spend a great deal of their time on trivial tasks that would polish Hoover's image. Senator Joseph M. Montoya (D–New Mexico) and Congressman Hale Boggs (D–Louisiana), the Majority Leader in the House, charged that their own telephones and those of other members of Congress had been wiretapped by the FBI. Senator Edmund Muskie of Maine, also a Democratic presidential contender at the time, citing Bureau surveillance of Earth Day as inappropriate, called for Hoover's replacement and the establishment of a domestic intelligence review board. Senator Gaylord Nelson (D–Wisconsin), picking up on that idea, introduced legislation to create a special governmental commission to investigate all domestic surveillance activities by the Bureau, the CIA, and military intelligence units. The Senate Majority Leader, Mike Mansfield of Montana, an unemotional Democrat who at first opposed the attacks on Hoover, announced that he too would support a congressional probe of the FBI. Several prominent Republicans in Congress also began to let it be known in discreet, off-the-record sessions that they thought the time for Hoover's retirement had come. A group of scholars, authors, commentators, former agents, and other ex-government officials, supported by the Committee for Public Justice and the Woodrow Wilson School of Public Affairs at Princeton University, convened a conference at Princeton to study the policies and practices of the Bureau. Another organization, a new one called Friends of the FBI, thought the challenge serious enough to commission a study on the other side by the Americans for Effective Law Enforcement.

Public opinion polls began to reflect a sharp slippage in popular esteem for the FBI. George Gallup's American Institute of Public Opinion reported in August 1970 that the percentage of those polled giving the Bureau a "highly favorable" rating had dropped to 71 percent from 84 percent in 1965. (Still, Gallup noted, the FBI fared better than most other government institutions; the Pentagon, for example, was rated "highly favorable" by only 28 percent of those polled in 1970.) Interestingly, the FBI was losing support among all segments of the population, classified on the basis of geography, age, and educational background; the decline was moderate only in the Midwest, the South, and among those with only a grammar school background.

Two polls released in May 1971 suggested that Hoover's personal prestige had also plunged. Despite uniformly high regard for the Director's past performance, pollster Louis Harris reported, Americans were split evenly — 43 percent saying yes and 43 percent no, with 14 percent undecided — on the question of whether Hoover should at last resign. The categories most in favor of his leaving the job were people under thirty, blacks, those with a college education, and people living on the East and West coasts. At the same time, a Gallup poll commissioned by *Newsweek* magazine showed 51 percent felt Hoover should resign, while 41 percent favored his continuing in office; nonetheless Hoover still had a rating of "excellent" from 36 percent of those polled and "good" from 34 percent. Whereas the Bureau once would have commanded overwhelming approval from virtually everyone in the country, the *Newsweek* survey showed only 49 percent saying they had a "highly favorable" opinion of the FBI; 31 percent marked their attitude as "moderately favorable." An accompanying *Newsweek* cover story, timed to coincide with Hoover's forty-seventh anniversary as head of the FBI, concluded that he was definitely on his way out.

When the Friends of the FBI weighed in with a survey conducted by Gilbert Youth Research in October and November of 1971 among 2,500 people between the ages of fourteen and twenty-five, it reported that 41 percent thought that the intense criticism of the FBI was unjustified, 27 percent agreed with it, and 31 percent said they did not know. But the glamorous G-man image among youth had apparently disappeared: only 21.5 percent of the young people questioned in the poll said they would like to become an FBI agent. More than 69 percent said they would not want to apply for a job as an agent. As the Friends put it, the results "underscored the need for a major information program among young Americans from fourteen through twenty-five."

Key White House aides during the Nixon administration eventually decided, for their own reasons, that Hoover would have to go. One day in July 1971, in fact, William C. Sullivan, who was in the midst of his bitter dispute with the Director, had a call from a friend in the Justice Department alerting him that "our problem is over . . . the albatross will be lifted from our neck, maybe even today." It seemed that Nixon had a meeting scheduled with Hoover during which the President was allegedly planning to suggest that Hoover retire and, in the words of the Justice Department official, "send him out in a blaze of glory" with compliments, honorific new titles, and sinecure advisory positions. There are conflicting versions of what actually happened during the visit between the President and the Director — some say that Nixon could not muster the courage to break the news to Hoover and just turned it into a social chat; others, that Nixon broached the subject but Hoover immediately resisted, making threats and veiled references to material about Nixon in the Director's private files — but the result was just another confirmation of the status quo. Hoover seemed as entrenched as ever.

Even within the Bureau the old spirit was deteriorating, as minor irritants grew to be festering problems. The Director's arbitrariness and viciousness in matters of discipline and transfers became worse than ever, and there were some surprising retirements within the upper ranks. Publicity about the circumstances under which William Sullivan left in October 1971 made the FBI look silly. Both in his internal comments and outside remarks, Hoover was reacting to the slightest criticism in a most peculiar — some said paranoid — manner. It was all rather embarrassing for an institution that had once been the object of envy and unstinting admiration. The Bureau was becoming a caricature of itself.

XXI

The Gray Year

I didn't care who it was. . . . I would have fallen behind a monkey as director . . . but it would have had to be a trained law-enforcement monkey.

— *The special-agent-in-charge*
of an FBI field office

J. EDGAR HOOVER'S DEATH on May 2, 1972, was an event that everyone should have expected, sooner or later, but for which no one was prepared. It hit the FBI rather like the Japanese attack on Pearl Harbor. At first the Bureau did not know quite what to do, and the reaction at headquarters was as if something subversive had occurred and further damage had to be prevented. For reasons that were obscure at the time and have never been clarified, one assistant director decided that all entrances to the Justice Department building had better be secured; agents were posted at the doors, and even people with permanent entry passes were stopped and questioned about their destination. (As soon as the Justice Department learned about this unrequested special service, several hours after it began, the agents were withdrawn.) The field was eventually advised by teletype of the Director's passing, and most work ground to a halt as the rank and file worried and speculated about the future.

Acting Attorney General Richard G. Kleindienst's first reaction was to summon John P. Mohr, assistant-to-the-director for the administrative side of Bureau operations, and ask that he secure Hoover's personal office suite, changing the locks on the doors and posting

495

guards so that nobody could get at the special personal files the Director kept there. When Mohr came to Kleindienst's office for that instruction, another man was sitting there silently whom Mohr did not know — L. Patrick Gray III, assistant attorney general for the Civil Division of the Justice Department and President Nixon's nominee to become deputy attorney general when Kleindienst moved up from the job of deputy to replace John Mitchell as attorney general. (Senate confirmation of both men had been delayed, however, during the long hearings before the Senate Judiciary Committee over the settlement of antitrust cases against the International Telephone and Telegraph Corporation.) But Kleindienst was too late. Certain items had been cleared out of Hoover's office immediately to be sure that they would stay in the orthodox FBI family. Some of the private files were removed to Hoover's home, which would be inherited by Associate Director Clyde Tolson; others were shredded and still more transferred to the office of Deputy Associate Director W. Mark Felt.

For a few people the Director's death totally deprived life and work of any meaning. Helen Gandy, his personal secretary, made it clear that she would leave as soon as she had an opportunity to pull Hoover's things together and move them out. Tolson, acting director for a day, resigned in a one-sentence letter even before the Director's funeral.* Some thought that Felt, as the loyal lieutenant most recently blessed with elevation into Hoover's personal court, would get the nod to take over the FBI, at least as a temporary custodian. A number of other members of the Bureau hierarchy hoped they might get the chance themselves. But as soon as the word was out that Hoover was gone, there were plenty of other contenders from the outside as well. By lunchtime, the public information officers for John Ingersoll, the director of the Bureau of Narcotics and Dangerous Drugs, had their boss's résumé well distributed among Washington newsmen in order to be sure that he would be "mentioned" in the speculation about

---

* Tolson's physical condition deteriorated further after Hoover's death and he went into virtual seclusion, refusing to see most people, including even Don Whitehead, who had been planning to write the authorized posthumous biography of the Director. John Mohr was one of the few whose visits Tolson would accept, and when the Senate Watergate Committee sent investigators out to interview Tolson, Mohr had to sit in and answer most of the questions for him. Mohr also helped Tolson write his will and became executor of his estate; much of his money was left to Mohr and other old Hoover faithfuls, and Tolson's brother Hillary went to court to contest the will as the product of an incompetent man manipulated by others. Although Tolson still fired off an occasional brief denial or rebuttal to nasty comments about Hoover that appeared in the press, he apparently spent most of his last days watching quiz programs and soap operas on television. Tolson never met Gray, although he formally addressed his letter of resignation to him on May 3.

Hoover's successor. Among the others on the inevitable lists of contenders were some old names, people who had once or twice been cited as possible replacements for the Director — including Supreme Court Justice Byron R. White and Jerris Leonard, the administrator of the Law Enforcement Assistance Administration — and some new ones, mostly people who held political appointments within the federal law enforcement establishment, including Myles Ambrose, head of the new Office of Drug Abuse Law Enforcement; and Eugene T. Rossides, like White a former star football player and an assistant secretary of the treasury responsible for enforcement activities. One theory had it that Nixon would name nobody for the time being and would leave day-to-day direction of the Bureau in the hands of a triumvirate of Hoover's aides until after the November 1972 presidential election. That would avoid the new procedure of confirmation hearings for the FBI director, which could provoke an early and unseemly review of Hoover's operation of the Bureau and exposure of some of its dark secrets.

But on Wednesday, May 3, the day after Hoover died and the day before his extravagant funeral, Nixon moved. Following a pattern established forty-eight years earlier almost to the day, when Attorney General Harlan Stone picked Hoover, the President named only an "acting" director of the FBI, promising that he would evaluate his performance later and decide on whether to nominate him for the permanent position.* Nixon's choice was Louis Patrick Gray III, the deputy attorney general–designate. The nearly unanimous reaction, inside the Bureau and out, was "Who's he?" and "Why?"

Pat Gray's name had not exactly figured prominently in the Hoover succession sweepstakes. It had already been a surprise, in fact, when he was nominated earlier in the year to be deputy attorney general, the second-ranking job in the Justice Department. Next to Kleindienst, a volatile and controversial character who was always talking himself into unfortunate headlines, Gray was a relatively unknown second-level political appointee, a plodding and methodical type, almost insipid. Whereas Kleindienst's nomination had stirred some interest and a few witnesses (even the first time around, before the ITT furor broke and he requested that his confirmation hearings be reopened), Gray's nomination to be deputy attorney general brought the bipartisan support of the two senators from his adopted home state

---

* Fond as he was of turning the minutest details of his own career into a model for others, Hoover often filled a vacancy in the Bureau's top ranks with an "acting" assistant director, who would get the full title only after a few months on the job.

of Connecticut, Abraham Ribicoff and Lowell P. Weicker, Jr., but little other comment. Again, this time, people hardly knew what to say about Gray, let alone what to expect from him.

The first quality that was invariably cited about Pat Gray by those who knew him was his well-developed sense of loyalty. He had come up the hard way and learned to appreciate the institutions and the people who helped him along. Born in 1916 in St. Louis, the first of four children of an Irish railroad worker for the Missouri Pacific, he moved at an early age to Houston when his father was transferred there. After graduating from a Catholic high school, he was admitted to the prestigious and tuition-free Rice Institute, where he studied engineering and business administration. Only after completing a full four-year course at Rice — and through the intercession of prominent people to whom he had delivered newspapers — did Gray win what he had always wanted: an appointment to the U.S. Naval Academy in Annapolis. In effect obtaining a second college education while he also plunged into service academy sports, including boxing, he finished 172nd in an Annapolis class of 476. Once commissioned, he attended submarine school and served in both the Atlantic and Pacific during World War II. After the war, he was given command first of one submarine and then of a division of six subs. Later he was sent to George Washington University Law School by the navy and worked in a number of legal and Pentagon staff jobs. But Gray's stint as a submarine commander was apparently the most important formative experience of his life; it seemed to type him, toughen him, excite him, and, some would argue, limit him. In various later important moments, whether crises or catharses, he could generally invoke the submarine spirit and ethic, if not to others then surely to himself.

By 1960 Captain Gray was serving as a military adviser on the staff of the Vice-President, Richard M. Nixon. Later that year, although he had been promoted to be an assistant to the chairman of the Joint Chiefs of Staff, Air Force General Nathan Twining, and was in a position to move further up the military hierarchy, Gray opted to retire from the navy and plunge into Nixon's presidential campaign against John F. Kennedy. He was assigned to work with Robert Finch, who was running the Nixon campaign in California, one of the states the Republican ticket would carry. Gray, as Finch's "right arm," showed what his boss called "an inordinate capacity for work" — an unusual self-discipline and an ability to stick with a job for hours after others had given up.

After Nixon's defeat, Gray settled in New London, Connecticut, near the submarine base where he had been stationed and as much home to his family as any of the places where they had lived. There he joined a small-town law firm, concentrating on taxes, trusts, and the chartering of small businesses. When the submarine *Thresher* disappeared in 1963, Gray devoted himself, without charge, to helping the families of the sailors who had been on board settle their estates; he established a scholarship fund for their children. But mostly he became a family man and spent a great deal of time with his four sons (two of them actually born to his wife Beatrice during her first marriage to a navy pilot, an Annapolis classmate of Gray's, who was killed in action over Okinawa in 1945). They went to some of the best private schools and universities, gaining the kind of head start that Gray would have liked himself but never had. The Grays built a home in the countryside in Stonington, atop a hill with a view along the coast into Rhode Island. There was room enough for Mrs. Gray's parents (her father was also a former navy officer who had settled in Hawaii) to come and live with them, and for a swimming pool in the backyard where Gray, something of a physical culturist, could swim laps to keep in shape.

Gray was a loner and a brooder who valued no advice more than that of his innermost self. He liked to read *The Federalist Papers* and other works about the early evolution of the American government. Some of his best thinking time, he would tell people, was when he jogged every morning — long before it became a fad — sometimes before dawn and preferably alone, without even one of his sons for company. In groups, there was a kind of locker-room congeniality and Rotarian sincerity about him, and he was capable of great warmth toward those he trusted; but he could also be mean and bitter toward someone he felt there was reason to doubt or distrust. Gray had an old-fashioned, corny side to his character; no book inspired him more (nor earned him more derision and scorn from hard-bitten old-timers in the FBI) than Richard Bach's *Jonathan Livingston Seagull*. Yet he prided himself on an openness to new ideas and enjoyed surrounding himself with younger people who would offer them. Some of those with whom he came into contact suggested that Gray suffered from a false humility, a kind of we-try-harder attitude that covered over a need for recognition and adulation.

He sat out the political turbulence that wracked the Republican party during the 1960s except for a peripheral involvement in local matters concerning the New London area. Pat Gray still saw himself as a member of the Nixon "team" in reserve, however — Nixon had written to him after the 1960 defeat, saying that "even though we lost, I shall forever be proud of those with whom it was my privilege to fight side by side" — and when his man ran again in 1968, Gray was ready to become involved. During the months leading up to that year's Republican National Convention, he helped pull together information on the strategy of Nixon's strongest rival, Nelson Rockefeller. Gray had no active campaigning role as he had had in 1960, however, and he was scarcely known to the new guard of Nixon counselors and confidants, John Mitchell, H. R. Haldeman, and John Ehrlichman. Only when Robert Finch was appointed secretary of health, education and welfare in the original Nixon cabinet, and learned that Gray had filled out a routine application for a job in the administration, was he brought into consideration.

Finch selected Gray as his executive assistant at HEW, a job that suited the navy man's talents for organization, discipline, and loyalty. After six months there, Gray gave an extraordinary speech to the department's political appointees that would repeatedly haunt him in the future. It was a pep talk of sorts, intended to stress that "we are here to serve, not to enhance our own perfectly normal, human selfish interests." He said, in part:

Each of us is possessed of our own desires, ambitions and goals. This is normal. This is commendable. At the same time, when we embark upon a career in the service of our government, whether that career is to be short term or long term, we must be quite willing to subjugate our own personal goals to a deep personal commitment to serve our President, our Secretary, and our Nation.

This commitment must be our homing beacon throughout our career in the service of our government.

Each one of us is here in HEW because Richard Nixon was elected to the high office of President of the United States. Further we are here because Secretary Finch has seen fit to place trust and confidence in us and to approve our selection to fill a position in HEW.

In short we owe our positions to the capability of the President to come off the mat, so to speak, and drive through hard, vigorous years of campaigning to win the nomination of the Republican Party, and then go on to win the Presidency of the United States with the valiant help of hundreds of thousands of dedicated, hardworking supporters, campaign workers, and contributors.

So also are we here because Secretary Finch has seen fit to ask us to serve with him and to help him move this Department forward as he and the President seek the solutions to the people problems which, if not solved, might well rupture and destroy the society which the people of our Nation have created.

Obviously, we are a chosen few, an elite group — make no mistake about it — there are thousands of Republicans who are knocking at the door and who would be pleased to be in our positions.

Appreciate this hard fact of life. Appreciate the fact that every single member of the opposite political party is working hard day and night to ensure that the President of the United States is hampered and harassed in carrying out his programs and that the President of the United States is not reelected to serve a second term.

This is a real hard political fact of life. This is in keeping with the nature of our political system. Without such a system, one party government could produce a totalitarian state. We accept this fact of life; so does the opposing party. Accordingly, do not retch or quiver when we insist that the preponderant majority of our colleagues — political appointees — be members of our own party.

. . .

Above all other qualities of character that we hold near and dear, we must have deep, abiding, sincere loyalty to our President and to our Secretary.

. . . I do not speak of blind, automatic loyalty. I speak of a sincere, an intelligent, a freely made decision to join President Nixon and Secretary Finch because we believe in them, trust them, understand the goals and objectives they hold, and desire to support them with the deepest sense of dedication and total commitment.

. . .

Loyalty includes also a dedication to your immediate superior and to those who work with you in our cause, on our team.

Loyalty includes an avoidance of criticism of our leaders and of our colleagues. Criticism which is destructive in nature is cancerous — it will destroy us and our entire team. Snide remarks and facetious comments lightly made often come back to haunt us. Too often have I heard this form of banter engaged in innocently. Too often have I seen the results published in newspapers or made the subject of remarks of the boob-tube word mashers.

Loyalty includes having the common sense and decency to deal with others in a manner calculated to bring credit to the President and the Secretary. . . .

Loyalty includes the touching of all required bases as we set out on our daily rounds to carry out the will of the Secretary. . . .

Why are we here?

A. Because we believe in President Nixon and Secretary Finch.

B. Because we are dedicated to them and their work.

C. Because we ask only to serve; not to be served.

D. Because we have no greed for personal aggrandizement.

E. Because we feel a deep sense of personal pride, honor and humility in being asked to serve.

. . .

Our objective — to assist to the fullest extent, the Secretary in his objective to make this the *best* Department in the Nixon Administration; to establish this Department as a Department on the move, a Department composed of compassionate and understanding people who are determined to generate and manage plans and programs designed to enrich the lives of all Americans; to make this Department so attractive and so meaningful in its work, that members of the civil service, and others not now in government, will be eager to join HEW and assist the Secretary to achieve his objectives. Imaginative, creative, dedicated, and competent people form the heart and flesh, the bone, sinew and muscle of any organization whether it be the corner grocery store, or a major Department of the Government of the United States. We must have them and we must work with them in such a manner that they can realize their full potential in the best interests of the people of the United States.

Gray was not particularly noticeable outside HEW during his work with Finch — except on one occasion when a copy was leaked to the press of an unusually long memorandum he had written, urging department employees to write shorter memoranda — but he clearly played a key role internally; for when he left in January 1970 and returned to his law practice in New London, Finch developed problems managing the sprawling HEW department.

Gray's departure came about for two reasons: There was built-in friction between him, as Finch's personal executive officer, and the undersecretary of the department, John Veneman, whom Gray considered to be pursuing his own personal political goals at HEW. Also, Gray's brother in Houston had died; he was taking on financial responsibility for some of the brother's family and thus wanted to return to his lucrative firm.

Although Gray had had relatively little contact with Nixon during his year at HEW, the President had obviously noticed him and heard about his work. He sent Gray an unusually effusive "Dear Pat" letter on January 30, 1970:

Throughout the years that you have been a member of the Nixon team it has been especially satisfying to me to know that I could depend on you to lend a hand whenever it was needed. We have gone through a number of battles together and have won some of them and lost others. In every instance the loyalty and dedication you have given so wholeheartedly have made victory sweeter and helped to take the sting out of defeat.

You brought a special understanding to your work in the Department of Health, Education and Welfare, and while I appreciate the responsibilities to your family which have caused you to leave the Administration and move from the Washington area, I deeply regret that we will lose the benefits of your courage as well as your ingenuity. To the gratitude all of us owe you for your faithful service to our country, I want to add my own particular thanks for all you have done to help my efforts and to carry our cause to the American people.

Before long, Gray was commuting back and forth to Washington from Connecticut, working on the staff of the cabinet-level committee Nixon had named, in a sensitive midterm election year, to work with southern states that had not yet desegregated their schools. Another lawyer who worked with that committee, having served as general counsel at HEW, was Robert C. Mardian. When Mardian, a close friend of Kleindienst from their days together in Senator Barry Goldwater's 1964 Republican presidential campaign, moved to the Justice Department late in 1970 to take over as assistant attorney general in charge of a newly revived Internal Security Division, Gray was persuaded to come back to Washington, too. He was named assistant attorney general for the Civil Division, succeeding William Ruckelshaus, who was leaving to take over the new Environmental Protection Agency.

The Civil Division is not an especially conspicuous niche at Justice. It has an important role in representing the government in cases dealing with major policy issues, but most of them are handled by career lawyers with expertise in the appropriate areas, such as admiralty law, customs regulations, and complex claims against the government. Few attract much attention among the public, as do some of the matters handled by the Criminal, Civil Rights and Antitrust divisions, for example. But to be assistant attorney general for any part of the Justice Department is a significant job, involving the occupant in major strategy sessions and planning efforts with both legal and political implications. Within a division, the assistant attorney general has considerable discretion over the allocation of resources to various pending matters, and whenever the government loses a major case he must decide whether to recommend an appeal to the solicitor general. Most assistant attorneys general, Gray among them, choose one or two important cases in which they will personally represent the federal government in oral arguments before the Supreme Court. Gray's single symbolic appearance before the justices came in a procedural case involving the Social Security laws. He was also given responsibility for the legal enforcement of the Economic Stabilization Act when Nixon instituted wage and price controls under its terms in 1971.

Gray first achieved prominence as assistant attorney general in the spring of 1971, when he coordinated the Justice Department's legal counterattack on antiwar demonstrators who were planning some of their biggest and most dramatic protests yet in the nation's capital. He handled the case in which the government tried to prevent the Vietnam Veterans Against the War (VVAW) from camping out on the Mall in front of the Capitol — feeling some frustration when the United States Court of Appeals for the District of Columbia Circuit ruled for the veterans even after Gray, arguing with emotion as an old-style veteran himself, claimed that some of the protesters had hoisted "a Viet Cong flag" above their tents. (It was actually the flag of the state of California.) Eventually the Justice Department won from the Supreme Court the injunction it had sought against the VVAW. But when the moment came to enforce it by evicting the veterans, some of them paraplegics, the White House lost its nerve, and Attorney General John Mitchell sent Gray back into court to ask that the injunction be lifted after all. In what was probably one of the most humiliating moments of his legal career, Gray stood red-faced before the bench as U.S. District Court Judge George L. Hart, Jr., berated him for the way the matter had been handled by the administration. "I don't think it could have been handled worse," Hart told him. Gray privately agreed, and the incident so bothered him that he contemplated resigning.

If Gray had wanted to leave the Justice Department at that point and return to Connecticut, he could have done so very graciously, especially since there were some federal judgeships open in the state that, under a Republican President, would ordinarily go to Republicans. On at least two occasions, the newly elected young Republican senator from Connecticut, Lowell P. Weicker, Jr., actually submitted Gray's name through Justice Department channels to be considered for a vacancy on the U.S. Court of Appeals for the Second Circuit. Gray took the matter seriously enough to prepare the detailed personal history — in his case, a compilation of documents more than an inch thick — that goes to the FBI and the American Bar Association, which perform a background investigation and review of the legal qualifications, respectively, of any federal judgeship nominee. But whenever the topic of the judgeship came up, Weicker recalls, Gray would balk and say, "The President has something else in mind. I don't know what it is, but I'd better wait and see."

The mystery was complicated somewhat by the fact that Gray had not settled in very comfortably on his return to Washington. Whereas he had lived in Annapolis while at HEW (and still managed to be in his office every morning by seven), he and his wife this time moved into a tiny efficiency apartment in a redeveloped area of Southwest Washington. His life-style also seemed to change. At HEW he had been a chain smoker, but now he quit entirely; and he also stopped drinking, taking only an occasional glass of wine. If he was not traveling elsewhere, the Grays took most opportunities to return to Stonington on the weekends.

When Gray was nominated to be deputy attorney general under Kleindienst, some people presumed that was the "something else" Nixon had held for him — a crucial job, perhaps the most important in the Justice Department, because under most attorneys general the deputy is responsible for the day-to-day supervision of the operating divisions and "bureaus" like the FBI and Federal Bureau of Prisons, as well as the United States attorneys around the country and the Office of Criminal Justice, a planning unit. But, even given Gray's reputation for administrative acumen, the appointment was unusual. Although they had worked together, Kleindienst and Gray were not particularly close. Nor did Gray have very broad experience in the law; he was not a scholar and, except for Finch, he had no known strong supporters or close friends in Nixon's inner circle — any of which might ordinarily be considered a qualification for the deputy's job. One theory was that Kleindienst, who liked to run things with a heavy hand, wanted a relatively submissive deputy who would take orders rather than try to innovate; another, held by the few who knew that Gray had been reluctant to accept a judgeship, was that the deputy attorney general-ship was a means of keeping him prominent but on a back burner, pending other developments.

Because of the hearings involving Kleindienst's handling of the ITT case, which lasted the entire spring of 1972, Gray never actually had an opportunity to hold the title of deputy attorney general. He served as an aide to Kleindienst during the hearings, helping rehearse him for the questions that the Senate Judiciary Committee might ask and passing on the committee's extensive requests for official Justice Department documents. Before that crisis was over, Hoover died. Late on the morning of May 3, Kleindienst phoned Gray and asked him to come to his office in the early afternoon. When Gray arrived, he found Ralph Erickson, assistant attorney general for the Justice Department's Office of Legal Counsel, poring through the statute books to review the rules governing temporary appointments. Kleindienst declared that Gray was to be named acting director of the Bureau, and that they would be going together immediately to the White House for the appropriate announcement. Gray, according to his own later accounts, was "just flabbergasted," at first suspecting that Kleindienst was only teasing him. Before the afternoon was out, however, his name was in the headlines.

The appointment was such a surprise to him, Gray has said, that it was only the next day, when he and his wife were at the White House after Hoover's funeral waiting for a car to the Justice Department, that he had an opportunity to discuss some of the terms and conditions. Nixon called both of the Grays into the Oval Office. As Gray later told it, the President lectured him about his respect for the FBI, his "close personal friendship" with Hoover, and the fact that he considered his relationship with Gray to be strictly a "professional" one. Supposedly, Nixon gave Gray instructions to run the FBI in a totally nonpolitical fashion; when Bea Gray spoke up to ask the President whether she might continue to work as a volunteer for his reelection committee, Nixon reportedly told her, "Absolutely not; you must resign immediately."

Months later, stories began to circulate in Washington suggesting that May 3, 1972, was not the first time that the subject of running the FBI had been broached to Pat Gray, but he always denied them. In fact, almost a year earlier, in June 1971, he had asked a member of his personal staff at the Civil Division to prepare a supersecret memorandum setting forth the most important source material about the Bureau, listing what the federal code said about the duties of the FBI and its director, and suggesting other things he could read about it. Was it just a routine matter, connected with the pending lawsuit demanding that women be hired as agents, which Assistant Attorney General Gray's Civil Division was handling in court? Had Gray had a premonition? Or was it merely a coincidence? One interpretation was that Pat Gray had been singled out way in advance, for whatever the reasons, as a replacement for Hoover, and that it was only Nixon's inability to talk the Director into retiring that prevented things from going ahead on schedule.

Gray had only limited contact with the FBI during his tenure at the Justice Department. One occasion was during the antiwar protests of the spring of 1971, when the Bureau channeled information to the Civil Division for use in the court effort to keep the VVAW from camping out on the Mall. During the Mayday demonstrations that followed, Gray met regularly with officials of the FBI's Domestic Intelligence Division to gather data that would contribute to the Justice Department's strategy for dealing with the protest. (Ultimately, the Department decided on a policy of sweep arrests by Washington's Metropolitan Police Department, a policy that came under serious criticism by the courts.)

One of the central points of contention during the Senate Judiciary Committee's hearings on Kleindienst's nomination and on the ITT case was the authenticity of a memorandum that had been published by syndicated columnist Jack Anderson. Allegedly written by ITT lobbyist Dita D. Beard, it linked settlement of antitrust cases against the conglomerate with a large ITT contribution to help underwrite the Republican National Convention of 1972, which was supposed to have been held in San Diego, where ITT's Sheraton subsidiary was opening a new hotel. It was in the Nixon administration's interest to have the controversial Beard memo declared a fraud. When FBI Laboratory tests were inconclusive, it was Gray who persuaded the Bureau quietly to release the original copy of the memo from its custody, despite an agreement between the Justice Department and the Senate committee that this would not be done. Initially the memo was lent to the White House. But before long, it ended up in the hands of private document experts hired by ITT. They examined it and declared it a forgery. (The issue was never resolved.)

Gray's most sustained communication with the FBI, however, concerned the lawsuit filed in federal court in Washington, with the support of the American Civil Liberties Union, by two young women who said they wanted to become special agents of the FBI but were being discriminated against by Hoover's men-only policy. The two women actually had no desire to join the Bureau themselves — Sandra Nemser was a legal aid attorney and Cynthia Edgar a staff worker for Democratic Representative Bella Abzug, the ornery congresswoman from New York City — but they hit the FBI where it had long been assumed to be vulnerable to make a point. One of the more surprising aspects of the legal action was that, in an era when barriers to women were crumbling, no one had thought of filing such a case sooner.

As soon as the case routinely arrived in the Civil Division for the filing of an official response in court, Gray called a meeting in his office, inviting Dwight Dalbey, the FBI's legal counsel, and other Bureau officials to discuss the issues. It was not a pleasant encounter for anyone involved. Dalbey presented the classic FBI position against accepting women, with which he himself personally agreed — asserting that they could probably not do the dangerous "combat" work sometimes required of agents, and that the Bureau should be exempt from the ordinary standards prohibiting employment discrimination on the basis of sex. Being an agent, the FBI believed, was a man's job. Gray, upon hearing that, exploded and, in what the Bureau representatives considered an insulting tone, gave them a lecture on constitutional law and jurisprudence. He suggested that the lawsuit should not even be contested and that women should be accepted as applicants. The FBI men responded in kind, telling Gray that he had no authority to push them around. If the Justice Department would not agree to represent the FBI position properly in court, or at least to listen to the Bureau's point of view before adopting a position, they said, then perhaps the FBI should hire a private attorney for the purpose of this case. Passions eventually cooled after Gray sheepishly said, "Well, now that L. Patrick Gray has made an ass of himself, I apologize." Still, the FBI people did not go away with happy feelings about the man, and as one Bureau official who attended that meeting put it later, "When I first learned that Pat Gray had been named acting director, I nearly choked."

The emotional issue of whether the FBI would permit female agents was still pending when Gray took over. In one of his first meetings with Hoover's Bureau hierarchy, he mentioned that question as one that he wanted to resolve quickly. It seemed clear to everyone there that Gray had made up his mind already to lower the barrier, but they asked him to withhold a final opinion until he read over some of the written arguments they had prepared. Several of the people who attended the session had the distinct impression that Gray had agreed to wait and at least to review the matter overnight. The next morning, however, they read in the *Washington Post* and the *New York Times* of Gray's determination that the traditional FBI attitude was unconstitutional and of his decision that women would be welcome to apply for jobs as agents. That was just the kind of tactic, some veteran Bureau officials say, that fueled resentment against a man already regarded as an interloper. If Gray had waited a few weeks and at least pretended to be considering the pros and cons — or better still, from the old-line Bureau standpoint, if he had let the matter ride until an inevitable federal court decision required that women be hired — it would have been easier for the FBI to swallow. "That way," said one veteran, "we could have blamed the court and reluctantly gone along, all the while realizing this was something whose time had come. . . . But no, he wanted to present an enlightened image. He wanted to bring the Bureau into the twentieth century, kicking and screaming, and this was one way."

There were many early confrontations of this sort as Gray found himself dropped in at the top of a closed, Byzantine subculture. One of the first crises he had to resolve on the afternoon he was named was a nasty conflict among the lieutenants over who would get to sit where at Hoover's funeral. Even as a former navy man, Gray had little patience for, let alone understanding of, the overdeveloped FBI sense of

protocol, discipline, and respect for tradition. As a result, he repeatedly violated the Bureau's unwritten rules.

One case in point was his early decision to reform the old restrictive dress and grooming regulations, immediately and dramatically.
The old Bureau way would have been to order up a "study," probably
in the Inspection or the Administrative Division, with instructions
specific enough so that the study would recommend exactly what he
intended; it might take a few weeks and it might have to go back for
revision a few times before the recommendations were on target, but it
almost surely would have worked. Instead, within days of Hoover's
death, Gray chose a route that, if not calculated to do so, certainly had
the effect of rubbing the Bureau's nose in its backwardness. He went
to the Washington Field Office, located just down Pennsylvania Avenue in the old Post Office building — an office where the regulations
were enforced with particular zeal because of its physical proximity to
headquarters and because the special-agent-in-charge at the time was
Robert Kunkel, former clerk and Hoover confidant — to announce that
agents could henceforth feel free to wear colored shirts, instead of only
white ones, and that their hair and sideburns could be grown a bit
longer. The announcement, to the sheer delight of Gray and to the
great embarrassment of Kunkel and other old-timers, was greeted with
resounding applause.*

These were frills, it could be and was argued, matters that stimulated various emotional responses but had little to do with the substance and the meaning of the FBI's work. But they were the vehicle
for Gray's attempt to have an early impact on the Bureau, to give it a
stamp of his own, something he felt he had to do if he was really to
take charge. It was not so much the actual changes he made but the
way he tended to make them that thoroughly offended the Old Guard.
"He was a great one to have conferences," recalled one official who
became disenchanted and who retired soon after Gray's arrival; "why,
I remember one great big conference in his office early on, when he
talked about what he wanted to do . . . well, it turned out he had
already provided a more detailed and elaborate discussion of his plans
to the press than he gave us. . . . if we wanted to embellish our notes,
we could always take a look at the newspaper. . . . We felt we were
being used." When Gray did consult people, he sometimes offended

---

* Had Gray checked, he probably would have learned that the Bureau's dress code
was less of an irritant outside of Washington; that except at annual inspection time
it was no longer taken very seriously in distant field offices. Nonetheless, its reform
was considered an important improvement.

them by overdoing it. For example, when John Mohr submitted a memorandum proposing a reevaluation of Hoover's unrealistically harsh "weight program," Gray offended Mohr by circulating the memorandum for comment by others, including some people who ranked below him. (The weight restrictions were relaxed in another of Gray's early reforms.) The early conclusion among Hoover's survivors in the FBI bureaucracy was that "he doesn't trust us." They were right.

It was little surprise, then, that the upper ranks began to empty of the old Hoover loyalists and deputies. Mohr's retirement was announced only six weeks after Gray's arrival. A gruff, sometimes brutally direct character, Mohr had instinctively reacted negatively to Gray's efforts to come on strong. On Gray's first day as acting director, he called Mohr to his office in the Civil Division and demanded, "Where are the secret files?" — apparently referring to the sensitive ones, including gossip about public officials, which Hoover had kept among the files in his own office. Mohr told him there were none, that this was just a widespread and unjustified myth. "You know, John, I'm a hard-headed Irishman that nobody pushes around," Gray reportedly said. "Well," came Mohr's retort, "I'm a hard-headed Dutchman and I feel the same way." With the departure of Mohr, who had been assistant-to-the-director in charge of administrative matters for more than twelve years (and an agent for almost thirty-three), and of Alex Rosen, who had only recently become assistant-to-the-director for the investigative side but had been an assistant director since World War II, Gray declared he would abolish those two key positions in order to shorten the chain of command.

All of the press releases announcing retirements by assistant directors indicated that the departures were voluntary, friendly, and in no respect unusual; but some of them papered over nasty circumstances. For example, when Joseph J. Casper, for nine years head of the Training Division, went in to see Gray to reveal his plans to retire, the acting director asked him what he thought of his performance so far. Casper was apparently candid, and negative — he accused the acting director of dishonesty — and the meeting deteriorated into a shouting match during which Gray suggested that Casper was sick and needed a rest.

The difficult relations between Gray and his inherited FBI hierarchy often seemed to be aggravated by the presence of three young assistants whom he had brought along with him from the Civil Division. It was heresy, of course, to put untrained "civilians" into positions that would ordinarily be occupied by agents who had worked their way up the career ladder for twenty years or more before attaining such lofty heights, but especially so in this case because Gray's "three stooges," as they were derisively called by some Bureau old-timers, were frequently interposed between Acting Director Gray and the members of the Bureau's executive conference — the assistant directors, who, according to tradition, met weekly with the associate director to discuss policy issues and pending cases.

Top-ranking among Gray's three personal aides was David D. Kinley, a displaced thirty-one-year-old Connecticut Republican who had settled in California to practice law before he came to Washington to work in the Nixon administration. He had met Gray at HEW. A sincere, intense, if somewhat humorless and supercilious man with a neatly knitted brow, Kinley served as executive assistant — in effect, as Gray's Gray. He generally controlled access to the director's office, and almost anyone who wanted to see Gray, even assistant directors who had been in the FBI for decades, had to go through this new arrival on the scene. Kinley handled most administrative matters coming in for Gray's attention, including requests for the installation of wiretaps in counterintelligence cases (a fact that particularly galled some of the veterans, who were not sure that Kinley could be trusted). As time went on and Gray became increasingly disenchanted with the old Crime Records Division (renamed the Crime Research Division for a time, to give it a more scholarly image), Kinley also took over dealing with the press on the acting director's behalf. It was a job he did well, and even without following all the old rules about who in the media was a Bureau "friend" and who an "enemy" — to the great dismay of Assistant Director Thomas E. Bishop and other traditionalists — Gray enjoyed an unusually favorable press. In Bureau tradition, Gray and Kinley were expert leakers, although they sometimes did not cover their tracks as carefully as they might have; they did not realize at first that all visits to the director's office and all phone calls in and out were routinely logged by secretaries.

Another of Gray's personal assistants was Daniel M. "Mac" Armstrong, a more jocular and relaxed type who handled staff work in the area of investigative policy. Armstrong had served as an assistant United States attorney in the Eastern District of New York (Brooklyn), and he had not only a feel for the prosecutor's viewpoint, but also friends in the agent ranks who could give him a sense of how opinion was running among the rank and file without worry on their part about what the director might want to hear. Armstrong's role was essentially low-key, and he did not seem to upset the career officials.

The special assistant who stirred up perhaps the greatest controversy and animosity was Armstrong's officemate, Barbara L. Herwig, at twenty-seven the youngest of the three and the first woman ever to participate in the business of the FBI in a role other than a traditional clerical or secretarial one. Herwig, a Californian with a reputation for a sharp legal mind, prided herself on having educated Gray on the issue of women's rights while working for him in the Civil Division — she was credited with bringing him around on the lawsuit filed by the ACLU — and now she brought the issue with her to the Bureau. Its symbol was her listing on the routing slips attached to documents for circulation: "Ms. Herwig," a form of address that she trained even the crustiest old unreformables to use. But the substance was a genuine inquiry into the status and treatment of women within the FBI. One rule Herwig managed to have changed immediately had decreed that women were not permitted to smoke at their desks, although men were free to do so. Another practice she attacked was that of not asking an unmarried woman to type anything connected with an "interstate transportation of obscene matter" violation. Although she never managed to achieve her goal of establishing a formal complaint procedure for women in the FBI who felt they were the victims of discrimination, as in some other federal agencies, Herwig certainly did set up an informal one. As her sources developed, she would hear of individual problems that women were having and would set about trying to correct them through her own channels. Later, when women were accepted for agent's training, Herwig looked in at Quantico to be sure that they were being treated fairly; when the first instances arose of male and female agents getting married, she made sure that the couple would be given appropriate consideration in the field assignment process. These aggressive activities did not endear her to the very traditional men running the FBI; as one summarized Herwig's assignment, "She got in people's hair. . . . She went around developing informants among the female employees, to find out what they were thinking and to stir up trouble." At one point Herwig, sensing such strong hostility from some members of the Bureau establishment, even had her phone swept to be sure that someone in the FBI was not wiretapping to check on her dangerous activities.

Kinley, Armstrong, and Herwig, also sometimes called "the kiddie corps" or "the mod squad," were resented most strongly because of what was taken as their total ignorance of FBI policy and operations. Eventually each one spent a week in a field office to familiarize himself with some important matters, but that hardly dispelled the widespread belief that they simply did not know what they were doing and talking about. One of the insults was that after the Administrative Division had developed its recommendations on how agents should be disciplined for infractions of the rules, it was the three of them who had the last word before Gray made his decisions. Invariably their influence was in the direction of leniency in the case of a lowly street agent or clerk and in the direction of harshness if a special-agent-in-charge or a high-ranking member of the hierarchy were involved. The three gained the reputation of being "bleeding hearts" who were egging Gray on to weaken the Bureau's tradition of military-style firmness with the personnel. Later, adding injury to insult, Gray also brought in a White House Fellow, Air Force Major John Fryer, as another member of his personal staff. He and "Herwig and Armstrong were mostly an annoyance," said one agent who watched them closely for a time; "but Kinley, now he was right in the middle. He was a real policymaker. In effect, he had the job of the associate director. He was bright, and he was powerful."

The man who was supposed to be functioning as second-in-command under Gray was W. Mark Felt, whom he named "acting associate director" almost immediately upon taking office himself. Felt had been Gray's FBI contact during the Kleindienst-ITT hearings, so he was the one member of the hierarchy whom the acting director actually knew personally. Others sometimes criticized Felt for the ease with which he could come down on both sides of a hotly disputed issue, such as whether the Bureau should accept women agents, but that was a quality that helped him perform a most unusual dual role — as the old Bureau's protector against Gray, and as Gray's protector against the old Bureau. There was also no disputing the fact that Felt knew the FBI from several valuable vantage points. Unlike many of the others in powerful positions at headquarters, he had run a number of field offices and returned to Washington as recently as ten years earlier; for seven years he had been in charge of the Inspection Division, so he also knew the strengths and weaknesses of some of the more obscure corners of FBI operations.

Gray was almost totally dependent upon Felt to handle the day-to-day routine matters that a new man could not learn overnight. The acting director was, after all, even more uninitiated and inexperienced in the Bureau's work than the average first-office agent; he had neither training nor relevant background for this job. When Gray traveled, he relied upon Felt to keep things under control and to keep him informed on major breaking cases; he regularly called upon him for advice. Felt, a smooth and charming man, tall and thin with silver-gray hair, was helpful and cooperative. Although he was sometimes reserved and businesslike, nowhere near as gregarious as some of the jovial assistant directors, Felt did create the impression that he was willing to throw his lot in with the new acting director. As one aide who worked closely with Gray put it, "We got the feeling that he [Felt] understood what we were trying to do. We came to see him as a sort of bridge between the old and the new." Felt seemed to be the one person who did not mind working directly with Gray's three young aides and who appeared willing to thrash out issues with them as if they were people whose opinions and ideas mattered, a courtesy that many others refused to extend.

But at the same time, as the interpreter of the strange new top man to the rest of the organization, Felt was showing himself to be skeptical and cautious. He passed along some of Gray's orders and instructions with a tone of "I know you won't believe this, but . . ." He complained to others that Gray was simply unable to handle the torrential paper flow that ordinarily came through the director's office. In short, Felt put himself in a position to agree with, and share in, any compliments given the Gray regime, but meanwhile to reinforce any criticisms of it. He was, as some Bureau observers suggested later, maneuvering himself into place so that if Gray were to succeed and win appointment and confirmation as permanent director of the FBI, Mark Felt could be named as his permanent associate director; and so that if Gray were to fail, Mark Felt might seem like the most logical choice as his replacement.

As acting director, Pat Gray faced some unenviable dilemmas. He had to convince a White House that was intent upon capturing in its grip what it saw as an enemy bureaucracy throughout the Executive Branch that he could be trusted with one of the most sensitive executive agencies of all. Yet he had to show Congress, including a Senate that might eventually be called upon to confirm him for the job, that he would be able to remain sufficiently independent of the Nixon administration or any other partisan masters to be effective. There was an obvious need, after decades of free-wheeling by the FBI, to make the Bureau more responsive to shifts in public policy and social priorities, but not so responsive that federal law enforcement came to be a mere adjunct of the election returns. Gray had to demonstrate independence, but he also had to be careful not to take the idea as far as Hoover had.

It was the Director's legacy and tradition — in effect, his ghost — that loomed as Gray's greatest problem. "No one can replace The Giant," he said disingenuously at a Flag Day ceremony in Washington six weeks after Hoover's death while accepting the 1972 Distinguished

Citizen's Award from the Washington Lions Club, presented to Hoover posthumously. But that was true. No successor could command the kind of knee-jerk respect and deference that the Director had had both from those in the Bureau and from the outside world. Nor could he get away with the exercise of such raw, unapologetic power to reorder the world when he did not like it the way it was. Whatever tricks he might pull, Pat Gray simply would not become the overnight hero of the policeman on the beat, a godlike symbol of Americanism ranking alongside Mom and apple pie, and a name synonymous around the world with law and order. And despite what they said, the more than twenty thousand employees of the FBI would not automatically transfer their loyalty to the new man in "Mr. Hoover's office"; that loyalty was something Gray would have to earn.

Publicly, Gray uttered all the obligatory words of elaborate praise for Hoover and his leadership; nearly every one of his early speeches began or ended with a paean to the Director. "By every definition of the word, his was a most distinguished career," Gray told the Fourth Annual Crime Control Conference of the governor of Mississippi; "those of us who carry on his work — the work of the FBI — will strive to merit the confidence and support of those who honored him, the vast majority of Americans who are law-abiding citizens of these United States." An "enlightened pioneer of professional law enforcement," Gray called Hoover at a national convention of the Veterans of Foreign Wars, one "whose distinguished career spanned one quarter of our Nation's history [and who] waged a lifelong battle against the forces of lawlessness, both criminal and subversive."

But while he was delivering these extended eulogies, Gray was also trying to untangle the chaos that Hoover had left behind inside the FBI. Under almost every rock was a problem. Although the Director had promised to commit hundreds of newly authorized agents to the fight against organized crime, he had actually assigned many of them elsewhere. Because of preoccupation with domestic protesters and black and student organizations, and because of restrictive procedures instituted by Hoover in his last years, some Bureau officials complained, the FBI was falling behind in its efforts to cope with its counterintelligence tasks. The existence of a "no-contact" list and the rupture of liaison with virtually all other federal agencies were hurting the FBI in its dealings inside government and with the public. There was an epidemic of airplane hijackings, but instead of developing a coherent policy for dealing with them, the Bureau was quibbling with the airlines and the pilots' association. The Bureau was lagging way behind most other government agencies and private companies in

L. Patrick Gray III, a political man with a well-developed sense of loyalty to his President, Richard M. Nixon, was named acting director of the FBI shortly after J. Edgar Hoover's death. In his initial efforts to wrench the Bureau out of its traditional ways, Gray ran into great trouble with the loyal Hoover lieutenants; later, as he fought for confirmation as the FBI's permanent director, the Congress, the press, and the public criticized him for granting special favors to the White House during the Watergate investigation.

Gray is shown presiding over one of his first meetings with the executive conference he inherited from Hoover. The three men to the immediate left of Gray are from left to right, Joseph J. Casper, long the head of the Training Division, whose resignation was marked by a shouting match in the director's office; Nicholas P. Callahan, then head of the Administrative Division and later Clarence Kelley's associate director; and W. Mark Felt, Gray's acting associate director who played both ends against the middle on the chance that he would be named to take over the Bureau when Gray failed. To the right of Gray is John P. Mohr, assistant-to-the-director for administrative matters and one of the most powerful men in FBI history, and, next to him, Alex Rosen, assistant-to-the-director for investigative matters, a Hoover stalwart since World War II. Mohr and Rosen soon resigned in disgust with Gray, and Gray immediately abolished the two traditionally important jobs. By 1975 the only man still holding the same job as when this picture was taken three years earlier was William V. Cleveland, assistant director for the Special Investigative Division, fourth from the right. Above the fireplace in the director's conference room is the formal portrait of Harlan Fiske Stone, the attorney general who named Hoover to run the FBI in 1924 and, therefore, the one most revered in the Bureau.

Gray arrives for his ill-fated confirmation hearings before the Senate Judiciary Committee and is greeted by Senator James O. Eastland (D-Mississippi), the committee chairman and a reliable protector of the Bureau for decades. (In the background is Senator Hugh Scott of Pennsylvania, the Senate Republican Leader.) Gray alienated both the Nixon administration and the Senate during his testimony, and when the committee appeared deadlocked his nomination was withdrawn. He later resigned in disgrace in April 1973, when it was learned that he had destroyed documents relating to the Watergate affair that were confided to him by White House aides.

minority employment policies. And a number of regional emperors held sway in the field as special-agents-in-charge, often terrorizing their agents into submission and ignoring the revision of old Bureau policies. Some authorities felt that FBI training was lagging way behind the times and criticized the Bureau leadership for its lack of sophistication and its ignorance of the latest thinking in the field of management. These difficulties, among many others, could not help but make Gray wonder how Hoover had had such a pure reputation. They gave him additional reasons, if he needed any, for resenting his predecessor.

The policy and administrative problems, while complicated, seemed solvable in the long run with appropriate analysis, shifts of manpower, and other management techniques. More vexing in the short run was the question of how to deal with the Hoover cult of personality, how to substitute some other feeling for the image of the holy Director in the minds of those thousands of employees going about their daily rounds. Curiously, Gray tried to eliminate the Hoover problem by emulating him. Shortly after settling in to his temporary job, he had an official full-color photograph taken of himself, reproduced in large numbers, and sent around to every FBI office in the world; there it was intended to take its place alongside Hoover's picture. When any FBI official visited Gray's office with his family, a Bureau photographer was invited in to record the occasion. Typically, the pictures were sent out with a patriotic inscription: "With deep appreciation for your dedicated service to our beloved country, Pat Gray." He adopted the regal life-style and attitude of a man of high position, enjoying the use of Hoover's chauffeured Cadillacs and the availability of a crew of office retainers to tend to his needs and run his errands. He hired a Filipino steward to prepare meals in the director's suite and ordered a new large conference table (although when he discovered that it had a Formica top he did not like, he sent it off to a storeroom). Frightened that he might be hijacked, he refused to take commercial flights for his extensive travels, instead chartering military aircraft at the Bureau's considerable expense.* At a rate of five hundred dollars an hour, the FBI was billed by the air force for about $100,000 worth of charter service within Gray's first eight months in office. "I finally got the idea," said one agent who watched Gray from afar, "that he wanted to set up a Court of King Patrick."

---

* Hoover's favorite way of traveling had always been by train, preferably in a coach whose temperature was constantly monitored and controlled. In his later years, however, the Director got in the habit of taking commercial flights for his annual visits to Florida and California.

Although he probably did not envision it in terms that crude, Gray did seem to have early delusions of grandeur and to dream of a glorious "Gray era" in the FBI's history. Whether it ever could have come about is doubtful, but the prospects were surely dimmed by his overt efforts to take over Hoover's place in the hearts and minds of the men and women of the Bureau. That place had been developed over nearly half a century; it involved an affection and adoration that was not available for facile transfer to somebody new. And the FBI was a far cry from the Department of Health, Education and Welfare. The employees at the highest level did not owe their jobs to the triumph of one political force over another; only one person in the Bureau did, and that was Gray. The FBI people's loyalty was as strong as that of which Gray had spoken so forcefully at HEW three years earlier. The loyalty was tireless, unstinting, often self-sacrificing, and sometimes blind. But with the Director gone, it was focused on an institution, not on any human being.

Pat Gray, like most other phenomena in FBI history, stirred distinctly different reactions and feelings at headquarters and in the field. In the eyes of most people in the field, especially the agents on the street, he was in many respects a hero. For a start, Gray made the average agent's life considerably easier. He loosened some of the petty rules and regulations — many of them honored only in the breach — that had so infuriated generations of Bureau men. Field offices no longer had to keep tiresome "time in office" statistics, and resident agencies were permitted to abandon the daily reports on which every agent's every moment had been accounted for. The permissible grounds for "hardship transfers" on the basis of illness or family problems were broadened. Under certain circumstances agents were permitted to take Bureau cars home, and they were for the first time granted advances of official funds to cover transportation in their own cars and temporary housing when they were under transfer orders. Gray instituted a "voluntary physical fitness program," under which agents were permitted, and encouraged, to take off up to three one-hour periods a week for physical exercise of their choice.* Besides cutting back the degree of Bureau control over an agent's weight, dress, and hair style, Gray also said it was acceptable for them to drink coffee or soft drinks, or even to eat chocolate bars, at their desks. As *Time* magazine quoted one career Bureau man, "The agents thought they had died and gone to heaven."

Gray also scored points among the people he liked to call "the troops" by lowering the boom on some of the more unpopular special-

* Clarence Kelley later suspended the physical fitness program.

agents-in-charge. His punishment of Wesley Grapp of Los Angeles, for financial improprieties, the interception of agents' phone calls, and refusing to accept some of Gray's minor reforms, was perhaps one of the most popular actions of Gray's entire tenure as acting director. Similarly, when agents' wives wrote in to complain about the arbitrary manner in which Richard Rogge, the SAC in Honolulu, was treating their husbands, Gray looked into the matter and transferred Rogge to Richmond. Another SAC who suffered the acting director's wrath was Robert Kunkel, who was demoted from running one of the Bureau's most important units, the Washington Field Office, to a medium-sized one in St. Louis. The official reason for Kunkel's punishment was that he had submitted a report to Gray that covered up the true circumstances behind an incident at the U.S. Capitol when two agents were disarmed by protesters during a scuffle; Kunkel, for his own part, insisted vehemently that he was really being punished by Gray for taking an overly aggressive role in pursuing the Watergate investigation. But whatever the actual basis, the SACs disciplined under Gray tended to be those who were roughest on the agents under their control.

One of Gray's most significant qualities, as far as many field agents were concerned, was his willingness to accept the ultimate responsibility for controversial decisions that came under attack, rather than passing the buck and looking for a scapegoat who could be held at fault, as Hoover was so often inclined to do. When a Southern Airways DC-9 jet was hijacked, for example, and flown around the country from one airport to another, the decision was finally made to have agents shoot out its tires at a military airfield in Orlando, Florida, in an effort to prevent it from taking off for Cuba. After the plane managed a dangerous takeoff even with flat tires, the FBI was severely criticized, by both the airline management and the Airline Pilots Association, for taking an action that allegedly endangered the lives of everyone on board. Gray, who had supervised the Bureau's handling of the weekend crisis from his study in Stonington, Connecticut, insisted that he himself should be held personally and directly responsible for the emergency decision, good or bad. He pointed out that the technical experts had been worried about the hijacked plane's dwindling oil supply and lack of maintenance, and that various airlines, including Southern, had assured the FBI that the DC-9 would not be able to take off with flat tires. That one incident earned Gray an enormous amount of respect among agents, who still cite it as a point in his favor. "Gray was able to say, 'I did it.' To me, that showed he was a man. He was able to accept responsibility," said one agent who was involved in that hijack case. "It proved him to be a stand-up guy," another said. A third agent, who had nothing to do with the Southern Airways case but who watched it from a distance, added, "He took the blame for what was obviously, in retrospect, a questionable decision. For once the brass was saying, 'I'm responsible,' instead of trying to pin it on someone else."

It might have happened under almost any new director after Hoover's long hold on the job, but Gray's arrival meant a new look at the qualifications of some agents who had felt doomed to obscurity and anonymity under the old regime. He reached out to the field to find people with proven talent in certain areas — for example, press relations and some aspects of security work — and brought them to headquarters in major supervisory roles, sometimes promoting them ahead of others who had been at headquarters for years. In a few instances that damaged morale while improving administration; but it also encouraged the idea that the old lockstep career development process could be short-circuited by people with genuine merit. Gray gave a few bright young agents already at headquarters unusually heavy responsibilities if they had impressed him or caught his atten-tion during routine meetings and planning sessions.* His accession also encouraged some agents, who were stars in the field but who had previously declined promotion in order to avoid the in-group at head-quarters, to apply for positions in Washington after all; some who came in under those circumstances were particularly innovative and original thinkers, and they advanced quickly once they had taken the first step out of their longtime role as street agents.

But the most dramatic gesture Gray made to the men in the field was to come see them. Sensing a hostility and closed atmosphere at FBI headquarters, Gray decided to fashion his own orientation pro-gram — and to look for supporters — by visiting the agents where they worked. Beginning only five days after he took office with a call on the field office in New Haven, near his adopted hometown, he launched a whirlwind tour of the Bureau's fifty-nine outposts, fitting them in with every available opportunity he had to make a speech. By November 14, 1972, Gray had looked in on fifty-eight offices, missing only Hono-lulu. (He never did make it there.) Some of the visits were brief and perfunctory, but in each case he at least delivered a little speech, shook hands, and surveyed the physical layout. The impact was extraordi-nary: agents and other employees who had often found the FBI

---

* To have been recognized and singled out for advancement by Gray came to be something of a liability after his demise; many of his favorites had to tread care-fully for a while, and some were later actually demoted.

leadership in Washington to be remote and aloof were impressed that a man in his position would travel so far just to see them; they took it as a personal compliment. For some, this might be the only opportunity in decades of employment by the Bureau actually to be in the same room with their ultimate boss, let alone to shake his hand or chat with him. Gray's speech was usually the same, and did not contain much beyond a routine assurance of his interest and commitment, but it nonetheless gave thousands of Bureau personnel a sense of direct involvement with someone who had previously been a mystery. "I want to know their problems because their problems are our problems," Gray said later in explaining the field office visits; "I seek their counsel; in fact, I demand their advice and counsel. I want to establish that personal rapport which builds confidence and enhances performance." The visits also served a number of other frank purposes for Gray. To some extent he actually managed to build a constituency in the field, which may have helped indirectly to improve his relations with the folks back at headquarters. Because he scheduled "press availabilities" in each city, Gray also became the subject of newspaper stories and television reports in places where he might otherwise have remained totally unknown. "I was stunned," said one close associate of Gray; "it suddenly dawned on me that what he was doing was trying to improve his chances for the permanent appointment. He was running for director." Because the tour was so frantic and hurried, however, there was some question about how much Gray actually managed to learn about field operations. Some suggested that like its apparent precedent, Richard Nixon's 1960 presidential campaign visits to all fifty states, Gray's traveling wasted a great deal of time and energy, not to say money, that could have been spent more wisely.

If Gray was considered a hero in the field, many of the powerful veterans at headquarters saw him as the devil incarnate. He simply went too far for their taste in his questioning of the traditional ways — the Hoover ways — that things had been done in the FBI. Over his first weekend as acting director, off in Connecticut, Gray drew up a list of thirteen "avenues of inquiry," which called for studies on topics ranging from an evaluation of the Bureau's contribution to the fight against drug abuse to the question of whether to establish a "Director's Advisory Committee" composed of outsiders. Gray's "avenues" also called for a new review of the "safeguards . . . to prevent the FBI from becoming a national police force" and of the Bureau's role in such areas as police training and protection of the nation's internal security. The process was institutionalized a few months later when Gray established the Office of Planning and Evaluation as a separate headquarters division. It had a charter to reevaluate a whole range of Bureau policies and practices, including administrative questions such as whether the largest field offices should have more than one assistant-special-agent-in-charge and issues such as whether the Bureau should help in the selection of police chiefs.* As Richard Baker, the first assistant director in charge of OPE, candidly put it later, the FBI would now be studying problems to determine the best solutions, whereas "in the past, we often looked for information to satisfy an advance conclusion."

Other assistant directors, for the most part, refused to take OPE seriously at first, considering it a waste of time and an unnecessary diversion of manpower. But they did take seriously Gray's abolition of the old Crime Records (alias Crime Research) Division, a favorite of Hoover and the vehicle for the Bureau's public relations and propaganda effort. Gray did not like the speeches the division prepared for him and felt that its hostile attitude toward some members of the press was doing the FBI more harm than good. After a number of bitter clashes with Thomas E. Bishop, the traditional assistant director for Crime Research, Gray forced Bishop's retirement, distributed some of the division's functions to other parts of the Bureau, and incorporated the FBI press and congressional relations duties into the acting director's office. That infuriated some of the old-timers, who saw it as tampering with the basic structure of the FBI and feared that the agency's public positions would now be forced through a meat grinder by David Kinley. They were already bitter over the fact that Gray's disciplining of SACs like Grapp, Kunkel, and Rogge had received widespread publicity, partly on the basis of what they suspected to be leaks from Gray's office. Whatever the merits of the actual decisions on discipline, they argued, there was certainly no reason for airing the Bureau's dirty linen in public. An SAC should not be preceded by negative press notices when he takes up a new assignment, they argued. Because they felt the acting director was doing that, they gave him the nickname of "Tattletale Gray." (Eventually Gray did put a tighter lid on information about his disciplinary actions when he became convinced that the publicity surrounding them was causing a morale problem.)

Another unkind sobriquet pinned on the acting director by the Bureau hierarchy was "Two-Day Gray," a reference to the fact that his barnstorming campaign travels from field office to field office kept him out of Washington. Gray would insist that he could always keep in

---

* Another early, temporary duty of OPE was to develop the necessary information and responses for Gray's confirmation hearings.

touch with Washington from the most distant field office. But that was just the point, the veterans would say; without being right on top of the paper flow one cannot really run the FBI. Invariably Gray would reject their advice, setting his critics off on another chorus of "Why won't he listen to us? We know best, we have been here for years. If he would only rely on us, we will pull him through. . . . We know how to run this place, and we could make him a success." When asked later to evaluate the reasons for Gray's eventual failure, one Bureau official after another repeated the same theme: "He didn't listen to those of us who could really help him and wanted to help him. He seemed to distrust anyone who had done well under Mr. Hoover."

Gray was stubbornly intent on charting his own course, part of which involved jerking the FBI out of its old isolation. Bureau officials were suspicious of him for trying to bring the agency more closely into the Justice Department family by urging FBI participation in department-wide programs and informal activities. They resisted his suggestion that the Bureau join in the annual Justice Department "service awards," which gave employees recognition for any special accomplishments; after all, the FBI men said, the Bureau has its own system that rewards both length of service and diligence. Gray encouraged direct communication between people on parallel levels in the FBI and the Criminal Division whenever a problem arose on a pending case, rather than insisting that the situation be "papered" with endless reports and other documents, eventually to be resolved only between the director and the attorney general. It was difficult for the Bureau people to talk with Gray about "the department," that evil place full of political appointees and ambitious young lawyers using government service to gain experience before entering a lucrative private practice, because that, after all, was the milieu from which Gray had most recently come.

Perhaps the greatest basis for ridicule of the acting director was his speeches. The Old Guard thought it was foolish of Gray to accept virtually every invitation he received to speak and then to race around the country keeping the engagements — from the annual convention of the Retired Armed Forces Association in Lowell, Massachusetts, to the Rotary Club of Butte, Montana — but they also scoffed at what he said. The "road show," as they called it, did provide an interesting picture of Gray the man and Gray the obsequious candidate for the permanent directorship. He would come off as a superpatriot, as in an address called "America Is Worth Fighting For" at the annual convention of the Veterans of Foreign Wars in Minneapolis:

As the visible symbol of our Nation, our flag continues to wave briskly in the crisp breeze of democracy. And while some have pledged their allegiance to the red flag of communist tyranny, the black flag of anarchy, or the white flag of surrender, I proudly share your obvious affection for the red, white and blue of America's banner.

Or angry with protest movements, as in his appearance in the "Great Issues Series" at Pepperdine University in Los Angeles:

Today we hear strident and bitter voices from a very small, though highly articulate minority that the historic institutions of America should be destroyed as completely as if the Huns or Vandals had passed through.

These voices, especially those of the extremist "New Left," assert that our democratic institutions are corrupt and not worth saving. We are told that our American way of life is repressive. These raucous voices proclaim there is no freedom in this country. They assert that there is no avenue for change within the existing political process. Reform is not good enough for them. They demand that the system itself be overturned.

. . .

I cannot envision what kind of rights and what kind of justice we would have if these calamity-howlers had their way. When they speak of justice, I am reminded of the words of the Great English jurist, Sir Edward Coke. "The worst oppression," he told us, ". . . is done by colour of justice."

Or boyishly idealistic, as in his discussion of "Fidelity to Perfection" before the Maine Bar Association in Bangor:

Presumptuous as it may be to take liberties with the long-cherished symbols of this great state, let me assert a guest's privilege. For this one day, I propose that the State of Maine be known as the home of the pine tree, the lobster — and the seagull!

I have in mind one particular seagull, "Jonathan Livingston" by name, and I offer him to you as the theme of my remarks. . . . he is symbolic of the liberated human spirit . . . soaring to ever greater heights . . seeking to conquer new worlds . . . pursuing excellence . . . and achieving the ultimate that lies within the grasp of his kind.

He represents the human imagination shaking itself free from the mundane and the mediocre, and thus the better able to address the problems of the real world and creatively resolve them. . . .

Let me illustrate this theme of human possibility by drawing on the latest chapter of my own autobiography, a chapter whose final lines are not yet written.

As you know, I was appointed Acting Director of the FBI in May of

1972, and I approached this assignment with a feeling of respect and admiration – bordering almost on awe – for the organization that John Edgar Hoover had built, and for the men and women who had shared with him in the creation.

. . .

I wanted to see what made this great organization "tick" . . . where were the sinews, muscles and nerves that held it together? Every American is a shareholder in the FBI. I wanted to see how good your investment actually was.

It is a rare tribute to Mr. Hoover . . . and to the men and women who built the FBI with him . . . for me to be able to stand before you today and tell you that this magnificent organization responded with a zest, an enthusiasm, with an all-consuming fidelity to perfection that is unparalleled in my experience.

(Gray took the same liberties with the symbols of the state of Wisconsin – and delivered the same speech extolling the example of the seagull – when he addressed its state bar association in Milwaukee a few weeks later.)

He could also wax eloquent as a defender of the Bureau he had taken over, as at a Student Conference on National Affairs at Texas A&M University:

The myths and legends being circulated about the FBI . . . that it is a national police force . . . that it has an eye in every bedroom . . . that it is an enemy of civil rights . . . need to be laid to rest.

In fact, the FBI, because of the training of its personnel, its guidelines for conducting investigations, its scrupulous respect for the rights of every citizen, is a vital force working against the type of controlled society we all so deeply detest.

But what bothered some people was that Gray could also sound somewhat political. That was the charge made about a speech Gray delivered on August 11, 1972, to the City Club of Cleveland. An advance memorandum warned him that the club "is dominated by liberals" and that Gray might expect "embarrassing questions" to be posed on "controversial subjects." He gave a tough talk in which he complained that "strident voices" were proclaiming that "American society is 'sick' and that law is used to repress freedom. . . . there are those who insist that our priceless liberties are being eroded – that freedom is increasingly in jeopardy across the United States." But he noted that the crime statistics had only recently begun to turn around and that "during the first quarter of 1972, crime registered its smallest increase — one percent — in eleven years." And he warned against "those who define their lawless activity as political expression."

Some people suggested that Gray's remarks about "strident voices" sounded as if he were referring to the Democratic presidential candidate for 1972, Senator George S. McGovern; that the citation of crime statistics was meant to boost the Nixon administration for keeping the streets safer than others could do; and that some of the "political expression" he found questionable included protest against American involvement in Southeast Asia. They were also suspicious of Gray's proclamation in the Cleveland speech that "we are on the threshold of the greatest growth pattern in our history — growth in the quality of life for all our citizens — growth in our total effort to eradicate the imperfections in human society (beginning, always, with our own)." These impressions of the speech as a political one were reinforced when it was revealed that Gray had addressed the Cleveland organization only after receiving a memorandum from a White House aide urging Gray to assign "some priority" to the City Club's invitation because of "Ohio being crucially vital to our hopes in November."

In a similar vein, it was later learned that the Bureau processed a request from the Nixon White House for "identification of the substantive issue problem areas in the criminal justice field" in several major states — "in order for John Ehrlichman to give the President maximum support during campaign trips over the next several weeks." When the request was received through the office of Deputy Attorney General Ralph Erickson, it was transmitted verbatim to twenty-one FBI offices in politically important states, with the approval of Gray's aide David Kinley and Acting Associate Director W. Mark Felt. When the incident became public, Gray noted that he had been out of Washington during the entire time when the political request was under consideration and was transmitted to the field, when the results came back, and when the answers were passed along to the White House. Some Bureau officials, in fact, insisted that exactly the same thing might well have happened under J. Edgar Hoover, but Gray's political background — and a growing fear that he might politicize the FBI — seemed to make people especially sensitive to such improprieties. Several SACs declined to respond to the request, and even White House aide John Ehrlichman, for reasons of his own, suggested publicly later that transmission of the memorandum through FBI channels had been an improper, political use of the Bureau.

With Gray overtly running for full-fledged appointment as permanent director, the suspicion grew that he felt that one of his most important responsibilities, not to say personal campaign tactics, was also to protect the exposed flanks of the Nixon administration. Nothing contributed to this suspicion as much as the Watergate scandals.

There are people in the FBI who argue persuasively that if J. Edgar Hoover had not died on May 2, 1972, the Watergate cover-up never could have succeeded as long as it did or might not have been attempted at all. Some take the argument even further, asserting that if Hoover had still been at the helm, the Watergate burglars working on President Nixon's behalf would not have broken into the headquarters of the Democratic National Committee that year. They would not have dared, because they would have feared detection by Hoover. If they did, according to this reasoning, the Director would have granted special consideration to no one and would have pressed the investigation to the hilt without the slightest hesitation. His motives would not have been purely those of the apolitical, vigilant guardian of the law; rather, he would have been reacting as the imperious bureaucrat whose turf had been trampled upon. He would have been furious, surely, to learn of the existence of the White House "plumbers," viewing them as an encroachment on the Bureau's prerogatives; and he would have been eager for revenge on the former FBI agents among the Watergate burglars, James W. McCord and G. Gordon Liddy, for so disgracing the Bureau's name — he would have done the job that needed doing. He might have entertained some conspiracy theories that his own worst enemy, the Central Intelligence Agency, was really responsible for the crime; but Hoover would have flooded the prosecutors with enough material to document any case they would want to make. How he would have reacted when he discovered just how high complicity in the cover-up went — and that the President himself was involved — is hard to say, the proponents of this Director-as-crime-stopper theory acknowledge, but he had certainly never hesitated in the past to defy and distress presidents, attorneys general, and mere White House aides, so why not this time, when it was all the more necessary?

What J. Edgar Hoover would have done is obviously an impossible issue to resolve. But it is almost as difficult to get the various authorities, inside the Bureau and out, to agree on exactly how the situation was handled by L. Patrick Gray, who was alive and well and running the FBI for most of the crucial period of the Watergate investigation.

Some extreme skeptics are prepared to believe that because Gray was in southern California (visiting the Los Angeles Field Office and giving two speeches at Pepperdine University) on the weekend of

June 16 and 17 — as were Nixon campaign aides John N. Mitchell, Robert C. Mardian, and Jeb Stuart Magruder — he was in on the cover-up plot from the very beginning. But the official FBI view, held to this day, is that the Bureau's investigation of the Watergate affair was a "full court press," a no-holds-barred effort from start to finish. According to this official view, even if Gray had tried — and he did not — he would have been unable to force the FBI to go easy or hold back. This is not ever done, and it was not done, goes the Bureau line: "Oh, I'm sure we all felt a certain deference toward the White House, something we would not feel if we had it to do over again," says one person who was involved with the case, now retired; "but we pushed, we really did. If there was a concerted effort to impede and interfere with the investigation, then the agents probably worked even harder than usual." Most of the men who helped run or coordinate the Watergate investigation have signed their names to statements, mostly solicited by Gray in his moments of tribulation or in preparation for his confirmation hearings, or otherwise given their word that there were no conscious, premeditated, successful pressures to prevent a full and conscientious inquiry. Field supervisors who directed the Bureau efforts in Florida, California, New York, and elsewhere also insist this is true; they say that they felt no restrictions on their efforts during the original Watergate investigation. Agents point with pride to references in the White House transcripts indicating the disgust of Nixon's aides over the fact that the FBI was "out of control" and had not been "used" to protect the White House as much as it could have been.

What then happened? Did a small conspiracy of men, vested with high office and political power, succeed in completely stumping and outwitting what is supposed to be one of the sharpest investigative agencies in the world? Were the lies so skillfully told to investigators, and was the obfuscation so meticulously cultivated, that it would have been impossible even for Sherlock Holmes to see through and solve the case? Or did the FBI, departing from its usual standard, put less than its best foot forward, and did its acting director, a political man who sounded obsessed at times with the notion of loyalty toward the President of the United States, do just enough to hold things back and give the conspiracy time to weave its web a little tighter now and then? The evidence, which will perhaps never be complete, points strongly to the latter conclusion. At the very least, the Bureau gave the holders of high office the benefit of some doubts. Gray, although he was not alone, made things easier for the conspirators in the White House and at the Nixon reelection committee. It is not entirely clear whether he realized what he was doing — the best that can be said is that he was naïve and easily tricked — but it seems obvious that the people who had something to hide realized what they were doing to him, and none of it was very good or very nice.

Some of the Bureau's work was simply sloppy and incomplete. As Bob Woodward and Carl Bernstein point out in their book, *All the President's Men,* the FBI did not manage to interview all of the people whose names and phone numbers were in the address books carried by the original Watergate burglars. The Bureau never sought even a pro forma interview with H. R. Haldeman, Nixon's chief of staff, to ask what he knew or theorized about the bizarre events. In many respects the FBI was apparently stymied by the Justice Department and the assistant United States attorneys handling the original Watergate prosecution for interception-of-communications and burglary: important leads concerning former Attorney General John Mitchell, which were coming out in grand jury proceedings, for example, were never passed along for the Bureau to follow up. The contents of a mysterious package shipped over to Justice from the CIA in December 1972 — including strange photographs (of Daniel Ellsberg's psychoanalyst's office) taken by E. Howard Hunt and Gordon Liddy during a trip to California on Labor Day weekend of 1971 — were not shared with the FBI. And Justice failed to authorize the Bureau to open a vigorous separate investigation into the "dirty tricks" side of the Watergate affair when details of it first began to trickle out (although the FBI probably could have gone further on its own than it did).

Gray extended courtesies to the people interviewed during the Watergate investigation that the FBI would not have granted in almost any other case. The Bureau often refuses to interview people who insist upon having a lawyer present. But attorneys at the Committee for the Re-election of the President (CRP, or, more irreverently, CREEP) were permitted to sit in on FBI agents' interviews with employees of the committee. When several of those employees called the Bureau back to say they had felt inhibited under the circumstances and to invite the agents to interview them again at home, they were soon confronted at work with information that had come up only in this second, supposedly confidential, session with the FBI; the FBI under Gray wired in CREEP's lawyers even when they were not present.

After long delays, Gray finally granted permission for agents to interview some fourteen White House aides, but he agreed to the demand that John W. Dean III, counsel to the President, be allowed to sit in and monitor what the people told the Bureau — supposedly because Dean was conducting his own inquiry for the President, but in reality becaue he was trying to keep the lid on the cover-up. The conditions were obviously not conducive to frankness on the part of the White House staff. Gray also repeatedly entertained suggestions from the CIA and the White House that FBI interviews with two men who had handled the money used to finance the Watergate burglary, and with a White House secretary who had worked for the "plumbers," might jeopardize confidential CIA sources and operations and other "national security" matters. Only after Mark Felt and the man who was then assistant director for the Bureau's General Investigation Division, Charles W. Bates, pressed Gray to demand an explanation in writing from the CIA, and the agency refused to provide it, did Gray tell his agents to go ahead with the interviews; in the meantime, progress on an important part of the investigation had been delayed. Gray apparently did not become suspicious when presidential assistant John Ehrlichman stepped in and abruptly canceled a meeting that Gray was to have with CIA Director Richard Helms to discuss the matter.

But probably the most egregious procedure Gray adopted was his agreement to give Dean copies of reams of Bureau documents concerning the Watergate case — not the Letterhead Memoranda (or summaries ordinarily used to disseminate information outside the FBI), but the actual "raw" unevaluated investigative materials, including "302 forms," on which individual interviews are reported. Also among the documents Gray transmitted to Dean were summaries of the telephone conversations that were originally intercepted with the electronic devices illegally installed at the Democratic headquarters in the Watergate complex; if the first copies had never arrived during all the confusion of arrests and court proceedings, now there would be an extra one that could be consulted by the Nixon strategists after all.

Later, as he sought to explain the provision of such sensitive material to Dean, Gray's navy instincts seemed to return: "You've got to operate on a basic presumption of regularity," he said. Dean, after all, "was counsel to the President of the United States." He was "within the official chain of command of the United States Government." But if regularity was to be presumed, it was curious that the acting director of the FBI also found it necessary and appropriate to handle the situation so surreptitiously. His initial meeting with Dean to discuss the materials wanted by the White House, in fact, took place during a walk around the apartment building in Southwest Washington where Gray lived, because Dean felt it would be too conspicuous if they met at the Justice Department building on a Sunday. For a time they sat and talked on a park bench. Whenever Gray did pass packets of mate-

rial on to Dean, he insisted that the presidential counsel come personally to pick them up rather than have them delivered by the regular
courier between the Justice Department and the White House.

Had Gray checked around about the propriety of turning over the
"302" interview reports — he eventually gave Dean about eighty-two
of them, covering almost half of all the interviews conducted by the
Bureau in its original Watergate investigation — he might have
learned that an identical request by Dean had already been turned
down by Kleindienst and Assistant Attorney General Henry E. Petersen before he had approached Gray. Some of the interview forms, of
course, later ended up in the wrong hands; while Dean promised that
they were only for the President's use, he freely copied and distributed
them. Although Gray was trying to be surreptitious and did not tell
anyone in the Bureau, not even his personal assistants, that he was
providing the material to Dean, he had already aroused suspicions by
ordering that he be furnished with a continuously updated copy of the
full Watergate investigative file for the stated purpose of remaining
"familiar" with all details of the case. Bureau officials found that order
most unusual, especially coming from a man who had complained that
he was unable to handle even the standard flow of memoranda and
reports through his office. Ordinarily, even in the biggest breaking
cases, the director would receive only summary teletypes, supple-
mented by any interview reports and other documents that were of
particular interest or importance.

Gray's continuing presumption of regularity and uprightness on
the part of the White House was all the more surprising, in retrospect,
in view of the fact that on June 28, 1972, he had met most secretly with
Dean and John Ehrlichman in Ehrlichman's White House office. Although the complete contents of Howard Hunt's safe at the White
House had supposedly already been turned over to the Bureau —
albeit after a substantial delay, to which Gray had consented — the
presidential aides now produced two manila envelopes containing
documents from Hunt's safe that, they said, had nothing to do with
Watergate, should not be incorporated into FBI files, and, in fact, were
"political dynamite" that "should not see the light of day." The envelopes, it was subsequently revealed, contained copies of State Department cables that had been doctored and fabricated by Hunt in order
to demonstrate that President John F. Kennedy had ordered the assassination of Ngo Dinh Diem, president of South Vietnam, during the
early stages of U.S. involvement in the Southeast Asian war. Gray
accepted the envelopes and never mentioned them to anyone at the
FBI for the next ten months. (Hoover, at the very least, would have

noted their existence in a memorandum for the record, say his former aides.)

The combined effect of these various gestures was a substantial obstruction of the FBI's officially aggressive Watergate investigation. Top-ranking Bureau officials were not privy to everything Gray was doing, but they grew increasingly suspicious — especially during meetings when the acting director created elaborate doodles to illustrate possible theories at the root of the Watergate case, most of which steered attention away from the White House and were considered highly implausible by the other men. That was one reason why people at various levels of the Bureau became such notorious leaks of information about the investigation, and about Gray's own exploits. Ehrlichman, Dean, and others at the White House repeatedly accused the FBI of being the source of some of the most damaging leaks about the case, and Gray, sometimes after meeting with the Bureau hierarchy to reassure himself, denied the accusations with a tone of outrage and insult. But the White House was right this time. Some FBI men believed that leaks were the only available means to be sure that the truth would eventually come out.*

After Nixon was reelected in November 1972, he moved slowly to name the new cabinet for his second term. The idea was to increase White House influence in all of the executive departments as much as possible, and the department that had to wait the longest before things were clarified was Justice. By the time Kleindienst was granted an extension of his tenure as attorney general — only after his old patron Barry Goldwater visited the President at Camp David and intervened on Kleindienst's behalf — he had been ordered to drop a number of key assistant attorneys general for committing such grave sins as expressing disagreement with the White House on matters of legal policy. But within the Justice Department, the last job to be filled was that of FBI director. Ehrlichman opposed Gray as an unfit blunderer. But there was a pretext for delaying the decision, in any event, because Gray had been incapacitated for several weeks as a result of surgery for an intestinal ailment, and the presidential aides could feign concern over his condition and about whether he would be physically capable of carrying on. Meanwhile, they looked around for other pos-

---

* Other, less noble motives for the leaks have been suggested: a desire to eliminate competition from such illegitimate groups as the White House "plumbers," an attempt to get the FBI credit for what it was doing, and a frank effort by people at Bureau headquarters to embarrass Pat Gray. Others, outside the FBI, were of course also responsible for many of the early leaks.

sible candidates: the various also-rans included such onetime good friends, now foes, as former Bureau officials Cartha DeLoach and William Sullivan; Nixon himself expressed a liking for Jerry V. Wilson, the Washington, D.C., police chief who had run plenty of errands for the White House. But Kleindienst strongly urged that Gray be retained, and Dean, for his part, was very happy with the arrangement he had had with him as the acting director. Finally, on February 16, 1973, Gray met first with Ehrlichman and then with the President.* Their discussion centered on Gray's health, the need to exercise "tough leadership" of the Bureau, and the continuing problem of leaks concerning the Watergate investigation. (They suggested that he use lie detector tests to find any culprits within the Bureau.) The next day Gray was announced as Nixon's choice as permanent FBI director.

By the time Gray's confirmation hearings, the first ever for an FBI director, opened on February 28, 1973, some influential senators had declared their opposition, including Robert C. Byrd of West Virginia, the Democratic whip. Byrd had been one of the keepers of the Hoover blind faith; now, in an about-face, he wanted to look hard at the Bureau. Byrd had apparently received some anti-Gray ammunition from old friends and contacts inside the Bureau, as well as from *Washington Post* reporters and airline pilots critical of him. But Gray felt very sure of himself, sure enough to reject all advice from Kleindienst and other Justice Department men on how to handle himself before the Senate Judiciary Committee. Meetings with Justice Department staff that were intended to be strategy sessions turned into angry shouting matches in which Gray asserted his intention to do things his "own way." Even David Kinley, who had full confidence in his boss, only now learning that Gray had provided extensive Watergate investigative files to John Dean, warned that the hearings might bog down on that issue; but Gray shrugged the concern away. As Dean put it to Nixon on the morning the hearings began, "Pat has had it tough. . . . He is ready. He is very comfortable in all of the decisions he has made, and I think he will be good."

The hearings were a disaster for Gray. They lasted for ten week-

---

* The White House transcripts showed that however close Gray might have presumed himself to be with the President, and others reported him to be, Nixon did not exactly share that view. "They say Gray is a political crony and a personal crony of the President's," Nixon said in a conversation with Dean; "Did you know that I have never seen him socially? . . . I think he has been to a couple White House events, but I have never seen him separately. . . . He has never been a social friend. Edgar Hoover, on the other hand, I have seen socially at least a hundred times. He and I were very close friends. . . . Hoover was my crony. He was closer to me than Johnson, actually although Johnson used him more. But as for Pat Gray [expletive deleted], I never saw him."

days over a three-week period, and with each committee session Gray's position seemed to grow weaker and more vulnerable. The senators not only used the occasion to review controversial areas of general FBI policy — including the handling of fingerprints and other arrest records, the Bureau's belated efforts against organized crime, its collection of information about congressmen, and the gathering of domestic intelligence — but they also set out on a minute review of how the Watergate case had been investigated. They exploded when they learned from Gray that he had so liberally shared FBI files with John Dean. Thinking he could appease the angry senators and ignoring the advice of Justice Department officials, Gray offered the members of the committee the same opportunity Dean had had — to peruse any of the "raw" materials of the investigation that would answer their specific questions and doubts. That, in turn, made several White House aides angry, and Kleindienst was ordered to pull the rug out from under Gray by forbidding him to make the files so widely available. The offer of liberal access to FBI files also got the American Civil Liberties Union upset over the harm that could be done to innocent people mentioned in them; and even the press, which Gray considered one of his allies, now seemed to turn against him. Gray also got himself in trouble with the White House by testifying that the Bureau files would show that dirty trickster Donald Segretti had been hired through Nixon's former appointments secretary, Dwight Chapin, and paid out of reelection committee funds by the President's personal attorney, Herbert Kalmbach.*

It did not take long for the administration to abandon the man it had just nominated to run the FBI. As the published White House transcripts later showed, by March 13 Nixon was saying, "Gray, in my opinion, should not be the head of the FBI. After going through the hell of the hearings, he will not be a good Director, as far as we are concerned." Dean stressed, however, that even if Gray were a "suspect director," he would "do what we want." Dean told the President that Gray was "still keeping in close touch with me. He is calling me. He has given me his hot line. We talk at night, how do you want me to handle this, et cetera? So he still stays in touch, and is still being involved, but he can't do it because he is going to be under such surveillance by his own people — every move he is making — that it would be a difficult thing for Pat. Not that Pat wouldn't want to play ball, but he may not be able to."

But Dean too dropped out of the ever-dwindling band of Gray

* Segretti, Chapin, and Kalmbach all eventually went to jail in connection with the scandals.

supporters on March 22, after the nominee testified that Senator Byrd was "probably . . . correct" in suggesting that Dean had lied to FBI agents when, in the initial stages of their Watergate investigation, he said he "would have to check" to find out whether Howard Hunt had an office in the White House. That day's testimony led Nixon to comment about Gray during a meeting with his top aides: "The problem with him is I think he is a little bit stupid." Nonetheless, the President called Gray the next day to offer his encouragement in the battle and to remind him that, should the issue come up again, Gray would not want to forget to point out that the President had urged him all along to conduct "a thorough and aggressive investigation" of the Watergate affair.

Increasingly, Gray became the hostage of the Judiciary Committee's eagerness to talk with Dean about why he had been poking into the investigation so much, and about other aspects of how the FBI had handled Watergate under Gray's leadership. Dean seemed to be the key. But the President was invoking "exclusive privilege" to prevent Dean from being required to testify, and Ehrlichman advocated leaving Gray to "twist slowly, slowly in the wind." Twist he did, and ignominiously at that. Absent Dean's appearance, the committee seemed to be split evenly on the issue of whether to send the Gray nomination to the Senate floor; but even if it were to reach the floor, it was becoming clear, the prospects there seemed very bleak. The committee never reconvened its hearings on Gray's fitness for the FBI job after the March 22 testimony. And Gray, his dreams shattered, wrote to the President in early April, asking that his name be withdrawn.

The plan was still that Gray would stay on as acting director until a suitable replacement could be found and confirmed, and then perhaps he could be slipped back into the running for a federal judgeship after all. It would be a reasonably graceful way for him to save face. But that plan would go awry also, as the secret of the documents from Hunt's safe that had been passed to Gray by Ehrlichman and Dean now began to unravel. During his confirmation hearings, Gray called Ehrlichman at one point (unaware that the White House aide was then taping his telephone conversations in order to protect himself) to warn that the committee, in discussing the contents of Hunt's safe, was "getting close" to the subject of the materials Gray had accepted for destruction. Gray urged that Dean, if asked, keep the story straight and say he "delivered everything he had [from the Hunt safe] to the FBI." As things evolved, the issue never was raised in the hearings; but by mid-April, with more people beginning to talk candidly with the prosecutors from the U.S. attorney's office in Washington, it seemed a likely prospect for a leak. On the night of April 15, 1973, Ehrlichman called Gray at home to warn him that Dean was suddenly talking to the prosecutors and, among other items of interest, was telling them about the Hunt files. Gray, who confirmed to Ehrlichman that the material had been destroyed, panicked. During a meeting with Henry Petersen, assistant attorney general for the Criminal Division, who had been put in charge of the Watergate investigation by the President, Gray at first pointedly denied that any envelopes full of documents had been confided to him; but then a day later he did an about-face and acknowledged to Petersen that they had been.

Early in the morning of Wednesday, April 25, 1973, Gray called Senator Lowell Weicker and told him he had urgent business to discuss. Weicker arrived at the Justice Department at 10 A.M. and was ushered through a back door into the director's office. Gray, looking white and drawn, poured his heart out to the senator about the occasion when Ehrlichman and Dean had given him the two envelopes of "political dynamite" that were "not to see the light of day." He recalled bringing the material to his office from the White House and then taking it to his home in Washington over the weekend while he made a trip to San Diego; on his return, Gray said, he took the envelopes back to the office and, without looking inside, tore them up and threw the pieces into the "burn bag." Asked by Weicker what was in the envelopes, Gray said he would have to ask Petersen, and he did. At a subsequent meeting in the afternoon, Gray told the senator Petersen had said the documents were fabricated cables dealing with the Diem assassination. Petersen was suggesting that Gray would have to go before a grand jury.

That night Weicker called an impromptu, embargoed press conference at his home for reporters who were his friends and revealed what Gray had told him. The senator discussed the significance of the revelations with the newsmen and pulled together their ideas of other questions that Gray should have to answer about the bizarre incident. On Thursday Weicker met again with his constituent, the acting director of the FBI, and argued that the story must come out immediately, told from Gray's point of view, for it was bound to appear soon anyway from a different perspective. Gray, still proud, resisted. Later in the day Weicker revealed to Gray that he had already talked with reporters and intended to lift the embargo that night. As the senator recalled the situation more than a year afterward, "I had a man's future in my hands. I couldn't just allow him to determine the solution himself. . . . He had hardly any reaction, just a perfunctory protest.

537

He put his arm around my shoulder as we walked to the elevator. He seemed bloody well relieved. I think that was what he wanted when he came to me — help in getting the story out." That same day, April 26, Henry Petersen warned Gray that they were both "expendable" and that Gray had better hire a lawyer.

The tale of Gray's burning of Howard Hunt's documents made banner headlines on Friday morning, April 27. Gray came into work at the usual time, reviewed some papers on his desk, and then met with David Kinley and Chuck Lichtenstein, a speechwriter he had brought in from the Federal Communications Commission for the period of his confirmation hearings. Gray still wanted to try to stay on, but the others persuaded him by noon that he had to resign. When he called the White House, there was resistance — but only, it soon became clear, because Nixon had already decided to dump him, along with Ehrlichman, Haldeman, Dean, and Kleindienst, the following Monday. Gray moved first and he left for Connecticut that same afternoon.

There was a peculiar epilogue. Some weeks later, when Pat Gray came back to Washington to testify before an executive session of the Senate Watergate Committee, he called Weicker early in the morning. He wanted the senator to know that this time he would tell the *whole* truth — he had actually taken the secret Hunt documents home to Connecticut in June of 1972, looked them over, stashed them among his shirts, and, only after six months had passed, had eventually burned them with the Christmas trash. Gray had told a different story the first time around, apparently because it made him seem a more innocent partner in the destruction of the material, just a public servant promptly carrying out orders from the White House. The new — and presumably true — version made it seem more like something he had thought through and done willfully. Gray would also reveal to the Watergate Committee for the first time that he had warned Nixon on July 6, 1972, barely three weeks after the Watergate break-in, that "people on your staff are trying to mortally wound you by using the CIA and FBI."

Naturally enough, Gray was an important witness before the grand jury that investigated the Watergate cover-up, and he also testified for the prosecution at the Washington trial in which Haldeman, Ehrlichman, Mitchell, and Mardian were convicted. But his most significant contribution may have been the hundreds of pages of documents and exhibits that he turned over to the Office of the Special Prosecutor for Watergate-related matters. Meanwhile, Gray waited for the eventual determination of his own lot. He was potentially vulnerable to prosecution on charges of obstructing justice or perjury before the Senate Judiciary Committee in connection with his destruction of the documents. "I justified my reticence not only because I then believed in the rectitude of the administration I was serving," he later told the Senate Watergate Committee, "but because my brief look at the file of State Department cables had confirmed for me what I thought were overwhelming considerations of national security." Gray also seemed liable to be charged with perjury for his denial during the confirmation hearings that he had any knowledge of the Nixon administration's "special program" of secret wiretaps against seventeen government officials and newsmen. Subsequent press reports suggested that Gray had been informed, both in documents and in personal conversations, about those wiretaps.*

Back home practicing law in New London, Gray seemed to some people to be a broken man, but to others he appeared only to be bitter. "I view my association with the men and women of the FBI as the high point in my life," he wrote in a letter. But Gray refused to go anywhere near the place again; a few months after he had left, two of his sons drove down from Connecticut one weekend and quietly picked up the personal possessions he had left behind in the office of the director.

Observers of the Bureau may ruminate for years in an effort to evaluate the impact and the character of Pat Gray's fifty-one weeks in office. The period included some events of which the FBI was not so proud — for example, the ill-advised effort, inappropriate for an investigative agency but insisted upon by the White House, to quell the Indian occupation of the village of Wounded Knee, South Dakota, in 1973;† and the arrest of Les Whitten, a colleague of syndicated columnist Jack Anderson, as he met with a source to pick up some documents that Indian protesters had taken from the Bureau of Indian Affairs and to return them to the government. (Both situations earned the FBI more ill will than technical success; the Indians from Wounded Knee proved impossible to convict and a grand jury declined to indict Whitten.)

Although Gray made a start on reordering the Bureau's priorities — for example, by ordering that more attention be paid to orga-

---

* Only in mid-1975 was Gray formally advised by the special prosecutor that he was in the clear.
† The Wounded Knee assignment, said the special-agents-in-charge who had served there in rotation, would have been more appropriately given to military troops. Whoever handled it, they contended, should have ended it promptly with force or else walked away from it rather than permit such a long siege with all of the attendant bad publicity.

nized crime — he attempted very few changes in investigative policy. Despite a few procedural revisions, such as the requirement of a token statement of jurisdiction for each case, the chaotic and overdeveloped state of the FBI's domestic intelligence collection was about the same when Gray left as when he arrived. One thing he did accomplish — by choice, and by fate — was the opening of a "window" on the Bureau, one that would not easily be closed again.

Pat Gray's idiosyncratic "LPG III" remains at the bottom of many FBI documents, but the huge photographs of him are gone from field office walls and his existence has been, in effect, eliminated from recent official Bureau history. Those who speak of him, even some of the agents in the field who were his strongest supporters and admirers, inevitably say they were ashamed and disillusioned by his destruction of some of the evidence from Hunt's safe. Other troublesome incidents they can forgive easily, but not that. Nonetheless, many agents kept in contact with him, sending him get-well wishes, for example, in 1975, when he underwent arterial surgery. "If only J. Edgar Hoover had died six months later," says one of Gray's admirers, "Pat Gray would now be director of the FBI . . . and he would be a good one, too." "Nonsense," scoffs a retiring assistant director, "Gray is nothing but an unhappy incident in the history of a great institution."

XXII

The Ruckelshaus Interlude

*The next thing we knew, there was this fellow named Ruckel-
something-or-other who had his coat off and his feet up on the
desk and was sitting in Mr. Hoover's chair. . . . I didn't know
who he was, and I really didn't give a damn, but he sure wasn't
the director of the FBI.*

— *A veteran FBI agent*

JILL RUCKELSHAUS ARRIVED AT HER SUBURBAN WASHINGTON HOME early
on Friday evening, April 27, 1973, from the White House, where she
worked as a special presidential assistant for women's programs. She
was expecting to find her husband Bill, who had taken the day off from
his job as administrator of the Environmental Protection Agency to
work in the garden. But he had gone out suddenly and left no message, so she had no idea where he was.

The phone rang shortly after she walked in. It was a real estate
agent calling. "Given your new situation, you'll undoubtedly want to
move to a home in a very secluded neighborhood," the agent said. Mrs.
Ruckelshaus was puzzled. "You will have to live on a quiet side street,
so that nobody really knows where you live," the caller continued.
"What are you talking about?" asked Mrs. Ruckelshaus. Came the
answer: "Well, your husband's the new head of the FBI, isn't he?"
That was how Jill Ruckelshaus found out about President Nixon's
short-term solution to the problems created by the dramatic departure
of L. Patrick Gray III from the Bureau.

Her husband had little more notice than she did. As he worked in
the yard, he received a call at about 1 P.M. from *Air Force One*, the

presidential airplane, asking him to meet Nixon at the White House later that afternoon when he returned from a trip to the South to dedicate a new dam. Even though Ruckelshaus was not yet even aware that Gray had resigned, he had a slight premonition about what might be on the President's mind: the previous December, while they were discussing whether Ruckelshaus should stay on at EPA during the second Nixon administration, the President had suddenly paused and asked Ruckelshaus directly whether he had any experience or interest in law enforcement. Gray's status was already uncertain at that point, and it occurred to Ruckelshaus that Nixon was perhaps hinting about the FBI job. But Ruckelshaus replied that while he had some interest, he did not feel that he had very much in the way of relevant background; five years in the office of the attorney general of the state of Indiana did not seem to him to be a sufficient qualification for a major law enforcement job. The conversation moved on and Ruckelshaus had heard nothing more on the subject.

Now Nixon was asking his help, talking about the "need to get somebody over there [to the FBI] in a hurry." As Ruckelshaus recalled it later, "He asked me very pointedly to do it on behalf of my country, as a request from my President. And my feeling is that if your President asks you to do something legitimate, in those terms, that you ought to do it." While agreeing to go to the Bureau temporarily, until a permanent successor for Hoover could be found, Ruckelshaus insisted that he had no desire to be there as a long-range assignment. Fully aware that he too would now be caught up in the web of Watergate, Ruckelshaus then turned to the President and asked him directly about his own involvement in the scandals. According to Ruckelshaus's later testimony before the Senate Judiciary Committee, Nixon replied "that it was a tragedy and that he wanted me to get to the bottom of it, he wanted to get to the bottom of it, and he was not in any way involved. He wanted me to go over there and do the best job I could and discharge the responsibilities of that office." As for Gray, the President discussed him, Ruckelshaus said later, "with some sympathy . . . he felt that it had really been a mistake to destroy those documents, and that was clearly something [Gray] was in trouble for." Then, after Ruckelshaus had drafted a brief statement for himself, he was trotted out into the White House press room — facing what he recalls as "a pack of snarling wolves" (relations between the Nixon administration and the media were especially bad at that time) — to be introduced as the new acting director of the FBI.

Ruckelshaus spent the weekend at home, except for a visit at the Justice Department Saturday with Attorney General Richard G. Kleindienst. He felt rather apprehensive about this sudden change in his governmental duties and wanted solid advice from someone who would be his superior and who was also a close friend. Ruckelshaus had no idea how he should or would handle the Bureau; the Bureau knew even less about what to expect.

Its initial reaction was negative, for on the surface William D. Ruckelshaus seemed to be only a Gray of a slightly different shade. He was a politician. Thirty-six in 1968, having served one two-year term in the Indiana state legislature (during which he was elected House majority leader by the Republicans), his party had sent him into the fray to try to capture the Senate seat held by Democrat Birch Bayh. Ruckelshaus lost, but he had fought a hard battle and done his duty for the Nixon-Agnew ticket, and with others who had done the same he was offered a comfortable job in Washington beginning in January 1969. As assistant attorney general in charge of the Justice Department's Civil Division (a job in which Gray, ironically, would succeed him in 1970), he enjoyed a fair amount of autonomy under Attorney General John Mitchell, who was busy advising the President and did not meddle in each division's affairs. Ruckelshaus developed a reputation as a droll, irreverent character who rarely hesitated to speak his piece, even in delicate circumstances. Those who worked with both Ruckelshaus and Gray in the Civil Division say they found Ruckelshaus to be a much looser and relaxed person — on occasion, seemingly unable to conjure up the seriousness necessary to deal with weighty matters — who did not try to impress others with the authority he held over them.

Late in 1970 Ruckelshaus became the first administrator of the newly created Environmental Protection Agency. It was a far more visible and creative job than the Civil Division, but also a more difficult one because of the powerful pressures he had to deal with daily. Automobile companies, local sewage authorities, and the Army Corps of Engineers, to name a few, sought constantly to soften the thrust of EPA's efforts, often through influential congressmen, but Ruckelshaus won bipartisan praise for his independence and his ability to confront and balance those forces off against each other. A tall, articulate man of good humor and irrepressible wit, a graduate of Princeton and the Harvard Law School who had also served two years in the army, he seemed a likely prospect to run for elected office again. He was ambitious. Ruckelshaus was frequently mentioned as a prospect for other jobs within the government. Kleindienst, when he succeeded Mitchell as attorney general in 1972, attempted on three occasions to name him as his deputy, but Nixon's powerful presidential aides refused to endorse Ruckelshaus for that slot. First they insisted upon Gray as deputy attorney general; then, when Gray was appointed to run the Bureau, they agreed to Ralph Erickson, already assistant attorney general for the Office of Legal Counsel, as a substitute; and finally they got rid of Erickson and forced the attorney general to accept Joseph T. Sneed, the dean of the President's alma mater, the Duke University Law School.

But however well respected and admired Ruckelshaus might have been, he was still a partisan politician and the influential barons of the FBI were not about to open their arms to another outsider in "Mr. Hoover's chair." W. Mark Felt, the acting associate director who was in charge of the Bureau on the weekend between Gray's departure and Ruckelshaus's actual arrival, had a busy two days on the phone to the field, taking the agency's pulse on its reaction to its new leader.

Ruckelshaus was hardly prepared for the events of Monday, April 30, 1973. After a brief stop at EPA to say good-bye, he arrived at the Justice Department building just in time for a 10 A.M. meeting in the attorney general's office that had been called by Kleindienst. There, with about thirty-five people gathered before him, the attorney general announced that he was resigning because his personal and professional closeness to some of the figures implicated in the Watergate case made it difficult for him to continue to run the Justice Department effectively. There had been no inkling of this new turn during Ruckelshaus's visit with him on Saturday. But Kleindienst had been to visit the President at Camp David on Sunday, and that was when the decision was made. Between the lines was a strong hint that he had been pressed to leave the cabinet. The Monday morning session was dramatic and emotional, and some of the people had tears in their eyes as the attorney general told of his departure and probable replacement by Defense Secretary Elliot L. Richardson. Kleindienst, for all his frontier brashness, had attracted a great deal of affection within the Justice Department — far more, for example, than the cold, businesslike Mitchell. One of the reasons for the sadness — and bitterness — in the room was the awareness that Kleindienst, who had not himself been tarred by the Watergate brush,* would be dealt with by the White House that day in the same breath and the same press release with presidential aides John D. Ehrlichman, H. R. Haldeman, and John W. Dean III,

---

* Kleindienst would later plead guilty to a misdemeanor charge for failing to admit during his confirmation hearings before the Senate Judiciary Committee that he had been pressured by Nixon in connection with antitrust cases against the International Telephone and Telegraph Corporation.

who were leaving (in Dean's case, forced out) because they were increasingly compromised by their own roles in the scandal. This deepening of the turmoil in the department, coming as it did only a few days after Gray's downfall, made Ruckelshaus feel even shakier.

No sooner did the FBI director arrive in his office than he found a copy of a telegram on his desk. He read it carefully:

THE HONORABLE RICHARD M. NIXON
PRESIDENT OF THE UNITED STATES
THE WHITE HOUSE
WASHINGTON, D.C.

MISTER PRESIDENT. THIS MESSAGE, BY UNANIMOUS ADOPTION, IS FROM THE ACTING ASSOCIATE DIRECTOR, ALL ASSISTANT DIRECTORS AND ALL SPECIAL AGENTS IN CHARGE OF FBI FIELD OFFICES THROUGHOUT THE UNITED STATES.* THE HALLMARKS OF FIDELITY, BRAVERY AND INTEGRITY AND OF DEDICATION TO CONSTITUTIONAL PRINCIPLES OF EQUAL JUSTICE AND PRESERVATION OF THE RIGHTS OF ALL CITIZENS HAVE MADE THE FBI A REVERED INSTITUTION OF OUR NATIONAL LIFE. J. EDGAR HOOVER'S PRECEPTS OF CAREFUL SELECTION OF AGENT PERSONNEL AMONG HIGHLY QUALIFIED CANDIDATES, RIGOROUS TRAINING, FIRM DISCIPLINE, AND PROMOTION SOLELY ON MERIT HAVE DEVELOPED WITHIN THE FBI LAW ENFORCEMENT LEADERS OF PROFESSIONAL STATURE RESPECTED WORLD-WIDE. IN THE SEARCH FOR A NOMINEE FOR THE FBI DIRECTORSHIP, WE URGE CONSIDERATION TO THE HIGHLY QUALIFIED PROFESSIONALS WITH IMPECCABLE CREDENTIALS OF INTEGRITY WITHIN THE ORGANIZATION ITSELF. WE DO NOT SUGGEST THERE ARE NOT MANY OTHER HIGHLY QUALIFIED LEADERS OF PROVEN INTEGRITY, BUT AT THIS CRITICAL TIME IT IS ESSENTIAL THAT THE FBI NOT FLOUNDER OR LOSE DIRECTION IN ITS SERVICE TO THE NATION BECAUSE OF LACK OF LAW ENFORCEMENT EXPERTISE OR OF OTHER QUALITIES ESSENTIAL TO THE FBI DIRECTORSHIP. NONE OF US SEEK PERSONAL GAIN — THERE IS A VAST RESERVOIR OF QUALIFIED EXECUTIVES WITHIN THE FBI'S OFFICIALDOM FROM WHICH A NOMINEE COULD BE SELECTED. WE ARE MOVED TO ADDRESS YOU THUSLY, BECAUSE OF OUR DEVOTION TO OUR SWORN DUTY TO THE PEOPLE OF THE NATION, BECAUSE OF OUR LOVE FOR THIS GREAT INSTITUTION, AND BECAUSE WE HAVE SEEN NO INDICATION OF CONSIDERATION OF FBI OFFICIALS, AMONG WHOM THERE IS AN INHERENT NONPARTISANSHIP AND A DEEP REVERENCE TO THE CALL OF DUTY TO ALL THE PEOPLE OF OUR NATION.

RESPECTFULLY,

ALL FBI OFFICIALS

* Actually, all special-agents-in-charge had signed the telegram except Wallace Estill, who was assigned to the Knoxville, Tennessee, Field Office. He was reportedly a long-time supporter of former Assistant-to-the-Director William C. Sullivan and suspected that the telegram was a ploy on behalf of the candidacy of an enemy of Sullivan, Mark Felt, who wanted very much to become director.

It was unusual, indeed unprecedented, for the Bureau hierarchy to take such a bold step — and to do so relatively publicly, as copies of the telegram were promptly leaked to the press. Whether or not the President actually noticed the telegram was not clear, but to send it had a very dramatic and cathartic effect within the FBI. "This [the appointment of Ruckelshaus as acting director] was really the straw that broke the camel's back," one of the instigators of the telegram explained later; "Mr. Ruckelshaus probably didn't feel very welcome when he saw it. . . . but it *was* kind of insulting to have a caretaker appointed." The bureaucracy was speaking up, and acting defiantly, to protect its interests and its instincts.

Ruckelshaus met with the assistant directors that afternoon. They sought to assure him that the telegram was not intended as a personal slap at him, a man whom they did not know, but rather as a general statement expressing their dismay over the apparent feeling that nobody within the Bureau, brought up under Hoover's tutelage, could be trusted to run the organization. Ruckelshaus, for his own part, said he did not feel they should take his temporary selection as an insult. Nixon had not purposefully excluded them from consideration, he argued; it was just that Hoover had dominated the FBI so completely and for so long that few other names from inside the Bureau had ever been able to surface and become known on the outside. They were a mystery.

The assistant directors showed some skepticism about Ruckelshaus's professed disinterest in holding on to the job; they could not believe that someone would not want it. But he reiterated that this was how he felt, and said he had two main goals for his brief tenure: "to find a good successor," with the promise that consideration would be given to people within the Bureau as well as outside; and "to conduct this Watergate investigation as vigorously as possible." At the same time, however, Ruckelshaus told them firmly that even though he was only temporary, "I expect to run it [the FBI] while I am here."

Two days later, the acting director had a meeting in Washington with the special-agents-in-charge, who were flown in from around the country; essentially the same messages were exchanged. The field people seemed less bitter about Gray and more accepting of Ruckelshaus, although many of them, like the assistant directors at headquarters, sounded the standard refrain to him that "if only [Gray] had taken our advice, he would have stayed out of trouble." They argued that instead of dealing independently with the White House, Gray should have taken the veteran officials into his confidence. This point would be made so often and so forcefully to Ruckelshaus that he

became convinced it was the vehicle for the Bureau men to assert a
normal human response of "don't blame me" — in this case, exonerat-
ing themselves of any responsibility or culpability for the disaster that
had just occurred in the FBI.

The best way to describe the seventy-day period when Ruckelshaus was acting director is to say that he and the Bureau were living
together, but never really felt at ease. In a word, each found the other
somewhat strange; but because Ruckelshaus was so temporary and did
encourage the candid airing of differences, the strangeness never
deteriorated into outright bureaucratic warfare. One problem Ruckelshaus found was that whenever he asked questions of some of the old-
time FBI officials — seeking to clarify or learn about procedures —
they tended to think that he was criticizing them and they would
become defensive. He attributed that attitude largely to the continuing
traumatic effect of having lost Hoover — "in some ways more traumatic than they would admit or realize." The questioning was difficult
for them, he supposed, because "some of those people who had been
in the FBI throughout their career judged the success of their effort
purely on the basis of their approval or approbation by Hoover. . . .
now the man who had been making that judgment for them was
suddenly gone," and the turbulent time under Gray had done little to
ease the pain and maladjustment. What the FBI needed now was
stability, and until it had that, even gentle inquiry was going to be
hard to take.

To the hard-boiled Bureau traditionalists, Ruckelshaus seemed
naïve, boyish, and playful about matters of moment and almost starry-
eyed in his conception of how policy could be formulated and tested.
In an early meeting with FBI executives, he tried out one of his own
favorite themes. While at EPA, he said, he had been pleasantly surprised to find how valuable it was to take some of the more difficult
issues out into the country for comment by ordinary people. One of the
best ideas on how to clean up the water had come from a woman's
testimony at a public hearing in Alabama, and some of the most original thinking he heard on the issue of pollution from automobile ex-
hausts was advanced by a housewife testifying in Los Angeles. Why
then, he asked, not solicit opinions and input from the people on issues
of concern to the Bureau, such as how to establish workable guidelines
to govern wiretapping? "Jesus Christ," said one member of the group
suddenly, "that is one of the worst ideas I have ever heard." Most of
the time the veterans just humored him, confident that he would not
be around long enough to put some of these bizarre ideas into effect.

And mostly Ruckelshaus accepted recommendations on administrative matters as they came up through the chain of command. Essentially, he let the Bureau run itself and, in fact, ordered that some of the minutiae that traditionally came through the director's office no longer be sent to him.

Ultimately, Ruckelshaus found himself in great awe of the FBI. Months later he told the Senate Judiciary Committee that the Bureau was, "in the experience I have had in government, the finest governmental organization I have ever been associated with. It runs better and is more responsive to the leadership at the top than any other organization I have ever been associated with." After what he said was a thorough study of the original Watergate investigation, he came eventually to believe that the FBI had done itself credit and that the holes in the investigation that later became obvious had not been intentional ones. Ruckelshaus accepted the Bureau position that, as he paraphrased it, "we did a good job and got a good result . . . that result has just been colored by the incidents that have been made public involving Gray . . . but there is no evidence that would tend to undermine the professionalism of the FBI itself." During his own brief tenure, there were no efforts by the White House or other political sources to interfere with the continuing Watergate probe, he insisted.

But it was the extraordinary responsiveness to the director, the availability of a vast bureaucracy to get a job done, that most impressed and overwhelmed Ruckelshaus. "In EPA, if I wanted to get people to do something," he joked later, "I used to make them think I wanted something else. Then I got it done! In the FBI, all I had to do was hint that I wanted something done, and it was done. It was almost like running downhill, for that group. I am not sure they were that eager to respond to me, but I was the director, and they were used to responding to the director all their lives and they could not stop." Ruckelshaus was astonished, for example, by the number of gestures that were automatically performed in his name because he was sitting — however temporarily — in the director's office. Once the laboratory had obtained the necessary samples of Ruckelshaus's signature, the standard flow of morale-boosting letters could start up again to mark weddings, births, deaths, anniversaries of joining the Bureau, and so on. As acting director, Ruckelshaus found that people he did not even know were "stopping me in the hall to say, 'Thanks a lot for the letter about my mother' " — in many cases a letter that he had never even seen or heard about himself.

This process of discovery and interchange occurred, however, against a backdrop of crisis and tension, especially at the White House. The tension became obvious from Ruckelshaus's first day on the job when, after the announcement that Haldeman, Ehrlichman, and Dean were leaving the White House, twelve FBI agents were sent to guard their files. The decision to send the agents in actually arose out of a discussion Ruckelshaus held with the new attorney general–designate, Elliot Richardson (whom Nixon had put in immediate charge of the Watergate investigation, supplanting Henry Petersen), and White House aide Leonard Garment, who was named to replace Dean, with the title of "special consultant" to the President. Clear in their memory was the fact that after Howard Hunt was arrested in connection with the original Watergate burglary, a substantial amount of material (including the cables Gray destroyed) was removed from his files before they were turned over to the FBI by Dean. Since it now seemed possible that the two top presidential aides and Dean might be charged with a crime (and indeed they were later), the concern was to prevent potential evidence from being spirited away. At the same time, though, since the files contained many items necessary for pending governmental business, they could not be sealed off completely, as evidence ordinarily would be. Agents were thus supposed to guard against actual removal of any of the files from a special secure room in the Executive Office Building next to the White House, but to permit those with access to the files to consult them and photocopy documents for a number of purposes, including the preparation of testimony or of a defense against any criminal charges that were later brought. But some of the agents on guard duty apparently misunderstood the ground rules, and they clashed with current and former White House employees who came into the room. Besides, the unseemly sight of the FBI guarding the nation's business from possible misuse by the President's own people was too much for Nixon and his aides. After a week the agents were withdrawn and replaced by a Secret Service contingent that was usually involved in helping protect the White House.

Before the end of Ruckelshaus's first week as acting director, there were renewed press reports about secret Nixon administration wiretaps on newsmen, including a suggestion that White House "plumbers" Hunt and Liddy had used electronic surveillance in the course of their own bizarre investigation into the publication of the Pentagon Papers in 1971. Defense attorneys for Daniel Ellsberg and Anthony Russo, who were then on trial in federal court in Los Angeles, charged with conspiracy, espionage, and theft of government property in connection with release of the controversial Defense Department study of the Vietnam war, immediately brought the reports to the

549

attention of the U.S. District Court Judge W. Matt Byrne, Jr. Almost a year earlier, in July 1972, Byrne had ordered the prosecutors in the case to reveal any electronic interceptions of conversations of the defendants, their lawyers, and consultants, so that he could determine whether those interceptions had tainted the evidence. The government did at one point admit privately to the judge that defense attorney Leonard Boudin had been overheard on a "national security" wiretap by the FBI on two of Boudin's clients, diplomatic missions in the United States of the governments of Cuba and Chile; disagreement over whether the defense was entitled to help the judge decide that wiretap's relevance to the case had gone to the Supreme Court and delayed the Ellsberg-Russo trial for several months. But the prosecutors had repeatedly said since then that searches of government records revealed no other such interceptions. Now the judge asked for a new search in light of the latest news stories.

The Ellsberg-Russo trial, nearing its end after months of testimony, had already been jolted only a few days earlier by the extraordinary disclosure that in September 1971, Hunt, Liddy, and some of their Cuban exile associates had broken into the Beverly Hills, California, office of a psychoanalyst who had once treated Ellsberg in the belief that they might find some juicy and damaging information about him. Byrne was in the midst of an inquiry into that situation and its possible effect on the case.* In the meantime, Byrne was seriously compromised himself by the revelation that he had met with Nixon and Ehrlichman at the Western White House in San Clemente, while the Pentagon Papers trial was in progress, to discuss the possibility of his appointment to an important new federal job. Eventually it became known that Byrne, on his own initiative, had met a second time with Ehrlichman in early April — in a park in Santa Monica — and that the job they were talking about was the directorship of the FBI. (The discussions took place after it became clear that Gray's chances of being confirmed for the post were doomed.) With a jury sitting in the Los Angeles trial that had been empaneled four months earlier and

* When President Nixon was first informed on April 18 that the Watergate prosecutors had learned about the Hunt-Liddy burglary at the office of Dr. Lewis Fielding, he told Assistant Attorney General Henry Petersen that "this is a national security matter" and that Petersen should "stay out of that." Only eight days later, after Attorney General Richard Kleindienst had intervened with Nixon, did the information go to the court in Los Angeles. It became clear that for more than a year and a half a number of government officials, including the President, had concealed facts that the defendants in the Pentagon Papers trial were entitled to know. Indeed, it could be argued that the illegal burglary by agents of the White House had irreparably tainted the prosecution.

550

with the case about to conclude, the pressure was also on now for full answers to be given in response to the newest allegations of wiretapping.

The usual check of indices at the Bureau and in other government investigative agencies had produced no new indications of wiretapping on Ellsberg, Russo, their lawyers, or their consultants. But Ruckelshaus, troubled by the press reports and increasingly skeptical of the administration he was serving, put out personal feelers in the Bureau for information and, as he later told it, "three employees" promptly came to him with "some recollection of the basic facts" about some seventeen secret wiretaps conducted between 1969 and 1971 on newsmen and government employees, supposedly in an effort to trace the sources of leaks of sensitive "national security" information from government councils. He called a meeting in his office on May 4 to order a full investigation into the special wiretaps and the disappearance of all records concerning them. Felt was to be off on vacation the next week, and Leonard M. Walters, assistant FBI director for the Inspection Division, was put in charge of the inquiry, which Ruckelshaus ordered be given top priority. As the meeting concluded, one agent lingered on and asked the acting director, "Do you really want to find out what happened to those records? Are you sure you want to know?" — hinting, it seemed, that the results of the investigation could themselves produce another scandal. Ruckelshaus said he did want the answers.

According to standard FBI procedure the investigation proceeded methodically, starting with the agents at the bottom who had been directly responsible for monitoring the wiretaps, moving up through their supervisors and the people who transmitted summaries of the overheard conversations to the White House office of Henry Kissinger. Kissinger was Nixon's national security adviser at the time of the wiretaps and the man who was especially agitated about the leaks of information. (During a subsequent inquiry by a Senate committee into the circumstances surrounding the wiretaps, Kissinger acknowledged in 1974 that he had provided the list of people to be investigated, but said he did not know what techniques the Bureau would use.) The point of the probe ordered now by Ruckelshaus was to establish what had happened at the lower echelons, so that they could not be blamed by higher-ups for loss or concealment of the wiretap tapes and logs. On Tuesday night, May 8, Ruckelshaus received a "preliminary report" that, according to its description in an official document filed two days later with Judge Byrne:

William D. Ruckelshaus, an Indiana Republican and the first head of the Environmental Protection Agency, was named acting director of the FBI on an interim basis after Gray's resignation. He presided over a particularly chaotic and demoralized interlude in the FBI's history, but during that time and later, when he served briefly as deputy attorney general, he initiated a thoroughgoing review of Bureau operations. Here, Ruckelshaus and Ron Ziegler, President Nixon's embattled press secretary, face hostile questions from reporters on the day Gray's resignation and Ruckelshaus's appointment were announced.

indicates that an FBI employee recalls that in late 1969 and early 1970 Mr. Ellsberg had been overheard talking from an electric surveillance of Dr. Morton Halperin's residence.* It is this employee's recollection that the surveillance was of Dr. Halperin and that Mr. Ellsberg was then a guest of Dr. Halperin.

I [Ruckelshaus] have no information concerning the substance of the conversation nor has the investigation to date been able to find any record of such a conversation. The investigation, of course, is not complete and further facts bearing upon the wire taps may be uncovered.

In Bureau terms, then, Ellsberg had "walked in" on a wiretap of somebody else. But the procedures for determining whether evidence had been tainted by such an "overhear" applied nonetheless, and the judge gave David Nissen, the chief prosecutor in the Ellsberg-Russo case, overnight to come up with the logs and records necessary to making that determination. The problem, Nissen pointed out, was that all records concerning the special wiretaps had been missing since mid-1971.

On Thursday evening, May 10, Ruckelshaus got a phone call from William Sullivan, the former Bureau official who, it turned out, had kept the records of these seventeen secret wiretaps in his own files for the sake of tight security, rather than mix them in with the general Bureau records and indices, or even with the special wiretap index of everyone who had been overheard in FBI electronic surveillances.† In either of those files the records might have been seen by ordinary agents and other employees in the course of their normal duties. Sullivan, stirred to speak up by the renewed public furor and by the fact that Ruckelshaus's investigation was leading in his direction, revealed that before leaving the FBI in October 1971, he had passed the material to Assistant Attorney General Robert C. Mardian, lest Hoover later try to use the wiretaps to "blackmail" the Nixon administration. Mardian had hinted, Sullivan said, that he delivered the records to the White House. That version was in conflict with a statement by former Attorney General John Mitchell that the documents and logs had been destroyed. Ruckelshaus directed that Mardian, who was

* Halperin, an official of the Defense Department during the Johnson administration, worked on the National Security Council staff under Kissinger for the first year and a half of Nixon's presidency; he was among the seventeen people wiretapped in the search for the leaks. Later Halperin was a consultant for the defense in the Ellsberg-Russo case. In 1969 Hoover scorned Halperin and two other aides to Kissinger at the NSC as "Kennedy-type Harvard professors" whom the FBI considered to be "security risks." (Halperin had taught at Harvard with Kissinger.) Kissinger hired them over Hoover's objections.
† See Chapter XII, "The Dukes," pp. 303–304.

already scheduled for an interview by FBI agents that same night, be asked if what Sullivan said was accurate. Mardian did confirm that he had transferred the records to the White House, and so the investigation turned there on Friday morning.

Meanwhile, in Los Angeles, when Nissen told Byrne that he still had nothing definite to report about the location of the records, the judge declared that he could wait no longer. Citing government misconduct in various aspects of the nearly two-year-old case, the judge granted a motion by Ellsberg and Russo for dismissal of all charges against them. Only an hour after Byrne had dismissed the case, Ehrlichman admitted in an interview with FBI agents that the missing logs and records had been tucked away in his White House files ever since Mardian had sent them over in order to minimize the risks of disclosure.

There would be speculation later that the sudden "discovery" that Ellsberg had been overheard on a secret FBI wiretap several years earlier was merely a device the government was using to try to abort its own prosecution of Ellsberg — to cut its losses. For the controversial, some said political, criminal prosecution had become more and more of a nuisance and a liability. One elaborate conspiracy theory had it that Ehrlichman* had met with Byrne and offered him a new job primarily for the purpose of preventing information about the burglary of the psychoanalyst's office from being disclosed; that Ehrlichman or somebody else leaked word of the judge's meetings to discuss the job offer as a reprisal against Byrne for disclosing the burglary in open court; and that the incidental "overhear" had been turned up as a means of ending the court procedures, which were bound to lead to further embarrassing revelations unless they were stopped. Part of this theory was that Ruckelshaus, in league with the others, had dragged out the FBI investigation into the lost wiretap records long enough so that the Ellsberg-Russo charges would be dismissed before the search became fruitful.

But Ruckelshaus insisted that there had been no foot-dragging at the Bureau. "We were, in our investigation, working as fast as we possibly could to find these records, to search them, to see if there were any further interceptions that should be revealed to the court involving Mr. Ellsberg or Mr. Halperin," he testified later. Forty-two

---

* It gradually became clear that Ehrlichman had directed the scheme to collect personal information about Ellsberg, which led ultimately to the burglary of his psychoanalyst's office. As a result, Ehrlichman was convicted of conspiracy to violate the civil rights of the psychoanalyst, Dr. Lewis Fielding, and of perjury in the "plumbers" trial in federal court in Washington.

separate interviews had been required and since many of them had to be conducted by the same few agents who developed the necessary background knowledge and expertise as the investigation proceeded, that took time. What was troubling, Ruckelshaus and the ranking Bureau faithful had to concede, was that a number of government officials, including some currently and formerly in the FBI, had known for years about these secret wiretaps and the fact that they were not included in the normal indices; but no one had spoken up to urge that they too be searched at the appropriate time for material that might have a bearing on the Ellsberg-Russo case, and possibly on other trials. If they had spoken up, if the Ellsberg "overhear" had been discovered sooner, and if a court hearing had shown it to be related to the evidence in the case, the long, expensive, and arduous trial might never have been necessary at all. The report submitted to Ruckelshaus also made the point that, despite his denials during his confirmation hearings, Gray had been informed about the secret wiretaps in a memorandum several months earlier.

It was all very embarrassing and upsetting to the FBI, but Ruckelshaus's next step was an unconventional one for the Bureau: he called a press conference at FBI headquarters on the following Monday to review the unsavory affair, including the fact that the missing records on the wiretaps had actually been found by agents on Saturday among the materials in Ehrlichman's former White House office. The disclosure raised serious questions about whether the Bureau and some of its leading officials had been involved in improper conduct, both in the installment of the wiretaps in the first place and later in their concealment.

The press conference itself caused some problems at the Bureau. When Ruckelshaus's personal press aide, Jack Conmy, whom he had brought along from EPA, asked the Bureau's press office to arrange to accommodate television cameras in an FBI conference room, he was greeted with astonished stares. This was something they did not really know how to do at headquarters, because it had never been done there before.

Mark Felt was notoriously adept at the old FBI headquarters game of playing various sides against the middle. One retired Bureau official recalls that when the American Civil Liberties Union filed its lawsuit to try to force the FBI to accept women as agents, Felt agreed to go along with John Mohr on an internal attempt to persuade Hoover to change his mind on the emotional issue. The suggestion was that if the Bureau processed applications from the two women who figured in the lawsuit, it might thereby avoid any court order and keep control over hiring policy in the FBI's exclusive hands. Even Tolson was said to have been lined up on Mohr's side. When it came time for formal discussion of the matter at a meeting in the Director's office, Mohr made his pitch; but Felt, who had done some checking around in the meantime, denounced the idea and said he agreed with Hoover that women should never be admitted to agent's training. That was that.

While Pat Gray was acting director, Felt supported and implemented Gray's decision that the Bureau would suspend the practice of pulling together information about congressional candidates from public sources and FBI files; but in conversations with old stalwarts in the field he also deplored Gray's alleged politicization of the Bureau. Yet on several occasions — including one when information came in concerning a paternity suit allegedly filed in Indiana against Democratic presidential candidate George McGovern — Felt urged Gray to use any juicy material that was available in order to earn "brownie points" at the White House.

As another former Bureau official put it, by the time Ruckelshaus had arrived on the scene, "anybody who wanted to be director of the FBI was willing to do some mighty strange things. It was interesting to see the lengths to which an otherwise decent human being would go." Mark Felt, as much as anybody, was now prepared to make his big push for the job, and after the telegram sent to Nixon, he sought to maneuver himself into the position of being the most logical and obvious candidate for director from within the Bureau ranks. What he apparently did not realize was the extent to which, with Ehrlichman and Haldeman gone from the White House and the administration in disarray, Richardson and Ruckelshaus would actually be responsible for managing the selection process.

Ruckelshaus found Felt to be helpful enough — indeed, sometimes Felt seemed to bend over backward to try to ingratiate himself with the new acting director — but he soon came to realize that one of Felt's techniques for promoting himself was to leak information that favored his position to the press. Word came to Ruckelshaus through Conmy's press grapevine that Felt had been responsible for a number of noticeable and controversial leaks, and there was even one rumor that John Crewdson, a young *New York Times* reporter, had been seen leaving Felt's office with his briefcase stuffed full of photocopied FBI documents. That was probably an exaggeration, but as one person who was close to the situation put it, "After all those years in Hoover's unreal world, Felt actually seemed to believe that this was how people got appointed to high positions. He would tell reporters, 'Remember,

I'm a candidate to become director of the FBI,' as if to say, 'You be good to me now, and I'll be good to you later.' He must have thought that if he gave the *Times* enough good stories, they would give him a big boost for the job." Ruckelshaus confronted Felt about the leaks, and he admitted talking with one of the reporters in question; but he said he had done so only to "set him straight" on some matters he was writing about.* The acting director felt sure that more than that was involved. The two men quarreled angrily, and Ruckelshaus accused Felt of undercutting him at a very difficult moment, when he was trying to help reestablish the credibility of the Bureau. Felt's conduct was, as far as Ruckelshaus was concerned at the time, "a violation of everything" — FBI regulations, standards of decent conduct, and perhaps the law.

The next day Felt came in with a letter of resignation, requesting retirement from the Bureau in late June. "It is my earnest hope that the standards of thoroughness, fairness, and impartiality that became the hallmark of the FBI during J. Edgar Hoover's forty-eight years as Director will continue to be maintained, and the the [*sic*] FBI will remain a career service staffed at all levels by law enforcement professionals," Felt wrote to Ruckelshaus. To Felt's apparent surprise, Ruckelshaus accepted his resignation. "There are very few men in this Bureau's history who have served in so many key positions and with such distinction," Ruckelshaus wrote back. "Your contributions have certainly added luster to this organization's reputation, and I want to express my appreciation for the capable and diligent manner in which you have discharged your duties. You have established a record of which you can indeed be proud."

Mark Felt retired to his comfortable home in the Virginia suburbs of Washington, a home that has one of the most complete collections anywhere of Hoover photographs and other Bureau memorabilia. He embarked on an extensive lecture tour, mostly of college campuses, during which he made a point of denouncing Pat Gray for mishandling the Watergate investigation and other delicate issues while at the FBI. Felt's retirement would be troubled only by the ignominy of being the subject of an extensive investigation by the Bureau of the leaks, a probe he called "a tempest in a teapot."

With Felt out of the running, Ruckelshaus embarked on what he billed as a search for a replacement as acting associate director. He

---

* One of the best-kept secrets of Watergate was sealed not by Nixon and Co., but by the star reporters, Woodward and Bernstein: the identity of their secret-weapon source, "Deep Throat." Inevitably speculation centered on Mark Felt, among others. Felt denies it; the author is inclined to believe him.

really had little intention of filling that vacancy, but wanted to leave it open so that whoever became the new permanent FBI director could choose his own man. What he was actually doing was looking for potential candidates for director among the Bureau's career people, but he thought that people might behave more normally if that were not directly stated. Ruckelshaus asked each of the assistant directors and the special-agents-in-charge of the largest field offices to nominate the three FBI men he thought would be best in the position of associate director. Altogether, taking account of overlap among the suggestions, the names of some twenty men were proposed, and Ruckelshaus interviewed them all. The interviews provided him with still further insights into how the Bureau operated, which people were most popular among their peers, and whether there was a serious morale problem in the field. There were also some amusing moments, for example, when he asked one of the men what he would do if he were testifying before the Senate Judiciary Committee and Senator Edward M. Kennedy of Massachusetts suddenly leaned forward and questioned him about whether he had ever participated in a surreptitious entry or other illegal activity on behalf of the FBI. "Well, sir," replied the prospective associate director without even a pause, "I would tell him that was none of his goddamn business."

"That was a marvelous response coming out of his stomach," Ruckelshaus remarked later. "It was reflective of the attitude of many people in the FBI. They feel that they are serving the public interest, and anybody who questions that really just doesn't know what is going on. And these things are not considered any of their business — that includes senators and a lot of other people, too. It does not necessarily occur to them that the public interest might include public knowledge of the kinds of techniques the FBI is using to go about fulfilling their function. They just really do not see that side of the public interest. . . . That is just a reflection of Hoover's beliefs and their own training."

Two of the people most frequently proposed by their colleagues in the field were Roy K. Moore and Charles W. Bates, the SACs in Jackson and San Francisco respectively. They were boosted as the type of agent who knew the investigative side of the work best and who would keep the FBI on the right track. But of all the Bureau candidates interviewed by Ruckelshaus, it was two others who were also sent to see Richardson, once he had been confirmed and sworn in as attorney general, and Alexander M. Haig, Jr., the career military man who had become Nixon's new chief of staff at the White House. They were James Adams, then serving a stint as special-agent-in-charge in

San Antonio after spending most of his career at Bureau headquarters in the Administrative Division, and "the other" William Sullivan — not William C. Sullivan of Hoover-feud fame, but rather SAC William A. Sullivan of Philadelphia, a tough-talking Hoover-loyalist type who had long experience in the field.* Both men had considerable support in the Bureau hierarchy and impressed Ruckelshaus with their potential for taking a strong grip on the FBI.

But a number of non-FBI people were also being considered seriously. Earlier, after it became clear that Gray could not be confirmed, the White House had still been focusing on candidates whom it thought could be counted upon to be politically responsive. The two men who had been considered leading prospects in April, before things fell apart, were, ironically, both Democrats, W. Matt Byrne and Henry Petersen. Judge Byrne, who had earlier been staff director of the commission that, under the chairmanship of former Pennsylvania Governor William W. Scranton, had studied growing campus unrest for the Nixon administration, was frequently advanced by Kleindienst as a good prospect for the FBI job. Petersen had come to know the President reasonably well as he took increasing responsibility for the Watergate investigation, and Nixon broached the subject of the Bureau directorship with him at a tense moment, in a manner that was no less compromising than the indiscreet approach to Byrne in California. The President had always wanted to get somebody in the FBI job who would be pliant; that was one reason Gray was picked in the first place, and it was a quality that both Byrne and Petersen had in their favor (according to the Nixon sense of values). But both of those candidates were now out of the question — Byrne, because of the publicity about his clandestine meetings with Ehrlichman; and Petersen, because his handling of various aspects of Watergate would be open to examination and criticism in confirmation hearings, leading to yet more carnage. The names of DeLoach and Sullivan came up again, but both were rejected as too likely to have a polarizing effect on the Bureau. As he had been before, Peter Pitchess, sheriff of Los Angeles County, California, was mentioned, along with a few other local law enforcement officials who were identified as close friends of the FBI.

By early June, however, with members of the Senate threatening

---

* This Sullivan, William A., later served as assistant-director-in-charge of the Los Angeles Field Office and was in the thick of the search for Patricia Hearst. After his retirement in July 1975, and acceptance of a job as chief of the Alcoholic Beverage Control Board of California, he became the first FBI official ever to appear on a Sunday network television interview program. On CBS's *Face the Nation,* he showed himself to be a dyed-in-the-wool loyalist, defending everything Hoover had ever done.

559

to go to court to have Ruckelshaus removed — on the grounds that his extended tenure might violate the Federal Vacancies Act of 1867, which states that temporary appointees who are normally subject to the confirmation process may hold office for only thirty days before they must undergo congressional hearings on their qualifications — he and Richardson had settled on their first choice. He was Clarence M. Kelley, a veteran of twenty-one years in the FBI until his retirement in 1961, including several assignments as special-agent-in-charge, and then for twelve years police chief of Kansas City, Missouri. Kelley had the advantage of a Bureau background, which would presumably mollify the people who had sent Nixon the telegram, but he was also fortunate enough to have been away from the FBI during Hoover's last turbulent years and during the Watergate scandals. The White House, which had also interviewed him, accepted that recommendation, with no ulterior motives apparent.

Ruckelshaus stayed at the Bureau only until the Senate could confirm Kelley, but it became clear that he had developed a deep and abiding interest in the problems and the prospects of the FBI. In a commencement address at Ohio State University on June 8, 1973, while he was still acting director, he discussed the problem of "a constant erosion of trust in government" and urged that the Bureau and its director no longer be left as free-wheeling and unchecked as they had been for half a century:

The FBI is not perfect. No institution created by men is. It has enormous power and thus can be a force for evil as well as good. If this power is to be used properly in a free society, the men and women who exercise it must have judgment, integrity and scope. The FBI does not exist aside from the people in it. More particularly it owes much of its force, effectiveness and tone to its Director.

The Director must be able to conceptualize how the FBI fits into our societal fabric at any given historical moment. He must recognize the permissible limits of investigative techniques — what is permissible in wartime or time of extreme emergency is impermissible when the threat to our country's security is minimal — and he must communicate forcefully those limits to FBI Agents. Needless to say, this takes an individual of considerable capacity.

Further, the necessity to America of our major Federal law enforcement agency's not exceeding a wise exercise of its power is too important to leave to the judgment of one man. There must be effective oversight of all FBI activities. This essential review and check should come from both the executive and legislative branches of our government. In my opinion neither the legislative nor the executive oversight or check is sufficient today and needs to be strengthened.

Later in the summer, Ruckelshaus was selected by Richardson (and this time approved by the White House) as deputy attorney general, with a special responsibility for working with the Bureau and helping it review fundamental areas of policy — including such basic questions as whether the intelligence-gathering and law enforcement functions of the FBI should be separated from each other and put in two distinct agencies; whether the Bureau should remain as part of the Justice Department or become an independent agency; how long a term any one director should serve; and what the basic guidelines should be that govern wiretapping. For a time these were known as "The Ruckelshaus Questions" — a name resented by the Bureau — and were the subject of intense study by joint FBI–Justice Department task forces. During his own confirmation hearings for the deputy's job, Ruckelshaus asserted that the Bureau desperately needed to be opened up "for public perusal so that [the public] can get a better understanding of how it functions." He urged review of the FBI's intelligence-gathering authority and its codification in either statutes or new executive orders, and stressed that a way must be found for the Bureau to strike a balance between "too much responsiveness" to higher authorities and "too much independence" from them. Above all, Ruckelshaus implored the Senate Judiciary Committee to get its newly established FBI Oversight Subcommittee working on scrutinizing Bureau operations.

It all sounded as if a new era were at hand, a new opportunity for constructive examination of the Bureau, with Ruckelshaus — the man who had been introduced to the FBI during a tense seventy-day period as its acting director and was now the second-ranking man in the Justice Department — serving as the crucial link. Then came the "Saturday Night Massacre" of October 20, 1973. Richardson and Ruckelshaus refused to fire Special Watergate Prosecutor Archibald Cox on Nixon's orders when Cox declined to back down on his demand for full access to the tapes of the President's Watergate-related conversations in the White House. Richardson resigned. The White House claimed that Nixon fired Ruckelshaus, but his version was that he managed to walk out the door just before he was to be thrown out.

Ruckelshaus, suddenly a folk hero for his defiance of Nixon, went on the lecture circuit. Later he opened a law practice in Washington.

Looking Ahead

XXIII

Enter Kelley

I know absolutely that I am not swayed by any ghost of J. Edgar Hoover. . . . The spectre of that man behind me never bothers me a bit. . . . I'm not saying that I'm better than he was, and I'm not saying that I'm worse than he was. I am my own man.
— *Clarence M. Kelley, in an interview with the author*

SWEAT BEADS ON CLARENCE KELLEY'S BROW, and he shifts uncomfortably in his chair. He picks up the top item from a neat stack of documents on his desk awaiting his initials, glances haphazardly at it, and then drops it as if nothing could interest him less. He flips with curiosity through a little deck of blue cards, clamped together at the top, that carries his appointments for the coming month or so; finding nothing that particularly excites his fancy, he tosses them aside too. "I don't know whether we're right or wrong," Kelley says with a sigh; "you get a very jaundiced view from here."

Right or wrong, Kelley would be on Capitol Hill in a few hours, facing a House subcommittee that is hopping mad over the latest revelations concerning the counterintelligence programs (COINTEL-PROs) once run by the FBI, especially those directed at New Left dissidents and "black extremists" during the 1960s. COINTELPRO is one of the uglier aspects of Kelley's inheritance from J. Edgar Hoover, and it is one of those scandals that, instead of dying down with the passage of time, keeps flaring up again, just beyond the Bureau's control. Fanning the flames this time is Attorney General William B. Saxbe, who has released publicly a report compiled by a task force of

FBI agents and lawyers from the Criminal Division of the Justice Department. Even after the Bureau has quibbled with department officials over particular words and has had the report sanitized as much as possible, it is still a devastating catalogue of disruptive, and perhaps illegal, actions taken by the FBI in the name of law and order.

Saxbe has a thing about COINTELPRO — there had been that speech to FBI National Academy graduates at Quantico the previous June, inappropriate from the Bureau's point of view, announcing that there would be no more "dirty tricks" from federal law enforcement officers — and despite the facade of a unified departmental policy that has been carefully hammered out, it is clear now that there is something of a schism on this issue. In a press conference, the attorney general has denounced some of the FBI's activities as "improper" and "abhorrent"; but at the same time the Bureau issued a statement for Kelley, saying that "the FBI employees involved in these programs acted entirely in good faith and within the bounds of what was expected of them by the President, the Attorney General, the Congress and the American people. . . . for the FBI to have done less under the circumstances would have been an abdication of its responsibilities to the American people." The justification given by Saxbe for releasing the report is simply that he had earlier promised inquiring reporters that he would do so. The FBI wonders, however, if there is not some other motive — perhaps a drive by the maverick attorney general to hold onto his job in the cabinet inherited by President Gerald R. Ford from Richard Nixon.*

"I don't feel any pressure, from within the Bureau or without," insists Kelley as he looks ahead to the hearing before the Subcommittee on Civil Rights and Constitutional Rights of the House Judiciary Committee. But pressure is implicit in the situation, with the Congress and a large segment of the public demanding a clear renunciation of the Hoover era, and with the Bureau old-timers needing to be defended no matter what was done in the past. It is, in some respects, the most serious crisis Kelley has faced in nearly a year and a half as director. "I wasn't here," he says plaintively in the privacy of his office, "I honestly don't know what the feeling was and what the information was that was coming in. . . . As for the great bulk of [COINTELPRO activities], there was nothing to them." But what about trying to ruin someone's credit rating, get him evicted from his apartment, or have him fired from his job on the basis of his political affiliations?

* If that was Saxbe's purpose, it did no good. A few weeks later he was named ambassador to India and replaced by Edward H. Levi as attorney general.

What of interference with an activist's candidacy for public office, or investigation of "the love life of a group leader for dissemination to the press"? Weren't some of these tactics purely and simply wrong? Kelley falls silent; he will not answer.

Kelley has a way of playing with a cigarette before he smokes it. He rolls it and squeezes it between his fingers until it looks as if it will fall apart and spill loose tobacco all over his desk blotter; then, at what seems like the last moment before this will happen, he puts the almost limp cigarette to his mouth and lights up with an old-fashioned flip-top lighter. He inhales the smoke in long, deep installments and flicks the ashes repeatedly, nervously. When he leaves the cigarette between his lips and continues talking as it dangles there, he is very much the tough cop out of Kansas City, a hired gun here to solve any problem that may be bothering the local people. When he tamps the cigarette out and leans forward, weighing each word as he plays with his black cameo ring, he is suddenly the man of reason and caution, here to analyze a situation with good sense and aplomb. When he is keyed up, he smokes a lot of cigarettes, and these images alternate hectically.

"Their motivation was to do what they thought was a good thing," Kelley says of the FBI people who administered and acted upon COINTELPRO. "Now, I'm not defending them all — some [actions] could be violations of civil rights, and they may properly be the subjects of civil suits." He has, in fact, urged that Assistant Attorney General Stanley Pottinger of the Justice Department's Civil Rights Division make a "full review" of the situation; the Bureau will "afford him full cooperation." But Kelley cannot really conceive of any of these COINTELPRO activities being considered a violation of any criminal statute because of the Bureau's intent at the time — to help the country, to deal with "revolutionary elements," to quiet things down in turbulent times. And besides, "all of them, or most of them, were approved by the Director"; if anyone is to be blamed, let it be Hoover, not those who were merely carrying out his orders and instructions.

Kelley is concerned to make it clear that whatever may have transpired before, this is a new era, and that he meant what he said in orders to all FBI personnel in December 1973:

FBI employees must not engage in any investigative activity which could abridge in any way the rights guaranteed to a citizen of the United States by the Constitution and under no circumstances shall employees of the FBI engage in any conduct which may result in defaming the character, reputation, integrity, or dignity of any citizen or organization of citizens of the United States.

He is worried that people are overlooking that unequivocal statement, and that as he is put in a position of defending, interpreting, or even just explaining things that went on under Hoover, his own identity will be lost in the shuffle. Kelley does not want to be thought of as "a redneck" and he is fighting hard to avoid that impression; he was heartened by favorable editorial comment that followed a recent speaking engagement at Yale University that had gone well.

"I have some very strong religious faith and principles, and these dictate to me on a number of occasions what I am going to do," he declares now. "So long as you're locked in by good principles, and can only be swayed by persuasive reasoning" — well, then the people have nothing to worry about with Kelley's FBI. It is a theme he thinks he may want to pursue later in the week in an address to a church group's annual convention in Kansas City. "If I can't, here in this job, do what I think is right for this country . . ." The sentence trails off; he is preoccupied by other thoughts, and for a moment Kelley muses that this problem would not exist at all if only the Justice Department had agreed in late 1973 to the FBI's recommendation for appeal of a lower federal court ruling that led to the release of the first official documents relating to COINTELPRO. The Bureau's estimate at that time had been that "we had better than a fifty percent chance of winning" on appeal; but then those were troubled days in the Justice Department in late 1973, and it had seemed to Solicitor General Robert Bork, then the acting attorney general, that a strong dose of openness and candor, rather than the usual tilt against disclosure, was in order.

"No, we're not always going to be right," says Kelley, getting back to the merits of COINTELPRO. "But now, you understand, I may do some things from time to time to sustain morale."

It is presumably that concern, to sustain morale, which governs and guides Kelley at the House subcommittee hearings later that same day. The hearing opens in a mood of nastiness. Some of the subcommittee members are angry not only over the substance of the COINTELPRO revelations, but also over the fact that they had not been briefed about the report in advance, as some of their Senate counterparts had been. "What is the attorney general prepared to give us besides this press release?" asks Congressman Charles B. Rangel (D–New York) derisively. The stated reason why they have not been briefed is that the Justice Department has been imploring the House Judiciary Committee to designate a particular group of congressmen, a special subcommittee that will have ongoing responsibility for oversight of the FBI; in the absence of such a designation, the Bureau has faced competing demands from this subcommittee and others for the same information. "Any number of subcommittees can assert jurisdiction. . . . Two subcommittees can study the same thing," says Congressman Paul Sarbanes (D-Maryland); "what's convenient for you is not the sole factor for us." But the point, says Deputy Attorney General Laurence Silberman, is to "minimize the number of people with access," since much of the information, especially in the COINTELPRO activities aimed at foreign intelligence agents, is "very highly classified." Silberman is there in Saxbe's place, and that is just another point of irritation. The Justice Department insists that the attorney general is off on a speaking engagement arranged long before this hearing was hastily convened, but the congressmen are suspicious that Saxbe has left town primarily to avoid confronting them on these sensitive issues.

Congressman Don Edwards of California, the subcommittee chairman, himself a former FBI agent who has become one of the Bureau's severest congressional critics, sets the tone in a prepared statement:

This Subcommittee is charged with legislative and oversight jurisdiction over the constitutional rights of American citizens. We take this responsibility most seriously. No provision of the Constitution, law enacted by Congress, or Presidential Executive Order — in my view — has authorized activities by the FBI such as those described in the . . . report. When I was an FBI agent many years ago, nothing in any manual or rule book authorized such conduct, and if they do today, they are without legal license.

Regardless of the unattractiveness or noisy militancy of some private citizens or organizations, the Constitution does not permit federal interference with their activities except through the criminal justice system, armed with its ancient safeguards. There are no exceptions. No federal agency, the CIA, the IRS, or the FBI, can be at the same time policeman, prosecutor, judge and jury. That is what constitutionally guaranteed due process is all about. It may sometimes be disorderly and unsatisfactory to some, but it is the essence of freedom.

I am disturbed by the spirited defense of the FBI's COINTELPRO program by Mr. Kelley. In his November 18 statement Mr. Kelley seemed to say that the mere invocation of the catch phrase "national security" justifies the COINTELPRO program's frightening litany of governmental violations of constitutional rights.

I suggest that the philosophy supporting COINTELPRO is the subversive notion that any public official, the President or a policeman, possesses a kind of inherent power to set aside the Constitution whenever he thinks the public interest, or "national security" warrants it. That notion is the postulate of tyranny.

Republican members of the subcommittee, supported by Silberman and Assistant Attorney General Henry E. Petersen, urge that the meeting go into executive session, as if to say that only then can some of the uglier aspects of COINTELPRO — and the names of victims — be freely discussed. Edwards and his fellow Democrats, however, insist upon keeping the meeting open, as if to say that only that way can the public be shown how truly repugnant the FBI activities were.

Kelley is caught in the middle of all this crossfire. He is accompanied by at least six other Bureau officials, but it is hard to tell whether some of them are there to help him or just to let him know that they are watching to be sure he says the right — i.e., loyal to the Bureau — things. The director seems to be at his inarticulate worst. In one colloquy with Congressman Jerome Waldie, a lame-duck Democrat from California, Kelley makes a forthright statement that "I do not think that we today should engage in this type of activity" (such as that embodied in COINTELPRO). If the Bureau did want to take such actions, he says, it would seek legislation authorizing it or go to the attorney general for advance permission. But would the FBI *ever* ask for approval of programs that would "violate rights," Waldie wants to know, "under any circumstances?" Kelley appears to say no, that the Bureau would not do such a thing, but then, in the confusion, it sounds as if he is adding a broad caveat — "unless we thought it a good idea." In an exchange with Sarbanes, Kelley tries to explain the origin of the programs with the statement that "in that time, with those troubles, there was a feeling that something should be done by somebody" to deal with the explosion of protest and disorder. Later, after hearing from Silberman that the Justice Department feels it has "ironclad assurances" that the FBI excesses will not be repeated, Waldie declares simply and insultingly that "I don't share your confidence in Mr. Kelley. He is a policeman."

Father Robert Drinan, a Democratic congressman from Massachusetts, appears to be reading the COINTELPRO report for the first time as the hearing proceeds, and he periodically erupts with outrage. He wants to know whether the Bureau and the department have any intention of advising the sixty-two "black extremists" referred to, but not named, in the report that the FBI had surreptitiously interfered with their private financial affairs; or the thirty-six "black extremists" whose employers or landlords were approached by the Bureau through "religious and civic leaders." Drinan rails about the "official anarchy" implicit in the FBI's actions and says that his constituents are "in horror" over the disclosures; he mocks Kelley's suggestion that emergency steps, not ordinarily justified, are sometimes appropriate under the President's "inherent power" to defend the Constitution in time of crisis.

"Why do you have to wave the flag?" Rangel wants to know, telling the director that it is "frightening" that he could even suggest that such tactics might be justified again in the future. He pleads with Kelley just to say of COINTELPRO, "It's wrong." But Kelley will not say it. During a break in the hearing and after it is over, the other FBI men on hand fend off spectators who want to ask questions of the director. At the end of the afternoon the Bureau delegation marches out as a phalanx, all in a huff and separate from the Justice Department people. Kelley retreats into the seclusion of his office with Associate Director Nicholas P. Callahan.

Meanwhile, back at Bureau headquarters, the External Affairs Division has been grinding out on plain white paper some "background material" for distribution to Bureau "friends" among the press. "The FBI's counterintelligence program was developed in response to needs at the time to quickly neutralize organizations and individuals who were advocating and fomenting urban violence and campus disorder," it says. "The riots which swept America's urban centers, beginning in 1965, were quickly followed by violent disorders which paralyzed college campuses. Both situations led to calls for action by alarmed Government leaders and a frightened citizenry." The Bureau's statement cites a string of past declarations and warnings about violence issued by prominent politicians; it notes the 1967 statement by Speaker of the House John W. McCormack that "public order is the first business of government." It quotes the finding of the President's Commission on Campus Unrest that "it is an undoubted fact that on some campuses there are men and women who plot, all too often successfully, to burn and bomb, and sometimes to maim and kill. The police must attempt to determine whether or not such a plot is in progress, and, if it is, they must attempt to thwart it." It refers to statements of enthusiastic endorsement of the FBI's COINTELPRO actions, after the first disclosures about them, from syndicated columnist Victor Riesel, the editorial writers of the *St. Louis Globe-Democrat*, and a senior editor of *Reader's Digest* — all conservatives.

Telegrams pour into the director's office that afternoon, mostly from special-agents-in-charge around the country who have heard about Kelley's statement and testimony, his refusal to go along with Saxbe's condemnation of the earlier Bureau tactics; for the most part they express thanks to Kelley for "standing up" for them. There is some reason to suspect that the telegrams were orchestrated by other people at headquarters.

571

"He would like to say COINTELPRO was wrong, because he knows it was wrong," says one Bureau official privately; "but he can't afford to offend his constituency."

"The good old days will not come back," Kelley says in a tone that is half warning and half frank description of the harsh realities of the new Bureau life. "We can no longer get something done with a simple 'yes' or 'no,' the way Mr. Hoover could. . . . I don't know if even he could have continued to do this under the current circumstances." The director's audience, seated at a small conference table with him, consists of two special-agents-in-charge, summoned for their turn to attend one in a long series of informal meetings that Kelley has convened with the Bureau's field commanders. The purpose is for the director to explain himself and his plans, to condition the people in the field to expect gradual changes and reevaluations of policy during his regime. But it is also intended that the SACs, and at some meetings, assistant-special-agents-in-charge, will offer their own thoughts and suggestions, and that Kelley will have an opportunity to size them up personally in a relatively loose, pressure-free atmosphere.

This session, like most of the others, is held on a Friday in Kansas City, which Kelley still considers home. It is where his children are — his daughter is a housewife and his son an accountant in management research with the Kansas City Life Insurance Company — and it is where his wife, Ruby, seriously ill with cancer, is. A miniature director's office has been established for him in the federal building above the central post office, just a few floors away from the FBI field office that covers the western half of Missouri and all of Kansas. There is nothing chic about this office, with its green carpet, harsh fluorescent lights, and standard government-issue furniture. In a typical week, Kelley flies to Kansas City from Washington by commercial aircraft on Thursday evening and stays until Sunday night or Monday morning. While in town, he is chauffeured about in one of Hoover's old bullet-proof Cadillac limousines (brought to Kansas City from Los Angeles, where it had been kept in reserve for the Director's annual visits) and generally attended to by one or the other of two agents whom he has personally selected as his aides. One a former New York City policeman and the other a former marine, they serve as a sounding board for Kelley and provide him with an entirely different view of the world, inside and outside the FBI, from the one that is pressed upon him daily in Washington.

Kansas City is a comfortable place for the director to be. There he has a stone and frame house in a neighborhood of well-manicured lawns, a cozy place with a drive-in garage underneath and a living room where he likes to settle in and watch football on television. (He is an avid fan of the Kansas City Chiefs, and enjoys going to their games when he has time.) Back home, he himself is still "Chief Kelley," admired and respected by the local leaders, welcomed by a circle of old friends at the Country Club Christian Church — an institution that provided most of the Kelleys' outside contacts and recreation during his years at the police department. Kelley is a man of simple tastes, never one to go out on the town unless it is for a light movie (preferably a comedy), and in Kansas City he can be peaceful, left alone by congressional critics and reporters and consulted by the Bureau on weekends only when absolutely necessary. He feels free to work in his yard or to wander into the field office on a Saturday afternoon, wearing an old sweater and galoshes, to see if anything of interest is happening. Kelley's presence has also meant a good deal of excitement for the field office, which under ordinary circumstances can be a rather dreary place; with the director coming in and out of town, the security squads, for example, have worked out elaborate means of protecting him, including the invention of a device capable of reaching and opening his car door from a great distance if a bomb is thought to be inside.

The SACs meeting with Kelley today were flown in from Savannah and Jacksonville, relatively small southern offices. These are men of the old school, faithful and obedient, long on fulsome praise and short on original ideas. When the director begins to tell them some of his views about how he wants to run the FBI and the directions he feels it should take, their pencils come out and they begin to take copious notes. Invariably they agree with him about everything under the sun, and it is quite a trick for Kelley to trap them into expressing their own opinions on a subject before he has given his. At one point he manages to do it, asking the SACs what they think of the occasional proposals floated in Washington to unify all federal investigative bodies into a single organization. The SAC from Jacksonville, William Alexander, a man of the South who has only recently returned there after long and lonely assignment up North, draws upon his long study of and indoctrination in the thoughts of Director Hoover to answer. He immediately pipes up to say in an ominous tone, "That's your first step toward a national police force." "Oh, I don't view it as that ominous," Kelley retorts; "if it had good leadership and administration, it might be all right. . . . But I am not sponsoring the idea." Alexander's face blanches like that of a child who has missed a word in a spelling bee, while a small smile of triumph — triumph at getting one of these people to express an attitude on his own — crosses Kelley's face.

The other SAC, J. T. Sylvester, Jr., from Savannah, a thirty-three-year FBI veteran, is originally from Maine and has been assigned to the South for many years. He is an old friend of Kelley, but the director apparently feels it is necessary and appropriate to reassure the two men of his dedication to the organization and his devotion to his new job. "Everything I have enjoyed in the way of success has come from the FBI," he tells them, stressing that even though he spent twelve years as a police chief he always continued to feel that he was part of the Bureau. As various issues come up in the discussion — the criticism the FBI took in connection with the Wounded Knee trial in St. Paul, proposed restrictions to be placed on the National Crime Information Center, the need for a more open attitude toward the press and the public — the director reassures his visitors that "in the months and years to come, we will continue to be faced with such problems. . . . I won't make any decision that is capricious or ill-advised. I'm not going to run off and do things which will harm the Bureau. I think there is a general acceptance of that. I'm not going to do anything to hurt the organization."

That said, Kelley notes frankly that "in the investigative field, I don't feel that we've had any good new techniques developed in a long time." He warns that legal decisions will probably begin to run against the acceptance of confessions in court and that "we may possibly lose some [cases] in the informant field." Court-authorized wiretaps under the provisions of the 1968 crime legislation and the nonauthorized ones in the "national security" field, he notes, must be kept to a minimum . . . "but my God, what results we're getting from them!" The Bureau's equipment, in some instances, is becoming obsolete, and because most field offices do not have "scrambling" devices for their two-way radio systems, their message traffic is vulnerable to being monitored by enterprising members of the press or the public. It is altogether a bleak picture, and what Kelley seems to be saying, albeit as gently as possible, is that the FBI had better wake up and find some new ways of solving its old problems, that it just might be in for some fairly far-reaching changes after all.

Many of the answers and comments from the visiting SACs indicate that the old emotional issues are still alive in the field. "I don't subscribe to this soft-pedaling on 'victimless crime,'" says Alexander; Sylvester agrees, complaining that it is often difficult to get the federal prosecutors to move on cases that seem to fall into the "victimless" category — including prostitution or gambling — even if they involve organized crime figures. There is a general feeling of disgust over the decline of interest in federal stolen car cases, which has meant that many auto thefts are prosecuted in state court on such charges as "joyriding" or "driving without a valid owner's registration card." Kelley deplores the fact that this retreat from prosecution is part of a national trend. Crime has become so bad in Detroit, he points out, that the police there have established an informal rule that they will not even respond to a theft complaint unless the loss is worth fifty dollars or more. If an auto theft charge is going to be "meaningless to a judge, then there is probably no point even bringing it up," the director says, noting that the Bureau's statistics for ITSMV cases (interstate transportation of a stolen motor vehicle) are way down. Alexander is disturbed by this apparent shift away from the old values; "the theft of an automobile is still a theft," he says defiantly. And all are agreed that even if society no longer regards this as a serious crime, it is certainly still a serious matter for any victim of an auto theft when it occurs.

But for the most part, the SACs' remarks are so long and so mundane that Kelley begins to look as if he is desperate for deliverance from it all. Deliverance does come occasionally in the form of phone calls — one from a man who is announcing to the boss that he has decided to retire after decades of service to the Bureau, another from one of Mrs. Kelley's doctors to propose a new form of treatment for her, a third from a young clerk at headquarters who was looking for a different agent named Kelley but was misrouted by the switchboard.* While the director is at his desk on the telephone, the SACs continue their own conversation, comparing notes and needs, reminiscing, wondering whether the public ever appreciated the extent of the Bureau's efforts to combat and solve the wave of airplane hijackings.

If Alexander and Sylvester thought they would be going to lunch at one of Kansas City's fancy new hotels, there is a surprise for them at noontime. Instead, Kelley has ordered up his old favorite barbecued-beef sandwiches from a local restaurant. An agent brings them in, wrapped in brown butcher's paper, spreads out blotters on the conference table at which everyone has been sitting, and the SAC of the Kansas City office, Paul Young, joins them for the meal. The discussion turns to lighter matters, including a television film a few nights earlier depicting the adventures of Melvin Purvis, the FBI agent who killed gangster John Dillinger in the 1930s. Kelley gives the others an opportunity to complain that the movie was offensive and a somewhat distorted version of events as seen by the FBI, then he weighs in diabolically with his own opinion that he found it amusing. They

---

* Kelley chuckles over the misdirected phone call and muses aloud that the clerk "will probably joke about this. In days gone by, she would have worried about where to hand in her resignation."

discuss the sons of SACs who have become agents, and Kelley remarks with a shrug that "I once had hopes for my son [joining the FBI], but then he got interested in making money instead." (One of his fondest hopes, in fact, was that they would at some time practice law together in Kansas City as "Kelley and Kelley.")

Back in session, Kelley, without getting too blunt about it, hints that Alexander and Sylvester are indulging in a common Bureau practice during their discussion of most of the issues — speculating on how the Bureau can better explain and justify itself to the public rather than on how it can actually improve its operations or increase dialogue with those outside the FBI. "We're saying all the time, 'People don't understand this,'" Kelley complains; "well — whose fault is it?" At one point the director touches on the tendency of many SACs to focus more heavily on their public relations role than on their responsibility to supervise the actual investigations conducted by their offices. "Maybe you fellows should cut down on your speeches, and only give one when you can make a point, not just as free entertainment. . . . When I was an SAC, I used to give some speeches that were nothing more than entertainment. . . . Maybe you should take on fewer speeches, but spend more time in preparation."

Kelley also wonders whether the Bureau has done as much as it could in the area of trying to prevent crime, rather than merely reacting to it: "How can we handle things in their incipient stages? . . . What could we do to stifle white-collar crimes before they become monumental in nature?" He notes that as soon as one kidnapping occurs — for example, that of newspaper heiress Patricia Hearst — there is bound to be a string of others; and he asks what can be done to warn potential victims and cut such epidemics short. Alexander points out that the Jacksonville Field Office got together "all of the officers and directors of a friendly bank" to give them guidelines for what to do in a kidnapping or extortion situation. "But how far can you carry this?" asks Sylvester; "do we extend it to supermarkets and other corporate people?"

Inevitably the conversation comes back time and again to Kelley the man, the void he is expected to fill, and his approach to running the Bureau. The director stresses repeatedly that he does not and cannot have the stature of J. Edgar Hoover. "His memory is sacred to me, to a considerable extent," Kelley insists; "he was a great administrator, but this cannot be duplicated." As for his own selection to run the FBI, it was "not on account of being Kelley or anything like that, but just because I fulfilled the requirements. . . . I fulfilled the qualifications: I was a lawyer, I had no political affiliations, I had local law enforcement experience, and I was a former agent." There are moments when Kelley sounds very defensive, perhaps even frightened: "So here we are, with a director who doesn't have the position that J. Edgar did. He is thought of as a 'former cop' in the job. . . . I have encountered very little new in the way of personnel problems or procedural problems. . . . I have made most of the mistakes once already, and I don't intend to repeat them. . . . I have been making a lot of speeches, and I try to use them to spotlight major problems . . . but I may have overexposed myself. I know I am not ready yet for *Meet the Press* or *Face the Nation*. I was caught flatfooted once recently [in a public appearance], and it was embarrassing. I have to learn more."

Eventually Kelley gives the SACs an opportunity to indulge extensively in their penchant for sycophancy: he asks them to evaluate his own performance, and to answer his basic question: "What can I do, without going back to the role of Hoover, to represent you better?" Sylvester's answer sums up their attitude: "I'm a firm believer in you as a man, and in what you can do for the Bureau. . . . You happen to be the right man at the right time. . . . If you were to go, for whatever the reason, it would hurt us." Alexander, for his own part, adds that although "we've had our ups and downs" — the recent downs, he says, were based primarily on people's failure to understand the Bureau's security work of the 1960s and on L. Patrick Gray's mistakes — "I think we've got a real wonderful organization. . . . I think the FBI will be regarded as one of the great law enforcement organizations in the world."

The director seems torn, as if he recognizes the role that such adulation and organizational self-praise serves in the FBI and, in fact, enjoys some of it himself; but at the same time, he seems thoroughly bored and restless with the platitudes and pats on the back. In one moment of particular impatience he stops the clichés short: "I say this without desecration . . . but we've got to forget about Hoover. We've got to climb . . . not just talk all the time. We've got to perform."

Even as the long reign of J. Edgar Hoover dragged on, from ten to twenty to thirty to forty to nearly fifty years, there were people outside the Federal Bureau of Investigation who dreamed with impunity that they might one day succeed the director in his exalted position. Mostly, they were children or chiefs of police. Both groups had an easier time keeping their fantasies alive than, say, people within the FBI hierarchy who knew that Hoover would not tolerate their having designs on his job. Clarence M. Kelley apparently missed out on the opportunity for such childhood dreams — the thought seems never to have occurred to him — but he made up for it later on, when he retired as an FBI agent and was serving as police chief in Kansas City. Once he was out of the Bureau, Kelley's aspiration to become director of the FBI was no sin, and it was certainly no secret. Among his friends in law enforcement circles, he spoke openly of the fact that he would love to have a crack at running the Bureau one day, a chance to turn it around and make its services more relevant to local police, to decentralize its structure and to modernize it. Kelley was widely known among the nation's police during the 1960s, but few people seriously thought that his name would be noticed in Washington when it came time to think about a replacement for Hoover; indeed, the most he dared to do, as one longtime friend and admirer put it, was to "harbor some futile hope that at the time Hoover died, maybe the wheel of fortune would spin in his direction."

Clarence Marion Kelley was born on October 24, 1911, in Fairmount, a hamlet in an unincorporated area between Kansas City and Independence, Missouri — the only child of Minnie Brown Kelley, who came originally from Whiting, Indiana, and Clarence Kelley, of Iola, Kansas, a man who had left school in the third grade but later began night school at age twenty and, after seventeen years of study, qualified as an electrical engineer. As a youngster, Kelley never had an opportunity to develop the usual childlike reverence for the local policeman because he never saw him. "I never was exposed to crime," he noted years later; "I don't recall there having been a single felony in my hometown." He was awed, in fact, when a man who worked for his father, who claimed to be a former bank robber, made speeches in the area about how he had seen the light and reformed. Kelley graduated from a high school in Kansas City, the University of Kansas, and then from the University of Kansas City Law School.

It was during his final year of law school, in 1940, that the special-agent-in-charge of the Kansas City Field Office spoke to Kelley's graduating class. As Kelley tells it: "My interest was stimulated because this man was very articulate and very interesting, and he painted a picture of a worthwhile dedicated service . . . I can recall well his statement that you never know what you are going to do that day when you go to work." Another factor was that given the nominal amount of money that young graduate lawyers were earning in those days, Kelley found the FBI's starting salary of $3,200 very attractive. He entered training in October of the same year, after passing the Missouri bar examination.

Kelley had not been particularly interested in criminal law during his studies — if anything, he leaned toward corporate law — but he

578

was as enthusiastic as any new recruit could be. "You have in me a typical special agent of the FBI," he is fond of saying; for it was in the Bureau that he formed his friendships, his feelings about life and work, and some conservative political attitudes. "The thing that probably impressed me more than anything else," he says, "was the caliber of the personnel. I had, of course, had classmates and fraternity brothers and the usual college career. But here you had a group of people who were completely trustworthy, who were all engaged in the same type of work and . . . I've often thought about this . . . probably this was to some extent a substitute for the brother that I did not have. I am sure that I didn't feel that at the time, but as I look back on those years, I had a deep interest in the fellow agents and developed, frankly, a deep affection for the men I was working with, plus the organization. It just seemed to me that this was almost home to me, without really realizing at the time what was occurring." Kelley followed the frenzied but methodical route of an agent who was ambitious to move along in the Bureau hierarchy. He was assigned at first to the resident agency in Huntington, West Virginia ("not an area charged with a lot of un-American activities," so the focus was on general criminal cases) and then did war-related security work in Pittsburgh, Erie, and Altoona, Pennsylvania. After a stint in Washington as a firearms instructor* for new agents and policemen attending the FBI National Academy, he was sent to Des Moines and then served in the navy for two years, mostly overseas. Returning to Bureau service in 1946, Kelley was assigned to Kansas City as a street agent, went to FBI headquarters as a desk supervisor, and then back to Kansas City as a field supervisor. He served in three consecutive offices as assistant-special-agent-in-charge, Houston, Seattle, and San Francisco. After a tour on the inspection staff, in 1957 Kelley was named SAC in Birmingham, where he served about three years before being transferred to run the Memphis Field Office.

"Clarence was a pleasant relief, the kind of guy you'd gladly work for," recalls one former agent who served under him on the West Coast: "he was a man's man kind of guy, as opposed to the shoe clerks who ran the Bureau." Kelley was apparently not much of a socializer, nor was he considered to be a dynamic leader; but one of his assets, as far as the street agents who worked for him were concerned, was that

---

* Kelley was not an instinctively good shot when he entered the Bureau; he had never handled a gun before and had to work hard to develop a proficiency. But eventually he became an expert. He still carries his gun, as director, but he has never once fired it on duty during all his years as an FBI agent or police chief, except when practicing.

he was believed to be independent of the hierarchy that toadied to Hoover and that ruled the FBI with an iron hand from headquarters.

"At the time I was in the Bureau," Kelley says, "you never thought of the need to examine the basis for doing things. . . . Hell, you did it!" Yet he recalls no instance in which he was personally involved with the installation of a wiretap, and the only tactic he remembers which "is now construed as offensive" was the use of mail covers in security cases and in the effort to locate fugitives. What sticks in his mind most vividly, however, is the fact that, as an agent, "you were received with open arms when you went to a citizen. You were well regarded throughout the community. . . . There was no investigation, or probe, or review of the operations of the Bureau. It was just that you were part of an organization that was generally well accepted." In those days, it never really occurred to Kelley that it could be any different, or that law enforcement techniques might come to be suspected for the threat they could pose to the civil liberties of the citizens.

Enjoyable as he found the Bureau, when Kelley reached the optional retirement age of fifty in 1961, he jumped at the opportunity to return to his hometown of Kansas City and take over its troubled police department. It was the sort of situation that many FBI career men regard as an ideal capstone to their career — a chance to run their own law enforcement operation and at the same time to escape the supervision of the many-layered bureaucracy at headquarters. Kelley's selection by the Kansas City Board of Police Commissioners came after a four-month search, during which he was recommended by, among others, Attorney General Robert F. Kennedy and various FBI officials.* One of his first tasks was to attempt to restore public confidence in the police department, which had been hit by a scandal that resulted in the indictment for corruption of the former police chief and four other high-ranking officers.

Something clicked, and within a short time Kelley the plodding, unexceptional Bureau official became Kelley the nationally known police leader, an innovator who made Kansas City a place to watch for experiments in law enforcement. He shook up the department slowly but continuously, until he had in effect demoted the corrupt elements and those who had opposed appointment of an outsider as chief; meanwhile, younger officers whom he felt he could trust gradually moved into positions of greater authority. By constantly reshuffling and (he said) rethinking — he reorganized the force seven times in almost twelve years — Kelley kept his opponents off balance, and the

---

* The SAC in Kansas City at the time, who was among those to recommend Kelley, was an up-and-coming Bureau executive named W. Mark Felt.

general feeling in Kansas City was that he was having a progressive effect on the department. When storefront police-community relations centers did not work, he tried putting the community relations officers in all precinct stations instead. He developed a twenty-four-hour-a-day helicopter patrol named Sky Alert; Metro Squad, a joint city-suburban investigative unit that worked in a six-county area on both sides of the Missouri-Kansas border; and Operation Barrier, which was intended to find fugitives before they escaped across that state line.

Kelley attracted attention because he seemed prepared to try almost any new idea, including programs to reevaluate the success of such traditional techniques as preventive police patrol. He encouraged his officers to discuss openly problems like police brutality, and despite criticism from within the department he welcomed a documentary filmmaker, Frederick Wiseman, into the ranks to make a television movie that provided a realistic view of police work, exciting and banal, attractive and ugly. Under his leadership, the Kansas City Police Department developed an early prototype of a sophisticated local computer network for circulating information among the various law enforcement units in a metropolitan area. (It was also one of the first to be subject to well-publicized abuses by suburban policemen interested in using their computer access to help out friends and make extra money.) Kelley's department welcomed the avant-garde Police Foundation to use Kansas City to test what one foundation official called "some of the most sacred assumptions of policing." As a direct result Kelley instituted a scheme of "participatory management," which abandoned the traditional paramilitary organization of the force in favor of a more informal decisionmaking process that welcomed input from the youngest officers.

"I don't believe in such activities as police roundups or vigilantes," Kelley said in an interview as early as 1963. "I do subscribe to the theory that society has to place some restrictions on the police. The police, after all, constantly are depriving people of liberty. But, the pendulum can swing too far the other way. There is no question that police activity can be hampered by a too-severe interpretation of constitutional rights. Sometimes this has made the job difficult." In 1972 he told a Washington meeting convened by the Law Enforcement Assistance Administration that "it borders on heresy to say that maybe police have never really been adequately attuned to the times or suitably administered," but that this was true. Throwing down the gauntlet before his own colleagues, he added, "I firmly believe that people in police fields have not recognized adequately that change is occurring around them at an unprecedented rate."

Through all this, Kelley somehow remained in the good graces of the country's powerful police establishment. He received the J. Edgar Hoover Gold Medal Award as Law Enforcement Officer of the Year in 1970, and he was appointed to the advisory board of the FBI's National Crime Information Center. In 1972, Kelley was named chairman of a five-man board selected by the Justice Department to supervise security arrangements for the Democratic and Republican National Conventions in Miami Beach; when a dispute arose among several law enforcement agencies in the Miami area over how to spend a special LEAA grant for convention-time peacekeeping measures, he was called in as the mediator.

Kelley's biggest problem during his twelve years as police chief in Kansas City was the oft-repeated allegation that he was insensitive to the problems and feelings of racial minorities. Indeed, even after a strenuous and sustained effort to recruit blacks to the police department in a city with a 20 percent black population, in 1973 there were still only about a hundred black officers on a force of 1,300; furthermore, there was feeling that an unusually large number of the white policemen, recruited from high school graduates in Kansas City and surrounding farm areas, were prejudiced against the city's minorities. Kelley was a frequent target of abuse by the local chapter of the Black Panther party, and at one point a Panther challenged him to a public duel. The strongest complaints came in 1968, when Kansas City, like many other major urban centers, suffered a serious outbreak of rioting after the assassination of Martin Luther King. According to his critics in the black community, Kelley used excessive force to control the riot, which contributed to its severity and led unnecessarily to the deaths of six black men suspected of being snipers. A city commission that investigated the handling of the riot noted the police department's poor record in minority hiring and suggested that the department's "human relations" and "public relations" desperately needed improvement, but it praised Kelley as "a capable and competent Chief of Police. He is honest and fair, has real integrity, and is highly respected generally by the policemen under his command, including the Negro policemen. . . . He has the capacity to adapt to changing times and demands, and is now demonstrating this. He is receptive to ideas and suggestions for improvement."

Kelley, for his own part, would later concede that it took special effort for him to understand the feelings and motivations of black people involved in civil rights demonstrations, and that his time as police chief included some on-the-job education in this regard. He tells one story on himself involving a protest against a segregated amuse-

Clarence M. Kelley, a twenty-year Bureau veteran who had served for twelve years as chief of police in his hometown of Kansas City, Missouri, was selected in 1973 to try to put the FBI back together again. A conservative man with modern ideas of organization and participatory management, Kelley was torn between pressures for change and the unrelenting efforts of the Old Guard to preserve the traditional FBI; most of all, he was haunted by the ghost and the image of J. Edgar Hoover, whose job, office, role and problems he had inherited. Kelley tried to strike a common touch by, for example, looking in on employees in different parts of the Bureau; once a firearms instructor for new agents, he struck a classic pose during a visit to a Bureau firing range.

WANTED

NATIONAL FIREARMS ACT

William Taylor Harris

Date photographs taken unknown
FBI No.: 308,668 L5
Aliases: Mike Andrews, Richard Frank Dennis, William Kinder, Jonathan Maris, Jonathan Mark Salamone, Teko
Age: 29, born January 22, 1945, Fort Sill, Oklahoma (not supported by birth records)

Height: 5'7"	**Eyes:** Hazel
Weight: 145 pounds	**Complexion:** Medium
Build: Medium	**Race:** White
Hair: Brown, short	**Nationality:** American

Occupation: Postal clerk
Remarks: Reportedly wears Fu Manchu type mustache, may wear glasses, upper right center tooth may be chipped, reportedly jogs, swims and rides bicycle for exercise, was last seen wearing army type boots and dark jacket
Social Security Numbers Used: 315-46-2467; 553-27-8400; 359-48-5467
Fingerprint Classification: 20 L 1 At 12
S 1 Ut

Emily Montague Harris

Date photographs taken unknown
FBI No.: 325,804 L2
Aliases: Mrs. William Taylor Harris, Mary Hensley, Joanne James, Anna Lindenberg, Cynthia Sue Mankins, Dorothy Ann Petri, Emily Montague Schwartz, Mary Schwartz, Yolanda
Age: 27, born February 11, 1947, Baltimore, Maryland (not supported by birth records)

Height: 5'3"	**Eyes:** Blue
Weight: 115 pounds	**Complexion:** Fair
Build: Small	**Race:** White
Hair: Blonde	**Nationality:** American

Occupations: Secretary, teacher
Remarks: Hair may be worn one inch below ear level, may wear glasses or contact lenses; reportedly has partial upper plate, pierced ears, is a natural food fadist, exercises by jogging, swimming and bicycle riding, usually wears slacks or street length dresses, was last seen wearing jeans and waist length shiny black leather coat; may wear wigs
Social Security Numbers Used: 327-42-2356; 429-42-8003

NATIONAL FIREARMS ACT; BANK ROBBERY

Patricia Campbell Hearst

FBI No.: 325,805 L10
Alias: Tania
Age: 20, born February 20, 1954, San Francisco, California

Height: 5'3"	**Eyes:** Brown
Weight: 110 pounds	**Complexion:** Fair
Build: Small	**Race:** White
Hair: Light brown	**Nationality:** American

Scars and Marks: Mole on lower right corner of mouth, scar near right ankle
Remarks: Hair naturally light brown, straight and worn about three inches below shoulders in length, however, may wear wigs, including Afro style, dark brown of medium length; was last seen wearing black sweater, plaid slacks, brown hiking boots and carrying a knife in her belt

Jan., 1971   Feb., 1972   Dec., 1973   April, 1974

THE ABOVE INDIVIDUALS ARE SELF-PROCLAIMED MEMBERS OF THE SYMBIONESE LIBERATION ARMY AND REPORTEDLY HAVE BEEN IN POSSESSION OF NUMEROUS FIREARMS INCLUDING AUTOMATIC WEAPONS. WILLIAM HARRIS AND PATRICIA HEARST ALLEGEDLY HAVE USED GUNS TO AVOID ARREST. ALL THREE SHOULD BE CONSIDERED ARMED AND VERY DANGEROUS.

Federal warrants were issued on May 20, 1974, at Los Angeles, California, charging the Harrises and Hearst with violation of the National Firearms Act. Hearst was also indicted by a Federal Grand Jury on June 6, 1974, at San Francisco, California, for bank robbery and use of a weapon during a felony.

IF YOU HAVE ANY INFORMATION CONCERNING THESE PERSONS, PLEASE NOTIFY ME OR CONTACT YOUR LOCAL FBI OFFICE, THE TELEPHONE NUMBER OF WHICH APPEARS ON THE FIRST PAGE OF MOST LOCAL DIRECTORIES.

C m Kelley
DIRECTOR
FEDERAL BUREAU OF INVESTIGATION
UNITED STATES DEPARTMENT OF JUSTICE
WASHINGTON, D. C. 20535
TELEPHONE: 202 324-3000

Entered NCIC
Wanted Flyer 475 A
(Rev. October 16, 1974)

One of the most widely publicized and mysterious cases in recent Bureau history was the 1974 kidnapping and conversion of newspaper heiress Patricia Hearst by a group of radical guerrillas who called themselves the Symbionese Liberation Army. After the group, including Hearst, allegedly robbed a San Francisco bank, the FBI distributed a wanted poster for Hearst and the two gang members she was believed to be traveling with. At one point Director Clarence Kelley acknowledged that the Bureau was simply "stumped" by the case, but the FBI continued the hunt. The three were arrested by agents in San Francisco on September 18, 1975, nineteen months after Hearst disappeared.

ment park in Kansas City. As the police moved in to arrest the demonstrators, one man intentionally went limp and had to be carried from the park to a nearby precinct station and then transported to police headquarters. "I followed the affair from the amusement park right on through," Kelley recalls. "And when he was prone on the floor, in the garage of the headquarters station, he was lying there crying and singing, in a very small voice, 'We Shall Overcome.' He obviously was embarrassed. He was a very fine-looking young black. He was dedicated to the cause of demonstrating his opposition to this discrimination, and personally, this was a very traumatic experience, and a lasting one, for me, which brought vividly to my attention that here was something that really troubled this young man. He was not a violator of the law, he was not a criminal, he was a concerned individual. I learned and grew as a result of that."

Another of Kelley's experiences, one that he relates quite often to special-agents-in-charge as an example of poor communication, concerned a protest in the Kansas City black community against the police department's widespread fingerprinting of criminal suspects. "A group of people, most of them ministers, came into the police department and demanded to have their fingerprints taken and then mixed in with the criminal fingerprint files," Kelley remembers. "There was some discussion on the subject, and I was countering with what I thought was a very logical explanation of why you just don't mix in noncriminal prints with the criminal prints. And a man in the back, who was white — I don't know whether he was a minister or who he was — said, 'He just doesn't understand.' It suddenly dawned on me that I perhaps didn't understand then about just what they were doing" — demonstrating their solidarity with those whose prints had been taken, almost all poor blacks, who would now probably be haunted by their new criminal records.

By 1972, the controversy over Chief Kelley's handling of the riot and of minority affairs in general had died down considerably. When the city of Boston was looking for a new police commissioner to solve especially difficult problems it was having, it turned to him; he was prepared to accept the job and make the move, but just then it was discovered that his wife was seriously ill. That was a factor again a year later, when he was offered the FBI job, but Mrs. Kelley persuaded him to accept it nonetheless. It was, said one Kelley intimate, "the old American dream actually happening. Here was a guy who really wanted that job for so many years, not an especially aggressive, grasping man — not avaricious — but just waiting. And fate struck." Financially, it was only a small step up for Kelley to accept the FBI directorship; between the director's salary ($42,000) and his Kansas City pension, he earned just short of $50,000 a year, and because of his wife's illness he had to maintain two homes.

No one suggested that this would be an easy assignment, especially given the Bureau's rocky ride through Watergate. What was needed, in fact, said Kelley's temporary predecessor, William Ruckelshaus, was somebody analogous to, and as good a mediator as, the late Pope John XXIII.

Alden McCray, the chief FBI Legat in London, was offering a toast to the dinner marking the end of a detectives training course at the Lancashire County Police Headquarters in Preston, England, on an early June night in 1973, when word came that the nomination for the FBI directorship had gone to Clarence Kelley. McCray didn't know Kelley from the man in the moon; but he did know that Kelley was a police chief who had spent more than twenty years in the FBI, and that, as far as he was concerned, was what really counted. The lone American in a room full of Englishmen, McCray nonetheless raised his glass to salute the "return to professionalism" that he envisioned for the Bureau if someone with such a background were taking charge. The reaction, he recalled later, was overwhelming — applause filled the banquet hall, and Lancashire's chief constable extended the group's congratulations to the FBI for surviving its crisis. "The Bureau had been kicked around," McCray notes, "and the British police were sympathetic; they understood how we felt, and they were as relieved as we were" that the new director would be a man with police credentials.

Kelley was probably correct when he told the visiting SACs in Kansas City that the important thing about his selection was not that he was Clarence Kelley, but that he fulfilled certain qualifications. The most common reaction to his selection, both inside the Bureau and among other departments of government and the public, was a great sense of relief — a feeling that somehow the FBI could now find its way back to "normal," a state of affairs that predated not only Gray and Ruckelshaus and the Watergate era, but also the turbulence of the late 1960s. Under the circumstances, though they did not know much about him personally, people tended to view the arrival of Kelley in the job as a sort of coming of the messiah, a wise sage who would set everything straight again. It was a most peculiar role in which to cast this very ordinary man from Kansas City.

The sense of relief extended to Capitol Hill. Senators who only a few months earlier were growling ferociously at Gray and, by reference, at the FBI, now cooed with satisfaction. When Kelley was taken around by legislative liaison officers from the White House and the Justice Department for private meetings with members of the Senate Judiciary Committee and other senators, the sessions were friendly to the point of effusiveness. Most committee members pronounced themselves impressed with Kelley's record as an FBI agent and police chief, said they would probably not ask many questions during the confirmation hearings, and indicated they were already prepared to vote in his favor. As Senator Strom Thurmond of South Carolina later summed up his attitude during the confirmation hearings, "I have no questions to propound to Chief Kelley. I have known him for a number of years. . . . I have heard others speak about his excellent work. . . . When one looks at Chief Kelley, he looks like an exemplary police officer and he acts like an exemplary police officer, and his record as Chief of Police in Kansas City, Missouri, is one of an exemplary police officer. I think the President is to be commended upon selecting this fine gentleman to head this position and he is the type of officer I would like to see on the police forces and in the law enforcement agencies as much as possible throughout the Nation."

Senator James O. Eastland of Mississippi, chairman of the Judiciary Committee, urged the Justice Department to generate telegrams and letters in support of the nomination from chiefs of police and black leaders, among others, that could be inserted in the hearing record right at the start, in the hope of building momentum in Kelley's favor. (The committee staff, in its enthusiasm, went overboard and threw in with the telegrams, ahead of schedule, a statement from Senator Hugh Scott, R-Pennsylvania, commending Kelley for his testimony before Kelley had had an opportunity to give much testimony.) Eastland also agreed to bring up Kelley's potential problems right at the start, including his handling of the 1968 riots in Kansas City and the turning over of surplus guns by the police department there to General Carl B. Turner, provost marshal of the army, who later sold them for his own profit.*

Opposition to Kelley did develop on the grounds of his alleged insensitivity to racial minorities. Senator Birch Bayh (D-Indiana) produced a memorandum to the director of the U.S. Community Rela-

---

* According to Kelley's explanation, his department was one of many solicited by Turner to provide firearms, supposedly for the use of himself and his staff in lectures before civic groups and for display in museums. Turner's contacts were especially good in Kansas City because he was an old friend of a man working under Kelley; as a result, the police department there gave him over a hundred weapons that had been discarded. Only later was it revealed that Turner had been selling them.

tions Service in Washington from the CRS field representative in Kansas City, discussing the racial tensions there. It noted a

lack of visible willingness on the part of the Kansas City Police Department (KCPD) either to penalize appropriately officers who have apparently brutalized minority citizens or to require positive results from efforts to recruit minority police officers. There have been several incidents in the last two years of perceived severe police brutality against minority citizens; no meaningful efforts have been made by the KCPD to show the public that the KCPD will not tolerate excessive use of force by its officers; indeed, the Chairman of the Board of Police Commissioners, in a recent public statement, suggested that he would support officers who use excessive force (on the ground that the offender "initiated" the incident which caused the force to be used). The officer force of KCPD is about 7% minority; the population of the city is about 23% minority.

Bruce R. Watkins, circuit court clerk of Jackson County, Missouri, and president of a black organization called Freedom, Inc., appeared to testify against the nomination. "Clarence M. Kelley, as a man," he said,

probably exemplifies, as much as anyone else, the stolid, amoral conservatism that seems to constitute the ranks of "police" officialdom of this country today. There is no question as to his loyalty, perseverance and faithfulness to those pristine principles that demand this adherence. There does exist numerous questions [sic] to his humanity. What I really mean is Clarence M. Kelley is the perfect "Big Brother" police official and the real tragedy is that he is merely symptomatic of a condition that permeates the whole country; that is, the poor, the black, are universally denied equality before the law.

At the same time, a black businessman from Kansas City was produced to testify in Kelley's favor. It became clear, however, that barring some sensational revelation, the committee was not going to judge the nominee on the basis of the 1968 riots and their aftermath.

But on the gut issues of current controversy concerning the Bureau — politicization of its investigative efforts, wiretapping, domestic intelligence activities, the problems posed by government data banks, and such — some members of the committee, especially the liberal Democrats, tried to draw out Kelley's opinions and attitudes during the public hearings. Kelley had been warned to expect as much, and the Justice Department gave him an advance list of thirty-five questions on difficult subjects that he could anticipate being confronted with, ranging from "What procedures, if any, would you make available for the receipt of critical comment from within FBI ranks?" (a reference to the severe punishment under Hoover of anyone who expressed views that dissented from official policy) to "What will you do when you encounter evidence of violations of one federal criminal statute while investigating violations of another statute? Will you consider it necessary to have any investigation into such other violations cleared by the attorney general or some other official in the Department of Justice?" (a reference to the Bureau's reluctance to explore the "dirty tricks" side of the Watergate affair without special authorization, after agents stumbled across it while investigating the burglary and bugging of the Democratic National Committee's headquarters).

So long away from the FBI, however, Kelley was fundamentally unprepared to address some of these issues. Encouraged by the Justice Department and the Bureau to avoid committing himself whenever possible, he capitalized on the fact of his twelve-year absence from the scene to plead ignorance in response to many of the questions posed by the senators. That was how he handled most of the questions from Senator Robert C. Byrd of West Virginia, the newly vigilant watchdog of the FBI. When Byrd solicited the nominee's opinion of his bill to take the Bureau out of the Justice Department and give it the status of an independent agency, for example, Kelley replied that he could see both sides of the issue:

> I have been chief of police for twelve years, and of course, traditionally in police circles, the prosecutive branch is separated from the investigative. The situation has been a very healthy one. I certainly see no objection to this.
> I would, however, want to know what was the executive intent behind the union of the Department of Justice and the FBI. I frankly never considered this in the past. It again [like other issues that arose in the hearings] was something that was never uncomfortable and I can visualize there possibly would be some economic reasons for the merging of them. I just am unprepared to answer you very well. I would see no disadvantage to it, however, so I would say . . . I would like to have more time to study it, to find out what would be the basis for these things.

On some issues Kelley seemed simply and painfully naïve. In an exchange with Senator Philip Hart (D-Michigan) on the subject of domestic intelligence, for example, he remarked that "I don't know this term 'domestic intelligence,' but general intelligence, you have that in the field of crime, you have it in the field of security or the violations of treason, sabotage and espionage. And that intelligence is gathered not just to be informed generally, but in contemplation of prosecution.

And I know of no intelligence effort which is not so directed." Hart seemed incredulous that Kelley could actually be unaware of the vast amount of FBI intelligence efforts that have no obvious relationship to prosecutions, but merely produce information that is stored in the files; the incredulousness was shared by many other people listening to the nominee's testimony, including some in the Justice Department.

But the Judiciary Committee was satisfied by Kelley's flat-out statements that he would not permit himself or the Bureau under his leadership to become entangled in politics. If pressure were exerted to try to hamper or hold back an FBI investigation, he said, "I would go to the attorney general and voice my protest and not having the satisfaction I would feel necessary, I would go to the President. . . . If I got no satisfaction from there, I would go out." Byrd noted in a tone of disappointment that Congress was not on the list of courts of resort to which Kelley would consider taking his appeal against pressure, and the senator suggested this was evidence of a need to establish a strong congressional oversight relationship with the FBI. Kelley agreed and said he was fully prepared to cooperate and work with any properly constituted committee that sought to exercise oversight, even though that would mean an invasion of the House Appropriations Committee's old claim to the exclusive right to review Bureau operations.

After hearings that lasted only three days, Kelley was warmly endorsed by the Judiciary Committee and enthusiastically confirmed by the Senate. President Nixon, looking for any attention-getting diversion he could find to distract the public from Watergate, flew to Kansas City to swear Kelley in on July 9, 1973.

The FBI had a permanent director for the first time in more than fourteen months. "I suppose you recognize," Senator Bayh had said to Kelley during his hearings, "that one of the most important jobs you have is to put the fellows on their feet again and instill pride in them that there is a purpose for quality investigative service for the country." "That is right," Kelley replied. "I don't feel that the problem of morale is as deep rooted as it might seem because they are real pros, and they are fine people. They won't take too long to get back on their feet, I think." That was the public posture, urged on Kelley by the Bureau hierarchy, which was eager to keep the FBI flag flying high. To be sure, the installation of a permanent director who did not have to worry about winning the favor of the White House or Congress would be a major boost to an organization ravaged by controversy. But Kelley was taking office at a time of anxiety over whether the repressive atmosphere of the Hoover era would return or whether some of the meaningful reforms launched by Gray would be carried forward. The idea of less independence for the FBI, closer links with the rest of the Justice Department, and scrutiny by Congress was a good one in the abstract, but it was also the source of considerable trauma for people who had become used to running their own show during their decades of service. There was an uneasy atmosphere within the Bureau.

If Kelley needed any additional evidence that the crises of recent years had taken their toll on the FBI, a Gallup poll published just a month after he was sworn in provided it. The decline in the Bureau's public image and popularity, which began in the late 1960s, had continued dramatically. Only 52 percent of those polled gave the FBI a "highly favorable" rating, Gallup reported, as compared with 84 percent in 1965 and 71 percent in 1970. Decreasing esteem for the Bureau was apparent in all segments of the population, but steepest among those under thirty, people with a college background, and those living on the East or West coasts. Even in the South, "highly favorable" opinions of the FBI had dropped to 59 percent, and among Republicans to 57 percent.* Since, as Kelley himself repeatedly noted, the Bureau's ability to perform successfully depends in large measure on the opinion the citizens have of it and the degree to which they are willing to cooperate with it, the implications of its decline in popularity were potentially serious.

From the moment Kelley's name surfaced as the leading candidate to become director, the Old Guard within the FBI set out to capture him and make him one of their own. There were, as Kelley likes to call them, plenty of "blandishments": offers of assistance with the simplest of things, efforts to convince him that he was the only person in the United States who could possibly have qualified to step into Hoover's shoes, effusive — sometimes outlandish — praise for his every little gesture. By the time Kelley was confirmed, of course, all of the elaborate services of the Bureau and its extraordinary responsiveness to the man at the top were at his command.

There are two competing ways to view Kelley's integration into the FBI upon arrival and his early handling of a powerful bureaucracy that can be devious or compliant. One could be labeled the "Simple Clarence" theory, which assumes that he has totally capitulated to the traditionalists and old-timers, in effect forgetting any perspective on the Bureau he might have gained since retiring as an agent, instead

---

* Interestingly, the same Gallup poll found that a far smaller number of people, only 23 percent, held a "highly favorable" opinion of the Central Intelligence Agency. Local police fared about the same as the Bureau, winning a "highly favorable" rating from 53 percent of those polled.

returning to the "old Bureau" syndrome. Propounded in some press accounts and in certain quarters of the Justice Department, this view has it that Kelley is not very clever and was easily fooled by people who had had years of experience with intrigue at FBI headquarters. Lending credence to this theory are some of the director's public appearances, when he has difficulty finding the words to express what he wants to say, appears to have been poorly briefed on major issues (or incapable of remembering his briefing), and finally settles upon clichés that have as their central element the belief that in the final analysis everybody still trusts and loves the Bureau. Kelley accepts whatever an assistant director tells him, according to this view, without taking account of the likelihood that some of them will be trying to promote themselves in his eyes or to expand their individual empires into new areas. Furthermore, the theory holds, Kelley is tricked by the Bureau's lip service responses to his declarations of openness and flexibility, whereas in fact very little has changed; the effort is actually to find ways to avoid fulfilling requests for information from Congress and other outsiders, sometimes while appearing to fulfill them. Kelley may have developed boards to evaluate the best people for promotion into certain Bureau positions, but the reform is meaningless, say the "Simple Clarence" theorists, because only people favored by the old powers within the Administrative Division are ever proposed for consideration by those boards. Many promotions, they insist, are still on the basis of sycophancy and avoidance of controversy rather than genuine merit and innovativeness.

The other view might be called the "Kelley as Machiavellian" theory. It holds that lurking behind the simple, policemanlike exterior of Clarence Kelley is a very clever, insightful man, who is an excellent judge of character and an expert at gradually bending an organization until it is responsive to him. The chief supporters of this interpretation are people who have known the director for many years and watched him in action in tense situations, as well as those, inside the Bureau or out, who have spent a considerable amount of time listening to his private ruminations about the FBI since he was sworn in. Kelley is often not good on his feet, they concede, but in more relaxed and intimate sessions, for example, with the House Appropriations Subcommittee, he is smooth, self-confident, and persuasive — without any need for the line-by-line revisions and corrections of transcript that were required in Hoover's days. According to this theory, the director also has a particular knack for evaluating objectively the recommendations of the hierarchy, and while he may sometimes appear to be accepting things uncritically, he is actually looking at them carefully and forming long-range judgments about whose advice should be trusted and whose not. Members of the Bureau's Old Guard have done so well, argue the "Kelley as Machiavellian" theorists, only because the director is using them for what they can provide — help in handling the bureaucracy and in easing the pressure on him — but discarding them whenever their helpfulness begins to run out or when they show any signs of making things more difficult for him. Kelley actually does not enjoy being "sucked up to," they point out, and he can readily distinguish approaches that are sincere and meaningful from efforts at self-promotion and self-aggrandizement. The most important thing in Kelley's initial period as director is to build a "climate for change" rather than to accomplish anything bold and dramatic, goes this view, and one day the traditionalists will wake up and find that he has managed to bring a great deal of reform to the institution.

Both theories find their support in the same body of evidence. One of Kelley's most important early decisions was his choice of Nicholas P. Callahan, the epitome of the veteran Hooverite in the FBI, as his associate director. Callahan had not served in the field in almost three decades, and he was a particularly ardent defender of the traditional way of performing most of the Bureau's responsibilities. One of the goals of the weekly meetings of the executive conference, he acknowledges, is to "keep the Bureau as free from criticism as possible." It was on the recommendation of Callahan, among others, that Kelley reestablished the two assistant-to-the-director jobs just below the associate director, as well as an External Affairs Division patterned exactly after the old Crime Records operation — thus putting the FBI back into its traditional structural shape (which, as the Bureau saw it, was conceived and ordained by Hoover) after it had been temporarily violated by Gray. Callahan insists that he is not part of a resistance group that is trying to prevent the Bureau from modernizing or adapting to new ideas. "Sure, I was a member of the Hoover staff, and you couldn't get me to say two words against him," Callahan says; "he gave due recognition to the workers in the Bureau. . . . It's because of him that it's an honor to be with the FBI." The degree of Callahan's entrenchment with the old faithful — led by his mentor John Mohr — is symbolized by the fact that he was a witness to some of the codicils to Clyde Tolson's contested will.

"It hurts me to hear the view that I'm old school or Old Guard," Callahan remarks in reflecting upon his role. "As far as I'm concerned, the FBI is not a one-man organization. You have got to depend on new people coming in to maintain the old traditions, the Bureau's efficiency and effectiveness. . . . Our job — the older guys staying around — is to stay in communication [with the new people] and furnish them with what they need. . . . Maybe it's my fault for not being able to get out and mingle with them, to go around and talk with them, and say 'Hi, fellas, what's your problem, and what can I do for you?' " Callahan's view of change is a simple one: "We have a well-organized and efficient operation now. We don't say it's a hundred percent, only ninety-eight." He pauses and laughs. "So how much room does that leave you to change or do things? If things are wrong, we're going to find out about them first ourselves and change them."

Other men commonly regarded as being part of the Old Guard were also given important jobs by Kelley. There was Thomas J. Jenkins, for example, who has been an FBI employee since 1934 (his first five years were spent as a clerk), a record that approaches that of Hoover. When Kelley reestablished the two assistant-to-the-director positions in December 1973, he gave the one on the administrative side to Jenkins; there, according to younger Bureau officials, he has managed to block or slow down a number of innovations as well as tried to continue running the Training Division, which was his previous assignment as an assistant director. Another view of Jenkins, however, is that he is an old-shoe type and a friend of long standing whom Kelley can count upon for factual reporting of problems and faithful implementation of programs. He puts up no resistance.

Some dissidents say (although never publicly) that Callahan and Jenkins are really the people running the FBI administratively under Kelley. Especially when the director is off in Kansas City or traveling elsewhere, it is said, they make major decisions — including personnel assignments — that would ordinarily be the director's prerogative. Some young supervisors at headquarters, desirous of attracting Kelley's personal attention to their work, have mastered the talent of sending important matters up through the chain of command only between Monday noon and Thursday noon, lest they never reach his desk otherwise.* At the same time Kelley apparently regards the presence of Callahan and Jenkins at the top as a valuable asset, because when they communicate down through the ranks at headquarters a policy that might otherwise be regarded as controversial — for example, Kelley's efforts to give special-agents-in-charge more latitude and independence in dealing with the press and other outsiders — it is more likely to be accepted than if it came from people who were not recognized as keepers of the faith. Kelley has exploited them for their

---

* Some of the old-timers, conversely, have learned to submit memos between Thursday and Monday to *avoid* Kelley and his aides.

connections and influence with more junior members of the Old Guard.

Other people initially advanced or listened to by Kelley did not last very long in their new positions. Edward S. Miller, for example, had served only six months as assistant-to-the-director for investigative operations when he was discreetly urged to retire; Kelley found him to be too much of a "zealot" who looked at every issue with the perspective of a man who had just been assistant director for the Intelligence Division. Another old-timer left the Bureau when the director failed to promote him to the second-ranking job in that division, which is in charge of all the FBI's counterintelligence and internal security operations; according to one source, Kelley considered that the man was "thinking with his experience rather than with his head." Kelley was frankly bored by some other assistant directors, feeling that they had specialized to the point of developing very narrow vision. The word went out that the kinds of men he sought as assistant directors were those who were all-around good managers, whom he could move among various divisions as he saw fit in order to solve problems and dilemmas as they came up.

It was sometimes difficult to read a pattern into the promotions and other personnel decisions made by Kelley. On the one hand, he removed responsibility for the Bureau's congressional relations from the Crime Records/External Affairs people, who tended to have a friends-and-enemies approach, and assigned it to John Hotis, a young agent widely respected for his knowledge of legislative and legal issues. But on the other hand, he sent Assistant Director Richard Baker back out into the field after he had barely managed to launch the Office of Planning and Evaluation into some crucial areas of FBI policy; and he brought in as SAC of the important Washington Field Office one Nick Stames, a man young in years but widely regarded as very traditional in his attitude toward the world outside the FBI, because of his long experience in the Administrative Division.

Two men emerged as people with particular influence on Kelley and therefore as bright prospects to succeed him one day. They were James B. Adams and John A. Mintz. After a varied early career that included service as a Japanese interpreter for the army and as a representative in the Texas state legislature, Adams chose to become an FBI agent in 1951. He advanced unusually quickly and within two years had become a supervisor in the powerful administrative apparatus at headquarters. There he stayed for much of his career, and in 1965 he was named the Bureau's personnel officer, a good spot from which to

595

gain a great deal of influence and leverage. In July 1972, Adams was sent out by Pat Gray for a perfunctory stint as SAC in San Antonio, an area he knew well; within a year and a half, Kelley had brought him back to headquarters as assistant director in charge of the Office of Planning and Evaluation. In the meantime, the fact that Adams had been one of only two FBI insiders considered for selection as director at the same time as Clarence Kelley substantially increased his stature within the Bureau. When Miller left in the summer of 1974, Adams moved up to become assistant-to-the-director for investigative operations. If Callahan and Jenkins could be said to run the administrative side of the FBI at times, it was Adams who became Kelley's surrogate on investigative matters. He was said to be calling the shots on a number of major, well-publicized cases. An enigmatic, ambitious man of the Old Guard little known outside the Bureau, except in Texas, Adams often accompanied Kelley on sensitive public appearances in Washington or substituted for him entirely.

Mintz's Bureau record is relatively brief. He became an agent only in 1961, just after completing the requirements for a Doctor of Law degree at the University of Chicago. After quick assignments to the field offices in Tampa, New York, Memphis, Jackson, and Washington, Mintz was transferred to the Office of Legal Counsel at headquarters in 1965. There ever since, he has been at the center of some of the FBI's most delicate legal crises — fights over whether to reveal the identity of informants, deliberations about what to say concerning the controversial COINTELPRO activities of the 1950s and 1960s, efforts to explain and rationalize legally the FBI's domestic intelligence programs, studies of how to set about recodifying altogether the Bureau's responsibilities in the security field. Mintz took over the Office of Legal Counsel in 1972 upon the retirement of longtime Hoover aide Dwight Dalbey, but he was so young (in Bureau terms) at the time, thirty-seven, that nobody got around to giving him the title of assistant director until April 1974. He is quiet, studious, good-humored, virtually unflappable under pressure, and, according to some, the man who has a better overall view of FBI operations and their legal and political ramifications than anyone else. Mintz is also one of the very few Bureau people whose legal judgment is respected — indeed, sometimes sought out — by attorneys in the Justice Department and other parts of the government. Kelley has gradually shifted more responsibilities into his once-tiny division.

Each man has a defect that is sometimes cited as blocking his path to the directorship. In Mintz's case it is that he has rather little field experience and has never been a special-agent-in-charge or even an assistant-special-agent-in-charge. As for Adams, incredibly, the complaint is that he is not really tall enough to be director. He is barely above the Bureau's old minimum height standard of five feet seven inches (some claim that he really isn't), and that is seen as a drawback by those who feel that the director of the FBI must be a large, sturdy-looking character whom criminals would not want to encounter in a dark alley. (Mintz does not have nearly as tough a visage as Adams, but he is taller.) Many people, including some in the Bureau, believe, in any event, that the next director will not come from within FBI ranks.

Even after Pat Gray's problems, Kelley committed the sin, unpardonable in some Bureau eyes, of bringing in outsiders to help him learn and run the FBI. William L. Reed, his personal executive assistant, left his job as director of the Florida Department of Law Enforcement to join Kelley in Washington. A personal friend and protégé of Kelley for years, he had been a college graduate patrolman on the Kansas City police force and later served on the faculty of his and Kelley's alma mater, the University of Kansas City Law School, and then on that of the University of Miami Law School. Reed, a rotund and jolly man who promptly made many friends in the Bureau hierarchy, came to act as the director's eyes, ears, and hands, especially during crisis situations when, for example, Kelley had to drop everything else and prepare for a confrontation with a congressional subcommittee angry over some new development. He came to Washington with a profound reverence and awe toward the FBI, based upon his early experiences and exposure elsewhere, when it was considered "the only federal agency we could trust," but also with a healthy skepticism of any large bureaucracy. Reed is capable when necessary of defending virtually any Bureau practice, but there are those who say that if Kelley has avoided being completely enveloped by the Old Guard, it was only because he had Reed's independent voice whispering over one of his shoulders.

Somewhat less successful at fading inconspicuously into the woodwork while also influencing Kelley was John Coleman, former director of training for the Kansas City Police Department. A kind of roving minister without portfolio, Coleman was given the task of examining old, time-honored Bureau practices — how many copies of every document must be kept and where, what rules must govern the storage and use of FBI cars, how the chief clerk in each field office organizes his or her staff, among other things — and making suggestions for modernization and cost-cutting. Coleman probably saved an entire forest from being converted into FBI letterhead memoranda, but in the process his abrasive and impatient manner irritated some of the people in the field offices he visited.

But most controversial among Kelley's three personal aides was William Ellingsworth, a young former newspaperman who had served as his public information officer at the Kansas City Police Department. The plan was for Ellingsworth to use Kelley's personal openness and comfortableness with the press as a vehicle for making the Bureau and its operations far more accessible to reporters. The days of "no-contact" lists and favored treatment for certain reporters who were established Bureauphiles were to be gone forever. No sooner had Kelley reestablished the External Affairs Division, however, than Ellingsworth was completely stymied in his efforts, sometimes even cut off from access to the director. One assistant director, Robert R. Franck, the first of several people tried by Kelley as head of External Affairs, so resented Ellingsworth's presence that he insisted upon listing him in the Bureau's telephone directory as a clerk. Whenever Ellingsworth managed to get a newsman in to see Kelley after he had already been denied an appointment by External Affairs, the top officials of the division might spend an entire afternoon fuming about it and working on new ways to try to neutralize Ellingsworth. At one point they even tried circulating rumors about his personal life.*

Kelley's experience with bringing outsiders into the Bureau was far less turbulent than Gray's; but then Kelley was a full-fledged director of the FBI, holding office with the advice and consent of the Senate, and there was not much the bureaucracy could do, short of trying to make the interlopers' lives miserable. Still, some old-timers were less angry about it than they were insulted. It seemed to imply something short of total trust by Kelley in the FBI professionals, and they simply could not understand why the director did not use bona fide agents in his office instead. As one person upset over this put it, "That's the way Mr. Hoover always did it, and it worked fine. If it was good enough for him, why isn't it good enough for Kelley?"

For a man who had taken dramatic control of the Kansas City Police Department and substantially changed it, Kelley found that he had to move much more slowly and deliberately at the FBI. He was privately disappointed that the vast majority of people in the Bureau were so suspicious of any departure from tradition. What revisions of policy and practice he did make were scarcely noticeable outside of the FBI, leading to a widespread public impression that Kelley was taking the Bureau back into the Hoover era rather than out of it. To some

---

* Ellingsworth resigned in the summer of 1975.

extent, after all the unfavorable publicity at the time of Gray's fall, that suited Kelley's purpose just fine; but after a time, it also became a problem that stood in the way of Kelley's achieving credibility as his own man. That was enough to lead some people to urge him to take bold steps that would make the point.

To be sure, there were some innovations that made plenty of waves within the Bureau. With the financial assistance of the Police Foundation (headed by that old Hoover archenemy, former New York City Police Commissioner Patrick V. Murphy), Kelley convened a series of regional management symposia for assistant directors, inspectors, SACs, and ASACs. Merely the fact that the meetings were held off Bureau premises in hotels and office buildings, and that the instructors and lecturers were not fully trained special agents was something of a shock, not to say a dangerous security risk, in the minds of some traditionalists. But when one of the lecturers, Richard Ross, a management consultant from Los Angeles, showed up with a beard and platform shoes and spoke of what sets off people's "freaky buttons," while another, Kansas City psychologist Marshall Saper, warned the Bureau executives against letting their "stress buckets" run over, it was clear that *something* in the FBI had changed. The purpose of the symposia was not only to expose the FBI leadership to some fairly sophisticated management techniques and ideas, but also to try to loosen up the old-timers and get them to consider new ways of solving old problems, such as the standoff between headquarters and the field.

In each of the eight cities where the symposia were held, Kelley also had a press conference. He would begin by circulating among the newsmen to introduce himself and shake their hands — some of the Bureau people could not believe their eyes: the director of the FBI was actually willing to touch a reporter — and then took questions on any subject, some of which he handled very well. Kelley failed in his effort to encourage the wives of Bureau executives also to ask him questions at these same press conferences; they sat terrified and mute in their chairs. He did not make headline splashes, but he did make a point within the Bureau: that the press need not be treated as lepers, that perhaps there was a legitimate public interest communications process that the FBI could take part in. At his other press conferences in Washington, with large delegations of headquarters officials looking on, Kelley sometimes seemed more reserved and cautious. If he had done nothing else to win widespread popularity among street agents, however, he earned a fond spot in their hearts on one occasion by acknowledging in response to a reporter's question that the Bureau was "stumped" in its efforts to solve the case involving Patricia Hearst.

599

The agents were gratified to have a public declaration from the top that, yes, the FBI is human and there are some situations in which it cannot work magic. They knew that had always been the truth; they were simply relieved that a director was finally willing to admit it.

To all appearances, this director sought to build no myth of infallibility around himself. He was often as much as fifteen or twenty minutes late for an appointment — an encouraging sign of humanity to some agents — and had no problem acknowledging that he is somewhat deaf in one ear, or that he had a benign tumor removed from his arm in the spring of 1975. SACs sometimes stumbled over themselves trying to do him special favors when he came to town, but were usually frustrated. If they had a bottle of Chivas Regal waiting in his hotel room, as some did, they would likely get it back unopened. (Kelley does drink scotch, but only very infrequently and well diluted with water — "flavored water," one aide says of the mix.)

Kelley had the Office of Planning and Evaluation run a Bureau-wide survey of agent attitudes toward the organization. Some agents, all too painfully aware of the old taboo on criticism from within the ranks, actually put on gloves to complete the OPE questionnaire, lest their answers be traceable by their fingerprints. The answers to certain questions would have encouraged any director — an overwhelming majority agreed, for example, that "if I had the choice to make over again, I would choose the FBI as a career" — but others pointed to real problems. Fewer than half of the street agents said they felt they had a strong voice "in changing the organization for the better"; many thought that discipline was not "handled in a fair and impartial manner" and complained that favoritism exists in promotion, assignment, and discipline.

According to some people in high Bureau positions, Kelley has managed to build a new spirit within the FBI — in the field, a far greater sense of independence from headquarters; and at headquarters, a genuine feeling of "participatory management" in which those at lower levels need not worry quite as much as before about expressing their own ideas, even if they are, as a favorite Bureau term puts it, "way out." Meetings of the executive conference have become more like those of a corporate board of directors than of the disciples of Christ. Kelley also claims to be conducting a major critical reevaluation of everything the FBI does, with the goal of redistributing manpower more effectively and setting clearer priorities than have ever existed in the past; with the press of daily events, however, and the Bureau in the midst of controversies, that is obviously a process that could take years to complete.

Actual Bureau policy on most matters has changed little, if at all, since Kelley took over. Although he may have come into office with some skepticism toward the growth of the FBI's security work, as some say he did, before very long and after a few intensive briefings from the appropriate people in the Intelligence Division, he was issuing alarmist statements about the foreign intelligence threat to the United States and calling for new agent authorizations to deal with it. It may be, of course, that these statements were thoroughly justified — since little of the evidence is made public, they are difficult to evaluate — but they were not accompanied by what some progressive elements in the Bureau had hoped they would be: a candid admission that while the counterintelligence problem may have remained serious, it was now possible to relax some of the unwarranted vigilance in the internal security field, a vigilance that in the late 1960s may have come to interfere with the First Amendment rights of the citizens. Some Bureau sources insist that the counterintelligence needs could be easily covered, and then some, merely by shifts of manpower from unnecessary internal security cases; but the bureaucratic roadblocks along that route are more than Kelley had been willing to risk.

One issue, the length of the director's term of office, a symbolically important question given Hoover's long tenure and Gray's short one, demonstrates an orientation process that Kelley went through upon taking over the job. During his confirmation hearings, Kelley said he had no objection to legislation setting a time limit on how long an FBI director would serve without undergoing reconfirmation for the post. His own suggestion was that a nine-year term might be appropriate (exactly the length of time between his appointment and his seventieth birthday). Before much time had passed after his confirmation, however, once the Old Guard had had a chance to work on him, Kelley issued a clarifying statement:

Since assuming the office of Director I have had an opportunity to afford further thought to this matter and appreciate that there are some substantial considerations that question whether the Director of the FBI should be restricted to a given term of office. We know of no clear-cut authority to remove an official who has received a Presidential appointment. However, in the absence of tenure, the Director of the FBI would be serving at the pleasure of whomever is President.

The heads of other investigative agencies; namely, Central Intelligence Agency, Drug Enforcement Administration and Secret Service are not restricted to a term of office. Accordingly, to single out the Directorship of the FBI would be in effect an exception. To provide tenure for the Director of the FBI would be tantamount to placing him in the same category as heads

and commissioners of regulatory bodies such as the Federal Power Commission, the Federal Trade Commission, and the Interstate Commerce
Commission who do serve for specific periods. The latter officials make
regulatory decisions affecting the Nation and specific terms of office have
the effect of assuring a continuing balance of political power. The office
of Director of the FBI is not political.

   . . . The office of Director, a non-political one, has been charged with
the responsibility of providing factual information upon which administrations of diverse political persuasions could formulate prosecutive policy and
look after the internal security interests of the country. Singling out the
position of Director of the FBI for a restricted term of office could suggest
that perhaps the confidence heretofore placed in the FBI is no longer
merited.

With the arguments against, and the insult felt by the traditionalists,
thus stated, Kelley proceeded to say that he was still in favor of a term-
limiting law and would "defer to the Congress" to accept Senator
Robert Byrd's proposal for a ten-year term. It was Kelley, but it certainly sounded like Hoover.

    Kelley's greatest opportunity for innovations obviously came while
Elliot L. Richardson and William D. Ruckelshaus, the men responsible
for choosing him, were still attorney general and deputy attorney general respectively. The three men had a warm personal relationship
which was expected to produce an unusually close consultation on
matters concerning the Bureau. Above all, Richardson and Ruckelshaus were committed to moving forward on the development of statutory standards for FBI activities. But when Richardson and Ruckelshaus fell victim to the "Saturday Night Massacre" of October 1973,
that era came abruptly to a halt. Robert Bork, the acting attorney
general, had many other things to worry about. William Saxbe, the
next attorney general, simply did not have the interest, the attention
span, or the stature to become deeply involved in such a project.
Besides, Saxbe lost the Bureau's confidence almost immediately with
his rash and ill-advised remarks about the Hearst case and other
matters the FBI was working on. By the time Edward H. Levi arrived
on the scene in early 1975, Kelley had to a considerable extent re-
treated into the FBI shell; he could not be blamed if by then he had
accepted the old Bureau saw that the Justice Department cannot be
relied upon because it is full of politicians and short-termers. There
was no evidence to convince Kelley that the revolving door would stop
turning — he had served under four attorneys general during his first
twenty months as director. As one former Justice Department official
put it, "Kelley was in an ideal position as long as Richardson and

Ruckelshaus were there. He could do almost anything and blame it on them. But once they were gone, he was on his own and at the mercy of the people who wanted to control him."

The director was cordial but not particularly intimate with the Levi regime, and he probably saw the new attorney general less than he had his two immediate predecessors. Levi, an aloof and professorial type, hardly seemed like someone who could roll up his sleeves and get involved with Bureau work. When Kelley mused about potential major changes in the future — even such heretical thoughts as wanting to incorporate DEA into the FBI or to have the Bureau give up its counterintelligence role completely — it was certain trusted SACs that he took into his confidence long before he would talk to the attorney general. Indeed, sometimes Levi and Kelley sounded as if they were on different teams. In the same week of August 1975 when Levi was telling the American Bar Association meeting in Montreal of the need to put carefully crafted restrictions on the FBI, Kelley made the well-publicized suggestion to the National Conference of Bar Presidents in the same city that Americans "must be willing to surrender a small measure of our liberties to preserve the great bulk of them" — a reference to his belief in the need for a certain measure of wiretapping and other surreptitious techniques to protect the national security.

Next to what was going on in the Justice Department until Levi's appointment, the minor turbulence in the Bureau was hardly noticed. But there was some turbulence that could not help but distract Kelley from time to time. Two consecutive assistant directors for the External Affairs Division failed to carry out the director's desire for a more open press policy, and so he tried a third one, and sent George Quinn, the division's number one man and its major link with the past, into the field as an SAC, taking some responsibilities away from External Affairs at the same time. He also gave people whom he personally trusted more responsibility in the division and moved Homer Boynton from the Intelligence Division into Quinn's job. The furor over COINTELPRO, allegations concerning files on congressmen, and fights about legislation and lawsuits all stirred bitter internal disputes over how they should be handled. Young agents in the field grew impatient "waiting for the other shoe to drop" and decided that perhaps Kelley was not going to lead them into an exciting new epoch after all.

Kelley often seemed a lonely man in the job. A stranger in Washington, he had few close outside friends to turn to. On Capitol Hill, he said, he felt particular warmth from only a handful of people, including Senator Edward Kennedy of Massachusetts — whose son's bout with cancer gave them something in common — and John Tunney of

California. There was little recreation or diversion (although he does Canadian Air Force exercises every morning to keep in shape), and he did not bother to enjoy the many perquisites available to the nation's "chief law enforcement officer." Even when he moved about in his limousine, he often sat in the front and chatted with chauffeur Tom Moten rather than affecting a grand style. Occasionally he had dinner at the home of Callahan or Jenkins, but mostly he poured his energies into his work. On the typical night he took a large stack of memoranda and other official reading matter home to his condominium apartment in suburban Bethesda, Maryland, a simple one-bedroom place. (Mrs. Kelley had selected the furniture for it, but her illness prevented her from living in Washington. One of the Kelleys' few major excursions together after he became director was a weekend fling in New York City to see some Broadway shows, accompanied by former Assistant-to-the-Director John Mohr, Assistant-Director-in-Charge John Malone, and other old-line Bureau people and their wives.)* Until Mrs. Kelley's death in November 1975, he continued commuting to Kansas City on the weekends.

Much of Kelley's time in the office was spent in a very traditional way — receiving visitors, presenting service keys to employees who had earned them through diligence (several hours a week were set aside for this), and the like. He did tend to worry about his image and, for all his protests to the contrary, about how he was stacking up alongside Hoover. He seemed to manage to hold on to his old-fashioned compassion — he sent a handwritten note to the wife or mother of every policeman killed on duty anywhere in the United States, for example — but at the same time, some of his friends in the Bureau noted that he was looking older and acting more irritable. Kelley felt fiercely proud of the FBI — "I don't know much about the CIA," he said at one point, "but if they're better, they're damn good" — but still something of a stranger in its midst.

---

* Some of Kelley's expenses for the New York trip, it was later revealed, were paid by the Prudential Insurance Company, which handles the Bureau's health insurance plan; the weekend theoretically included some discussion of its terms with company officials.

XXIV

Big Brother

During the past few decades the demands by Government for personal and sensitive information about its citizens have escalated. This insatiable appetite for information among Government policymakers and administrators is closely related to the increasing responsibility which we have placed upon government, especially the Federal Government, for our health, safety, and well-being. . . . Most Americans are willing to cooperate by divulging information about virtually every aspect of their lives if they believe it will help the Government fulfill these responsibilities.

Yet if we have learned anything in this last year of Watergate, it is that there must be limits upon what the Government can know about each of its citizens. Each time we give up a bit of information about ourselves to the Government, we give up some of our freedom. For the more the Government or any institution knows about us, the more power it has over us. When the Government knows all of our secrets, we stand naked before official power. Stripped of our privacy, we lose our rights and privileges. The Bill of Rights then becomes just so many words.

. . .

Privacy, like many of the other attributes of freedom, can be easiest appreciated when it no longer exists. A complacent citizenry only becomes outraged about its loss of integrity and individuality when the aggrandizement of power in the Government becomes excessive. By then it may be too late. We should not have to conjure up 1984 or a Russian-style totalitarianism to justify protecting our liberties against Government encroachment. Nor should we wait until there is such a threat before we address this problem. Protecting against the loss of a little liberty is the best means of safeguarding ourselves against the loss of all our freedom.

. . .

605

If traditional Government recordkeeping practices and records policies have not yet posed an intolerable threat to personal privacy or reputations, it is only because of the benign inefficiency of these file-drawer record systems. Until very recently, significant amounts of information were not collected about individuals and therefore were not available to others. Use of information collected and kept on a decentralized basis is slow, inefficient, and frustrating. It requires an immense effort to collect information on a specific individual from a variety of different agencies, and then to have it sent out to the agency requesting it. It is ironic but true that what has thus far saved much of our privacy and our liberty has been the complacency, inefficiency, and intra-agency jealousies of the Government and its personnel.

> — *Senator Sam J. Ervin, Jr., Democrat of North Carolina, introducing the Criminal Justice Information Control and Protection of Privacy Act on February 5, 1974*

DAVID HARKNESS WAS ARRESTED on a traffic charge in Des Moines, Iowa, on May 28, 1973. He was taken to a police station and told he would be free to leave as soon as he paid a fifteen-dollar fine. But after a short time, according to a report of the incident in the weekly newspaper *Computerworld*, an officer told him, "Bud, you're not going anywhere. The Marine Corps got a hold on you." The "hold" had turned up when the Des Moines police ran a routine check on Harkness's name through the FBI's National Crime Information Center (NCIC); the computer printout showed him to be a deserter from the marines, absent without official leave (AWOL) since January 1972. The same thing had happened once before: the Des Moines police had arrested him in June 1972 because, according to the computer, he was AWOL from the marines.

There was one major problem — the computer was wrong. Harkness had once actually been AWOL while in the marines, and he was disciplined as a result. Since then, he had been discharged from the service on May 3, 1972, but somehow the NCIC computer was never told about that, or it had forgotten, misplaced, or misdirected the information. The young man was obviously no saint. After his discharge, he was convicted of stealing auto repair equipment belonging to the government and put on probation. Now, however, he had a job and was making progress. But almost everywhere he turned, the computer's designation of him as a deserter from the marines was there to haunt him. Any time his name was entered and matched against the

606

computerized national files, the Marine Corps "hold," even though no longer valid, would crop up. It could prevent him from obtaining a federal job or being licensed by Iowa and other states to practice certain professions.

The Des Moines police disclaimed any responsibility for the foulup. All they could know about the matter was what the NCIC computer said. The FBI also said it could not be held responsible. The only information it had was what the Marine Corps gave it; and the marines, like anyone else using the services of NCIC, were expected to update every entry made with the "disposition" of the case. The Des Moines police could notify the Bureau and the Bureau could notify the marines; but, said an FBI official, "they [the marines] have to remove the charge. We can't." In the meantime, Harkness would have no choice but to excuse the inconvenience and wait.

The President's Commission on Law Enforcement and Administration of Justice suggested in its 1967 report that one way the federal government could attempt to cope with the relentless increase in the crime rate was to apply the latest in computer technology to criminal justice information systems. Just as Congress had once passed laws to bring certain criminal offenses under its jurisdiction, the Executive Branch could now speed the processing and dissemination of information about fugitives and stolen property to make the job of policemen much easier. The hope was that criminals could thus be caught faster. The Crime Commission cautioned that special care was necessary to be sure that individual rights would not be violated in the process, and it urged that even if federal initiative came into play, control over the computerized systems be kept at the local and state level if possible so that federal authorities would not be tempted with a centralized control that was subject to abuse.

No agency on the federal level, or anywhere else for that matter, was as well equipped as the FBI to launch any new coordinated criminal justice information network, whatever the ground rules. Since 1924, the Identification Division had maintained manual fingerprint files and kept records of all arrests reported to it by local law enforcement agencies. The reporting of arrests gradually became universal, either because of state laws that required it or because it was mutually convenient for local agencies and the Bureau. As a result, the FBI had "rap sheets" on most criminal offenders in the country, local and federal, listing the dates of their arrests, the nature of the charges against them, and sometimes the disposition of each case. It also had comprehensive lists of fugitives from the law who were believed to have fled interstate, and of cars and other vehicles that were thought to have been taken across state lines after being stolen.

J. Edgar Hoover, according to some of his survivors in the FBI, was at first distinctly unenthusiastic about the prospect of converting the Bureau's manual records into computerized files. He was proud of the files as they were, and he had an old-timer's distrust of newfangled technology, fearing it would cause the Bureau more trouble than it was worth. But eventually the Director was brought around in the mid-1960s, especially when he realized that if the FBI did not do it, someone else might. As one of the Bureau's informational pamphlets on NCIC euphemistically puts it, "The FBI, in conjunction with the Advisory Group to the Committee on Uniform Crime Records, International Association of Chiefs of Police (IACP), which group is made up of law enforcement representatives from local, state and Federal agencies, recognized the advantages a computerized index of information could offer law enforcement."

Launched on January 27, 1967, the National Crime Information Center initially operated for only two hours a day and linked fifteen law enforcement agencies and one Bureau field office to computerized records in Washington. It was billed by the FBI as another of its many "services" to local law enforcement. At the outset there were five separate files in the computer: wanted persons, stolen vehicles, license plates, firearms, and stolen identifiable articles. Later, separate files were added on stolen securities and stolen boats; and the vehicle file was expanded to include aircraft, snowmobiles, and dune buggies. The first direct connection with another computer, a "computer-to-computer interface," was established with the California Highway Patrol in April 1967, and shortly thereafter another was accomplished with the St. Louis Police Department. NCIC's original data base was 23,000 records, and by the end of 1967 the system was handling an average of 15,000 transactions — an entry of a record, an inquiry, clearance of a record, and so on — a day. Eventually it expanded to cover all fifty states and Puerto Rico. By June 1, 1974, the system contained four and a half million records; the average number of daily transactions was up to 147,220, with a "single day high" of 180,580. Seven months later, on January 1, 1975, the Bureau reported, the total number of records in NCIC was almost 5.7 million — including 1.6 million stolen securities, 1.2 million stolen articles, and almost a million stolen motor vehicles. Some 158,851 wanted persons were listed, accounting for only about 3 percent of the NCIC records, and many of them were military deserters. The number of computer terminals linked up to NCIC grew dramatically and then began to decline as the

Bureau pursued its policy of having all entries and inquiries directed through central terminals located in state capitals or at major metropolitan police departments.

From the start, NCIC seemed to be a law enforcement miracle. Communication processes that once had taken days or even weeks were now telescoped into hours, minutes, even seconds. The Bureau itself was astonished by some of its early successes; as it reported in one pamphlet:

A few weeks after the NCIC became operational, a detective requested his headquarters to check a New York license tag number of an automobile parked at the curb of a Philadelphia street. Using their NCIC terminal, the Philadelphia Police Department made inquiry of the FBI computer in Washington, D.C., and was advised of a record of a stolen vehicle with the same license number. The Philadelphia Police Department confirmed the theft with the New York City Police Department and impounded the automobile, and the owner was identified and notified of the location of his car. From the inquiry on the street in Philadelphia through police headquarters, over communication lines to the FBI computer, back to the officer on the street with the message, the total elapsed time was 90 seconds.

The number of NCIC "hits" — successful matches of inquiries with records in the computerized file — climbed steadily, reaching an estimated 850 a day by 1974. Although that figure fell below the Bureau's goal of achieving success on 1 to 2 percent of each day's queries, the FBI always pointed out that there were also intangible benefits, including "the inestimable savings of investigative time accrued through the rapid apprehension of wanted persons who probably would have committed additional crimes" and "the safety of patrol personnel when, for instance, they are able to determine before approaching a suspect vehicle, that (1) the vehicle is stolen or, more importantly, (2) that a wanted individual known to be armed and dangerous may be driving the vehicle." Regardless of percentages, the higher the absolute number of "hits" through the NCIC system, the more police agencies seemed to use it. The lore of NCIC was constantly built upon by success stories:

• A driver is routinely stopped by state police at Hope, Arkansas, for illegally passing a school bus. The arresting officer notes the vehicle identification number visible through the windshield and, when he arrives at the station, where the driver is to post bond, he runs the car's serial number through the NCIC computer. The car turns out to be recorded as stolen from Oak Park, Illinois. On the basis of that computer "hit" the officer searches the car; he finds that the ignition and door have been tampered with and discovers the original Illinois license plates under the seat.

• A new municipal employee in a southern city is being shown how the NCIC system works and as part of the demonstration a police officer makes a hypothetical inquiry using the name and date of birth of the employee. The reply indicates that there is a criminal warrant out for the man, and so the policeman arrests him immediately. As the FBI later told it in a magazine article for prosecutors, "The man's career was terminated after 60 minutes on the job."

• A New York State Police officer, having stopped a car with Indiana license plates, notices ammunition in the glove compartment while he is talking with the driver. When he searches the car he discovers four guns, and a quick check of their serial numbers through NCIC establishes that at least three of them were reported stolen in North Carolina and Florida. A further search, after the five people in the car are arrested, uncovers thirty-eight payroll checks stolen from Indiana and another seventy-five from Florida. A subsequent inquiry of NCIC reveals that all of the men are wanted in Indiana on a felony charge of larceny and that one is on parole from both Indiana and California. The stop of the car eventually touches on thirty-three felony and ten misdemeanor charges.

• In a southeastern Pennsylvania town, four young men drive into a supermarket parking lot. Three of them go inside and wander around suspiciously; the manager discreetly calls the police. When the officers arrive, they run a check on the license number of the car (in which one of the youths is sitting and waiting) over the police radio through NCIC and Pennsylvania's Commonwealth Law Enforcement Assistance Network (CLEAN) — only to learn that one of the men, to whom the car is registered, is wanted for bank robbery. Before the apparent plan for robbery of the supermarket can come off, the fugitive bank robber is identified, arrested, and turned over to the FBI.

• A private pilot prepares to use his small airplane one Sunday afternoon, when he suddenly discovers that it has been stripped of all its avionics equipment. He calls the local sheriff's office, which dusts for fingerprints and sends descriptions and serial numbers (which the owner had carefully noted) of the equipment to NCIC for inclusion in the "stolen article file." Within a few days a man shows up, at another airport, offering equipment with the same numbers for sale at bargain rates. His fingerprints turn out to match those on the stripped plane. The pilot gets his equipment back, and the thief goes to jail.

The initial planning and development of NCIC was done with the help of a group of advisers from local and state agencies that already had advanced computerized systems or were well along in planning them. But in 1969 that group was replaced by a new NCIC Advisory Policy Board, which, in a semblance of democracy, was elected by the agencies that had computer terminals connected to NCIC, with representatives to come from each of four geographical regions defined by the FBI. The board would come to include important and influential figures in the police world, including the state police or highway patrol directors from New York, Rhode Island, Ohio, Michigan, Missouri, West Virginia, and Arizona, the commissioner of the Florida Department of Law Enforcement and the director of the Texas Department of Police Safety, and police chiefs from, among other places, Cincinnati, Santa Monica, and Kansas City — one Clarence Kelley. The idea was that the "users" of NCIC at the state and local level would thus have a great deal of input on how the system was developed, even with control in the hands of the FBI. With no other part of the executive branch of the federal government or Congress paying any particular attention, it was left to these police officials to help the FBI develop whatever guidelines and ground rules its computer network was to have.

The original NCIC came to look like a primitive, minor league operation next to what became possible. While NCIC was getting started, several states — the number eventually grew to twenty — embarked on their own experimental efforts to design and develop a computerized system for the sharing of criminal histories, called the System for Electronic Analysis and Retrieval of Criminal Histories (Project SEARCH). Beginning in 1969, SEARCH received support funds, in the millions of dollars, from the new Law Enforcement Assistance Administration (LEAA). It developed a standard format for storing individual criminal histories in a computer, summaries of which would also be available in a central national index. The idea was that whenever the subject of a query was listed in the central index, the inquiring agency would be referred, by the computer, to the appropriate state for the subject's complete criminal history. The need seemed clear: criminal mobility was increasing, and many people who were arrested were successful at concealing their criminal records in other jurisdictions elsewhere in the country. The concept of SEARCH was that accurate, updated criminal history information would be valuable not only to law enforcement agencies, but also, in the long run, to other members of the "criminal justice family" — courts, corrections, parole, and other officials. The early thinking of Project

SEARCH devoted considerable attention to problems of privacy and security; a proposed "code of ethics" for the system included a clear-cut statement that:

the participants should make a continuous effort to refine every step of the criminal justice information system provided by SEARCH to assure that the most sophisticated measures are employed and the most perceptive judgments are made in the development and operation of the System to optimize the protection of individual privacy.

The proposed code also included regular auditing procedures to verify the accuracy of data in the SEARCH records, the purging of any record of a first offender whose case was resolved in his favor, and the establishment of procedures whereby an individual could "learn the contents of the arrest record kept about him" and correct any "inaccuracies or prejudicial omissions."

Once SEARCH had shown that a computerized system dealing with criminal histories was feasible, the question in 1970 was how, when, and under whose supervision it would become operational. Since LEAA within the Justice Department had provided most of the original development money for SEARCH, it fell to the attorney general, then John N. Mitchell, to make some critical decisions.

The FBI had originally declined to take any part in the testing of SEARCH, but now that the system's potential was clear it became very interested indeed. The Bureau battled with LEAA, in fact, for control of a national computerized criminal history (CCH) system. It was one of J. Edgar Hoover's last hard-fought and successful battles. The Director sent Mitchell a memorandum on July 23, 1970, asserting that the Bureau should take control of CCH because of its "experience and expertise in three functions, namely, identification, the setting of standards, and computerized information systems. . . . In addition, the FBI's long-standing working relationships with the local, state and Federal enforcement agencies is [sic] vital to the successful operation of a central index." Hoover argued that:

to place the central index in an agency other than the FBI would result in enormous duplication of expenditures, not only at the Federal level, but also at the state level. Rather than build a new system, the FBI already has a proven system of computers, communications, and personnel which can be expanded to meet the requirements for a computerized exchange of criminal identification records with the states.

He attached resolutions supporting the Bureau's role which had been passed by the IACP and the International Association for Identification. (The latter put the association "on record as praying for the continued leadership of John Edgar Hoover, Director of the Federal Bureau of Investigation, in all such efforts.")

Clarence M. Coster and Richard W. Velde, then associate administrators of LEAA, wrote to Mitchell on August 3, 1970, with a candid discussion of the alternatives, as the attorney general had requested. Control of a CCH system might overtax the FBI's facilities, they suggested, but more to the point, there were "possible legal and political implications":

If SEARCH were no longer a decentralized, state-controlled system, the national data bank could loom as an issue. The existence or even hint of such a data bank could arouse certain members of Congress and the public. Although manual records are presently maintained by the FBI and have been for years, detailed arrest information available centrally in computerized form does present questions of privacy.

LEAA would need to develop a computer capability in the near future anyway, Coster and Velde argued, and it would be competent to provide a mere administrative service function without being suspected of attempts at turning a state-run system into a national data bank. Besides, they noted frankly, "LEAA is a new agency seeking to establish its identity. The provision of this service to the states would enhance its prestige both in the criminal justice community and with the public. Finally, since LEAA is not oriented toward any component of the criminal justice system, there could be more likelihood that the entire criminal justice community would be involved." The FBI, on the other hand, was oriented primarily toward law enforcement agencies, the LEAA associate administrators said.

LEAA offered to share administration of the CCH program with the FBI. But Hoover wrote back to Mitchell on August 17 that any such arrangement would ignore "the principle of fixed responsibility. In my opinion, the management of an operating system cannot be divided between two agencies. This amounts to management by 'committee' resulting in conflicting interests, delays in decision-making, and other problems." He insisted that there was no threat of a national data bank because a decision about what would be placed in the computerized system would be made only "in coordination with the states. This Bureau plans no greater detail in the computerized crimi-

nal history record than is presently frequently available in the manu-
ally operated criminal identification record function." The Director
took offense at LEAA's suggestion that the FBI was oriented toward the police to the exclusion of others; "for over 45 years this
Bureau has been providing a service to the courts, prosecutors, and
correctional agencies in the exchange of criminal identification records
[criminal history information]," he said.

Mitchell sought the advice of the Office of Management and Budget (OMB) on the problem, and Arnold R. Weber, associate director
of OMB, reported back on September 3, 1970:

> The test States take pride in having developed an apparently successful
> and workable system, and they are justifiably reluctant to turn the system
> over to total Federal control. (This is a particularly sensitive point since in
> the early stages of the project the FBI was asked by the States to help lead
> the project and declined the invitation.) This can be overcome by giving
> the States an equal voice in establishing the policy of a national system
> based on confederation of the individual State system.
>
> . . . The central data bank is not wanted by the States. They voice
> their concern about "invasion of privacy" and the concept of "Big Brother"
> watching over the country. These concerns can be overcome. Such informa-
> tion is already collected and stored by the FBI, and the Internal Revenue
> Service has an extensive data bank of corporate and individual income tax
> returns. However, if only the central index were maintained at the Federal
> level, this would be much less of a problem.

At the same time, Weber noted that the CCH plans were essentially
"a refinement" of what the Bureau was already doing, that it was
questionable whether LEAA had legal authority to operate systems or
only to develop projects, and that, in any event, it did seem wasteful
to establish duplicate federal law enforcement computer networks.
Weber recommended that:

• Authority to operate the system go to the FBI, but "on a limited
record length basis," with the states continuing to develop their own
automated criminal history systems, which would be compatible with
the central index maintained by the Bureau;

• A strong "Policy Control Board" be named, reporting directly to
the attorney general rather than through the FBI bureaucracy, to decide upon future development and operation of the program. The
board was to include "high level officials" from the FBI, LEAA, and
the states, including representatives from all elements of the criminal
justice system, such as police, prosecutors, courts, corrections, and
parole. "Membership should be structured," Weber said, "so that the

States have an equal voice with the Federal Government in recommending policies for the future direction" of the system. The NCIC advisory policy board might be represented on the new group, but not until later should consideration be given to merger of the two committees; and

• Planning should begin for development of "an integrated criminal justice system" that would combine the computerized criminal history work, NCIC, and the FBI's fingerprint identification activities, all under the jurisdiction of the new policy board but not necessarily under the direction of the Bureau.

On December 10, 1970, the attorney general authorized the FBI to operate the CCH system, and the Bureau immediately moved to incorporate it into NCIC. But perhaps because Mitchell knew the kind of bureaucratic uproar that could result from circulating a document that contained criticism of Hoover's FBI to the Bureau and to others, he did not share Weber's other comments and recommendations with the FBI or LEAA; not did he establish any policy board that would be directly responsible to him rather than to the Bureau.

The NCIC board, made up entirely of law enforcement representatives, moved decisively to assert its own authority over the CCH system. In March 1971, it approved various ground rules and decided, among other things, that the central file would not merely direct those who query the system to the appropriate state, but would include a detailed criminal history of every offender entered into the system by any of the states. It would contain the same information that the FBI always kept on its "rap" sheets in the Identification Division. Theoretically, this was to be a temporary situation, until all the states had an opportunity to establish their own identification bureaus, fingerprint identification capability, information flow, and appropriate computer systems. In the long run, the NCIC board said, the central CCH file would keep only "summary data" on those whose offenses all occurred within the same state; the more detailed records for those people would be maintained at the state level (when the states were ready and able to accept them back) and queries would be directed there in keeping with the original concept. But in the case of "multi-state offenders" and those with federal criminal records, the complete record would be maintained by the FBI. The original deadline for full-scale operation of the CCH system — and therefore the return of most of the complete records to the states — was July 1, 1975, but developments fell far behind schedule, and it seemed likely that the Bureau would be holding on to the "single-state offender" records much longer than initially indicated.

In fact, although CCH went into formal operation on November 30, 1971, its progress was very slow indeed. By 1974, only six states (Arizona, California, Florida, Illinois, New York, and Pennsylvania), the District of Columbia, and the Bureau itself had fully entered their records into the CCH file within NCIC. Then things began regressing. The New York State records had to be withdrawn because they had not been properly updated, and the Pennsylvania records were taken out when the state police reported that "fiscal considerations" prevented them from continuing full participation. Most states, whether ready to submit their own records or not, had one-way access to the files already in CCH regardless. But the one-way access of Louisiana, for example, was suspended for a time in 1974 because, contrary to NCIC regulation, there was no "criminal justice agency control over the computer equipment and personnel by which and through whom CCH data was being processed." For the most part, however, these were regarded as minor setbacks in the onward march of CCH, and the NCIC board pledged itself to expanding two-way participation across the country.*

The Bureau did not have to look far to find another computer system to add to its growing collection. In 1966, a consortium of states, acting independently of the federal government, had established the National Law Enforcement Telecommunications System (NLETS) as a nonprofit corporation to manage the exchange of administrative messages between criminal justice agencies across the country. NLETS had no data bank of its own, just a teletype system operating in conjunction with a central message-switching terminal in Phoenix. The FBI was connected to NLETS only insofar as any state was; it could use the system to communicate securely with others about news of arrests or thefts. When concern developed that NLETS was too slow and would not meet the needs of the future — such as state-to-state communications about computerized criminal histories — LEAA gave the Jet Propulsion Laboratory of the California Institute of Technology half a million dollars to study other feasible telecommunications systems that could handle the drastically increased needs of criminal justice agencies through 1983. In the meantime, LEAA also provided $1.5 million in June 1973 for the upgrading of NLETS so that it could operate faster and more efficiently.

Some FBI officials began to view NLETS as a logical adjunct to

---

* By late 1975 Michigan and Virginia had taken the place of New York and Pennsylvania as fully participating members of the CCH system. But still there were only six states, and the FBI's new, more modest goal was to have states representing "half of the population" — if not half of the states — enrolled in a two-way exchange by late 1976.

NCIC, because the prompt switching of messages among the states would be an essential component of the fully developed and operative CCH system. They pointed out that the Bureau would be able to handle virtually all of these needs for law enforcement across the country with only a few more communications lines and slightly improved computer hardware beyond what NCIC already had. No initiative was launched during the confused period when L. Patrick Gray III was leaving the Bureau and losing his grip on it and when William Ruckelshaus was serving as a caretaker in the job. But only two days after Clarence Kelley took office, he signed a letter the Bureau had prepared asking the attorney general, Elliot Richardson, to endorse the FBI view that its statutory authority to operate NCIC include the authority to expand communications support for the entire system — for example, by taking over the switching of administrative and substantive interstate criminal justice messages. The FBI wanted to incorporate NLETS in the name of another "service" to local law enforcement.

It was not a clear question for the Justice Department or for other concerned agencies. The department's Office of Legal Counsel told Richardson it was not certain that there was sufficient legislative authority to support the FBI's request. One question was whether NLETS would even need to exist as an entity at all if the Bureau became capable of switching the message traffic among state and local agencies. LEAA, now under the leadership of an ambitious administrator, Donald E. Santarelli, vehemently opposed the Bureau's move, asserting that "federal control over message switching would be inconsistent with security and privacy considerations at this time" and that it "would be contrary to the principle of state and local government self-sufficiency and their possessing their own capabilities in the criminal justice telecommunications field." Others, like Clay T. Whitehead, director of the Office of Telecommunications Policy in the White House, warned that this further expansion of NCIC could "result in the absorption of state and local criminal data systems into a nationwide, Federally controlled communications and computer information system." One concern expressed by some opponents of the proposal was that the Bureau would, if it took over NLETS, have the capacity to monitor anything that state or local enforcement agencies said to each other — a capacity that, even if it were not exercised in the short run, could become a threat in the future.

Yet on October 1, 1974, only a short time after the latest annual convention of the IACP had come down in the Bureau's favor on the issue, the man who was by then attorney general, William Saxbe, granted the FBI authority to prepare a plan for taking over limited message switching, covering traffic between NCIC and state and local agencies and also any "NCIC-related" traffic among the state and local agencies themselves. The plan would require review and approval at several levels. It was only a partial victory for the Bureau, but, in the view of FBI officials, another major step in their direction. Harold R. Tyler, Jr., the new deputy attorney general under Edward H. Levi, made other decisions in the Bureau's favor, but Levi delayed action on the FBI plan, pending congressional consideration of the issues.

The fear, increasingly, was that the FBI, with its well-established emphasis on centralized control and responsibility, could now become the central repository for too much information and the operator of too extensive a computer capability. For all its disclaimers about not wanting ever to be a national police force, the Bureau would have an extraordinary potential, if not actual, authority. Already it was becoming far more efficient. The development of the automated fingerprint scanner meant that any incoming fingerprint card could be searched against all Bureau files and records in a matter of seconds, and the prospect was that this capacity might eventually be extended to terminals in the police stations or even in individual patrol cars. Ultimately it was conceivable that a single fingerprint at the roadside could become enough to bring retrieval of a person's entire criminal history — and more — in a few seconds. It was a policeman's dream and a civil libertarian's nightmare.

One concern was that the Bureau's computerized data banks would be hooked up to the many other data banks that exist both in and out of government. A survey by the staff of the Senate Subcommittee on Constitutional Rights, while Senator Sam Ervin was its chairman, found 858 separate data banks in fifty-four federal agencies, some of them containing hundreds of millions of entries. One, maintained by the Defense Supply Agency, was a catalogue merely of allegations of wrongdoing against people that were later determined to be unfounded. Some data banks, such as those maintained by the Internal Revenue Service and the Selective Service System, were found to disseminate information to other agencies despite explicit promises of confidentiality. The National Institute of Mental Health maintains a system called the Client Oriented Data Acquisition Project (CODAP), which set out to develop a profile of everyone who had ever participated in a federally funded drug treatment program. The Drug Abuse Warning Network (DAWN), launched by the Drug Enforcement Administration, paid hospitals and other institutions one dollar apiece for access to the records of patients who were known or thought to have abused drugs. In those systems, as in the Treasury Enforcement Computer System (TECS), which includes records from the several law enforcement agencies housed in the Treasury Department, it may be difficult to separate out criminal data from noncriminal information.

In the mid-1960s a public and political uproar prevented significant progress on an executive branch proposal, supported by many scholars, to create a "National Data Center" that would collect and centralize planning and research data on the entire American population. Even so, the Subcommittee on Administrative Procedure and Practice of the Senate Judiciary Committee found that federal files contained more than three billion records on individual citizens, including 27.2 million names, 2.3 million addresses, 264.5 million criminal histories, 279.6 million mental health records, 916.4 million profiles on alcoholism and drug addiction, and more than 1.2 billion financial records. By mid-1972, the General Services Administration, unknown to Congress or other parts of the government, was preparing to establish a massive computerized data bank, "FEDNET," which was to bring together the data-processing and telecommunications operations of several federal agencies. With its information storage capabilities, FEDNET looked like a revival of the National Data Center concept. Once again, a furor appeared to prevent its development, at least temporarily.

Outside the scope of the federal government, enormous data banks are maintained by credit bureaus and the insurance and banking industries. The entry of an individual's Social Security number into them, as into many government data banks, is liable to produce lengthy printouts of information that is allegedly confidential when it is provided by a citizen. In the name of better government, the National League of Cities (supported by LEAA, the U.S. Department of Housing and Urban Development, and other federal agencies) has sponsored the development of "integrated municipal information systems" (IMIS) for individual cities. They would bring information into a central file from all urban service departments, including the police, schools, and welfare department, as well as basic census data. One man involved in developing the IMIS plans, Robert Knisely, has warned that pulling all that information together could pose serious problems: a teacher could learn that a child is illegitimate, which — if this upset either the teacher or the child or both — could lead to poor grades, which might prevent him from getting a job later, which could lead him to crime; efficient criminal justice records could then keep him permanently unemployed.

By no means does the capacity, technology, or the will exist for the FBI to plug in to all available data banks. For one thing, many of them do not have their data in formats that are compatible with each other. But already some state information systems, in Iowa, California, and elsewhere, are mixing records from schools and other service institutions with computerized criminal justice files. The NCIC Advisory Policy Board rejected a proposal to create a credit card index in the central files, but on October 1, 1975, it launched a "missing persons" file, which could throw the records of youthful runaways in with those of serious criminal types. LEAA has funded the development of state and regional computerized intelligence files on organized crime, as well as more general ones on civil disorders, militants, and extremists. If those files are centralized nationally — and why not? — they could pose a serious threat to free speech and the expression of minority political views. The Senate Constitutional Rights Subcommittee, now under Senator John V. Tunney (D-California), found evidence in 1975 that NCIC had been used to "flag" people of interest to the Bureau, possibly including prominent politicians; thus if ever they were stopped on a routine traffic violation, the FBI would learn where they were.

Any fears and worries about the data banks were only intensified by the growing knowledge and awareness of errors and abuses that had already occurred. Arrest records, even in manual, nonautomated form, have long been a problem. The case of one Dale B. Menard drew particular national attention to potential abuses. Menard, while he was a nineteen-year-old student in Los Angeles, was arrested by that city's police department on August 10, 1965, on suspicion of burglary, when he was found lying on a park bench at 4 A.M. not far from a wallet belonging to someone else that contained ten dollars. He claimed to have a good explanation for his presence there, corroborated by a friend, but he was nonetheless held for two days while police investigated and then released him. The fingerprint card that the Los Angeles Police Department sent to the FBI, following normal procedures, noted that the police had been "unable to connect [him] with any felony or misdemeanor at this time." Claiming that his arrest had been without probable cause, Menard and his family tried for months to have the record of it expunged from police files, and therefore from FBI files, but the police department insisted that records could be removed only on court order. The FBI, similarly, said it could not remove the record simply at the arrested person's request. Menard felt that the existence of the arrest record could hurt him in the future. It did not say he was guilty of a crime, but then neither did it say that he was not guilty — only that the investigating officers had been unable to come up with anything. The record, ambiguous at best, lay in the Bureau files for potential dissemination to anyone who queried the records system for a check of Menard's name. It was later found to have been passed along to the Marine Corps, among others. But it was the potential scope of its dissemination that was particularly troubling. For if Menard by chance applied to be a real estate salesman in Idaho, to practice medicine in Nevada or law in North Carolina, or, for that matter, to drive a taxicab in Glendale, Arizona, run a bowling alley in the District of Columbia, or just to have a summer job in Province-town, Massachusetts — to mention only a few of the circumstances in which the Bureau would be required to run checks on any job or license applicant — he would have to be fingerprinted and have his arrest record summoned up from the FBI files for comparison of the prints. The consequences were quite unpredictable.

Menard became the plaintiff in a major lawsuit brought by the American Civil Liberties Union, and after long and arduous litigation, U.S. District Court Judge Gerhard A. Gesell in Washington ruled in 1971 that the FBI had no legal authority to disseminate arrest records outside the federal government for non–law enforcement purposes.* Gesell noted that the Identification Division of the FBI "has little opportunity to supervise what is actually done with the arrest records it disseminates. It requires that a proper purpose be stated by the agency requesting information but what is in fact done with the infor-mation as a practical matter cannot be constantly checked. It is appar-ent that local agencies may on occasion pass on arrest information to private employers." The judge, complaining of the "increasing com-plexity of our society and technological advances which facilitate massive accumulation and ready regurgitation of far-flung data," appealed for government restraint:

A heavy burden is placed on all branches of Government to maintain a proper equilibrium between the acquisition of information and the necessity to safeguard privacy. Systematic recordation and dissemination of informa-tion about individual citizens is a form of surveillance and control which may easily inhibit freedom to speak, to work, and to move about in this land. If information available to Government is misused to publicize past incidents in the lives of its citizens the pressures for conformity will be irresistible.

* The judge refused, however, to order the expungement of Menard's actual record. Menard appealed that part of the decision, and in April 1974 the U.S. Court of Appeals for the District of Columbia Circuit finally ruled that the FBI could not retain the records of the young man's "police encounter" in its criminal files (although it could leave them in its "neutral identification records").

Initiative and individuality can be suffocated and a resulting dullness of mind and conduct will become the norm. We are far from having reached this condition today, but surely history teaches that inroads are most likely to occur during unsettled times like these where fear or the passions of the moment can lead to excesses. The present controversy, limited as it is, must be viewed in this broadest context. In short, the overwhelming power of the Federal Government to expose must be held in proper check.

The FBI's influence in government circles must never be underestimated. Before long Senator Alan Bible, Democrat of Nevada, was sponsoring a rider to the FBI appropriations bill that specifically and indefinitely restored the Bureau's authority to make fingerprint checks for employment and licensing purposes whenever the practice was established under state law and local ordinances. (Bible apparently became involved because casino operators in Las Vegas were concerned that they would no longer be able to depend upon FBI checks of the people they hired. Others, including banks, also protested that they were being denied a valid service that protected the public.) The Bureau proudly and defiantly resumed its procedures. In a major concession to critics, however, Clarence Kelley announced on July 1, 1974, that the FBI would no longer distribute "raw arrest data" more than a year old to non–law enforcement agencies. The arrest records would still be disseminated, Kelley said, if they included a conviction for a crime or if the arrest had taken place within a year of the request for the check of the files, regardless of whether a disposition of the case had been entered on the Bureau's "rap sheet."

Dale Menard was a rare exception, in that he and his family pursued the issue and found out what had happened with the records of his arrest in Los Angeles. Less aware, less aggressive, or less articulate people, particularly members of disadvantaged minorities who have uneasy relations with the police, are subject to the same abuses and problems, but are unlikely to risk the confrontations or venture the costs necessary to set things right. One study showed that 75 percent of the employment agencies in the New York area would not accept for referral a job applicant with an arrest record. Another showed that of seventy-five employers surveyed, sixty-six would not even consider a man who had been arrested for assault, even if he had been tried and acquitted on the charge.

The annals of congressional committees and legal organizations are full of tales of horrifying problems caused by arrest records that are not updated or are simply in error. One young black man in Washington was arrested while a senior in high school in May 1970; then in

January 1971 he was acquitted of a robbery charge that was apparently based on a case of mistaken identity. Although he later enrolled in college under a National Merit Scholarship, the police on several occasions showed his photograph in neighborhoods where they were investigating crime and also came back each time to quiz his family and friends. In California, a man was fired from his job with a company that installed alarm systems in banks after the local police did a "security check" with the FBI for the company and found that the man had an arrest record. His two arrests, it turned out, were for being a "public nuisance" and for possession of marijuana. In the first instance he had been tried and acquitted, and in the second the charges were dismissed; but those outcomes had apparently never been reported to the FBI by the local police or California state authorities, and so the arrests continued to haunt him. Another California man, a schoolteacher, approached Claude Brinegar, then the U.S. secretary of transportation, during Brinegar's tour of one of the stations of the new Bay Area Rapid Transit (BART) system in San Francisco; in full view of television cameras, the man asked Brinegar whether he thought President Nixon should be impeached. Although Brinegar ignored the man, four BART policemen promptly arrested him; later the city police fingerprinted him and charged him with assaulting a cabinet officer and resisting arrest. When he was arraigned, the judge suggested that the whole case was foolish, but the man soon discovered that the state board of education had been informed of his arrest and was considering whether it should revoke his teaching credentials.

Bureau officials have frequently asserted that they are interested in having the fullest, most accurate records possible, that by no means do they want to circulate unreliable information. But the FBI has little capacity — and, it often seems, little will — to compel the agencies that submit fingerprints and arrest records to update them with dispositions. As state and local governments have come under fire for some of the same abuses pinned on the federal system, their record has improved substantially, but thousands of cases remain in the Bureau files with little prospect that they will be updated, and the FBI disseminates them anyway. Similarly, the Bureau has applied only the mildest of sanctions against those agencies that have violated the rules concerning use of fingerprints and arrest records, and it never holds the individual officers responsible to account for their violations. During the trial of the *Menard* case, the FBI revealed that only two police agencies — the Cabazon, California, Police Department and the Northumberland County Sheriff's Office in Sunbury, Pennsylvania — were then on the "restricted list" because of abuses. It produced only four other instances of restrictions during the previous ten years — one lasting for two weeks, another for a month, the third for six months, and the other for just over a year. In late 1974, the Identification Division said that no police agencies were then on its restricted list because none were known to be abusing the records provided to them by the FBI.

With the computerization of the Bureau's vast records, the risks became even greater and the issues requiring examination more serious. Transactions would be faster and probably more difficult to trace afterward. The Bureau would have to count upon the good faith of police agencies about how carefully they restricted access to their NCIC terminals; and even when NCIC was queried by somebody authorized to have access, it would be impossible to know whether he might be exercising that authority for unauthorized purposes — such as helping out a friend or picking up some extra money by checking out job applicants. Try though it might to set standards, the Bureau would surely be unable to monitor the compliance with its standards of fifty different computerized criminal history systems operated by the states. The states were perfectly entitled, of course, to make their own decisions about what crimes they considered to fall into NCIC's category of "serious and significant violations." Theoretically, certain arrests would be excluded — juvenile offenders, drunkenness, public order offenses such as disturbing the peace, and the simplest traffic violations — but in other areas there were differences among the states. Some, for example, consider that "serious" crimes include non-support, adultery, simple gambling charges, and homosexuality; and so records on those charges might well be distributed through the CCH network. Those not noted in the central index might be available within the state files as a supplement, to be drawn upon by those who were referred from the index.

The General Accounting Office (GAO), investigating how criminal justice agencies use criminal history information at the request of Senator Ervin's subcommittee in 1974, found serious problems in two states that were presumed to be among the most sophisticated in their handling of computerized criminal justice data, Florida and Massachusetts. In Florida, according to a GAO report, at least thirteen state agencies failed to comply with the state's own dissemination practices for criminal history information, either by allowing unauthorized access to the files — for example, by city agencies and local employers — or by supplying data to other agencies that were not entitled to receive it. One Florida police agency's criminal history files were discovered to be open to the general public, and several said that they regularly provided material to military recruiters. In Massachusetts, it was impossible to identify the source of about 10 percent of the requests for criminal history information made of the state probation department because requests were accepted by telephone without any verification of the identities of the callers; it seemed clear that unauthorized private parties were thus drawing upon the department's files. (Both states promised to correct their procedures.)

The GAO report also showed that there was relatively little research or knowledge available on how criminal justice agencies use the arrest record information available to them. GAO's limited survey in Florida, Massachusetts, and California showed, however, that the most frequent use seemed to be after arrest rather than before it, and that other parts of the system, such as prosecutors, courts, probation, and parole officials, might have a greater actual need for the information in the decisions they make than do the police. Those findings gave rise to some questions concerning the basic assumptions of the CCH system — such as whether it really needed to be so fast and streamlined, and whether the terminals and access should be located primarily in the hands of police agencies.

For several years the FBI churned along virtually without outside interference in its development of efficient computerized information systems. In the summer of 1973, however, Governor Francis W. Sargent of Massachusetts declared that his state would refuse to enter its records into the CCH system because its operating standards, as approved by the NCIC board, were inadequate. The Bureau failed to require the updating of arrest records with the ultimate disposition of cases, Sargent complained in a petition to the Justice Department requesting better rules (a petition joined by, among others, Senators Edward W. Brooke of Massachusetts and Harold E. Hughes of Iowa, and Congressman Barry Goldwater, Jr., of California). The existence in the files of incomplete and inaccurate records, they said, "can violate the individual's rights to privacy, equal protection, due process, freedom from cruel and unusual punishment, the presumption of innocence principle, and the 'beyond a reasonable doubt' standard of proof." The petition also objected that the CCH standards "fail to require periodic review and expungement of files"; "fail to properly control access to CCH files, permitting dissemination of file material for purposes unrelated to legitimate law enforcement needs"; "fail to insure adequate opportunity for file subjects to have notice of and opportunity to challenge the contents of their files"; and "fail to specify what offenses will result in the introduction into the national file of an individual's name and record."

Sargent made Massachusetts an example for the rest of the nation. Alone with Alaska and Iowa, it had adopted laws putting stringent safeguards on the information kept by the state itself and restricting how it could be used. In Massachusetts, a Criminal History Systems Board was established to pass on the question of who might have access to the records, along with a Privacy and Security Council intended to serve as a citizens' watchdog and prevent abuses. For a time, the state house in Boston did battle with the federal government; the federal Small Business Administration threatened to cut off funds to Massachusetts because of what it considered an overly restrictive attitude toward the criminal justice files, and the Justice Department, through the U.S. attorney in Boston, sued the state in an effort to force Massachusetts to become a fully participating member of the CCH system. (Elliot Richardson, while attorney general, dropped the lawsuit pending congressional efforts to develop more thorough standards for the computerized network.)

But Massachusetts was not alone. Increasing public concern over the issue of data banks, coming as it did during the Watergate era, created what was in effect a privacy lobby determined to put the Bureau on the defensive. Newspapers editorialized on the issue, congressmen who had previously ignored or praised the development of the Bureau's computerized systems began to speak out; and the New Mexico branch of the American Civil Liberties Union mounted an ambitious public relations campaign, featuring eyes staring from balloons and billboards and numbers hung around the necks of children, to dramatize the threat to individual rights.

Strong sentiment developed on the issue of purging or sealing criminal history files once a certain period of time had elapsed. In California, for example, a new policy was adopted that permitted records of misdemeanor arrests to be kept for only five years when they resulted in no conviction, and for seven years when there was a conviction. But the Bureau remained adamant on that subject. "I am completely opposed to sealing any criminal justice information against criminal justice agencies," Clarence Kelley told the Senate Constitutional Rights Subcommittee during hearings in the spring of 1974. "The likelihood of abuse of such information, as long as it is confined within criminal justice agencies, appears to be so minimal in contrast to the value of this information for criminal justice purposes that I unequivocally urge you to omit any restrictions on criminal justice agency access to any type of criminal justice information," he said. To do otherwise, Kelley argued, would "hamstring law enforcement." He asked: "If only ten murderers or kidnappers repeated their crime outside the statutory time frame, is not this enough to warrant criminal justice agencies access to offender records which may provide leads in subsequent murder or kidnapping investigations?" The furthest the Bureau would go was to continue a reform instituted by Pat Gray — the elimination from the files of the arrest records of anyone eighty or older. (In California, the records were purged when the person became seventy, provided he had been in no trouble with the law since the age of sixty.)

The Bureau acted most of the time as if it were being persecuted on the issue. "Our only stake in this entire matter," said Assistant Director Wason G. Campbell, for a time the man in charge of the FBI's Computer Systems Division, at the 1974 hearings, "is to provide service to the law enforcement community at the lowest cost to the taxpayer." Why not go after newspaper morgues, some Bureau officials asked, only half facetiously, arguing that they contain much of the same raw arrest data and unevaluated information that is in law enforcement computers.

There were a few grudging nods by the FBI to the concern for privacy. The paper printouts or cathode-ray-tube monitors at NCIC terminals began to carry a legend warning against unauthorized dissemination of the information provided. Yielding to pressure from the attorney general, the Office of Management and Budget, and others, the Bureau appointed six non–law enforcement "criminal justice community representatives" to the NCIC board to serve alongside the twenty representatives of police agencies; the board itself voted against expanding to include "public sector" representatives, whom they considered unnecessary. The FBI made it slightly easier for people to challenge and correct their records, but took no steps to provide information about how to do so to a broad spectrum of the public.

Most of the changes and reforms that did come were forced upon the Bureau, however. Congress passed the Privacy Act of 1974 and, in the same year, major amendments to the Freedom of Information Act. Although there were some conflicting provisions in the two laws, they had the combined effect of making FBI files more vulnerable to outside inquiry. The special section established to handle administration of them for the Bureau, moved from the Office of Legal Counsel to the Files and Communications Division, grew to have 160 employees by October 1975 — with half of them occupied full-time for about three months with the exclusive task of complying with a court order to turn over substantial Bureau files to the sons of Julius and Ethel Rosenberg. During the first nine months of 1975 the Bureau received 10,200 requests from citizens under the Freedom of Information Act to see their files, 2,000 of them in August alone; fulfillment of a routine request, including review of the file and deletion of the names of sources and other material, came to take at least two months. (The Bureau said officially that it would give no special treatment to requests from members of Congress, but discreet checks were run, for example, for members of the various committees investigating the FBI.) The Privacy Act established a Privacy Protection Study Commission, empowered to look into data banks and information systems like the FBI's. And both houses of Congress, meanwhile, were working on additional legislation to deal specifically with the handling of criminal justice records.

The fundamental question has become whether it is too late, whether the FBI has already created such a mass of centralized and computerized information that no amount of tampering, adjusting, and controlling would eliminate the basic threat. If that amount of information about citizens and their possible wrongdoings is concentrated in a single agency and is so easily retrievable, the potential is there for a government to make judgments about their future behavior or to try new experiments in social control. It could be only a matter of putting the appropriately angry or ambitious man in charge.

XXV

The Rules Change

Everyone wants everything pronto. . . . They have the capacity to tie us up tremendously. . . . In fact, sometimes I think they are going to strangle us."
— *An FBI official, complaining of the new demands being placed on the Bureau*

IT IS DIFFICULT FOR ANYONE TO GIVE UP A POSITION of special privilege and begin to be treated just like everyone else. In that sense, the FBI — as an institution and as a group of human beings — is in a situation not unlike the survivors of a European revolution, the impoverished old white aristocracy of the American South, or a pack of animals that once enjoyed an unchallenged territorial imperative but suddenly must fend for themselves among the other species. The group that has lost its privilege generally clings for a while to some vestige of its power, but eventually it comes to the recognition that times are changing and it had better adapt as gracefully as possible. Those who deal with the former privileged class are likely to be rough, to gloat and growl and show little mercy. It is, above all, a process of humiliation.

One of the most painful things the Bureau has had to do, unaccustomed though it may be, is to recognize its own failings and sometimes even to talk about them publicly. With society no longer prepared to respect the institution primarily on the basis of its razzle-dazzle exploits from the 1930s, of security in times of Red scares, or of the inexplicable reputation of one man who became a symbol, the FBI must substitute genuine self-evaluation for ritualized self-congratulation. Inspections that punish agents for keeping too many bullets in their desks or for failing to open enough new cases satisfy for only so long before they are recognized as a fraud; meaningless statistics ultimately become a tiresome diversion from the actual substance of an agency's work. If the Bureau had trouble recognizing these facts of life, plenty of people suddenly appeared on the sidelines to administer the necessary shock treatment.

Beyond the things that the FBI overdid during the volatile 1960s — especially its fanatical and sometimes simple-minded ventures in the internal security field — it became clear that there were several areas in which the Bureau failed to meet the challenges facing it:

• Despite several spurts of attention and intensified investigation, the FBI never managed to cripple the operations of the organized crime syndicates that are estimated to squeeze hundreds of millions of dollars annually out of the American economy. There were some disruptions, to be sure, and substantial increases in the number of convictions of organized crime figures, but nothing that could be called a major victory.

• Whether connected to the syndicates or not, white-collar crime — consumer frauds, embezzlements, swindles of vast sums of money from the government, stock manipulations, and such — grew dramatically while the FBI stood idly by. Many of the most clever and practiced white-collar criminals came to believe that they had more to fear from some state and local investigators than from those at the federal level.

• At the same time it was obvious that the Bureau, for all its attention to internal security, had been unable to cope with domestic terrorism. Bombs exploded sometimes right within view of a field office, but the FBI often did not have a single lead to go on. Until early 1975, when a number of young fugitives wanted in connection with bombings and bank robberies turned themselves in or were captured, it was unable to penetrate the radical underground. It took more than nineteen months for agents to locate Patricia Hearst, the kidnap victim turned urban guerrilla.

In all three categories, mavericks in the Bureau argued, one of the main problems was the FBI's reluctance to adjust old investigative techniques to unusual circumstances and to develop new ones where necessary. In the case of organized crime, it was unwilling to make the necessary commitment to long-range, dangerous undercover work, relying instead (once electronic surveillance was cut back) on the desperate cooperation mostly of lower-level "button men," who defected from the ranks because they sensed themselves to be in trouble.

Officials in the investigative divisions at Bureau headquarters in Washington generally did not understand the issues and ploys involved in many white-collar crime schemes, so they rarely encouraged agents in the field to develop the necessary sophistication. Only in a few offices, for example, were there agents who understood the computer technology that has become a useful tool in cracking many cases; instead, most of the computer-wise agents were concentrated at headquarters, working on NCIC and other Bureau administrative operations. As for the underground terrorists, the FBI was often stumped as soon as it realized there were no old-fashioned membership lists or easily infiltrated meetings that could become the focus of an investigation. In the face of a life-style that did not depend upon credit cards, bank accounts, and telephones, whose confidentiality could always be violated, the Bureau was helpless. For years the fugitives managed to build false identities without being detected, much in the manner of "illegal" international espionage agents. By the time of the heavily publicized adventures of Patricia Hearst, the FBI had actually improved in this area, but one would hardly know it from outward appearances. The Bureau just looked silly as the ragtag radical "army" she had joined managed to evade hundreds of agents — living at one point just a few blocks from the San Francisco Field Office, later spending months as conspicuous outsiders in a small northeastern Pennsylvania farm area — and when the FBI and the Los Angeles Police Department reacted with such extraordinary firepower when some members of the band were trapped inside a ghetto house in Los Angeles.

But give an agent a car case or a check case and it was like asking him to tie his shoelaces. That was just the point — the FBI had never remeasured and realigned its priorities from the good old days and so it had never reallocated its manpower to suit changing times. Now Clarence Kelley was obliged to state the obvious to his SACs: every case is not equal after all, despite what Mr. Hoover always said. Some are very much more important than others and must be given earlier and much more serious attention; others are more properly left to local authorities or a later date.

When Attorney General Edward H. Levi took office in early 1975, Kelley, in briefing his new boss, actually acknowledged the existence of a category of "special emphasis investigations" that included aircraft hijacking, "top thieves," and white-collar crime. "In addition to promptly reacting to and vigorously investigating [hijackings] 'after the fact,' " Kelley told Levi, "the FBI continually plans for and devises methods to thwart the hijacker." Even with airport security precautions up and hijacking incidents substantially down, the FBI remained vigilant, the director said. The "top thief" program, which Kelley said involved twenty-three agents and nineteen support personnel, was described as "a national activity [of the Bureau] with regional emphasis on those individuals considered to be major thieves and fences in each particular geographical area." Once any subject of the program is identified, he explained, "background, including description, associates, travel habits and modus operandi, is gathered to permit concentrated coverage and establish culpability in crimes of interest to the FBI and state and local law enforcement agencies." Kelley asserted that the Bureau was also involved in "increased research, detection and resolution" of white-collar crime cases, with more than a thousand agents on the task and nearly nine hundred support employees helping. Already in Fiscal Year 1974, the director noted, convictions in the area of white-collar crime and computer fraud had almost doubled. Growing out of a special seminar on the issue for U.S. attorneys in May 1974, Kelley added, white-collar crime would be "targeted for intensified investigation and prosecution on a nationwide basis throughout the coming decade."

But anyone who had watched the FBI for some time could not help asking whether this would be a significant and meaningful change or just a temporary shift of emphasis to deal with the passions of the moment and to keep the critics at bay. If it had to make a choice, would the Bureau pursue with a new enthusiasm the kind of high-flying fraud perpetrated by financier Robert Vesco, or would it really prefer to spend its time and hundreds of agents on Patricia Hearst and other latter-day, headline-catching heirs to John Dillinger? Would it plunge into antitrust investigations, as promised, or would its heart always belong to the Dyer Act? Can the FBI make the necessary adaptations itself, or must they be imposed from outside?

There could be no doubt that things were different now, that a new scrutiny was being directed at the Bureau — by Congress, within the executive branch and the judicial system, by the press, and among the general public. The scrutiny did not really come from the FBI Oversight Subcommittee of the Senate Judiciary Committee. Senator James Eastland made certain that it would be a sweetheart panel, a rubber stamp, by naming himself chairman of the subcommittee and stacking it with unquestioning Bureau friends like Roman Hruska, John McClellan, and Strom Thurmond. (Hruska emerged from one of the earliest closed-door executive sessions of the subcommittee — at which Kelley and Assistant-to-the-Director James Adams had appeared — and told waiting reporters, "You realize, of course, we can't tell them how to run their agency.") The oversight subcommittee had only one full-time staff member and half the time of another; even if they were aggressive, there was only so much the two could do. Instead, the initial arrangement was that two young agents from the Research Section of the FBI's Intelligence Division would help the subcommittee out on any special needs it had. The earliest public hearings of the subcommittee confirmed the projections: only a few of the senators attended and they seemed utterly unprepared; Senator Robert Byrd of West Virginia alone showed any intention of turning the hearings into a meaningful inquiry into Bureau affairs.

But the fact that the new Senate oversight subcommittee promised to be such an insignificant force only encouraged others to try to do the job instead. The House Judiciary Committee ordered up an audit of the Bureau's domestic intelligence-gathering activity by the General Accounting Office, the investigative arm of Congress. Congressman Don Edwards's Subcommittee on Civil Rights and Constitutional Rights pressed forward with its inquiry into COINTELPRO and other controversial FBI programs, while different House Judiciary subcommittees launched their own probes into wiretapping and other Bureau information-gathering techniques. The Senate established a new select committee, under the chairmanship of Senator Frank Church (D-Idaho), to investigate the CIA and FBI and other intelligence agencies, with a view toward determining whether and to what extent they had overstepped their legal bounds. The House, although it was beset by internal bickering over how to proceed, did much the same. The climate was one of inquiry instead of coziness, and it was obvious that dealing with Don Edwards, the newly concerned Robert Byrd, and others showing a genuine interest in examining the FBI would be a different game from the Bureau's comfortable old relationship with the likes of John Rooney and James Eastland. The ranks of the FBI's uncritical, submissive defenders were thinning down all the time.

Within the Justice Department, too, the Bureau was losing ground; the tolerance for its cocky independence and self-assuredness was ebbing. When Elliot Richardson, writing a memorandum to all Justice Department employees, included the FBI's people for the first time, he was saying that they were welcome in the family; but he was also tacitly saying that certain responsibilities and attitudes of cooperation must come along with family membership. Richardson and his successors, William Saxbe and Edward Levi, pressed to make the Justice Department's official organization chart — on which the Bureau is but one of many constituent parts reporting to the attorney general — a reality. Inside the FBI, these efforts were viewed rather like the invasion of a foreign aggressor. There was muttering at headquarters over the fact that the department was pushing to "take control" of the Bureau — not a bad description, actually — and in the field, individual agents were shocked to find that U.S. attorneys and other Justice Department representatives were, as one put it, "trying to tell us what to do . . . trying to tell us how to handle our cases."

To an extent, the effort seemed to be working. Justice Department officials pronounced themselves far happier with their relationships with the Bureau than they had been during the Hoover era, when they felt a need for constant vigilance to prevent the FBI from playing dirty tricks and pulling bureaucratic end runs on them. Where FBI officials had once behaved like adversaries, they now seemed to be making genuine efforts to cooperate. And yet, only in April 1975 was it revealed that the FBI — Kelley included — had kept the secret inventory of Hoover's "official and confidential" files from Richardson and Saxbe. When it came time to face the question of those files squarely before a congressional subcommittee, Levi had to pry additional details out of the Bureau as if with a crowbar. The Bureau had planned, and written, a typically defensive, obfuscating presentation for Kelley on the subject of FBI files on congressmen; Levi's people had to take it over and construct their own more thorough and candid statement.

Later in the spring of 1975 the Bureau told Levi, with some embarrassment, that it had "discovered" in the files records of another five previously unrevealed COINTELPROs from the 1960s. One was an effort to frustrate the plans and activities of Puerto Rican independence groups in the United States, and another, code-named "Operation Hoodwink," was a rather hilarious — Levi called it "foolish" — attempt to confound and disrupt the Mafia and the American Communist party by trying to make them angry with each other. Two involved disruptive tactics against the American-based representatives of foreign governments, Yugoslavia and Cuba. The fifth, called the "Mexican border program," involved the FBI in cooperative actions with the Mexican police to interfere with the relationship between the American and Mexican Communist parties. In one instance, when the Bureau learned that the wife of a Mexican communist had a permit to cross the border and work in the United States, it arranged to have her permit revoked; other disruptive actions extended well beyond the border, deep into Mexico. When Levi and his aides learned about these matters, they did not wait for a court suit or congressional hearing, but volunteered the information to the House Judiciary Committee. One troublesome, un-

634

answered question was why, when so many FBI people must have known about them, these COINTELPROs were not revealed earlier.

In assessing the Bureau's attitude toward those seeking information about it, both from inside the Justice Department and outside, the words of one alumnus of the Kleindienst and Richardson administrations at Justice seemed apropos: "They don't exactly lie to you, they just mislead you. . . . You have to learn: unless you know exactly the right questions to ask the Bureau, you will never get a complete and truthful answer." The arrival of Clarence Kelley seemed to have done little to change that fact of life with the FBI.

As the last quarter of the twentieth century began, the Bureau had developed into a senior citizen of the law enforcement world and of the American government, one that stood for professionalism in police work and — all the warnings and promises notwithstanding — that had in effect become a national police force. Born in an era of crime waves and Red scares, it had grown in size, stature, and influence during a major showdown with totalitarianism and then flourished further under more crime waves and more Red scares. It had a peculiar legacy from a single powerful man — a mixture of honesty and efficiency, pettiness and foolishness, and a penchant for arousing fear and loathing. The FBI stirred strong feelings in one direction or another on the part of most Americans: its agents were disdained as thugs or worshiped as heroes, miscast and exaggerated to be either Gestapo-style storm troopers or all-powerful supermen. Most people, defenders and critics alike, were confident that the Bureau was capable and equipped to do virtually anything.

The dissipation and decline of the image, then, was bound to be a disappointment all around. Under the new microscope in use after the Watergate scandals had passed, the Bureau looked neither as good nor as bad as anyone had feared or expected. Its Hooverian facade stripped away at last, it did look a great deal more human. But in any event, its future seemed uncertain, and there were serious proposals for imposing major structural changes on an organization and bureaucracy that had once seemed invulnerable and immutable.

One plan offered was to take the FBI out of the Justice Department entirely, making it an independent investigative agency outside the chain of political command and responsiveness. That way, argue the proponents of such an arrangement, directors of the FBI and career officials would not worry about having to please a succession of attorneys general and presidents, but could be motivated first and

Nicholas P. Callahan

Thomas J. Jenkins

Among Clarence Kelley's aides were some unswerving Hooverites like Nicholas P. Callahan, his associate director. Callahan followed John P. Mohr through the ranks at the "seat of government" (FBI headquarters), and when Hoover's longtime side-kick Clyde Tolson made out his will with Mohr's assistance, Callahan was on hand as a witness. Kelley reestablished the traditional jobs of assistants-to-the-director, and on the administrative side he named Thomas J. Jenkins, an Old Guard old-shoe type known less for his innovations than for his willingness to follow his boss's

James B. Adams   John A. Mintz

orders. On the investigative side he appointed James B. Adams, a traditionalist and a product of the powerful Administrative Division, but also a man with some field experience and respect among younger agents. Adams and John A. Mintz were thought by some to have the inside track as possible successors to Kelley. Mintz, who became chief legal counsel for the Bureau in his mid-thirties, was widely respected for his legal talents in other parts of the Justice Department and elsewhere in Washington.

The J. Edgar Hoover FBI Building (so named immediately after the Director's death), built at a cost of 126 million dollars, loomed ominously over Pennsylvania Avenue in Washington and seemed an appropriate physical symbol of the monolithic institution Hoover built.

foremost by the public interest; they could function as full-time law enforcement professionals unhindered by considerations of practical politics. There would be no confusion, and little overlap, between the prosecutive and investigative functions, and cases would proceed according to guidelines that have been carefully thought out and objectively developed. But critics of the proposal argue that the cure might be worse than the problem, because it could make the Bureau altogether too independent — free from outside supervision and resistant to changes in popular sentiment and shifting public priorities on law enforcement issues. While it might solve the conflicts felt by someone in the position of L. Patrick Gray III, it could at the same time create a super J. Edgar Hoover, who builds his own power base and wields a clout that is not even tempered by the need to get along with other members of the government.

Another suggestion, advanced by former Assistant-to-the-Director William C. Sullivan and others, is to split the FBI into two separate agencies, one concerned with its classic criminal jurisdiction and the other with the "security" side of its work. Such a division of authority, it is suggested, would permit more appropriate recruitment practices and assignment policies: people with the necessary background and interests could be channeled into a new agency handling most of the police-type work on the federal level; the more intellectual, studious sorts, capable of making and understanding subtle distinctions and possessing the patience for long-range work with few tangible results, would be separated out into an agency that handles counterintelligence and internal security assignments. Both tasks would probably be better accomplished under such a system, say its supporters, and the country would be less likely to experience the overdone domestic intelligence efforts that have been characteristic of the FBI. On the criminal side, agents and supervisors could develop the necessary specialties that they are lacking today. But there are also strong arguments against such a division of the responsibilities between two agencies: neither one would be capable by itself of handling the crimes with an ideological background, including bombings and other terrorist acts, that have become so common. And the security agency could pose special problems, developing the same kind of haughtiness toward the criminal agency that the CIA has shown toward the FBI, and coming up with its own exclusive definitions of which groups and ideas pose a threat to the nation's stability. Once so specialized, it could become a danger in itself.

A third option would simply put far more severe controls and restrictions on the Bureau than have ever existed before. The laws and rules governing its operations would be rewritten, more tightly and strictly. Its budget would be scrutinized with greater attention to every line item and its personnel standards and appointments subject to more meaningful supervision from outside the agency. Determination of policies and priorities would no longer be left so substantially in the hands of the FBI, but would be determined outside and then presented to the Bureau as a fait accompli. Agents would have greater protection from arbitrary disciplinary and transfer policies, and they would play a more important role in a democratized bureaucratic structure. Promotion and advancement would be based more genuinely on merit and achievement, measured by objective criteria instead of sycophantic abilities and internal political maneuvering. In a word, what Harlan Stone and J. Edgar Hoover claimed, and to some degree managed, to do in 1924 would be done again, in a manner relevant and meaningful to the times.

Whichever, the good old days were gone. The rules were changing.

Afterword

The Director, had he been there, could not have asked for a better day for the dedication of his $126 million palace than September 30, 1975. The sun was shining and the sky was a clear autumn blue. The courtyard was decked out in red-white-and-blue bunting and filled with the Bureau faithful of past and present, smiling and happy as they heard the United States Marine Band play monumental selections, including the "J. Edgar Hoover March," a creation of Special Agent Al Nencioni of the Alexandria Field Office. Only the night before workmen had finished putting up the glittering letters along Pennsylvania Avenue that marked it as the J. Edgar Hoover FBI Building.

Architecture critics were having a field day, calling it a monstrosity that fit in poorly with its austere, neo-Gothic neighbors. Agents and visitors were regularly getting lost in its labyrinthine, sterile-white, endless corridors that were uninterrupted by any dash of color and indistinguishable each from the next. Justice Department officials were complaining that the Bureau had triumphed again, carefully restricting access to the building — only a red stripe across a Justice Department identification card would do — and rationing out the parking spaces in its cavernous garage. Rumor had it that some of the stairwells were inhabited by uninvited rats; in Hoover's day that might have meant criminals, but now it meant rodents.

But never mind all that, this is a festive and glorious occasion. The invocation seeks divine endorsement for the FBI's effort to give the country "order and peace." The administrator of the General Services Administration, Arthur Sampson, hopes that the Hoover Building will be a fitting attraction for the Bicentennial year. Clarence Kelley notes that the unification of all Bureau functions under one roof at last will permit its work to be done more smoothly; and Attorney General Edward H. Levi finds some words of faint praise to say about Hoover, noting the Director's bold moves to clean up a corrupt bureaucracy in the 1920s and his plunge into the fight against crime in the 1930s. President Gerald R. Ford is on hand, too, and reveals that he once had a "great [but unfulfilled] ambition" to be an FBI agent. He calls this a "truly magnificent building" and praises the agent force for being "legendary symbols" to the American people; what better time than this, he asks, for "a renewed commitment to the rule of law in America."

The dedication, though, is like an oasis of joy in a bleak and monotonous desert of criticism for the Bureau, extending for the moment as far and as long as the weariest pessimist can imagine. On Capitol Hill, the Senate Select Committee on Intelligence, headed by Frank Church (D-Idaho), is probing into the events surrounding the "Huston plan" of 1970, the COINTELPROs, and other FBI misadventures. On the other side of the Capitol, the House Select Committee on Intelligence, after a puppydoglike start under Congressman Lucien Nedzi (D-Michigan), has a new eye-catching, publicity-seeking chairman in Congressman Otis Pike (D–New York). Pike means business, and he is probing the costs of intelligence-gathering and uncovering weird arrangements like the Bureau's purchase of vast quantities of electronic surveillance equipment through the "U.S. Recording Company" at a high markup. Other committees are scrambling for a piece of the action, crowding each other for a chance to scrutinize some corner of the FBI. There are weeks when the investigations and revelations seem like a cascade: Did the Dallas Field Office destroy Lee Harvey Oswald's threatening note, and on whose orders? How long did the Security Index remain in operation? How much private mail did the Bureau open, where and when and why? At the Justice Department, a special committee meets almost every day, hammering out new "guidelines" — perhaps the seed for new statutes — to govern FBI operations. Advance word is that the guidelines will be a hard-nosed structure for Bureau accountability, that they will set out narrowly drawn criteria for the FBI's domestic intelligence activities, substituting consultation for free-lance innovations by the Bureau and requiring strict advance approval for any "preventive" actions of the COINTELPRO sort.

Domestic intelligence is much in the news again, in part because of a report by the General Accounting Office that barely 3 percent of FBI investigations in that field lead to actual prosecutions. Bureau documents are surfacing, less through leaks than in response to subpoenas. One is a particular classic: Addressed to Cartha DeLoach by William C. Sullivan and dated July 19, 1966, it sets out the DO NOT

FILE procedure for materials connected with the FBI's "black bag jobs," which are acknowledged to be "clearly illegal." The only reason such a memo ever became available, apparently, is that Hoover broke his own rule and filed it among his "official and confidential" papers. But if little else was filed, how then can anyone trust the official statistic, provided by the Bureau to the Church Committee, that "at least fourteen domestic subversive targets were the subject of at least 238 [surreptitious] entries from 1942 to April, 1968." Just what about the Bureau is to be believed? And how to explain Hoover's extraordinary hatred for Martin Luther King, now revealed in even more grotesque detail — efforts to prevent him from receiving honorary degrees and seeing the pope; an anonymous letter that King interpreted as an invitation to commit suicide; lobbying with Congress even after King had been killed to prevent his birthday from being declared a national holiday? Assistant-to-the-Director James Adams cannot explain; he admits to the Senate committee that the crusade against King was improper and had no legal basis.

Even in Superior Court of the District of Columbia, an FBI controversy rages — an unseemly and embarrassing public contest to the last will and testament of Clyde Tolson. Will Hoover ever really be able to rest in peace?

But the Bureau presses forward, believing that its image will survive the storm (although some wonder whether Clarence Kelley will, unless he makes a dramatic break from the past). Belief in that image is strong enough for the FBI's half-a-billion-dollar annual budget to include enough money to provide tours for the half a million visitors now expected annually. The tour they will have is a slick new one, with organized crime taking the place of the old Rosenberg spy case and talk about white-collar crime substituting for boilerplate warnings about the menace of communism. Yet, some things change slowly, almost imperceptibly — at the insistence of John Mohr, the high priest of Hooverdom in retirement, the tour includes a replica of J. Edgar Hoover's office, faithful down to his actual desk lamp and his rug embroidered with the FBI seal.

Appendix

One of the most dramatic confrontations in the history of the FBI was the extended conflict in 1971 between J. Edgar Hoover and a man long considered a leading prospect to succeed him, William C. Sullivan (see Chapter XII, The Dukes). Sullivan was a controversial Bureau figure who developed many of its counterintelligence and antisubversive techniques; he quarreled often with his colleagues in the hierarchy, but sometimes he was the only one who dared to express the complaints and criticisms that many others felt. As things became more bitter, Sullivan, assistant-to-the-director for all investigative matters, listed his grievances in brutally frank letters to the Director — one on August 28, 1971, and another, longer one on October 6, 1971, after he had been forced out of the Bureau by Hoover. The letters are unique in the annals of the FBI. The entire text of the August letter and excerpts from the October one are presented here, for what they reveal about the tension inside the Bureau in Hoover's last months, the evolution of controversial FBI policies, and about one man's anguished break with an organization to which he had given his life.

Saturday A.M.
August 28, 1971

PERSONAL

Dear Mr. Hoover:

It is regretted by me that this letter is necessary. What I will set forth below is being said for your own good and for the FBI as a whole of which I am very fond. The premise from which I write is this, from diverse sources I have received the impression that you consider me to be disloyal to you but not to the FBI. If this is correct it is a serious matter that ought to be discussed.

First, I wish to direct your attention to my 30 year record in the FBI. It is well documented and I don't need to present it to you here with its letters of commendation and awards given by you. You have access to all this. If this record of three decades is not conclusive evidence of loyalty what is? You have said that I consistently put the work of this Bureau above personal considerations. My family certainly will attest to this for they have year in and year out suffered from my neglect. This I now realize was a mistake on my part. Countless others have also put the Bureau above all other considerations.

Second, you and I recognized years ago that we do not possess the same philosophical view or the same approach to FBI operations. We have disagreed but we worked together and I have carried out your instructions even when I disagreed with them strongly. This is as it should be because any organization must have an authority capable of making the final decision and invested with the power to implement all such decisions.

Third, during the past year in particular you have made it evident to me that you do not want me to disagree with you on anything. As one official of the FBI has said you claim you do not want "yes men" but you become furious at any employee who says "no" to you. I think this observation has much truth in it. If you are going to equate loyalty with "yes men," "rubber stamps," "apple polishers," flatterers, self-promoters and timid, cringing, frightened sycophants you are not only departing from the meaning of loyalty you are in addition harming yourself and the organization. There is no substitute for incisive, independent, free, probing, original, creative thinking. I have brought up my children to believe and act upon this truth. They disagree with me regularly. But, they are not disloyal to me. In fact I think their loyalty is more deep, strong and lasting because of this kind of thinking.

Fourth, ever since I spoke before the UPI Conference on October 12, 1970 you have made it quite clear you are very displeased with me because, according to you, I downgraded the Communist Party, USA. My answer to the question raised was accurate, factual, truthful. As I pointed later to Mr. Tolson in Executive Conference I would give the very same answer again and again if it was asked. You know as well as I do that the Communist Party, USA is not the cause of and does not direct and control the unrest and violence in this Nation. The UPI was wholly accurate in reporting what I said. Some papers were incomplete in reporting my remarks and there may have been a headline here and there that was not entirely correct. However, I repeat what I said was correct and I cannot understand your hostile reaction to it which has continued to this day.

Fifth, you are incensed because I have disagreed with you on opening new foreign liaison offices around the world and adding more men to those already in existence. It seems to me you should welcome different viewpoints. On this subject I want to say this here. I grew up in a farming community where all people in a family had to literally work from the darkness of the morning to the darkness of the night in order to make a living and pay their taxes. It could be that this is what causes me to be so sensitive about how the taxpayers' money is spent. Hence, I want to say once more that I regard it to be a serious waste of taxpayers' money to keep increasing the number of these offices, to continue with all that we now have and to be adding more and more manpower to these offices. Our primary responsibility is within the United States and here is where we need to spend the taxpayers' dollar combating crime. And, as our own statistics show we are not doing too well at it here. Why, then, should we spread ourselves around the world unnecessarily? You keep telling me that President Nixon has ordered you to do it and therefore you must carry out his orders. I am positive that if President Nixon knew the limitations of our foreign liaison operations and was given all the facts relative to intelligence matters he would reverse these orders if such have been clearly given. A few liaison offices can be justified but this expansion program cannot be no matter what kind of "reports" your inspectors bring back to you. Do you think many (if any) will disagree with you? What would happen if they did?

Sixth, I would like to convince you (but I am almost certain to fail in this) that those of us who disagree with *you are trying to help you and not hurt you.* For example, you were opposed in the Shaw case. This man should have been allowed to resign without stigmatizing him with the phrase "dismissal with prejudice." This was wrong. It cost us $13,000 I am told. On August 28 in a memorandum from Mr. Toldon [*sic*] to you we have been instructed to have no conversation or give any answers to representatives of certain papers and two broadcasting companies. Mr. Hoover this is wrong and also it will sooner or later hurt us. You cannot do this kind of thing in a free, democratic society. It matters not whether we like or dislike certain papers or broadcasting companies they are entitled to equal treatment. Again, your decision to keep Mr. Roy Moore in Philadelphia is in my judgment both wrong and unjust. This man has been there since April. He has done brilliant work. It is definitely not necessary to keep him there any longer. He should be sent back to his office and family. I wish you would change your mind in both these cases. Again, I want to say those of us who disagree with you are trying to help you. May I suggest that we are more loyal than those who are constantly saying "yes, yes, yes" to you and behind your back talk about "the need to play the game" in order to get the paycheck regularly and not be demoted or transferred.

Seventh, you have refused to give Assistant Director C. D. Brennan and myself any more annual leave. The reason you give is not valid and you know it. All it amounts to is this: you dislike us and you intend to use your absolute power in this manner as a form of "punishment." I am hardened to all this and can take it. But my family cannot. My oldest son is registering for college in New Hampshire this coming Tuesday. Naturally he wanted me to be with him and is extremely disappointed that I cannot be. Of course, I want to be with him and find out what kind of a roommate he has, talk to his professors, etc. My wife, in addition to respiratory trouble is now ill with colitus and cannot handle the situation (if you doubt this I will submit to you the doctors bills for the past three years and will give you their names and you can send out one or two of your global circling inspectors to talk to them and this time they will have to bring back what the doctors say and not what you want to hear). But even more serious is this: My son who has been staying with me has not driven a car a great deal and is not a good driver. Yet, because you refuse to give me any leave I had to tell him he must drive all the way to norther [*sic*] New Hampshire (well over 600 miles) alone today. He left at 5:30 A.M. this morning. Mr. Hoover, I want to tell you very simply but with deadly seriousness that I am hoping and praying for all involved in this that my adolescent son makes this long and dangerous trip today without any harm coming to him. Surely, I don't need to explain to you why my wife and three children regard you, to put it mildly, as a very strange man.

Eighth, what I have said here is not designed to irritate or anger you but it probably will. What I am trying to get across to you in my blunt, tactless way is that a number of your decisions this year have not been good ones; that you should take a good, cold, impartial inventory of your ideas, policies, etc. You will not believe this but it is true: I do not want to see your reputation built up over these many years destroyed by your own decision and actions. When you elect to retire I want to see you go out in a blaze of glory with full recognition from all those concerned. I do not want to see this FBI organization which I have gladly given 30 years of my life to along with untold numbers of other men fall apart or become tainted in any manner. We have a fine group of men in the FBI and we need to think of every one of them also.

Ninth, as I have indicated this letter will probably anger you. When you are angered you can take some mighty drastic action. You have absolute power in the FBI (I hope the man who one day takes over your position will not have such absolute power for we humans are simply not saintly enough to possess and handle

647

it properly in every instance). In view of your absolute power you can fire me, or do away with my position (as you once did) or transfer me or in some other way work out your displeasure with me. So be it. I am fond of the FBI and I have told you exactly what I think about certain matters affecting you and this Bureau and as you know I have always been willing to accept the consequences of my ideas and actions.

Respectfully submitted,
[signed] Wm. C. Sullivan

◆

2810 64th Avenue
Cheverly, Maryland
October 6, 1971

Mr. J. Edgar Hoover
4936 Thirtieth Place, N.W.
Washington, D.C.

Dear Mr. Hoover:

Please refer to your letters to me of September 3 and September 30, 1971. You state that I have not replied to your letter of September 3. In the light of our conversations this letter did not require a reply. However, as long as you want a response I will give you one now even though it is after the fact. This letter I am sending to your home in order that you may hold it privately for as you are aware the Bureau has become a bit of a sieve and this letter if seen would be the subject of gossip which, I am sure, we both wish to avoid.

First, I wish to say this complete break with you has been truly an agonizing one for me. You well know how fond I am of the Bureau and its work. To some degree this is the paradox for it is over this fact the rupture has risen. By this I mean the damage you are doing the Bureau and its work has brought all this on, but more of this later. At this time I want to again thank you for the support you have given me in the past and in particular when I was quite ill in Arizona years ago from a respiratory ailment. In the years now gone we have enjoyed some good conversations and some hearty laughter. I think you will agree I have with enthusiasm always, as time mounted, accepted every special assignment, dangerous or non-dangerous given me by you and carried them out to the best of my ability. We have had a reasonably close relationship and this is why it is so tragic for it to have ended as it did. It is regretted changes could not have been made to prevent it.

I will now turn to your letter of September 30, 1971, in which you say you are, in substance, forcing me into retirement for the sake of "public interest." May I suggest this is one of your minor faults — overstatement and overkill. More relevant is your charge that I have been unwilling to accept "final administrative decisions." This is not true and you know it. You cannot cite one instance where I have refused to carry out your instructions even when I disagreed with them vigorously and wholly. But, this leads to larger issues which I wish to discuss with you.

Many times I have told you what I think is right and good about the FBI, but now I will set forth what I think is wrong about it hoping that something worthwhile will come out of it. I want to make it clear that I am not blaming all these faults upon you. All of us in high places around you must also bear our share of the blame. One might call it a collective responsibility.

No. 1 *Concealment of the Truth and All the Facts from the People of this Nation who have a Right to Know*

A very good and serious example of this is the Communist Party of the United States. In the mid-forties when the membership of the Party was about 80,000 and it had many front organizations you publicized this widely month and month out. In fact it was far too widely publicized to the point where you caused a Communist scare in the Nation which was entirely unwarranted. You had your staff of writers in the Crime Records Division (a "front" of your own to conceal our huge public relations and propaganda operations which no government Bureau should have) turning out hundreds of articles on the great "dangers of" and "serious threat" of Communism to our national security. You never seemed to be that concerned with organized crime. I am just as much opposed to Communism as you but I knew then and I know now that it was not the danger you claimed it was and that it never warranted the huge amounts of the taxpayer's dollar spent upon it. I stand condemned for not making an issue of it at that time. What happened when the Communist Party went into a rapid decline? You kept the scare campaign going just the same for some years. However, when the membership figures kept dropping lower and lower you instructed us not to give them out to the public any more and not even to the Justice Department. I told you at one time we should publish the low figures and let the Bureau get credit for a job well done and point out how successfully Communism can be met in a democratic society but you would have none of it. At the time of my leaving the Bureau this week the membership figures of the Communist Party are down to an amazing 2800 in a nation of over 200 million people and you still conceal this from the people. Of the 2800 only about half are active and wholly ineffective. I think it is a terrible injustice to the citizens and an unethical thing for you to do to conceal this important truth from the public. You keep complaining that in my lectures I downgrade the Communist Party. Had I remained in the Bureau any longer I would, contrary to your instructions, have told the public about the tiny 2800 membership of the Communist Party. I stand condemned for not doing so before, despite your instructions not to do so. You will recall that on October 12, 1970, speaking before the conference of UPI Editors at Williamsburg I told them the Party was not the cause of and did not direct or control the racial and student unrest in the Nation. On my return to Headquarters you were furious and gave me hell for what you called "downgrading the Communist Party" and you raised with me how were you going to get appropriations wanted if I kept doing that. We do not need to get appropriations that way. Further, if there is no longer a Communist problem we should not spend money on it. In fact, I have for some years been taking men of [sic] Communist work in the field and here at Headquarters and putting them on some important work.

. . .

No. 4 *Senator Joseph McCarthy and Yourself*
More than one of us at the Bureau were disturbed when you identified yourself with Senator McCarthy and his irresponsible anti-Communist campaign. His method was not the method which should be used to combat Communism and he did grave damage to national security in the sense that reflective men said if this is anti-Communism I want none of it. Yet, you had us preparing material for him regularly, kept furnishing it to him while you denied publicly that we were helping him. And you have done the same thing with others. This is wrong and one day the "chickens may come home to roost."

. . .

No. 7 *FBI and the Police Departments*
As you must know, we are not at all well-liked by the police departments around the country with some exceptions. They complain that it is a one-way street. We take everything from them and give nothing, that we steal credit from them, deliberately overshadow them, etc. If it was not for the excellent person friendships built up by our field office special agents with the police, conditions

would be far worse. When I say disliked, I mean the official policy of the FBI toward the police, our headquarters' attitude, not the special agent in the field. The FBI National Academy to train police is one of the finest things you have done, yet until recent years it was not regarded highly by police who came in from large departments. When I was single I roomed at the same place with many of them when they were in Washington. Almost without exception they had a low opinion as to its practical worth for them. I remember a man from Los Angeles saying they had a far better training school than the FBI Academy. But, he said he was satisfied to come here because the FBI diploma from our Academy was valuable to him and would help to promote him. He laughed and said he was certainly not going to let out the "secret" of its low quality instruction and hurt himself and fellow class members, who, according to him felt the same as he did. He pointed out that men from very small police departments might get some practical value from the course but not any person from medium sized departments up. With our new quarters and training facilities at Quantico this has all been corrected. But, why was the old inadequate situation allowed to prevail for so many years? It was the same with the few officers from foreign nations who attended. I talked to some of them. They complained no special courses were set up for them; that courses geared only to police needs in the United States had very limited use for them. This, too, recently has been corrected but more needs to be done here if we are to train any large numbers of them. Lastly, and the most important point, is this: the FBI should not try to dominate the police (as we were repeatedly told to do in our In-Training class) but should cooperate and treat them as equals and wherever possible let them take the credit and publicity for cases worked in common. We should stay in the background. Why do we need to grab the headlines? If we did this, we would find police departments all over the nation anxious to give us all possible help and our war against crime would be far more effective than it is now. One more point, the police never liked recovering stolen automobiles then having our men on your instructions go down to where the cars were, take down all the basic statistics, set a recovery value (the highest possible) then have you, at the end of the year, total all this and take claim for so many cars recovered that were stolen, and the total value of them. Here was the FBI taking credit for what the police had actually done.

. . .

No. 10 *FBI and Illegal Agents in the United States*

This is one of our most serious and harmful security problems in the United States today. Yet you abolished our main programs designed to identify and neutralize the enemy agents. I just cannot understand this. It simply is not a rational thing to do. This is one of your acts that led me to take a strong stand against you for I am convinced you are seriously damaging our national security. You know the high number of illegal agents operating along the east coast alone. As of this week, the week I am leaving the FBI for good, we have not identified *even one of them*. These illegal agents, as you know, are engaged, among other things, in securing the secrets of our defense in the event of a military attack so that our defense will amount to nothing. Mr. Hoover are you thinking? Are you really capable of thinking this through? Don't you realize we are betraying our government and people by abolishing programs to protect them from enemy illegal agents? Now that I am gone you do not have to save face anymore by holding out against what I recommend. Please reconsider and start those programs again. I must say again I just cannot understand you. I do not know what is the matter with you that you should do such a thing.

No. 11 *FBI and Security Investigations*

I think we have been conducting far too many investigations called security which are actually political. This is our policy and it should be changed at once. What I mean is investigations mainly of students, professors, intellectuals and their organizations concerned with peace, anti-war, etc. We have no business doing this. Now, if there are definitely subversives (a word that always bothered me, hard to define) among them seeking to violate our laws, all well and good, investigate them as individuals but with great care so as not [to] smear the organization they are with. Just think of the time and money we have wasted on nothing but political investigations. Is it any wonder so many students and professors detest the FBI. I am not the only one who thinks this. Many, many field office agents think the same and some have resigned and commented about it.

. . .

No. 14 *FBI and our Statistics*

We all know they have never been either definitive or wholly reliable. More than one scholar has pointed this out down through the years and instead of appreciating their interest we looked upon them as enemies to be attacked. Why do we have such an attitude? Is it because long years ago you projected the image of infallibility and now you are stuck with it? No one is infallible and he who takes this position is doomed to be exposed and taken apart sooner or later. To return to our statistics, in many instances we came up with about any thing you wanted. The story has long been told in the FBI that one year when you were testifying you were asked the cost of crime in the United States and you replied 22 billion. According to the account, it was 11 billion based on our scanty statistics. The men said now what will we do for the Director is wrong. Our enterprising young supervisor said we have no problem here at all. Just multiply the 11 billion by two and you have established the correctness of the Director's figures. So 22 billion it was for years until some taxpayer wrote in and said he noted that for some years the cost of crime remained constant at 22 billion and how could that be? Needless to say it started to change and move up from that time on. What the new figures were based on I do not know. It is suggested that we get some of the most brilliant statisticians in the country on contract and set a real and useful statistical system.

. . .

No. 21 *FBI and Infallibility*

I mentioned this once before briefly. Here I want to say this. Our effort (though you may deny it) to create the impression in the mind of the American people that we are infallible, perfect and sort of superhuman has over the years done us far more harm than good. Why can't we take a cold, factual, sensible position and set forth where necessary what we have done that is right and good, and also set forth our mistakes when we make them and what was wrong with our action. We would be respected far more. Often we have gone into long-winded explanations as to why we were not wrong when actually we were. Truth needs no lengthy explanation. We have wasted much time and money arguing and defending ourselves when a brief, simple statement of our error would have paid us richer dividends. Let us get away from infallibility and present ourselves as ordinary human beings trying to do the best job possible but not always succeeding.

. . .

No. 25 *Military Leave*

A few years ago I could see the beginning of the breakup of the FBI. At first I did not admit even to myself. I made excuses. I rationalized. I turned aside from the obvious. At last I had to face up to reality. You had abolished vital programs, your decisions were fouling up other operations and I decided I could better serve my country in the army and I wrote to you and said I would like military leave to go to Vietnam. This was a time when many of our young soldiers were getting ambushed and killed because of a lack of good intelligence, I was told. You made it clear you did not want me to take military leave so I dropped the idea. I wonder how much different it all would have been if you said "yes go ahead." No use now of speculating about it.

651

APPENDIX

No. 26 *Leaks of Sensitive Material*

Mr. Hoover, you have regularly told the public FBI files are secure, inviolate, almost sacred. Years ago when I first discovered this was not true at all I was stunned. But, we had created in time a certain atmosphere in the FBI difficult to describe and one learns to live with what one learns, both good and bad. We have leaked information improperly, as you know, on both persons and organizations. My first recollection was leaking information about Mrs. Eleanor Roosevelt whom you detested. And so it was year after year right up to our leaking the investigation on the killing of President John F. Kennedy and thereafter to the present. This should also stop.

No. 27 *FBI and Politics*

This topic I have saved until the last because it has done more than anything else to bring on my disillusionment with the FBI. Like so many young men before I entered the FBI I thought the FBI was the epitome of purity and that you were about as flawless a leader that can be found. I held on to this belief while I was in the field offices despite stories told me by old agents. I held on to it for a long time after I returned to Headquarters as a supervisor. This again despite stories circulated that the FBI was the most political agency in government and that you were completely immersed with politics with every administration. I do not have to go into detail. I saw example after example of how you willingly served any powerful figure in an influential office. While you are extremely conservative yourself I noticed it did not matter whether the political figure was liberal or conservative, if it served your ends, you were eager to act. It did not matter whether it was a Republican or a Democrat or whether the Administration in power was Republican or Democrat. I saw clearly at last that the FBI always presented to the American public as non-political, as being outside, above and beyond politics, was just the contrary. It was immersed in politics and even went so far as to conduct purely political investigations and inquiries. At times, it seemed that when we were not asked to perform politically we sought opportunities to do so. I was so concerned about this under Mr. Johnson's administration that I wrote you a letter and expressed my concern and urged that the FBI not be used politically. Again, you are not the sole blame here. We who helped you inside the Bureau to carry out such activities must share the blame. And, the politicians who used [sic] must also share the blame.

FINAL OBSERVATION

Mr. Hoover, you know this was not an easy letter for me to write, both physically and psychologically. The first is true because as you can see I am no typist so please pardon the mistakes and organization. The second is true because we have been friends and worked together for years even though our views often differed. The hardest decision I have ever made in my lifetime was the decision in July to take a stand and break with you hoping that some good would come out of it for the Bureau, not for me because I would be leaving. It was a last resot [sic]. You know well I tried in every proper way to bring about the badly needed changes. You did away with vital programs. You falsely accused me of writing the two fine letters which Sam J. Papich, former liaison with CIA, had written trying to prevent you from further damaging the Bureau. I never wrote these letters but I would have been proud to have done so and had you listened to Mr. Papich, one of the finest and most able men this Bureau ever had, we would not be in the horrible condition we are in today and there would have been no need of my writing this letter to you. Like myself, Mr. Papich was most fond of the Bureau but he saw it was deteriorating and tried to prevent it. After the reception his two fine letters received he knew the cause was hopeless and retired. Perhaps I should have done the same thing at the time but I still clung to the hope that changes could be brought about orderly and quietly and once more the Bureau would be moving ahead and doing what the people thought it had been doing all along.

Once again I want to say, Mr. Hoover, we are not blaming you alone. We were all part of your staff for years. We all share the blame and responsibility. This is no time for anger, recriminations or vindictiveness. There is still time to bring about the progressive changes needed. I am gone now so you do not have me any longer as a "thorn in your flesh." Why don't you sit down quietly by yourself and think this all over and then get some of the men together and work out a plan to reform, reorganize and modernize the Bureau. If you do not give reality to what to some degree has become a bubble that bubble will burst and it will be bad for all. You can still do it if you will only see the situation as it actually is and then act. It is an internal situation and it need not even get into the press. Just handle it quietly in a professional manner. This is what I hope you will do.

Mr. Hoover, if for reasons of your own you cannot or will not do this may I gently suggest you retire for your good, that of the Bureau, the intelligence community and law enforcement. More than once I told you never to retire; to stay on to the last, that you would live longer being active. It looks now that I may have been wrong. For if you cannot do what is suggested above you really ought to retire and be given the recognition due you after such a long and remarkable career in government.

Sincerely yours,

[signed]   William C. Sullivan

Glossary

This is a list of terms, phrases, acronyms, organizations, and Bureau euphemisms that appear in this book and other materials concerning the FBI.

administrative advancement — one choice available to new agents in the Bureau, it involves a series of desk jobs and transfers while working one's way up through the hierarchy. The alternative is to remain a "street agent" who works "on the bricks."

airtel — an internal FBI communication, urgent enough that it must be typed on the day it is dictated, but routine enough to be sent by air mail rather than teletype.

APL — American Protective League, a voluntary patriotic organization that engaged in vigilante-type activities during World War I. Launched with the blessings of the Justice Department, it assisted the Bureau with the notorious "slacker raids," during which thousands of people were arrested for allegedly evading the draft.

applicant work — the Bureau's investigation of the background of people who are applying for jobs with it or with certain other federal agencies or who are under consideration for appointment to high federal positions. Applicant work expanded and flourished during the Red Scare of the late 1940s and early 1950s.

ASAC — pronounced *ay*-sack, assistant-special-agent-in-charge, the person who is second in command of an FBI field office or, in the largest offices, one of several second-ranking officials.

BNDD — Bureau of Narcotics and Dangerous Drugs. Formed by merging several other agencies and placed in the Justice Department, it became the chief federal narcotics–law enforcement agency in the 1960s.

Bureau — in traditional FBI usage, headquarters in Washington. Also used to refer generally to the FBI.

Bureau supervisor — an FBI agent assigned to headquarters who coordinates the work on particular categories of cases from a geographical region or a grouping of field offices. Although the job is generally a step up the FBI career ladder, it can be a boring and uninspiring position.

Career Development Program — the method, frequently revised and tinkered with, by which FBI agents are promoted. Traditionally, it has required about twenty years to complete it and reach the point of running a field office.

CCH — Computerized Criminal Histories, the controversial file within the National Crime Information Center that permits immediate mechanical retrieval of an individual's entire criminal record.

CID — Criminal Investigation Division, the part of Scotland Yard with which the FBI has its closest ties in Great Britain.

classifications — the categories, all precisely numbered, into which the Bureau divides its investigative responsibilities — e.g., "crime on a government reservation" or "interstate transportation of stolen property."

COFO — Council of Federated Organizations, a coalition of civil rights groups active in the South in the 1960s, which was intensively investigated by the Bureau.

COINTELPRO — counterintelligence program, used by the Bureau, first against the Communist party and foreign agents and later against domestic groups ranging from the Ku Klux Klan to the Black Panther party, to disrupt and discredit those it was investigating.

CPUSA — Communist party of the United States, which J. Edgar Hoover continued to detest and to investigate long after it had been rendered impotent.

CRP, or CREEP — Committee for the Re-election of the President, which worked on behalf of Richard Nixon in 1972 and was at the center of the Watergate scandals.

CRS — Community Relations Service, created by the Civil Rights Act of 1964 and housed first in the Commerce Department and later in the Justice Department. Its mandate was to seek peaceful solutions to racial and other community crises.

DEA — Drug Enforcement Administration. The product of a reorganization of narcotics enforcement agencies by the Nixon administration, it was wracked by scandals. Officially parallel to the FBI within the Justice Department, it is much distrusted and disliked by the Bureau.

DST — Direction de la Surveillance du Territoire, the French equivalent to the internal security side of the FBI.

executive conference — the members of the FBI hierarchy (associate director, assistants-to-the-director, and assistant directors) who meet regularly to advise the director on policy matters. Under J. Edgar Hoover, they rubber-stamped his every decision and whim.

FBI Academy — the physical complex of buildings on the U.S. Marine base in Quantico, Virginia, used for FBI training of agents and local policemen as well as for some Bureau conferences.

FBI National Academy — the FBI's training school, generally twelve weeks long, for members of local and state law enforcement agencies and, more recently, some from overseas. The NA was long the vehicle for the Bureau's efforts to build up credit with local police who would then help the FBI solve cases.

FBIRA — the FBI Recreation Association, to which nearly every Bureau employee makes a voluntary contribution of two dollars a year. It buys the service keys that are awarded to employees at regular intervals for length of service.

FBN — Federal Bureau of Narcotics. Long located in the Treasury Department and run by Harry Anslinger, it was the FBI's archrival and investigated the Mafia long before the Bureau did.

field division — the territory covered by a field office, which usually includes one or more federal judicial districts.

field office — one of fifty-nine regional units of the FBI (see endpapers), regarded by most agents as being locked in an eternal struggle with headquarters.

field supervisor — an agent who manages the efforts of a "squad" within a field office. A supervisor, often on his way up the Bureau career ladder, is paid more than most "street agents," but is generally confined to his desk.

form 302 — the standard interview report form, on which an agent records all of his impressions and on which he is often cross-examined in court.

The Grapevine — the monthly publication of the Society of Former Special Agents of the Federal Bureau of Investigation.

GID — General Intelligence Division, established as a separate part of the Justice Department in 1919 by Attorney General A. Mitchell Palmer. Run by J. Edgar Hoover, then a twenty-four-year-old special assistant to the attorney general, it compiled files on "subversives" and was later incorporated into the Bureau of Investigation.

GRU — Glavnoye Razvedyvatelnoye Upravleniye, Soviet military intelligence organization.

headquarters city — the location of any field office, i.e., "headquarters" for that field division.

HILEV — code name for the Bureau's intensified intelligence-collection program overseas, after the Legats were expanded in 1970 at Hoover's insistence.

HISC — House Internal Security Committee, the new name given to the House Un-American Activities Committee in the early 1970s in an effort to make it sound more acceptable.

HUAC — House Un-American Activities Committee. A leader in decades of Red scares and witch-hunts, it often traded information on "subversives" with the Bureau and egged the FBI on to more ambitious efforts in the internal security field.

IACP — International Association of Chiefs of Police, long manipulated and controlled by the Bureau, but declared an "enemy" by Hoover in the 1960s under its aggressive director, Quinn Tamm, himself a former Bureau official.

IDIU — Interdivisional Information Unit, formed by Attorney General Ramsey Clark in the late 1960s to monitor the potential for urban racial disturbances and later used by the Nixon administration, with its name changed to Interdivisional Intelligence Unit, to coordinate the flow of information about antiwar demonstrations and other purportedly "subversive" activities into the Internal Security Division of the Justice Department.

IEC — Intelligence Evaluation Committee, a group formed within the Justice Department by the Nixon administration to bring together available intelligence on such subjects as "foreign influence in the antiwar movement." Its formation was one of several indications of White House dissatisfaction with domestic intelligence efforts of the Bureau during J. Edgar Hoover's last years.

indices — the alphabetized card file in each field office that refers to every name mentioned in any document in its files. At FBI headquarters there is a central index, as well as special indices of people of "security interest" to the Bureau or who have been overheard in wiretaps. The first step in most FBI investigations is an "indices check."

INS — Immigration and Naturalization Service, a rival of the Bureau although also in the Justice Department.

inspection — the annual (or, in the event of a crisis or controversy, more frequent) visit to a field office by a group of senior agents, sometimes known as "the goon squad," to evaluate the performance of the office and agents and to determine their compliance with hundreds of minute rules and regulations. Inspections were long an instrument of Hoover's iron-handed control of the Bureau.

inspector — the highest FBI rank below assistant director or special-agent-in-charge. An inspector either helps run a headquarters division or travels on the inspection staff. Most SACs are drawn from the ranks of the inspectors.

inspectors' aide — a junior member of the traveling inspection staff. He has usually already served a stint as a Bureau supervisor and will, as his next step of advancement, become an ASAC.

INTERPOL — the International Criminal Police Organization, with headquarters in Paris, which facilitates the exchange of identification and investigative information among its members. J. Edgar Hoover pulled the FBI out of INTERPOL in 1950, and later the Treasury Department became the official U.S. representative.

The Investigator — the monthly publication of the FBI Recreation Association. Frequently featuring photographs of Bureau employees at work, play, and award ceremonies, it is an important part of the FBI's efforts to maintain high morale and devotion to the agency among its staff.

ITOM — interstate transportation of obscene matter, a Bureau classification.

ITSMV — interstate transportation of a stolen motor vehicle, the crime banned by the Dyer Act of 1919, long a favorite FBI preoccupation because of its value for annual statistics.

ITSP — interstate transportation of stolen property, a Bureau classification which has become a frequent method of prosecuting stock thefts and other "white-collar crimes."

IVI — Independent Voters of Illinois, an early subject of Bureau investigation on the grounds that — like other liberal organizations — it might be a target for communist infiltration.

KGB — Komitet Gosudarstvennoy Bezopasnosti (Committee for State Security), the Soviet agency that combines the functions of the FBI, CIA, National Security Agency and other American government institutions into one.

LEAA — Law Enforcement Assistance Administration, the agency established by Congress within the Justice Department in the late 1960s to channel federal funds for the improvement and strengthening of local police and other law enforcement and criminal justice agencies. It became a bureaucratic rival of the FBI and was suspected of wanting to take away some of the Bureau's functions, including fingerprint identification and the NCIC.

legal attaché — the title given to most Bureau agents assigned to work overseas. Based in an American embassy or consulate, he is theoretically only a "liaison" with foreign police, but in fact has come to perform many other functions.

Legat — the shorthand term for an overseas FBI office and for an agent assigned to work in one (e.g., "He is a Legat in Bonn" or "He is assigned to the Bonn Legat").

LHM — letterhead memorandum, the summary report used to disseminate information about a Bureau case outside the FBI. Sources are generally concealed carefully in an LHM.

MEDBURG — FBI code name for its investigation of the burglary of its resident agency in Media, Pennsylvania, in 1971.

MIBURN — FBI code name for its investigation of the killing of three civil rights workers in Philadelphia, Mississippi, in 1964. (The case was captioned under an earlier probe into the burning of a church.)

MI-5 — the British Security Service, which handles counterintelligence work parallel to that of the FBI.

MI-6 — the British Intelligence Service parallel to the CIA.

NA — FBI National Academy. Its graduates become "NA associates."

NCIC — National Crime Information Center, the FBI's computerized criminal information file that has revolutionized law enforcement, making it possible, for example, for local policemen to determine within minutes whether a car they have stopped or a gun they have recovered is stolen.

nitel — a Bureau communication that is important enough to go by teletype, but routine enough to wait for transmittal overnight at cheaper rates.

NKVD — a forerunner of the Soviet KGB.

NLETS — National Law Enforcement Telecommunications System, a teletype network on which state and local agencies exchange messages. The Bureau has sought to take over all NLETS message-switching as a "service" to local agencies.

"number one" man — the top aide to an assistant director or other high-ranking Bureau official, in effect second in line in his division.

"number two" man — the second-ranking aide to an assistant director or other key Bureau official, in effect third in line in his division.

number three card — the index card on which the FBI agent keeps his field office informed of his whereabouts.

ODALE — Office of Drug Abuse Law Enforcement, created by the Nixon administration as part of its fight against illegal narcotics traffic but later merged into the Drug Enforcement Administration. One of the flashier agencies in the drug field, ODALE for a time maintained a "heroin hotline" on which citizens could call in anonymous reports of drug activity.

OGPU — a forerunner of the Soviet KGB.

OMB — Office of Management and Budget, successor to the old Bureau of the Budget. Under J. Edgar Hoover, the FBI generally managed to avoid undue interference by OMB and its predecessors, but after he died it began to assert some control over FBI budget priorities.

ONNI — Office of National Narcotics Intelligence. Created by the Nixon administration to coordinate all available intelligence in the drug field, it never accomplished very much; its major importance was as a means for William C. Sullivan, a deposed aide to Hoover, to return to Washington after the Director's death.

OO — office of origin, the field office that does the first investigation on any particular Bureau case and then continues to receive copies of all further reports on it.

OP — office of preference. Bureau agents traditionally listed three offices where they would like to be assigned; with seniority, good behavior, and prudent selections, they would have a fair chance of getting there. Agents now select only one office, and the Bureau attempts to assign them within a reasonable radius of it, but the same factors still govern.

OPE — the FBI's Office of Planning and Evaluation, established by Acting Director L. Patrick Gray III shortly after he took over in 1972.

OSS — Office of Strategic Services, the World War II clandestine intelligence agency that was a forerunner of the CIA.

PAC — Polish-American Congress, an early subject of Bureau investigation.

PINAP — FBI code name for its investigation of the kidnapping of Virginia Piper of Minneapolis in 1972.

RA — Bureau abbreviation for both resident agent and resident agency.

RCMP — Royal Canadian Mounted Police, the Canadian counterpart of the FBI.

relief supervisor — an agent who fills in for his superior when he is away; he does it without any extra compensation, but it is a first step toward "administrative advancement" in the Bureau.

resident agencies — the smaller FBI offices, scattered across the country (see endpapers), which are generally responsible for covering geographical areas distant from the main field offices; in recent years they have also been established in suburbs and at airports. Always distrusted by Hoover, the resident agencies are favored by some as the best place to work in the FBI.

resident agent — an agent assigned to a resident agency.

SAC — pronounced by enunciating the three letters, never "sack," special-agent-in-charge, the agent in command of one of the Bureau's field offices or, in the largest offices, one of several top-ranking people.

SACB — Subversive Activities Control Board, established by the Internal Security Act of 1950 to ferret out "communist action" and "communist front" organizations, but eventually denied funds by Congress and abolished in the 1970s after the federal courts had curbed its powers.

SDS — Students for a Democratic Society, the radical organization that, along with the rest of the New Left, became a major FBI preoccupation in the late 1960s.

SEARCH — System for Electronic Analysis and Retrieval of Criminal Histories, a cooperative project among several states that led to the FBI's Computerized Criminal History file in NCIC.

serial — an individual document within an FBI file. Each document has its own unique number, composed of the classification, the case number, and the serial number.

SIS — Special Intelligence Service, the FBI's clandestine intelligence-gathering operation during World War II, which functioned primarily in Latin America.

SLA — Symbionese Liberation Army, the group that kidnapped and then converted newspaper heiress Patricia Hearst in 1974, foiling the FBI along the way.

SMUN — Soviet Mission to the United Nations, a major focus of concern and investigation for the FBI's New York Field Office.

SOG — seat of government, the traditional name for FBI headquarters in Washington.

special — any case that is singled out by headquarters for special attention and resources, particularly kidnappings or dramatic cases in which a policeman or other victim is killed.

special agent — any FBI agent.

Special Branch — the part of Scotland Yard that handles "security" cases and intelligence matters, especially on assignment from MI-5.

squad — a group of agents who work together on cases under a single supervisor, anywhere from a half a dozen to twenty-five, depending on the field office. In the largest offices the squads are narrowly specialized; in the smallest ones they may handle a variety of classifications at once.

SRA — senior resident agent. Although the SRA is responsible for coordinating a resident agency's assignments and in large RAs earns more than his colleagues, he has no formal authority over them as the SAC and ASAC do over all agents in the field division. The SRA designation is determined strictly on the basis of seniority in the Bureau.

street agent — an agent who opts to continue investigating cases throughout his Bureau career, rather than following the path of "administrative advancement."

SWAT team — group of agents, at least one group per field office, that has been trained in the use of "special weapons and tactics," especially in confrontations with urban guerrillas and other terrorists.

SWP — Socialist Workers party, an "Old Left" organization that has been the subject of intensive Bureau investigation for decades because of its adherence to the views of Russian revolutionary Leon Trotsky.

teletype — the secure, encrypted communications network maintained by the Bureau, with a terminal in every field office. Also used to refer to an urgent FBI communication sent over that network.

TFIS — theft from an interstate shipment, a Bureau classification.

TIO — time in office, or the amount of time any agent spends at his desk rather than out on an investigation. Hoover required for years that field offices maintain and report TIO statistics for every agent. Too much time in the office was a basis for punishment, and so many agents took their paperwork to a public library rather than risk discipline.

UFAC — unlawful flight to avoid confinement, a Bureau classification that is used as the basis for tracking down people who escape from state and local prisons.

UFAP — unlawful flight to avoid prosecution, a Bureau classification. UFAP warrants are used as the basis for the FBI's capture of many fugitives wanted by state courts; once they are captured, however, the federal charge is rarely pressed.

U.S. attorney — one of the ninety-four regional federal prosecutors to whom the FBI refers cases.

VOT — voluntary overtime, required of all agents. An old Hoover gimmick for obtaining adequate appropriations from Congress, it was always precisely kept track of. Agents must now work an average of one hour and forty-nine minutes of overtime every day in order to qualify for certain fringe benefits beyond their basic salary.

VVAW — Vietnam Veterans Against the War, an organization that participated in the antiwar demonstrations of the early 1970s and was intensely investigated and infiltrated by the FBI.

Weatherman — the militant, terroristic faction that split off from Students for a Democratic Society and claimed responsibility for many bombings of the late 1960s and early 1970s.

Bibliography

The bulk of the material in this book is based upon primary research — reporting, interviews, and observation of the FBI in the field and at headquarters in Washington. But there already exists a vast literature on the Bureau and on related agencies and topics, and I relied heavily on some of it, especially in trying to establish the historical context for my own explorations. What follows is a partial list of books that may be useful references, or at least starting points, for those who wish to explore various aspects of the FBI further.

Barron, John. *KGB: The Secret Work of Soviet Secret Agents.* New York: Reader's Digest Press, 1974.
> An authoritative look at the Soviet superagency, its authority coming in part from extensive FBI cooperation with and approval of the manuscript. Some of the Bureau's most successful and exciting counterintelligence work is described in detail.

Bernstein, Carl, and Woodward, Bob. *All the President's Men.* New York: Simon & Schuster, 1974.
> The story of how two *Washington Post* reporters undid the Watergate cover-up, in which the FBI and its acting director, L. Patrick Gray III, look none too good.

Bontecou, Eleanor. *The Federal Loyalty-Security Program.* Ithaca: Cornell University Press, 1953.
> An exhaustive and skeptical review of the program that plunged the Bureau and other government agencies into the business of examining the "loyalty" of actual and prospective federal employees.

Brown, Ralph S. *Loyalty and Security.* New Haven: Yale University Press, 1958.
> An examination of the federal loyalty-security program that focuses on the wrongs done some of its victims.

Clark, Ramsey. *Crime in America: Observations on Its Nature, Causes, Prevention and Control.* New York: Simon & Schuster, 1970.
> A sort of memoir with prescriptions, including some biting comments about the FBI, by J. Edgar Hoover's least favorite attorney general.

Collins, Frederick L. *The FBI in Peace and War.* Introduction by J. Edgar Hoover. New York: Books, Inc., 1943.

    An early example of the slavish and unstinting praise that built the Bureau's image. As Hoover puts it in his introduction, "You cannot condemn a friend for the sin of overfriendliness."

Conners, Bernard F. *Don't Embarrass the Bureau.* Indianapolis: Bobbs-Merrill Co., 1972.

    A novel revolving around the outrages of life in the FBI of Hoover's last years, by a former agent. Farfetched but funny.

Cook, Fred J. *The FBI Nobody Knows.* New York: Macmillan, 1964.

    An important book for its efforts to puncture the FBI balloon at a critical time in its history. Heir to Max Lowenthal's book (see below), it is also a useful antidote to the official history of Don Whitehead. Cook, like others, became the object of FBI vilification after his book was published.

Cummings, Homer, and McFarland, Carl. *Federal Justice: Chapters in the History of Justice and the Federal Executive.* New York: Macmillan, 1937.

    With a collaborator, the attorney general most responsible for the expansion of the Bureau in the criminal field tells the story of how the federal government at first didn't, and later did, get involved. Useful for an opposing view is an article by William Seagle, "The American National Police: The Dangers of Federal Crime Control," in *Harper's,* November 1934, pp. 751–761.

de Gramont, Sanche. *The Secret War: The Story of International Espionage Since World War II.* New York: G. P. Putnam's Sons, 1962.

    Chronicles of some important cases, including Coplon, Abel, and others, in which the FBI does not measure up to its image of perfection.

Demaris, Ovid. *The Director: An Oral Biography of J. Edgar Hoover.* New York: Harper's Magazine Press, 1975.

    Interviews with former Bureau officials and others on matters of Hooverian controversy.

de Toledano, Ralph. *J. Edgar Hoover: The Man in His Time.* New Rochelle, N.Y.: Arlington House, 1973.

    A stab at biography, from an admirer of the Director, which shows that you can put a good twist on all the negative stories if you really try.

Divale, William Tulio, with James Joseph. *I Lived Inside the Campus Revolution.* Cowles Book Company, 1970.

    The memoir of a man who for a time informed on the New Left and old for the FBI.

Elliff, John T. *Crime, Dissent, and the Attorney General: The Justice Department in the 1960s.* Beverly Hills: Sage Publications, 1971.

    An academic student of the Bureau looks at structural and political developments during an important period. Elliff's other published articles and book chapters about the FBI, especially on its domestic intelligence-gathering operations, are also useful.

Federal Bureau of Investigation. *Annual Reports.*

———. *The FBI Law Enforcement Bulletin.*

———. *Uniform Crime Reports.*

    As long as they are not taken too seriously, all of these Bureau publications are essential to an understanding of the institution and its evolution over a half-century.

Fooner, Michael. *INTERPOL: The Inside Story of the International Crime-Fighting Organization.* Chicago: Henry Regnery, 1973.

    An adoring light touch.

Guthman, Edwin. *We Band of Brothers.* New York: Harper & Row, 1971.

    A sympathetic look at the Justice Department as run by Robert F. Kennedy, by his chief of public information; therefore, unsympathetic to Hoover and the Bureau.

Harris, Richard. *Justice: The Crisis of Law, Order and Freedom in America*. New York: Dutton, 1970.

In chronicling the transfer of power from the Kennedy-Johnson administrations' regime at the Justice Department to the Nixon administration, Harris makes some perceptive observations about the law-and-order mentality of the late 1960s that so profoundly affected the FBI.

Hoover, J. Edgar. *Masters of Deceit: The Story of Communism in America and How to Fight It*. New York: Henry Holt, 1958.

The ghostwritten gospel on which Hoover made a fortune while stirring up the forces of anticommunism.

Hyde, H. Montgomery. *Room 3603: The Story of the British Intelligence Center in New York During World War II*. New York: Farrar, Straus, 1963.

Dramatic tales of how the British and Americans fought German spies.

Karpis, Alvin, with Bill Trent. *The Alvin Karpis Story*. New York: Coward, McCann & Geoghegan, 1971.

One of the busted gangsters tells the story from his side.

Lowenthal, Max. *The Federal Bureau of Investigation*. William Sloane Associates, Inc., 1950 (Harvest paperback edition, Harcourt Brace Jovanovich).

A skeptical view of the Bureau's history, painstakingly documented with references to early hearings and other public records. Originally doomed to obscurity, in part because of the Bureau's efforts to discredit the author's patriotism, it enjoyed a revival twenty years after its original publication — but is still open to the charge of stacking the deck with biased and selective quotation.

Manchester, William. *The Death of a President: November 20–November 25, 1963*. New York: Harper & Row, 1967.

Interesting on the cool relationship between J. Edgar Hoover and Robert Kennedy, but more so today for the absence of any information at the time of the Kennedy assassination about the Bureau's relationship with Lee Harvey Oswald.

Messick, Hank. *John Edgar Hoover: An Inquiry into the Life and Times of John Edgar Hoover and his Relationship to the Continuing Partnership of Crime, Business and Politics*. New York: David McKay, 1972.

A thin, negative book about the Director.

Miller, Arthur R. *The Assault on Privacy: Computers, Data Banks, and Dossiers*. Ann Arbor: University of Michigan Press, 1971 (New American Library paperback edition, 1972).

One of a number of poignant warnings about the threat from computerized information systems maintained by law enforcement and other government agencies.

Millspaugh, Arthur C. *Crime Control by the National Government*. Washington: The Brookings Institution, 1937.

Includes some early criticism of the Bureau, somewhat out of step with its times.

Nash, Jay Robert. *Citizen Hoover: A Critical Study of the Life and Times of J. Edgar Hoover and his FBI*. Chicago: Nelson-Hall, 1972.

Another negative book about the Director, the publication of which coincided with his death.

Navasky, Victor S. *Kennedy Justice*. New York: Atheneum, 1971.

Apart from other valuable material, it includes a detailed look at some of the conflicts between Hoover and Robert Kennedy and some objective conclusions.

Nelson, Jack, and Ostrow, Ronald J. *The FBI and the Berrigans*. New York: Coward, McCann & Geoghegan, 1972.

A detailed narrative of one of the Director's more extraordinary and outrageous crusades.

Nelson, Jack, and Bass, Jack. *The Orangeburg Massacre*. New York: World, 1970.

Chronology of an episode when the Bureau took sides with racist South Carolina police forces in a major civil rights case.

Ollestad, Norman. *Inside the FBI*. New York: Lyle Stuart, 1967.

Acid memoir of an ex-agent who was in the Bureau for a short while.

Overstreet, Harry and Bonaro. *The FBI in Our Open Society*. New York: Norton, 1969.

Commentary and critique on FBI controversies (and on others' books on same) as spoon-fed to a husband and wife team by the Bureau itself.

Pearson, Drew. *Diaries 1949–1959*, edited by Tyler Abell. New York: Holt, Rinehart and Winston, 1974.

Tidbits on how it was in the good old days, when J. Edgar Hoover and powerful journalists worked hand-in-glove.

Perkus, Cathy, ed. *COINTELPRO: The FBI's Secret War on Political Freedom*. Introduction by Noam Chomsky. New York: Monad Press, 1976.

Includes Bureau documents concerning its controversial counterintelligence programs, revealed in the course of a lawsuit brought by the Political Rights Defense Fund on behalf of the Socialist Workers party.

Russell, Francis. *The Shadow of Blooming Grove: Warren G. Harding in His Times*. New York: McGraw-Hill, 1968.

Includes some excellent material on the pre-Hoover Bureau and the corruption that affected it during the Harding administration.

Schneir, Walter and Miriam. *Invitation to an Inquest: Reopening the Rosenberg "Atom Spy" Case*. New York: Doubleday, 1965.

Raises some troubling questions about the Bureau's role in the case.

Schott, Joseph L. *No Left Turns: The FBI in Peace and War*. New York: Praeger, 1975.

A good collection of outrageous tales of life with and under Hoover, by a former agent who retired in good standing.

The Story of the FBI: The Official Picture History of the Federal Bureau of Investigation. Compiled by the Editors of *Look*. Introduction by J. Edgar Hoover. New York: Dutton, 1947.

Pure propaganda, but interesting look at the Bureau image after World War II.

Tully, Andrew. *The FBI's Most Famous Cases*. Introduction and Comments by J. Edgar Hoover. New York: William Morrow, 1965.

Another of Hoover's favorite journalists gives the Bureau's side, with research and editing courtesy of the FBI.

Turner, William W. *Hoover's FBI: The Men and the Myth*. New York: Dell, 1971.

An ex-agent's scathing but fairly well documented look at recent Bureau history. Turner tends to overrate, and overwrite about, his own personal conflict with Hoover and the hierarchy, which went to the Supreme Court, but on some other matters he has excellent perspective.

U.S. Congress. *J. Edgar Hoover: Memorial Tributes in the Congress of the United States and Various Articles and Editorials Relating to His Life and Work*. Washington: Government Printing Office, 1974.

A good indication of the esteem in which Hoover was held and the way he managed to fool the public for half a century; some revealing and not so laudatory anecdotes slipped past the editors' eyes.

U.S. Department of Health, Education and Welfare. *Records, Computers and the Rights of Citizens*. Report of the Secretary's Advisory Committee on Automated Personal Data Systems. Cambridge: MIT Press, 1973.

An excellent look at the issues and the hard questions concerning government record-keeping, in law enforcement and other areas.

Watters, Pat, and Gillers, Stephen, eds. *Investigating the FBI: A Tough, Fair Look at the Powerful Bureau, Its Present and Its Future*. New York: Doubleday, 1973.

The proceedings of the conference on the FBI that was convened at Princeton University in 1971. Some of the chapters are far better than others, but it is generally a good, well-documented review of the complaints about the Bureau in the last years before Hoover's death.

Westin, Alan F. *Privacy and Freedom*. New York: Atheneum, 1967.

An early warning about the dangers of government records systems.

Wheeler, Burton K., with Paul F. Healy. *Yankee from the West: The Candid, Turbulent Life Story of the Yankee-Born U.S. Senator from Montana*. New York: Doubleday, 1962.

A man who was involved in many controversies with Hoover and the FBI tells at least a part of his story. Agents once hid in the bushes outside Wheeler's home to spy on him, but later he became a certified "friend."

Whitehead, Don. *The FBI Story: A Report to the People*. New York: Random House, 1956.

The classic work on the Bureau, reciting chapter and verse exactly as the FBI wanted it told. For all its partisanship and self-serving material on Hoover, it is a fascinating period piece and still a good source on some of the subjects, including wartime activity, which Hoover discussed for the first time with Whitehead.

————. *Attack on Terror: The FBI Against the Ku Klux Klan in Mississippi*. New York: Funk and Wagnalls, 1970.

More spoon-fed Bureau material, this time going overboard to try to cover up some FBI excesses and negligence.

Wise, David, and Ross, Thomas B. *The Espionage Establishment*. New York: Random House, 1967.

A good overview.

Wright, Richard O., ed. *Whose FBI?* Introduction by Clark Mollenhoff. Chicago: Open Court Publishers, 1974.

Meant as an answer to the Princeton conference (*Investigating the FBI*), it goes a bit far in defending the Bureau.

Those studying the Bureau will also find it useful to consult books recently published about the Central Intelligence Agency, especially *The CIA and the Cult of Intelligence,* by Victor Marchetti and John D. Marks (Knopf, 1974), and *Without Cloak or Dagger: The Truth About the New Espionage,* by Miles Copeland (Simon & Schuster, 1974), for what they reveal about relations among agencies in the intelligence community. Other invaluable sources include the annual hearings on the FBI budget, since 1924, before the House Appropriations Subcommittee on the Departments of State, Justice, and Commerce, the Judiciary and Related Agencies; hearings before the Senate Constitutional Rights Subcommittee on criminal justice data banks and other potential threats to privacy; the Senate Judiciary Committee's confirmation hearings on the nominations of L. Patrick Gray III and Clarence M. Kelley to be FBI director, Elliot L. Richardson to be attorney general, William D. Ruckelshaus to be deputy attorney general, and the various versions of the Nixon administration "White House Transcripts."

Index